Praise for Jill Watts and ___

"Jill Watts' timely, deeply absorbing narrative unravels the little known but highly significant behind-the-scenes account of Franklin D. Roosevelt's unofficial Black Cabinet, and their relentless determination that New Deal socio-economic justice include Black Americans. The voices of the historical actors come right through the pages and give a flavor to the narrative as though you were actually on the scene . . . A powerful piece of scholarship and a great story."
—Margaret Washington, author of *Sojourner Truth's America*

"A well-researched, urgent, and necessary history of black folks during the New Deal that excavates the too often ignored history of black female genius behind racial progress." —Michael Eric Dyson, *New York Times* bestselling author of *What Truth Sounds Like*

"Meticulously researched and beautifully written . . . This absorbing look at a pivotal point in civil rights activity before the 1950s and '60s is well done and should be of interest to us all." —*BookPage*

"My great-uncle Frank Horne, a poet, a doctor and an educator, was a member of FDR's so-called 'Black Cabinet.' For the first time, this fascinating new book tells the whole story of the victories and defeats of these brilliant black New Dealers and the dynamic, charismatic black woman, Mary McLeod Bethune, who was their leader." —Gail Lumet Buckley, author of *The Black Calhouns: From Civil War to Civil Rights with One African American Family*

"Important and timely. One comes away from this deeply researched and engaging narrative with a rich and textured sense of the work the members of the Black Cabinet accomplished in the decades before the modern Civil Rights Movement and the stakes and significance of their efforts."
—Judith Weisenfeld, author of *New World A-Coming: Black Religion and Racial Identity during the Great Migration*

"This sweeping history looks at how a core group took on the racist machinations of post-Reconstruction government to give Black communities a chance to influence one of the most powerful men in the world. Though they never achieved official recognition, they still helped change the course of history . . . A dramatic piece of nonfiction." —*Library Journal*

"Making her subjects come alive for the reader, [Jill Watts] portrays [the Black Cabinet] as courageous individuals motivated by a combination of personal ambition and principled devotion to the cause of black rights, which the New Deal by no means embraced with enthusiasm. These crusaders paved the way for the political transformation of the African-American community from Republican to Democrat, and prefigured the Black Civil Rights Movement."
—Daniel Walker Howe, author of Pulitzer-Prize winning, *What Hath God Wrought: The Transformation of America, 1815-1848*

Also by Jill Watts

Hattie McDaniel:
Black Ambition, White Hollywood

Mae West:
An Icon in Black and White

God, Harlem U.S.A.:
The Father Divine Story

THE BLACK CABINET

The Untold Story of African Americans and Politics During the Age of Roosevelt

JILL WATTS

Grove Press
New York

Published simultaneously in Canada
Printed in Canada

First Grove Atlantic hardcover edition: May 2020
First Grove Atlantic paperback edition: January 2021

This book was designed by Norman Tuttle of Alpha Design & Composition.
This book set in 13-point Centaur MT by Alpha Design & Composition of Pirttsfield, NH.

Library of Congress Cataloging-in-Publication data is available for this title.

ISBN 978-0-8021-4866-7
eISBN 978-0-8021-4692-2

Grove Press
an imprint of Grove Atlantic
154 West 14th Street
New York, NY 10011

Distributed by Publishers Group West

groveatlantic.com

21 22 23 24   10 9 8 7 6 5 4 3 2 1

For my mom
Doris Ruth Watts

For my nieces
Sarah and Abby Woo

In Memoriam

George Armstrong

Frazier Baker and his one-year-old daughter, Julia

Anne Bostwick

John Lee Eberhart

Thomas P. Foster

Gus

Felix Hall

Robert Hall

Paul Mayo

Claude Neal

William Norman

Odell Waller

And other victims of lynching and racial violence
who have lost their lives

CONTENTS

NOTE TO READER

Some of the language in this book was and is offensive. It is quoted here from the original sources to offer insight into historical realities that African Americans of the era faced and to illuminate the struggles of Black Cabinet members in their fight for equality.

PROLOGUE

In the middle of January 1940, Mary McLeod Bethune awoke early in her Washington, D.C., home. A dry wheezing, punctuated by a breathless cough, often stirred her, and she would rise, sometimes well before dawn. She grabbed the doctor's latest remedy, then made her way to the kitchen for a hot cup of tea. For much of her life, she had suffered asthma attacks, and this winter they seemed worse. And now, at sixty-four, she was also plagued by arthritis and had to use a cane to get about. Yet, she refused to be stilled and seemed to possess a reserve of boundless energy. Her life had been filled with hard work, and no matter what obstacle she faced, she would not—could not—rest.

Born in Mayesville, South Carolina, in 1875, Mary McLeod Bethune was the daughter of parents who had both endured slavery. Freed after the Civil War, her family sharecropped for a time, and as a youth, Bethune had worked alongside her mother, father, and siblings in cotton fields and cold, swampy rice paddies. But she hungered for a better life; she fought for an education, received a scholarship, and left home. During summer breaks, to help pay for her schooling, Bethune took jobs as a cook and a maid in white homes. Drive and industry and, she insisted, "faith and prayer" brought her out of poverty and took her to the heights of success. By the 1930s, Bethune had become one of the African American community's most revered figures. She was the founder of Bethune-Cookman College, a driving force in the black women's club movement, and a celebrated civil rights activist. In 1936, President Franklin Delano Roosevelt personally offered her a position in the New Deal, his administration's massive collection of federal agencies and programs aimed at healing America's Great Depression, the most serious economic crisis in the nation's history. Mary McLeod Bethune accepted an appointment to head up a work program for African American youth, and with that, she became the first African American woman to lead a federal division.

Almost immediately after settling into her new post, Bethune took command of an informal group of black federal employees known as "FDR's Black Cabinet." Before her arrival, they had, for the most part, operated independently in their various programs, fighting for equal inclusion for African Americans in the New Deal. From diverse backgrounds, the group's members were often divided by internal rivalries and personal conflicts. But with a single-minded determination, Bethune began to channel their individual campaigns against discrimination and transform them into an unofficial lobby for African American concerns. She was both irrepressible and irresistible. In personal encounters she radiated a winning charm. In front of audiences she possessed a spellbinding charisma. African Americans of the era would celebrate Mary McLeod Bethune as the "First Lady of Our Negro Nation."

What she had achieved was not lost on her. "I know what it is to yearn for a chance to do something, to be something better," she remarked in one interview. "When I was very young I resolved to lift myself, somehow, out of the confusion and misery of those . . . [post-Civil War] days, and in lifting myself I found a higher motive, that of lifting others." By winter 1940, she had been battling for African American equality in the federal government for almost six years, and she continued to drive hard. Much was at stake. The Great Depression had gripped the nation for more than a decade. Although the economy had begun to turn around, homelessness and poverty persisted in parts of the nation. Hitler and Nazism had moved throughout Europe, and on the other side of the world, tensions had grown with Japan.

While these threats loomed large over the nation, much of the African American community remained destitute. In 1933, when Franklin Delano Roosevelt first took office, unemployment in many African American communities ran at 50 percent or higher, twice the national average. Of the nearly twelve million African Americans living in the United States counted in the 1930 census (who composed almost 10 percent of the entire population), 73 percent lived in the rural South and faced dire poverty and the threat of starvation. The vast majority of black southerners were denied the right to vote. Overall the outlook for African American citizens during the Great Depression was grave. Segregated in communities across the country, subjected to racial violence, and denied equal access to education, social and legal justice, health care, and jobs, many African Americans, rather than recovering by 1940, continued to fall desperately further and further behind. Black people and their sufferings were never far from Bethune's mind. She believed that she had been brought into the world with a special purpose—and that was to end the brutalities against the African American people and lead them to equality. Deeply devout, she began every morning in prayer. These cold January winter mornings were no different.

By the second week of the month, rain had turned to snow and then to rain again. Bethune's doctors had cautioned her to slow down, but she refused. New anti-lynching legislation known as the Gavagan bill, named for its sponsor, New York congressman Joseph A. Gavagan, was making its way through the House of Representatives. Bethune steeled herself for the fight to get it passed. Since emancipation and the end of the Civil War in 1865, lynching as a means to terrorize the black population had become a public ritual, especially below the Mason-Dixon Line that historically designated the geographic division between North and South. Unchecked by local and state authorities, white mobs took the law into their own hands and tortured, mutilated, and killed black men, women, and children. Lynch mobs were brazen. White crowds posed for photographs—arrogantly grinning and laughing as black bodies were hung from trees, were riddled to shreds by bullets, were stabbed, and were set on fire.

No black family in the South was immune from the horrors. According to one study, between 1882 and 1940 more than three thousand African Americans had been lynched in the United States. And that figure did not take into account the numerous murders and mob slayings of black citizens that had gone unreported. Bethune carried with her a childhood memory of Gus, a family acquaintance who, in the streets of Mayesville, had refused to obey a white man's demand he blow out a lit match. When ordered a second time, Gus threw a punch and leveled that white man. A white crowd began to circle around Gus. Someone yelled, "string him up." Bethune remembered her father grabbing her, hustling her away, and commanding, "Don't look backward." When they arrived home, her mother immediately sent her to bed. But she never forgot the haunting voices and angry shouts of the white mob. She had nothing against white people; the "shock and fear" had long passed, she explained later. But her loathing of the brutal injustice had not.

When the Gavagan anti-lynching bill reached the House floor, Bethune summoned three core members of the Black Cabinet to join her in the gallery to observe as Congress debated it. They were all young men of professional accomplishment—the pride of the black community. The serious and diligent Robert Clifton Weaver had been the first African American to earn a PhD in economics from Harvard University; he worked for the Federal Housing Administration. The bookish and quiet William H. Hastie had served as a solicitor in the Department of the Interior and was the first African American to hold a federal judgeship. The outspoken and clever Al Smith was an alumnus of Howard University; he was an administrator in the Works Progress Administration and headed up the largest African American jobs programs in the New Deal.

Together the group made a striking team. Bethune often dressed in somber Victorian fashion—the lace and long dresses, sensible shoes, and draping jewelry that had been popular two generations before. With her cane, she cut a stately figure. Her Black Cabinet colleagues were dapper; lean, handsome, and urbane, they sported wing tips, fedoras, and tailored suits. Behind Bethune's back, they called her "Ma." (She usually didn't approve of such informalities—to most, she was "Mrs. Bethune.") They would lay claim to their title as "her boys." Although black men resented the disparagement conveyed by the term "boy," in this case it was an inside joke—an outlandish reference to Ma Barker and her boys, the era's infamous gang of white outlaws headed up by a ruthless matriarch.

Perched in the House gallery, Bethune and her three Black Cabinet colleagues watched as a fiery debate over the Gavagan bill raged on the House floor over three days. In the past, white southern Democrats had repeatedly blocked legislation that would make lynching a federal crime. It was superfluous, they contended. Murder was already illegal—and the constitution delegated the power to enforce such laws exclusively to local police and state courts. But the Gavagan bill's supporters countered forcefully: to leave the prosecution of lynch mobs in the hands of white local and state authorities, who notoriously looked the other way, only protected murderers and their accomplices. Tempers flared and passions rose on the House floor. One congressman stood and offered an emotional defense of the anti-lynching bill. As he finished, many in the gallery, including Bethune, broke into hearty applause. Such demonstrations from visitors violated House rules, and a sergeant at arms marched down the aisle. Singling out Bethune, he warned her, "If you do that again, I'll have to ask you to leave the gallery." Bethune remained "quiet and dignified" but defiant. According to the *Pittsburgh Courier*, one of the nation's most influential black newspapers, she "nodded" and replied, "Thank you, sonny."

As the anti-lynching bill's debates wrapped up, Bethune made her way over to the White House for a private meeting with the president. Most of the Black Cabinet never interacted with FDR, but Bethune had special access through First Lady Eleanor Roosevelt. The two women had been acquainted since the 1920s, and once Bethune joined the

New Deal, their friendship was sealed. Although Eleanor Roosevelt brought to the White House a spirit of compassion and tolerance, she had grown up among New York's old moneyed elite and was blithely unaware of the stark realities of African American life. Bethune awakened her to the seriousness of American racism and the injustices of inequality and transformed the First Lady into a vocal advocate for civil and human rights.

Yet Eleanor Roosevelt's equally privileged husband was not as dependable. FDR embraced the game of politics. He was a wily figure, always maneuvering to advance his agenda, protect his programs, and further his reelection ambitions. Despite the president's promise to uplift the common American—so that there would be no more "forgotten man"—immediately out of the gate the New Deal had failed to reach the vast majority of black citizens. Throughout his years in office, FDR remained reluctant to speak openly on racial affairs. He was a Democrat, and historically the white South controlled his party. To keep white southerners in the fold, the president catered to their whims, traditions, and demands. Many—in fact most—of Roosevelt's Oval Office staff members were white southerners. Press secretary Stephen Early, a Virginian, a descendant of Confederates, and a longtime Roosevelt booster, anchored the group. Early was chummy with the president, joining him for cocktails and an occasional hand of poker. Along with other advisers, Early routinely dismissed, obstructed, or outright denied African American requests to meet with FDR. Fraternizing with or showing too much sympathy toward black citizens was political dynamite, Early insisted. The president never indicated that he disagreed.

However, Eleanor Roosevelt did not accept the bigotry displayed by Early and other staffers. In the face of their indignation over her support for African American equality, she circumvented them and routinely arranged for Bethune, and other black leaders, to meet with the president. For almost three years, the First Lady had publicly condemned lynching and supported the proposed legislation to end it. Yet her husband had remained silent, even as black lives continued to be lost. FDR privately confessed to Walter White, the executive secretary of the National Association for the Advancement of Colored People (NAACP), that his reticence came because he feared that if he endorsed anti-lynching bills, white southerners would retaliate by dismantling the New Deal.

But on January 12, the president granted Bethune fifteen minutes just before noon, as rain gave way to snow. Bethune claimed to have a warm and open relationship with Roosevelt, and it is certain that she tried to persuade him to publicly support the Gavagan bill. But when Bethune emerged, she whisked past waiting reporters with no comment. She had met with the president on many occasions and likely left knowing that he would have nothing to say either for or against anti-lynching legislation. Later, when journalists clamored for a scoop, Bethune issued her own noncommittal statement. "Each time I go to see him [Roosevelt]," it read, "I return with greater courage to continue my fight for my people."

A version of the Gavagan bill eventually made its way through the House only to die in the Senate. But despite this defeat, the Black Cabinet's appearance at the congressional debates and Bethune's trip to the White House carried a special meaning for the black community. It was a reminder of the presence of African Americans in the Roosevelt administration, their unwillingness to remain silent, and their resolve to continually challenge white oppression and authority. Bethune's actions, as well as those of her colleagues, embodied efforts to force the executive branch not only to take notice of and address African American concerns but also to recognize that the racial dynamics of American politics were in flux. Under Roosevelt, African Americans were abandoning the Republicans, the party of Lincoln, and voting for Democrats. A presidential election loomed ahead, in the fall of 1940. Black votes and black lives mattered. Roosevelt had to be reminded of that fact.

Bethune and her team also faced the reality that FDR hardly embraced them; racial issues were often the third rail of American Depression-era politics. The president did not sanction the Black Cabinet; in fact, he never even acknowledged its existence. African American New Dealers had independently established the Black Cabinet. Although eventually it included more than one hundred African American federal employees, its core members, in addition to Bethune, were Weaver, Hastie, Smith, and Robert Vann, the firebrand editor of the *Pittsburgh Courier*. A group of predominantly Ivy League–educated members of the black elite gathered around District of Columbia native Weaver and his childhood friend Bill Hastie. They were a scholarly crowd with impeccable credentials, who relaxed regularly at poker games in the basement of Weaver's home. Al Smith never felt welcome in Weaver's circle, and he often operated alone. He had grown up in tough circumstances in the South and put himself through Howard University while working at the post office. Robert Vann was one of black America's most recognizable names. Known not only for his militant journalism, he had been for years a confirmed player in national party politics—an influencer of black votes. Like Bethune, he was only one generation removed from slavery and much older than other members of the nearly exclusively male Black Cabinet.

Early on, this diversity in age and background sparked conflict among African Americans in the Roosevelt administration. But when the venerated Mary McLeod Bethune appeared, she demanded they unify. Despite their differences, they all agreed that just securing an equal share of the New Deal was not enough. The time had come for African Americans to be granted their long overdue rights as citizens. Together the Black Cabinet pushed and pulled, battled and bargained, using their positions to commence the modern struggle for African American civil rights. Fundamentally, they were never Roosevelt's Black Cabinet. They were their own Black Cabinet—self-generated, self-sustaining, and self-directed.

In Mary McLeod Bethune's vision, the Black Cabinet was at the forefront of a radical remaking of the United States—one that had the potential to compel the nation to live up to its constitutional promise to extend equal rights to all Americans. "The principle of justice is fundamental and must be exercised if the peoples of this country are to rise to the highest and best," she lectured one audience, "for there can be neither freedom, peace, true democracy or real development without justice." The time to fight had come, and she demanded Black Cabinet members follow her example and work tirelessly—through victories and through defeats—to improve African American lives. "Then armed with the pride and courage . . . conscious of his positive contribution to American life, and enabled to face clear-eyed and unabashed the actual situation before him, the Negro may gird his loins and go forth to battle to return 'with their shields or on them.'"

Black Cabinet members answered her call to action. Together they would sacrifice family, friends, careers, and health in frustrating, sometimes dangerous, and almost always impossible jobs. They became the unsung heroes of the age of Roosevelt; they helped shape an era and a philosophy that indeed transformed the nation.

This is their story.

PART ONE

Of People and Politics, 1908–1932

Chapter One

Remembrance

THE STORY of the Black Cabinet in the era of Franklin Delano Roosevelt begins a generation earlier, with a cadre of African American federal officeholders who came to Washington, D.C., as appointees under another President Roosevelt. More than three decades before FDR moved into the White House, his fifth cousin Theodore Roosevelt assumed the presidency and while in office appointed a number of African Americans to key positions. Over lunches at Gray's Café, Washington's handsomely appointed, upscale black-owned eatery, this group of black federal officials began to forge close bonds. By 1908 their "talkfests," as they were known, had become routine. While dining on a menu that mixed the best of turn-of-the-century American haute cuisine with home-style southern favorites, they strategized on how to protect and promote the advancement of the race. The United States in 1908 was a brutal place for black citizens. Most African Americans lived in southern states, where they were disenfranchised, impoverished, and denied equal access to the justice system. In 1907 and 1908, according to Tuskegee Institute, white lynch mobs took the lives of 147 African Americans. The vast majority of these murderers were never arrested, much less held for prosecution.

In 1908, while the first Black Cabinet was forming, a thirty-two-year-old Mary McLeod Bethune was teaching class at her Daytona Beach school for African American girls. Driving hard through endless days and nights, she had increased her enrollment from five pupils to 250 pupils in four short years. Her husband left her that year. "He could not understand that my soul was on fire to do things for my people," Bethune later reflected.

Miles away, in Pittsburgh, Robert Vann was a second-year law student at the University of Pittsburgh. A native of Ahoskie, North Carolina, in 1908 he was twenty-nine and supporting his education by working nights and weekends as a dining-car waiter on the Pittsburgh and Lake Erie Railroad. Already an active Republican stalwart, he cashed in a few political favors later in the year to secure a position as a clerk in a city government office.

In 1908, Alfred Edgar Smith was a five-year-old growing up in the segregated resort town of Hot Springs, Arkansas. He started school in 1908, and on his first day, as he walked to Hot Springs' segregated black schoolhouse, a group of white boys ambushed him with a hail of rocks and racial slurs. Smith turned and hurled the rocks right back at his white assailants.

That same year, in Knoxville, Tennessee, four-year-old Bill Hastie was also beginning to learn to fight back. He came from a family of pride and accomplishment. His father, a graduate of Howard University, worked at the local branch of the U.S. pension office, and his mother, a teacher, was well known as "a race woman"—the black community's term for African American female leaders who encouraged pride in race and womanhood and who pursued civil rights activism. "Most of our neighbors were white," he recalled later. "Their children soon learned that to me 'nigger' was a fighting word. So, we became friends and playmates in mutual respect."

Robert Weaver was not even a year old in 1908. He had been born into one of Washington, D.C.'s most distinguished black families— his grandfather was Robert Tanner Freeman, an early black Harvard graduate and the nation's first college-trained African American dentist. Weaver's father had a well-paying government job in the U.S. post office and the family often socialized with friends who held federal positions. As a member of the black elite, it was expected that the young Weaver would join the "the talented tenth," identified by NAACP founder W. E. B. Du Bois as the select children who would be nurtured to lead the African American community. Robert Weaver remembered that it was assumed that someday he, too, like his father and family acquaintances, would work for the government.

Most certainly, on occasion, the Weavers dined at Gray's Café. Everyone who was anyone in black Washington, D.C., did. And no doubt there were times that nearby sat those very men who were in the process of forming the first Black Cabinet.

In March 1908, as Bethune and Vann chased their adult ambitions, and as the joys and trials of black childhood preoccupied Smith, Hastie, and Weaver, more than one hundred of America's most prominent black leaders turned out for an extravagant banquet at Gray's Café. The purpose of the evening was to celebrate Ralph W. Tyler, who the previous year, at the invitation of Theodore Roosevelt, had assumed the position of the auditor of the Department of the Navy. Of all the African American appointments made by the president to date, Tyler's was the most powerful and prestigious. At his post, he oversaw the U.S. Navy's complicated bookkeeping system, keeping a watchful eye on the department's $110 million budget. Known for his quiet yet forceful presence, he had executed his duties with precision and adeptness—winning praise from his white supervisors and from African American leaders.

It was the efficient and determined Tyler who issued the call for upper-level African American federal jobholders to rally over lunches at Gray's. He was usually joined by James A. Cobb, special assistant to Washington, D.C.'s district attorney; Robert H. Terrell, Washington's first African American judge; John C. Dancy, the city's recorder of deeds; and R. W. Thompson, who clerked in several government offices. Newspaper editor Calvin Chase, Howard University professor Kelly

Miller, and attorney and former politician P. B. S. Pinchback were also regulars. Thompson, who also wrote for Chase's newspaper, christened the group the "Black Cabinet" in 1908. And with that, the first informal and internal governmental African American advisory body was born.

That evening in March, the Black Cabinet turned out in force at Gray's to fete Tyler in the most extravagant style. An elegant and old establishment, Gray's catered to the black high society in a segregated city that offered few upscale dining options for African Americans. The café was lavishly outfitted; fine liquors and quality cigars were sold on the first floor, and in several small salons women could dine respectably or patrons could enjoy privacy. (One of these became the first Black Cabinet's regular meeting place.) On Gray's second floor, Washington, D.C.'s celebrated mixologist Wash Wood held forth at a bar that opened onto two large dining rooms.

Gray's had reserved the largest of these dining rooms for Tyler's tribute and put on a feast that the *New York Age*, an African American newspaper, rated "epicurean" in its "gastronomic delicacies." White-coated waiters swept in and out with oysters on the half shell, Roquefort salad, sherry, Gray's famous terrapin soup, fillet of beef in mushroom sauce, and Parisienne potatoes. Dinner was finished off with a glass of claret, some coffee, and cigars. Then the speeches began, with Robert H. Terrell serving as the toastmaster. "The addresses were all of an unusually high character touching more seriously upon the vital problems of the hour than is customary on a festive occasion," the *Age* reported. But there was also "a flow of 'innocent merriment,' effervescent humor, and incidents of 'infinite variety.'" At the end of the evening, Ralph Tyler rose and expressed his gratitude. "I came among you to add my mite [contribution], to assist in propagating all and everything that may contribute to the proper advancement of our interests as a race," he remarked, "and you have cordially accepted my mite." Work with white Americas to promote racial harmony, Tyler urged his audience, and he complimented the president for growing the ranks of African Americans in government. His mood was reflective as he observed, "Today we enjoy a representation not dreamed of twenty-five years ago."

No doubt many others in the room that night nodded with approval. Almost all of them, especially the members of the Black Cabinet, had not only witnessed but participated in the many battles African Americans had waged in the forty-three years since slavery had been outlawed in the United States. Most of the members of this first Black Cabinet had come of age during Reconstruction, the period stretching from 1865 to 1877, when the nation attempted to rise from the ashes of its bitter civil war. Reconstruction had been led by a Republican-dominated Congress that passed constitutional amendments guaranteeing the civil and voting rights of American citizens regardless of race. (At the time, the amendments protecting suffrage were understood to apply only to men. Politics was regarded as a masculine domain.) Republicans also mandated the deployment of federal troops to the South to protect African Americans from the white backlash to emancipation and from intimidation at the polls. The result was what the Republicans, declaring themselves postwar as the Grand Old Party (GOP), had hoped for: esteem for the widely proclaimed "Party of Lincoln" grew rapidly in black communities. Black men registered as Republicans, giving the party a foothold in the South.

Dominated by former slaveholders and secessionists, post–Civil War Democrats were synonymous with the old Confederacy in the eyes of most African Americans. As the Republicans became the party of choice for African American voters, white southern Democrats, along with vigilante groups like the Ku Klux Klan, blocked black men from the polls. Democratic leaders openly denounced the extension of voting rights to African Americans as an "evil." In the South, determined to preserve the political arena exclusively for white southern men, the Klan and its sympathizers terrorized the black population with violence, brutality, and lynchings. They burned black churches, schoolhouses, homes, and farms; they attacked, beat, and murdered African Americans trying to forge a path in politics or business. With members of the KKK in their ranks and their antiblack rhetoric, Democrats emerged as the party of segregation, disenfranchisement, and racial violence.

To a man, every member of Theodore Roosevelt's Black Cabinet had started his political life as a devout Republican. With the support of the GOP, African American men in the South proudly and bravely registered to vote. Several were elected to local, state, and federal offices. The Black Cabinet's elder statesman P. B. S. Pinchback was one of those who had served in political office during Reconstruction. Born to a free woman of color in Georgia in 1833, he had fought for the Union during the Civil War. He made his way to Louisiana, and after the war swiftly rose through Republican Party ranks there. He was elected to the state senate in 1868 and in 1872 was sworn in as Louisiana's acting governor when his predecessor was suspended from office for purported election fraud.

But the open doors of political opportunity for men like P. B. S. Pinchback closed quickly. White southerners resented the empowerment of black men and vehemently defied the mandates of Congressional Reconstruction. They escalated their campaigns of bullying and violence. They also fervidly alleged that their rights were being denied, that they were an oppressed majority, and that the traditions of the old South—slavery and plantation life—benefited both the nation and black people. Economic realities played directly into the white South's refusal to share power and its determination to consign African Americans to a status as close to enslavement as possible. Black people had labored in slavery without wages for generations; now freedom came with no compensation and no reparations. With no money, no homes, and no land, most black families were forced into sharecropping.

It was a difficult, nearly impossible existence; in exchange for housing, land, tools, seed, and other farming supplies, families turned over crops as payment in kind. Ultimately sharecropping locked African Americans into an economic dependency that, in turn, became a new form of bondage. Unable to pay off the accumulating debts owed to landowners who cooked the books, sharecroppers became tied to the land and condemned to perpetual labor. Entire families had to work on these farms. There was little time for children to be formally educated—and the schools that existed were few and grossly underfunded. Within the decade after emancipation, the majority of African Americans in the South had become trapped in the sharecropping system. It consigned generation after generation of African Americans to lives of perpetual destitution.

In the 1870s, the new leadership of the Republican Party became determined to make peace with southern Democrats. Believing that the ongoing divisions between the North and South hindered the nation's economy, the GOP backed away from politically empowering African Americans. Gradually the U.S. military pulled out of the South, leaving African Americans with less and less protection. Using nearly impossible literacy tests or charging exorbitant poll taxes (voter-registration fees), white southern election officials blocked black voters from the ballot box. African Americans were voted out of or prevented from running for office. The reversal of the political tide directly affected Pinchback. He was elected to the U.S. Senate, but Louisiana's white Democrats made certain he was never officially seated in Washington.

The final blow to the postwar gains of African Americans in the South came in 1876. To secure the White House for Republican Rutherford B. Hayes in a disputed election, the GOP agreed to completely and finally abandon Reconstruction. No more would the federal government interfere with the white South's internal affairs. Over the next two decades, African American men effectively lost the vote; segregations became the rule, enforced by a system of discriminatory laws and expectations that came to be known as Jim Crow; and African Americans languished even further in a poverty perpetuated by sharecropping.

Ironically, the end of Reconstruction and the Republicans' abandonment of their black constituents laid the groundwork for the emergence of African Americans in the ranks of Washington's federal employees. Determined to maintain black support, in 1877 Hayes offered the

renowned African American abolitionist Frederick Douglass the position of marshal of the District of Columbia. Douglass had escaped
slavery before the Civil War and had risen to become one of the nation's
most outspoken civil rights activists. The marshal's job was a prestigious
patronage post that had traditionally gone to the president's closest
friends. Such appointments were rewards to supporters for their political
fidelity and to assure their future allegiance. Despite his serious reservations about Hayes, Douglass accepted the post. It was the highest
federal appointment ever offered to an African American and allowed
Douglass to build up a core of black federal employees in professional
positions in Washington.

Douglass had even more opportunity to increase the ranks of black
federal workers under Hayes's successor, James Garfield, who appointed
Douglass as the recorder of deeds for the District of Columbia. Consequently, the recorder's position became an appointment traditionally
awarded to African American party loyalists. A number of other positions, including the ambassadorships to Liberia and Haiti, were also
reserved for African Americans. White GOP leaders believed that ear-
marking these as "black posts" guaranteed African American support.

The numbers of African Americans serving in Washington, D.C.,
continued to inch up during the 1880s and 1890s. Much of this
growth came through the establishment of the Civil Service Commission in 1884. The goal of the civil service was to reduce the number of
patronage jobs going to party regulars as spoils of political victories.
That practice had not only produced some incompetent hires but also
aroused bitterness—the most extreme case had driven a frustrated
office seeker to assassinate Garfield in 1881. A portion of federal jobs,
which would grow with each presidency, was placed under control of
the Civil Service Commission. These included diverse positions ranging
from clerical and janitorial employment to jobs with the postal service
and appointments as lower-level administrators in various branches
of the federal government. Those seeking civil service jobs had to
take and pass an examination. Federal employers were required to hire

one of the top three scorers for openings in their divisions, and since test takers' races were not listed, this resulted in the selection of a significant number of African Americans for non-patronage posts.

In 1884, arriving fresh from the countryside with a bare-bones scholarship to Howard University, future Black Cabinet member Kelly Miller took the civil service exam. He had been born in 1863 into slavery in Winnsboro, South Carolina, and had worked in cotton fields as a child. A product of the freedmen's schools set up to educate African Americans during Reconstruction, Miller had been a standout student. Able to cipher complex math problems quickly in his head, he was known around his hometown as "the Lightning Calculator." Even with his scholarship, Miller lacked enough funds to cover his education at Howard and needed a job. He passed the civil service examination with extraordinarily high marks and was hired as a clerk in the D.C. pension office. He was thus able to earn his bachelor's degree, and the job helped him pay for postgraduate work.

Despite the addition of some African Americans to the federal job force, the increasing denial of voting rights in their home districts meant the possibilities remained limited for black citizens to be genuinely included in the nation's political affairs. The presidency of William McKinley, a Republican who won the White House in 1896, confirmed that African Americans would not have much of a political voice. In an effort to court white votes below the Mason-Dixon Line, McKinley pushed for a final healing of the still-festering animosities between the North and the South. His stance reflected the increasing influence within the GOP of a group known as the "Lily Whites." Instead of expanding the party's base by protecting black voters, Lily Whites demanded that Republicans court the South's white independents and fence-sitting Democrats. Although a minority, Lily Whites took center stage in the party—vocal and aggressive, they ardently opposed African American suffrage, civil rights, and anti-lynching legislation.

The ambitious mainstream GOP leaders, hardly racial liberals themselves, eagerly adopted the Lily White strategy. The party's hierarchy generally assumed that those African Americans who could still vote would stick with the Republicans; after all, the GOP had given the country Lincoln, and he had purportedly freed the enslaved. (The celebrated Emancipation Proclamation had only declared freedom for bondpersons in the Confederacy, leaving slavery untouched in the upper South's border states.) A smattering of political patronage appointments would testify to the Republicans' appreciation for black votes. Some cash would also help, the party thought. With virtually no campaign finance regulations, payola was common in turn-of-the-twentieth-century hardball politics, and both parties practiced it. Republicans believed that throwing a little more money in the direction of African American newspapers and compensating key black loyalists would keep African Americans voting a straight GOP ticket. In any event, Democrats were unlikely to net many black ballots.

Political choices for African Americans were few, and with their votes, William McKinley won two terms. Under the thumb of lily-whitism, he did nothing to reverse or check the disenfranchisement of black Americans. In 1898, when a deadly race riot broke out in Wilmington, North Carolina, he retreated without a word to the White House. Often black federal officials were targets of white supremacists, and John C. Dancy, who was Wilmington's collector of customs at the time, refused to give in to threats against him and leave his post. That same year, in Lake City, South Carolina, local white residents demanded that the town's newly installed African American postmaster, Frazier Baker, resign from his federal position. Baker rebuffed them. On February 22, in the middle of the night, a mob of more than two hundred white men encircled his home, set it on fire, and then shot Baker and his family as they tried to escape. Baker died immediately. His wife and four of their children were wounded. His one-year-old daughter, Julia, died in her mother's arms. The White House offered no comment, as African American leaders lodged complaints against local officials' refusal to act after the heartless murder of a federal employee and his daughter. The assault on the Bakers testified to the dire need for federal anti-lynching legislation—mob killings of any nature constituted lynchings and, activists insisted, only federal laws could stop such brutalities. Although he ordered the Justice Department to investigate, McKinley never publicly condemned the attack on the Baker family. In the end, the Bakers' murderers went free.

In 1901, William McKinley also lost his life to an assassin's bullet, to be succeeded by his bold and colorful vice president, Theodore Roosevelt. Known as an energetic supporter of reform, regarded in his time as a political progressive, Roosevelt declared his determination to use the tools of governmental regulation to curb big business, protect natural resources, and uplift society in general. The McKinley wing of the GOP disdained Roosevelt for his zealous reformism and what seemed like reckless impulsiveness. Some African Americans also maintained suspicions about the "Rough Rider" president, who bragged about taking San Juan Hill in Cuba during the Spanish-American War while never acknowledging the black troops who deserved credit for that victory. But many African Americans wagered that the race might fare better with Roosevelt. One of these was Kelly Miller, now a Howard University professor, who led the chorus of those predicting Roosevelt would be friendly. The new president was, Miller noted, a model "of the strenuous life" and a man of "high moral courage."

Shortly after Roosevelt took office, Booker T. Washington received an invitation to dine with the president at the White House. At that moment, Washington was the nation's most respected African American leader. Born in slavery, he had founded Tuskegee Institute, which became the nation's premier vocational school for African Americans. An advocate of a conservative approach to race relations, Washington urged African Americans to accommodate segregation and disenfranchisement and instead concentrate on economic empowerment. Tuskegee's mission was to train black men in agriculture and manual arts, and black women in domestic science. Washington was staid, with a formal bearing, and his acceptance of the racial status quo won him many white supporters. The invitation to dine with the Roosevelts at the White House was a milestone. Racial codes generally prohibited blacks and whites from breaking bread together, since it implied equality between the races. But Washington was about to challenge that tradition as the first African American White House dinner guest.

On October I, 1901, Washington arrived at the White House at eight o'clock in the evening. He was escorted into the dining room, where around the table sat the president and First Lady, Colorado businessman and family friend Phillip Stewart, Roosevelt's daughter Alice, and several raucous grandchildren. Always talkative, Theodore Roosevelt no doubt, on this evening as on others, dominated the conversation with his lively wit and tales of adventure.

After dinner, the president invited Washington and Stewart to the Red Room for coffee and to talk politics. Roosevelt immediately got down to business. The Republican Party needed to expand its influence. He believed the South could be turned decidedly for the Republicans and "talked at considerable length concerning plans about the south," Washington recalled. He would need to count on Washington to help him hold black voters, the president confided. To demonstrate his appreciation, Roosevelt declared his intention to expand the influence of African Americans in upper-level federal posts and asked Washington to help him select the right men for these positions.

Washington was a keen political operator himself and certainly detected the president's true intentions. Of course, Roosevelt needed to solidify his standing among African Americans. But the president was also concerned that holdovers from the previous administration might obstruct his upcoming run for the White House. With Washington's assistance, he could get rid of black McKinleyites. The savvy Washington immediately sensed the opportunity Roosevelt's proposition presented. Most of McKinley's appointees had not been Tuskegee men, but by playing along with Roosevelt, Washington could place his own people in federal posts and boost his power. At ten o'clock he left the White House, mulling over which of his associates could best represent the race as well as advance Tuskegee's interests.

The immediate aftermath of the dinner proved disappointing to Washington and his allies. When news that a black man had dined with the president in the White House broke, an avalanche of complaints came from both white Democrats and white Republicans. White pro-Roosevelt journalists, likely working at the president's behest, insisted that Washington had not been invited to dinner: it had been an informal, impromptu working lunch. Appalled at the faked reports, African Americans demanded that the president correct the record. The White House refused. In turn, the black community continued to protest and rejected the attempts to obscure the truth. A lithograph entitled "Equality" circulated; it showed the president and Washington seated together at a table with a portrait of Abraham Lincoln looking on approvingly.

Despite the discouraging turn of events, Washington began to forward his recommendations for black federal appointments to the White House. During Theodore Roosevelt's two terms, most African Americans serving in federal jobs in the capital, and many in other parts of the nation, came with Washington's endorsement. With that, Washington emerged as black America's political boss, trading and collecting political favors. His home base became known as "the Tuskegee Machine," and to get ahead, an office seeker needed its blessing. "Booker T. Washington was recognized . . . as the unchallenged spokesman for his race," Kelly Miller later recalled. "Whatever patronage . . . accorded to the race was dispensed by him." But these appointments came with a price. Those men occupying the posts had to sacrifice their independence to "the master hand of the great Tuskegeean," Miller observed.

Although yoked to the Tuskegee Machine, black appointees serving in Theodore Roosevelt's administration were accomplished and influential figures in their own right. James A. Cobb, the special assistant to Washington, D.C.'s district attorney, had been raised in extreme poverty in Louisiana but held degrees from both Fisk and Howard Universities. He had a thriving law practice in Washington. Judge Robert H.

Terrell, a Virginian and a longtime Republican, had been born free before slavery's end. After the Civil War, he headed north and worked his way through Harvard. Washington, D.C., recorder of deeds John C. Dancy was a former educator and newspaperman. Dancy previously held federal appointments in both his home state of North Carolina and Washington. Navy auditor Ralph Tyler had written for both black and white newspapers, a rare accomplishment for an African American journalist of the time. He established a commanding presence among his D.C. counterparts, black and white alike. "Ralph Tyler always had sand in him," observed Kelly Miller.

The most trusted of Booker T. Washington's lieutenants, Tyler was responsible for keeping tabs on William T. Vernon, Roosevelt's pick for register of the U.S. Treasury. For that post, the president had gone outside of Tuskegee circles, in a nod to Washington's opponents. A minister and the president of Kansas's Western University, Vernon was neutral—neither friend nor foe of Washington. He seemed like a safe choice and came with the endorsement of the African Methodist Episcopal (AME) Church, one of black America's oldest and most respected religious denominations. Yet, Vernon's inclusion was a disappointment to Washington, and Roosevelt's other black appointees would hold Vernon at arm's length.

Washington's partnership with Roosevelt definitely benefited the Tuskegee Machine. With regular and direct access to the president, Tuskegee's head consolidated his position as a leader, recognized nationally by both black and white Americans. GOP chiefs gave Washington control over Republican campaign funds earmarked for advertising in black newspapers. This allowed him to exert considerable influence over the black press. He maintained several black reporters on retainer and had enough muscle to silence at least some of his critics.

At the same time that Washington was amassing considerable personal power, those settling into impressive posts in the District of Columbia quickly realized the obstacles they faced in using their positions to fight black poverty, lynching, and Jim Crow. Almost all white administration officials viewed African American federal jobholders as little more than boosters for Roosevelt and the GOP. Most African American appointees found themselves pushing paper at their desks. They were excluded from supervisory positions because whites refused to take orders from black men. Only Ralph Tyler successfully defied the unspoken rule that African Americans were simply figureheads. "He knew how to run his office and never failed to let those over him know it," observed Kelly Miller.

Other factors conspired to not only block but also eliminate African American influence in the federal government. Within a few years, Washington and his associates realized that rather than building up the ranks of African Americans in patronage appointments, Roosevelt was reducing the overall number in both the capital and other parts of the nation. The president cut some positions outright and in others replaced African Americans with whites.

Those who hung on to Washington, D.C., jobs faced increased antagonism and marginalization. Since Reconstruction, African Americans in federal service, despite facing racism on the job, worked side by side with their white counterparts. But during the early years of the twentieth century, a handful of white lower-level federal administrators mandated that black and white employees be segregated. Several government cafeterias limited service to whites only. In one of the Treasury Department's divisions, African Americans were assigned to sit in what one writer has called a "Jim Crow corner." When African American federal workers protested, the White House claimed the president was ignorant of attempts to segregate black employees. Shortly afterward, some, but not all, departments lifted segregationist orders. When Ralph Tyler's white secretary publicly announced she would not serve a black man and demanded a transfer, the White House denied her request, warning all employees against making similar demands. But separate bathrooms and lockers in the Departments of the Interior and the Treasury remained the norm, and African American jobholders continued to experience racial hostility in the workplace.

The truth was that Theodore Roosevelt's overall record on race was far from progressive. In late 1906, two major White House decisions dramatically eroded the president's reputation with black Americans. In September, a riot broke out in Atlanta, and despite pleas from African American leaders, Roosevelt refused to send in federal troops to protect the black population there from violent white mobs. An estimated forty African Americans were killed. In a separate incident a few months later, Roosevelt announced his decision to issue dishonorable discharges to 167 black soldiers who had been accused of inciting a racial disturbance that had resulted in the death of a white man in Brownsville, Texas. The charges against the men were false, and many were veterans with distinguished service records nearing retirement.

As some African Americans grew vocally impatient with the president, Booker T. Washington urged him to deliver a speech that at least condemned the Atlanta riot. Roosevelt did make an address, to Congress. But rather than heeding Washington's advice and defending black citizens, he blamed African Americans for the violence in both Atlanta and Brownsville, asserting the clashes resulted from black "criminality." Furthermore, the president excused lynching, maintaining that it was an understandable white impulse rooted in what he claimed to be a need to protect the virtue of white women. "This message is calculated to do the Negro more harm than any other state paper issued from the White House," Kelly Miller fumed. Hopes that the presidency of Theodore Roosevelt would be transformative were dying and fast.

Facing the federal government's open racism and the reality that even Booker T. Washington had little influence over the president, the core of Roosevelt's black appointees increasingly turned to one another for support. Gray's Café had always been a popular gathering spot for black federal employees, and Ralph Tyler specifically recruited James Cobb, Robert Terrell, John Dancy, R. W. Thompson, and even outsider William Vernon for regular lunches there. Professor Kelly Miller, publisher Calvin Chase, and the venerated P. B. S. Pinchback gladly sat in. Washington, the group's hidden hand, made sure to join them when he was in town.

Monday through Friday at noon, Tyler and his colleagues would trickle into Gray's and order lunch and drinks. While topics ranged widely and included the weather and Gray's much-talked-about terrapin soup, most discussions centered on the needs of African Americans and black appointees' struggles within the federal government. When R. W. Thompson first identified the group as the Black Cabinet in the summer of 1908, he offered the name in jest. Originally, "Le Cabinet Noir" referred to an unpopular and clandestine group established by the French crown in the eighteenth century to secretly suppress political dissidents. For some the label *black* was regarded as offensive—*Negro* and *Afro-American* were the preferred terms. "*The [Washington] Bee* respectfully suggests that they look up the definition and decide among themselves if they wish that appellation to be continued by this correspondent," Thompson wrote in one column, taking a good-natured jab at his colleagues. But reports of the Black Cabinet began appearing in other African American news sources, drawing the attention of African American political watchers. The name stuck.

Black Cabinet members came to be regarded as the stars of Washington, D.C.'s black upper crust, and they began to appear regularly in the society columns of African American newspapers. On Saturday nights, they often gathered for cards, "sans respect for fleeting hours," at the home of attorney William L. Houston, Bill Hastie's uncle, who had founded the first black law firm in the nation's capital. As word of the Black Cabinet spread, gawkers began turning up at Gray's and booking tables just to catch a glimpse of these black political pioneers and Washington power brokers.

That the Black Cabinet emerged publicly in 1908 was probably no coincidence—it was a presidential election year. Early on, Booker T. Washington had begun seeking African American support for William Howard Taft, the Republican nominee handpicked by Roosevelt himself. Taft was hard to sell to black Americans. As secretary of war, he had initiated the dismissal of the Brownsville soldiers. He also supported the disenfranchisement of African American voters in the South, arguing that they were too ignorant to vote. Taft's camp openly courted Lily Whites, and many black political pundits believed that a Taft presidency would only further impede African American campaigns for social justice and equality. The NAACP's W. E. B. Du Bois was so disenchanted that he threw his support behind Democrat William Jennings Bryan. "If . . . you can prefer the party who perpetuated Brownsville, well and good," he wrote in the summer of 1908. "But I shall vote for Bryan."

To protect his position and that of his D.C. surrogates, Washington focused his efforts on getting Taft into the White House. Black Cabinet members hit the campaign trail to support the GOP's nominee. Ralph Tyler was dispatched with kickback for black newspapers. "IS IT TRUE?" teased Calvin Chase's *Washington Bee*, "that Taft, if elected president, will make several big appointments to colored men?" In his syndicated column, R. W. Thompson played up what he could. "He is a friend of the labor element and will poll the bulk of the votes of the workingmen who work with their hands instead of their mouths," he wrote. When the election results were in they showed that Taft had won the presidency with the help of the African American vote. But some wondered: Would black loyalty to the Republicans be rewarded?

On inauguration day in March 1909, a blizzard hit Washington, D.C., and the customary outdoor rites were canceled. Taft and outgoing president Theodore Roosevelt rode together from the White House to the U.S. Capitol through streets drifted high with snow. Inside the Senate chamber, Taft took the oath of office and rather than read his speech, delivered its highlights and then dispatched a courier to release the complete text to the press. When African Americans picked up their newspapers the next day, they discovered that the new president's speech followed nearly perfectly a Lily White line. The time was far overdue for the nation to move past the divisions that had festered since the Civil War, it read. The incoming administration pledged to honor southern self-determination. To African Americans, Taft promised political appointments: "Any recognition of their distinguished men, any appointment to office from among their number, is properly taken as an encouragement and an appreciation of their progress." But Taft qualified his pledge, stating that such positions would only "be pursued when suitable occasion offers." African Americans knew that "suitable" implied that blacks would not be placed in federal posts if whites objected, as Taft knew they would.

Only a few weeks later, black Republican loyalist Douglas Wetmore arrived in Washington seeking a federal job. By chance, as the *Baltimore Afro-American* reported, Wetmore ran into Taft. Attempting to make his case to the president quickly, he boasted that he had the Black Cabinet's endorsement:

"Black what?" the president snapped.

"Black Cabinet," Wetmore stated.

"And who and what is that?" Taft huffed.

The *Afro-American* observed, "The surprising feature of this colloquy is that for the first time it gives evidence of the astounding fact that the President was sadly ignorant of so important an entity as his 'Black Cabinet.'"

Some speculated that the Black Cabinet was on its deathbed. One African American political observer remarked that it did not matter much: black federal appointees had been wholly ineffective—more concerned with personal advancement and their bank accounts than racial progress. An editorial in the *Afro-American* agreed, dismissing the group as not only incompetent but also "imaginary."

Determined to save the Black Cabinet, Washington went directly to Taft. It would be in the White House's best interests, he insisted, to not only maintain but increase black federal appointments. Taft seemed won over and made some promises, but events soon clarified that he had little intention of following Washington's counsel. While the total number of African Americans in federal patronage positions both in Washington, D.C., and the nation had dipped under Roosevelt, it plummeted once Taft took office. This was particularly conspicuous in the South. Washington sent off urgent appeals for Taft to halt the attrition. "I believe in your own time and in your own manner you will do whatever is necessary to let colored people see that you are not inclined to decrease materially the number of Negroes holding office throughout the country," Washington wrote to the president in summer 1909, enclosing a list he titled, "Negroes who have Disappeared from Office." In response, the president advised caution and patience: "The matter of appointments and filling places is a most difficult one to carry out, for reasons that the places are so few and vacancies come so rarely that it is difficult to shape a plan of action."

In early 1910, almost a year into his first term, Taft finally acted. While outside of Washington, D.C., African American federal patronage appointments continued to decline, in the nation's capital many of the officeholders held on. The Tuskegee Machine no doubt sighed with relief when it became clear that Robert Terrell, James Cobb, and Ralph Tyler would stay. Taft replaced William Vernon as register of the Treasury Department with James C. Napier, a black Nashville attorney who was a faithful Tuskegee supporter. Another member of Washington's inner circle, Whitefield McKinlay, a prominent black D.C. realtor, received the post of Georgetown's port collector. Later in the year, Taft made his most publicized appointment, nominating William H. Lewis as an assistant attorney general in the Justice Department. A Bostonian, Lewis was a former collegiate all-American football hero who held a Harvard law degree. After a behind-the-scenes duel with southern senators, Lewis won confirmation and assumed the highest federal appointment ever held by an African American.

Yet Booker T. Washington still had good reason to worry. The president had dismissed Tuskegee loyalist John Dancy from the recorder's office and, in his place, installed Henry Lincoln Johnson. An African American GOP activist and attorney from Georgia, Johnson was cozy with some of Washington's most ardent critics. Additionally, his benefactor was Republican National Committee chair Frank Hitchcock, who had clashed with Ralph Tyler and was a well-known panderer to the Lily Whites. Members of the Black Cabinet distrusted Johnson for his blatant political ambitions. Some believed that he aspired not only to displace Tyler as the Black Cabinet's head but also to unseat Washington as Taft's lead adviser on black America. When Johnson took his seat at Gray's, tension filled the room.

Taft's actions left Kelly Miller deeply disenchanted. Writing in the *Washington Bee* under a *nom de plume*, as "the Sage of the Potomac," he railed at his Black Cabinet colleagues for not being more militant. "Outside of dining on terrapin and old musty ale," he despaired, they had offered "no service" to the race. In 1910, when the group's meetings became increasingly irregular, Miller demanded that they get back to it. "Politically there is a dead calm," he wrote, declaring that black appointees had become "merely figurative." It was time to "resume their talkfest and make a noise as if they figure in the equation."

The *Indianapolis Freeman*, a black weekly, accused Miller of being "grouchy and dyspeptic." But his caustic remarks reflected the frustration felt by many who had become exasperated by the Black Cabinet's inability to challenge the White House's racism. The president seemed to draw closer to Lily Whites, and he dodged pleas for federal intervention against lynching and disenfranchisement. The segregation the Black Cabinet had battled back under Roosevelt began to spread again. The Department of the Interior, determined to separate black and white employees, assigned African Americans to irregular hours and graveyard shifts while allowing white employees to remain on a standard nine-to-five work schedule. In the dining hall there, black employees would be served only at separate tables. African American federal workers watched as they were passed over for hard-earned promotions and received lower pay than white colleagues.

By late 1910, the Black Cabinet decided the federal workplace was one area where its members might be able to wage a successful battle. Ralph Tyler initiated a campaign to lodge complaint after complaint on behalf of black federal employees experiencing discrimination in

D.C. offices. In January 1911, the *Washington Bee* joined in and called for Taft to act directly against the unfair treatment of black employees in federal service. Taft remained silent. With the election year of 1912 approaching, Whitefield McKinlay applied more pressure. He sent Taft a report documenting and protesting numerous incidents of Jim Crowism throughout the federal government. Still the president offered no response.

Nonetheless Taft presumed that black federal appointees would be in his corner for his reelection bid, and he desperately needed them. The presidential race turned into an in-house Republican slugfest. Dissatisfied with Taft's record on conservation and political reform, Theodore Roosevelt announced he would run again for the White House. Panicking, Taft's camp began consolidating delegate support and decided that African Americans were critical to securing the GOP nomination. In early 1912, hoping to lock down the black vote, Taft called five members of the Black Cabinet—Tyler, Lewis, Napier, Johnson, and McKinlay—to the Oval Office.

What would it take, Taft asked, to ensure African American support for his reelection? The Black Cabinet responded bluntly. "Practically all the time last evening was devoted to discussing [Taft's] Southern policy," Ralph Tyler wrote to Booker T. Washington, "which we made plain to him was distasteful to every Negro." Black voters felt betrayed by the president's allegiance to Lily Whites. To win them over, he must declare a dedication to civil rights, restore African Americans to federal posts in the South, and endorse anti-lynching legislation. The Black Cabinet also objected strongly to the discriminatory policies that had crept throughout federal offices. In unison, they warned Taft that they could not credibly campaign for him. Tyler reported to Washington that all of those present "told him that the Negroes could not defend his Southern policy as now carried out." Taft listened, seemed receptive, and asked Tyler to draft a speech on race relations for him to deliver later.

After the meeting, Tyler sent the president a memorandum summarizing the Black Cabinet's recommendations. Over the next couple of months, he drafted two speeches for the president, both crafted so Taft could unequivocally declare his commitment to equality and to protecting the lives of black Americans. Eventually the president responded. "I can't come out with such a speech," he replied coldly to the first one. On the second, the president contemptuously scribbled, "I am not going to say anything on many of the subjects set out. I think it cheeky to ask it."

Finally, in April, Taft made a speech of his own to a black audience at Washington, D.C.'s Metropolitan AME Church. After an introduction by Kelly Miller, Taft rose to weak applause. The president condemned lynching as "disgraceful" but stopped short of supporting federal legislation to outlaw it. He stumbled through with some platitudes but avoided criticizing Jim Crow, disenfranchisement, and the decline of African Americans in federal posts. As he closed, gloom descended in the sanctuary. It was clear: Taft was not going to modify his position on race. "The address here is regarded as a disappointment," reported the *Baltimore Afro-American*.

Yet, as the campaign season heated up, Taft made a misstep that created an opportunity for the Black Cabinet to push back. In February 1912, the president announced the nomination of William C. Hook for a seat on the Supreme Court. As a federal appeals judge, Hook had been unsympathetic to black causes and had upheld segregation in public transportation. The NAACP, the *Washington Bee*, the Black Cabinet, and other African American leaders speedily joined together to block Hook. Eventually, Taft dropped the nomination, and many credited the Black Cabinet for that victory, the press reporting that the group "revolted and told him frankly that . . . no colored man would be found to speak for him in the campaign." African American political watchers regarded Hook's derailed nomination as the crowning achievement of the Black Cabinet of the Taft era. But in exchange for Hook's withdrawal, the Gray's lunch crowd had to hit the road and get the president reelected.

As the GOP's convention finally got underway, there was only faint enthusiasm among African American leaders for Taft's candidacy. To counter growing disgruntlement within the black electorate, Washington dispatched the reliable Tyler to buy positive coverage for Taft in black newspapers. Henry Lincoln Johnson rallied Georgia's black delegates to side with the president on the convention floor, allegedly making payoffs as high as fifty dollars per vote. While using money to capture votes may have been unseemly, it was not unheard of, and it worked. In the end, Taft won the Republican nomination for a second time.

Unwilling to concede, Theodore Roosevelt bolted from the Republicans to organize the Progressive ("Bull Moose") Party. Some African Americans, including former Black Cabinet member John Dancy, followed him out. But much to the dismay of Dancy and other black Roosevelt enthusiasts, when they arrived at the Progressive Party convention, officials refused to seat them, a decision approved by the former president himself. As the election neared, a small faction of African Americans, including W. E. B. Du Bois, decided to back the Democratic challenger, Woodrow Wilson. Rumors in black leadership circles suggested that Wilson had promised to be color-blind in dispensing federal posts and that he would block discriminatory laws. Du Bois did not completely trust reports of Wilson's alleged racial tolerance; after all, Wilson was both a Democrat and Virginian-born. Yet, along with several other black leaders, Du Bois reasoned that the Democratic candidate could not be any worse than Roosevelt or Taft.

As the November election neared, Wilson's support among African Americans, while not broad, became notable. It was the first time a critical mass of black leaders had backed a Democrat for president. In the Republican corner, Taft's African American spokesmen struggled to make the argument for the president's reelection. The *Baltimore Afro-American* noted that on the campaign trail, Black Cabinet members focused on why Roosevelt and Wilson should not be elected more than why Taft deserved a second term. At one stop, Henry Lincoln Johnson predicted disaster if Roosevelt and his Bull Moosers won. "I hope that the race will not be foolish enough to forsake the Republicans this time," he warned in one interview. Yet, the split in the

Republican Party proved lethal, and Woodrow Wilson triumphed. For the first time since Reconstruction, a southern Democrat would occupy the White House.

On November 21, 1912, a few weeks after Wilson's victory, the Black Cabinet gathered at Gray's for what Booker T. Washington declared a "consolation dinner." Tuskegee's leader was preoccupied with business elsewhere but sent a gift of two southern delicacies: gravy-slathered opossum and Alabama sweet potatoes. Gray's supplied oysters on the half shell, hominy, coleslaw, cider, and coffee. Despite the election's disappointing outcome, the evening was merry. All the Tuskegee faithful were there—Lewis, Terrell, Napier, McKinlay, and Cobb. Ralph Tyler served as the master of ceremonies to a crowd that included many of Washington's most prominent African Americans. The *Washington Bee* reported that "all reveled in enjoyment" as Black Cabinet members toasted and roasted each other; barbs were directed at the absent Henry Lincoln Johnson, whom many blamed for splitting the black Republican vote. During the festivities, a bogus telegram arrived. Democrat Wilson, it read, would dump all of the Black Cabinet except Johnson: "[Wilson] feels he owes his election more to Col. Johnson than any other one man." The room roared. But the festivities were bittersweet. All knew that the Black Cabinet was gasping its last breath.

Wilson revealed his true racial attitudes quickly. The White House issued sweeping decrees that segregated most of Washington's federal workplaces. Black employees were isolated, confined to separate offices, or sequestered behind newly erected barriers and curtains. At the D.C. post office, where Robert Weaver's father worked, most black employees arrived one morning to find they had been assigned to desks behind a ten-foot wall of lockers separating them from the rest of the office. Dining areas in most government cafeterias were declared off-limits to African Americans—some allowed black employees to eat in back rooms or kitchens. Lavatories in many federal buildings were designated for either whites or blacks.

Washington was a southern city, and Wilson's support of segregation in the federal government brought to the surface the racism that had historically haunted the district. In the antebellum era, slave markets operated openly in the city's streets. During and after the Civil War, the African American population grew; many black people were drawn to Washington by the democratic symbolism of the nation's capital, federal job opportunities, and the educational excellence of the historically black Howard University. As a result, by 1900, Washington, D.C., had proportionally the largest African American population of any city in the country. The community was robust, with numerous black churches, schools, newspapers, social clubs, theaters, businesses, and activist organizations. Most white-owned businesses located outside the black community refused service to African Americans. Although there were no municipal Jim Crow laws, segregation was customary, and the majority of blacks and whites lived in separate neighborhoods; most African Americans settled in the northwestern area of the city.

Wilson's support of segregation emboldened local white efforts to hasten housing restrictions and other forms of discrimination in private employment and commercial trade. Residential segregation was increasingly institutionalized in the form of restrictive covenants written into property deeds and banning African Americans from purchasing homes in various parts of the city. The district's white population also proposed legislation formalizing Jim Crow throughout the capital, segregating public transportation and prohibiting interracial marriages. While these bills were defeated, the attempt to push them through reflected the tacit permission that Wilson's White House gave white racists to impose white-supremacist control over the city.

Racial violence also increased after Wilson's election. The Washington, D.C., police were known for their brutal treatment of African Americans. Tensions rose in the city when the black population started to grow even more during World War I. Beginning in 1915, African Americans left the South for wartime industrial jobs in northern and midwestern cities. Known as the Great Migration, the surge of African

Americans toward urban areas increased when the United States entered the war in 1917 and continued after the war's end in 1918. Competition for employment and racial animosity led to a summer of violent riots in 1919; one occurred in the District of Columbia. Howard University history professor Carter G. Woodson witnessed the disturbance firsthand as he walked along Pennsylvania Avenue. "There ran by me a Negro yelling for mercy . . . pursued by hundreds of [white] soldiers, sailors, and marines, assisted by men in civilian attire," he recalled. The mob "caught the Negro and deliberately held him as one would a beef for slaughter, and when they had conveniently adjusted him for lynching, they shot him. I heard him groaning in his struggle as I hurried away as fast as I could without running, expecting every moment to be lynched myself."

Few voices within the federal government spoke against the insurgent racism that came to dominate the city once Wilson took office. After the president was inaugurated, the White House swiftly eliminated as many African Americans in government jobs as possible. Civil service regulations protected some black workers, but Wilson staffers rammed through new procedures that gravely disadvantaged African American applicants for new positions. Job seekers were now required to submit photographs, making them identifiable by race. The administration also quickly cleared out African Americans already working in government patronage posts. Robert Terrell and James Cobb escaped the ax, but within weeks of Wilson taking office, most Black Cabinet members received termination notices. Some believed that D.C. recorder of deeds Henry Lincoln Johnson might survive. But eventually he was also asked to step down, and for the first time since Frederick Douglass accepted the post in 1881, the recorder's position went to a white man.

Over in the Department of the Navy, Ralph Tyler, who had held on, grew increasingly furious as he watched his colleagues being pushed out and Jim Crow taking over. In the spring of 1913, Tyler sent the president a letter stridently protesting the increase in barefaced inequalities spreading throughout the government: "As an American citizen first, and secondly as a Negro, and finally as an official serving this government, I appeal to you, as President of these United States, as president of all the people, to discourage the segregation of Negro employees of this government." Tyler insisted that it was time for Wilson to step up and denounce "foul play" and replace it with "fair play." His objections went unanswered. By summer Tyler had reached the limits of his patience and, through a friend, leaked his letter to the black press. It ran verbatim in the widely circulated *New York Age*.

Within days, Ralph W. Tyler was sent packing.

One night in June 1913, Kelly Miller stopped in at Gray's Café for dinner. "I peeped in the room where the Black Cabinet used to hold its daily sessions," he wrote. "There wasn't even a reminder of those has-beens. The room that once knew them knows them no longer." Most former Black Cabinet members had already left town—they were now "scattered to the four winds." The *Washington Bee* waxed sentimental. "For the Black Cabinet," read one editorial, "here's rosemary—that's for remembrance."

By 1915 the Black Cabinet's patron, Booker T. Washington, was dead. A year later, Wilson won a second term. Kelly Miller lamented: "Well, there will be no resurrection of the Black Cabinet."

Miller was right—for a time. The era of the first Black Cabinet had ended. For a brief moment, in 1920, hope for its revival rose. The Republicans, their wounds mostly healed, retook the White House with their candidate Warren G. Harding. Only a few weeks after the election, Kelly Miller announced with some confidence that the Black Cabinet was about to be reborn. Ralph Tyler, long exiled from Washington, D.C., agreed that "the famine" of the Wilson era was over.

But shortly after Harding took office, it became apparent that the reunified Republican Party had gladly collected black votes with little intention of offering anything in return. Right away, white Republican leaders drastically cut the size of southern delegations, which often included African Americans, to national conventions. Serving as representatives to local, state, and national GOP meetings had been the last remaining opportunity for disenfranchised southern blacks to participate in the electoral process. The move was a major triumph for the Lily Whites and almost completely eradicated black southerners from American politics.

The crisis for black Americans only worsened throughout the 1920s with the emergence of a new Republicanism based on a philosophy of antireform and anti–governmental regulation. Beginning with Harding and extending into the presidencies of Calvin Coolidge and Herbert Hoover, the White House focused on pro-business policies that created a financial boom. But it was a surface prosperity that left behind many economically vulnerable populations, including African Americans. And in terms of race, lily-whitism echoed through the GOP's policies and rhetoric. In a Birmingham, Alabama, speech in 1921, President Harding endorsed Jim Crow laws, stating that "racial amalgamation, there cannot be." Additionally, black federal appointments, already drastically reduced in number, continued to disappear. Federal and diplomatic positions that had traditionally been doled out to African Americans went to white Republicans. More civil service jobs went to whites, and even more federal office spaces became segregated. The GOP presidents of the 1920s also ignored pleas for equal rights and refused to support anti-lynching legislation. The Ku Klux Klan, which had gone dormant after the U.S. government abandoned Reconstruction in the 1870s, experienced a rebirth in 1915, continuing through the 1920s. This time the organization went national. While its targets included anyone who was not white, Anglo-Saxon, and Protestant, in many areas African Americans remained the main focus of the Klan's campaigns of harassment, discrimination, and murder. Although Harding condemned the KKK, he and his successors declined to use federal power to curtail the Klan's terrorist activities.

The party presumed that, in place of political posts and social policies promoting equality, it could still ensure African American support by conjuring up the ghost of Lincoln or, in some cases, purchasing it for the right amount of cash. The *Indianapolis Freeman* observed that in the 1920s the Republicans came to realize that while paying for black votes was "expensive," it was also "indispensable." The irony of it all, the paper pointed out, was that buying African American allegiance was unnecessary; the Democrats, the party favored by the many members of the KKK, remained so brazenly hostile it seemed unthinkable that they might ever attract African American supporters.

Yet, as the Roaring Twenties came to an end, major transformations shook the American economy and politics. With the stock market crash in 1929 and the onset of the Great Depression, economic turmoil strangled the entire country. President Herbert Hoover, who was just over six months into his term, seemed at a loss as to how to remedy it. Republican policies of laissez-faire economics and Hoover's refusal to support federal assistance to the poor and unemployed hurt vast sectors of American society. As jobs disappeared, Americans lost their homes and farms. In some places, they starved. Tent cities—called Hoover-villes, as a rebuke to the president—filled with the homeless sprang up on the edges of urban centers. Soup kitchens and breadlines spread nationwide. Yet Hoover claimed that federal intervention would inhibit recovery, undermine democracy, and threaten individualism. Despite worsening conditions, the president seemed deaf to cries for help.

As the Depression deepened, the African American populace, which historically had existed in a state of economic despair, sank into even more desperate poverty. Help came only through private charities or local and state governments, which favored whites and turned African Americans away. In the cities, thousands of African American families were packed into overcrowded housing. Sharecroppers saw the price of agricultural goods plummet; their debts piled higher, and their ability to eke out a living evaporated. "To supplement our scanty rations, we take our buckets and roam the hillsides for berries, nuts, or wild greens; sometimes we fish in the creeks, at other times our black women tramp the fields looking for bits of firewood, piling their aprons high, coming back to our cabins slowly, like laden donkeys," wrote author Richard Wright. "When Queen Cotton dies . . . how many of us will die with her?"

Hoover's administration underscored the tacit acceptance of racism with an avalanche of insults. The White House approved a plan to segregate World War I African American Gold Star mothers during a state-sponsored visit to France. The War Department demoted two black cavalry units to noncombatant status, reclassifying them as military servants. By nominating Judge John J. Parker, an aggressive foe of black suffrage, to the Supreme Court, Hoover signaled his opposition to civil rights and his political loyalty to Lily Whites. The president repeatedly declined to be photographed with African Americans. Kelly Miller stridently condemned Hoover: "During his whole public career he has never uttered one word concerning the Negro as a separate entity nor engaged to deal with his separate problems as such."

By 1932, Miller was not alone in his disgust with Hoover. With the economy careening downward, many Americans had lost patience with the president and his administration. The alienation was especially keen among African Americans; they had seen the party of Lincoln turn its back on them. With almost no voice left in Washington, with starvation and mass destitution spreading throughout the black community, African Americans watched the bridges of hope wash away. It was a great slide downward from what Ralph Tyler identified as "the halcyon years" of the first Black Cabinet. With a Republican Party dominated by white racism and operating under the assumption that African American voters would remain forever in its pocket, the Black Cabinet was now only a romanticized and distant memory.

In 1932, as the country slid deeper into an economic abyss, a presidential race loomed ahead. By this time, Mary McLeod Bethune's women's boarding school in Daytona Beach had been transformed into the coeducational Bethune-Cookman College. While the Great Depression placed Bethune's institution in fiscal jeopardy, she had emerged as a national figure. Named by reformer Ida Tarbell as one of America's fifty most important women, Bethune was "a woman to be proud of." As the embattled Herbert Hoover struggled to charge up his Republican base, Bethune weighed her options. She knew her endorsement could contribute mightily to Hoover's reelection efforts with black voters.

At the beginning of the 1932 presidential campaign, Robert Vann sat pensively on the sidelines, contemplating where to throw his support. Over the years, he had built a thriving law practice and was celebrated for saving eighty African American men from the death penalty. He had become editor of the *Pittsburgh Courier* in 1910 and transformed it into one of the nation's leading African American newspapers. Increasing in prominence in the GOP, he had used the *Courier* to whip up support for GOP candidates. But Republicans had repeatedly passed him over for patronage positions, and he was simmering over their broken promises.

By 1932, Al Smith had made his way to Washington, D.C., where he enrolled in Howard University, got married, and pursued his degree while holding down a job at the post office. That spring, after twelve years at Howard, he completed a bachelor's degree in liberal arts. To celebrate, he quit his job, borrowed a car, and headed to Los Angeles to attend the Olympic Games, where he met track stars Jesse Owens and Ralph Metcalfe. At summer's end, he returned to Washington and began substitute teaching. Smith was only an observer of the presidential contest. As a D.C. resident, he was prohibited from voting in national elections because the District of Columbia was not a state.

The same applied to William Hastie, who now also called the capital home. His family moved there in 1916, when his father was transferred to the D.C. pension office. By 1932, Hastie, who held a doctorate in jurisprudence from Harvard, was a man of considerable note. A top student in his law class, Hastie had served as an editor of the prestigious *Harvard Law Review*. Deeply committed to civil rights, he became active in Washington's NAACP and began practicing law in the firm run by his uncle William Houston and his older cousin Charles H. Houston. Hastie had joined the faculty of Howard University's School of Law, where he was mentoring future Supreme Court justice Thurgood Marshall.

After moving to Washington, D.C., in 1916, Hastie had formed a fast friendship with Robert Weaver. At Harvard the two had lived in the same boardinghouse and regularly played poker together. While working on his dissertation, Weaver had accepted a faculty position at North Carolina Agriculture and Technical (A&T) College in Greensboro. But he had little passion for teaching there and abhorred the segregation of the South. So in the fall of 1932, he took a leave of absence and headed back to Cambridge to work on his thesis. Weaver was the scholarly type and poured himself into his studies. The presidential race, he remarked later, seemed nearly irrelevant to him. And his permanent address was the District of Columbia, so he too could not vote.

By 1932, many of the original members of the first Black Cabinet were dead. But two new generations of leaders, represented by the older Bethune and Vann on the one side and the younger Smith, Hastie, and Weaver on the other, had begun their rise. And in 1918 the *Topeka Plaindealer* had predicted their future. "We long to see the return of the 'Black Cabinet' in Washington," the paper remarked. "It's on furlough but will be back someday. And when it does, it will be a young one too. We believe in young blood."

Chapter Two

Turning the Picture of Lincoln to the Wall

EVA DEBOE Jones earned her living as a manicurist doing white women's nails. On workdays she journeyed from her black Pittsburgh neighborhood to the exclusive estates of some of the city's wealthiest white families. Jones and her husband, William, a waiter in a local restaurant, lived modestly. But she was an excellent manicurist and in high demand with members of white society's wealthy elite. Her clients recalled her as "pleasant," "sensible," and very precise.

Jones had worked hard all of her life. Born in 1877 in a rural area of Wilson County, Tennessee, she had been sent north as a child to live with relatives in Pittsburgh. Soon after arriving, she was hired as a servant in the home of George W. Guthrie, a prominent local attorney and politician. Eventually, she became a personal maid to Guthrie's wife, who taught her manicuring. Jones was so talented that other Guthrie family members and friends began seeking her services. By 1900, she had established her own business, traveling a circuit of white beauty shops and private homes. A proud and independent woman, she was active in the Maids and Butlers Club, a social and political organization for Pittsburgh's domestic workers. Like most African American voters, Eva DeBoe Jones was a registered Republican.

But by the 1930s, Jones had grown disillusioned with the GOP. When the Great Depression hit Pittsburgh, her neighborhood felt it especially acutely. Before the stock market crash, Pittsburgh's black residents, like other African Americans in cities around the nation, lived in substandard housing in segregated and overcrowded communities. Most African Americans in northern and midwestern cities like Pittsburgh had arrived from the South during the Great Migration, which had begun in 1915 and continued until 1930. During that period more than one and a half million African Americans left the South looking for a better life, even though the job boom of World War I had ended by 1919. The financial meltdown of the late 1920s halted this first Great Migration and also intensified African American poverty. Black unemployment in the Steel City, averaging almost 40 percent, ran significantly higher than white unemployment. African Americans there struggled to survive by any means. Some resorted to hunting in backwoods or fishing in rivers polluted by industrial waste. Others sifted through city dumps for coal to keep warm and for bottles and cans to sell. Despite Hoover's insistence that relief be locally based, private charities and city governments could do little to help; they were also cash-strapped. The president's stubborn refusal to use federal aid to help the poor and homeless left the impression that the White House and the Republicans were indifferent to the suffering.

Yet Jones was discouraged with her party for reasons that went beyond the economy. Her disillusionment arose from the GOP's conduct during the election of 1928. The party had centered its campaign against the Irish Catholic New York Democrat Alfred Emanuel "Al" Smith (no relation to the Black Cabinet member) on allegations that if he were elected, the country would be ruled by the Pope. In Jones's view, the Republicans' visceral and intolerant political rhetoric sprang from the same well of bigotry that fueled white persecution of African Americans. She had proudly cast her vote for Smith, who went down in a decisive defeat to Hoover. Her dissatisfaction with the GOP continued to intensify. In 1932, she declared open support for the Democratic governor of New York, Franklin Delano Roosevelt. He promised a New Deal for the American people, and his buoyant optimism (his campaign song was "Happy Days Are Here Again") stood starkly against Hoover's stubborn aloofness.

One summer day, as the presidential campaigns geared up, Eva DeBoe Jones made her rounds in eastern Pittsburgh's affluent Shadyside neighborhood. She had an appointment with Emma Guffey Miller, who resided in a stately two-story brick mansion with three live-in servants. Miller's family had investments in oil and coal, and Emma Miller was politically well connected. She was one of Jones's few Democratic customers, and her brother was Pennsylvania's mighty political boss, Joe Guffey.

When Jones arrived, she unpacked her nail files, clippers, cream, and polish and took Miller's hand in hers. They chatted. Jones waited for the right moment. When it came, she said, "Mrs. Miller, Mr. Vann'd like to meet your brother."

Emma Guffey Miller was stunned.

It was well known that Robert Vann was a mover and shaker among black Republicans. While the GOP leadership had repeatedly snubbed him for appointments, it was assumed that he would continue to deliver votes—and that the Democrats were irredeemable in the eyes of African Americans. Surely the Republicans would not want to lose the support of Vann's robust *Pittsburgh Courier*, which by the 1930s was one of the nation's most influential black newspapers. A man of rock-solid confidence, Vann was a respected figure within Pittsburgh's African American community. Successful at business and in his law practice, he had a hand in almost all aspects of black Pittsburgh—its politics, activist causes, and social affairs. Vann was personally ambitious, but he viewed as his life's calling the battle for the rights of African American people. He maintained that the best route for change was through the American political system. To further that end, he organized Pittsburgh's Butlers and Maids Club (where he met Eva DeBoe Jones), which served as his base for mobilizing the black vote.

Many knew Vann's personal story of hard toil and success; it was heralded as a classic rags-to-riches tale. That a black man born in the small southern town of Ahoskie, North Carolina, in 1879 would rise to become prominent and powerful, even in the African American community, was remarkable. Whether or not his mother, Lucy Peoples, had been enslaved was unclear, but his grandparents certainly had been. Raised by his single mother, who was a domestic worker, Vann never spoke of his father. But because he was light-skinned and had straight hair, many speculated he was the son of a white man. He did admit that his mother had named him for one of her white employers, who hailed from a respected local family; she had hoped that tie would help her son advance in the world. A few friends urged Vann to get ahead by passing, if not as a white man then as a Native American. He consistently and vehemently rejected even the thought.

Robert Vann's early life was spent following his mother as she moved among plantations, cooking and cleaning for white families. While he often worked as a houseboy and sometimes in the fields, he also was able to attend school during parts of the year. Lucy Peoples reared her son strictly, applying a switch for bad behavior and marching him to the Baptist church on Sundays. By the time Vann reached the age of twelve, his mother had taken a husband. Vann's stepfather, whom he despised, hired him out as a farmhand. The young Vann plowed, tended, and picked tobacco and cotton. But rather than accept a life of hard manual labor, he aspired to get as much education as possible. By age sixteen, he had saved enough of his own earnings to enroll at a residential high school for a few months. To cut boarding costs, each weekend he walked twenty-two miles, round-trip, to his home and back. During one of these treks, a fierce winter storm hit the area, and Vann braved the walk back to school. Soaked to the skin, freezing, and already ill, he stumbled into a classroom and fainted. The school's principal gave the determined young Vann a job so he could pay to board through the weekends.

Despite his disadvantages, Vann proved himself a promising scholar and was admitted to Richmond's Virginia Union University. Although drawn more to the social and political life of the campus than to his studies, Vann still demonstrated an incredible drive for education. "Once having found what he is best suited for," Vann later wrote, "the individual should pursue aggressively his goal. Opportunity would then almost inevitably come his way." Vann fit in nicely at Virginia Union and began courting a local woman. He was a frequent visitor at the home of Professor Joseph E. Jones, a star faculty member who chaired the Department of Homiletics and Greek Studies. Jones's home was a gathering place for conversation and debate among Richmond's black activists and intellectuals. Robert Vann developed a deep admiration for Professor Jones and a fast friendship with his son, Eugene Kinckle Jones.

But determined to succeed at all costs, when he got an opportunity to go north to complete college, Vann broke off his engagement to his Richmond sweetheart, bid goodbye to the Joneses, and headed to Pittsburgh.

In 1903, Vann enrolled at the University of Pittsburgh, where he finished his bachelor's degree and then continued on at the university's law school. Those who knew Vann remembered him as tireless, strait-laced (he did not drink and only rarely accepted a cigar), persuasive, and completely focused. Some described him as a "good fellow"—the friendly, talkative sort. Others thought him thoroughly opportunistic, portraying him as "shrewd and calculating."

Although Vann pursued law school with diligence, his passion was politics. As soon as he arrived in Pittsburgh, he registered to vote, an opportunity denied to him in the South. He joined the Republican Party and, in 1906, threw himself into a local political campaign, participating in rallies, grassroots meetings, and parades. He was hooked and subsequently maneuvered himself into positions of increasing influence within the state GOP, developing into a savvy political operative. Seemingly inexhaustible, he traveled miles and miles, making speeches on behalf of Republican candidates and the party.

Despite receiving assurances that he would be rewarded for his fidelity to the party, Vann was repeatedly passed over for choice patronage posts. In 1928, he continued to support the Republicans, but only halfheartedly. After the election, the party skipped over him again—this time GOP insiders told him it was punishment for his running ads for both the Democratic and the Republican candidates in the *Pittsburgh Courier*. Vann's temper flared. "I'll see you in 1932," he snorted at one GOP handler. As that election neared, the party eyed him warily. A confidential internal Republican National Committee (RNC) report described his newspaper as "disloyal and bitter."

With a nudge from Dr. Joseph Johnson, an African American lifelong Democrat who had served as Woodrow Wilson's ambassador to Liberia, Vann decided to approach the Roosevelt camp. Knowing that political boss Joe Guffey opposed investing resources and energy in the black vote, Vann had asked Eva DeBoe Jones to be his go-between, wagering her close connection to Emma Guffey Miller might open doors.

It did. Miller was elated at the possibility that Vann might desert the GOP. Over the previous decade, she had emerged as a major player in the Democratic Party. A leader in the women's suffrage movement, Miller had worked for passage of the Nineteenth Amendment, which in 1920 gave women the right to vote in national elections. She denounced the KKK and supported a number of reform causes, including education and public aid for the poor. She had seconded Franklin D. Roosevelt's nomination at the 1932 Democratic National Convention. Although she enjoyed all the privileges of the upper class and had graduated from Bryn Mawr, she could be tough and frank, and she liked her whiskey nearly straight. Miller was eager to recruit Vann for the Democrats as quickly as possible. Nevertheless, her brother initially rejected even the idea of meeting the *Courier*'s editor. "You can't take the colored vote away from the Republicans, Emma," Joe Guffey contended. "You've got to have money to get the colored vote and we haven't a cent to spare in this campaign."

Emma Guffey Miller refused to hear the word *no*. She continued to pressure her brother until he gave in.

In August 1932, Joe Guffey arrived at his sister's house to meet Vann. After introductions, the *Courier*'s editor got right to the point.

For seventy years, he declared, Republicans had taken advantage of the black vote. The GOP had arrogantly assumed that vote would be forever theirs and had never made a sincere effort at improving African American lives. Vann's fiery and open resentment surprised the Democratic Party boss. What would it take, Guffey asked, for the Democrats to win the publisher's support for their candidate? Vann had his answer ready. First, he wanted a position of influence within the campaign. Second, should Roosevelt win, he wanted a Washington, D.C., appointment, and a prestigious one at that.

Hungrily eyeing a choice opportunity, Guffey now had to convince James A. (Jim) Farley, Roosevelt's campaign manager, and Louis McHenry Howe, Roosevelt's closest adviser, that the African American vote was up for grabs. Farley and Howe resisted—successfully attracting black voters to the Democrats was a long shot, they argued, and the campaign was on a shoestring budget. Guffey persisted: African Americans had been brutally impacted by the Depression, and the Republicans appeared completely callous to their suffering. The GOP could not now, for any price, he contended, buy the black vote. Although not entirely convinced, Farley and Howe did agree to establish a "Negro division" and selected Dr. Joseph Johnson to lead it. Kicking in $10,000 of his own to fund it, Johnson created four regional subdivisions charged with targeting precincts that had substantial black voting blocs. Vann received an appointment as the leader of the Democrats' national African American publicity efforts. Then Guffey and Vann hatched a plan for the newsman to make a very public defection from the Republican Party as the first step in a full-scale effort to bring African Americans into FDR's camp.

As a journalist, Vann knew exactly how to spin it.

On Saturday, September 11, 1932, the African American community of Cleveland, Ohio, packed the Saint James African Methodist Episcopal Church to hear the famous Robert Vann deliver a speech entitled "The Patriot and the Partisan." Citizens' highest call, he told the audience, was to love and protect their country—to put patriotism ahead of "blind" partisanship. It was time for African Americans to wake up and take up their patriotic duty. "The Republican Party under Harding absolutely deserted us. The Republican Party under Mr. Coolidge was a lifeless, voiceless thing. The Republican Party under Mr. Hoover has been the saddest failure known to political history," he thundered. "The only true gauge by which to judge an individual or a party or a government is not by what is proclaimed or promised, but by what is done." Vann charged that the Republicans had been complicit in erasing many of the gains made by black citizens just after emancipation. No longer could the party presume it would receive unearned African American votes by attempting to cash in on the purported achievements of the long-dead Abraham Lincoln. "I see millions of Negroes turning the picture of Lincoln to the wall. This year I see Negroes voting a Democratic ticket," Vann announced. "I, for one, shall join the ranks of this new army of fearless, courageous, patriotic Negroes who know the difference between blind partisanism and patriotism."

Across the nation, headlines in black newspapers reported Robert Vann's defection to the Roosevelt camp, featuring quotations from his speech. Throughout the fall of 1932, he recited "The Patriot and the Partisan" at various stops. Operatives on both sides viewed it as a brilliant piece of media manipulation.

Attempts to convince African Americans that the Republicans had betrayed them were not enough. Black voters also had to be persuaded to cast their lot with the Democrats, the party of the white South and the old Confederacy. This meant that strategists had to demonstrate that Democrats had undergone a change of heart on the issue of race. To that end, the Democratic National Committee (DNC) announced the appointment of what the black press called "the Big Four." It included eleventh-hour convert Robert Vann, Democratic stalwart Joseph Johnson, and two other African American party regulars: William J. Thompkins, a Missouri physician and newspaper publisher, and Julian Rainey, a high-powered attorney for Boston's public transportation department. Collectively the group cut an image of distinction and accomplishment. The party sent out publicity blasts as members of the Big Four hit the campaign trail.

The idea of using these four front men to promote FDR and the Democrats was the brainchild of Manuel Roque, an engineer turned journalist. Of Afro-Cuban heritage, Roque had migrated to the United States in 1921 to attend college. He later settled in Indiana, where he became immersed in that state's Democratic Party circles. Multilingual (he spoke five languages), Roque was an inspiring speaker and gifted writer. In the fall of 1932, he began churning out articles and press releases in an effort to promote the Big Four as a sign of new things to come from the Democrats. Not only did the black press run his stories, the Big Four made the pages of the *New York Times*. While the Big Four was hardly a Black Cabinet, its organization intimated that Roosevelt, if elected, would assemble a team of African American advisers.

One of the biggest hurdles the Democrats faced was selling the party's presidential ticket to the black electorate. As governor of New York, Roosevelt had a troubling record on race. He had remained mum on civil rights and had done very little to ameliorate black poverty in his state. Although born and bred in New York, FDR spent considerable time at his Warm Springs, Georgia, vacation home, complete with a twelve-hundred-acre farm and a black household staff. Roosevelt was regarded by some (and regarded himself) as an "adopted son" of the South. As a result, his New Deal for the forgotten man rang suspiciously disingenuous to African Americans.

Roosevelt's choice of Texas congressman and Speaker of the House John Nance Garner as his running mate only underscored the Democrats' lack of understanding of African American concerns. Unlike Roosevelt, whose racial attitudes were cloaked in his hushed neglect and southern fantasies, Garner aggressively used his power to extend discrimination and protect white supremacy. As an influential member of the South's congressional delegation, Garner had blocked anti-lynching legislation and opposed civil rights policies. He had also supported poll taxes. Roosevelt chose Garner specifically to court the white South, and that decision alarmed African Americans.

But Robert Vann had hired Manuel Roque as the *Pittsburgh Courier's* lead political correspondent and, in October 1932, dispatched him to Washington for an exclusive interview with the Democratic vice presidential hopeful. In a feature-length article, Roque profiled what he claimed was the true John Nance Garner. There was "nothing to be afraid of," he assured black readers: the Speaker was "a man whose tenderness of heart is only matched by the resoluteness of his stalwart spirit." In fact, Garner was, according to Rogue, a friend of the African American community and supporter of civil rights. "I believe in equal opportunity for every American citizen, regardless of race," the powerful Texan reportedly stated. The vice presidential candidate was described as direct, honest, and "the last of the log cabin tribe," an heir to Lincoln. Roque echoed Vann's insistence that it was time for a switch. "For most of us, this is our first Democratic vote," he wrote. "But we know it is time for a change and beg members of our race to vote for him."

Anxiety rapidly set in among Republicans as the Democrats intensified their efforts to grab black votes. In the final weeks of the presidential race, the RNC redirected resources toward a last-ditch effort to court African Americans for Hoover. Journalistic partisanship was not uncommon in this era, and the GOP diverted some funds to black newspaper publishers in hope that they would redouble positive coverage for Hoover. Salaries and travel stipends went to influential African American Republicans to finance their efforts to get out the black vote, which Republicans assumed would be loyal to the party. The GOP also announced it had convened its own special black advisory committee. A number of prominent black Republicans were wined and dined at a planning session where the president made a special appearance. In early October, Hoover also invited one hundred black Republicans to the White House for a conference. They emerged warmly endorsing the president. A photographer snapped a picture of Hoover with the black delegates on the White House lawn. It was reportedly the only photograph taken of Hoover with African Americans during his years in office. The RNC reprinted and circulated it with a title that unashamedly borrowed from FDR's campaign. PRESIDENT HOOVER OFFERS NEW DEAL TO COLORED RACE, it declared.

Fanning out, prominent black Republicans worked feverishly to rally the ranks. Mary Church Terrell, the widow of the first Black Cabinet's Robert H. Terrell, poured herself into the campaign. She wrote to Mary McLeod Bethune, urging her to release a public statement backing the Republican ticket. Terrell had reason to worry about the celebrated educator's allegiances. Bethune's ties to the Democratic candidate's wife, Eleanor Roosevelt, and his mother, Sara Delano Roosevelt, were no secret. The three had first met in 1927, when Eleanor Roosevelt invited Bethune, the sole African American attendee, to a national meeting of women's club leaders held in her mother-in-law's New York home. When lunch was served, the white delegates made it clear that they would refuse to sit with Bethune. Aghast at the rudeness, Sara Delano Roosevelt guided Bethune, arm in arm, to sit with her and Eleanor. Bethune admired both Roosevelt women for their kindness and defiance of white racist customs. Never passing up an opportunity to advance her causes and her school, she subsequently eagerly cultivated ties to both women.

In Daytona Beach, where Bethune-Cookman College stood, Mary McLeod Bethune was a registered Republican and a staunch supporter of the GOP. (Despite being disenfranchised in other parts of the South, African Americans had preserved their right to vote in Daytona Beach.) And her devotion to the party of Lincoln had paid off. In the mid-1920s, President Calvin Coolidge had appointed her to the national Commission on Child Welfare, and in 1928, she had enthusiastically endorsed his successor, Hoover. During that presidential race, she had even served as Florida's statewide chair of the Republican Colored Voters League. Her reports from the field were glowing: "Florida Negroes are standing solid for the GOP. Men are immovable; women are doing their part."

Under Hoover, Bethune retained her seat on the child welfare commission. In the fall of 1930, he invited her to the White House to attend a national conference on children's health and education. While she was thrilled to receive the invitation, its hastiness—the event was just a few days away—left her "slightly appalled."

She immediately caught a train to New York. She traveled for hours in a run-down, segregated Jim Crow car. As was the custom, when the train crossed the Mason-Dixon Line, she joined other black passengers and moved forward to take a seat in the tidy and comfortable coach section where whites rode. Arriving in Manhattan, she headed to the home of Elizabeth Frothingham, a wealthy white socialite and Bethune-Cookman supporter. With access to the city's most exclusive boutiques—which all refused service to African American women—Frothingham had a ready selection of dresses, hats, shoes, gloves, and other accessories appropriate for a White House visit. Bethune studied them carefully. A dress made of black velvet would do, she decided. It would convey gravity and taste. She added a fur scarf to affect a look of accomplishment.

Then she was off, rushing to board a train headed south for the District of Columbia. Arriving early in the morning on the day of the conference, she hailed a cab at Washington's Union Station. Looking out the window as she sped to the White House, she felt "excited at being in the citadel of her country."

The taxi left Bethune at the White House portico. With her invitation in hand, as she crossed the executive mansion's well-manicured grounds, headed toward the East Wing entrance, she heard a white groundskeeper call out: "Hey there, Auntie, where y'all think you're going?" Bethune claimed she stopped, walked over to him, studied his face, and then answered, "I don't recognize you. Which one of my sister's children are you?" She then marched confidently into the White House, a place where, outside of the black domestic staff, African Americans were rarely admitted.

Bethune would recount her first visit to the White House many times over the years. While she regarded it with pride, she never let listeners forget the reality of what it meant to be a black woman in a nation dominated by white men and white racism. She also proclaimed her fearless determination to resist discrimination.

The election of 1932 put Mary McLeod Bethune in a bind. Caught between Hoover and Roosevelt, she certainly did not want to alienate either camp. But as a national African American leader at a time when the black populace suffered so intensely, she could not remain neutral. Late in the campaign cycle, she decided to lend the full force of her celebrity in support of Hoover. The GOP highlighted her endorsement by publicizing her appointment by President Coolidge to the Commission on Child Welfare and by President Hoover to a committee planning a memorial building that would celebrate African American accomplishments. "I want you to know that I am doing all that I possibly can for our party," Bethune wrote to Mary Church Terrell shortly before election day.

While a Hoover supporter, Bethune carefully sidestepped criticism of Roosevelt and focused on his running mate's tremendous shortcomings. "She predicted calamity if John Garner of Texas were elected Vice President of the U.S.," reported the *Baltimore Afro-American*. Garner's hostile record on civil rights was inexcusable. "I am using my influence in every section I touch," she assured Terrell. "I feel confident that the best efforts will bring forth the best results."

Despite the determined labor of black Republicans like Bethune, Herbert Hoover lost badly to Franklin Delano Roosevelt in the November election. The popular vote went decidedly to Roosevelt, who netted 57.4 percent to Hoover's 39.7 percent; the New York governor won an electoral college landslide, taking forty-six out of forty-eight states. The stunning results testified to the widespread dissatisfaction of Americans from all backgrounds with Hoover and the Republican Party's policies. "The country was voting a 'national grouch' against three years of business stagnation, against farm foreclosures, bank failures, unemployment and the Republican argument that 'things could have been worse,'" remarked the *New York Times*. Roosevelt resonated with many Americans. While he had come from wealth and privilege, he had conquered his own challenge; in the 1920s he had survived a nearly fatal case of polio that had left him paralyzed below the waist. Americans were unaware that the president was wheelchair-bound; all they saw was a robust and exuberant leader. His can-do attitude and optimism brought encouragement and comfort to those suffering during the Great Depression. These traits compelled a sizable number of Republicans to abandon the GOP and support FDR.

Yet, for Robert Vann, his Big Four colleagues, and some Democratic Party bosses, the question was: How many of those crossovers were African Americans?

Just how many African Americans contributed to Roosevelt's win was hard to get an exact fix on. Determining black voting trends was tricky business. Most election watchers were interested in tracking votes by party and region but not by ethnicity and race. The numbers in the South were clear; most African Americans had been disenfranchised below the Mason-Dixon Line. But in the North, Midwest, and the West, black voting patterns could be estimated only by examining the results in predominantly African American precincts. While early on, many in the black press declared that African Americans had forsaken Hoover for Roosevelt, later others thought there was not really much change.

Still, several commentators agreed that the Democratic National Committee's effort to reach out to black voters in 1932 was meaningful, if not entirely successful. While FDR's campaign seemingly failed to draw a flood of black votes, it did prove that a significant proportion of black Republicans were ready to support a Democrat. Just before the election, the head of the Associated Negro Press wire service, Claude Barnett, surveyed a sampling of black leaders on their opinions of both parties and President Hoover. Most responded that they were loyal Republicans but intended to vote for Roosevelt. One of the few surviving members of Taft's Black Cabinet, James Napier, explained that he remained a Republican because, in his view, the GOP was "the only organization that has ever done or accomplished anything for the advancement of the Negro." Yet for this election he supported the Roosevelt ticket, because "President Hoover has done nothing in a political way to raise the standard of Negro citizenship in this country but on the other hand he has subscribed to the policy of white supremacy in all of his dealings with the Negro."

Furthermore, Democratic handlers realized that while blacks had not crossed over at the same rate as other constituencies, a significant surge had still taken place in regions of critical influence. Although a few estimates indicated that in some areas Hoover netted more black votes than he had in 1928, the numbers also showed that Roosevelt made impressive gains among African Americans in Pittsburgh, New York, Indianapolis, Kansas City, and Saint Louis. Many thought such pronouncements were premature, but some analysts heralded the end of the Republican monopoly over the black ballot. "For the first time in a great national election there was marked dissention in the ranks of the colored voters," observed an editorial in Kansas City's *Plaindealer*. "The Negro voter could not be made to forget what he considered the studied indifference of the President and his advisers and the impressive list of the administration's definite sins of commission."

Once the black press had declared that African Americans played a significant role in the Roosevelt win, the real numbers became immaterial. "Negro Ballot Seen as Key to Victory," read the headline in Harlem's nationally circulated *New York Amsterdam News*. African American journalists sensed a swing in black votes and, by documenting and magnifying it, elevated its importance. Writing in the *Journal of Negro Life*, white journalist Arthur B. Krock labeled the shift in the African American electorate as "a splendid revolt."

Krock also warned against interpreting the trend as the beginning of a permanent migration of African Americans out of the Republican Party. Rather, he speculated, it represented a shift toward independent voting. Whether or not he realized it, Krock had stumbled upon a strategy advocated for years by Kelly Miller (a member of the first Black

Cabinet) and several other African American leaders. They had come to believe that if black voters broke from the GOP and helped seat a Democrat during a major election, white politicians on both sides would be forced to recognize the power of the black ballot. This would compel the parties not just to court African Americans but to work toward remedying the wrongs suffered by black citizens to keep them in the fold. As swing voters, the black community would gain power in a political system that had either taken them for granted or passed them by. Many nonpartisan African Americans cheered the 1932 election results as a definitive step toward forming a black voting bloc that would be party-neutral. "One thing is for sure, our vote has been split as never before," Kelly Miller wrote after it was all over. "No longer can any political party lay claim to this vote as its exclusive possession."

However, in the haze of postelection punditry, African American political observers also conveyed ambivalence over the incoming administration's willingness to work to maintain the black vote. "It is an open question as to whether or not the Democrats *nationally* will do much for the Negro," wrote the NAACP's executive secretary Walter White. "I doubt that they will attempt to do very much against him, which will be a vast improvement over the last four years." Kansas City's *Plaindealer* warned Roosevelt that he would be subjected to a series of important "tests" of his commitment to black citizens. "I, for a long time, maintained that it makes little material difference to the Negro as to what white man occupies the White House or which political party is in national power," declared Kelly Miller. But now that the muscle of the African American ballot had been revealed, he was optimistic that white political leaders would support equality and "a fair, impartial enforcement of the law."

Two days after the election, Joe Guffey trekked to Franklin Delano Roosevelt's Hyde Park, New York, home. Located on the Hudson River, the elegant mansion and expansive lush grounds had been in the Roosevelt family for several generations. Roosevelt was always jovial when receiving guests, but on that day he was especially cheerful as he basked in his election victory. In appreciation for Guffey's brilliant political maneuvering, the president-elect offered to grant his top requests for patronage appointments on the spot. Guffey first asked for and got a nice ambassadorship for a generous DNC contributor. Then he proposed a ranking post in the Justice Department for Robert Vann.

"Before you say anything about Bob Vann," Guffey interjected, "I ought to tell you he's colored."

"Will I have to have him confirmed by the Senate?" Roosevelt asked, mindful of the southern wing of his party.

"No," Guffey responded.

"The job's yours, Joe," Roosevelt replied.

The wooing of black voters had just begun, and Joe Guffey was certain that with continued effort, the payoff could be rich in 1936.

Some of this depended on the Big Four and the genius behind their image, Manuel Roque. However, troubling reports of infighting surfaced immediately after the election, when rumors arose about resentment over Vann's meteoric rise in the party. Internally, divisions between Vann, Johnson, and Thompkins flared. While Rainey wanted nothing, and Roque was angling for a civil service job, an unidentified source hinted in the press that Johnson and Thompkins also expected to receive important posts. African American journalists pressed the incoming administration to make good on its debt to black voters with patronage, as a signal that Roosevelt was serious about forging a reciprocal relationship with the community. Those members of the Big Four interested in serving seemed like the logical choice for prime positions.

As tensions among the Big Four increased, other African American leaders began preinaugural attempts at building bridges to the administration. In the forefront was the NAACP, hopeful that it would be able to open a channel to the Roosevelt White House. In early January 1933, NAACP officials Walter White and Joel Spingarn, one of the early white supporters of the organization, requested a meeting with the president-elect. In late February, White and Spingarn received a response: Roosevelt was too busy to see them.

Although Roosevelt may have been purposefully dodging the nation's leading civil rights organization, he was certainly preoccupied. Between the November 1932 election and the inauguration in March 1933, he watched along with the rest of America as the country sank further into economic chaos. More businesses and banks failed, and unemployment continued to escalate. Hunger and homelessness spread across the country. For African Americans, the situation grew graver. One survey showed that 64 percent of black men in Harlem were out of work, and the Urban League, another prominent civil rights organization, reported that its files were teeming with applications for relief. "From end to end, there is a moving throng during the daytime," the *Pittsburgh Courier* reported. "Men with families up early in the morning, seeking an opportunity to earn something, anything. Willing to be paid in money, food, clothing, coal, or other necessities." OUR ECONOMIC SYSTEM HAS FAILED, one headline in a black weekly exclaimed, adding: "The Nation Is at Suspense."

Meanwhile, both the incoming and outgoing administrations seemed completely uninterested in the worsening conditions in black communities. Neither Hoover nor Roosevelt accepted African American leaders' assertions that continued racial discrimination hurt national recovery efforts. A lasting economic solution required policies that addressed the diverse realities for all Americans—leaving any group jobless and without spending power weakened attempts to revive the economy. While Hoover considered federal assistance to any sector of society unthinkable, Roosevelt was eager to marshal Washington's resources to end the Depression. Preparing to assume office, he assembled a group of American intellectuals, several of them drawn from the faculty at Columbia University, which the press nicknamed "FDR's brain trust." The group advised the president-elect to pour government dollars into saving the economy. But these were plans designed by whites for whites. The New Deal, in its original form, made no allowances for

the unique circumstances faced by African Americans or other marginalized groups. One brain truster, Columbia University economist
Rexford Tugwell, later recalled that dealing with the complexities of
racism and discrimination was a low priority for the president and his
administration. "I wouldn't say he [FDR] took no interest in the race
problem," he later recalled. "But he didn't consider it was important
politically, never as far as I knew."

Although Roosevelt appeared oblivious to race matters, some Democratic leaders fixated on the potential bounty to be reaped from black
votes. Joe Guffey successfully persuaded Jim Farley to plant African
American Democratic grassroots organizations in eleven states with
large black electorates. The party also promised African American partisans control over hiring for local and state patronage posts previously
occupied by black Republicans. Jim Farley and Louis Howe charged
the Big Four with developing a blueprint to address the vast needs of
African Americans. The party honored Manuel Roque with a position
on the inauguration's prestigious publicity committee on the assumption he would provide pro-Roosevelt press coverage.

The weather was dreary on inauguration day, but Roque's report,
which ran in the *Pittsburgh Courier*, was spirited and merry. Roosevelt's
admonition that "the only thing we have to fear is fear itself" captured
what Roque called "the hope that rose in the heart of man." As the
president spoke, Roque alleged, "a shaft of bright sunshine fell at the
capitol steps as if wanting to disperse the clouds of economic difficulties." The day's celebrations demonstrated that a brighter future
was surely ahead. Roque estimated that 150,000 African Americans
attended the swearing-in ceremony—a figure he most certainly inflated.
He also noted the visible black presence in the inaugural procession.
Despite its members' recent reclassification as military servants, the
black Tenth Cavalry, in full dress uniform, led the inaugural parade
with a display of precision riding. African American youths marched
with the presidential vanguard and black Boy Scouts lined parts of the
parade route. Interspersed throughout the procession were additional

black military units, Howard University's Reserve Officers' Training Corps (ROTC) cadets, black American legionnaires, and a number of African American fraternal organizations. Roque reported that "when these colored contingents passed the court of honor," America's new president offered "a snappy salute of recognition which brought thunderous applause from the dignitaries seated on the Presidential flanks and across the street."

Once in office, Roosevelt soared into action, demanding that Congress quickly approve New Deal legislation to commence economic relief, recovery, and reform within the first one hundred days. His press secretary, Stephen Early, who had left a career in journalism, arranged for the president to take to the airwaves and explain the administration's plans in regular weekly radio broadcasts that became known as "fireside chats." The driving philosophy behind the New Deal rested on massive federal spending on an abundance of government programs to stimulate the economy. Businesses and banks needed to be jump-started—they would get loans and federal support—as well as some stiff regulation. For the American worker, the White House was determined to generate as many jobs as possible to put money quickly into consumers' pockets, so they would begin spending again. The brisk expansion of government programs required an equally hurried growth of federal agencies. Newly hired advisers and staffers poured into the capital. They were young and old, men and women, many Democrats and some Republicans. A number were politicians; others were educators, activists, and social workers. Roosevelt's brain trust swelled with national authorities, all white, brought in from universities and social-work circles.

But a conspicuous absence existed among the new corps of experts pouring into Washington. Almost sixty days into the new administration, despite the massive growth of federal advisory posts, not a single African American had been hired. In fact, the White House was in the process of dismissing most of Hoover's diminutive cadre of black Republican appointees. New applications for civil service posts from African Americans went ignored. Myra Colson Callis, with degrees from both Fisk University and the University of Chicago, had passed her civil service examination in 1927. During the Republican years she had been repeatedly turned down for government jobs. And when she tried for a Department of Labor position in the Roosevelt administration, the answer again was no. Some began to wonder whether Democrats were about to eliminate African Americans from all federal posts. None of the Big Four, including Robert Vann, had been called to serve in the new administration. Despite the much-ballyhooed deal with Guffey, Vann was still waiting on the sidelines at home in Pittsburgh.

No one even mentioned the possibility of resurrecting a Black Cabinet.

There was good cause for concern that African Americans would be entirely left out of the New Deal. Observers soon realized that one of the administration's hallmark programs, the National Recovery Administration (NRA), had completely bypassed the country's black population. The NRA was far-reaching and encouraged businesses and industries to keep prices steady, pay workers a minimum wage, and follow fair codes of competition to fight deflation and bankruptcy. Those employers who cooperated with the NRA were allowed to post signs or imprint their products with the government's blue eagle symbol, bearing the words "We Do Our Part." The NRA also pumped money into a jobs program to combat unemployment. But African Americans quickly discovered that they were repeatedly turned down for NRA-generated jobs. "I would not insult your intelligence by trying to cite figures and give facts to show that we are not faring well under the NRA," remarked a *Baltimore Afro-American* columnist urging black leaders to pressure the White House before it was too late. "Since a few months from now it will be useless to crack down on our responsible leaders in Washington because of the discrimination which might develop. . . . I take the liberty to ask them now, what they are doing to insure the rank and file a better deal?"

By spring, the Big Four had called a truce and began pushing the president to act. In mid-April, Julian Rainey wrote to Roosevelt's adviser

Louis Howe indicating that apprehension was setting in as "the colored people of the nation are waiting hopefully for some sign of administrative recognition." He suggested that a White House meeting between the Big Four and the president would put minds at ease and give black citizens "assurance that they were not 'forgotten.'" Howe responded that the president was "not seeing any delegation of this kind" until he was able to get the country past the worst of the economic crisis.

In April, the Big Four met in Washington, D.C., to discuss glaring New Deal neglect and the organization of a permanent national African American division within the Democratic Party. They reconvened there again in May 1933 to talk directly with Jim Farley, pressing him on the necessity for the administration to step up and include black Americans in the New Deal. As he exited that meeting, Vann waved off prying reporters. "No news now, boys," he remarked. "We will make a statement later."

The reality was that the Big Four had no intention of making any statement at all. As they retreated to Washington's Mu-So-Lit Club, a private men's club founded decades earlier by Ralph Tyler and other members of the first Black Cabinet, a secret memorandum containing recommendations from the group was being delivered to the president. Vann, Johnson, Thompkins, and Rainey agreed to suppress its contents so they could save face should their demands be ignored. Their list was extensive. Roosevelt must restore the "black posts" that had been lost under previous administrations and place African Americans in some positions that historically had gone to whites only. Immediate appointments must be made of Vann to the Justice Department, Thompkins to the governorship of the Virgin Islands, Johnson to his former position as the ambassador to Liberia, and Roque to a Commerce Department job. In addition, sixty-six other posts must be given to African Americans. Furthermore, the Big Four added, Roosevelt must mandate that all government offices be integrated, that federal bosses desist in using photographs to weed out black civil service applicants, and that all black military regiments be restored to combat rank.

The administration offered no response to the memorandum.

Then in June, an Oval Office spokesman announced the appointment of Robert Vann as an attorney in the claims division of the Department of Justice.

But that was it.

Although almost all of the Big Four's requests had died on Roosevelt's desk, Vann was elated. In Pittsburgh, the Democratic Party and Joe Guffey honored him at not one but two elaborate ceremonial dinners. By mid-July, Vann had arrived in the District of Columbia. On Friday, July 14, 1933, he took the oath of office, with his wife, Jessie; Dr. Joseph Johnson; and Joe Guffey by his side. Mrs. Vann, who despised the capital city—steeped as it was in white southern racism and segregation—quickly headed home to Pittsburgh.

On Monday, July 16, Robert Vann proudly arrived at the Justice Department, ready to make good in what was regarded as a pathbreaking, prestigious appointment. But reality soon set in. On day one, he searched for his office until someone informed him that he had not been assigned one. Nor had anyone designated a desk for him. He also soon discovered that none of the department's white female stenographers would work for him; they refused to accept a black boss. For the first few weeks, Vann tried to carry out his duties wherever he could find space. Eventually he was given a tiny, isolated office and assigned a male clerk to attend to his secretarial needs. He received very few assignments, and those sent his way were ordinary title searches. The attorney general, who had skipped Vann's swearing in, declined his requests for a meeting. Besieged by black office seekers and their surrogates, Vann began collecting patronage requests. With his Justice Department duties so thin, Vann bought a new Packard and began commuting home to Pittsburgh each weekend to oversee the *Courier* and continue his law practice. He rapidly became disheartened. Julian Rainey urged him to keep his chin up, to recognize that he could contribute to the race in his position by pressuring the administration to increase African American appointments. That was not enough for Vann. Emma Guffey Miller remembered his rapidly deepening despair, stating that she had "never seen such a dejected man in my life."

Despite his widespread reputation as a self-promoter, Vann considered himself first and foremost a race man—dutifully committed to the advancement of the African American people. To a great degree, his despondency resulted from his realization that the Big Four had had absolutely no sway over the White House, a sign that Roosevelt's presidency would be impervious to the crisis in black America. As well, it suggested that the African American alliance with Democrats was, as it had been with Republicans, a one-way street that benefited the party only. This was underscored by the growing economic desperation of black citizens as they watched New Deal aid speed past and disappear into white communities. "Is the Negro getting a 'New Deal' or only a 'New Shuffle?'" asked Kansas City's *Plaindealer*.

As concern built that the African American population would become the most forgotten of forgotten Americans, one of the earliest attempts to redress inequalities came from the prestigious and very powerful Rosenwald Fund. Founded in Chicago by Sears, Roebuck, and Company head Julius Rosenwald, the organization had dedicated many philanthropic initiatives to African American education, health, and economic uplift. Disturbed by the intensifying crisis in the black community, the fund sponsored a conference in Washington, D.C., in early May 1933. The purpose was to solve the problem of massive black unemployment by bringing together African American leaders and representatives from white businesses and labor unions. However, out of the five hundred invitations sent to businessmen and industry heads, only one was accepted. Not a single white labor union agreed to attend. According to the NAACP journal the *Crisis*, the American Federation of Labor (AFL) openly bristled at the idea of "sitting at a conference with the Negroes."

In the end, the Rosenwald conference drew representatives from the Rosenwald Fund, a smattering of federal government employees, and

some of the era's most important black leaders. W. E. B Du Bois, the
nation's foremost African American activist, gave the opening address
before an audience that contained, among others, Mary McLeod
Bethune, Kelly Miller, Walter White, and Robert Vann's old friend
from Virginia Union, Eugene Kinckle Jones, who now led the National
Urban League. Also in attendance were several white race-relations
specialists, including the fund's head, Edwin Embree, and his associate Will W. Alexander, a white minister who also headed up Atlanta's
Commission on Interracial Cooperation.

For three days in May, conference attendees heard reports on the
shocking destitution in black urban communities nationwide. Economist Joseph Willits presented a study revealing that unemployment
for African Americans in Philadelphia ran at 56 percent while that of
whites was at 40 percent. Several participants spoke on the precarious
nature of black urban life. Howard University sociologist E. Franklin
Frazier offered evidence on the spread of malnutrition and illness in
black urban communities, which had become increasingly overcrowded.
Jobs, education, and training opportunities were almost nonexistent.
Frazier argued that poverty literally trapped African Americans in inner
cities, leaving them no way out.

Other speakers revealed that African Americans in the South and
in the farm belt found themselves in equally dire circumstances. In
some areas, white people, fearing a loss of labor, barred indebted and
struggling tenant farmers from taking on second jobs in order to feed
their families. Insisting that everything on their properties belonged to
them, white landlords confiscated and kept any food and clothes the
Red Cross distributed to destitute black sharecroppers. The few black
farmers able to obtain relief checks discovered that banks frequently
refused to cash them.

During open forums, conferencegoers debated various solutions to
the problems facing Depression-weary black Americans. While opinions diverged, a consensus emerged around Eugene Kinckle Jones's
proposal that the White House recruit African American advisers to

serve in various departments and agencies throughout the New Deal constellation of programs. While the NAACP rated the conference as disappointing and maintained that the informational sessions and interracial lunch gatherings were its highlights, the meeting did plant Jones's idea in the attendees' minds. The federal government could only effectively help African Americans by incorporating black voices into the New Deal.

Throughout the summer of 1933, calls for Roosevelt to bring African Americans into his administration as New Deal advisers grew louder from the black community. The demand was echoed at the NAACP's national convention in late June, where delegates demanded the organization's leadership accelerate pressure on the federal government to address civil rights and the black community's economic needs. At the conference's end, Walter White emerged with a list of resolutions. It called for increased taxes on those in the upper income brackets, as well as national health-care coverage, retirement pensions, and unemployment benefits. The list included firm demands that the White House take immediate steps to incorporate African Americans fully into the New Deal, not only by expediting aid and assistance but also by putting black consultants to work at the federal level. African Americans desperately needed policy advocates in agricultural agencies, in the Reconstruction Finance Corporation, a division that provided loans to businesses and banks, and in the National Recovery Administration's jobs programs.

That spring and summer, discrimination within the National Recovery Administration came under fire from two young African American Harvard graduates, Robert Weaver and his childhood friend, attorney John P. Davis. Together they had founded the Negro Industrial League in Washington, D.C., in 1933. In many ways, the pair was a study in contrasts. Davis, short and heavyset, was outspoken and known as uncompromising. A champion college debater, he was dynamic and persuasive, and although he could be domineering, many people found him captivating. Weaver, on the other hand, with a pencil-thin mustache and lean athletic build, cut a gallant and handsome figure. He had an Ivy League self-assuredness, and while he could be "a stuffed shirt," he was also calm, measured, and very credible. That summer, Weaver had crunched numbers and uncovered evidence not only that the New Deal was neglecting African Americans but also that policies reinforcing racial inequalities were indeed hindering the national recovery overall. Davis succeeded in getting the Negro Industrial League on the docket to testify at several Capitol Hill hearings, where it rolled out Weaver's findings for congressional representatives.

In addition to the hard fact that very few African Americans had secured jobs under New Deal relief, it was also disturbing that the National Recovery Administration had proposed differential wages and hours for workers based on region and job classification. The racial implications of the policy were obvious to black leaders. The NRA permitted employers to pay southern workers in many industries the lowest of all wages. Since most African Americans lived in the south and their employment opportunities were restricted to certain segregated blue-collar jobs, the NRA's guidelines allowed white employers to pay blacks far lower wages than whites in similar positions in other areas of the country and in other southern workplaces. It was clear evidence that the agency intended to collude with the South's white population to perpetuate and federally institutionalize brazen racial discrimination. White citizens and lawmakers in the South had obstinately opposed equal pay for equal work, insisting that African Americans were less efficient employees and could survive on lower wages because their cost of living was much lower than that of the white population. If the federal government forced them to stop shorting black paychecks, then, white southern employers warned, they would lay off all black workers.

Weaver provided a brilliant counter to the NRA's plan to institute race-based asymmetrical wages. He statistically demonstrated that black labor was just as productive as white. Drawing from his surveys, as well as other scholarly studies, he documented that black household expenses were indeed lower than white household expenses—not because African

Americans needed less to live on but rather because they had been historically forced to subsist at far below poverty level. Weaver also proved that differential wages would impede general recovery by blocking the purchasing power of black Americans. His numbers confirmed that paying African American workers equal wages would increase the demand for goods and services and stimulate the production of more jobs for all. Davis did most of the talking at the hearings, but when Weaver presented his findings solo, the *Pittsburgh Courier* rated his delivery "masterful."

Although Weaver's reports addressed several businesses and trades, his testimony resulted in wage increases only for African Americans in the timber industry. Neither Weaver nor Davis regarded it as much of a victory, as NRA administrators began implementing unequal wages throughout several jobs programs. But they had succeeded in detailing New Deal inequalities before congressional subcommittees and were gaining notice in the black press. J. Finley Wilson, the national leader of the African American Elks lodges, praised the Negro Industrial League's work. "Throughout the nation, as we travel," he telegrammed Roosevelt, "we will see the mystic sign emblazoned everywhere, N.R.A. the symbol of cooperation with the National Recovery Administration. We propose to organize so that this N.R.A. will signify 'NEGRO RECOVERY ALSO!'" The significance of Weaver and Davis's findings was underscored by NAACP official William Pickens, who announced that the NRA was doing nothing to advance African American recovery. In his estimation, *NRA* stood for "Negro Removal Act."

While Weaver and Davis continued lobbying, in August 1933, young activists and intellectuals joined with veteran NAACP leaders for a four-day retreat at Troutbeck, Joel Spingarn's posh rural estate in Amenia, New York. Since it was the second time the NAACP would confer there, attendees popularly referred to the meeting as the "Second Amenia." The purpose was to bring together the younger and older generations to discuss the revitalization of the NAACP and its fight for equal rights during the Depression. The younger attendees were a high-powered group that included, among others, Harvard-educated Ralph Bunche, Bill Hastie, and Howard University School of Law dean Charles H. Houston; University of Chicago graduate student Mabel Byrd; and Harlem Renaissance poet Sterling Brown. Du Bois and Spingarn presided over the conference. Weaver and Davis, toiling away in the nation's capital, were absent. While their revelations about the New Deal's weaknesses had drawn the NAACP's attention, the organization regarded the two young men with suspicion. Du Bois alleged that their Negro Industrial League existed "chiefly on paper" and warned that while Weaver and Davis were "individuals of intelligence," they were "not representative of any mass movement." Roy Wilkins, the NAACP's assistant executive secretary, added, "I am told these men are in the proposition for what they can get out of it, or for the prestige which can be turned into jobs later."

Despite his omission from Du Bois's list of the up-and-coming, Weaver later credited the Second Amenia as the catalyst that set into motion the events that would eventually result in the rebirth of the Black Cabinet. Those present at Amenia engaged in four days of intense discussion, mixed with hiking in Troutbeck's dense woods and fishing in its crystal lake. The general consensus was that the weekend was energizing and productive. "When anyone got the floor," remarked Du Bois, "they really took hold of the thought and did something with it." Despite differences of opinion that ranged from radical to conservative, the participants agreed that the times called for a unified push for a "reformed Democracy" that would offer "full and indiscriminatory integration of the Negro into every phase of American life." Something had to change, and the New Deal presented the opportunity to propel forward the American civil rights revolution.

The Second Amenia's turning point came when Henry Morgenthau—the head of the Farm Credit Administration, a Roosevelt brain truster, and Spingarn's neighbor and friend—dropped in unannounced. He arrived just in time to listen in on a discussion of poverty in rural black America. He claimed he was shocked to learn about sharecropping and professed he was unaware that such a practice existed in the United States. Vowing to tackle the problems of African Americans in the Cotton Belt, he pledged to appoint an African American adviser to the Farm Credit Administration and asked that the conference send him a name for the job.

Attendees were invigorated by Morgenthau. It seemed as if at least someone inside Roosevelt's inner circle finally recognized the administration's obligation to African American citizens. Additionally, the inclusion of the NAACP in the selection process for black posts indicated a willingness to break from the tradition of naming partisan cronies to important jobs with the expectation that they act as mere figureheads. But all agreed, one adviser was not enough. As Second Amenia closed, delegates issued a demand that FDR incorporate African American representatives into all phases of the New Deal.

After Second Amenia, Kelly Miller, writing in the *New York Amsterdam News*, dubbed the attendees the "Young Negro Brain Trust." He remarked that the conference made the case that "the demands of a swiftly changing age call for a new deal for the new day." Robert Vann, slogging along at his job in the Justice Department, ran an editorial in the *Pittsburgh Courier*, remarking that "certainly the Negroes, the worst sufferers from the depression, hail the turn of tide" represented by the potential contained within FDR's New Deal.

While the president rolled out the New Deal, while young black intellectuals called for an African American voice in the federal government, and while Robert Vann fought to become a force in the Justice Department, Eva DeBoe Jones, the woman who originally opened the door to the Roosevelt camp, continued to make the trip from her segregated community to the lavish homes of her white employers. As word of her role in the defection of black voters to the Democrats began to circulate, she watched quietly as her Republican clients, one by one, began to drop away.

PART TWO

Called to Washington, 1933–1935

Chapter Three

Will the New Deal Be a Fair Deal?

IN AUGUST 1933, Robert Weaver returned to his academic post at Greensboro's North Carolina Agriculture and Technical College. He dreaded going back. While he was a popular professor, he found teaching there a chore. He felt smothered by Greensboro's omnipresent segregationist traditions and laws; he isolated himself, refusing to patronize segregated stores and entertainment venues. His colleagues chided him for turning down opportunities to socialize. But he much preferred to be lonely than to accommodate Jim Crow.

There in Greensboro and its surroundings, Robert Weaver became exposed to the rawest versions of white southern racism. He had endured discrimination as a member of Washington, D.C.'s African American community and then later as one of the few black students at Harvard. But as a member of the black elite, he knew his experiences were unique. His move deeper into the South forced him to directly confront the realities lived by most black Americans. As he traveled in and out of Greensboro, he passed sharecroppers' shacks and the cotton and tobacco fields where black farmers barely scratched out a living. The Depression had hit North Carolina hard. By fall 1933, 25 percent of all families there depended on some kind of public or private assistance; the NAACP estimated that the rate was far, far higher for the African American rural population. And poverty haunted not only rural areas but also the cities. The textile industry was one of North Carolina's largest employers, and it had collapsed with the Depression's onset. Large textile mills stood on the hills surrounding Greensboro—they had dominated the city's economic life. As the economy deteriorated, black mill workers were laid off or cut back to starvation wages at a far, far greater rate than white workers.

At night, in his room, Weaver meticulously pored over the numbers again and again, mining them for irrefutable proof that black communities were in a downward spiral. That summer he tracked the data of twelve thousand black cotton-mill workers nationwide who had managed to hang on to their jobs. He determined that 75 percent of them were grossly underpaid and overworked, despite the National Recovery Administration's mandates regarding minimum wages and maximum hours. Times were hard and people took any job they could get—even if they earned almost nothing. This was, as Kansas City's *Plaindealer* pointed out, a "new kind of slavery."

As Weaver walked Greensboro's black neighborhoods, he witnessed firsthand the impact of the Great Depression and the suffering it caused. Families were homeless; children went hungry. For Weaver, the experience marked the beginning of a transformation. His determination to resist American racism grew. "The lash of prejudice is not the overt lash; it's the subtle lash of feeling yourself up against an iron block of prejudice that is the most cutting. Because I had been protected, I felt the cut more deeply," he reflected. "I have not brooded about discrimination, but I have never ceased to resent it." Robert Weaver believed he had the tools to fight against racial prejudice and discrimination; all he needed was the chance to use them.

The Robert Weaver who came to Greensboro was a man of limited but rare privileges. In 1933, he was only twenty-six, but he was impressive in nearly every way. Handsome, with a chiseled jaw and a sly smile, Weaver radiated confidence, pride, and dignity. His family history was remarkable and distinctive. His celebrated grandfather, D.C. dentist Robert Tanner Freeman, remained a prominent figure in the District of

Columbia's black community. His grandmother, Rachel Turner, born out of wedlock to white parents, had been raised by an African American family and lived her life as a black woman. She had one daughter with Freeman, Weaver's mother, Florence, who was born shortly before her father's early death. A widow for nearly fifteen years, Rachel Freeman remarried in 1890—and well at that. Her second husband, Albert J. Farley, was a clerk for the Supreme Court, and his salary enabled the family to move to the middle class, interracial Washington, D.C., suburb of Brookland. Florence received the best education available to black women in the era; she was well trained in Latin and classical poetry. She was a proud and principled woman who demanded that her son achieve. "The way to offset color prejudice," Weaver recalled his mother saying, "was to be awfully good at whatever you do."

Robert Weaver's father, Mortimer Grover Weaver, came from far humbler origins. He was born about 1870 on a farm in Fauquier County, Virginia. His mother was a domestic, and his father was a white man, a former slaveholder who had sided with the Confederacy during the Civil War. As a child, Mortimer worked in the fields. But when he reached his teens, he was sent to off to attend high school in the District of Columbia. A few years after graduation, he secured a prized position in the city's post office. Robert Weaver described his father as extremely quiet, "a puritan, who didn't smoke, drink, or gamble." A careful guardian of his earnings, Mortimer Weaver saved his money and, in 1901, married Florence Freeman. He purchased a home in Brookland near her parents' house and, eventually, a seaside cottage for weekend getaways. The Weavers quickly added two sons to their family, Mortimer Grover Jr. and Robert Clifton.

The Weavers were intensely proud of their sons and were determined that they should have the finest that could be offered to African American children. While Brookland's neighborhood may have been integrated, its schools were not. But the closest black secondary school was the top in the country—Paul Laurence Dunbar High School. Dunbar was rigorous and challenging, requiring students to master all academic disciplines. In Weaver's era, 80 percent of the school's graduates attended northern colleges; many were admitted to the most prestigious in the nation. The pressure to succeed at Dunbar was enormous. Robert Weaver recalled that there was "no question" children of the District of Columbia's black elite "would do well in school, go to college, and enter a profession."

While Robert Weaver performed admirably in high school, his older brother was an academic star. Mortimer Weaver Jr. was extremely serious, much like his father. A valedictorian at Dunbar, he excelled in all academic disciplines and, after graduating with honors from Williams College in 1925, entered Harvard to pursue a master of arts degree in literature. Within a couple of years, he had finished his MA and joined the faculty at North Carolina A&T.

Although less of a standout than his brother, Robert Weaver graduated near the top of his class at Dunbar. In 1925, he joined Mortimer Jr. at Harvard and declared a major in economics. African Americans were unwelcome in the university's dormitories so, like other black Harvard men, Weaver lived off campus in an African American–owned boardinghouse. He roomed first with Mortimer and later with Louis Redding, a law student. Next door were two Dunbar alumni, Bill Hastie and John P. Davis, both also pursuing law degrees. Hastie and Davis later added a third roommate, a doctoral student in political science named Ralph Bunche. The bond among these five men was strong. They lived, ate, and studied together, and played poker on Saturdays. Bunche recalled their straitlaced landlord bursting into their room shouting, "Stop that evil game." But most Saturday nights consisted of more talk than cards; these poker parties were dominated by long and fervid debates over the advancement of the race. Weaver would credit this group of young men and their late-night discussions for broadening his intellectual understanding of American racism and the African American fight for equal rights.

Weaver's first few years at Harvard were exhilarating and challenging. He enjoyed the social life and courted a number of young women.

When Harlem Renaissance poet Countee Cullen married W. E. B. Du Bois's daughter, Yolande, Weaver served as one of the groomsmen, in what was regarded in the African American community as the wedding of the decade. Weaver was barely interested in his studies, and his grades suffered.

But in Weaver's senior year, his life took a turn. Shortly after accepting a prestigious professorship in Howard University's literature department, his older brother, Mortimer, died suddenly. The cause of death was never revealed—the family would only say that it was sudden.

For Robert Weaver the loss was a colossal blow. He admired his brother and had lived in his shadow. He emerged from the tragedy determined to meet the expectations that his parents had set not only for him but also for his brother. Friends worried about his intense pursuit of success. Thoroughly focused and resolute, Robert Weaver left behind the frivolities of campus life and finished his bachelor's degree with honors. He then immediately attempted to do what no African American had ever done before—earn a PhD from Harvard's extremely conservative economics department. It was not a welcoming environment. Weaver remembered that the department's most influential scholar, Frank Taussig, "didn't think that black men had aptitude for economics." Nonetheless, Weaver excelled. After passing his comprehensive examinations with high marks, he focused on crafting his thesis, entitled "The High Wage Theory of Prosperity." In 1931, he followed in his brother's footsteps and headed to Greensboro to teach.

But Robert Weaver realized quickly that he could not faithfully tread his brother's academic path. While at North Carolina A&T, he yearned for a job in Washington, D.C.—someplace more cosmopolitan, more intellectually exciting, where he could be in the thick of the struggle. On weekends, he often headed back to Brookland to work with John P. Davis, who had returned to the capital city. Their organization, the Negro Industrial League, had two members, Weaver and Davis, and one secretary, Davis's wife, Marguerite DeMond Davis, and was dedicated to exposing the weaknesses becoming alarmingly apparent in the New

Deal's main jobs program under the National Recovery Administration. Testifying before congressional committees throughout 1933, Davis and Weaver gained increasing attention in the black press. Davis emerged as the charismatic leader who occupied the limelight of their crusade, while Weaver played the cool head, the dignified academician with the facts and figures. By late summer, the two had begun reaching out to the nation's civil rights organizations and leaders in hope of transforming the Negro Industrial League into an umbrella network of activists. The *Pittsburgh Courier* praised Davis and Weaver for their attempt to assemble an external "Brain Trust" that was "ready to work" on New Deal problems and forward recommendations to the federal government.

But Weaver had also set his sights on a government job. In the spring of 1933, just after Roosevelt took office, he had begun attempts at securing a federal post. Government work had been a tradition in the Weaver family and among their social set. "I had grown up in Washington and my father was in government . . . [my] step-grandfather was in government," Weaver later commented. "I had known . . . a reasonable number of black Americans who were in government." Yet, like other African Americans seeking federal employment as the New Deal dawned, Weaver was repeatedly rejected. In the summer of 1933, after the Negro Industrial League made its first splash, Davis began lobbying for the National Recovery Administration to give his partner a position. The agency's answer was a flat no.

Discouraged, Weaver felt that he had hit a brick wall. "Although there is grave need of carrying out of special work upon the position of the Negro under the National Recovery Administration, the Government has taken little account of this problem," he wrote to John Henry Williams, one of his Harvard professors. "Past experiences with the limitation placed upon me as a Negro have caused me to give up all hopes in that direction."

In late August 1933, Robert Weaver picked up his newspaper and learned, like other Americans, that the Roosevelt administration had established the Office of the Special Adviser on the Economic Status of Negroes. The idea had originated with the Rosenwald Fund's Edwin Embree and Will Alexander, who had been peddling it around Washington throughout the summer. Alexander had become convinced that Roosevelt "was a sort of messiah" and that "perhaps the next stage in race relations in this country would sort of center around what happened in Washington, D.C." The Rosenwald Fund proposed to underwrite the special adviser's salary and office expenses for the first few years. That would allow Roosevelt to avoid a confirmation process that might trigger retaliation against the New Deal by southern Democrats, who consistently opposed any kind of support for African Americans.

Reportedly, the secretary of the interior, Harold L. Ickes, a Chicagoan with Rosenwald ties, finally got the plan in front of the president. The interior secretary could be irascible, but as the past president of the Windy City's NAACP, he had established a reputation for being liberal on the issue of race. Roosevelt approved the proposal and placed the office under Ickes, allowing him to choose the man to occupy the special adviser's position. Rather than consult with the many African American leaders he knew personally, Ickes demanded Alexander and Embree provide him with a list of names.

Ickes picked the last name on their list—Clark Foreman, a white southerner.

Although he was too guarded to ever say so, Robert Weaver must have been exasperated to hear that a white man would become the federal government's first and only special adviser on the economic status of Negroes. The overall reaction from the black community was shock and dismay. "We are frank to admit there is no 'New Deal' for us in Secretary Harold D. [sic] Ickes's appointment of [Clark Foreman]," protested the Baltimore Afro-American. "That is the 'Old Deal,' such as we have had for years in naming white supervisors of Negro schools, white officers in Negro regiments, and white candidates for political offices in Negro districts." The NAACP telegrammed Ickes, protesting that there were numerous African Americans, with equal or superior educational credentials, better suited for the job. The *Chicago Defender* observed, "It was certainly bad enough to select any white man for this particular post, but to select one from Georgia was certainly adding insult to injury." The choice of Clark Foreman, in part, led the Urban League's journal, *Opportunity*, to ask, "Will the New Deal be a Square Deal for the Negro?"

After Foreman's selection was announced, the NAACP's Roy Wilkins confided to the Associated Negro Press's wire-service editor Claude Barnett that the Rosenwald Fund had intentionally made an end run around the NAACP. "The people who planned it evidently were certain that we would oppose such an appointment [of a white man] and therefore they did not show their hands in time for any opposition to be stirred prior to the actual announcement," Wilkins remarked. In his opinion, the special adviser would accomplish nothing; the naïve Foreman had been put in to block, rather than to address, black grievances. Wilkins declared that the NAACP would call for the appointment to be "bitterly fought by all Negro organizations, especially the Negro press, not on the grounds that Foreman is personally objectionable, but that no white man can speak for Negroes in this time of stress."

This was the message the NAACP's lead Washington attorney, Charles H. Houston, carried directly to Ickes. The son of respected black District of Columbia lawyer William Houston, Charles Houston had known many of the members of the first Black Cabinet, who had been frequent guests at his childhood home, and was well acquainted with the inner workings of Washington politics from an early age. A Harvard graduate, the younger Houston had risen to become dean of Howard University's School of Law and was respected for his nononsense tough-mindedness. Face-to-face with Ickes, he argued that an African American appointee was far more qualified to be a special adviser on issues critical to black Americans. Ickes emphatically disagreed. The "time" was "not ripe" for a black appointment, he sputtered. A white man had access to people and places, both on Capitol Hill and in the South, that were off-limits to blacks. Ickes maintained that he was so certain the specialist had to be white that he had not considered a single African American for the position.

Houston next confronted Foreman, who, after some waffling, admitted that he too believed there were more capable African Americans who could have filled the special adviser's job. In an attempt to demonstrate his commitment to black inclusion, Foreman pledged to fill out his staff with African American assistants and secretaries. He would carry his fight against discrimination beyond the Interior Department, he promised Houston, and battle it in agencies throughout the federal government.

The African American community had good reason to be skeptical of Clark Foreman. While he was an eager champion of black causes and had worked on racial affairs for both the Rosenwald Foundation and Will Alexander's Commission on Interracial Cooperation, Foreman's Georgian roots ran deep and were tied to the slaveholding past. His grandfather had fought for the Confederacy and had been a leader among southern Democrats. His uncle edited the *Atlanta Constitution*, which opposed black suffrage and equal treatment for African Americans under the New Deal. Foreman was raised in the traditions of the white South, where racial divisions were a given and African Americans were presumed naturally to occupy an inferior position in society.

Foreman pointed to two experiences that had awakened him to the immoral and illogical nature of the South's white supremacist ideology. As a college student in Georgia, he had witnessed, as a member of the crowd, a frenzied lynch mob torture and burn a black man named John Lee Eberhart to death. In a letter home to his parents, Foreman stated he was sickened by the murder and decried lynching as a "terrible, barbaric" act. A few years later, while attending Harvard, Foreman received an invitation to join his classmates for dinner with W. E. B. Du Bois. He refused, indignant over the idea of dining with a black man as a social equal. But his friends' scorn forced him to give in. The evening was transformative. Foreman was awestruck by Du Bois's towering intellect and moved deeply by the lecture the celebrated civil rights pioneer delivered to a large audience. "That was my break, so to speak," he later recalled, "from the southern tradition."

By the time Roosevelt entered office, the thirty-one-year-old Foreman had amassed an impressive résumé. He had studied in the North and in Europe, finished a doctoral dissertation on African American education at Columbia University, and worked for Will Alexander. Despite his accomplishments, Foreman had not been the top choice of either Alexander or Embree for the special adviser post. He possessed an abundance of youthful energy and a fervent commitment to battling racism that some found insufferably brash and overbearing. Will Alexander regarded him as fanatical: "If he [Foreman] waked up some night in a nightmare dreaming that he was not a liberal . . . he wouldn't have slept for a month." One former African American colleague described him as patronizing, believing that his intensity smacked more of a prideful stubbornness than of a genuine understanding of African American concerns and challenges. Foreman was a "billy goat" when it came to solving problems, Alexander warned Ickes—"just butt right into them and keep butting until you're through." Much to Alexander's surprise, the interior secretary was not dissuaded: "That young fellow's the man I want. I think he's the only one who can do any good in a job like this."

When Foreman landed in the Department of the Interior in August 1933, he found plenty of problems to "billy goat." He confirmed that the studies Weaver and Davis had produced were true: the National Recovery Administration's jobs programs were either turning African Americans away or paying black workers disastrously low wages. "Many white people in the South are dogmatically opposed to Negroes participating [equally] . . . with white people in any beneficial measures," the Urban League reported. Foreman also discovered that racial bias ran rife throughout the New Deal. The Civilian Conservation Corps (CCC), another major program, was as prejudicial as the National Recovery Administration. Administered by the U.S. Army, the CCC provided work relief to teens and young men by enrolling them in military-style camps to perform conservation duties in local, state, and national parks. Although it was promoted as open to all races, the CCC rejected most black applicants. In camps that admitted African Americans, they were usually segregated and assigned to the lowest-paid, unskilled jobs. Beyond this, the CCC's leadership was exclusively drawn from white army personnel, leaving African American youths at the mercy of white officers, many from the South, who treated them abusively and contemptuously.

In addition to the reports of the CCC's racial hostility, other factors deterred African American youth from seeking help from the program. Some worried that in joining, they would be conscripted into the military. Black northerners feared assignment to CCC programs in the racially hostile and violent South. Furthermore, CCC regulations required participants to live in work camps under the constant supervision of white military overseers. Army rules were imposed, and enrollees were not permitted to leave camp unless they were granted special passes from program administrators. It all carried alarming echoes of the slave past.

New Deal discrimination was increasingly institutionalizing racist practices into programs and policies at the federal level, and Clark Foreman embraced the fight to end it as his personal mission. One of his first acts was to decline to accept a secretary from the all-white federal pool and demand that Ickes allow him to hire an African American woman. The interior secretary agreed and said he knew just the right person—a fellow Chicagoan, Lucia Mae Pitts. A highly experienced professional, she was a frank and proud "race woman" who did not suffer fools. She was, by her own admission, a perfectionist and a "stoic."

Besides being a top-notch secretary, Pitts brought to the special adviser's office the much-needed perspective of a black woman. Born in Chattanooga, Tennessee, in 1904, Pitts had moved to Chicago as a child with her widowed mother, who was a domestic worker. Pitts attended one of the city's best high schools, where the student body was overwhelmingly white, and she endured racism's constant sting. But rather than discourage her, the experience drove her forward. "My ambition had been further fired, I think, by some racial hurts," she observed. "Most Negroes have felt them; they affect different people, different ways. As for me, they made me determined to prove a Negro girl could be as good as any other girl—perhaps better."

Before coming to Washington, D.C., Lucia Pitts had worked in a variety of positions. In Chicago, while she studied stenography, she took jobs as a maid and as an office temp and in a pool hall. She also wrote for the popular black newspaper the *Chicago Defender*. After completing her secretarial degree, Pitts worked for the Tuskegee Institute, a New York theater, Atlanta's African American newspaper syndicate, and the Federal Council of Churches. In the early 1930s, she landed a job in the Illinois House of Representatives' stenographic pool. The pool's only African American secretary, Pitts endured the frigidity of her white coworkers and elected officials. But one figure welcomed her, Anna Wilmarth Ickes, a representative from Winnetka, Illinois, and the wife of Harold Ickes, who was then a crusading local reformer.

When Foreman came calling, Pitts had fallen victim to the state of Illinois's Depression-era layoffs and lost her job. She jumped at his offer. After a screening by the Rosenwald Fund, she boarded a train for the nation's capital and was at her desk by September 5, 1933. On that day, Lucia Pitts became the first African American woman to serve as a secretary to a white federal administrator in Washington, D.C.

Pitts was eager to work, and the Department of the Interior publicized her appointment in the black press. But she refused to be flattered and, like other African Americans, harbored serious reservations about Clark Foreman. At the beginning, she maintained a cool, yet professional distance from her new boss. Foreman later described her attitude as "rude," while she characterized it as "unbending." She would not be an accomplice to a ruse targeting black people. "I felt it was my duty to be the Negro's watch dog and see that nothing was put over on us," she later wrote. "I did not know [Foreman] . . . and I did not intend to let him think that his employment of me automatically put me on his side—not until he proved himself."

Pitts remembered the New Deal's formative period as "hectic and busy." Relief and recovery programs were organized and reorganized rapidly. Some were housed within preexisting divisions in cabinet departments; others were new, independent agencies whose purpose required oversight from one or more cabinet secretaries. There was competition among programs and cabinet secretaries, especially for funding. But all those serving in the New Deal realized the seriousness of their charge; they were there to rescue the nation from economic catastrophe. Clark Foreman had already rushed into battle. He spent long days trying to pressure cabinet officials and New Deal heads to appoint African Americans to their divisions. Pitts remembered Foreman's determination as almost feverish: "He walks the floor up and down when dictating, flicking the furniture, picking up a pencil or rubber band or what not, to put them down again; occasionally dropping into a chair, to rise and walk again."

The iciness between Pitts and Foreman quickly thawed, as she became convinced of his sincerity. He spent long hours in the office receiving individuals and delegations asking for help for themselves or economically devastated black communities. (Robert Vann was also increasingly deluged by visitors with the same pleas.) Pitts not only witnessed but also contributed to the expansion of African American federal appointments, as Foreman sought her recommendations for expanding the black secretarial corps. He also immediately added "field representative" to her list of duties and dispatched her to Virginia Beach to survey the damage from a deadly hurricane that had left numerous African American families homeless. Pitts also watched as the white South slapped the label of "race traitor" on Foreman, rebuking him for selecting an African American woman as his secretary. No black woman was capable of handling such an important job, white racists contended. They recoiled at the idea that a white man and a black woman shared office space. Later, one southern publication attempted to smear Foreman by alleging that he was having affairs with two black secretaries. Foreman later claimed that Georgia's Democratic governor and New Deal foe Eugene Talmadge took to the radio "twice a day" to denounce his decision to hire Pitts. This probably was overstated, but Talmadge was well known for boldly trumpeting white-supremacist views to fan racial resentments.

While Foreman may have earned Pitts's respect, he still had a long way to go with the black public. He knew that with each passing day, African Americans were tumbling deeper into economic despair. He tenaciously charged ahead pushing for jobs and resources for black citizens. He aggressively buttonholed Roosevelt's cabinet heads and became an unwelcome figure in cabinet and New Deal offices. Foreman "got kicked out of the War Department when he went over to find out what they were doing," Will Alexander remembered. Harry L. Hopkins (the head of the Federal Emergency Relief Administration and one of Roosevelt's closest advisers) "kicked him out when he went over to see him."

Foreman also received a chilly reception when he showed up at the office of the CCC's head administrator, Colonel Duncan K. Major.

"Well now, Mr. Foreman, I leave here usually at 4:30 and it is now 4:20," the colonel barked.

"Well, . . . what I have to say won't take more than ten minutes," Foreman responded. "Why can't we have Negro officers in the Negro CCC camps?"

"It would never work," scoffed the northern-born colonel, admonishing the Georgia native for knowing so little about white southern traditions.

Foreman stormed out of the office. "The Colonel showed nothing but scorn for me," he complained to Ickes. Will Alexander recalled that overall, Foreman "had a rather rough time, but that made it interesting. He liked to have a rough time."

Foreman eventually stumbled onto one official willing to hear him out, Secretary of Commerce Daniel C. Roper. A fellow southerner,

Roper was eager to do damage control on race relations. The Commerce Department was a major player in the National Recovery Administration, and Roper had taken much of the heat for that program's bigoted practices. Roper had compounded his problems by dismissing a respected African American appointee, a Republican holdover who advised the department on black-owned businesses. Then he made an unpopular decision even worse by abolishing that position. African Americans demanded the secretary restore the post and either rehire its previous occupant or find a replacement. So when Foreman came calling in the late summer, Roper seized the chance to fix his public image.

At Foreman's suggestion, Roper agreed to sponsor a conference on the economic problems of African Americans. The Justice Department's Robert Vann was recruited to chair the meeting, which included black intellectuals, leaders, and activists from across the nation. They met in Washington in September 1933 and for two days discussed strategies to speed up relief to black communities. There was some hope that those assembled would endorse Clark Foreman, but that disappeared when reportedly they drummed him out of one of the conference's sessions.

The high point of the conference came when Roper, while addressing the gathering, announced his plan to restore the recently eliminated African American post. He then asked the group to put forward names for the position. While the delegates may have been encouraged to hear that Commerce would hire a black adviser, they agreed that no one person could handle the overwhelming needs of black America. At the end of the meeting, they informed Roper that they had organized themselves into an official advisory committee. Although they insisted on being based in the Commerce Department, they demanded review power over all decisions affecting African Americans throughout the New Deal. John P. Davis seized the opportunity and lobbied for the department to include Robert Weaver on the advisory committee. He was told no.

While some noted that the Commerce Department's advisory committee on African American affairs threatened to compete with

Foreman's office, no doubt many realized that it also had the potential to emerge as the New Deal's Black Cabinet. But that hope died quickly. Protests immediately came from William Thompkins and Joseph Johnson, members of the now nearly forgotten Big Four, who were still waiting for their political payback. They had remained sidelined during the conference while Vann had assumed a central role, and that seemed to them like a selfish power grab. Then when it came to naming the Commerce Department's new African American adviser, Vann clashed not only with Johnson and Thompkins but also with some members of the new black advisory committee. The verbal brawls subsided briefly when Vann was in a head-on automobile collision while en route to Pittsburgh. Although he suffered a skull fracture, he was soon back in the thick, issuing fighting orders from his hospital bed.

In the end, despite opposition from Joseph Johnson, who badly wanted the appointment, Roper named the Urban League's Eugene Kinckle Jones to the Commerce post. The selection of Jones, whose close friendship with Vann dated back to their days at Virginia Union University, only heightened already existing tensions. "The appointment of Jones was one of the fundamental causes in the break in the ranks of the famous 'Big Four,'" reported the Associated Negro Press (ANP) wire service. According to the ANP, Vann was to blame for this unseemly situation: "[Jones] had nothing to do with this tempest in the teapot."

Jones's efforts to avoid infighting were characteristic of his calm, affable, and diplomatic manner. Tall, charming, and athletic (he had been a tennis champ and collegiate star pitcher), the Urban League executive, at the age of forty-eight, was strikingly fit and distinguished. Raised in Richmond, Virginia, the son of two respected and race-conscious college professors, Jones had been given many opportunities, and he embraced the responsibility of challenging American racism. After finishing at Virginia Union, Jones earned a master of arts degree in sociology at Cornell University and helped found Alpha Phi Alpha, the nation's first African American fraternity. After teaching for a few years, he took a job as a field inspector for the Urban League in 1911. The organization was only a year old and he fully embraced the opportunity to shape the Urban League's programs dedicated to addressing the conditions faced by African Americans in the cities. As the Great Migration began and poverty spread, Jones advocated for the deployment of social workers into black neighborhoods to assist residents in job hunting and economic advancement. In 1917, the Urban League had selected Jones as its executive secretary, and he guided the organization from New York City as it grew throughout the 1920s. Although a registered Republican, disillusioned by the damage resulting from the racial policies of the Harding, Coolidge, and Hoover administrations, Jones had broken ranks and voted Democrat in 1928 and 1932.

Eugene Kinckle Jones's addition to the New Deal team was received with applause, in part prompted by Commerce Department press releases. "Credit to Race," remarked the *New York Daily News* on Jones's appointment. The *New York Times* celebrated Jones as "one of the foremost authorities on the problems of Negro life in the cities." Jones's achievement was certainly a milestone. When he arrived on the job in late October 1933, he became the first upper-level leader of a national civil rights organization to occupy an advisory post in the federal government.

Yet for Jones, the transition from Urban League head to Commerce Department adviser was rough. Despite his efforts to rise above the quarrels over his appointment, he entered office under a cloud of suspicion. He suffered from his connection to Vann, which was only highlighted by reports that the two roomed together in Washington. Some charged that Jones was nothing more than a patronage appointee, the administration's attempt to appease Vann and to derail growing criticism from the black community. Additionally, to some Jones seemed a bad fit. A nationally recognized specialist in black labor, he now headed a division dedicated to the recovery and expansion of black businesses. The *New York Age* wagered that Jones's real talents would be wasted: "Some may question whether the acute problems affecting the race have not more to do with labor than commerce."

Although Eugene Kinckle Jones was hired at $5,600 a year (a respectable salary although lower than that of other New Deal officials) and given a spacious suite with two offices, he had no staff and no authority to pursue projects or investigations. It quickly appeared that his role in New Deal relief, outside of serving as the subject of a publicity campaign, was murky at best. Jones soon found himself under a mountain of complaints regarding New Deal inequalities, many from the Urban League itself. With no resources, he was blocked from offering any response. The press was told that his role was "the study of Negro problems." Yet there was never any mention of actually solving them.

The fanfare around Jones's appointment was certainly not enough to satisfy those demanding that Roosevelt respond to the crises in black America. Stories of African Americans struggling against poverty filled the pages of the nation's black newspapers. Learning that his family was starving, Ed Nash, a prisoner in the Oklahoma City jail, escaped, found a few days' work, got his earnings to his wife, and then voluntarily surrendered to authorities. In Kansas City, Kansas, a charitable group lobbied for a soup kitchen to be located near a local black elementary school, because so many of its students were going hungry. Already cash-poor communities watched helplessly as food and fuel prices started to rise, when National Recovery Administration wage and price regulations kicked in. "The burden is still on the poor," remarked the Wichita, Kansas–based *Negro Star*. "If he makes more he must pay more." As the cost of living increased, black incomes continued to plummet. One African American journalist reported that "a conservative estimate would place 90 percent of Harlem's population in the breadline."

The first Black Cabinet's Kelly Miller urged African Americans to abandon cities and return to the countryside, where they might make a living off the land. "The city Negro has no definite function or assured status," he told the *New York Times*. "The farm is the Negro's best chance and the best help the government can render him in this emergency is to aid him to avail himself of this chance." Clark Foreman agreed and began to advocate for African Americans to be admitted to the programs run by the Division of Subsistence Homesteads, which placed families on collective farms to communally work the land. Those programs had only accepted white applicants and turned away African Americans seeking aid. Far from making him more popular, Foreman's proposal actually damaged his reputation further. He did not advocate for African Americans to be integrated into preexisting projects. Instead he called for separate blacks-only collective farms. Such plans convinced some African American leaders that the white southerner was really in the business of promoting segregation. Even though Foreman defended the idea of racially separate farms as the only safe option for black southerners, his critics viewed it as yet more evidence that Washington was in the process of creating and enforcing a federal form of Jim Crow policies.

Furthermore, the justice system continued to fail black citizens in the most horrific ways. Throughout the summer and fall of 1933, the national media was filled with stories of the "Scottsboro Boys," nine African American youths, ranging in age from thirteen to twenty, who had been arrested for allegedly gang-raping two young white women. While there were Americans of both races who spoke out on behalf of the accused, exposing the charges as groundless, in late fall two of the nine were tried before an Alabama jury, found guilty, and sentenced to die in the electric chair. (All nine were much later exonerated.) About the same time, George Armstrong of Princess Anne, Maryland, was jailed for an alleged assault of a white woman. While he awaited a hearing, a white mob pushed past twenty-five state police officers assigned to protect him, dragged him through the town, hung him, and then burned his body. The leaders of the mob cut up and passed out pieces of the rope used to lynch Armstrong as keepsakes.

Just over 130 miles away from Princess Anne, Maryland, in Washington, D.C., President Roosevelt sat silent in the White House.

On October 18, 1933, Clark Foreman strode through the stately, white-columned entrance of Washington, D.C.'s Whitelaw Hotel. A five-story brick structure opened in 1919, the Whitelaw was the only hotel in the city that accommodated African American visitors. The interior was elegant—tastefully decorated and accented with classical-style molding and decorative windows. Over the years, the hotel's ballroom had hosted many affairs—parties, weddings, testimonial dinners, and political meetings. But on this chilly fall night, the Whitelaw was the site of a banquet celebrating the organization of the new Joint Committee on National Recovery. Led by John P. Davis and Robert Weaver, the Joint Committee was a rebranded version of their Negro Industrial League, which assumed the goal of uniting civil rights organizations, black churches, and benevolent societies from around the country to collaborate on a sweeping campaign to pressure the federal government to address New Deal discrimination. That night, representatives from the African American community and the Roosevelt administration dined on the Whitelaw's celebrated cuisine and listened to a carefully researched report on the state of black America offered by Robert Weaver. John P. Davis dramatically closed the session: "The work of Negro organizations united in effort to free black labor from economic slavery will not be done until real dollars find their way into the pockets of black workers, and hungry Negro men and women no longer wander the streets jobless."

Although Davis's comments were electrifying, Clark Foreman was fixated on the impressive Weaver. At the end of the banquet, Foreman made his way over to Weaver, introduced himself, and remarked that he was searching for an associate adviser in his office. Would Weaver be interested in interviewing for the position? The young economist said yes.

On November 3, 1933, at ten o'clock in the morning, Robert Weaver arrived at the Department of the Interior building. He made his way down the long hall on the first floor and found the office of the special adviser. When he opened the door, he discovered a small room with Lucia Mae Pitts at her desk in one corner and Clark Foreman at his desk in the other.

Lucia Mae Pitts witnessed most of Weaver's interview.

Foreman immediately began talking, laying out ambitious plans to fight for complete African American inclusion in all federal relief and recovery programs. The associate adviser, he explained, would carry out statistical research—collect the hard data that he could use to prove to skeptical administrators that African Americans faced persistent discrimination within all New Deal programs. Additionally, the position would carry with it the opportunity to consult on policy as well as the expectation that the office's activities would be promoted within the black public. Then, without pausing, Foreman asked Weaver: "Will you take the job?" As Pitts remembered, Weaver seemed surprised. The young economist fell silent and started to "pace the floor." Foreman did the same but "in the opposite direction." Pitts grew impatient. "Will you two please sit down?" She commanded. "You're driving me crazy."

Weaver and Foreman obediently took their seats, and then talked for almost two hours. When noon approached, Foreman invited Weaver to the Interior Department's cafeteria for lunch. The two had just seated themselves at a table when a hostess accosted them.

"Do you work in the Department [of the Interior]?" She demanded of Weaver. Foreman interceded, telling her they both did.

"Where?" She shot back. Foreman gave his office number, and she scribbled it down as she hustled away.

Foreman knew that the department's executive dining room did not serve black people and realized the stir Weaver's presence would cause.

And Weaver knew as well. When the Wilson administration mandated segregated cafeterias, his father had refused to eat in the post office's blacks-only dining room and protested by brown-bagging at his desk for years.

Lucia Mae Pitts was working alone when Weaver and Foreman returned to the office discussing the hypocrisy of Jim Crowism in a building that was owned and operated by the federal government. Foreman pleaded with Weaver to take the job—to recognize the higher purpose that could be achieved in government service, even in challenging segregation in the federal workplace. Pitts remembered Weaver was torn, concerned that the associate adviser's job would compromise his position as an activist. Weaver recalled it very differently. Desperate to get out of Greensboro and eager to make his mark, he claimed he accepted the position immediately.

Three days after his interview he wrote John P. Davis a letter breaking the news that he was about to become a New Dealer. "I believe that such a position will offer an opportunity to influence the operation of the recovery program as it affects Negroes," Weaver told Davis, pledging to continue his support for activism outside of the government. Shortly afterward, Foreman also wrote to Davis, asking that the Joint Committee on National Recovery grant Weaver a leave of absence to pursue his research for the special adviser's office.

Davis was furious. He sent Foreman a blistering response, declaring Weaver's appointment thoroughly illegitimate. The special adviser had not consulted with a single African American leader about the appointment, Davis pointed out. Bringing Weaver into the Interior Department would critically impede the Joint Committee's work, allowing the administration to monopolize, and by implication control—or, even worse, suppress—Weaver's quantitative surveys. Privately and publicly, Davis denied Foreman's request. He proclaimed Weaver's selection was "no more than a makeshift palliative which fails to remove the original and basic ill." That "ill" was Clark Foreman.

Davis also responded to Weaver in writing, pressing him not to take the post and arguing that it would co-opt his contributions to the struggle. Weaver was not persuaded. He had made up his mind, he told Davis; to turn down the opportunity would be a strategic blunder. As a New Dealer, he could feed Davis and other civil rights leaders with inside information. Davis fired back: "We are anxious that you do not become either the creature of a system, the stamp of an advisory office, or the burden bearer of an administrator's errors in regard to race." And with that, the two childhood friends parted ways. Although Weaver would continue to support the Joint Committee, he grew increasingly disenchanted with Davis, later dismissing him as "a little, short guy" who was "sort of pompous" and "liked to speak."

The Department of the Interior moved two more desks into the already cramped special adviser's office—one for Weaver and another for his secretary, Corienne Robinson, handpicked for the position by Lucia Mae Pitts. When Robert Weaver showed up for his first day of work on Monday, November 13, he became, along with Robert Vann and Eugene Kinckle Jones, one of the few African Americans who occupied advisory positions in the Roosevelt administration.

It was likely that the young Weaver had never met either Vann or Jones before joining the New Deal. Both men were well-established black leaders of the older generation, and Weaver was a young Harvard-educated upstart. In addition, when he arrived, Weaver came bearing a certain attitude. To his mind, Vann and Jones were purely patronage appointments; they were selected not for their expertise but rather to, as he put it, "pay off political debts." Cronyism had nothing to do with his recruitment, he believed. He had won his job because of his academic credentials and rigorous scholarly aptitude.

Foreman indeed had enlisted Weaver for his training as an economist and for his impressively researched assessments of the New Deal's toxic impact on the black community. But Weaver also had to pass the

Rosenwald test—he had to be approved by the group that funded the special adviser's office. This required that Weaver profess a certain brand of liberalism, one that maintained a faith that interracial accord could be achieved through the apparatus of American democracy, middle-class values, and capitalism. The New Deal sought to repair the American economic system, not by overthrowing it but by using the tools of the U.S. federal government. That approach, so buoyantly proclaimed by Roosevelt, matched the Rosenwald Fund's view, that such a federally driven philosophy could be applied in reforming American race relations. Only those who would further that political vision, like Clark Foreman, Lucia Mae Pitts, and now Robert Weaver, would be allowed through the door.

Still, Weaver was right: Vann was a seasoned, old-style political hack, and Jones, to a great degree, had ridden in on his old friend's coattails. But Weaver would discover that he had more in common with these men than he would care to admit. Both Vann and Jones had been aggressive advocates for African American rights throughout their careers. And like Weaver, they were alarmed at seeing the New Deal leaving black citizens further and further behind. In fact, while Vann personally made no criticisms of the Roosevelt administration, his *Pittsburgh Courier* and his investigative reporters devoted significant space to exposing New Deal neglect. The same week Weaver arrived on the job, the *Courier* carried stories on a strike against the meatpacking industry by African Americans who were forced to labor long hours for unfair wages despite the White House's professed concern for the "forgotten man"; demands that the National Recovery Administration pay black and white workers in the shipping industry equally; and a complaint filed by the Urban League with the Commerce Department over the obstruction of black workers from employment by Saint Louis's white labor unions. Like Weaver, Vann's *Courier* was in the business of documenting and exposing flaws in the New Deal by getting the information out to the public.

Weaver had even more in common with Eugene Kinckle Jones. As members of the black bourgeoisie, Ivy League graduates, and believers in the methods of social science, both early on recognized the potential advantages as well as disadvantages posed by the New Deal's lassoing of federal power to heal the economy. "Here you had the federal government assuming responsibilities that it had never assumed before," Weaver later observed. "This meant that the economic structure of the country would be impacted to a degree that it had never been impacted before by the federal government. . . . I was frightened by the dangers of this . . . not coming with a philosophy and a policy of involvement and somewhat equitable activity for the minority group of which I was a member." Jones had a nearly identical concern. Just after Roosevelt had taken office, Jones, as the head of the Urban League, had written to the president and sent him a report on conditions in black America. "Too often when steps are taken to ameliorate social conditions, Negroes are not given equitable consideration," Jones had warned FDR. As the White House restructured and expanded the federal government's role in the life of the individual, Jones continued, it could not ignore its responsibilities to African Americans. The federal government granted U.S. citizenship, he pointed out. Therefore, it fell to Washington, not the states or the localities, to safeguard all constitutional rights—civil, economic, and political—for all citizens regardless of race. When those rights were threatened in any form, Washington had not only the legal duty but also the moral obligation to step in to protect all Americans and their well-being.

Even before they joined the Roosevelt administration, Vann, Jones, and Weaver had begun the process of pushing the White House to redefine the New Deal. They all recognized that Roosevelt's recovery programs were more than just remedies for the country's economic woes—collectively they presented an opportunity to reformulate the federal government's approach to the welfare of American citizens. Embedded within Roosevelt's programs and expansion of federal power was the opportunity to extend civil and human rights to every American—to make real the ideals of democracy. Under the New Deal, early racial-affairs advisers believed, the American Dream could be expanded beyond its promise of economic opportunity and material success to include the guarantee of equality and human rights for all citizens.

About the time Weaver started his new job, the government announced the selection of three prominent African Americans for posts in the administration. Foreman hired the Big Four stalwart Dr. Joseph Johnson as a field representative. It was purely a political appointment, and Johnson would primarily be used to travel the country to extol the benefits of the New Deal to African Americans. Further, the Interior Department named Hampton Institute graduate Alonzo Moron the commissioner of public welfare for the Virgin Islands. But the most celebrated addition came when Secretary of the Treasury Henry Morgenthau, fulfilling the pledge he had made at Second Amenia, announced that the president of Georgia's Fort Valley High and Industrial School, Henry A. Hunt, had accepted his invitation to head up a new African American division of the Farm Credit Administration. This would bring the esteemed Hunt, who had a national reputation as a committed and diligent black leader, directly into the New Deal orbit.

Understanding full well that the recent African American appointments, including his own, were calculated for show, Robert Weaver was determined to rapidly establish that he intended to be an agent for change, a real New Deal brain truster, not just a publicity tool. The confident Weaver would give his advice, solicited or not. Pitts remembered him working long hours into the night, chain-smoking Lucky Strikes, and loudly dictating pages and pages of letters, reports, and memos. Despite Weaver's personal and intellectual fastidiousness, piles of paperwork on his desk grew higher and higher.

Within a couple of weeks, Weaver had compiled a memorandum for Clark Foreman assessing the strengths and weaknesses of not only their office but all New Deal agencies. Not surprisingly, it revealed gross inequities and deeply ingrained institutional racialism. The Interior Department's hallmark jobs program, the Public Works Administration (PWA), had failed almost as badly as the National Recovery

Administration. Work projects in African American neighborhoods were glaringly few, allocations for such programs were disproportionately low, and local black residents were routinely turned away from relief jobs. A good share of PWA projects focused on the construction or renovation of public infrastructure, including buildings, roads, bridges, and power plants. But in many areas, local PWA administrators selected contractors who hired from unions that denied black workers membership. Weaver urged Foreman to move faster to secure jobs for African Americans across New Deal programs and to lodge public protests against agencies that practiced racial discrimination. He also called for all proposed Interior Department projects and contracts to be sent to their office for evaluation and comment before receiving a go-ahead from the department's chiefs.

Weaver also made one last recommendation, which was probably the most important. Since September 1933, responding to pressure from "a national Negro organization" (likely the NAACP), Ickes had required that all PWA agreements carry a clause prohibiting "discrimination exercised against any person because of color or religious affiliation." Such a mandate was pathbreaking; never before had any federal government agency or program instituted official restrictions against racial or religious bias in hiring. Yet Weaver's report revealed that the added clause had been worthless, that flagrant discrimination remained the norm. Ickes's order, he pointed out, lacked an enforcement mandate and did not stipulate a process through which violators could be flagged and penalized. Weaver recommended that the Interior Department take the next step and commit to terminating all contracts undertaken for any project when cases of proven racial discrimination came forward. This would require the department to hire legal experts to investigate claims that work relief had been denied because of racism.

Weaver had to feel a bit of pride as well as satisfaction when he received word that Ickes had approved his recommendations. He immediately and successfully advocated for his old friend William H. Hastie to be recruited as an Interior Department legal investigator. But Hastie initially hesitated to accept the post. A dedicated activist, he recoiled at the idea of becoming a pawn in the administration's public relations efforts to deflect African American criticism of the New Deal. And he was preoccupied with teaching at Howard, working with civil rights organizations, and practicing law. He was also serving as lead attorney for the New Negro Alliance (NNA), an organization that challenged segregation both in court and through direct protest. The NNA was in the middle of its "Don't Buy Where You Can't Work" campaign, which targeted white businesses in black neighborhoods that refused to employ African Americans. Yet the pressure on Hastie to sign up with the New Deal was enormous. In addition to Weaver, Felix Frankfurter, Hastie's former mentor at Harvard (who would soon be appointed to the Supreme Court), urged him to take the Interior Department job. Hastie acquiesced. By late November, he had joined the department as a solicitor. In his spare hours, he continued to teach at Howard and walk the picket line at a store in the black community notorious for its discriminatory hiring practices.

The ranks of African Americans in the Roosevelt administration still remained extremely thin. And black appointments seemingly did nothing to put bread on tables in black homes. As disappointment and desperation intensified, Tuskegee's president, Robert R. Moton, came forward with an idea. What the president badly needed, Moton argued, was a separate "advisory committee" to consult "with the government as to the needs of colored people." He sidestepped the mention of a Black Cabinet—that was political dynamite, especially in the South, and would undoubtedly be rejected—but he laid out a plan for a group that would function as one.

Tuskegee's Booker T. Washington had led the establishment of the first Black Cabinet, and Moton, not surprisingly, emerged as an advocate for its restoration. Like his predecessor, he was an accommodationist. Regarded by many as a "strong, sensible, and tactful man," he was the one black leader who enjoyed wide acceptance from both blacks and whites. As Booker T. Washington had done, Moton pursued opportunities to advance Tuskegee as well as his position among Washington, D.C.'s decision makers. Although he had supported the establishment of the Office of the Special Adviser on the Economic Status of Negroes and the appointment of a white man as its head, Moton had grown impatient by the fall of 1933. The black press was filled with dreadful accounts of New Deal failures and white racist neglect. Nothing was getting done, and something had to change.

Moton's call for his version of a Black Cabinet came with endorsements from many black leaders, including the Associated Negro Press editor Claude Barnett and other members of the African American press. Additionally, New Deal racial-affairs advisers Eugene Kinckle Jones, Robert Weaver, and Clark Foreman offered their support. In mid-December, Moton sent his request for a black advisory committee to Ickes. The New Deal had failed black Americans, Moton told the Department of the Interior's chief. "It is no fiction to say that only indirectly and sometimes only casually and as often not at all, does the welfare of the Negro become a concern to the government," he wrote. "And when the evidence is overwhelming that he is ignored and neglected because he is a Negro, there are those who urge for the same reason—because he is a Negro—the government not take account of his condition and provide for his interests." Requests for placing advisers throughout the New Deal had largely been ignored. Ickes must push Roosevelt to accept the plan for a central black advisory committee and assign it oversight of all black recovery. Placing black relief in the hands of African Americans would give the New Deal credibility and black advisers unity of purpose, addressing profound weaknesses within the structure that already existed. "With a multitude of counselors," Moton continued, "the public is at a loss to know through whom the government can be approached concerning the things that vitally affect the welfare of the twelve million of America's most neglected citizens."

The day after Moton's recommendation landed on Ickes's desk, Foreman followed up with a memorandum to the interior secretary. He
cited the many barriers that blocked African Americans from receiving
equal New Deal assistance. Appointing an African American advisory
committee, he asserted, would have a "very great psychological effect
on the Negroes and would do a great deal to offset the unfavorable
propaganda that has gone out." Such a group must not be relegated to
window dressing for the Democrats' political aims, Foreman cautioned.
Ickes must take Moton's plan directly to the president, who needed
to appoint a "carefully selected" committee unfettered by political
patronage, one that would be "as much as possible a planning group"
for reforms in New Deal policy.

Moton's and Foreman's letters to Ickes went out just before Christmas 1933.

On Christmas Eve, the relentless Robert Weaver wrote up a report
for Foreman on a PWA proposed housing project in Atlanta named
Techwood. The plan was calamitous, Weaver had concluded. It would
bulldoze an African American neighborhood and replace it with whites-
only housing. Hundreds of African Americans would be left homeless.
The outcome, Weaver also pointed out, would use federal dollars to
worsen black poverty and validate Jim Crow segregation.

Weaver's advice was exactly what the federal government needed.
But to get the Roosevelt administration to listen, what Weaver needed
was more African American voices to join in and pressure the White
House to respond to the realities of life in black America.

Christmas came and went. The Techwood project proceeded. And
there was no word from the White House regarding Moton's proposal
to resurrect what would in reality, if not in name, be a Black Cabinet.

Much like the first Black Cabinet members, Robert Weaver and Bill
Hastie decided they would make a stand and challenge discrimination
within the federal workplace. Not too long after Hastie accepted his
position, they met for lunch and headed to the Department of the

Interior's segregated cafeteria. On their way, they flipped a coin. Weaver lost. It meant he not only had to pay for lunch but also had to be the one to request to be seated.

"Do you work here?" the hostess asked Weaver and Hastie.

"Yes," Weaver replied.

"Would you mind giving me your name?" she responded.

"No. This is William Hastie and I am Robert Weaver. Now would you mind giving me your name?" Weaver asked.

"She looked as if she were about to have a stroke [but] she gave her name," Weaver recalled. He wrote it down, and she showed the pair to their table.

They had broken a barrier by being seated in the whites-only dining room. Now the success of their protest rested with a single African American woman, waitress Dorothy Roane. The cafeteria's rules prohibited her from serving Weaver and Hastie. To do so could mean she would lose her job.

"What can I get you?" she bravely asked.

While Weaver and Hastie ate their lunch, a delegation of white female cafeteria workers made its way to Ickes's office.

Without looking up from his work, Ickes greeted them: "Good afternoon, ladies. What can I do for you?"

"Mr. Secretary, do you know that Negroes are eating in the lunchroom?" they asked.

"Yes," he replied.

"What are you going to do about it?" they demanded.

"Not a damned thing, ladies," he responded.

Shortly afterward Ickes issued a formal order directing that all of Interior's dining facilities be fully integrated. It was a victory for Weaver and Hastie and the first step in ending the discrimination that had spread throughout federal buildings since the Wilson years.

Chapter Four

A Black Cabinet

BILL HASTIE was a quiet man who preferred to listen rather than talk. In part, this may have been because he had been hearing impaired since childhood. But more so, it was because Bill Hastie was contemplative by nature. Pensive and serious, he was, as everyone agreed, a genius. One associate described him as having "a mind that can see around corners." Like his close friend Robert Weaver, he bore an Ivy League formality. Unlike Weaver, who was worldly and pridefully self-confident, Hastie possessed a nearly ethereal humility. The two men shared a devoted friendship and complemented one another. Weaver was a firm believer in numbers and quantitative analysis. Hastie had a great faith in ideas, specifically in the democratic ideals underlying American law.

When Bill Hastie joined the New Deal in the fall of 1933, he had already emerged in the D.C. community as a brilliant strategist in the civil rights struggle. His family had lived in the capital city since 1916, and the Hasties had a long legacy of militant activism. In addition to his outspoken mother, Roberta, who frequently reminded her son "they can't Jim Crow us," Hastie drew inspiration from his father, William H. Hastie Sr., who had been raised by a grandmother born into slavery. Known for his extreme reserve, the senior Hastie was a much less vibrant figure than his wife, but he shared her commitment to actively rejecting second-class citizenship. "After all," he wrote to the young Bill Hastie, "no deeper satisfaction can come to us than the feeling that we have fought against wrong—and won."

Although the Hasties had been newcomers to Washington, they were quickly embraced by the city's black elite, an acceptance facilitated by their family ties to the venerated Houstons. Bill Hastie greatly admired his older and very accomplished cousin, attorney and civil rights activist Charles H. Houston. Endeavoring to follow in his cousin's footsteps, Hastie early on aimed at a career in law. Tall, lean, and bookish, he graduated as Dunbar High's class valedictorian in 1921 and won a scholarship to Houston's alma mater, Amherst College. Finishing his BA there at the top of his class, after a brief stint teaching high school, Hastie enrolled in Harvard Law School in 1927 and was reunited with the Weaver brothers. His friendship with Robert was cemented there and grew only more steadfast after Mortimer Jr.'s sudden death.

At Harvard, Professor Felix Frankfurter ranked Hastie as one of the law school's best students ever. On Frankfurter's recommendation, Hastie became the second African American to join the *Harvard Law Review*'s staff. (Charles H. Houston had been the first.) Hastie diligently pursued his studies, establishing a reputation for stern aloofness. Classmates remembered him as extremely private, and although he spoke rarely, when the occasion arose, he would unflinchingly stand up for principle.

Hastie's solemn determination was spurred in part by his family's view that his education—his legal training—was part of a greater obligation to contribute to the uplift of the African American community. The notion that the practice of law could be a tool in the reconstruction of American society motivated Bill Hastie, who drew inspiration from his cousin. "It is where the pressure is the greatest and racial antagonisms most acute," Houston would later write, "that the services of the Negro lawyer as a social engineer are needed."

Bill Hastie entered government service with the intention of using his position to reengineer American society. Much like Robert Weaver, he viewed the New Deal as infused with transformative possibilities. The broadening powers of the federal government as it intervened in the economy could be deployed to end not only economic discrimination against black citizens but also the denial of political rights and social justice. Dire consequences awaited African Americans if the New Deal was not redirected, Hastie believed. Black Americans would not only be left behind economically if federal policies sanctioning segregation, inequality, and disenfranchisement were not blocked, they would also see all hope of claiming their constitutional rights vanish.

On the evening of December 12, 1933, Bill Hastie made his way across the Howard University campus to the library. He headed up the stairs and into the Moorland Room, which housed the nation's first archives dedicated to preserving African American history. The room was filled with books, file cabinets, card catalogs, and desks, and it also had meeting space. Hastie had been summoned by the Urban League to arrive at seven thirty sharp to join a select group of invitees for what was described as a "secret meeting." The topic of the discussion was not specified.

Hastie discovered that about fifty people had been invited to the meeting, including almost all of the African American New Dealers. (Robert Weaver and Robert Vann were away on business.) Seated around the room were Professor Kelly Miller; Howard's president, Mordecai Johnson; T. Arnold Hill of the Urban League; Weaver's former partner John P. Davis; and a dozen other representatives of the black community. Clark Foreman appeared and took a seat. The remaining thirty attendees were white federal employees from various New Deal agencies. Like other African Americans in the room that night, Hastie must have wondered why a meeting of so many government employees had not been scheduled at a federal office.

The Urban League's Hill gaveled the group to order and immediately turned the meeting over to Labor Department official Isador Lubin. The discussion for the evening, Lubin announced, would focus solely on the National Recovery Administration (NRA) and race-based wage differentials. He would not entertain comments on any other topic. All remarks would remain strictly confidential. "I assume no members of the press are present," he added, as the crowd sat in silence. It was now obvious—the meeting was being held at Howard to placate African American leaders and New Dealers who had criticized the NRA. White federal representatives were there to convince them that they were wrong.

African American attendees immediately reiterated their position that paying inequitable wages to any group of laborers, regardless of race, would hinder an overall recovery. The white representatives then made their pitch: African Americans actually benefited from the NRA as it was structured, they declared. White employers in the South would never agree to pay black and white workers equally, and, they alleged, it was well known that African Americans were less productive and less able workers than whites. To force equal pay for equal work would result in job losses for African Americans and would cut into employers' profits. This was the best the agency could do. The NRA's advocates were so blindly confident of their argument that when they finished, they asked those African Americans present to unconditionally endorse the program and its lopsided practices.

Bill Hastie, Eugene Kinckle Jones, Henry Hunt, and all other black attendees were aghast. Clark Foreman joined in as they voiced unanimous disapproval. "No Negro supported the contention that a differential discriminatory wage, because of subnormal ability . . . or under any other guise, would be advantageous for Negroes," Clark Foreman reported later to Ickes. "All Negroes who spoke agreed that such attempts at discrimination were reprehensible and unacceptable for Negroes."

As John P. Davis rose to speak, tension in the room escalated. He had just returned from an investigatory trip through the South, he reported. Then he placed on a table piles of pay stubs he had collected. Here was documentation that a vast majority of black workers under the NRA toiled long hours in the most difficult of jobs for wages on which no one could survive. Local NRA officials often looked the other way, he testified, which allowed employers to pay black workers even less than the already discriminatory rates.

Davis then recounted chilling examples. Instead of the required twenty-five cents an hour for a forty-hour workweek, one South Carolina fertilizer factory paid black men ten cents an hour for a mandatory seventy-eight-hour workweek. Black women at Georgia's Southland Pecan Company labored sixty hours a week for fifty-seven cents total. For white employers, who had always paid inadequate wages, the Depression became an excuse to cut black earnings even more. There were "thousands of forgotten 'forgotten men' in the south living on starvation wages," Davis observed, and it was courtesy of the NRA.

But Davis was not done. Racial discrimination in the NRA was not confined to local offices: it originated at its top. He produced copies of confidential minutes taken during a September 1933 closed-door meeting of high-level New Deal officials. He began reading verbatim.

"Are you also situated that every day brings a group of demands from a group of Negroes to be appointed to something?" Secretary of Labor Frances Perkins asked, complaining that her one African American adviser, a Republican holdover, was "not very satisfactory." She sighed, "I don't know how we are going to deal with them."

Ickes chimed in. "I do not see how we can appoint them as Negroes," he said, still stinging from the criticism he had received over Foreman. "If we did that, we would have to appoint women as women and nationalities as nationalities."

Perkins's tone then changed, and she stridently disagreed with Ickes: "The Negroes are treated differently as workers than any other group of people, and it is just possible that one who has exhibited discrimination against Negroes . . . is not qualified to follow up on their complaints."

Perkins was usually regarded as sympathetic toward black Americans, and despite her support for hiring African American advisers, the overall exchange was troubling. It revealed that two of the administration's most progressive cabinet secretaries regarded African American inclusion as burdensome.

Yet, far more alarming were the remarks that came from the NRA's Hugh Johnson. He grumbled about Mabel Byrd, a Second Amenia alumna and University of Chicago graduate who had been hired by one of his deputies to investigate racial inequality in the administration's work programs. Curiously, despite mounting complaints from African Americans, Byrd had sat idle at her desk for weeks, given no budget to carry out her work, before being inexplicably laid off. "Dr. [Alexander] Sachs has appointed a Negress to look into certain matters with respect to Negro labor. I questioned the wisdom of it and the extent of authority he has given her," Johnson sputtered. "This was crazy. It gave her authority to go in and interrogate employers and all that kind of thing."

A representative from the Department of Agriculture concurred: "We would be playing with fire to send a Northern trained Negro to the South [to investigate white employers' practices]."

This may have been real concern for Byrd's safety—African Americans who traveled in the South, even for leisure, were always in harm's way. But the comments also revealed that New Deal advisers not only worried about offending southern sensibilities but also subscribed to them. Johnson both couldn't remember Byrd's name and identified her using the despised racial slur *Negress*. John P. Davis declared that the minutes demonstrated "an indication of the callous indifference exhibited by President Roosevelt's official family" for black citizens.

Black racial-affairs advisers who attended the Howard meeting couldn't have been completely surprised. They had all experienced the internal racism that pulsed throughout the federal government. But to hear it coming from the administration's highest-level leaders made the fight against New Deal exclusion seem even more daunting. They left the meeting disgusted and discouraged. When he heard about what had transpired, Robert Vann sent a memo to Roosevelt adviser Louis Howe: "I cannot believe the President shares the spirit which the minutes convey. . . . To my mind, the whole thing is unpardonable."

Clark Foreman felt the same way. He shot off a blazing letter to Ickes, demanding it be forwarded to Commerce Secretary Daniel C. Roper. The minutes, Foreman seethed, revealed that the administration's core leaders were prejudiced against African Americans in general, and the Howard meeting proved that the New Deal's architects were adherents to the southern myth that African Americans were inferior and undeserving of comparable pay. It was outrageous that the National Recovery Administration believed it could lure black racial-affairs advisers and civil rights leaders to a meeting and then assume that they would happily endorse the agency's racist policies. Outside of publicity stunts, some high-profile appointments, and empty pronouncements, the New Deal had done nothing but harm African Americans, Foreman charged.

Despite Isador Lubin's hope that the press had not been present at the Howard meeting, among those in attendance were two black community leaders who were also newsmen. Quickly, the story of the leaked minutes appeared in African American newspapers. What had been suspected by many in the black community seemed to be confirmed. Racism and paternalism infected the National Recovery Administration, as well as other New Deal and cabinet departments, all the way up to its highest level. News stories appeared to confirm that the Roosevelt camp had grabbed the black vote and now had left African Americans to go it alone.

To make matters worse, the Department of the Interior, rather than responding to the needs of African Americans, was harassing John P. Davis. Ickes ordered a probe to determine the source of the leaked minutes. When an Interior Department investigator grilled him, Davis tersely recommended that Ickes stop persecuting black critics of the New Deal and concentrate on investigating racial discrimination across a variety of New Deal programs, including those directly under Ickes. In the end, it turned out that lots of people, from lower-ranking officials to the president, had seen the minutes, so nobody could pinpoint how they had made their way to Davis. But Ickes's heavy-handed response only heightened African American alienation within the administration.

By the end of 1933, it seemed to many African Americans that Roosevelt's policies were well on their way to cementing American racist ideology into federal practice. The *Baltimore Afro-American* quoted

Southern Tenant Farmers Union representative Howard Kester's assessment that the New Deal was nothing more than a "raw deal" for black
citizens. In his letter to Ickes, Foreman implored the cabinet official to
make good on his promises to treat black Americans fairly. The secretary
must intercede with Roper and force him to assert control over the
National Recovery Administration, he insisted. Someone had to get to
Roosevelt and demand that the president step in and stop the damage,
not only to preserve his image but to save the African American people.

By the night of the meeting at Howard University, Franklin Delano
Roosevelt had been in office for nine months. Although much of the
country had embraced his buoyant optimism, the economy had shown
only slight improvement. The Great Depression was far from over, and
that was especially true for African Americans. Although Roosevelt
was not actively hostile to African Americans, race was an issue that he
evaded as much as possible. "I think there is no doubt that President
Roosevelt had made a calculated determination . . . to hold the support
of the southern Democratic leadership, including the most reactionary
and prejudiced of that leadership," Bill Hastie reflected.

As part of that effort, FDR and the Democrats had dispensed choice
White House patronage positions to many white loyalists from below
the Mason-Dixon Line. This placed Roosevelt behind a solid barrier of white southerners who controlled the Oval Office. Roosevelt's
press secretary, Stephen Early, of Virginia, led this group. Early and
Roosevelt's senior aides—fellow Virginian General Edwin M. Watson
and Kentuckian Marvin H. McIntyre—had been nurtured in southern racism and Jim Crow customs. Together this trio of White House
advisers, who oversaw FDR's appointment calendar, vigilantly denied
African Americans access to the president. The NAACP's executive
secretary, Walter White, recalled being repeatedly stonewalled by the
White House staff, which refused to forward his letters and telegrams
to FDR. When Charles H. Houston and a black reporter attempted to
see Louis Howe at the White House, a white secretary curtly greeted

them with, "What do you boys want?" Early excluded black journalists from White House press conferences. He even denied Eleanor Roosevelt's request that an African American female reporter be admitted to her press briefings.

But Roosevelt did have contact with African Americans, and on a daily basis. For years, Roosevelt had employed black servants at his Hyde Park estate and at his second home in Warm Springs. When he moved into the White House, he brought along his own staff, which joined many career White House maids, butlers, and cooks who were black. The First Lady shuddered when she discovered that the black and white domestic staff dined in separate and starkly unequal quarters. She didn't demand integration, fearful of alienating white voters, but instead discharged most of the white help and opened up the whites-only dining room to all black household employees.

For the permanent African American White House domestic staff, the arrival of the Roosevelts marked a new era. Longtime maid and seamstress Lillian Rogers Parks recalled that Herbert Hoover required household workers to remain, as much as possible, invisible, separate, and silent. Franklin and Eleanor Roosevelt's White House was the opposite. "Under the Roosevelts, doors stood open, and happy voices rang out, and there was no more popping into closets, and no more hiding when the President or the First Lady took the elevator," Parks remembered. "You were invited to 'come in and ride along.' We walked freely down the halls."

The First Lady generally disliked and circumvented, when she could, White House hierarchies and traditions. At the inaugural lunch, Eleanor Roosevelt joined the staff and helped serve the guests. She often scrambled eggs for the family herself (it was, in truth, the only dish she could make). Butlers were no longer required to stand at attention during informal dinners or family meals. When she heard that head doorman John Mays's wife had passed away suddenly, the First Lady canceled all of her appointments and spent the rest of the day with him at his home. While Eleanor Roosevelt did not speak out openly against racism, her acquaintance with Mary McLeod Bethune as well as with the NAACP's Walter White won her respect in the black community.

Although the Roosevelt White House seemed more relaxed, the domestic staff's jobs, in many ways, became increasingly demanding. The Roosevelts' large family, live-in confidants, dogs, and endless stream of guests made for long days and nights. On the one hand, the president and his kin "weren't hard to please," according to one butler. But on the other, the executive mansion seemed to be in a perpetual state of chaos. African American staff members recalled the Roosevelts often working tirelessly into the night as they struggled against the Great Depression. Eleanor Roosevelt came and went constantly and unpredictably, sent out on trips to survey conditions in the United States and to speak on behalf of her husband.

Both Franklin and Eleanor Roosevelt agreed that the White House had to set an example. Although born to wealth and privilege, Franklin wore frayed shirts, sweaters with holes in them, and old suits. Eleanor banned extravagant, multicourse dinners and insisted that all leftovers be served to the family. While it was admirable that the First Family imposed frugality on themselves, at the same time this penchant for austerity severely impacted White House employees. When he assumed office, Roosevelt cut the salaries of all federal workers, which included White House domestic staff members who already often took outside employment just to get by. Even those who had come with the Roosevelts from Hyde Park found the pace taxing and the compensation inadequate. But the Roosevelts' head butler, James Reynolds, counseled the staff not to complain to the First Lady; long hours were her norm, and she would not be sympathetic.

Among the White House domestic staffers, none worked harder than Irvin McDuffie and his wife, Elizabeth. College-educated and a gregarious conversationalist, Irvin McDuffie was working as a barber in Atlanta in 1927 when he was called to Warm Springs to cut FDR's hair. Roosevelt, who always enjoyed a good talk, took to McDuffie immediately, and recruited him as his personal valet. Over the years, McDuffie was by Roosevelt's side day and night, taking off only one afternoon a week. He was completely loyal to FDR. "I didn't know anyone could have a disposition as good as his, there's no other man like [Roosevelt]," he told one reporter in 1933.

Elizabeth McDuffie was even more outgoing than her husband. Although born into a sharecropping family in Georgia, she had graduated with a major in theater from Morris Brown College, where she forged a friendship with classmate Walter White. Despite holding a college degree, she found herself confined to domestic jobs and followed her husband to the White House, where she served as a maid. The career staff there found Lizzie McDuffie, as she was known, to be somewhat shocking. She rejected the stiff deferential propriety that was customary for those who served the president and First Family. Vivacious and possessed of a boisterous sense of humor, McDuffie was startlingly chummy with the president. "Lizzie treated FDR like one of her own family, kidding him and teasing him by kissing the bald spot on top of his head," Lillian Rogers Parks remembered. Roosevelt seemed to welcome the attention, and addressed Elizabeth McDuffie as "Doll." Like her husband, she was intensely devoted to the president. While some definitely disagreed, Elizabeth McDuffie later maintained that Franklin Roosevelt "was democratic without posing and a true friend of the Negro race without paternalism."

FDR depended heavily on the McDuffies. The couple lived in the White House and was on call twenty-four hours a day. It was common knowledge that Roosevelt had contracted polio in 1921. But the public wasn't aware that the president was paralyzed below the waist and required constant assistance. The McDuffies, along with other members of FDR's inner circle, played a significant role in keeping the president's disability hidden. Irvin McDuffie was responsible for seeing to all of FDR's needs—getting him up in the morning, putting on his heavy iron leg braces, lifting him into a wheelchair, and attending him throughout the day. Each night, McDuffie helped the president wash, remove his leg braces, and prepare for bed.

Additionally, Elizabeth McDuffie was the only White House maid who had complete access to the president's bedroom. "He [FDR] had no secrets from her," Parks claimed. White House domestic staff members were required to maintain strict confidentiality, and this was especially important with the Roosevelts. The president's marriage had been compromised by earlier infidelities, and by the time he arrived at the White House, his relationship with the First Lady had become almost exclusively a political and intellectual partnership. There were also whispers that Eleanor Roosevelt, in turn, had her lovers. The domestic staff carried the burden of covering up any such dalliances for both Roosevelts. But it was the McDuffies who assumed most of the responsibilities for protecting the president.

Irvin and Lizzie McDuffie not only saw to FDR's personal and household needs, they also helped manage the White House's relationship with the black community. Lizzie McDuffie later claimed she had informed the president that she would act as his "SASOCPA"—his "self-appointed-secretary-on-colored-people's-affairs." Later she insisted that she had pressured Roosevelt behind the scenes—compelling him to pardon three black World War I veterans imprisoned for their alleged participation in a riot and making him aware of the plight of the nine youths falsely accused in Scottsboro, Alabama. In private, both McDuffies joined the chorus of voices critical of the New Deal, informing the president of discrimination in jobs programs and the Civilian Conservation Corps. Black leaders inside and outside of the New Deal administration realized that even though Stephen Early blocked them from getting information and requests to the president through normal channels, the McDuffies were glad to act behind the scenes as couriers to both the president and the First Lady. Certainly the McDuffies were in the know about the

Howard University meeting and its fallout. That the talkative couple did not at least mention it to the president seems unlikely.

On December 27, 1933, Harold Ickes was ushered into the Oval Office for a meeting with Franklin Delano Roosevelt. White House secretaries had allotted Ickes fifteen minutes at noon. With the clock ticking, the next appointment pacing outside, and lunch waiting, the notoriously direct interior secretary made it quick. The policies of the National Recovery Administration and other New Deal programs had been disasters for black Americans and were eroding their support for the administration. A midterm campaign was fast approaching, and Democrats would need every vote they could get to protect their efforts to heal the national economy. Ickes briefed FDR about Robert Moton's proposal for an advisory committee to offer counsel on African American affairs. That might appeal to African American voters, Ickes allowed, but in his opinion, the idea was "a mistake," because it would "establish a precedent for the setting up of committees representing different races, nationalities, and other groups."

Roosevelt agreed and nixed Moton's proposal. What would be acceptable, Roosevelt told Ickes, was for all cabinet and New Deal programs to be asked but not required to dedicate at least one adviser, black or white, full- or part-time, to African American concerns. There would be no separate committee, FDR stressed, but Ickes could go ahead and facilitate a meeting in which racial-affairs advisers could "correlate their work" by sharing information and discussing problems. Policy making, however, was strictly off-limits.

The cunning FDR was always carefully navigating political waters. Somehow, in that meeting with Ickes, he had both rejected and accepted the formation of a Black Cabinet.

On January 2, 1934, Ickes informed Clark Foreman of the president's decision. Foreman immediately began working with Robert Weaver to organize a meeting of government officials to assess the status of black recovery. Naming it the Inter-Departmental Group Concerned with the Special Problems of the Negro, Foreman and Weaver both knew they had a hard fight ahead. Very few federal agencies had anyone assigned to serve African American needs. Most New Deal and cabinet department heads felt either that they had done enough for African Americans or that the black community did not merit any singular attention. But Weaver and Foreman believed that the establishment of the Inter-Departmental Group might compel most, if not all, programs to appoint at least one adviser dedicated to addressing conditions in black America. Although Ickes had warned Foreman away from developing policy, the audacious special adviser, when he issued the call to meet, informed invitees that the purpose of the group was to help "formulate general principles of action" to lift African Americans out of the Depression.

As Foreman and Weaver worked on getting the Inter-Departmental Group off the ground, the White House began taking other steps to improve its image among African Americans. Shortly after the New Year, encouraging stories of more black appointments began to appear in the African American press. The government's messenger corps, a main conduit for communication within Washington, D.C., had long been primarily African American—and its ranks had expanded vastly to meet the needs created by the rapid growth of the New Deal. Although in the past, black applications for civil service and clerical posts had been shuffled to the bottom of the pile, now more African Americans were receiving federal jobs throughout the nation's capital.

But black newspapers devoted most of their attention to the addition of African Americans to upper-level advisory positions in the New Deal administration, most certainly a calculated effort by the White House to court black voters. The Department of Agriculture, the Public Works Administration, and the Federal Emergency Relief Administration (FERA) recruited African Americans for key posts—several of the selectees were big names among black leaders. Forrester Washington, the highly respected head of Atlanta University's School of Social Work, was appointed as FERA's lead racial-affairs adviser.

Lawrence Oxley, the director of North Carolina's black welfare division, secured a choice position with the title "Commissioner of
Conciliation for Negro Labor" in Frances Perkins's Department of
Labor. And finally, William Thompkins received his long-anticipated
reward: thirty years of loyalty to the Democratic Party had won him
the position of the recorder of deeds of the District of Columbia,
the post once occupied by the iconic abolitionist and civil rights
activist Frederick Douglass.

The increasing number of African Americans in New Deal posts
and word that the government was setting up the Inter-Departmental
Group Concerned with the Special Problems of the Negro produced
considerable excitement within the African American community. In
January 1934, the Associated Negro Press editor Claude Barnett asked
his Washington bureau chief, Eugene C. Davidson, to produce a series
of profiles on African American government officials. Davidson was
a Washington, D.C., native and a member of the city's black elite; his
father was an attorney and famous for patenting a number of innovations to the adding machine. A Harvard graduate, Eugene Davidson
had been drafted during World War I and, serving in 369th Infantry
Regiment—the "Harlem Hellfighters"—he had fought 191 days in the
trenches and at the decisive Second Battle of the Marne. He returned
home a hero and, well-positioned, he came to know many African
Americans in the federal government personally.

Yet, Davidson was also a hard-hitting journalist and initially rejected
Barnett's proposal, worried he would be forced to write fluff that would
promote the administration and plug the careers of black New Dealers.
But shortly afterward, as enthusiasm for the new appointments grew
and hope for the Inter-Departmental Group rose, Davidson changed
his mind. He believed that by using his pen, he too could contribute
to redirecting the New Deal.

In March 1934, the first installment of Davidson's syndicated column, entitled "The Black Cabinet in the New Deal," ran in African

American newspapers nationwide. In it, Davidson announced that a Black Cabinet had been born:

> Roosevelt is the hub of our wheel of progress. . . . Connected by spokes is another wheel, a cabinet of the president and heads of his alphabetical administrations. On the outside of this wheel is the outer circle, the rim, the iron rim that takes all the hard knocks of the uneven road. . . . This rim, this outer circle, is the Black Cabinet.

In Davidson's opinion, African Americans had reached a watershed moment. "The New Deal is a revolution, and if you and I do not realize it, we are asleep as history is in the making," he declared. His assessment of FDR was positive: The president was "a cool, collected, courageous radical . . . who firmly translates his promises for the forgotten man into vigorous and unprecedented action." With this shift in government, he wrote, had come a team of African Americans hired by New Deal agencies and cabinet departments. It included, most notably, Robert Vann, Henry Hunt, Eugene Kinckle Jones, Forrester Washington, Lawrence Oxley, William Thompkins, Bill Hastie, and Robert Weaver. (Davidson also named several other lower-level black appointees, along with Clark Foreman, as Black Cabinet members.) Davidson posed a question for the Black Cabinet: "Where is the Negro during this revolution? . . . Is he fighting for his prize in the sun or is he hopefully and prayerfully taking what is handed him with promises that when it is all over, he will be taken care of?" He also provided the answer—it was the Black Cabinet's responsibility to lead and make sure that this opportunity for transformation was not lost.

With Davidson's column, the "Black Cabinet" was reborn. He promised his readers a frank, insider's appraisal of its members.

Over the next several weeks, Davidson profiled various members, and his assessments were not flattering. Robert Vann was a single-minded political opportunist, in Davidson's view: "He has the illusions that he is the greatest race politician that ever came along, but [he] likes to play a lone hand of influence." Vann was a cutthroat willing to sell out others to advance himself. Henry Hunt of the Farm Credit Adminis- tration understood "the sharecroppers' woes and their struggles to get ahead under conditions similar to peonage," Davidson acknowledged. But at the same time, he asserted, Hunt's grasp of the black American experience was tenuous at best. The sixty-seven-year-old Hunt was so light-skinned he was commonly presumed to be white. To Davidson, Hunt was "a colorless old gentleman, colorless both literally and figu- ratively." Eugene Kinckle Jones was lauded as "honest," "statesmanlike," and "race-interested." But Davidson charged it was "absurd and illogi- cal" for the former Urban League head to accept a post as a Commerce Department adviser. Jones had grabbed whatever position he could: "He likes too well, it seems, the title of advisor, which means but little in this revolution where dynamic direction of a program is needed and an enthusiastic sponsorship of an unpopular idea is essential."

Davidson's articles certainly established the Black Cabinet in the minds of his readers. But it was not the image that either the admin- istration or racial-affairs advisers desired. The journalist's strident criticism of Black Cabinet members raised public concerns about their commitment and competency. His columns endangered these advisers' internal battles to reform the New Deal and threatened to erode external support for African Americans who had broken into the federal ranks.

To do damage control, someone inside the New Deal administra- tion assigned Clark Foreman's secretary, Lucia Mae Pitts, to counter Davidson with a series entitled "New Deal Personalities." Pitts was an experienced journalist, and she knew how to craft human-interest articles that appealed to readers. Robert Vann's life was presented as a model rags-to-riches story; he was an inspirational activist, lawyer, crusading editor, and devoted family man. Pitts judged Henry Hunt as "quite distinguished looking" and emphasized his unquestioned com- mitment to the African American cause as well as his love of sports, especially baseball. She highlighted Eugene Kinckle Jones's impressive qualifications and remarkable physical fitness, and readers learned of his fondness for "all southern cooking." Robert Weaver was celebrated as brilliant and conscientious. "He has a keen mind and the ability generally to see all sides of a question, as well as the consequences of all points of view," Pitts noted. And she made sure to mention that he was not only "good looking" but also single.

As Pitts rolled out her series, Davidson continued to pound away at the Black Cabinet in his columns. His fourth profile zeroed in on Clark Foreman. Like many African Americans, the journalist felt that Foreman's selection as special adviser was a catastrophic blunder. "Dr. Foreman, sincere, immature, and bashful, cannot," he argued, "no matter how hard he tries . . . [free himself from] his southern background." He specifically condemned Foreman's support for racially separate homestead subsistence farming projects. Foreman's contention that the policy "protected" African Americans from hostile white southerners was only an excuse for spreading federally sanctioned Jim Crowism. "As a leader of the race," Davidson warned, "he is most dangerous to its future emancipation."

When Claude Barnett received Davidson's Foreman column, he personally edited the draft and then sent the column off under Davidson's byline. The revised Foreman profile that appeared in various African American newspapers around the nation was packed with praise. The special adviser was a "team player" who sought advice from African Americans and who had the potential to bring about the "establishment of a new faith" by providing African American people "unusual service."

Davidson was furious when he saw how Barnett had scissored out and varnished over the criticism in his original submission. He protested to the editor by letter and then released his original version to the press. It ran in several papers along with the journalist's allegations that Barnett had suppressed the truth and succumbed to "powerful influences."

In response, Barnett canceled the Black Cabinet series. He wrote to Davidson heartily denying that he had bent to the will of the White House, or to anyone else. Dismissing Davidson and his charges, Barnett insisted he was unbothered and that the columnist's accusations were "far from the truth, so we won't worry."

In the midst of the dustup over the Foreman profile and to counter what had become extremely toxic publicity, Lucia Mae Pitts fired back with a generous appreciation of her boss. Making it clear that she worked closely with him, she praised Foreman's work on behalf of interracial cooperation and stated that in her view, his commitment to African Americans was sincere. While Foreman was "youthful," serious matters were never far from his mind, and he spent hours working for African American advancement.

Although Pitts had the last word, it was Davidson's columns, which the Associated Negro Press circulated widely, that spread the news about the Black Cabinet. Despite his pronounced skepticism, Davidson had planted in the black public's mind the idea that the Roosevelt administration housed a Black Cabinet and that the group, despite its flaws, was dedicated to rescuing African American people from the Great Depression and taking on the fight for civil rights. This was reinforced as other journalists began to mention the New Deal's Black Cabinet.

Watching as the African American press resurrected the term "Black Cabinet," Kelly Miller joined in to spread the word. In a syndicated article, "'FDR's Negro Brain Trust'—What Will It Do?" he compared the newcomers to his comrades who had served under Theodore Roosevelt and William Howard Taft. But there was a dramatic difference, he told his readers. These Black Cabinet, or brain trust, members were far better equipped for the fight. The new members were men of exceptional merit, "a body of highly trained Negro experts and specialists such as has never been known before." Miller also hailed this as the beginning of a second Reconstruction of the nation—one in which African Americans would finally achieve equal citizenship. "The Negro stands in the most critical position which he has occupied since emancipation," he wrote. The responsibility to push forward and fulfill the promises made to black Americans by the Constitution would fall to the new Black Cabinet. Not only must they forcefully advocate for African Americans to receive their equal share of the New Deal, they must also lead the battle for human rights and social justice in America. "They must blaze the way," Miller decreed, "and show the race how to walk therein."

As a Washington insider and longtime friend of the Hastie-Houston family, Kelly Miller was aware of the fierce internal wars the Black Cabinet members had begun to wage on behalf of the African American people. Like racial-affairs advisers of the past, they encountered bitter contempt and resentment within the federal government. Many divisions within the executive branch resisted appointing black advisers or assigning officials to deal with African American affairs. Most agencies that hired African Americans assigned them to report to lower-level administrators, who were often dismissive and refused to forward information or complaints up the chain of command. John P. Davis was right; racial animosity extended into the upper ranks of the Roosevelt administration. It was impossible to forget that the worst of racial slurs was used by ranking government officials, including a treasury department official, in public statements. The *Baltimore Afro-American* reported that Democratic leaders Joe Guffey and James Farley had demanded the president fire the Justice Department's narcotics commissioner Harry J. Anslinger for circulating an official and open memorandum containing the term "ginger-colored n-----." Anslinger escaped termination; he was protected by a powerful Democrat, the newspaper publisher William Randolph Hearst.

Furthermore, Jim Crow continued to dominate the federal workplace. Government washrooms were segregated by race, and many elevators were reserved for whites only. African American appointees were prohibited from using the recreational facilities provided for federal workers. Despite Weaver and Hastie's efforts, most government dining rooms refused to serve African American advisers. Frances Perkins eventually integrated her cafeteria but mostly because the

Labor Department had been infested with vermin, and she wanted to stop employees from eating at their desks. When Bill Hastie arrived at his job, he discovered that the all-white and all-female Interior Department clerical pool had unanimously decided it would not work for him. Eventually, the department hired and assigned him an African American stenographer—and placed her desk in an area that was separate from her white counterparts.

Hastie may have had hope that such flagrant racism would not be tolerated for long in his division. His immediate boss was Nathan Margold, one of his Harvard law professors, who had urged him to take the Interior Department job. But Hastie soon discovered that Margold refused to confront the racism that existed in his own division and avoided assigning him to cases directly related to African American concerns. Instead, Hastie's initial tasks focused on title disputes on Native American reservations. In an interview with a black reporter, Margold claimed that Hastie would eventually be given cases where he would "be able to serve your people," which, in his mind, included residents of American Pacific island protectorates, "Alaska, Howard University, Indians, etc." Eventually Hastie was brought in to consult on the Virgin Islands. But outside of Howard University issues, none of his assignments had any relation to Interior Department policies affecting African Americans.

Like other members of the Black Cabinet, Hastie found serving in the Roosevelt administration an isolating experience. Scattered throughout federal agencies, most racial-affairs advisers had little opportunity to interact or develop relationships—in fact, the Black Cabinet of the early New Deal was more a concept than a collective effort. Most black officials spent time away from Washington conducting field investigations and speaking in black communities across the nation on behalf of the White House and its programs. Vann and Jones had a long friendship but often headed home to their families on the weekends. Henry Hunt and Forrester Washington were overloaded not only by their government jobs but also with their continuing responsibilities at their respective colleges. And everyone knew Lawrence Oxley had a reputation as a lone wolf who pandered to whites.

Robert Weaver and Bill Hastie, as they had done at Harvard, looked to each other for support. In 1934, Weaver purchased a row house near Howard University and moved out of his parents' home. There, in his basement, Weaver and Hastie revived the poker sessions of their college years. "We met frequently in my recreation room for all-night bull sessions," Weaver recalled. At first the group was small. Charles H. Houston was a regular, as was old Harvard pal Ralph Bunche, who was teaching in the political science department at Howard. When they were in town, Walter White and Roy Wilkins of the NAACP dropped in. The group grew as the government started to add more black advisers. It was a highly select crowd of young black New Dealers, eventually including, among others, William J. Trent Jr., a Wharton alumnus; respected journalists Henry Lee Moon and Ted Poston; educator Frank Horne (who was the uncle of entertainer Lena Horne); and Weaver's assistant, Booker T. McGraw, another Harvard graduate, who had a newly minted PhD in economics.

An evening at Weaver's included drinks, cigars, some serious poker playing, and a lot of manly joshing. Always stiffly professional at work, Weaver relaxed during poker nights. He ruled the room with his quick wit and "sometimes earthy, sometimes sly" sense of humor. The Harvard crowd was intense and competitive. "They wiped me out," stated Truman Gibson, a later War Department appointee. "Bunche taught me how not to play poker."

But poker nights were not just about cards. As the hour grew late and as the room filled with smoke and talk, the discussion turned solemn. How could American racism be fought and civil rights finally secured? What was the best and fastest strategy to end the suffering in black communities around the nation? How could those determined to block African Americans from participation in the New Deal be outsmarted? These nights were dominated by "feverish discussions of how faster progress could be made in achieving equal opportunity for Negroes."

Deep bonds developed among the group. "There were obvious advantages in these friendships," recalled Bill Hastie, who played his cards quietly and spoke thoughtfully. "We shared ideas *and* information."

Robert Weaver's poker nights would play an important role in how the Black Cabinet negotiated for just treatment of African Americans by the federal government. The mutual support the gatherings provided became crucial as the Inter-Departmental Group Concerned with the Special Problems of the Negro began to meet in early 1934, about the same time Davidson was introducing the Black Cabinet to the public. Although the black press reported on the organization of the Inter-Departmental Group, details about its activities were sparse, since its meetings were strictly confidential. But behind those closed doors, Black Cabinet members quickly realized what they were up against. From the beginning, most of the group's white members were either blithely ignorant of African American realities (and determined to remain so) or openly hostile to black equality.

The first meeting took place on February 7, 1934, when seventeen men, only six of them black, and Lucia Mae Pitts as minute taker, assembled in a Department of the Interior conference room. Robert Vann, who chaired the meeting, wasted no time and immediately demanded members report on the status of black relief in their divisions. Most of the white attendees rushed to speak first. The Department of Agriculture representative boasted that its relief programs, especially those established by the Agricultural Adjustment Act, were resoundingly successful. W. D. Searle, of the War Department, which oversaw the segregated armed forces as well as the Civilian Conservation Corps, declared that he strongly "doubted that anyone could say . . . [his division] has a race problem." The Treasury Department, which participated in numerous New Deal programs, claimed to be confused as to why it had been invited, since it claimed that it "had very little to do with the Negro problem."

The few white representatives who admitted that discrimination existed in their programs dismissed the idea that it could be any other way. Assistant Secretary of Labor Edward McGrady maintained that he personally believed in equal pay for equal work, but it was unfeasible, in his opinion, since it would stir aggressive white resistance. The National Recovery Administration's Charles Roos acknowledged that black workers suffered disproportionately under his program. He admitted that the administration's codes had resulted in "displacement of Negro workers" and "violations . . . and intimidation of Negroes for economic reasons." But he concurred with McGrady—white racial assumptions could not be contested. These problems were impossible to fix.

But most white delegates argued that their programs had reasonably served the black population. Some cited their agencies' use of hiring quotas based on the 1930 census, which showed African Americans were about 10 percent of the nation's population. The spokesman for the multistate Tennessee Valley Authority (TVA) contended that the Wheeler Dam project did not discriminate, because nearly one-tenth of its labor force was black. While he conceded that the number of African Americans working on the Muscle Shoals Dam was far below the 10 percent mark, he argued it was still fair. Blacks composed only a small proportion of the population in the vicinity, he claimed. In reality, as black members pointed out, both projects were in regions of Alabama with black populations that numbered far greater than the national average. What emerged but went unsaid was that the TVA manipulated the data and invoked quotas when they worked in favor of white laborers.

When confronted about the disparities in the program, the TVA representative shrugged. African Americans in the region inexplicably refused to apply for the program's jobs, he insisted. It couldn't be because of prejudicial treatment, because no one had complained of it. Perhaps "illiteracy" was a deterrent for some, he mused. Yet, he added, curiously African Americans in the area seemed to be restrained by some unspecified "fear." Black advisers around the table knew exactly what that meant; African Americans in the Tennessee River valley were being kept away from relief work under the threat of violent white retribution.

The meeting's tone changed as Black Cabinet members offered numerous examples of the New Deal's gross inadequacies and widespread discrimination. Henry Hunt questioned the cheerful claims about Agricultural Adjustment Act programs, which offered landowners incentives to cut production and take land out of cultivation, with the goal of driving up prices of farm goods. Reports from the South revealed that African American sharecroppers were being driven from their farms under the policy. The program, which offered loans under the Farm Credit Administration, was thoroughly impractical for black people, Hunt pointed out. Participation required property ownership, and most African Americans were landless. Robert Weaver offered statistical evidence proving New Deal urban renewal and housing programs forced African Americans from their homes. Almost all new federal housing was reserved for whites, and the only way to halt the spreading of black homelessness, Weaver asserted, would be to integrate these projects. Forrester Washington of the Federal Emergency Relief Administration declared that his office files were teeming with letters from desperate African Americans needing jobs. Ignoring the president's restriction against policy making, he announced his intention was not just to answer these letters but also to develop a "creative program" to get African Americans relief work.

After nearly three hours, the group was at an impasse. Black advisers had made clear the New Deal's deficiencies and the urgent need to redress them. But their reports were met with incredulity and even open hostility from several white representatives. Foreman and Black Cabinet members made a motion to establish subcommittees to compile statistics on the impact of the New Deal on the African American population. It was blocked. The mood was gloomy. Eugene Kinckle Jones suggested that the Inter-Departmental Group meet again in March to focus solely on black industrial labor. That idea passed unanimously.

The next meeting was even more volatile than the first. Weaver and Hunt had been dispatched to the field, leaving only four Black Cabinet members at the table. But they came armed with loads of documentation confirming New Deal racism. Forrester Washington presented comprehensive evidence "of discrimination and other irregularities in both the Civilian Works Administration and the Federal Emergency Relief Administration." Eugene Kinckle Jones followed with statistics that proved black poverty during Roosevelt's first year in office had risen at an alarming rate. Clark Foreman offered a report demonstrating that New Deal legislation protecting unions severely hurt black workers. Under the new policy, the American Federation of Labor (AFL)—a national alliance of labor unions—had emerged as the go-to proxy for the execution of all New Deal labor contracts. Since most local AFL chapters refused to admit black workers, vesting so much power in a single union placed yet another barrier between African Americans and federal work relief.

At the end of Foreman's report, resentment from several white members spilled into the open. The Civilian Conservation Corps' James McEntee and Labor Department official Edward J. Tracy, both former AFL men, vigorously denied the charges that the union practiced discrimination. The AFL's national charter prohibited racial bias, blustered McEntee. But local AFL chapters maintained independence, Eugene Kinckle Jones countered. It was common knowledge that the locals actively banned black workers. McEntee and Tracy bristled. Forrester Washington cited reports that the AFL refused to admit African Americans to metal, stone, and wood workers unions. "Can you deny that?" he thundered.

McEntee and Tracy could not, and the scuffle over labor continued, until the War Department's W. D. Searle interrupted. Union practices were beyond the group's purview, he maintained. The group had been restricted from advising on policy, he argued, scolding Black Cabinet members for straying from their charge. Foreman pointed out that *advice* was exactly what racial-affairs *advisers* had been hired to provide. He also argued that it was the responsibility of the group to bring the consequences of union legislation to the White House's attention. There was no good reason to keep cabinet officials and the White House in the dark, Robert Vann asserted. The president, he stated, "would be amazed if he knew the facts." For criticism of the New Deal to reach even a cabinet secretary was simply unthinkable, Searle said. All that would do was hurt the entire effort to heal the country's economy. Cabinet chiefs would just pass the information back to agency heads, and FDR would never see it anyway, he added, dismissively.

Black Cabinet members refused to back down. Over Searle's strident opposition, the group organized two committees. One would investigate black industrial labor, and the other would report on conditions in black rural America.

On March 30, with Weaver and Hunt back from the field, the Inter-Departmental Group reconvened. This time, of nineteen in attendance, eight were African American. The agricultural subcommittee took the floor first. Its study proved that Henry Hunt's assertions were correct: the Agricultural Adjustment Act (AAA) had only intensified economic misery for African Americans, most of whom were sharecroppers. Under the AAA, landholders who let farms lie fallow or destroyed crops and livestock were given federal subsidies that were supposed to be split with their tenants—but most kept the funds for themselves. Although the AAA prohibited it, many white planters evicted sharecroppers from their farms, leaving entire families without a place to live or any means of support. Reports revealed that white planters showed up at New Deal field offices "demanding jobs and relief" for their African Americans tenants. In some places, local agencies complied. But their administrators often paid black wages directly to white landlords, and hence many African American tenants never saw a single penny. Racism and discrimination permeated all aspects of farm aid. It was controlled by local officials and white planters who colluded not only to prevent black recovery but also to rob African Americans of any progress made in the nearly seventy years since emancipation. Assistance programs were not enough; recovery demanded major economic and social reform.

The situation for black labor was not much better. Eugene Kinckle Jones presented data showing that New Deal programs were leaving

African Americans further and further behind. Jobs in cities and towns that had traditionally been occupied by African Americans, ranging from elevator operators to sanitation workers, had gone increasingly to whites. In addition to the closing off of employment opportunities, the wage gap between black and white workers was growing. Disturbingly, Jones reported, his committee's investigation revealed that white "intimidation of the Negroes" had risen in urban areas across the country. The future promised more marginalization, more violence and threats, and increased poverty.

Bravely and solemnly, Robert Weaver rose to anchor the most controversial portion of the labor report. He had compiled statistics on African Americans and labor unions. The numbers spoke for themselves, he declared. Nationwide, only a small portion of African American workers belonged to unions, because almost all unions, including the AFL, allowed white locals to vote down African American applicants. Making life even more difficult for black workers, New Deal legislation carried provisions that forbade employment to strikebreakers. Since scabbing had been one route through which African Americans entered the industrial labor force, these new federal restrictions barred them for life from employment in many trades. As structured, the New Deal's attempts to protect and empower unions only disadvantaged black workers, Weaver asserted, observing that "it allowed them to be exploited as a sub-marginal group and it accentuated the racial discrimination to which they ordinarily are subjected."

As Weaver finished, James McEntee, Edward Tracy, and other white representatives from the Labor Department sat fuming. Immediately, one Labor Department official spoke up; the labor committee's report was too combative, and it must be revised to emphasize "cooperation." Weaver's assertions were "superfluous" and patently wrong, McEntee declared. The committee must delete all the sections that "acknowledge that there is any attempt to discriminate against Negro labor." The unflappable Robert Weaver objected—to redact those portions, he said, would render the report meaningless by erasing its most important findings. In the end, Weaver triumphed; the Inter-Departmental Group allowed his conclusions regarding racism and American labor to stand.

For the first time, hard evidence documented by government officials proved that Roosevelt's recovery programs had set back African Americans. It preserved for time and for history the experiences of millions of forgotten black workers crushed by racism and economic upheaval. As the meeting ended, tension hung heavy in the room. Sullenly, the Inter-Departmental Group members dispersed without scheduling a follow-up meeting.

In the meantime, Robert Weaver had begun attempts to recast New Deal policy to address black America's problems. Since the fall, he and Bill Hastie had deliberated on how to increase the number of African Americans employed in Interior Department work-relief programs. Weaver had successfully exposed the failures of Ickes's nondiscrimination clause; it had no teeth—no mechanism by which it could be enforced. Charges of discrimination continued to stream into the special adviser's office. But proving government contractors were violating Ickes's order required costly and time-consuming case-by-case field investigations. In the end, evidence gathered for a single instance did not demonstrate the reality that African Americans en masse were subjected to prejudicial treatment. Additionally, when confronted, noncompliant contractors hid behind New Deal legislation, arguing that they were restricted to hiring only union labor, which was usually exclusively white.

But by the early months of 1934, Weaver and Hastie had devised a plan. At the first Inter-Departmental Group meeting, the TVA had cited quotas (based on contrived numbers) to protect the lion's share of relief jobs for white workers. Weaver had concluded that these same statistics, when accurately applied, actually proved that black workers had been subjected to prejudicial treatment. Weaver wondered: If a program did not employ African Americans in proportion to their population and their skills in an area, then wasn't it evidence of discrimination not just against an individual but also against the entire group? Of course it was, Bill Hastie replied. Such statistical data fit the legal category of prima facie evidence—which "establishes fact"—and it would prove that racial bias affected black workers as a whole. Contractors could be required to hire African Americans even if unions refused their membership, Hastie advised. When deviations were discovered, the government was obliged to cancel the contract, under Interior Department rules.

At Weaver's urging, the Interior Department had begun using prima facie evidence to watchdog jobs programs for racial bias. It "caused some resentment," Weaver admitted, but overall it was a "positive" and successful solution. What Weaver and Hastie did not realize was that they had innovated a pathbreaking policy that would become the foundation for other federal antidiscrimination regulations—and the pioneering affirmative action legislation of the 1960s.

But in 1934, the challenge was to get other New Deal agencies and cabinet departments to adopt the prima facie model to prove discrimination against African Americans in their programs. Weaver and Clark Foreman decided that if the Inter-Departmental Group met again, they would try it out there.

They got their chance when the group finally reassembled on June 1. Isador Lubin, who had presided over the calamitous Howard University meeting in December, was present on behalf of the Labor Department. Unwittingly, he provided an opportunity for Weaver and Foreman to introduce the prima facie concept when he remarked that the Labor Department was unable to require antidiscrimination clauses in all government contracts. Since each governmental agency was free to draft its own contracts, Lubin announced, the department had no legal right to intervene. Nothing could be done; federal law did not prohibit racial bias in hiring, and there could not be "a revolution in thought and social habits overnight" that would compel equal opportunity.

Clark Foreman disagreed. "It occurred to us," he remarked, almost offhandedly, "that a possible solution is saying that any variation in the [proportion of African Americans in the] various trades from that of the 1930s census can be considered prima facie discrimination unless a good reason is given for it."

Lubin was stunned. Wouldn't it be impossible to find skilled African Americans in trades like carpentry to fill all needed positions on construction projects? he stammered. Not at all, responded Robert Weaver. The data showed quite the contrary. According to the 1930 census, there were plenty of skilled black laborers available throughout the nation.

Lubin remained skeptical. Never one to back away from a fight, Foreman refused to let it go. The labor official had to concede, Foreman said, that there was "special pressure of the Ku Klux Klan and other unions . . . to employ [only] white labor" and that the only way to protect black workers was for the government to step in. Lubin grew anxious, but he seemed to agree as he dashed off for another obligation.

Then the raw feelings festering among members of the Inter-Departmental Group surfaced openly. When Eugene Kinckle Jones called for a study of the demotion of black combat soldiers to the servant ranks, African American Labor Department appointee (and army veteran) Lawrence Oxley forcefully objected. That subject, he blustered, was completely outside of the group's charge. The War Department's W. D. Searle jumped in, warning that Jones's proposal was inappropriate as it was "touching on politics tremendously." Robert Vann refused to let that comment pass. A discussion of inequality in the military was not "touching on politics," he retorted, it was "touching on policies."

The verbal scuffle raged on. Eventually, the gracious Eugene Kinckle Jones got the floor again and reminded the Inter-Departmental Group members of their grave responsibility:

> After all, some of us are representatives of the people and they are interpreting our position here as being . . . interested in all their American life. We know this is the most difficult problem—the race problem—the American people have faced; but if, as President Roosevelt says, the whole idea is toward a fuller life, every black man is expecting to have a little fuller life tomorrow than today. . . . If we narrow ourselves, not

carrying ourselves outside certain problems that relate only to immediate recovery, then we are denying ourselves the opportunity to discuss here things that will contribute toward a general, fuller life.

Jones articulated what had become the Black Cabinet's mission. The members were more than advocates for Depression-era assistance; they were the vanguard of a new civil rights movement.

There would be no investigation of the military, and the Inter-Departmental Group never met again. Still, Foreman and Weaver viewed the group as a success. They believed that the establishment of quantifiable evidence of racial discrimination within the New Deal was itself a victory—even if it did not make it all the way up through the chain of command to the president.

For the powerful team of Bill Hastie and Robert Weaver, the Inter-Departmental Group had provided a forum that allowed them to introduce the practice of using prima facie evidence as a test of racial discrimination. They believed it had the potential to open up opportunities, not only in employment but also in other aspects of society, that could radically alter the lives of African Americans. But as the year progressed, none of the federal divisions outside of the Department of the Interior were willing to adopt it.

Later in 1934, Bill Hastie stood before an NAACP audience in North Carolina. As always, he measured his words carefully. By this point, he had found working for the government discouraging. But he maintained a profound faith in the legal ideals upon which the country was built. He urged his listeners "to take advantage of all constitutional guarantees" offered through the justice system as they battled against the Great Depression and American racism. "The Negro has got to fight now with all the power he has against every denial of those rights that appears," Hastie urged.

Bill Hastie was a reflective man. Certainly, he knew that he was speaking as much to himself as he was to his audience.

Chapter Five

Factions

IN 1934, like other victims of the Great Depression, Alfred Edgar "Al" Smith was desperate for steady work. The national unemployment rate had improved somewhat; it was down to 21 percent from its peak at about 25 percent the year before. Yet African Americans, including those in the nation's capital, saw very little of that extremely modest recovery. Living with his wife, Leona, in her mother's boardinghouse in Washington, D.C., Smith was just scraping by. Leona was pursuing a degree in education, and he had enrolled in a master's program at Howard University. He earned what he could by substitute teaching and freelancing as a journalist. When finances got really tight, his mentor at Howard, Alain Locke, loaned him a few dollars.

What Al Smith needed was a stable job, and what he wanted was one with the government. He was caught up in the excitement of the New Deal. In early 1934, in a *Pittsburgh Courier* column, he cheered: "The Democrats are in! We remember when this was a signal for our parents to assume an air of tragedy . . . [but] consider[ing] the present-day appointments of Negroes to office under the Roosevelt Administration, and listen[ing] as two Democratic Congressmen introduce an anti-lynching bill, we find reason for our belief that times have truly changed." The task ahead, as the midterm elections neared, was to keep the Democrats in power so the country could be healed. Al Smith was anxious, and hungry, to become a part of that mission.

Yet a job in the Roosevelt administration seemed like a long shot. Most of the government jobs were going to big names like Robert Vann, Eugene Kinckle Jones, Henry Hunt, and Forrester Washington. The Rosenwald Fund controlled the majority of the remaining posts and allotted them to appointees like Robert Weaver—men possessing advanced degrees, primarily from the Ivy Leagues, and from distinguished families. Al Smith came from a solidly working-class background. He had a BA from Howard, the top historically black university in the country, but for the Rosenwald crowd, that was not quite enough.

That kind of pretension aggravated Smith, but nonetheless he pushed ahead. The thirty-one-year-old Arkansan had come up the hard way— "I'm an Ozark hillbilly . . . lean and mean and tough as a ten-penny nail," was how he described himself.

Al Smith was proud of his humble roots. His father, Jesse R. Smith, had been enslaved in Virginia and eventually made his way to Hot Springs, Arkansas, where he married Mamie Johnston. Born in 1903, Al was the youngest of their four children, and his early life was one of austerity. Jesse and Mamie Smith worked at the renowned Arlington Hotel mineral baths, earning a dollar a day plus tips. They were frugal and carefully saved their earnings so they could purchase a home and some acreage. The Smiths were strict and had no patience for "foolishness"; they expected all their children to work hard. As a youth, Al Smith "fed all the livestock, took out the ashes, split kindling and sawed wood, laid and made fires, gathered eggs, weeded." It toughened him: "If you never sawed a cord of oak wood with a buck saw greased with a bacon rind, you never worked hard."

Smith also remembered constantly facing white bigotry, claiming that even as a child, he had his own way to resist it. When white dignitaries visited his school, the teacher demanded that the children sing spirituals. Smith silently protested by only mouthing the lyrics.

But racism in Hot Springs was often overt and violent. Undoubtedly, Al Smith remembered twenty-year-old William Norman. In

1913, Norman was accused of assaulting a fourteen-year-old white girl. A mob—numbering, by some reports, more than one thousand—kidnapped him from the city jail. As Norman professed his innocence and begged for mercy, his assailants took him to the city center, stripped him naked, tied him to the crossbars of an electric pole, and used him for target practice, riddling him with bullets until he was dead. Then his body was "cut down, thrown onto a blazing bonfire and burned," reported one paper. Local authorities claimed that "the great number of persons in the mob makes fixing of responsibility unusually difficult." No one was ever prosecuted for Norman's lynching.

Al Smith was determined to break free from the Jim Crow South, and with his mother's encouragement, he set his sights on Howard University. But his father's sudden death, in 1916, drove the family into destitution and forced the teenager to go to work to help support the family. Over the next four years, at nights, on weekends, and during summer breaks, Smith worked as a hotel bellhop and elevator operator. When his mother died in 1920, he lied about his age and applied to Howard. He was accepted, left Hot Springs, and headed to Washington, D.C., for a better life.

Howard was, as Smith recalled, "a new world." He studied under some of the era's most notable black intellectuals, taking courses from the famous Kelly Miller, the revered historian Carter G. Woodson, and the literary giant Alain Locke, who was regarded as the father of the Harlem Renaissance. Smith became a popular man-about-campus. He was striking—almost six feet tall, very thin, light-skinned, with blue-gray eyes. A raconteur with a rollicking sense of humor, he joined a fraternity (Omega Psi Phi), managed and appeared with the Howard Players, and, after an encounter with an up-and-coming Duke Ellington, started his own band. He met W. E. B. Du Bois, and he wrote for the NAACP's *Crisis* and the Urban League's *Opportunity*.

After his postgraduation trek to California in 1932, Smith returned to Washington to begin research on his master's thesis in U.S. history entitled "The Elimination of the Negro from Politics, 1870–1908."

Studying nights at Howard and working during the day, he trolled Washington, D.C., offices for a federal job. In the spring of 1934, Forrester Washington, the Federal Emergency Relief Administration's racial-affairs adviser, announced he was looking for an assistant. Smith wanted the post badly and asked Locke for help. The professor interceded, and in March, Al Smith joined the New Deal.

On his first day, Smith was escorted into an office furnished with only one chair and two tables that were stacked high with thousands of letters from African Americans pleading for aid. "Do something with these," he was told. Mrs. Roosevelt had demanded each receive a personal response.

The letters told an anguishing story of black lives during the Great Depression.

An elderly woman in Shreveport, Louisiana, wrote: "Mister Roosevelt, Dear Colonel and Dear Sir, Here I sit with borrowed pencil, borrowed stamp, borrowed paper, borrowed envelope, and tears in my eyes." There was widespread starvation and death in her community, she testified. Another letter pleaded with the president to send rent money before its writer was out on the streets: "I ain't got nowhere to go, so you better hurry up." W. B. Smith, who had a relief job at a Louisiana mill, told of the discrimination black workers faced. "The feeling the white race have against the colored race" was so intense that local officials had assigned guards to protect black people working on New Deal projects. His federal boss paid out the prescribed wages to black workers, but deducted rent for uninhabitable lodgings. Jake Adams of Selma, Alabama, protested the state's practice of ignoring the National Recovery Administration's minimum wage requirement; he made only ten cents an hour. "Please tell me what to do? I will have to have something to take care of my people," wrote Adams. "I know the United States Government is putting this money out here for us laboring men. This is what the President says. So, I am willing to do my part, that is as far as I am able—but I'm not willing to work for nothing."

When Al Smith looked out the window of his office, he could see across the Potomac, where Robert E. Lee's estate stood, "with its old slave quarters on the distant hills of Arlington." On nice days, the office was filled with warm afternoon sun. But the view of the Lee plantation, standing as a relic of slavery, the Civil War, and the unreconstructed nation, served as a daily reminder of the gravity of Smith's task. This wasn't just a job. It was a fight against the legacy left by enslavement.

Al Smith sat down and began answering each letter, one by one.

As Elizabeth McDuffie told the story, her husband was just bringing the president into his private office when the White House phone began jangling. It was an evening in February 1934, and calls normally were screened by White House secretaries. But that night, the secretary on duty was late. The line rang and rang. According to Elizabeth McDuffie, the president finally grabbed the phone himself.

"I'm Sylvester Harris, down in Mississippi," said a voice on the other end. "A man is getting ready to take my land and I want to know what to do. The papers say to call you and here I am."

McDuffie recalled that Roosevelt was in an especially cheerful mood. "Sylvester, I'll investigate, and you'll hear from me," FDR promised.

Within a few weeks, with help from a government representative, Harris's farm was saved.

The personal appeal of an African American farmer to the president offered the Democrats a choice opportunity for midterm campaign publicity. Stephen Early, who had worked for both the Associated Press (AP) and Paramount Pictures News, made sure Harris's story appeared in national newspapers and in movie newsreels for months afterward. The white media gobbled it up but also used it to reinforce the most negative of stereotypes in its coverage. An AP dispatch claimed that Harris identified himself as "a nigger down here in Mississippi," and alleged the farmer complained that before he reached FDR, "de White House gentleman what answered the phone up ther got mad and said, 'Quit calling de president.'" The black press also ran accounts of Harris's appeal, but they protested the disparagement and inaccuracies circulated by the white media. The *Pittsburgh Courier* declared that the AP had "misquoted" Harris, and the *New York Age* ran the farmer's interview without putting it in dialect. The *Chicago Defender*'s report revealed that Harris was far from a countrified rube; his farm was one of the most productive in the region.

The Sylvester Harris story seemed to confirm that FDR really was a down-to-earth champion of common Americans. Such an image was critical to the Democrats as the midterm election cycle started to grind forward. The survival of the New Deal depended on maintaining, if not growing, the party's majority in the House and Senate. Anything less would mean the end of Roosevelt's recovery programs and jeopardize his efforts to resuscitate the American economy. A faction within the Democratic National Committee was convinced black votes could protect the New Deal. At least some Democrats, among them political boss Joe Guffey and FDR's close adviser Louis Howe, were anxious to see the party and the president portrayed as friendly to the black community. They believed that in addition to Sylvester Harris, the Black Cabinet could also be an asset in reaching out to African American communities.

In July, as the campaigns heated up, New York congressman Joseph A. Gavagan took to the House floor to make a speech. A Democrat, Gavagan was Irish Catholic and had been raised in Hell's Kitchen, one of Manhattan's poorest neighborhoods. Education had helped him climb out of poverty, and he held a law degree from Fordham University. Representing upper Manhattan, including parts of Harlem, he was an outspoken advocate for the New Deal, FDR, and civil rights. Earlier in the year, he had introduced an anti-lynching bill only to see it die in committee, in part because of rock-solid opposition from southern Democrats. He would not give up and continued to reintroduce the anti-lynching legislation. Gavagan, who genuinely despised lynching, was up for reelection in 1934, and he desperately needed his African American constituents' support.

"Mr. Speaker," Gavagan began, "I . . . take peculiar pride in setting forth in the Congressional Record as I see it just how the colored citizen has fared under the New Deal." He hailed both the president and the First Lady for bringing a new attitude to the White House. "It has been increasingly evident that President Roosevelt, unlike his predecessor, as well as Mrs. Roosevelt have drawn no 'color line' at the White House." FDR had offered Haiti's black president the same courtesies extended to white world leaders. The First Lady had been photographed holding the hand of a six-year-old African American boy at the annual Easter egg roll. She had vocally condemned inequality in black education, saying that "we can have no group beaten down, underprivileged, without reaction on the rest." Gavagan hinted that the president had supported his anti-lynching bill and had even made efforts to get the bill to the House floor. And the congressman claimed that "well-known colored leaders and highly trained social experts" had been recruited to serve in the New Deal. They formed a "little cabinet" (a reference to the unsanctioned Black Cabinet) and advised the administration on issues of race.

Gavagan's address ran verbatim in the black press. It implied that the Black Cabinet was FDR's idea and that the president sought the group's guidance. Of course, African American federal officials knew the real story—the president had vetoed the creation of a Black Cabinet and had no intention of consulting with its members.

But the battle for the black vote was on, and Democrats hungrily exploited whatever they could to gain an advantage. That included calling up members of the Black Cabinet and sending them out as spokespeople for the New Deal. Their investigatory trips and speech-making were absorbed into the Democrats' midterm campaign strategy and used to buttress the party's ambitions for a fall election sweep. It placed the black brain trust in an awkward position. Several cringed at the idea of sugarcoating White House policies. But at the same time, most agreed that the New Deal was the black community's best hope. At one stop, Eugene Kinckle Jones conceded that relief programs suffered from inequalities but, he insisted, the Roosevelt plan was still a "better deal" than any previous administration had offered the African American people. "Despite the shortcomings of the Federal Emergency Relief," Forrester Washington remarked, at a social workers' conference in late spring, "without it the colored race could hardly have survived."

When they appeared together at a symposium on black labor, Clark Foreman and Lawrence Oxley tried to sound upbeat. "The immediate effect of the NRA [National Recovery Administration]," Foreman declared, has brought "more benefit than harm to the Negro." When some listeners groaned in disagreement, Oxley shouted: "President Roosevelt is no fairy with a magic wand." When several audience members alleged that Black Cabinet members were covering up the administration's failures, Oxley shot back: "The colored workers serving under the New Deal in Washington are no buffers or wastebaskets, and the NRA is beneficial to the colored man."

Robert Vann also encountered deep skepticism on the road. Speaking to an adult education group in New York, he praised the Roosevelt White House for forging "a new and more favorable mental attitude towards the colored man." The black citizen had "refused to be licked," Vann announced, and was "smiling through his rags." Hearing that, one audience member couldn't hold back his disgust. "Do not go back to Washington," he admonished Vann, "and tell Mr. Roosevelt that the Harlem Negro is smiling through his rags. . . . The Harlem unemployed are serious and in a fighting mood."

For Forrester Washington, pretending enthusiasm for the New Deal was almost unbearable. He had grown increasingly impatient with the administration's apathetic attitude toward the needs of black Americans. He had also come to view his Black Cabinet colleagues as too tentative and too accommodating. Believing that external pressure might help racial-affairs advisers make their cases to federal chiefs, he issued a press release, probably written by Al Smith, calling for "colored welfare and citizens' committees to visit their local FERA [Federal Emergency Relief Administration] headquarters and make their needs known." That strategy, calling on the black public to lobby local, state, and even federal administrators, eventually was adopted by most Black Cabinet members.

In the spring of 1934, Washington also announced in black newspapers his plan for each "destitute Negro family" to receive a government loan in the form of a farm with livestock and seed. Participants would pay off their debt with surplus crops and by working on New Deal infrastructure projects. Then he fired off a memorandum to FERA chief Harry L. Hopkins, demanding that the plan be implemented immediately. He added that black women needed to be included in relief programs and charged that confining black workers to unskilled positions in jobs programs was as bad as the dole.

Hopkins never replied.

In late July, fed up with the administration's indifference and neglect, Washington dropped a bombshell. He announced he would resign from FERA the following month. With the midterm campaigns gaining more momentum, the declaration could not have come at a worse time for the Democrats. In interviews with black journalists, Washington denied any discontent and said that he simply wanted to return to his post at Atlanta University. But rumors of his frustrations circulated extensively. Many observers interpreted Washington's departure as a vote of no confidence in both the New Deal and FDR. They hailed his act as a "protest resignation."

Almost immediately, the fight began over who would succeed Washington. It brought the tensions growing within the Black Cabinet into public view. Hunkered down in various agencies, racial-affairs advisers found themselves pitted against one another in competing divisions. Their efforts were affected by the turbulent and transitory nature of the New Deal. The administration's many programs were quickly assembled, disassembled, and then reassembled; some overlapped, and upper-level officials fought over the same and often scarce resources. Loyalty to one's division and boss was the unspoken rule within the culture of federal government workers. Divisive workplace politics that flared among high-ranking white New Deal chiefs further complicated the efforts of African American federal officials.

Additionally, by this point, clear factions, divided by generation, education, and position, had emerged within the Black Cabinet. Each camp had its own favorite for the FERA position. It was a choice job; it had the potential to add a key member to one of the black New Deal cliques.

In early August, Eugene Kinckle Jones invited a group of black federal officials to the Commerce Department to hash out who would take over Washington's job. It's likely that no one was surprised when Jones opened the meeting and declared he wanted the FERA position. Robert Vann immediately seconded the idea. Jones was a nationally recognized expert in black jobs creation. What more needed to be discussed?

"Mr. Jones' bid . . . was said to have been received very coolly by the younger brain trusters," reported the *Chicago Defender*. At the table were J. Victor Cools and J. P. Murchison, two black Department of the Interior employees who were allies of Robert Weaver. It was time for "new blood," they protested. The appointment must go to someone unfettered by political cronyism, someone with fresh ideas. "Nothing had been done by the 'older heads,'" and it was time to push energetically ahead for change.

District of Columbia recorder of deeds William Thompkins, also present, opposed Eugene Kinckle Jones, but he didn't like the "new blood" idea either. The post must go to a Democratic Party loyalist as a sign of good faith by the Democratic National Committee to black voters. Jones was a Republican, Thompkins pointed out; it would be a political blunder to put him forward. And, he added, Robert Vann should not dictate who should get the post.

Vann was furious.

Thompkins continued, brandishing what he told the group was the secret memorandum of May 1933 sent by the Big Four to President Roosevelt. None of the recommendations had been fulfilled, except the appointment of Vann to the Justice Department, he observed. He began reading directly from the document. Vann protested vigorously and demanded he stop. "I'm not used to being hushed," retorted the D.C. recorder, and he resumed reading. Vann grabbed a hat and stormed out of the room. Quickly realizing he had the wrong hat, Vann headed back to retrieve his own. A black reporter lurking outside in the hall suspected that something was up.

Before long, accounts of the dispute over Forrester Washington's successor filled black newspapers. It did not look good for either the Black Cabinet or the White House.

In the end, the job went to a FERA insider—Harry Hopkins picked Al Smith. As Washington's assistant, he had loads of experience, and he was free from ties to any of the Black Cabinet's warring parties. Some African American leaders complained that Smith was the wrong man for the job. He was too green; he was an unknown, they charged. Smith brushed off the criticism; he was enormously proud of being chosen—it was a personal triumph and a chance to create opportunities for others. FERA issued press releases announcing Smith's promotion. Surely the news would help the Democrats' efforts to court black voters and protect the New Deal.

As congressional campaigns launched into full swing in the fall of 1934, African American Republicans urged the GOP to exploit the Black Cabinet's squabbling in order to undermine the Democrats' attempts to snare the black vote. Much to their shock, the GOP's leaders were not at all interested. "In my mind the most important thing that the colored voter should realize is that the Republican Party is their friend," wrote one Republican congressman to Associated Negro Press editor Claude Barnett, evoking the GOP's status as the party of Lincoln. "I believe that colored voters realize [that] . . . and that the Republican Party can rightfully depend on their support."

Claude Barnett, a GOP stalwart, did not share the leadership's confidence. Despite widespread disappointment in federal aid programs, African Americans did not blame the president, he argued. Rather, they believed New Deal failures rested with local authorities who refused to enforce FDR's will. The "glitter and glamor of the New Deal," which Roosevelt had grounded in the rhetoric of the "common man," and the presence of a Black Cabinet appealed to black voters, Barnett contended. He could lend a hand by publishing stories exposing the administration's many flaws. Not necessary, GOP leadership replied. There was no budget for that kind of publicity push anyway, they claimed.

A few African American Republican editors still made an effort to block the Democrats from collecting black votes, concerned that African Americans would be lured into a self-serving party dominated by the bigoted, unrepentant white South. They agreed with Barnett; the Black Cabinet, now one of the Democrats' main selling points, made a perfect target in Republican attempts to undercut the White House. As the election neared, the *Kansas City Call* planted a rumor, reporting that a "reliable" source had confirmed that the president would "disband" the Black Cabinet after the midterms. Other papers picked up the story. The *New York Amsterdam News* asserted that "the President is not in favor of a special set-up for Negroes . . . and [now believes] that their problems should be approached from the same conception of general public welfare as those of other citizens." Job titles identifying advisers as specialists on race would be dropped, it stated.

The claims that the black brain trust would soon be dead forced the Democrats into a defensive mode. The Black Cabinet was "Not on Way Out in Washington," proclaimed one source. In fact, it was more robust than ever, asserted another. Black appointees had increased over the past several months. The *Baltimore Afro-American* listed twenty-one African Americans holding advisory jobs in cabinet departments and New Deal agencies. By denying accusations that the Black Cabinet was being dismantled, the African American press helped to further cement it into the imagination of the African American public.

In many ways, at this point, the Black Cabinet existed mostly on paper, since there was so little collaboration among its members. But through African American journalists, it was increasingly becoming a reality. The black press was powerful. For black communities, it functioned as a lifeline of information. Racism and segregation restricted the gathering and dissemination of news. Traditionally the mainstream white press, in print, on radio, and in movie newsreels, either ignored or distorted events related to black lives. When African Americans did receive attention, it was almost always disparaging coverage that perpetuated degrading black stereotypes: it sensationalized purported black criminal activity; it highlighted embarrassing episodes; it normalized racial discrimination; it promoted white supremacist thought. White American journalism focused on white people and reinforced white attitudes and privilege. It ultimately and, sometimes purposefully, blocked African American access to important news and information related to black lives. In turn, the black press shouldered the responsibility of filling in the gaps. Black newspapers not only highlighted black interests, achievements, and activism; they also exposed lynching, police brutality, and the persistent denial of African American rights. Ultimately black reporters, newspapers, and wire services played an important role in educating, inspiring, influencing, and empowering African Americans.

White House and government officials were generally oblivious to the reporting done by black journalists, and very few white Americans read black newspapers. But some in the Democratic Party leadership were at least aware of the importance of the African American press to the black community. And despite the Democratic National Committee's best efforts to plant positive stories, as the November election neared, much of the news related to black America continued to be discouraging. Discrimination persisted in jobs programs. Agricultural relief still bypassed black farmers. Housing projects rejected African American applicants. Some critics in the black media began to protest more loudly, placing the blame for the lack of action on African American New Dealers. The Black Cabinet needed to step up quickly because, as the *Baltimore Afro-American* pointed out, "young people are . . . expressing lack of faith in leaders."

On October 19, 1934, Claude Neal, a twenty-three-year-old African American farm laborer in Jackson County, Florida, was arrested for the murder of a white woman. A week later, vigilantes broke into the jail where he was imprisoned, forced him from his cell, and tortured him. He was stabbed. He was choked. He was burned. Members of the mob severed parts of his body and forced him to eat his genitals. Finally, they killed him. Neal's body was dragged behind a car to another location, where a mob numbering in the thousands further mutilated the corpse before hanging it in a tree and posing for photos with it. The mob then raced over to Neal's mother's home (she had been arrested as an accessory but incarcerated in another jail) and burned it to the ground.

News of Neal's lynching spread throughout the nation's white and black media outlets. "It is a revolting and revealing story," read an editorial in the *Pittsburgh Courier*. "Revolting because of the unbelievable savagery of the dehumanized wretches who tortured the youth to death and dismembered his body and revealing because [of] the conditions, social and economic, which it exposes." Such violence, the paper asserted, operated to perpetuate black "economic exploitation" through fear and trap "terrified Negroes in a condition little better than chattel slavery." Pushed to respond publicly, Franklin Roosevelt stalled. Receiving a request from the NAACP that she speak out against lynching, Eleanor Roosevelt left a note on the president's nightstand asking his permission to do so. It was denied. Walter White wrote to Harold Ickes urging him to read the NAACP's report on the Neal lynching, warning that "the effect of such an outbreak" of mob violence threatened "the whole Recovery program."

On October 25, 1934, the night before Claude Neal's life was taken, Clark Foreman announced his resignation at a banquet for John P. Davis's Joint Committee on National Recovery. He had negotiated with Ickes to have Robert Weaver replace him.

"I considered jobs to be the prime essential for improved economic status and that I would try to get as many for Negros as possible, including my own," he chuckled. "I meant what I said, and I am happy to announce that an extremely well qualified Negro, whose attitude on problems affecting colored people is one which merits your confidence, now has my job." As he concluded his remarks, he praised the Black Cabinet. "Advisers can do much to fight segregation, discrimination, and general injustice," he assured the crowd. "There are numerous instances which I could cite where foresight on the part of an adviser and a memorandum to the right person have greatly improved conditions."

Shortly after Weaver took over Foreman's spot, Americans went to the polls and handed the Democratic National Committee a nice victory. The party swept contests across the country, earning a sizable majority in both the House and the Senate. African Americans played a role in the Democrats' win. Despite the New Deal's failings and the White House's silence on the nightmarish Neal lynching, black voters didn't hold the president responsible for their troubles. For many, FDR had become an icon. His portrait appeared in black homes. "Where a large number of blacks lived, during fireside chats you could hear [the broadcasts]. . . . Walking down the street, you didn't have to worry about getting home . . . because it would be turned on all the way," Robert Weaver recalled. "[The president] made listeners feel as though he were talking to them and to them individually, and alone." Just before the election, the Democratic National Committee brought Sylvester Harris, the farmer who had telephoned FDR, to Chicago to speak for the party and the president. "Folks flocked to see him," reported the *Pittsburgh Courier*. "A lot of them, moved by his homely philosophy, were to some extent guided by him." The Republicans just could not compete. The New Deal might have been flawed, but many black citizens believed in Roosevelt—and that he was a president for all forgotten Americans.

What had started as a trickle of black voters into the Democrats' fold two years earlier became a stream in 1934. Reflecting on the election, Robert Vann praised the black community for "awakening." This time, black citizens did not need to turn Lincoln's portrait to the wall; it was obvious, Vann said, that "if Abraham Lincoln were alive today he would have to be a liberal and a Democrat." The DNC's scheme for courting black voters had worked, and the party owed some of that success to the Black Cabinet.

Shortly after the midterm races, political reimbursement for black loyalty started to flow. "Race Gains Posts in Democratic Landslide," the *Pittsburgh Courier* announced, as more African Americans received federal appointments. Al Smith and Robert Weaver saw increases in their budgets and hired more assistants. As a concession to Robert Vann, the federal government added five million government dollars to Pennsylvania's budget; a portion went to railroads as incentives to hire black workers. Black New Dealer and education specialist Ambrose Caliver told reporters that local federal administrators had been instructed to disseminate federal funds to black and white schools equally. Later in November, President and Mrs. Roosevelt visited Nashville's Fisk University, one of the nation's most notable historically black colleges. The famous Fisk Jubilee Singers sang "Hand Me Down the Silver Trumpet, Gabriel." The students gave the Roosevelts a standing ovation.

While the White House basked in its midterm victory, the Black Cabinet struggled against a dense barrier of internal white resistance to its quest for reforms that would better the lives of black citizens. Its members doggedly chipped away at the system, circulating reports on discrimination to anyone who would read them; wresting money to fund their programs; building prima facie cases to stop discrimination when they could. They used the White House domestic staff to get messages and information to the Roosevelts and relied on African American allies in the federal messenger service for access to information on high-level discussions impacting black people. When they couldn't make headway from the inside, they leaked information to the black press and to other African American leaders. But the Black Cabinet's progress was painfully slow, and by necessity its activities were generally hidden from the public.

Some community leaders and African American journalists grew increasingly impatient with what seemed like a lack of action by the black brain trust. The *Chicago Defender* blasted African American New

Dealers, especially those under Ickes, as "spineless," "political parasites," and "intellectual flies." Without naming him, the *Defender* accused
Weaver of not possessing "the courage and manhood to champion
the economic and industrial rights" of the African American people.
The Black Cabinet had accomplished "NOTHING," it charged, and was
obstructed by in-house divisiveness and backstabbing. The *New Journal
and Guide* of Norfolk, Virginia, published a letter blaming black officials
for "sleeping at [the] switch" while black schools floundered. In the
New York Age, Forrester Washington finally expressed his true opinion
openly: President Roosevelt was false-hearted, and his New Deal had
purposefully excluded African Americans. Black Cabinet members
needed to stand up and confront the administration. "The only thing
that works upon Washington is political pressure from the outside and
pitiless publicity," he warned his former colleagues. "The job of the
Negro advisor is to do something besides praising."

Robert Weaver found the criticism distressing. As the head of the
Office of the Special Adviser on the Economic Status of Negroes,
he had been working around the clock for change. The Rosenwald
funding had reached its limit, and now his division relied entirely on
federal dollars. He received a larger office which, with a firm hand, he
led according to his personal work style: it was hectic, operating at a
nonstop pace, yet efficient, logical, and rigidly professional. In addition to compiling statistics and undertaking various studies, including
a comprehensive investigation of racism within the Tennessee Valley
Authority, Weaver succeeded in securing government aid for black colleges. The office kept a watchful eye on federal contractors and flagged
pay stubs revealing black people had been bypassed for jobs as prima
facie evidence of discrimination. Weaver also vigorously advocated for
an increase in hiring of African Americans in both advisory and secretarial posts throughout the Interior Department. While not flashy,
these were pioneering advancements.

In fact, by 1935, Weaver was earnestly convinced that the Black
Cabinet's labors had resulted in several victories. Programs targeting

African Americans were receiving more support and more funds. The number of black federal appointees continued to expand, with new experts joining the administration throughout the year. Local agencies had also hired black advisers, clerical workers, and consultants. In the South, the federal government had provided more funding for teachers' salaries in black schools. That not only increased employment but also gave African American children more access to education. Black employment on New Deal work projects overseen by the Department of the Interior and Al Smith's program in the Federal Emergency Relief Administration had begun to grow incrementally.

Weaver also cited federal housing projects as another area of success. He had pushed for African Americans to get their fair share of both public housing and the jobs that came with the construction of new projects. Early on, he had taken his case directly to Ickes. During an appointment with the interior secretary, he demanded that the special adviser's office be given a central role in public housing. "Young man, what do you know about housing?" barked Ickes. Weaver confessed he knew nothing about it at all but, he pointed out, the federal government had never undertaken housing redevelopment before. "You'll do fine. None of those sons of bitches know anything about it either," Ickes chortled.

Weaver was a quick study and rapidly emerged as one of the New Deal's foremost experts in housing and urban renewal. His first and main project had been Techwood, in Atlanta, where he compelled local officials to hire African Americans as part of the site's construction workforce. His figures showed that black craftsmen made up almost 13 percent of all trained workers on the project, and black laborers comprised 90 percent of those in the unskilled ranks. Weaver proclaimed it a New Deal triumph for African Americans.

However, Weaver and other Black Cabinet members knew that such successes were bright spots among many disappointments. Although national employment had inched up, a study from Florida Agricultural and Mechanical (A&M) College for Negroes suggested that recovery was proceeding much more slowly for blacks than for other Americans. Despite racial-affairs advisers' testimony at government hearings on the harm caused by race-based wage differentials, the National Recovery Administration granted permission to several manufacturers and businesses to pay black workers less. The percentage of black skilled workers at Weaver's Techwood housing project, though an improvement, was still far below the fair proportion. Weaver had been forced by white leaders to accept a lower number; he knew that reporting the prima facie evidence of discrimination would only ignite racial tensions and bring the project to a halt. Additionally, a black neighborhood had been bulldozed to make room for Techwood, and the city's segregationist codes restricted the new housing to whites only. Former residents, the black urban poor who desperately needed better housing, were forced to scramble for homes in deteriorating neighborhoods elsewhere.

Despite these disappointments, Weaver worked ceaselessly. He was a tough boss with exceptionally high expectations for himself as well as his staff. Later, those under his supervision spoke of enduring the "Weaver treatment"—reprimands "marked by a politeness so unrelieved in its iciness that its victims felt they would be warmer if they curled up in a refrigerator." In Weaver's view, running a tight ship was necessary. For him, the early Roosevelt years were an era of "yeast, excitement, and dedication," with extremely high stakes and tremendous possibilities. "I had all of the enthusiasm of youth and I had all of the self-confidence that youth sometimes has, or at least it affects having if it doesn't have," he recalled. "I was very, very much involved in the job, in the potential of it, and in the hopes of it, so I felt that this was a real opportunity."

All those who knew him remembered Robert Weaver sacrificing everything for his job. Outside of Saturday night poker and occasionally joining Bill Hastie for a movie or dinner, he socialized very little. Weaver cultivated such strict privacy that even some of his closest friends were surprised when, in the summer of 1935, he announced that he had gotten married. His bride was Ella Haith, originally of North Carolina. Weaver first met her in the 1920s, when she was dating his older brother, Mortimer. After Mortimer died, Haith had gone north and had passed for white to attend college. While earning degrees from both Carnegie Mellon and the University of Michigan, she began corresponding with Weaver. She eventually landed a teaching job in Baltimore, and after courting her for a short time, Weaver popped the question. It was a perfect match of two members of the "talented tenth," both from the best of families.

Bill Hastie also got married in 1935. His new wife, Alma Syphax, was a Howard graduate who hailed from an old and established D.C. family—her ancestors had been enslaved on the Lee plantation. Hastie bought a home just a few blocks from the university and not too far from Robert Weaver's house.

Although the poker crowd was settling down, that didn't end the regular Saturday night gatherings. In some ways, as federal advisers' jobs became more challenging, the poker nights played an increasingly central role in the men's lives. These gatherings provided a chance to blow off steam, a chance to speak openly, and the opportunity for black New Dealers to seek advice from intellectuals and external leaders like Hastie's cousin Charles H. Houston, the NAACP's Walter White, and Ralph Bunche.

While poker nights encouraged collaboration among Weaver's friends, they drove a deep wedge between Black Cabinet members. Weaver's circle was exclusive and welcomed those with the best degrees, with the most notable accomplishments, and from the finest families. A Rosenwald connection was almost always required. Older advisers who owed their positions to political patronage were snubbed; Robert Vann, Eugene Kinckle Jones, Lawrence Oxley, and William Thompkins were never included, nor were other, younger black New Dealers with less prestigious degrees, jobs, or backgrounds. Despite being well placed in the Federal Emergency Relief Administration, Al Smith was never fully accepted by Weaver and his associates. Smith was rarely, if ever, invited to poker night. He resented the "Rosenwald list" and what he felt was the group's insufferable pompousness.

Smith was not alone in his opinion. Many years later, a former Black Cabinet member anonymously remarked, "Weaver's boys were more sophisticated; they fancied themselves a cut above the others." Some Black Cabinet elders dismissed the group as arrogant snobs and inexperienced upstarts. Weaver was aware of their antipathy. Most of the older generation, he recalled, "considered us children and . . . would have been happy to have had us come in as their office boys." But in his opinion that crowd was "interested in mainly self-advancement."

It was well known among African American political insiders and journalists that rifts among Black Cabinet members were deepening. Some observers attributed the deterioration of any bonds they may have initially forged to a clash of personalities fed by ambitious self-centeredness. "Bickerings and petty jealousies had split the so-called 'Black Cabinet' into many factions," Norfolk's *New Journal and Guide* later recalled. "Each had become more or less content to do his own special job without bothering about 'larger things' affecting the race as a whole."

Some of the members of the Black Cabinet were self-interested. Many of the divisions were indeed personal. But all members were also deeply committed to uplift—and their dedication grew more intense the longer they were in their jobs. The major impediments to forming stronger working relationships stemmed from the obstacles they confronted in the chaos of the New Deal and its institutionalized racism. Still, their internal divisions festered and were further aggravated by a couple of larger-than-life personalities that made cooperation harder.

The Labor Department's Lawrence Oxley was probably one of the most divisive members of the black brain trust. Oxley certainly believed in civil rights as a long-term objective. But he often supported accommodation to segregation and disenfranchisement. His inconsistency was attributed to what many felt was a thinly concealed desire to please whites. Oxley also was temperamental—he had a short fuse.

Like Forrester Washington and Eugene Kinckle Jones, he had made his name in social work. But unlike Washington and Jones, he had come to the field through a far less direct route and, as many suspected, with no formal training.

Lawrence Oxley was born in 1887 in Boston, Massachusetts, and he came from relatively comfortable circumstances; his stepfather was a coachman for a wealthy white Boston family and, with his earnings, had invested in real estate. Oxley's educational history was always sketchy; he attended public schools, but it was never clear whether he had graduated. As an adult, he enrolled briefly at the Prospect Union Association, founded to provide education for working-class men and staffed by Harvard faculty. But he decided against an academic route and initially pursued a career in entertainment. In the 1910s he toured England as "the Coloured Serenader" and headed his own orchestra. During World War I, he avoided being shipped to Europe to fight by wrangling an appointment as a morale officer for the U.S. military. He spent the war stateside, and for the rest of his life he insisted on being formally addressed as Lieutenant Oxley.

After the war, Oxley bounced between jobs. He inspected training facilities for the War Department; he worked for an organization that studied black welfare programs. In 1922, he landed in North Carolina and, claiming to be a Harvard graduate, obtained a teaching position. After questions about his degree surfaced, he was fired. But using connections within the Episcopal Church (he was a lifelong member), he was appointed director of the Negro division of North Carolina's Board of Charities and Public Welfare. It was in that position he made his mark by developing a conciliatory philosophy of community uplift. Based on Booker T. Washington's self-help ideology, Oxley's approach to remedying African American poverty and unemployment focused on black self-reliance and self-improvement. He earned praise for organizing grassroots welfare programs in North Carolina run independently by African American communities. His model became known as "locality development" and was adopted throughout the nation.

After Roosevelt's election, Oxley began lobbying for a federal position. He approached Robert Vann first; Vann turned him away. Next Oxley appealed to John P. Davis for help; Davis also refused him. Eventually he convinced North Carolina's Josephus Daniels, the former secretary of the navy under Woodrow Wilson, to support him. Daniels maintained strong ties to the White House; his assistant secretary during the Wilson years had been Franklin Delano Roosevelt. According to Will Alexander, Daniels wrote to Labor Secretary Frances Perkins, assuring her that by hiring Oxley she would "never have any more trouble over the race problem in the South or hardly anything else." Perkins jumped at the chance and brought Oxley on board as fast as she could.

But Lawrence Oxley was hardly a figure to lessen black concerns. It was well known that he could be irascible and brittle. It was also common knowledge that he continued to falsely claim to have a Harvard degree. That alone was an unpardonable offense to most Black Cabinet members, especially Robert Weaver and other Harvard alumni. Ralph Bunche detested Oxley, calling him the "head S.O.B. of all S.O.B.s," whose only concern was "buttering his own bread." John P. Davis condemned his "indiscreet" and obsequious relationship with white people, declaring him "unfit for office." The Rosenwald Fund's Will Alexander regarded Oxley as a self-interested charlatan; according to him, the man's only talent was that he "knew how to talk to white people."

Yet, in his own way, Oxley was committed to fighting for black America. In 1935, word spread that African American messengers, elevator operators, and custodians would not be hired to work in the new Department of Labor headquarters. Oxley protested their exclusion directly to Perkins: "It is important that there shall be no loss of these traditional jobs in this period of reconstruction when the Negro continues to be the last hired and the first fired." Perkins agreed and reversed the order. (It was a limited victory, since it did little to expand the African American presence beyond blue-collar ranks.) Later, privately, Oxley warned Labor Department officials to choose their words carefully when addressing black Americans. "If you are making a speech before negroes, there are three phrases which you must never use," he cautioned a department spokesperson. Those phrases were: "you must be patient," "this is a condition which has gone on for generations and which it will take a long time to rectify," and "you people."

Oxley's relationships with Black Cabinet members rapidly grew worse. Most African American New Dealers distrusted him. Once he sided with the military at an Inter-Departmental Group meeting, and after that his fellow members were never certain what position he would take. Although Robert Weaver and Bill Hastie continued to support John P. Davis's Joint Committee on National Recovery, when Oxley received his Labor Department appointment he withdrew from the activist organization. But curiously, after resigning, he continued to show up at Joint Committee meetings. Davis didn't protest, thinking that by tolerating the Labor Department official he might eventually open a channel to Perkins.

What Davis didn't realize was that Oxley was attending Joint Committee meetings with the purpose of feeding information back to the Labor Department. Initially, his reports were inconsequential; they contained intelligence that could be obtained easily by anyone, since Joint Committee gatherings were public. But in the spring of 1935, Oxley began to pass on serious allegations. After a Joint Committee conference in May, he sent an urgent memo to his Labor Department superiors, charging that the meeting was "distinctly communistic in character" and that most of those on the platform "seemed to be concerned first with making an attack on not only the present administration but American ideals and institutions." While notable African American communists such as James Ford attended, black leaders representing a wide spectrum of other viewpoints were present as well. This included several Black Cabinet members—and although none of them spoke, two poker night regulars, Ralph Bunche and Charles H. Houston, did.

Oxley's accusations impugned the reputations of Bunche and Houston and, by association, the rest of Weaver's circle. While the others held their tongues, Ralph Bunche did not. "I come from the nation's capital and I awake every morning with the sickening stench of pussy-footing, sophisticated Uncle Tom, pseudo Negro leadership in my nostrils," he told one audience, indirectly referring to Oxley. "There the race has some highly paid, so called Negro leaders many of whom hold their positions by carrying tales about other Negroes to the white folks. There Negroes attempt . . . to ingratiate themselves with their white superiors by labeling every Negro who demands justice for his group a 'red.'" There would never be much trust or respect for Oxley among the vast majority of Black Cabinet members.

Another unwelcome addition to the ranks of black New Dealers was journalist Edgar G. Brown. He was unforgettable—strikingly dapper and athletic, sporting a Vandyke beard and heavily pomaded hair. Unlike Oxley, Brown was no accommodationist—in fact, he was a ferocious warrior against bigotry. But his quarrelsome style, combined with his absolute obstinacy, alienated many. Associated Negro Press editor Claude Barnett described Brown as possessing "remarkable courage—some call it nerve. Will brave anything, cannot be discouraged, cannot be embarrassed." But many, both black and white, agreed that Brown's stridency was often over the top. Years later the *Pittsburgh Courier* wrote that his "rantings did more harm than good to the cause for which he professed to fight."

Edgar G. Brown was born in 1898 in the gritty, mostly white mining town of Sandoval, Illinois. His father drove wagons, hauling goods and coal around the area. Sandoval was a "sundown town"—it was understood that African Americans still on the street after dark were risking their lives. Opportunities for black youths there were limited. In 1913, Brown's talent for tennis, a sport of the elites, won him admission to Sumner High, an exclusive black boarding school in Saint Louis, Missouri. That opened the doors to Chicago's Northwestern University, where Brown majored in business while working as a baggage handler at the city's train depot. After a stint in the army, he began a career in journalism in the early 1920s. He also worked as a publicist for the Madam C. J. Walker beauty supply company and played tennis on the black circuit, winning four national championships. Temperamental, he received several suspensions by African American tennis associations, once for using his newspaper columns to attack his opponents.

In 1932 Brown left the Republican Party, hitched his wagon to the Roosevelt campaign, and made a run for Congress as a Democrat. He lost, but after Roosevelt's victory, he began pushing for a New Deal post. Brown possessed a compelling connection—he was the brother-in-law of FDR's trusted valet, Irvin McDuffie. In the fall of 1934, Brown received a position at the Federal Emergency Relief Administration. Al Smith assigned him to do publicity for the program, but Brown wanted something more hands-on. With the president's support, he was transferred to the Civilian Conservation Corps (CCC) in March 1935.

There Brown threw himself head-on into a fight with one of the New Deal's most racially antagonistic agencies. The program's civilian chief, Robert Fechner, was a southerner and a former American Federation of Labor head, and he was stubbornly determined to conserve the program's resources for white Americans. Despite pressure from Clark Foreman and others, Fechner refused requests for the appointment of black officers and initially balked at enrolling African American youths in the program.

But negative publicity had mounted in the black press, hurting the White House and forcing Fechner to accept a few African Americans into the CCC. However, he remained a committed segregationist, and most black teens and young adults who joined the program were assigned to blacks-only camps headed by hostile white officers. At Camp Kane, in Pennsylvania's Allegheny Mountains, the commander used racial slurs while reprimanding African American corps members. At another location, a white officer ordered one young man to stand at attention and fan flies off him. In both cases, the youths complained. In turn, they were discharged.

Although he had been appointed to consult on the CCC's educational programs and oversee black public relations, Brown swiftly redefined his responsibilities and began lodging protests against the mistreatment of black enlistees. He called for the appointment of black officers and demanded that the CCC hire African American medical personnel. Taken aback by Brown's assertiveness, Fechner developed a pronounced dislike for his racial-affairs appointee. The CCC head complained to FDR that when Brown visited one site, "his conduct was so objectionable and so detrimental to discipline and morale that the Camp Officer had to ask for his removal." Brown was also reported to have posed as Fechner and fooled a receptionist into putting his call directly through to Agriculture Secretary Henry A. Wallace. It was whispered that Wallace was not at all amused.

After only a few weeks on the job, Brown was forced out.

He appealed to Roosevelt. "I hope you can keep Brown, the colored man in the CCC," the president wrote to Fechner. "He is, in addition to his duties with you, writing about farm work and his information service is quite valuable." Fechner grudgingly complied. Brown was reinstated in June but warned to restrict his activities to public relations tasks. "I agree with you," Roosevelt assured Fechner. "Brown should confine himself to preparing newspaper materials on what Negro CCC camps are doing."

Brown returned slugging. He continued to document the program's rampant discrimination and to file complaints with administration officials. His approach seemed to work. In August, the CCC announced the addition of more black educational advisers, and by October, eight African American chaplains and nine black medics had been recruited for black camps. About that time, Interior Secretary Harold Ickes sent off a letter to Fechner, likely at the urging of both Brown and Clark Foreman, who was working in Ickes's office, demanding the appointment of black officers and administrators. "I am quite certain that Negroes can function in supervisory capacities just as efficiently as can white men," Ickes wrote, "and I do not think that they should be discriminated against merely on the account of color." Fechner gave in, agreeing to bring in black officers. But he continually refused to yield to calls for integration. He asserted to one NAACP leader, "Segregation is not discrimination and cannot be so construed."

Although dismayed by Fechner and the practices of the CCC, Brown remained publicly supportive of FDR and the New Deal. He produced articles extolling the CCC's virtues, and he undertook speaking tours on behalf of the administration. Behind the scenes, he also came in handy for needed damage control. After a racial clash at a New York CCC camp, he persuaded the *New York Amsterdam News* to stop printing negative stories about the program. He also composed promotional radio spots, one act plays, and other press releases for the CCC. He orchestrated a letter-writing campaign encouraging black enlistees to send in glowing reports about camp life to various black media sources.

Fechner's dislike for Brown only increased. The CCC director banned him from visiting camps without advance approval from his office. "He seems to be obsessed with the feeling that he should constitute himself the personal representative of every Negro in our CCC organization," Fechner complained. He also banished Brown to an extremely small office at the end of a hallway with a plank for a desk.

Nonetheless, Brown appeared to be the one Black Cabinet member who could get things done. And that only estranged him further from fellow racial-affairs advisers, who had held him at arm's length. He was well known for exaggerating; many believed his claims about his contributions to the CCC reforms were overblown. Brown's entrance into government, through family ties, consigned him to the black brain trust's periphery—all factions were wary of him. Their suspicions only increased when Brown founded the United Government Employees (UGE), a union designed to represent black federal workers in the District of Columbia. He kicked it off with a membership drive that succeeded in drawing in some lower-level black federal jobholders. He eventually succeeded in negotiating a small salary boost for D.C. custodians, but little more came of his efforts. The UGE turned out to be a one-man operation, with Brown serving as president, treasurer, and sole lobbyist. It never held formal meetings, but it seemed to collect plenty of dues. Al Smith remembered Brown as clever but not above using deception; in Smith's opinion, Edgar G. Brown was a "bull thrower."

Despite their many differences, Black Cabinet members did share similar experiences. Riding on what journalist Eugene Davidson had described as the "iron rim" of the New Deal's "wheel of progress" was both emotionally and physically taxing. Unlike many of their white counterparts in similar posts, black government officials were required to travel extensively. Several journeyed thousands of miles each year, which isolated them from their family and friends and also diluted their influence in the Washington workplace. Field assignments were exhausting and could be dangerous, especially in the South, where confronting whites about racial discrimination in regional New Deal programs might trigger violence.

Interactions with local white New Dealers were almost always tense. Throughout the country, white state and local officials routinely rejected or redirected resources designated for African Americans. Many, especially those below the Mason-Dixon Line, did not hesitate to express open resentment against black inclusion. Eugene Talmadge, Georgia's defiant governor, consistently turned down relief for black citizens. One black New Dealer, James Atkins of the Works Progress Administration (WPA), recalled that when he attempted a simple survey of a South Carolina adult education program, a white state official blocked it. Arguing that the survey tampered with "relations of the races," the official warned he would terminate all New Deal educational programs for both blacks and whites unless the study was dropped. Atkins acquiesced. Like others in the black brain trust, he knew that defying white southerners could carry dire consequences and that blacks, as well as poor whites, badly needed the federal government's financial support for their schools.

Since he was light-skinned, Al Smith sometimes found his way around white southern obstinacy by passing as white. Using that ruse, when he discovered African Americans were being short-changed in an area, he gave local officials a scolding. In some cases, he turned the tables on white administrators and warned them that if African Americans weren't given equal consideration, he would be the one to ax the area's New Deal projects, both black and white. Al Smith was shrewd, and he was brazen; he knew he lacked the power to cut New Deal programs. He also knew the risks he was taking and that if his true racial identity were revealed, he might not make it home. His Washington bosses were so concerned for his safety that they required him to report in every night while on the road in the South.

Retaliation by white terrorist organizations was a constant danger. The Ku Klux Klan operated throughout the country, and its loathing for the New Deal and Roosevelt was no secret. One training program for black youths later reported that the group's participants had been targets of vigilantes who were "night riding"—making after-sundown attacks on African Americans who were receiving New Deal assistance. Before leaving his post at the Federal Emergency Relief Administration, Forrester Washington reported that Atlanta's white supremacist Black Shirts paraded through the streets with signs reading "Employ White Men and Let Niggers Go" as a protest against African American inclusion in federal job programs.

These constant and menacing forms of white racism led many African Americans in the South to fear rather than seek help from the New Deal. Al Smith recalled that during field investigations, African American women working on federally funded sewing projects begged him not to push for equal wages, worried that once he departed, white employers would retaliate against them. Despite their unfair salaries, they claimed they were making more than they had as maids and cooks. A letter addressed to the "Hon. Franklin D. Roosevelt" arrived in Smith's office testifying to the desperation and fear in Georgia. "Mr. President . . . hard as it is to believe the [white] releaf [sic] officials are using up almost everything that you send for them self + their friends," the anonymous author wrote.

"Cant sign my name Mr. President—they will beat me up and run me away from here and this is my home."

Black Cabinet members had a tough time finding food and lodging while traveling. Throughout the nation, many restaurants and hotels refused to serve black people. African American New Dealers had to seek out black-friendly eating establishments or, where none existed, rely on black community members for meals. Black Cabinet members may have relied on a directory for black travelers such as *The Green Book* (1936–67) to book black hotels or find private homes that hosted African Americans on the road. Lodging with local residents had its benefits. During one Mississippi trip, James Atkins stayed with distant relatives of his in-laws. Such contacts, he acknowledged, helped him better understand and address the needs of local black communities.

Transportation presented yet another challenge. While driving from Baltimore to Washington, Robert Weaver was stopped by the police for speeding. When he protested his innocence, he was handcuffed and carted off to jail. Friends bailed him out, and the case was dropped. For longer trips, most African American New Dealers traveled by train. Although as government employees they were provided with first-class vouchers, Black Cabinet members were booked into segregated cars on southbound trains. "You gather your luggage and stumble forward to the Jim Crow car, which has been switched on at the station," recalled journalist Ted Poston, who later joined the Black Cabinet. "The car you are leaving is air-conditioned. Its dual seats are comfortable. It is clean and well-lighted, and all its equipment is modern. The Jim Crow car is filthy."

Often Black Cabinet members demanded to be accommodated in what was known as the "Lower 13." Since the South's segregation prohibited blacks from occupying overnight Pullman sleeping cars, as required by the government's first-class vouchers, trainmen could be forced to set up private night quarters for Black Cabinet members in the spacious lounge cars. At daybreak, however, Black Cabinet members were expected to return to their seats in the Jim Crow car.

Some Black Cabinet members encountered skepticism from white railroad employees who found it hard to believe that African Americans held such high-level government posts. One white conductor in Mississippi escorted the WPA adviser James Atkins to a seat in the whites-only car. When Atkins got off at his stop, an African American porter pulled him aside. "You know what that conductor said?" he chuckled. "'That light-complexioned man—he must be from the islands. He couldn't be a nigger, because no nigger has a job like that.'"

In Washington, D.C., as the number of African American federal employees increased, so did discrimination in federal buildings. When forced to hire their first black employees, some administrators rushed to segregate toilets and lunchrooms. In some buildings, if African Americans could not be assigned to separate offices, managers hid their desks behind shelves, cabinets, or screens. There were constant reminders of white prejudice. Lucia Mae Pitts, who remained Clark Foreman's secretary, recalled the "shock, disbelief, sometimes outrage" that she encountered from whites when they entered the office and found an African American secretary. Across the board, even among the highest level of African American advisers, blacks earned less than whites in comparable positions. "The United States Government buildings, by way of analogy, constitute just one big O'Hara plantation, shot through with all the patronizing attitudes of the South," stated one *Baltimore Afro-American* columnist. "Conditions on the job are rotten," he observed, adding that the black federal workers' "blood boils with indignation as they resent . . . discrimination and race prejudice in Uncle Sam's service."

Despite the hardships of serving in the Roosevelt administration, most Black Cabinet members hung on. They all must have watched with grave concern as the conservative-dominated Supreme Court began striking down New Deal programs in the late spring of 1935. Both the National Recovery Act and the Agricultural Adjustment Act were ruled unconstitutional, cited as examples of overreach by the executive branch.

Although those programs had not helped black Americans much, the court's attack on FDR's relief plans suggested that the entire New Deal could be in trouble. If key programs were nullified, and federal intervention by the nation's chief executive weakened, the possibilities for addressing black needs would be constricted. African American advisers, most of whom served in temporary agencies set up to address problems resulting from the Depression, would disappear from the federal ranks. From the perspective of Black Cabinet members, a New Deal was better than no deal.

Of the core Black Cabinet members, Al Smith was the most in danger of losing his job. The bill that created the Federal Emergency Relief Administration expired in the spring of 1935, and amid the jitters created by the Supreme Court's attack on the New Deal, it wasn't going to be renewed. Over the previous year, Smith had built up his division, first as an assistant and then as its head. He generated reports for his superiors; they hadn't asked for them, and he believed they didn't read them. But he wrote them anyway—and then released them, often clandestinely, to the black press. If he couldn't get exact figures, which was often the case because local white administrators refused to supply them, he guessed at the numbers—sometimes intentionally deflating or inflating them. If he couldn't get action, he leaked information to the NAACP and the Urban League.

To a degree, Smith's strategy worked. He got African Americans hired on local New Deal projects, some as caseworkers to help document the plight of black Americans. Smith also created some white-collar projects—one would eventually evolve into an effort to collect the oral histories of African Americans who had lived through slavery. He claimed the White House tapped him to ghostwrite letters for FDR and craft speeches for White House officials. Like others, Smith was disappointed in the administration and the New Deal. But he was willing to play on both teams; he seized every opportunity and looked for every loophole to advance the African American people. He did much of that covertly while attempting to maintain a good relationship with the white New Deal leadership.

In May, as the Federal Emergency Relief Administration was being shuttered, Smith along with his staff followed Harry Hopkins to the Works Progress Administration, the New Deal's largest jobs program. It was a big step up for Smith. Just over two years before, he had been struggling to make a living. Now, as the head of the African American division of the WPA, he was part of one of the most expansive work-relief programs in the nation. It confirmed the self-proclaimed Ozark hillbilly's status as a member of the black federal elite. Smith's position was just as important as the one Robert Weaver occupied; this only increased the strain between the two men. Smith began rubbing elbows with the nation's most notable African Americans as well as top white New Deal leaders. His position allowed him to act as a bridge between blacks and whites both inside and outside the New Deal administration. Al Smith was a bit of a gadfly, and because of it, without knowing he was doing so, he would bring a very dramatic change to the Black Cabinet.

About the time he joined the WPA, Al Smith ran into Aubrey W. Williams, Harry Hopkins's assistant, at a gathering. Williams was in the process of setting up the National Youth Administration, he told Smith; it was a work and educational program for teens and young adults. Smith insisted there was someone at the gathering Williams must meet.

That person was a woman, elegant, regal, and poised.

She was Mrs. Mary McLeod Bethune.

PART THREE

Thinking and Planning Together, 1935–1939

Chapter Six

Star-Led

O N TUESDAY night, June 25, 1935, in Saint Louis, Missouri, as a massive storm hit the city, more than two hundred delegates to the NAACP's annual conference crowded into the auditorium of Vashon High School. A segregated school built to serve teenagers of the black community, Vashon had been selected to host the NAACP's six-day conference. Voter discrimination, Jim Crow, black unemployment, the plight of the sharecropper, the Italian invasion of Ethiopia, black education, inequalities in the justice system, lynching, and the weaknesses of the New Deal were among the many urgent topics on the agenda. As the rain pounded down outside, delegates took their seats in anticipation. The conference would open with a speech from Mary McLeod Bethune, that year's recipient of the NAACP's highest honor, the Spingarn Medal, named for founding member Joel Spingarn. Bethune had been chosen for her thirty-plus years of trailblazing in African American education, the black women's club movement, and civil rights activism. "Mrs. Bethune has always spoken out against injustice, in the South as well as the North, without compromise or fear," the award's selection committee declared.

When Bethune's name was announced that evening, the crowd stood, and the roar of applause filled the room as she crossed the stage to receive the medal. She then took the podium and surveyed the assembly. When she came into the world, as a sharecropper's daughter, almost sixty years earlier, it would have been unthinkable that she would one day stand before such a crowd, which included the top African American leaders of the country as well as many noted white Americans, some of whom were representatives of the federal government.

Most of black America was familiar with the life story of Mary McLeod Bethune. It resonated deeply with the experiences of many, especially the poor and the working class. She was one generation away from slavery, and the horrors of living in bondage were still fresh in her family's memories. Born in 1875 to Patsy and Samuel McLeod, she had been the fifteenth of seventeen children. Both of her parents and eight of her siblings had been enslaved. Several of her brothers and sisters had been sold away before the Civil War. During slavery, her mother and father had lived apart until Samuel McLeod's master purchased Patsy and put her to work on his plantation. Bethune remembered both her mother and her grandmother telling of living under the constant threat of sexual abuse. When an overseer attempted to rape Patsy McLeod, she battled back. She was branded on her breast as punishment for her defiance. Patsy's mother, Sophie, bore deep welts across her back, the result of whippings she received for fighting off a white man. Bethune claimed her maternal line descended from African royalty, and she credited it for her independence, her inner strength, and her pride in womanhood and race.

Bethune also emphasized her uniqueness. Her mother had encouraged her to develop confidence and forceful resolve—as well as to embrace her special purpose. "My mother said when I was born I was entirely different than the rest," Bethune told an interviewer. "My ideas were different. My mother was proud of it. She felt: here comes one of the children who is going to do something. My father felt the same way."

Such a destiny seemed a very distant dream for an impoverished African American child in Jim Crow America. The McLeods barely made enough to live on. Bethune's hometown of Mayesville, South Carolina, was rigidly segregated and provided few educational opportunities for African American children. Racial violence, or the threat of it, was a daily reality. Still, Bethune claimed that at a young age she set her sights on a different life. One day, while working in a white home with her mother, she discovered a book. She had never seen one before; she opened it up and looked through it. "Put that down. You can't read," commanded the daughter of her mother's employer. "I thought, 'Maybe the difference between white folks and colored is just this matter of reading and writing,'" Bethune recalled. "I made up my mind I would know my letters before I ever visited the big house again."

She declared that while working in the fields, she prayed for the chance to go to school. It came when she was eleven. A local teacher, organizing a new school sponsored by the Presbyterian Church, appeared at their farm and asked the McLeods which of their children could be spared to attend. They chose the young Mary. She was eager to start, and she loved learning—it opened up a new world for her. She became one of the school's most dedicated pupils, and by age fifteen she had soaked up all it had to offer.

Then she returned to the fields.

About a year later, with the help of her teacher and a sponsor, Mary McLeod enrolled in an African American all-girls school, Scotia Seminary. A residential program, Scotia offered a rigorous curriculum that combined Christian instruction with secondary-level mathematics, English, history, and geography. To cover her expenses, Bethune took jobs as a domestic over summer breaks. Her enthusiasm for her studies and her strict work ethic won her a scholarship to Chicago's Moody Bible Institute in 1894. She excelled there. A woman of magnetic personality, striking beauty, and quick intelligence, she won high marks. She excelled in evangelism and was praised for her rich singing voice and magnificent oratorical skills. After finishing Moody's two-year program, Mary McLeod applied to be sent as a Presbyterian missionary to Africa. Church fathers turned her down. Only white people received mission calls to Africa. It was, she said, a "bitter disappointment."

At age twenty-two, Mary McLeod returned to Mayesville to teach. The following year, she moved on to a position at the Haines Institute, in Augusta, Georgia, where she worked under Lucy Croft Laney, the school's African American founder. Laney believed that the progress of the race depended on black women. If properly trained in basic skills and Christian values, black women would pass on what they learned to their families. This would have a chain effect and uplift African American communities. Laney urged her faculty to reach out to people in Augusta's poorest black neighborhoods and model exemplary female leadership. McLeod was entranced and inspired by Laney. She came to believe that she too could, and should, open a school of her own.

Over the next few years, Mary McLeod held various teaching posts in different schools in the South. In 1897, while working in Sumter, South Carolina, she met and married Albertus Bethune. Two years into marriage she gave birth to their first and only child, Albert. She retired from teaching, gave up her dream of building a school, and began to devote herself to being a full-time wife and mother. Yet she quickly realized that she was unsuited for a life of conventional domesticity. Before Albert turned a year old, she had accepted another teaching job—this time in Palatka, Florida. "This married life was not intended to impede things I had in mind to do," she later explained. "The birth of my boy had no tendency whatever to dim my ardor and determination."

In 1899, the family arrived in Palatka, where Bethune immersed herself in a whirlwind of activities. She taught on weekdays and devoted Saturdays and Sundays to building her own school. Albertus Bethune tried his hand at business, but he floundered. His energetic wife took on more work, selling policies for the Afro-American Life Insurance Company.

But Palatka soon seemed too small and too limiting. In 1904, Bethune uprooted the family again and headed for Daytona Beach, thinking it might be a better location for her school. Soon after, Albertus Bethune decided he was done; he left Daytona Beach without his wife and young son and returned home to South Carolina. The couple never divorced, and Albertus Bethune died in 1919. Mary McLeod Bethune never remarried.

In Daytona Beach, Bethune finally saw her vision become a reality. The city had a large African American community and was also a vacation spot, filled with rich white philanthropists. Seeking support for her school, Bethune targeted these white donors; her fund-raising efforts furnished her with connections to the country's financial elite. Grants came in from the Carnegie Foundation, the Rosenwald Fund, and John D. Rockefeller. Although she steered toward Booker T. Washington's philosophy of vocational education, which appealed to many whites, she also devised a broad curriculum that offered classes in math, science, literature, history, and languages. In 1923, after a merger with the Cookman Institute, Florida's oldest historically black college, she renamed her school Bethune-Cookman College. She ran it with an iron fist—with an unwavering resolve that it offer an education that was comprehensive, vocational, and Christian. "Mrs. Bethune was tough here at school and out there in the white world," recalled one Bethune-Cookman acquaintance. "You learned early *not* to cross her. One did exactly as told while working for her."

Bethune emerged as a powerhouse. By the 1920s, she was touring the country, speaking on behalf of her college, expanding her donor base, and appearing at teachers' conferences and meetings sponsored by women's organizations. While Bethune-Cookman furthered her contacts in educational, business, and Republican political circles, her power base was rooted in black women's clubs. Emerging just after the Civil War, American women's clubs served as social organizations in which women could build relationships and explore concerns ranging from domestic arts to suffrage. Their membership was composed primarily of educated middle- and upper-class women. Often clubs engaged in various forms of community service, with the goal of reforming society based on middle-class ideals, which included strict discipline, temperance, Christian notions of virtuousness, and an ambitious pursuit of success through hard work, self-denial, and independence.

White women's clubs refused membership to black women, and by the turn of the twentieth century, African American women began establishing their own clubs. Like white women, black women were interested in promoting the advancement of women overall as well as uplifting society by spreading middle-class values and propriety. But in addition, the black women's club movement made the fight for racial equality a top priority; the motto for the National Association of Colored Women (NACW), an umbrella organization for all black women's clubs, was "Lifting as We Climb." For years, Mary McLeod Bethune had been moving up through the ranks in black women's clubs, and in 1924 she was elected president of the NACW. In that position, she amassed even more support from black women around the country, which provided her with grassroots energy that she could activate when she needed it.

Bethune's rise to leadership in black America had made her endorsement prized among white American politicians. And like many other African Americans, she had been a solid Republican and had served the party diligently. In turn, while the Republicans were in power in Washington, she courted them, always mindful of the potential benefits to Bethune-Cookman, the NACW, and African Americans in general.

Although in 1932 Bethune endorsed Herbert Hoover and the Republicans, her loyalty to the party of Lincoln had already begun to wane. No doubt this shift had been helped along by her ongoing relationship with Eleanor Roosevelt and Sarah Delano Roosevelt. For FDR's first inauguration day, Bethune penned an article for the *Pittsburgh Courier*, calling for the new administration to "adopt as its policy the fundamental principle of justice to all classes and races." Slowly, over the next year, she began to reposition herself as a supporter of the new president.

The opportunity for Bethune to make a definitive political realignment came in the fall of 1933. Despite pressure from the NAACP, Franklin Roosevelt had said and done nothing when Maryland's George Armstrong had been brutally lynched and his body desecrated that November. Several weeks after Armstrong's murder, two white men were lynched in California. Shortly afterward, in a speech broadcast over the CBS and NBC radio networks, without mentioning any specific cases,

President Roosevelt condemned lynching as a "vile form of collective murder." Characterizing it as a "deliberate and definite disobedience of the commandment of 'Thou shalt not kill,'" Roosevelt denounced "those in high places or in low, who condone the lynch law." There was a "new generation," he told listeners, who expected "action by collective government and by individual education, toward the ending of practices such as these." Although Roosevelt had stopped short of endorsing a federal anti-lynching law and his public denunciation occurred after two white men were murdered, his public rejection of this type of vigilante killings gave many African American leaders cause for hope.

These included Mary McLeod Bethune. "President Roosevelt has touched, in my mind, the most vital problem of American life—mob rule, in denouncing lynching. We have been waiting patiently to hear his voice on this growing spirit of barbarism in our country," she told the press. "It looks like we are getting somewhere." Several months later, she joined other black leaders and signed a declaration praising FDR for supporting the black community. "President Roosevelt deserves the tribute you have in mind," she wrote in an endorsement. "May I thank you for the privilege of participating in this splendid effort."

Public admiration was also growing on the Roosevelt side. In May 1934, Eleanor Roosevelt made a special appearance at a Commerce Department meeting on African American education. After a warm introduction from Howard University president Mordecai Johnson, the always direct First Lady didn't mince words. The funding of black schools was both grossly inequitable and unacceptable. "When I read those figures, I couldn't help but think how stupid we are," she declared. "We must learn to work together—all of us regardless of race, creed, or color. We must wipe out the feeling of intolerance whenever we find it—or belief that any other group can go ahead alone. We must go ahead together, or we go down together." The auditorium roared with "the thunder of applause," and the First Lady "rushed over to Mrs. Mary McLeod Bethune with a gracious smile and hand extended in greeting." She then shook hands with Johnson and the rest of the

African American guests on the platform. With that, Eleanor Roosevelt had broken one of racism's strictest codes—one that forbade even the most formal physical contact between whites and blacks. It affirmed in many people's minds that a friendship, unique for its era, had developed between the First Lady and America's most celebrated African American female leader.

"There is a great happiness in my heart tonight," Mary McLeod Bethune began her Spingarn Medal acceptance speech on that stormy June night in 1935, her deep voice resonating throughout the hall. "Not a selfish, personal happiness, but a happiness and satisfaction that comes to one who has labored in the heat of the day for the common good, and now as the shadows of life begin to lengthen comes to receive a 'Well Done.'" Tonight, she announced, she would speak on brotherhood, cooperation, and unity, the essential elements of the African American struggle. "Equality of opportunity is necessary to brotherhood," she told the crowd. "We stand in adoration for those who, regardless of the section of the country in which they live, have been big enough, courageous enough, to stand for social justice and equality of opportunity, even at the risk of their lives."

But the key to achieving brotherhood was interracial cooperation. White Americans must clean out their "dead branches of misunderstanding and lack of appreciation [that] have kept our existence clouded with prejudice." Brotherhood rested on "human understanding," she told the crowd. Yet, she cautioned, racial progress also demanded that African Americans put aside their differences and unite. "If we would make way for social and political justice and a larger brotherhood, we must cooperate," she admonished the audience, which no doubt included feuding members of the Black Cabinet. Locking arms and battling for equality was not a task for the ordinary or the faint-hearted. She asked those gathered if they had the fortitude and the bravery to join the struggle. It would not be easy: "I would call tonight upon those who are star-led, who have clearly in mind a purpose in life; who do not fear the struggle and the work which must needs be the lot of those who dare to live above the cloud of popular thought and limited desire."

The crowd was electrified, and as Bethune concluded, listeners burst into resounding applause. Assistant Secretary of the Treasury Josephine Roche, who was attending the conference on behalf of the White House, was spellbound. Joining Bethune onstage, she presented her with a bouquet of flowers and then embraced the educator. "The two women stood with their with arms about each other," reported Walter White to a white acquaintance. "You will understand how Josephine's action was obviously an unconscious expression of that human brotherhood of which [Bethune] had just spoken."

Once she got back to Washington, D.C., Roche immediately contacted the National Youth Administration's chief, Aubrey Williams, demanding that he give Bethune a seat on his advisory board. Williams had received similar pressure from Al Smith, who had introduced him to Bethune with the idea she be recruited as a consultant on black youth. The First Lady, who regarded the National Youth Administration (NYA) as one of her pet projects, added her voice, extolling the value that Bethune would have to the program. Certainly, Bethune's expertise in African American education would be a big plus for expanding the program's reach. The incorporation of the acclaimed educator into the New Deal had definite public relations benefits—it would boost the White House's credibility with African Americans. Bethune was a woman of the people, admired by the people. Actor William Warfield remembered the elation her visits brought to his hometown. "The black heroes like Frederick Douglass were remote from me when I was growing up. We didn't see them," he explained. "But Mary McLeod Bethune was there. She used to come to my town to speak. My father was a self-educated man, a minister, and so what that great lady said was very important to him."

Aubrey Williams needed little convincing. He had grown up poor in Alabama and had struggled for an education. Unlike most of his white southern contemporaries, early on he had developed a revulsion for racism and discrimination. In the summer of 1935, he not only named Bethune to his advisory committee but also invited Howard University's president, Mordecai Johnson, to join. The appointments made the NYA unique. Very few New Deal advisory boards had one black member, much less two.

The role of the NYA's advisory board was to supply advice and information to Williams and his subordinates. Board members' duties were light—they had to attend, at most, two meetings a year at the Capitol. Policy making was off the table. Most programs had similar groups of consultants, and New Deal higher-ups regarded them as merely for show.

Mary McLeod Bethune did not share that view and had no intention of being restricted to a symbolic role.

As she began her term, Bethune was also in the process of establishing the National Council of Negro Women (NCNW), designed to unite all black women's clubs and other African American women's groups—including black sororities, social service organizations, the black YWCA, and women's activist leagues—under one banner. The NCNW's goal was to advance the cause of African American women through information-gathering and lobbying efforts. As the council came together under Bethune's leadership, one of its top priorities was to provide black women better access to New Deal resources. They had been largely left out of relief and recovery efforts, and Bethune was determined to reverse that practice as rapidly as possible. She arranged for the NCNW's headquarters to be located in Washington, D.C., and made its upper floors her second home.

Bethune's frequent visits to the capital on NCNW business allowed her to extend her role in the NYA beyond its biannual meetings. She immediately began lobbying vigorously for the broader inclusion of African Americans in the NYA's programs, especially those in her home state of Florida. By the fall of 1935, she had successfully secured two black appointments to Florida's NYA advisory board, helped establish youth recreational projects in rural areas, and procured funding for four of the state's historically black colleges, including her own school. No doubt she had a role in the selection of Bethune-Cookman alumnus Edward R. Rodriguez as the state's first African American NYA assistant supervisor. Bethune had raised Rodriguez and regarded him as an adopted son. Her efforts in Florida paid off. By late 1935, the *New York Age* praised the state's black NYA programs for "progressing rapidly."

Bethune also pushed for the nationwide expansion of African American NYA programs, for black administrative appointments, and for an increase in federal support for black higher education. Learning that in some locations, agents had declared African American teens ineligible for the NYA because, ironically, they were not receiving aid from other programs, she protested. These were some of the neediest youths, and to appease Bethune, federal NYA officials overrode local exclusion in several cases.

Among Mary McLeod Bethune's many strengths, which included a brilliant mind for organizational politics, was her profound certitude. For many, she offered a model of a completely self-assured and confident African American woman. "I have no inferiority complex," she claimed in one interview. The Rosenwald Fund's Edwin Embree observed that she was entirely aware of "her worth and the righteousness of her cause" and that she possessed a "determination and assurance that brook[ed] no interference." Clark Foreman, who first met her in the 1920s, remarked on her "spiritual power" and "eloquence." "Few people," he wrote, "combine her understanding with her forceful leadership." Bill Hastie remembered his earliest encounter with Bethune, when he was teaching at a New Jersey school: "I looked out across the campus and there was this smartly dressed elegant woman striding across campus with a swagger stick. They were all the rage among the fashionable ladies of the time." At a later reception, he had a long talk with the famous educator. "It was at that time I was introduced to her strength. She was a most impressive person."

Bethune believed that strong and steady leadership was an essential ingredient in achieving tangible victories in the war against racism.

Centralized power that coordinated and demanded cooperation, in her estimation, was the most effective tool in driving along progress in social movements. Some accused Bethune of operating in a unilateral and autocratic manner. She insisted that those who accepted the responsibility of leadership derived their power from the grassroots. "Those of us who accept some measure of responsibility for leadership," she explained, "must realize that in such people's movements, the real leadership comes up out of the people themselves."

The incorporation of African Americans who were "star-led" into the New Deal decision-making process was essential. Outside activism had long been the only alternative for black protest. Now, the era of Franklin Delano Roosevelt and the New Deal presented the opportunity to work from inside. Her mission, as Bethune viewed it, was to both hasten economic recovery and redeem a nation ravaged by a history of bitter racism and discrimination.

What the New Deal needed, Bethune had determined, was a stronger black presence. Earlier in 1935, African American congressman Arthur Mitchell, an Illinois Democrat who had won his seat during the previous midterms, put forward a bill calling for a single body to represent African American needs directly to the president. The model of positioning advisers throughout the New Deal had been a failure, Mitchell argued. For a summer congressional hearing on his proposal, among the documents he submitted were letters from Bethune, Tuskegee's Robert Moton, and Howard's Alain Locke. Bethune was so enthusiastic that she declared the plan "vitally important" and offered her "genuine approval," urging that "the Cabinet" include at least one African American woman.

The NAACP and Charles H. Houston mounted strident opposition to the bill. Since it did not allocate any specific powers to the cabinet, it would have no tools to fight within the government, Houston argued. In fact, if the bill passed, it would give various departments and agencies an excuse to terminate their racial-affairs advisers, since they would insist the cabinet provided plenty of black representation. The overall impact, Houston predicted, would be to decrease the presence of African Americans in the federal government. But there was another grave danger that lurked in establishing an entirely separate division for African Americans, something that seemed uncomfortably similar to the Bureau of Indian Affairs. Through it, African Americans would be consigned to the status of "wards of the Government," Houston maintained, pointing out that "Negroes are not wards; they are citizens." African Americans' history and resources differed from those of indigenous peoples, who were members of sovereign nations. Black Americans deserved, Houston said, to have "their problems considered and acted upon . . . just the same as the problems of any other group of citizens in the United States."

The Black Cabinet bill died in committee before it could come to a vote.

Bethune wasn't satisfied. She began to press Aubrey Williams to do more than include African Americans on his NYA advisory board. In her view, Williams needed his own Black Cabinet to guide him, and she told him so. He rejected her suggestion. Yet, in December 1935, he agreed to hire an administrative assistant in charge of "Negro Affairs" for the NYA. With enthusiastic recommendations from Bethune and Howard University's Mordecai Johnson, he selected Juanita Saddler to serve.

Texas-born and Oklahoma-raised, Saddler came from a civil rights family. Her father, Eugene Saddler, practiced law and was president of the Oklahoma State Negro Bar Association. He battled against lynching, segregation in public transportation, and the state's attempts to deny African Americans the vote. He sent his daughter off for the best education available, and Juanita Saddler earned degrees from Fisk and Columbia Universities. She served as a field secretary for the YWCA, and in 1933, she returned to Fisk as its first dean of women. Efficient, disciplined, and highly experienced, Saddler was also a groundbreaker in race relations and had drafted plans for the future integration of the YWCA. In many ways, the forty-three-year-old Saddler was a perfect fit for the National Youth Administration.

In early December, Saddler arrived in Washington, D.C., eager to get down to business. The first day on the job, she discovered that she had no office and no one could tell her what her duties were. Finally, after two weeks, she was able to secure an appointment with a lower-level NYA administrator. He wasn't sure what she could do, he said, shrugging her off. She sent a list of recommended actions she could spearhead. Agency officials took it under consideration. Several weeks passed, and she was finally assigned an office and a secretary but no tasks.

Refusing to be sidelined by the NYA's indifference, Saddler decided to create her own assignments. Studying a pile of letters from local black NYA officials requesting help, she decided she needed to conduct field investigations. Over the next six months, she toured black programs in the North and the West (the South was absent from her itinerary, likely for safety reasons). She forwarded to her superiors in Washington her assessments of the NYA's weaknesses and her recommendations for transforming the program into a more potent force for black youth.

For a time, Saddler and Bethune worked together as a team. Bethune applied pressure using the public limelight, while Saddler labored quietly on the inside, leaning on national and local agency heads for NYA improvements. She agreed with Bethune; the ineffectiveness of the NYA in black communities largely resulted because it lacked local African American administrators to lead programs. "The failure to have, not only one, but several Negroes as staff members, is really a form of segregation," Saddler wrote in an internal report. "As long as our society provides a dual [segregated] system, even though it means duplication, economic waste, and is divisive," she continued, "adequate provision similar to that made for the white group must also be made for the Negro." Saddler also recognized one of the great flaws in the New Deal: it was temporary—once prosperity returned, it would end. The future of any population, such as African Americans, that failed to recover from the Great Depression's effects would be gravely endangered when programs were terminated. Hoping to make some of her efforts permanent, Saddler began advocating for the reassignment of the NYA's African American school programs to the Department of Education. She was ignored.

Saddler did not hesitate to speak her mind to white people during field investigations. At local NYA sites, she often suggested ways to fine-tune activities and advised white officials on navigating black communities' delicate internal politics. She urged black leaders and civil rights organizations to use external pressure to secure increased benefits from the NYA—and she didn't hide from her Washington bosses that she had told local leaders they needed to complain more. She was also vocal about her abhorrence of segregation. She wrote to the Texas NYA director, Lyndon B. Johnson, demanding that he allocate more resources to African Americans, hire black administrators, and implement interracial collaboration: "The fact that the Government is aiding and now supporting various projects in the State, seems to me to allow leeway for liberal and tolerant groups and individuals in the community to make the social patterns more just and equitable for all the people in the community." Johnson rejected most of her demands. But the future U.S. president did eventually agree to appoint a committee of black consultants—his own Black Cabinet—to advise him on state programs. It fell far short of her objectives, but when Saddler could not achieve integration, she usually secured concessions.

Many of the victories hard won by Saddler and Bethune became realities in the early part of 1936. With Roosevelt's reelection bid looming in the distance, the White House was determined to help the Democrats snatch the black vote from the GOP once and for all. Building up black NYA programs provided great press and spread goodwill among African American voters.

But the year opened with worrisome news. Throughout the previous fall, Robert Vann, the administration's senior black brain truster, had been battling with a white newspaper, the *Georgia Woman's World.*

Its editor had denounced him for defying the color line, charging that he employed two white female secretaries. Published by the Women's National Association for the Preservation of the White Race, the paper was supported by Georgia's Democratic governor, Eugene Talmadge. This was not the paper's only attack on the administration and African Americans. It had also directly assailed the Black Cabinet as well as condemned Eleanor Roosevelt for speaking at an NAACP gathering.

Vann was incensed and fired back with a scathing letter to the paper, stating he employed only black male secretaries. He then accused its editor, Mrs. James Rogers Wakefield, as well as Governor Talmadge, of not having "a very high I.Q." and issued an ominous warning to white southern Democrats. "The Negro vote of the border and Northern States helped put the Democrats in power," he pointed out. "It is highly probable that the same vote will someday take them out of power." There were whispers that the administration was unhappy that Vann had not just let the insult pass and that his response planted a threat to pull black support from the Democrats.

In January 1936, disenchanted with the New Deal and seeing his dream of emerging as a power within American politics die, Robert Vann resigned from his position in the Justice Department. He refrained from criticizing the New Deal and publicly remained a Roosevelt supporter. But he had come to believe that the New Deal leadership had intentionally stymied the African American struggle by hiring many of black America's most gifted activists and then muzzling them. Before leaving the capital, while cleaning out his office, he grumbled to a friend, "I'm not doing anything down here. It looks like they put me down here in Washington to shut me up."

Robert Vann was one of the Roosevelt administration's most notable black officials, and after his resignation, not surprisingly, the spotlight increasingly fell on Mary McLeod Bethune. And her public presence grew as her bond with the First Lady deepened. Spending more and more time in Washington, D.C., she became a familiar visitor to the

White House. Chief usher J. B. West recalled the First Lady "running down the driveway to meet" Bethune, and the two women "walking arm and arm into the mansion." These defiant displays of interracial affection raised eyebrows of Secret Service agents and administration staffers. "In those days, that was just something you didn't do," remarked one White House butler. But Eleanor Roosevelt's warm welcomes not only served as a declaration of her friendship and commitment to equality, they also protected Bethune from the hostility of white secretaries and other officials who felt that the only African Americans who belonged in the White House were servants.

As their friendship blossomed, it became clear that Roosevelt and Bethune had much in common. Although Bethune was ten years older, both belonged to the post–Civil War generation of American women drawn to the progressive movement. As they reached adulthood, they both actively embraced the turn-of-the-twentieth-century reform impulses. While Mary McLeod Bethune had labored to launch her school for black girls and women, Eleanor Roosevelt was working in a settlement house on New York's Lower East Side. Bethune and Roosevelt shared a common dedication to early twentieth-century feminism, middle-class values, education, and national uplift. They also had difficult, even restraining marriages, and they both bonded comfortably with other women.

Bethune and Roosevelt were also passionate about politics. They had come of age at a time when women had fought for and won the right to vote (although most black women across the South remained disenfranchised). Regardless of the advances women had made, politics and governing remained the domain of men, and very few women were able to attain elective office or achieve direct political power. Yet Bethune and Roosevelt found back channels that allowed them to exert influence. For Bethune it had been through her heralded status in the black community and her use of that reputation for political leverage. The far more privileged Roosevelt found her entrance through her husband; his political victories permitted her to rise within the Democratic Party as well as in national politics. Roosevelt and Bethune, and FDR for that matter, enjoyed political partnerships just as much as (and perhaps more than) they did personal and intimate connections.

Mary McLeod Bethune and Eleanor Roosevelt both understood that the political side of their friendship required some give-and-take. Roosevelt called on Bethune for advice and support. Bethune gladly gave it, but she also expected a return, including backing for her school (which struggled financially during the Depression), advancement of her causes, and access to the president. Later Ralph Bunche noted that Bethune had advised him, "*Contact* is *the thing.*" Eleanor Roosevelt certainly recognized the advantages that her relationship with Bethune held for the president, the Democratic Party's attempts to recruit black voters, and the overall success of the New Deal. As much as anyone, the First Lady was mindful of the pending 1936 presidential campaign and the role that Bethune could play in FDR's reelection. As Bethune's status with the Roosevelts rose, she received a much-coveted invitation to dinner at the White House, an opportunity that very few black citizens had ever enjoyed.

During these years, Eleanor Roosevelt began her own personal journey. As an upper-class white woman, she had been raised isolated from African American realities. She later claimed that as a child, her first contact with black Americans had been through the exaggerated stories of Uncle Remus. Although she had been to the South, the United States was so firmly segregated she did not directly interact with a person of African descent until she was a teenager traveling in Europe. Into adulthood, she remained ignorant, later confessing, "I never dreamed they had a special problem of any kind."

According to White House servant Lillian Rogers Parks, Eleanor Roosevelt was awakened to the brutalities of American racism through Mary McLeod Bethune—the educator "greatly influenced Eleanor Roosevelt and taught her to fight segregation." The First Lady herself credited the charismatic Bethune with forcing her to confront the depths of her own racial prejudice. The First Lady greeted close friends—all but Bethune—with a kiss. Although Roosevelt claimed she recognized that this was a result of her still deeply rooted racism, all she could bring herself to do at first was make a studied effort to "give Bethune a peck on the cheek." As their bond grew, her discomfort began to melt. Eventually she finally kissed Bethune without a thought, and she marked the moment as her liberation from bigotry. Yet, this indicated that Roosevelt remained oblivious to racism's complexities. The kiss was a superficial deed, one through which the First Lady could assuage her own guilt. Bill Hastie later praised the First Lady's open-mindedness, but he also insisted that her grasp of prejudice during the New Deal years was simplistic. "Eleanor Roosevelt was a supporter but at that time, really very naïve," he commented.

Some questioned the genuineness of the friendship between Roosevelt and Bethune. There were those who regarded Bethune as a savvy "opportunist," while others observed that Bethune played to white expectations to achieve her purposes—that her rhetoric was much more acquiescent in front of whites than it was before African Americans. This duplicity, a few charged, lurked within Bethune's interactions with the First Lady. Indeed, Bethune could be fawning. In a later letter requesting that Eleanor Roosevelt head up a Bethune-Cookman fund-raising campaign, she gushed: "My thoughts are of you and my prayers are for you. You are a great symbol in this world for the spirit of good. Please don't overtax yourself." Roosevelt's response was terse and impersonal: "Dear Mrs. Bethune: I am willing to be Honorary Chairman of the committee to raise funds for your school but not Chairman. Every good wishes [sic] for success."

Nevertheless, many testified to the closeness of the friendship. Mariagnes Lattimer, whose father was a White House butler, described the bond between Bethune and the First Lady as "warm and intimate." Dovey Johnson Roundtree, who later worked for Bethune in the NYA, witnessed the mutual devotion shared by the two women. "Always, of course, there was a great rush and hush when Mrs. Roosevelt's secretary, Malvina Thompson, phoned the office, but when the First Lady got on the line, Mrs. Bethune relaxed," she recalled. "She laid down the sword she had wielded all day long, stopped fighting, and spoke in the way one does to a trusted ally." Roundtree pointed out that the friendship between Roosevelt and Bethune was "ahead of its time" and that it "threatened both races."

While some African Americans may have been threatened, whites were generally the ones who reacted with hostility to the Bethune-Roosevelt connection. The *Georgia Woman's World* reprinted photos of Bethune and Roosevelt together, alleging that African Americans were "taking over the White House." The president's press secretary, Stephen Early, was alarmed by the affection shared by the black educator and the First Lady. White House southern relations rested in his hands, and in 1936 he ordered Eleanor Roosevelt to *"NOT* visit the colored school with which a Mrs. Bethune is associated." Florida's Democrats, he reported, had informed the White House that "such a visit would be 'most unfortunate'" and would hinder their attempts to maintain white support for the party and the president. Anyway, it would also be a conflict of interest, he added, because Bethune-Cookman College had applied for a federal loan. The loan was hardly the problem; many schools with ties to the Roosevelts were seeking assistance. Rather it was the specter of an interracial friendship that disturbed Early, a southerner dedicated to preserving the racial status quo. With a reelection campaign on the horizon, any positive relationship between the White House and African Americans was, in his view, a pronounced liability.

Under the White House's thumb, Eleanor Roosevelt had no choice but to comply. Many of FDR's advisers worried over what they viewed as her extreme liberalism, especially on race relations. They fought to rein her in. Realizing the first priority was to keep her husband in power, she compromised, though she pushed back when she felt she could do so without harming the president.

In the spring of 1936, Mary McLeod Bethune marched into Washington, D.C.'s Union Station and through the gate to board an express train to the Roosevelts' home in Hyde Park. A young African American porter stopped her.

"You can't get on this train," he warned. "This is a special party going to see the President."

Bethune paused and, always the educator, decided to deliver a lesson on race pride.

"Do you know," she lectured him, "that the day has come—is here now—when colored persons are included in special parties? This is a special party going to Hyde Park to see the President of the United States and I am in that special party and I am going on this train."

She then continued past him and boarded a waiting passenger car.

The train steamed north toward Hyde Park, the site of FDR's estate on the Hudson River. Aubrey Williams had decided that his National Youth Administration advisory board's unwieldy size and infrequent meetings had made it ineffective and was determined to have Roosevelt hear directly from a small subset of board members. Bethune was there to represent black Americans, and this was to be her first formal meeting with the president. Williams cautioned her to report, not advocate.

That wouldn't do, decided Bethune. When her turn came, she spoke directly. For the youth of black America, the NYA had done much good, she remarked. African American teens and young adults working on NYA projects earned between fifteen and twenty-nine dollars a month and that "meant real salvation for thousands of Negro young people." There had been a combined effort between the NYA and the WPA (facilitated in part by Al Smith) to give parents of black NYA youths access to education and training in marketable skills. But this simply was not enough, Bethune insisted. African Americans needed to be more fully incorporated into NYA programs across the country, and the White House needed to expeditiously approve more funding to hire black officials at the local and state level. Time was of the essence: "We are bringing life and spirit to those many thousands who for so long have been in the darkness. I speak, Mr. President, not as Mrs. Bethune, but as the voice of 14,000,000 Americans who seek full citizenship. We want to continue to open doors for these millions." Bethune later told of seeing FDR's eyes well up with tears. He reached across the table, she claimed, and he took her hands. "Mrs. Bethune," he began, "I am glad I am able to contribute something to help make a better life for your people. I want to assure you that I will continue to do my best for them in every way." The room went quiet, and the meeting was adjourned.

Several weeks after the Hyde Park meeting, Aubrey Williams informed Bethune that FDR had agreed that there was a need for an increased African American presence within the NYA and had directed him to organize the Office of Minority Affairs. The president wanted her to lead it, Williams revealed. Bethune claimed the invitation was a complete surprise. No, she had her college to think of, she told Williams. "Think of serving millions instead of hundreds," he responded. No black woman had ever led a federal division; she would be the first. If she turned it down, he warned, it would go to a man. "I visualized dozens of Negro women coming after me filling positions of high trust and strategic importance," she remembered.

At a face-to-face meeting with Roosevelt and Williams, Bethune accepted the position. The president, according to her, was "beaming" and remarked, "Aubrey . . . Mrs. Bethune is a great woman. I believe in her because she has her feet on the ground—not only on the ground but deep down in the ploughed soil."

Now occupying a principal position within the New Deal administration, Bethune drove ahead, pushing for change—her way—in the National Youth Administration, the New Deal, and society at large. In the summer of 1936, she began building her staff and petitioning for more resources. She immediately lost Juanita Saddler, who told Lawrence Oxley that she could not bear to be a subordinate in the office that had resulted, to a great deal, from her hard work. At Robert Weaver's suggestion, Bethune invited educator Frank Horne to serve as her assistant. A New York native, Horne had passed for white to obtain an ophthalmology degree from Central Illinois University. In the 1920s, he had established a successful practice in Harlem, received acclaim as a poet, and then landed a job at Fort Valley (Georgia) High and Industrial School, where he later took over the position of president when it was vacated by the Farm Credit Administration's Henry Hunt.

Horne, who had prominent ties to the NAACP, initially turned Bethune down. He had been critical of the New Deal, sending Harold Ickes a blistering thirteen-page condemnation of the federal government's tolerance of substandard segregated black schools, which he called a "Dog House Education." Driving the back roads of Georgia, he reported how the "fine, brick school house on a hill" that served white children contrasted with the "cracker box" in a "bare and rain-eroded gully" where black children were educated. Horne was dedicated to remedying the inequalities and injustices in Georgia's public schools.

Bethune turned on her powers of persuasion. "There is a big job to be done. . . . There are twelve million Negroes in America depending upon the kind of program we shall send out," she wrote to Horne. (Her accounting of the size of the black population often varied.) "Your service to the race and the nation will be greatly enlarged. . . . The program of the National Youth Administration is a challenge to the best that there is in us at this time."

Horne later remarked, "When she [Bethune] asks you to do something, you *want* to do it." He reported for duty in her office within weeks.

Rounding out her staff, Bethune also brought along her personal secretary, Arabella Denniston, an alumna of Bethune-Cookman and a former Urban Leaguer. She would later add a second stenographer, Harriet West; social work professional Pauline Redmond Coggs; educator R. O'Hara Lanier; and journalist Harry McAlpin, who anchored publicity and ghostwrote some of her speeches.

Right off, Williams arranged for Bethune to travel to NYA sites and speak on behalf of the program and the president. At a Fisk University conference, she assured her listeners that Washington, with "its great beehive of minds," was working tirelessly to "make plans and give employment so that America might stand on its feet." She urged black leaders to work with whites in positions of power for equal inclusion in relief programs and to create a nation based on "brotherly love." Back again in Washington, Bethune demanded a bigger budget. Over time, probably with some help from Eleanor Roosevelt, most of her requests were granted. Of all the New Deal programs addressing African American needs, hers received the most funds and the most publicity.

Bethune rose to power in the New Deal at a critical moment in its history. During the summer of 1936, the presidential race heated up and she knew that it was the right time to strike. Certainly she wagered that if she could help deliver African American votes for Roosevelt, the Democratic National Committee would have a hefty debt to pay to both her and the black community. While a significant number of African Americans had voted Democratic in 1932, and even more had crossed over in 1934, Bethune's goal was to help transform the entire African American electorate from loyal Republicans to supporters of Roosevelt and the Democrats. Party affiliation wasn't important; she had remained a Republican. In her view, other African Americans could do the same and, like her, vote Democrat as long as FDR and his party addressed their needs. It was a political balancing act that Bethune embraced enthusiastically; she possessed a strategic cleverness and organizational acumen that well prepared her for the rough-and-tumble world of politics. African American scholar John Hope Franklin recalled his first encounter with Bethune, in 1936: "I was in awe of her. . . . I doubt that I spoke a word as she talked about her work with the Roosevelt administration and as a college president and her struggle to decide between a career as an educator and one as a politician." Although shut out by race and gender, Bethune had found a door that allowed her to enter national politics.

Deploying Bethune quickly and as fully as possible was important to FDR's reelection hopes. By the end of June 1936, the Republicans' convention had come and gone. The GOP had chosen a candidate with reformist roots—Kansas governor Alfred "Alf" Landon. A former Bull Mooser, an old-line Republican of the Theodore Roosevelt stripe, Landon had his liabilities and was regarded as devoid of all charisma.

But Kansas had started a nice bounce back from the Depression, and he could also boast of some achievements in the area of race relations. He had spoken out against the Ku Klux Klan in the 1920s. He had appointed an African American to the Kansas attorney general's office and several black Republicans to leadership positions in the state GOP.

The Republicans kicked off their campaign for black votes with direct attacks on the New Deal. The Roosevelt administration, they charged, served the whims of the white southern Democrats. White House programs like the National Youth Administration and the Civilian Conservation Corps favored whites over blacks. Yet again, the party conjured up Lincoln's ghost, insisting that the Republicans remained the "Great Emancipator's" heirs. THE CONTINUATION OF THE NEW DEAL MEANS: THE GHETTO, THE RESERVATION, JIM CROW, SERFDOM AND EXTINCTION FOR THE NEGRO, bellowed one ad for Alf Landon. "I'd rather vote for a dog on the Republican ticket than the best Democrat who ever lived," thundered Roscoe Conkling Simmons, a black party spokesman, at a campaign stop. He charged that "any black man who votes for a Democrat is placing a curse on the soul of Abraham Lincoln."

Roosevelt certainly had his disadvantages. While he was generally popular, the New Deal's overall track record was hardly spectacular. After almost four years, in 1936 unemployment nationwide averaged almost 17 percent—a sluggish recovery at best. The Roosevelt camp seemed to be either snoozing or just plain uninterested in the black vote. Dr. Joseph Johnson, of the Big Four—the 1932 campaign's core black leaders—had implored the Democratic National Committee to set up a permanent black division, but to no avail. The Associated Negro Press's Claude Barnett, fed up with the GOP, expressed willingness to secretly help the DNC get Roosevelt reelected. No one took him up on his offer. Early in the year, Eleanor Roosevelt sent a memo to FDR's chief strategist, Louis Howe, with a list of suggestions for the campaign. Among them was one that encouraged the party to concentrate efforts in African American communities. "The *negroes* of this country are in a more definitely friendly attitude toward the

Administration than I have ever known them to be to a Democratic Administration and we should add to our organization . . . a unit that will supervise and keep in touch with them," she wrote. A committee including William Thompkins, Eugene Kinckle Jones, and Robert Vann, among others, she urged, should be organized and sent out to speak. Her recommendations ended up sitting in a pile of papers somewhere.

Inside the Roosevelt White House, alarm grew. Louis Howe died in the spring, and by summer the Democrats were nearly broke. Although his reelection chances were seemingly in jeopardy, the perpetually jovial FDR appeared unfazed. He left in July for a vacation with his sons. Eleanor Roosevelt and Harold Ickes fretted; Roosevelt's campaign manager, Jim Farley, started to worry. FDR, they all feared, was too certain, too convinced that his charm and magnetism would crush the famously dull Landon.

While the president was off fishing, the First Lady decided she would push the campaign forward. She organized a women's division for the party, demanded Democratic bosses come up with a clear reelection strategy, and insisted the DNC undertake a serious drive for black votes. On the final issue, she peppered Stephen Early and Farley with suggestions; one was another plea that they dispatch FDR's black supporters to stump for the president. Mary McLeod Bethune would be especially effective, she suggested. Early ignored the mention of African Americans; he informed her that the party couldn't afford to undertake an elaborate campaign because of lack of funds. Farley was a little more receptive. He assured the First Lady that by mid-August the reelection effort would be in full swing. He had plans in place already to consult with the Rosenwald Fund's Will Alexander, who wanted to set up an African American wing within the party. "I know about Mrs. Bethune," Farley remarked. "I will have another conference with Mr. Alexander next week in Washington and go over with him at that time the organization he has in mind."

Most African Americans loyal to the president had already begun discussing their plans—they did not need Alexander's guidance, and it was patronizing to assume they did. However, rallying African American Democrats, independent black voters, and disgruntled black Republicans promised to be somewhat tricky. The ongoing feuds among the original Big Four made it especially complicated. The intense dislike between longtime rivals Robert Vann and William Thompkins had deepened as the two battled to lead a new national division of African American Democrats. Just before the Democratic convention, Thompkins called a separate meeting of black party members to solidify his claim as the party's top black leader. Vann lashed out at Thompkins, accusing him of promoting segregation. The *Pittsburgh Courier* editor then announced to the press that he would be the Democrats' African American point man.

Jim Farley tried to sidestep the clash by appointing Boston's Julian Rainey and Congressman Arthur Mitchell as cochairs of the DNC's black division. Thompkins and Vann were assigned to head up the efforts in their own states, which made them even angrier. Left completely out in the cold was longtime Democrat Dr. Joseph Johnson. Livid, he bolted and publicly endorsed the GOP. The Big Four's original idea man, Manuel Roque, also exited and not quietly. "They [the Democrats] do not now intend to and never will play fair with the colored group," he charged. "They are compelled to bow to their Southern constituency which dominates the party." The turmoil seemed to play right into the GOP's hands.

As they had done during the 1934 midterm election, Democrats highlighted their claim that FDR was personally responsible for the increase of African Americans in federal service. "Roosevelt has given the Negro larger recognition by way of appointive positions than any other administration Democratic or Republican since Theodore Roosevelt," insisted Kelly Miller, now solidly in FDR's camp. The president's appointment of Mary McLeod Bethune was probably the most frequently noted example of his purportedly sincere commitment to African American citizens. "Distinguished leaders of our own race like Mrs. Mary McLeod Bethune . . . have been called to Washington,"

White House maid Elizabeth McDuffie told one cheering crowd while campaigning for FDR. "She has seen to it that more than 30,000 of our own boys and girls benefited from the federal government's student-aid program under the NYA." According to McDuffie, FDR was committed to "economic improvement to all people" and had recruited "hundreds of our brightest young men" for jobs "of high authority, in every major department of the government."

The reality was that there weren't "hundreds" of new black appointees and that the "brightest young men" who made up the Black Cabinet constantly encountered obstructions "in every major department of the government." They had no "authority," and the White House had little interest in their advice. Additionally, they remained fundamentally divided—their differences both personal and professional raged on. Progress was painfully slow. The job title of racial-affairs adviser may have been impressive, but the actual work was flat-out disheartening. The Black Cabinet made good campaign talk, but the reality was that there was no unity among its members, and it was a mostly symbolic group.

But where others saw adversity, Mary McLeod Bethune saw opportunity.

At her command, on Friday evening, August 7, 1936, seven black federal officials, among them Robert Weaver, Al Smith, Lawrence Oxley, and Frank Horne, arrived at her Washington, D.C., home. She had brought them together, she announced, to discuss "plans for the full integration and participation of Negroes" in the New Deal. The black population still languished in poverty and faced persistent discrimination. The remedy for this had to come from the federal government; it was the only American institution that possessed enough power to achieve black recovery and secure equal rights, she pointed out. It was the Black Cabinet's obligation to fight this battle, and that demanded complete and harmonious collaboration among the members. "The responsibility rests on us. We can get better results thinking and planning together. We must think about each other's problems. Let us band together and work together as one big brotherhood and give momentum to the great ball that is starting to roll for Negroes," she implored. "I feel helpless without the fellowship, interest, and cooperation of all of you."

Bethune insisted they meet regularly and share information, strategize, and support each other in their individual quests within the New Deal. "We must think in terms of strategic attacks at this time. Let us forget the particular office each one of us holds and think how we might, in a cooperative way, get over to the masses the things that are being done and the things that need to be done."

Almost immediately, the group began quarreling. The New Deal had benefited African Americans, Lawrence Oxley insisted, citing as an example the first all-black homestead project in Newport News, Virginia. Not all was well at Newport News, Al Smith sighed; it was under construction, and his office was fighting off efforts there to replace black workers with whites. Robert Weaver spoke to the difficulty of coordinating the various and divergent black programs. "Three years ago, I attempted to organize the Negro heads of various departments for the same purpose," he stated, referring to the Inter-Departmental Group Concerned with the Special Problems of the Negro. Despite the energy that body put into generating carefully researched reports, the information had never made it all the way up the chain of command. When the findings were released to the public, they had been misused or distorted, hindering the black cause. Yet, perhaps another attempt at gathering data and formulating syntheses might be worth a try, he conceded.

There was no time for discord. Bethune reminded the members of the black brain trust of "their responsibility for the promotion of Negro interests." She felt this responsibility "to the burning point of my soul," and she insisted that in their positions they were obligated to feel it too. "Let us forget where we are and work for the greatest interest and greatest good of Negroes," urged Dewey Jones, one of Al Smith's assistants. Discussion turned to what could be done. All agreed that information needed to be gathered, shared, and somehow conveyed to the public, the upper-level New Deal leaders, and the White House.

That evening Mary McLeod Bethune had succeeded in uniting the badly fractured Black Cabinet under her leadership. It would cautiously remain an informal body, but it was intended to function as an organized internal lobby for African American needs within the federal government. Pledging to work together as one, that night the members decided to call themselves the Federal Council on Negro Affairs. Outside their circle, the title was rarely used, and the African American public persisted in identifying them as the Black Cabinet. That name had already become iconic.

Those present that night left the meeting with a renewed spirit of determination and commitment. And it was a woman who took the reins and began driving the men toward securing a voice for black people within the federal government. In Bethune's mind, there was no question she would succeed and her male colleagues would follow.

Indeed, Kelly Miller observed, "Mrs. Bethune has few equals."

Chapter Seven

We Belong Here

As the presidential race headed into its final months, Mary McLeod Bethune shifted into high gear and made it the Black Cabinet's central task to get FDR reelected. She was resolved, Kelly Miller observed, to leave "no stone unturned to retain the New Deal in power." The preservation of the New Deal and its philosophy of federal intervention, as well as the perpetuation of the Black Cabinet, rested on keeping the Roosevelts in the White House. In September 1936, Bethune announced she would make a "Good Will" tour of the nation.

Suddenly she seemed to be everywhere at once. Just one leg of her travels took her from Washington, D.C., to Chicago, to West Virginia, home to Daytona Beach, and north to Ohio, Pennsylvania, and New Jersey, with several other stops along the way. She dropped in for a well-publicized visit with the First Lady in the Roosevelts' New York City apartment. Later she endorsed the president on a CBS radio broadcast; it was the first time an African American woman had participated in a discussion of politics over the national airwaves. Eager to see the famous Bethune, large crowds, mostly black but some of them integrated, came out to hear her on the campaign trail. "In all her talks Mrs. Bethune analyzed the economic situation of the Negro in America and stressed the need of Negro youth for training of the hand as well as of the head," the *New York Age* reported. "She also emphasized the extraordinary possibilities of the program of the National Youth Administration."

At an appearance at a black college in North Carolina, Bethune urged African American students and faculty to embrace the New Deal and federal relief—it was not a handout, as some White House critics alleged. "I believe in the dignity of work," she stated. "Do your work with efficiency, regardless of the task, earn what the Government is paying you and it will not be charity." The White House's accomplishments on behalf of black people were impressive, she told her audiences. The administration had provided educational stipends to African American children from grades one to twelve, college scholarships to black students, and Civilian Conservation Corps jobs to black youth. Stopping in at her Washington, D.C., office, she announced that the National Youth Administration (NYA) had awarded African American graduate students over $50,000 in grants.

With far less splash, Bethune's Black Cabinet colleagues also stumped for the president. Some still regarded electioneering with distaste; they were not political appointees and cringed at the task of selling the deeply flawed New Deal to the black public. While they may have been compelled to participate by Bethune's inspiring call to arms, Al Smith observed, they also didn't have much choice. There was direct pressure on Black Cabinet members to campaign for the president. "Do what you can to get [Roosevelt] reelected," were the orders from the administration. Several racial-affairs advisers supported the FDR camp with speeches, newspaper interviews, and personal appearances, highlighting what they described as Roosevelt's genuine commitment to African Americans.

Lawrence Oxley was eager to get on the campaign trail. In August 1936, he commenced a lengthy, multistate trip to pump up support for FDR while also collecting data on African American unemployment. He told a Memphis audience that he was "optimistic in his outlook on the prospects of Negroes," provided they did their part "to realize and grasp their opportunities." Although Robert Weaver found politicking crude and was far from charismatic, he pitched in too. The African American press featured him and Bethune as star black appointments.

Accounts of Weaver's brilliant rise in the government appeared in black newspapers, and he too made speeches plugging New Deal successes. Weaver also published a careful assessment of the administration's achievements in housing and labor. It was academic and formal, not fare for the casual reader but for a more scholarly audience; it precisely documented the effectiveness of public housing programs and antidiscrimination clauses built into federal contracts.

As a former journalist, Al Smith knew what played well with the public. In late summer and early fall 1936, he churned out publicity featuring purported Works Progress Administration (WPA) triumphs. He generated press releases, sent reports to black leaders, and authored a booklet entitled *Interesting Facts About the Negro and the WPA*. Smith also collaborated with the Pathé newsreel company on *We Work Again*, a film promoting work relief for black Americans. The sixteen-minute short dramatized the impact of the WPA on African American communities. It opened with scenes of black urban destitution and poverty, men on the street, and families standing in breadlines. As the music swelled, the camera panned over the same people and revealed their transformation into joyful and gratified workers, employed courtesy of the federal government. A parade of proud, well-dressed teachers, secretaries, factory laborers, doctors, nurses, and construction workers appeared. Handsome building projects and the revitalization of the black inner city testified to the happy consequences of Roosevelt-generated jobs. Black children, who benefited from better school facilities and newly trained teachers, played gleefully in new parks and community pools. The film ended with classical and gospel music performed by a choir and scenes from a government-sponsored, all-black Harlem production of *Macbeth*.

When Smith screened *We Work Again* in October 1936, New Deal chiefs were impressed. They ordered its immediate release. It played around the country, mostly in black schools and churches as well as in African American movie houses. Although it was a glossy and radically overblown portrayal of African American recovery, Smith's film was pioneering. African Americans in Hollywood movies almost always appeared as ignorant and childlike servants—black screen characters that reinforced negative racial stereotypes. But in *We Work Again*, African Americans, even the unemployed, were portrayed with dignity. They were well dressed and many of those depicted were middle-class professionals. The film emphasized the theme of African American accomplishments and progress. The *Saturday Evening Post* hailed it as a vital contribution to FDR's campaign.

Former Black Cabinet member Robert Vann, despite his disaffection with both the administration and the Democrats, also threw all his energy behind the effort to reelect Roosevelt. He was focused on the possibility of obtaining another political post, thinking he might reap either a federal judgeship or, better yet, an appointment as the first black governor of the Virgin Islands. In addition to coordinating black voter outreach in his home state of Pennsylvania, he convinced the Democratic National Committee to use him as a liaison to African American newspapers. In an interview with the *Baltimore Afro-American*, he warned that the Republicans' efforts to retain and recapture black votes would fail. "The money does not persuade this year as it once did, because the party of Landon . . . is not the party of Lincoln," Vann asserted. "The colored voter knows the difference."

Certainly Vann had a hand in composing many of the DNC's press releases, including those that promoted the Black Cabinet as one of the most compelling reasons for African American voters to jump on the Roosevelt bandwagon. "As the campaign gets under way colored voters should remember there are certain basic points to the credit of the New Deal," one read, pointing out that the number of African Americans in federal posts was at a historic high. The appointments of Weaver and Bethune were undeniable evidence, it claimed, of the president's "humane attitude toward the citizens of the country, regardless of race, creed, or color." The African American public read that "not only have hundreds of trained race people been called by the Roosevelt administration to serve their country, but their opinions have been accepted in reference to federal work among the Negro citizens."

The DNC also offered generous payouts to some African American news sources for political advertising. Although the majority of black newspaper editors were leaning toward FDR anyway, the funds helped seal the deal on their endorsements.

As the election neared, the White House pumped more funding into African American relief efforts. The administration allocated $2 million for studies on black joblessness, with the goal of putting more African Americans back to work. More than $50 million had gone to federal housing projects and more was coming, thanks to Robert Weaver. The Civilian Conservation Corps finally opened a camp headed exclusively by African American officers. Al Smith's office was distributing more WPA jobs in black communities, though in some areas, they came with pressure to vote for Roosevelt and the Democrats. THE WAY TO JUDGE A MAN'S FUTURE IS BY HIS PAST, blared a full-page ad for Roosevelt in Vann's *Pittsburgh Courier*. It presented heartening New Deal "Facts and Figures"—26,000 young people were receiving stipends from Bethune's NYA, black schools and hospitals saw increased funding, and "300,000 Negroes [have been] taught to read through government grants for adult education." A man of the people, the president was "Right and Regular" and had been "the most considerate friend the Negro has had in the White House since Theodore Roosevelt."

While more resources had started to flow, inside the black New Deal, the big picture was not as rosy. Relief programs for African Americans, in comparison with those for white Americans, remained drastically unequal and inadequate in relationship to the disproportionate poverty suffered in black communities. In his October report to his WPA bosses, Al Smith cited numerous complaints from African Americans unable to secure New Deal aid. With the arrival of the harvest season, white southern planters had pressured local WPA supervisors to fire black workers from relief jobs in order to force them back into the fields. African American women also found themselves driven out of New Deal work. "Negro women . . . are being unfairly cut off WPA sewing projects and forced to take domestic service employment at starvation wages," Smith reported. Behind the scenes, Black Cabinet members also reported on continued and rampant discrimination against African Americans within the New Deal administration. In general, they reported, many immediate supervisors refused to forward their reports to higher authorities who could act.

Even though the GOP continued to hammer away at these New Deal inadequacies, the party's efforts with African Americans seemed to lose steam as the November election neared. The Republicans had superior financial resources and dispersed their usual cash flow to black newspapers, but it had little effect. Alf Landon had a rocky campaign, and in the eyes of African Americans, he looked increasingly less like an heir of Lincoln and more like the progeny of the old Confederacy. When he announced his support for states' rights, alarms went off in the black community. His position signaled to the white South that he would not use federal power to protect African Americans. Consequently, when he declared his opposition to lynching, it rang as disingenuous; most African Americans and anti-lynching activists agreed that such mob murders would never be stopped by state authorities. It would take the full power of Washington, they argued, to end the lynching of black people.

Landon also opposed most federal relief programs, insisting that the New Deal eroded individualism, spread dependency, and—in the case of African Americans—enslaved them, making them "ward[s] of the federal government." The Republican presidential candidate contended that the economic crisis could be overcome only if all economic relief was devolved to the states. That only caused more consternation among black voters. Past discrimination by white state and local relief officials was well known in the black community. Many African Americans had been converted to FDR's brand of federal intervention, which they believed was essential in protecting all marginalized citizens. Government assistance was not an end for its recipients. It was a means by which Americans could climb out of financial ruin and achieve success within the system.

The Landon campaign also had to compete with the growing reputation of the Roosevelts as friends to the black community. Robert Vann's *Pittsburgh Courier* highlighted the First Lady's popularity with the African American masses and emphasized the Roosevelts' human touch. The paper recounted how Hattie Mosley, a leader in Ohio's black women's political clubs, "made her way" to the front of a crowd in Springfield and presented the president with a bouquet. Both Franklin and Eleanor Roosevelt welcomed her with "broad smiles and friendly handshakes." During a campaign stop at Howard University, Roosevelt for the first time publicly pledged support for the black community. "Among American citizens," he told the audience, "there should be no forgotten men and no forgotten races." In a newspaper interview, Crystal Bird Fauset, an African American WPA official from Philadelphia, dismissed Republican charges that the New Deal threatened to put African Americans back in bondage. It was the other way around, she contended: "The leaders of the Republican Party are determined to protect only the interests of the capitalists of the country, thereby keeping the workers of the country in a state of virtual economic slavery." It had been an uphill battle for the Republicans throughout the campaign. When the *Baltimore Afro-American* reported in the summer that Alf Landon's African American cook announced that in her opinion "President Roosevelt is the man for the job," no doubt the Democrats rejoiced.

On election day, 1936, FDR took a decisive 60.8 percent of the votes, the largest margin ever won by a presidential candidate. The outcome represented a seismic shift among African Americans. In areas where black people could vote, most chose Roosevelt. Although political watchers still struggled with ambiguous figures regarding black voting trends, using what data was available they estimated that between 1932 and 1936, FDR had increased his take of black votes by margins ranging from 60 percent to 250 percent. Of Harlem's black voters, 81 percent went for Roosevelt. In Pittsburgh, Vann's territory, 75 percent of African Americans cast their ballot for the president. "The Negro vote stood like a stone wall against Landon in every one of the pivotal states," proclaimed the *Pittsburgh Courier*. African Americans may not have officially reregistered as Democrats, but their voting allegiances were now with Roosevelt and his party. The changeover was historic. During the election of 1936, for the first time, both major American political parties had entered into an out-and-out battle for the black vote. The African American electorate had secured its role in the body politic, thanks in great part to the Black Cabinet's efforts.

Yet, an important question lingered: Would African American voters remain in the Democratic fold? "The new mobility of the Negro vote with the attendant attention paid to it in pivotal states, can mean a new deal politically for the Negro," the NAACP's Walter White observed. "Negroes, however, must wisely and unselfishly utilize this new power and these new situations. They must let the Democratic Party know that all elections will not be won by the overwhelming majority of 1936 . . . [and] that Negroes want something done about lynching, discrimination in jobs, and relief and in the civil service." To maintain African American backing, the Democrats needed to make good on their debts.

Payback started right away. A few weeks after FDR won his second term came the announcement that his mother, Sarah Delano Roosevelt, would lead a massive fund-raising campaign for Bethune-Cookman College.

But Mary McLeod Bethune was interested in far more than personal favors.

In early December 1936, she headed to the NAACP's national headquarters in New York City for a meeting with Walter White. Several weeks before, she had informed White that she was planning to call African American leaders and civil rights organizations from around the country to Washington, D.C., for a massive conference under the banner of the National Youth Administration. The goal would be to examine the crises in black America and formulate solutions to the problems the African American people faced daily. While the needs of black youths would be discussed, the conference would address the uplift of the entire community. Whites were certainly welcome to attend, she remarked, although subcommittees appointed during the conference would be exclusively African American because the identification of problems and solutions had to come from the black community. She would insist, she revealed, that the federal government not only endorse the NYA conference but also pay for it. It was a gutsy idea that White found "provocative." And he was always up for a fight.

That day, the two spent several hours discussing "the minimum basic objectives which the Negro asks for in the next four years." They created a list of demands that included more funding for the NYA, more support for black education, and increased assistance to "farm tenants and sharecroppers." The original Social Security Act of 1935 had omitted domestic and agricultural workers, and the conference would demand that be remedied. The White House had to be pressured to support federal anti-lynching laws, the inclusion of nondiscrimination clauses in all government contracts, an end to unfair civil service practices, the integration of national parks, and the expansion of African Americans in the military, especially in the newly emerging air corps. A top priority, Bethune and White agreed, was to expand the Black Cabinet with "more federal appointments, especially in executive positions, of qualified Negroes." Bethune then departed and returned to Washington to begin preparations.

Bethune's goal was to seize the moment to build on the successes of the Black Cabinet. After almost four years, the group could claim some hard-won victories. Its members had established an African American voice within the federal government, one that was growing as black appointments increased. Using their influence, they had wrangled New Deal relief for many African Americans, and although the aid fell far short of what was needed or fair, had it not been for the constant pressure applied by Black Cabinet members, relief would have bypassed almost all black citizens. The nondiscrimination clauses in Interior Department contracts helped make this possible and stood as a model for other divisions committed to fighting racial bias.

The black brain trust had also documented the African American experience under the New Deal and tracked the impact that racism had on the black community. Whites had often charged that African American complaints of unequal treatment were overblown and that blacks should blame themselves for their lack of progress. But the studies generated by Black Cabinet members provided indisputable proof that America was not the land of open opportunity for African Americans and that the community had been impeded by the Jim Crow system, the denial of a political voice, educational inequalities, and economic repression. Black Cabinet members had also nudged FDR's New Deal to go beyond simple fiscal recovery. Under their influence the concept of the American Dream and its relationship to the federal government expanded. The New Deal was not just about repairing a country's economy to facilitate individual material success; it was about nourishing a new nation where all could enjoy the promises of democracy and human rights.

Racial-affairs advisers were aware of their contribution to reorienting American political culture to take into consideration issues of race. And they realized that because of the changes, the Democratic Party had to execute a delicate balancing act. The DNC faced the complicated task of preserving a new, yet extremely divergent base that included white southerners, African Americans, farmers, industrial workers, union members, and urbanites. The challenge for the Black Cabinet was to force the party to honor the black community's needs and continue to recognize the power of African Americans at the ballot box. The pressure had to be steady, clear, and relentless.

As many in the Black Cabinet agreed, leveraging the white party leadership was not enough. They needed access to the president.

Led by Stephen Early, a protective wall of White House staffers, almost wholly unsympathetic to the African American cause, continued to act as the first and formidable hurdle. Although Eleanor Roosevelt had begun to experience an awakening in her attitudes toward race, most of the rest of the White House had not. And it was a mystery where FDR really stood. He was chummy with the black domestic help but gave Early, who was deeply bound to southern decorum, substantial control over public relations even in the area of the White House's interactions with black Americans. Robert Weaver believed the president was not a dependable ally in the black struggle. "He had lived in Georgia. He had accustomed himself and accommodated himself to the Southern race relations," Weaver explained later. "He did not have the feeling that Mrs. Roosevelt had of the fact that it was something that should be changed or could be changed." In Weaver's view, FDR "was not a champion of civil rights and . . . he did not have this high on his priority."

Most agreed that this was because FDR continued to calibrate his actions to appease the powerful southern wing of his party. Bethune later affirmed that the president approached African American affairs with extreme caution. "More than once I proposed pretty drastic steps to end the hideous discriminations and second-class citizenship which make the South a blot upon our democracy," she revealed. "But FDR usually demurred, pointing out that a New Reconstruction in the South would have to keep pace with democratic progress on a national scale." When Walter White pressed the president for a public endorsement of a federal anti-lynching law, FDR refused. "I did not choose the tools with which I must work," Roosevelt told White. "The Southerners by reason of the seniority rule in Congress are chairmen or occupy strategic places on most of the Senate and House committees. If I come out for the anti-lynching bill now, they will block every bill I ask Congress to pass to keep America from collapsing."

Still Mary McLeod Bethune was convinced that the president was, deep down, a genuine supporter of African American rights. "You know, Mrs. Bethune, people like you and me are fighting and must continue to fight for the day when a man will be regarded as a man regardless of his race or faith or country," she claimed he had confided to her. "That day will come but we must pass through some perilous times before we realize it. . . . Justice must and will prevail." Her optimism about Roosevelt led her to trust that he could be steered in the right direction.

While Bethune credited FDR with tutoring her on "practical politics and how important it is that we understand their meaning if we are to make progress in the political arena," she had arrived in Washington, D.C., with a well-developed political shrewdness. She also realized that the African American cause needed to be sold to the president and the Congress. The case for black citizens needed to go beyond academic documentation based on dry social scientific methods used by her colleagues: to get the attention of those in power, it had to be dramatized with courage and passion. She was determined to apply so much pressure on Roosevelt that he would have to act; she believed she could lay the groundwork for him to use his constitutional and moral authority to advance African American people, which in her mind was what he really wanted to do anyway. Her NYA conference would give the president a good excuse to act expeditiously.

She announced the NYA conference in the *Pittsburgh Courier*: "With a President planning and working for the welfare of all the people . . . the opportunity had arrived for the definition of an all-embracing plan to promote the integration of the Negro into national life . . . under the guidance of the federal government." She called for representatives from diverse sectors of black America to join together "with one mind to draw up a set of definitive recommendations and with one voice to ask our President and our government, which we love and serve, for their help in achieving our objectives." Aubrey Williams and several other New Deal administrators agreed to cover the conference's costs. Frances Perkins volunteered to host it at the Labor Department and provide meals in its dining room. The press reported that all of the Black Cabinet would be there, including former members Robert Vann and Forrester Washington.

In early January 1937, delegates to Bethune's National Conference on the Problems of the Negro and Negro Youth began arriving in town. The Whitelaw, the only hotel in Washington that accommodated African Americans, quickly filled to capacity. Bethune's staff scrambled to arrange lodging for overflow attendees in private homes and boarding-houses. On the morning of Wednesday, January 6, more than one hundred delegates gathered in the Labor Department's stylishly appointed auditorium for the opening session. Aubrey Williams called the conference to order and introduced the agenda, which covered, among other issues, jobs, poverty, education, health care, housing, policing, politics, and social justice. The goal, he announced, was to develop policies and programs to remedy black destitution and American racism. At Mrs. Bethune's direction, he cautioned, no information would be released to the press during the proceedings. A full report, speaking for the whole, would be circulated after the conference concluded.

Just before noon, there was a stir in the back of the auditorium, and Eleanor Roosevelt marched in. The crowd stood and "roared with applause." The First Lady made her way to the front, shook hands with Mary McLeod Bethune, and got right to her remarks. "This may be your problem as a race, but it is not your problem alone," she assured the audience, stating that the desperately "low standard" of living endured by most black Americans was intolerable. Her main concern was with children, she told the crowd. To uplift the nation as a whole, all children must receive comparable attention and the nation's care. "We are all equal citizens together. We should have equal responsibility for everyone in the community." As she finished, a smiling Eleanor Roosevelt took her seat between Bethune and Harold Ickes. The audience was thrilled.

Bethune then took over and, for the remainder of the three days, steered the meeting with steely resolve—she introduced speakers, summarized main points, refereed debates, and drove the conversation forward toward solutions. Hers was a firm hand, and when dissent rose, she rapidly extinguished it. When one squabble broke out on the floor, she pounded the lectern, warning, "You have somebody holding the gavel, see? Now let's keep the spirit. We are here thinking together. Let us differ in the right spirit."

The Black Cabinet played a prominent role during the gathering. Conferees heard reports from Lawrence Oxley, Robert Weaver, Al

Smith, Edgar Brown, and William Hastie. Addresses also came from
Commerce Secretary Daniel Roper, the Civilian Conservation Corps'
Robert Fechner, Treasury's Josephine Roche, Agriculture Secretary
Henry Wallace, and Will Alexander, now working in one of the rural
divisions of the Resettlement Administration. Each evening the con-
ferees broke into smaller committees and, in consultation with Black
Cabinet members, worked until midnight crafting recommendations
for their assigned topics.

During the Friday session, the conference reconvened to hear committee reports and discuss next steps. The results were exhaustive and
covered all aspects of African American life; the final draft of the
conference's recommendations ran thirty pages long. The conference
endorsed all the proposals formulated by White and Bethune at their
December 1936 meeting.

But the subcommittees went much further. The economics and
employment group called not only for parity in New Deal relief but
also for the revision of labor laws and increased assistance to black
tenant farmers. The education committee recommended that both the
National Youth Administration and the Civilian Conservation Corps
become permanent programs and that federal dollars be distributed
equally to black and white schools. They also demanded the integration of youth recreational and training programs, of the military
academies, and of all national parks. Those discussing health care
called for the establishment of more hospitals and clinics to serve
black citizens, for all African American veterans to receive the same
military benefits enjoyed by whites, and for government-funded well-
ness programs in black communities. Advised by Weaver, the housing
committee endorsed the administration's new low-income projects
but rejected the policy of racially separate programs, "because of the
danger of federal segregation being accepted as patterns for private
community development." The social justice subcommittee emphatically condemned police brutality, which, its members pointed out,
ran unchecked in black neighborhoods. They urged the president and

Congress to quickly pass legislation prohibiting lynching, Jim Crow on public transportation, and race-based disenfranchisement.

Late Friday afternoon, after the committees finished their reports, when Bethune called for a vote on their recommendations, those present overwhelmingly shouted *aye*. Then she spoke. She was inspired, she told the audience. "I feel that colored citizens who have been under ether all these years are waking up and that the injustices which we have suffered can no longer be meted out to us so easily." The results of the conference would be conveyed to cabinet officials, to New Deal heads, to the press, and, without delay, to the president. "I have a feeling," she continued. "I don't know whether it is of an Esther or Deborah, that the time has come to march forward. I want you to feel that we are going to present your ideas, unreservedly, before the President, that we want your prayers, that we will get results."

Two days before the president's second inauguration, Bethune sent Roosevelt a copy of the conference's agenda, a list of participants, and the committees' recommendations. In a cover letter, she praised the administration for creating, for the first time in history, an opportunity for black citizens to collectively lay their case for equal treatment before the federal government. But she also condemned the nation for continuing its flagrant denials of social justice and human rights: "The Country opens wide the door of opportunity to the youth of the world but slams it shut in the faces of its Negro citizenry." The conference report echoed the voices of "twelve million American negroes." The meeting's results offered "a challenge to the social consciousness of the present national administration." Roosevelt must forward these materials to his cabinet and Congress for action, Bethune insisted. She declared that she would soon be seeking a face-to-face appointment where, on behalf of the conferees and the African American people, she would personally place the conference's recommendations in the president's hands. At that time, she promised, she would convey the gathering's "loyalty" to the administration.

Bethune's message wasn't veiled. If the president, and the Democrats, expected continued black support, a "loyalty" that recently helped hold the White House, the conference's proposals were going to require attention and response. Bethune had three thousand copies of the proceedings printed, bound in blue, and distributed across the nation. Known as the Blue Book, the publication was regarded by conferencegoers as the definitive plan for change—the first-ever cooperatively generated, comprehensive, unvarnished delineation of and prescription for the problems facing black Americans. It became the vehicle through which the Black Cabinet was finally able to directly deliver its findings to the president and the public.

There was optimism in the air after Bethune's NYA conference. The NAACP praised the gathering as a clear break from the past. "The recommendations . . . are of a tone not usually found in government-sponsored conventions," the *Crisis* observed. "There was no mincing of words and no 'pulling of punches' and no smoothing down of condemnation of present practices." In a letter to Charles H. Houston, Bethune celebrated the gathering as pathbreaking: "Let us clearly understand that this is the first time in the history of America that a conference of this type has been held in connection with the Government of our country representing all angles of Negro life and finally uniting in its recommendations as one voice." Houston agreed. He wrote to Aubrey Williams insisting that if the NYA conference's demands became policy, not only would African Americans be lifted out of economic despair but also "race relations and the country would generally be much improved."

One of the Blue Book's most significant contributions was its rejection of the assumption that aid for black Americans and integration were mutually exclusive in Depression-era relief. Since the beginning of the New Deal, an unspoken rule had dominated negotiations over African American assistance: some relief might be granted if the racial status quo, Jim Crow, and disenfranchisement were not questioned. Housing, education, and farming projects had to be segregated; job training and employment should not challenge traditional, mostly manual black labor. In the South, where Jim Crow was law, administrators insisted that the federal government could not defy local ordinances. In other areas, in parts of the North, Midwest, and West, where segregation was de facto, local authorities maintained that integration and parity would infuriate whites and threaten all relief. Racial separatism was too charged to be contested and, in the minds of many white New Dealers, unrelated to national economic recovery. Choices had to be made— African Americans either asked for food or they asked for fairness.

The Blue Book made clear that the Black Cabinet and the conference's other representatives expected both. They rejected the notion that economic relief could be achieved separately from reform in race relations, which would demand integration. "Despite the tremendous efforts of the Government agencies during the past three to four years to rescue the country from the destroying effects of the depression," the Blue Book stated, "the mass Negro population is living on the lowest levels of existence, with attendant hunger and misery." While New Deal racism worsened the Depression for the black population, it endangered the nation's long-term economic health. Conferees underscored what Weaver had been saying for years—that it was impossible to hold on to the racial divide and achieve a widespread and sustaining recovery.

Bethune later conceded that the Black Cabinet had struggled to get the conference's messages across. But she continued to argue that the NYA conference and the Blue Book represented a new "technique" and a "forward step." The efforts of those who attended the meeting in early 1937 represented the culmination of arduous labor carried out by black federal officials. As the Blue Book circulated, one black newspaper singled out the Black Cabinet for praise because its members had produced, for the first time in the history of the struggle, "a single, clearly stated program for the Federal government as it touches upon each phase of Negro life—a program that is simple and yet complete, thoroughly concrete."

On January 20, 1937, people began gathering on the National Mall to witness the second inauguration of Franklin Delano Roosevelt. Although Washington, D.C., was in the grip of a cold snap, and it poured rain, the crowd swelled to forty thousand. It would be the first oath of office taken by a president in January. (The inauguration had been moved up from March to trim down the lame-duck period.) The Roosevelt camp had made some efforts to include African American supporters in the festivities. The president's Harvard classmate, the African American educator G. David Houston, of Massachusetts, had been appointed to the inauguration committee and had secured, for the first time, equal access to all the day's events for black reporters. During the inaugural parade, Houston and his wife and daughter sat in the reviewing stand. At his recommendation, an African American soldier, George H. Wanton, who held the Congressional Medal of Honor, served in the parade's Honor Guard. Houston also arranged for tickets to the swearing-in ceremony for a number of African American leaders. These included Bethune, who received an invitation to sit in the section nearest the presidential stand.

Carrying an umbrella instead of her usual cane and wearing a fur coat and "old-fashion galoshes," Bethune braved the pounding rain. She arrived two hours early and presented her ticket, which was stamped "Reserved." A surprised white usher studied it and then commanded her to "just take one of those seats back there," waving her toward the last row of seats. Although they were marked reserved, they were the farthest away. Almost all the seats near the presidential podium were empty. "I do not necessarily need to have a reserved seat," Bethune said coolly. "I will just go up here and take one of the general seats." She pushed past the usher and joined others filing in. She then took the seat closest to the presidential podium she could find. All those around her were white and, she recounted, were "gracious" and welcoming.

In the driving rain, together they sat, watching as Roosevelt took the oath of office and then delivered his second inaugural speech. "I see one-third of a nation ill-housed, ill-clad, ill-nourished," he observed, acknowledging that enormous trials still lay ahead. As he spoke, the rain came down harder; the vigorous Roosevelt wiped his brow and tried to smooth his rain-soaked notes. "We are determined to make every

American citizen the subject of his country's interest and concern; and we will never regard any faithful law-abiding group within our borders as superfluous," he promised. "The test of our progress is not whether we add more to the abundance of those who have much; it is whether we provide enough for those who have too little."

"The inauguration address was a great tonic. It was filled with fair play and justice to all," Bethune declared. The parade also embodied her hopes for the nation. Her "dream was realized," she claimed, when the interracial delegation representing the NYA marched past: "They were not in separate groups. There was a white girl, then a Negro girl; a white boy and a Negro boy, a very fine unit of American youths marching together . . . a marvelous example of the integration of Negroes into the program of American life."

Despite the elation she felt, she could not forget the usher's attempt to subject her to Jim Crow at the swearing-in ceremony. In fact, reminders of American racism, slavery, and segregation ran throughout the festivities. The inaugural parade's presidential reviewing stand was a replica of the Hermitage, the plantation home of the Democratic Party's forefather, President Andrew Jackson. For African Americans, Jackson, a slaveholder, symbolized the old South and bondage, not democratic political ideals. Bethune and G. David Houston were the only African Americans invited to the White House's official inauguration reception. Without naming names, the *Chicago Defender* alleged that some Black Cabinet members had skipped the day's events. They "stayed at home playing poker, pokeno, or pool, so convinced were they that it was not a 'Race affair at all.'" Those in the know immediately recognized that the *Defender* was referring to Weaver and his circle.

After the inauguration, Bethune pushed for time with Roosevelt to go over the details of the NYA conference. Although she would later insist that he never denied her requests for appointments, she spent several weeks trying to arrange to see him. It is likely that Stephen Early blocked Bethune. FDR's press secretary was not won over at all by the Bethune magnetism. And she was not particularly impressed by him and did not hesitate to let the press secretary know it. She recalled how during a phone conversation with Early, he addressed her as "Mary." She bristled. "We have never seen each other, Mr. Early," she commented. "I am Mrs. Mary McLeod Bethune." In the South, "we are not so formal," Early replied, reminding her of his privilege as a white man to call her by her first name. She corrected him. "Did we know each other better I might call you Steve and you might call me Mary," she remarked.

Finally, in mid-February, Bethune secured an opportunity to meet face-to-face with the president. Coincidence or not, the *Pittsburgh Courier* had just run an interview with her detailing the discriminatory treatment she had received at the inauguration.

Bethune arrived for her appointment at the White House on February 18, 1937, to discover that a *Baltimore Afro-American* reporter had beaten her there. He broke the news to her that not only was she absent from the president's callers' list, but Roosevelt's secretaries had no idea who she was. Confidently, Bethune assured him that "there had been no mix-up." She "smiled," posed for a photo, and ascended the steps to the White House.

The president had agreed to see Bethune in his private office after dinner. This would become his way of handling meetings with her—after hours and in his private quarters. This way, FDR bypassed his Oval Office staffers, dominated by Early and other white southerners. It also kept such appointments off the books and, generally, out of the public record.

Bethune disappeared into the East Wing, where she was escorted up by elevator and into the president's office. It would be the first time a Black Cabinet member had personally brought requests to FDR. "There was no one in that private office but the President of the United States, Mary McLeod Bethune, and God," she remarked. "I spoke to the President candidly and directly about the needs of Negro youth and what we felt the government could do to help." The meeting lasted just over twenty minutes, and when Bethune emerged, the *Chicago Defender* asked for a comment. "I found the President very much interested in the findings of the conference . . . and anxious to discuss the problems presented," she responded. "He was well informed and demonstrated a sympathetic interest." She reported that Roosevelt accepted a second copy of the conference's proceedings and promised to study it thoroughly. Bethune offered no specifics about what, if anything, the president promised to do. But she was confident that the outlook was good: "I feel that our people are on their way to a better integration into the affairs of the government than ever before."

If the January 1937 National Youth Administration conference did anything, it was to confirm that Mary McLeod Bethune was the indisputable leader of the Black Cabinet. She had long received honors and accolades, but after the conference, praise for her leadership grew even more lavish. One women's club leader told the *Baltimore Afro-American* that "the conference to me in reality is an epoch-making occasion. . . . I believe that unborn generations will arise and bless the personality and name of Dr. Mary McLeod Bethune as our national leader." An African American minister compared Bethune to both Harriet Tubman and Joan of Arc. The *Literary Digest*, in an article entitled "Negro Angel," asserted that with Bethune, "never before in American History has the Negroes' future seemed so secure." One source reported that she had become "the most sought after Black Cabinet member" for personal appearances. Kelly Miller claimed that for the first time since Theodore Roosevelt's Black Cabinet, African American advisers were positioned to make substantial contributions. Almost thirty years before, he noted, it had been "the Booker T. Washington Black Cabinet"; now it was "Mary McLeod Bethune's Black Cabinet."

Miller's declaration was no exaggeration. In just over six months, Bethune had marshaled nearly complete control over the Black Cabinet. She had accomplished what seemed impossible; she had united the bitterly divided factions. "Our greatest hope is that the Negro representatives in these fields see the problem as a whole and try to eliminate individual selfishness," she explained to Howard University graduate student Laurence Hayes, who was preparing a study on black federal employees. "Our only objective is to keep the Negroes connected in an official capacity with the government constantly in tune with each other for the common good, to eliminate personal jealousies, political chicanery and work for the common good." She had banished internal quarreling and "backbiting," demanding cooperation and reminding cabinet members of their higher duty to black people. "All for one and one for all" became the rule under Bethune, according to Al Smith. She was a master at mediating disputes. "Strong wills and fiery tempers make meetings interesting and tempestuous. Some members . . . filibuster on favorite topics and have to be ruled from the floor," Smith recounted. "Only the tact of Chairman Bethune, who is accorded absolute author-ity and respect, keeps things smooth and members smiling. Previous to her coming, the council flew apart from internal explosions."

Bethune's success came from her extraordinary self-confidence and determination, as well as her healthy ego. But much of her ability to broker a truce between the Black Cabinet's warring parties derived from her rural upbringing. Most of the younger members of the Black Cabinet held advanced degrees in social sciences from the nation's best universities. As scholars they were trained to trust in numbers and to work in isolation. Other members of the black brain trust had been long immersed in the game of politics, where jostling for individual power was the dominant mode of operation. Bethune sought power, but she maintained that it was achieved by working with and on behalf of the whole. She later reminisced about how, when she was a child, sharecroppers relied on each other during harvest time. No one family had enough hands to get its crops picked and to market in time to satisfy the white landlord. So neighbors organized "cotton picking parties." Residents far and near came together to harvest crops, often within a twenty-four-hour window. Bethune remembered fondly the camaraderie that came from working side by side, day and night, as well as the large communal dinners where everyone celebrated a job well done.

"Those cotton picking, cornhusking, and fodder stripping parties gave to us a great spirit of helpfulness," she told one interviewer. The cooperative nature of agricultural labor taught her to appreciate the importance of "social relationships" to achieving success. "I was always happy when the evening was over to see that great pile of cotton that we had picked for the neighbors," she recalled. She insisted that this inspired her to serve for and with others, shaped her understanding of group dynamics, and influenced her philosophy of collective action. "During those stages of my development, this laid the basic principles of the things I do today," she reflected. A group was stronger when its members were working in unison rather than separately.

But a group also needed strong leadership, and it was in this spirit that Bethune convened the Black Cabinet. She demanded that Black Cabinet meetings be both civil and meaningful—focusing on clear objectives. Since the meetings took place in her home, she had considerable leverage. Although they occurred once a month throughout 1937, later they would become more intermittent and often occurred on an emergency basis. Regardless, she remained at the center. The Black Cabinet would gather, according to Al Smith, "only on the call from its chairman Mary Bethune."

Despite their newfound unanimity, Black Cabinet members still split off into factions, gathering separately after hours in their offices, meeting over lunch or dinner, and socializing with their own cliques in their homes. Weaver's Saturday night poker parties continued to be exclusive. Inviting Bethune, of course, was out of the question. She was a woman and far too prim; her disapproval of liquor, tobacco, and gambling was no secret. Other older black appointees, like Lawrence Oxley, Eugene Kinckle Jones, William Thompkins, and Henry Hunt, were focused on their families and friends outside of the government. Always too rough around the edges for Weaver's crowd, Al Smith had his own set of associates—many from his alma mater, Howard University. Affable and well connected, Bethune's assistant, Frank Horne, circulated among all the groups, carrying information from his NYA office to Weaver's basement over to Henry Hunt in the Farm Credit Administration and then to Smith at the WPA.

When Bethune called, African American brain trusters snapped to attention and reached across their divides. New black federal officials were admitted to the Black Cabinet without exclusion and while there was no official membership list, occasionally membership dues were collected to offset modest expenses. As the group grew, often ad hoc committees were assembled to tackle specific cases or special problems. Sometimes a subgroup (usually including Weaver and Hastie) would meet at the home of Charles H. Houston, who acted as the Black Cabinet's unofficial legal counsel. When needed, black racial-affairs advisers also sought outside assistance from the NAACP, the Urban League, the black press, and the American Civil Liberties Union.

But the most important business was transacted when the Black Cabinet convened under Bethune's watchful eye, which assured everyone's "opinion was sought and respected." Frank Horne recalled that Weaver played a dominant role in debates and discussions: "He was a thorough scholar, diplomatic, conservative, incisive, no faking; he always knew what he was talking about. In meetings he often asked pointed questions no one could answer." The Black Cabinet was, Weaver remembered, "a forum where problems could be discussed, and potential solutions developed. Members often made concrete decisions and carried out assignments . . . such as preparing memorandums for future meetings, presenting ideas to government officials or black leaders, and assembling information for release to the press." Often the group drafted documents jointly. It became, as Al Smith described it, "a counsel of strategy" that shared "confidential inside information" as "necessary ammunition for fighting the Negroes' cause." Members sought and got advice about projects and problems, then agitated for change in their individual programs. Larger, cooperative efforts across divisions were also planned. Bethune encouraged amicable debate. Lawrence Oxley recalled that meetings usually closed with a common agreement: "That's the answer we'll give." The brilliance of Bethune's leadership lay in her ability to take the fractured nature of the Black Cabinet and make it an asset rather than a liability.

By assuming a more structured form, the Black Cabinet members actually put themselves in jeopardy. For federal employees to organize an internal, unsanctioned group, which had been prohibited earlier by the president, was perilous. It was imperative that the Black Cabinet not be viewed as official or its members as insubordinate to their federal bosses. In the 1970s, Lawrence Oxley observed: "They probably would call it treason today if we'd do it." Black Cabinet members were not only clandestinely collaborating to defy their immediate supervisors; they were also often joining forces in opposition to the administration. If African American advisers were seen as a lobby for black interests (which was exactly what they had always been), then it would not only result in the loss of their jobs but also endanger African American inclusion throughout the New Deal. To protect the group, at Black Cabinet meetings, minutes were generally not taken or preserved. A paper trail could fall into the wrong hands, and sensitive discussions might be leaked. With no documentation to prove otherwise, gatherings could be explained as social affairs for black federal employees or as planning sessions for government-sanctioned activities like the NYA conference.

The Black Cabinet flew under the radar, and very few white federal administrators were aware of its existence, despite its mention over the years in the African American press. But given the First Lady's close relationship with Bethune, the president must have known that the group had crystalized within the New Deal ranks. Still, always calculating his political advantage with the white South, FDR never publicly acknowledged or mentioned the Black Cabinet. Those rare New Deal chiefs who were conscious of the group reportedly accepted its existence without comment. Bethune admitted confidentially to Laurence Hayes that the Black Cabinet was "trying to do a job in a quiet but effective manner."

Being a Black Cabinet member, according to Al Smith, was like having "two pairs of eye glasses." One pair was for the federal workplace, where black brain trusters masked their true thoughts in front of their white bosses. The other pair was worn "at home" in the black community, where the group could be authentic and openly express opinions. The Black Cabinet gave African American New Dealers a chance to wear that second pair together, as they formulated strategies to combat prejudice in the government and in society at large.

Throughout 1937, the roles of the Black Cabinet members became more defined. Bethune led the group; Robert Weaver emerged as her second in command. Weaver and his circle, all young and university-educated, generated statistics and translated numbers into reports and position papers. Bethune then stepped in. Drawing from her long experience as an activist and evangelist, she translated the Black Cabinet findings into vivid appeals, made on behalf of the African American people, that she shared with New Deal heads, the president, and the public. "To us she was Mrs. Bethune, or . . . Mother Superior, and we were her boys," Weaver recalled. "She had contacts; she was a dramatic person. It would have been foolish for somebody to have attempted to replace her."

One of Bethune's greatest contributions was her access to Eleanor Roosevelt. They worked "practically hand in glove," recalled Frank Horne. "You tell me what needs to be done," he remembered Bethune saying. "I'll see that it gets in touch with Mrs. Roosevelt." Even the NAACP's Walter White often relied on Bethune to get to the First Lady. As Bethune solidified her position at the NYA and within the African American brain trust, the list of demands that she submitted to Eleanor Roosevelt grew longer. It was understood that the First Lady kept the president up to date on the African American situation. And if she could not talk directly to her husband, then it was well known among Black Cabinet members that she left notes with their requests on his nightstand.

Working with Bethune did open a channel to the White House, a critical step forward in the Black Cabinet's struggle. Still, some male members resented her. A few would complain about her stubbornness, her domineering presence, and what struck them as an overbearing personality. She was "a dictator, a potentate," remarked one Black Cabinet member anonymously in the 1960s. Despite being willing to admit to her weaknesses—in some skills and areas of knowledge—Bethune displayed an imperiousness mixed with an enormous sense of self-importance. She was demanding and, if disappointed, did not hesitate to issue a scorching reprimand. She could be witheringly judgmental. "There is something about the intensity of her gaze which makes one just a little ill at ease," one interviewer commented. "One is conscious of an examination that is more than casual." Her authoritarian ways, Bethune insisted, came from her West African royal ancestry. In many parts of West Africa, power was matrilineal, and so it would be natural, Bethune reasoned, that she should be a leader and that others should follow. Intensely proud of her heritage and her dark skin, she boasted that she possessed "not a drop of any blood but Africa." A good portion of Black Cabinet members had significant European ancestry, and at least some of them felt she disregarded them because of it.

Indeed, a great gulf existed between Bethune and many of her Black Cabinet associates. Those who passed for or were mistaken for white could take advantage of white privileges that Bethune could never experience. Additionally, many African American New Dealers had been raised among the black bourgeoisie. With the exception of Lawrence Oxley, all had advanced degrees. Bethune's educational history was far less stellar—at Moody Bible Institute she had completed only a two-year postsecondary program. Hailing from some of the most distinguished black families in the country, those who gathered around Weaver viewed problems academically and remained invested in their status as members of the black elite. Bethune, who had worked in the fields and as a maid, continued to identify with the African American masses—and they identified with her.

That resonance that Bethune felt with the people was reflected in her daily interactions. Chief White House usher Alonzo Fields recalled that most visitors, black and white, ignored the African American domestic staff. But Bethune "would always bow and say hello to you." Never forgetting her roots, she stayed true to the values and practices of her community. The teachings of the black church, a powerful force in the lives of many African Americans, remained her foundation, and she often testified to her deep Christian faith. Every morning when she arrived at her office, her first task was to call her staff together for a morning prayer.

Bethune also faced resistance from some male Black Cabinet colleagues who chafed under the command of a woman. Assertiveness, regarded as admirable and shrewd in men, was seen as unbecoming and aggravatingly bossy when it came from a woman. However, during her lifetime, not one of the core black federal officials breathed a word of public disrespect for Bethune. At worst, when she was out of earshot, they called her "Ma Bethune," with a sexist and ageist familiarity that was often not intended as a compliment. And after Bethune's death, several Black Cabinet members openly grumbled about her leadership. The most vocal was Robert Weaver, who claimed that he was the Black Cabinet's hidden hand and that Bethune, as the public face, depended heavily on him. She was, he maintained, "the titular head, and I was more or less the operating head of it."

Weaver also repeated the allegation originally made by Urban League head Lester Granger that Bethune had "the most marvelous gift of affecting feminine helplessness in order to attain her ends with masculine ruthlessness." Weaver—and he wasn't alone—regarded Bethune as less capable than her male counterparts. Although Bethune grounded her campaigns for change in her experiential knowledge, Weaver dismissed her as too emotional and not enough of an intellectual. He viewed her tactics as based purely in theatrics, "flattery," and "shame." Her success came from her White House contacts, he would argue, which the male members of the Black Cabinet were willing to exploit.

The perceptive Bethune was certainly aware of their attitudes. A key player in the African American women's club movement, Bethune came to Washington after years of fighting both racism and male chauvinism.

Bethune absolutely refused to acquiesce to male authority, white or black. "I chat and deal with men just as I chat and deal with women," she insisted. "I never felt any inferiority with men." And her prominence and power made Mary McLeod Bethune untouchable, something she did not shy away from asserting. "A lot of people have asked 'why are we here?'" she remarked at a later gathering of black leaders—mostly male and including many African American New Dealers. "You are here because I called you to come. And whenever I want you to come I will call you, and I expect you to come whether I want anything important or not."

For black women, Bethune represented the supreme role model. Through the National Council of Negro Women, Bethune had a built-in and loyal following. Just after the 1936 election, she also started to push for the larger presence of African American women in government specifically and in the public sphere in general. "There is today a most intense need," she told the *Pittsburgh Courier*, "for the Negro women of America to stand shoulder to shoulder in a solid phalanx to fight the battle of the Negro masses and promote their integration into the fabric of American democracy." Rachel Robinson, wife of baseball star Jackie Robinson, remembered the empowerment that Bethune conveyed: "We saw in her the strength of our mothers and the effective leadership that black women can epitomize."

On a cold December day in 1937, Mary McLeod Bethune arrived at the White House promptly at five o'clock. Eleanor Roosevelt had invited her to an afternoon tea for female government administrators and wives of New Deal chiefs. The First Lady greeted her and then hurried her off for a short private chat. When the two emerged, Eleanor Roosevelt personally introduced Bethune to each guest, likely in order to head off the racial hostility borne by some of the white guests present that evening.

Bethune scanned the room. The only other African Americans there were the black members of the White House domestic staff, who, she later told the press, "served with such competence and distinction as to honor themselves and all of us." She also recounted that she was "received with increasing courtesy and graciousness by many groups to whom it is a new experience to share social amenities with a Negro woman."

One African American journalist described the White House on the afternoon of the tea as "resplendent with sparkling lights, fresh flowers," and "a veritable banquet of varied types of sandwiches, relishes, cakes, nuts, candies." Despite these delights, Bethune could not forget the suffering of the African American people and their exclusion from all the goodness and justice of American life. "In all that great group I felt a sense of being quite alone," she confided to her diary. "So, while I sip tea in the brilliance of the White House, my heart reaches out to the delta land and the bottom land. I know why I *must* be here, *must* go to tea at the White House. To remind them always that we belong here, we are a part of this America."

Chapter Eight

Things Are Happening

THE BLACK Cabinet members' jobs had always been demanding, and as Franklin D. Roosevelt's second term unfolded, they grew even more so. With the Democrats and the White House awakened to the power of the black vote, the time seemed ripe to push forward. Racial-affairs advisers rushed to expand their projects to reach as many African Americans as possible. The New Deal, now in its second phase, had begun to shift away from recovery to focus on permanent financial and legal reforms aimed at preventing future depressions. In turn, the Black Cabinet sought to ramp up African American relief: it remained a matter of life or death in many communities. But racial-affairs advisers also pressed for institutional changes to ensure the black community was not left behind once the nation's economy healed.

As they fought for transformation within federal institutions, they found that they were themselves transformed. Black Cabinet appointments became far more than just nine-to-five jobs. Being a Black Cabinet member was a lifestyle requiring around-the-clock battles against American racism both inside and outside the U.S. government. Witnessing firsthand the destitution and despair caused by discrimination, racial violence, poverty, and social injustice took a heavy toll on Black Cabinet members. Dedication had drawn most to answer the call to serve in the New Deal. Each reacted differently to his or her individual circumstances. But for all, despite the hardships, the commitment burned more intensely the longer they struggled.

Henry Hunt of the Farm Credit Administration met his challenges as a Black Cabinet member with his characteristically quiet but gracious resolve. Described as "straight-forward" and "self-effacing," he was the oldest member of the African American brain trust; he turned seventy the year FDR was reelected. Hunt cut a striking figure, with dark hair and a gray Vandyke beard, but his tall frame was slumped from years of hard labor. Black Cabinet members held deep respect for the soft-spoken, measured, and highly accomplished Hunt. As an educational pathbreaker in Georgia, he had headed up Fort Valley Industrial and Training School for almost thirty years before joining the New Deal. In addition to offering degrees in scientific farming, the domestic arts, and teacher training, Fort Valley was famous for its conferences and traveling workshops on the latest agricultural innovations. With old-fashioned southern cordiality and an elegant, upper-crust Georgian drawl, Hunt had been able to work with whites in some of the most dangerously racist parts of his state. W. E. B. Du Bois had nominated him for the appointment in the Farm Credit Administration, insisting there was "no one [else] in the United States who had such wide and intimate knowledge of the black rural South and such devoted personal interest in its betterment."

Henry Hunt had been raised by a single mother in the red hills of Georgia, and he loved the land—he wrote passionately about "feeling a kinship for the very soil itself." The son of a white Confederate soldier (and former slaveholder) and a free woman of color, he had begun working in the fields as a child. Although his mother owned their small farm, Hunt's family, along with other southerners, struggled in poverty during the years just following the Civil War. Extremely light-skinned and always presumed be to white by strangers, he learned, as a child of a black woman, that his African heritage consigned him to second-class citizenship and a life of hard labor. There was no need for much education; the school year for black children in his hometown was only three months long. Their place was in the fields for the rest of the year.

One of Hunt's brothers cut his ties to the family and passed for white to get his education. But Du Bois recalled that for Hunt "to take a stand in America as anything but a Negro would have made him supremely unhappy." Henry Hunt could not and would not forsake his family, his friends, the South, or the African American people. He recognized that his choice presented "an opportunity for . . . battle on the highest plane," Du Bois said. Those who knew Hunt remarked on his steadfast sincerity and integrity. Frank Horne described him as the embodiment "of culture, of accuracy, of thoroughness, [and] of genuineness."

With help from some of his siblings and his earnings as a manual laborer, Hunt worked his way through Atlanta University. At the age of twenty-four, in 1890, he graduated with honors and immediately embarked on a teaching career. In 1904, he was hired at Fort Valley. The school had been failing for years, but Hunt rapidly turned it around. He boosted enrollment while winning over hostile local whites by revamping the curriculum. Cutting back on the liberal arts and the sciences, he introduced a new focus on farming and carpentry for men and domestic science for women.

Some sharply criticized Henry Hunt for being an accommodationist. It was true, he would admit, his model for Fort Valley was entirely compatible with Booker T. Washington's approach. Washington was a family friend, and one of Hunt's sisters taught at Tuskegee. Hunt contended that a conservative educational philosophy was the most practical approach to black education in the climate of southern white resentment. The town of Fort Valley was a dangerous place; white supremacy dictated the relations between the races. In 1912, an African American domestic worker named Anne Bostwick was abducted by a white mob from her Fort Valley jail cell. She had purportedly admitted to murdering her female employer. (It was the victim's husband who first reported Bostwick's alleged confession to authorities.) "The negress was lynched from an auto," the *Cincinnati Enquirer* reported. "The machine in which she was sitting was driven under a tree, a rope placed about her neck and the other end tied to a limb of the tree. The machine was started at high speed and the Negress left hanging. Her body was then shot to pieces. Her eyes were shot out and such a fusillade directed at her waist that she was cut in two."

Some remarked it was a miracle that Hunt was able to sustain any kind of school for the black community in the midst of such potent white racism. "Those who do not live in the deep South can have no conception of the difficulty of his task, nor of the risks involved," one Urban League official commented on Hunt's accomplishments. "It is not a question of financial support, it is a question of community sanction of Negro education, and that sanction is not easy to get."

Despite his conciliatory disposition, Hunt could also be a forceful critic of the United States' racial caste system and the country's economic exploitation of the forced cheap labor of black Americans. In an article written before he arrived at Fort Valley, he argued that after the Civil War, African Americans "had arisen, if at all, only from the position of the master's farm animal in slavery to that of his less cared for farm hand in freedom." Sharecropping was simply a new type of bondage. It had to end everywhere if black people were to advance in any area of American life.

In Hunt's opinion, the key to African American liberation was right before everyone's eyes: it rested in agriculture. Land empowered people. Nature's energy could be harnessed for purposes beyond sustenance and economic profit. The same fields that tied African Americans to debt and destitution could become a path to freedom, he contended, if property ownership could somehow be extended to black southerners. By farming their own land, African Americans would rise and contribute to one of the nation's greatest enterprises, farming for national and international markets. "There must be that love for the farm itself, its rocks, its woods, its hills, its shady rills, and its meadows, that can come no other way than through the proud sense of ownership," he emphasized. This economic independence would not only create self-sufficiency, it would also produce the resources out of which African American "institutions for social reform" could grow and multiply.

A trip to Denmark in 1931 on a Rosenwald grant and a tour of collective farms there only confirmed Hunt's beliefs. The Danish cooperative model extended beyond agriculture and had impacted the country's business and industry. Ideally, it held the potential to create a society of equals. "Instead of big fortunes being amassed by a few magnates, the capital is distributed in small amounts among the masses of people. The Danes accepted many years ago the theory that the people of a country are happiest when there are few who have too much and fewer still who have too little," he observed. In Hunt's mind, collective farming could be more than just the answer to black rural poverty—it could help end American racism.

Henry Hunt assumed his post as a racial-affairs adviser with a clear vision for what he hoped to accomplish: to end the abuses of the sharecropping system by increasing African American farm ownership. But like his colleagues, he had faced enormous resistance. He was immediately straitjacketed in the Farm Credit Administration. He had repeated his criticism that the farm loan program he oversaw was useless to most black Americans; participation required property ownership, and 77 percent of African American agricultural workers were landless. Hunt had also protested against New Deal agricultural policies that continued to force African American sharecroppers off individual farms and into migrant labor. Hunt's bosses had also dispatched him to the field to organize credit unions in black Cotton Belt communities, but even though government guidelines required only seven investors to open a credit union, establishing one among a cash-poor people was impossible. It wasn't the kind of help impoverished Americans needed. Most of the letters that came into his office were from unemployed black farmers who asked for jobs or even direct relief. His advice: seek aid from other New Deal programs.

Hunt did what he could. Knowledgeable about all aspects of agriculture, he offered to counsel African Americans interested in farming and, while traveling, gave hands-on instruction. Hunt also established connections with other agencies and external organizations that dealt with rural African American issues. At conferences, in governmental meetings, and with farmer alliances, he shared his expertise, while at the same time soliciting support for his office. He toured black schools and reviewed their agricultural programs. When he attempted to compile a comprehensive study of African American farming, federal agencies turned down his request for data. Instead, he secured it from the NAACP. As thanks, he began to supply W. E. B. Du Bois with whatever inside information he could gather.

But Henry Hunt had come to Washington with much bigger plans. When he toured the country, he did not confine himself to lecturing on the New Deal and its programs; he also spoke extensively on the benefits of collective agriculture. In a modern economy, farming required a hefty outlay of cash. State-of-the-art equipment, the best seed, and up-to-date fertilizers were essential to compete in commodities markets. But the outlay for these innovations was beyond the reach of most sharecroppers. Such hurdles could be cleared, Hunt suggested, if farmers pooled their earnings and invested together in equipment, livestock, and other necessities. These acquisitions would increase their yields, and with the profits, they could purchase their land. The *Fort Valley Message* reported that after hearing Hunt talk, a group of black tenant farmers and sharecroppers had taken out a loan together and bought a reaper. By the fall of 1937, they had almost paid it off.

As early as 1935, Hunt began pushing for resources to set up a Fort Valley agricultural collective that he hoped would become a model for other African American–led projects. Unable to secure support within his own agency, he turned to the New Deal's Resettlement Administration, overseen by the somewhat more sympathetic Department of the Interior. Although over the program's four years the Resettlement Administration had established collective farms throughout the country, only twenty-six of 150 farming projects were interracial (with whites the majority of the participants), while nine were exclusively black. Usually white communities raised strident opposition to proposed nearby resettlement projects that included African Americans, even if they were segregated. The government normally acquiesced and canceled them. Newport News, Virginia, was home to one of the few black projects that had moved forward despite white protests. The government had refused to scratch the project but did place it behind a densely forested area to screen it away from local whites.

Despite Hunt's long history of goodwill with local residents, Fort Valley whites raised stubborn opposition to his proposal for an all-black collective farm. Their reaction was so bitter that in the heat of the 1936 campaign, funding for the project was cut. But in early 1937, once FDR was again securely in office, Hunt's budget was reinstated. To appease Fort Valley residents, the project was relocated about twenty-five miles south to Montezuma, Georgia. Once word got out about the project, named Flint River Farms, whites in Montezuma launched a crusade to block it. A massive black collective farm would bring down their property values, they alleged. Flint River Farms would generate unrest among the African Americans who could not be accommodated by the project, and black farmhands would demand higher wages from their white employers. The result would be a drastic collapse of the local economy.

Despite the shrill resistance, several well-to-do white landholders supported the proposal for Flint River Farms. They anticipated making a tidy profit from selling their property to the government and emerged as some of project's strongest advocates. Well positioned, moneyed, and powerful, they prevailed, and in the spring of 1937, the Montezuma city council, with support from the local Kiwanis Club, gave Hunt's project the go-ahead.

Henry Hunt was elated; he would finally see his aspirations for black rural America translated into practice. Now busier than ever, he maintained a hand in the affairs of Fort Valley School and tended to his post at the Farm Credit Administration while he poured himself into overseeing the organization and construction of the massive Flint River project. The federal government, at his recommendation, purchased eleven thousand acres of former plantation land and began dividing it into more than one hundred farmsteads. Hunt planned it so that each family received a plot of land with home, barn, outhouse, and chicken coop as well as livestock (two mules, cows, chickens, and pigs). Property was distributed under a lease-to-own agreement, and participants paid for it with low-interest government loans. Flint River residents were cautioned against planting cotton, a mono-crop that had exhausted the land, and retrained to cultivate vegetables, fruits, and grains.

Hunt was proudest of the eighteen hundred acres set aside specifically for a farming cooperative. Named Flint River Farms Incorporated, it was to be run jointly by forty African American married couples. Each was provided with a home and a small plot of land, with the understanding that they would farm the rest of the acreage together. By laboring cooperatively and splitting the profits, participants could eventually purchase their own farms. Hunt's dream of African Americans freed from sharecropping through collective farming and experiencing the independence of working for themselves would become a reality.

By the spring of 1938, Hunt began to see his efforts pay off. The first twenty-five homesteads were ready; families moved in and began to put in crops. Despite his plea for black autonomy (he had proposed the entire project be run by African Americans alone), New Deal chiefs insisted that a white manager supervise Flint River. But the rest of the project's staff was black. Students began to make the trek from Fort Valley, to instruct the residents on advancements in agricultural techniques and modern homemaking skills. It was a mammoth and complex undertaking—and Hunt confessed it was stressful. But it had been his life's goal. The Flint River project steamed ahead toward its formal opening, scheduled for the fall of 1938.

At the Department of the Interior, Bill Hastie also found his experiences taxing but, unlike Hunt's, not particularly fulfilling. He had hesitated to enter government service, worried that his skills would be wasted and his efforts on behalf of African American people thwarted. His worries were soon confirmed. Early on, Hastie had made a major contribution in developing the department's prima facie antidiscrimination policy. But beyond that, he was mostly consigned to pushing paper, a tremendous frustration for a brilliant legal mind. While he played a role in the Black Cabinet, he channeled most of his activism outside of the workplace. He remained active in the NAACP, participated in anti-lynching campaigns, and continued on as the New Negro Alliance's legal counsel in its fight against discriminatory hiring practices. He walked the picket line in front of white businesses targeted by the "Don't Buy Where You Can't Work" campaign and helped successfully fight back attempts in the courts to declare picketing illegal.

Hastie may very well have considered resigning. But an assignment came to his desk that he found challenging and important. By 1935, the Virgin Islands had begun drafting a new constitution. Since the islands were a U.S. protectorate, many of their affairs were handled in the Department of the Interior. As a solicitor, and likely because he was black, Hastie was called upon to work with Virgin Islanders on the legal issues surrounding their governance. He earned the admiration of both his supervisors and the islands' residents for his brilliance, diplomacy, and mastery of the law. In recognition of his service and his talents, Ickes recommended, and FDR agreed, that Hastie be nominated for the federal bench of the Virgin Islands' district court. If confirmed, Hastie would become the nation's first African American federal judge.

Hastie's nomination was first put forward in 1935. But he faced persistent opposition from Robert Vann's former boss, Attorney General Homer Cummings, whose duties included overseeing the island's judicial affairs. Cummings insisted that Virgin Islanders would accept only a white judge and would resent being placed under a black appointee. President Roosevelt attempted to intercede, arguing that Hastie's selection "would be an extremely interesting experiment and if it does not work we can always bring him back to the department." The attorney general refused to budge.

Previously Roosevelt had avoided the confirmation process when it came to African American appointments, wagering that white southerners would reject all black nominees regardless of their qualifications and annihilate the New Deal in retaliation. During his first four years in office, FDR had forwarded only one African American name—that of William Thompkins, to the position of recorder of deeds, which had traditionally been awarded to black political loyalists. The president's reluctance had thus confined African Americans to advisory appointments, civil service posts, secretarial positions, or blue-collar jobs as custodians, messengers, elevator operators, cafeteria workers, or manual laborers.

Yet Roosevelt felt he had a good chance of getting Hastie through. Widely respected among black Americans, Hastie also had a good relationship with the Virgin Islands' leaders. Furthermore, the president believed white southern reaction might be surmountable since the appointment would be outside of the continental United States and serve a predominantly black population. The British tradition of recruiting colonial judges from native-born populations set a precedent for Hastie's selection, the president insisted. But Hastie was not a native of the Virgin Islands, and the president knew that. Likely Roosevelt hoped that since Hastie was of African heritage, Congress would view him as interchangeable with any black islander and therefore acceptable. Such a rationale offered a stark glimpse into how FDR's decisions were framed by racist assumptions and how top-level racial barriers operated to deny African Americans equal acceptance as native-born U.S. citizens.

In February 1937, Roosevelt sent Hastie's name forward to the Senate. About a month later, Bill Hastie arrived before the Senate Judiciary Committee for his confirmation hearing. He entered the room surrounded by supporters, including his former student Thurgood Marshall; his uncle, pioneering black D.C. attorney William L. Houston; and his wife, Alma Syphax Hastie. Before the hearings, Ickes had assured

Hastie that he had paved the way by glad-handing Utah senator and judiciary chair William H. King. But as the proceedings got under way, King immediately went on the attack. Declaring Hastie's nomination a "blunder," the Senate chair insisted that Virgin Islanders opposed the appointment. Hastie was unqualified—an amateurish trial attorney with no foreign policy experience who would be unable to maintain "a judicial point of view." The implication was clear: in King's view, Hastie's dedication to civil rights activism meant he was unqualified to hold a judicial post. According to King's logic, no one who supported black equality could ever receive a judgeship.

King wasn't alone in his opposition. Maryland senator Millard Tydings, who chaired the Committee on Territories and Insular Affairs, joined the battle against Hastie's appointment. His objections grew from his virulent racial hostility combined with a spiteful dislike for Harold Ickes. The Interior Department managed the Virgin Islands' administration, and Ickes had dueled with the senator over who maintained jurisdiction over the territories. Furthermore, Tydings was an anti–New Deal Democrat who had been a nasty thorn in FDR's side. "He was not only a bitter antagonist," Ickes commented on Tydings, "he was arrogant and the possessor of a biting tongue that his colleagues had come to fear." The powerful Maryland senator's resistance ensnared Hastie in a seemingly impassable political gridlock.

Ickes decided to play political hardball. He dispatched black journalist and sometime Interior Department investigator Melvin Chisum to Maryland. Chisum's instructions were to visit the black communities in Tydings' district and spread word of the senator's attack on Hastie. Baltimore had an especially sizable black electorate, and the senator was up for reelection. Ickes knew that Tydings depended on those votes to retain his seat.

Not too long after Chisum's visit, protest letters flooded into Tydings's office. According to Ickes, the senator began to receive visits from "imposing delegations" of disgruntled African American voters. One even included the head of Maryland's black Democrats' division. The syndicated column Washington Merry-Go-Round, which appeared in white newspapers nationwide, observed that in Maryland, Tydings's "holding up the appointment of a colored judge to the Virgin Islands is the next thing to political suicide."

On Friday, March 26, 1937, Ickes wrote in his diary with great satisfaction that Hastie had won confirmation.

Kelly Miller was elated. "The appointment of William H. Hastie as Federal Judge of the Virgin Islands indicates President Roosevelt's broad-minded interest in the welfare of the race," he wrote in the *Baltimore Afro-American*. "Under President F. D. Roosevelt's administration the Negro has received more generous treatment than under any of his predecessors since his distant kinsman." Publicly, Hastie expressed optimism about his new appointment. Privately, he despaired. Of all Black Cabinet members, he had remained the most militant and open in his activism. He believed that his appointment, one that could not be refused given its pathbreaking importance, was not intended to advance the race but rather "to remove me from action."

Although Hastie would be exiled to an outpost, Robert Weaver remained in the thick of the fight. About the time his old friend won confirmation, Weaver was being considered for a transfer to the newly formed United States Housing Authority (USHA), established under the Housing Act of 1937, sometimes known as the Wagner-Steagall Act. The Housing Authority's mandate was to ensure that New Deal housing programs for low-income Americans became permanent after national recovery. Since African Americans composed a large sector of the urban underclass, they stood to benefit significantly from the institutionalization of public housing programs.

Because he had pioneered urban residential and redevelopment programs, Weaver was the logical choice to become the Housing Authority's lead racial-affairs adviser. Nonetheless, Harold Ickes refused to approve the move. Despite his great affinity and respect for Weaver, he was disgruntled because the Housing Authority had not been placed under his control. Some viewed that with relief—the interior secretary was domineering and hot-tempered. But to African Americans, Ickes had emerged as one of the more sympathetic New Dealers, and to see housing become the domain of an unknown and untested administrator raised concerns. Additionally, the Wagner-Steagall Act allowed local officials oversight of public housing. Since many cities and states had already demonstrated their open opposition to the inclusion of African Americans in housing projects, it was critical the Housing Authority have a federal administrator who could advocate strongly for black interests.

In early 1938, Walter White and other black leaders pushing for Weaver's transfer to the Housing Authority finally prevailed over Ickes, and the interior secretary released Weaver. With Mary McLeod Bethune's blessing, Frank Horne also made his way over to the Housing Authority, to become Weaver's assistant. The new position promised Weaver a chance to influence federal housing policy, an opportunity he eagerly embraced. In his mind, it was not enough to demand more public housing for the black population; the real objective was to push for integrated public housing and contest the American tradition of residential segregation. Weaver had been raised in a middle class, interracial community with the comforts (and tensions) of white suburbia. As a black New Dealer, he toured black communities in cities nationwide, and this had opened his eyes to the effects of urban poverty. He became convinced that social environments shaped their residents. Integrated public housing was a crucial step in uplifting black people as well as American society as a whole. "Not only does the person develop more fully if he is given better surroundings, but society benefits because a better citizen is produced," he concluded. The bonds formed between those living together in interracial neighborhoods would lead the way to reform in American race relations.

Weaver realized that massive challenges loomed before him. The substandard living conditions endured by the majority of African Americans had continued to worsen in many communities during

FDR's presidency. Jim Crow laws, restrictive covenants (neighborhood agreements that prevented nonwhites from purchasing property), and de facto segregation had been left intact by the administration. This limited where African Americans, even those with resources, could live. In urban areas, the black poor were crammed into the decaying parts of cities and towns; they lived in densely confined neighborhoods. Segregation forced African Americans to pay impossibly high rents for small, dilapidated tenements that white landlords refused to maintain. Author Richard Wright described one black apartment building as filled "with filth and foul air, with its one toilet for thirty or more tenants, it kills our black babies so fast that in many cities twice as many of them die as white babies." Black citizens were some of the neediest Americans in urban cores, and it was imperative to see that the Housing Authority did not pass them by.

One of Weaver's first acts was to demand that all USHA building contracts carry a fair employment clause based on the one he originally developed with Hastie in the Interior Department. Since many of the projects would go up in inner-city neighborhoods occupied by African Americans, this meant more jobs for black workmen. Drawing from his experiences at Techwood (which ended up reserved for whites only) and other early projects, Weaver convinced the agency to order that slum-clearance programs in African American communities either accommodate black residents or provide them with comparable housing in the vicinity.

But these safeguards could reach only so far. They were mandated by the Housing Authority, not the Wagner-Steagall Act. Weaver knew if challenged in court, they would not hold. Furthermore, the Housing Authority had no real power to implement any watchdog procedures. It fell to Weaver and his staff to ensure that African Americans received fair treatment. Knowing that local housing authorities would be obstinate, he lobbied hard for the inclusion of African Americans on housing boards in areas with sizable black populations—they would become his first line of defense. While the Housing Authority had no administrative control over localities, it did hold the purse strings, and in some cases, Weaver used them to force city and state administrators to cooperate. Field visits would be another weapon. Conscious they had no real authority, Weaver's staffers contrived a ruse. They had badges engraved and flashed them to none-the-wiser local officials when investigating projects and complaints.

Although able to seat only twenty African Americans on the nation's three hundred local housing boards, Weaver bragged that the housing program was "one of the outstanding examples of equity of treatment between white and black Americans." When interviewed by Swedish economist Gunnar Myrdal, who was studying American race relations, Weaver offered an upbeat assessment of his accomplishments. One-third of the housing projects under the old Public Works Administration (Ickes's program) and the new Housing Authority were designated for African Americans. A number of local housing authorities had hired African Americans for posts in management, engineering and architecture, legal affairs, clerical support, and social work. Some construction jobs had gone to black workers, although he admitted the majority of those were low-paying, unskilled positions. Although by 1940, only fifty of 468 projects were integrated, Weaver considered it a step forward. Myrdal agreed: "Indeed, the USHA has given [the black citizen] . . . a better deal than has any other major federal public welfare agency."

But Myrdal also uncovered another side to the Housing Authority, revealing shortcomings that Weaver agreed were flaws. Overall, public housing failed to provide the broad assistance so badly needed by the most impoverished sector of the black community. Families admitted to low-income housing had to demonstrate they could pay rent, and this excluded most unemployed black city dwellers. Generally, public housing remained segregated. At some integrated sites, blacks and whites lived at opposite ends of the developments. Weaver reported that in one interracial project in the South, the city hired guards to make sure that black and white residents used different sidewalks. Many local USHA administrators refused to establish any public housing for African Americans, segregated or not. Some expressed fear that better housing would attract African Americans to their communities, undermining their efforts to keep their towns and cities white. In Memphis, white women appeared before local officials to oppose a planned African American housing project. One spokesperson for the group insisted that just the thought of living near African Americans had already caused the death of one neighbor and was "worrying the rest of us sick."

Weaver was mainly concerned that if the opposition were not countered, public housing would not only increase residential segregation but also normalize it as federally sanctioned practice. The time to establish integrated projects was now, he argued: "It will not be easy to change the type of racial occupancy if a definite pattern of separate facilities has been established, for such a pattern creates vested interests which resist change." Extolling the virtues of reconstructing society through housing policy, he spoke out against those who resisted. "The initial approach of those who would postpone deciding this matter is the statement that 'public housing cannot solve the race problem,'" Weaver wrote. "Though one may accept this point of view, one must realize that public housing can either complicate or ease the problem, and that, in any event, it cannot avoid it."

During Weaver's tenure, one of the Housing Authority's earliest attempts at establishing an integrated project was Pittsburgh's Terrace Village. It was Pennsylvania's first public housing program and a massive undertaking: it would be one of the largest constructed during the New Deal and cost over $13 million. The project covered 130 acres of hilltop land, much of it previously home to a significant portion of the city's African American population; its master plan included housing for 2,635 families. One side of the project was adjacent to the black community's business district, and other parts offered direct access to jobs in downtown Pittsburgh as well as in local factories and mills.

In 1938, two years before it was scheduled to open, the government began taking applications for Terrace Village housing. One of the first to arrive was from Eva DeBoe Jones, the woman who had arranged the initial meeting between Robert Vann and Joe Guffey in 1932. Her role in the migration of black voters into the Democratic Party had been publicized in the *Saturday Evening Post* during the 1936 presidential contest, and the subsequent rapid drop-off in her clientele had left her financially destitute. But she remained faithful to Roosevelt and his party. "Eva Jones has stuck by the Democrats, though it practically cost her her living," Emma Guffey Miller revealed. The competition for apartments at Terrace Village was stiff, but Jones got one, likely with some pressure applied by local Democrats on the housing board. In the fall of 1940, she was selected to serve on the committee that welcomed Roosevelt when he came to Pittsburgh to dedicate the project. "This kind of work has got to go on," FDR told a crowd that roared with approval. The president celebrated this as "another phase of democracy at work."

Robert Weaver agreed. He was proud of his role in harnessing the power of the federal government through the New Deal for the good of dispossessed American citizens. For him, the New Deal had provided a place to channel both his academic interests and his desire to transform American race relations. In many ways, government work was a perfect fit for the man who had emerged as the nation's foremost expert on federal housing and race.

Mary McLeod Bethune embraced all that came with being a black New Dealer—she loved attending the meetings and conferences, giving speeches, taking calls and appointments at her office, and issuing orders to her staff and Black Cabinet colleagues. She also found field investigations exhilarating, albeit exhausting. She was energized by meeting people and reviewing the results of New Deal programs. Moving from site to site, she marveled at the arresting beauty of the American countryside. She decided that her experiences must be shared and that she would write a newspaper column recounting her travels and her efforts in Washington. She would call it Day to Day—it became black

America's alternative to Eleanor Roosevelt's popular syndicated column *My Day*. It would be uplifting. It would promote the National Youth Administration and the New Deal. It would also do its part in fighting American racism. Throughout 1937 and 1938, Bethune's column appeared in the *Pittsburgh Courier*.

"The beautiful 'daylight train' of the Southern Pacific sped on and took us through San Luis Obispo," Bethune reported from California, stunned by the Golden State's "orange groves, lemon groves, wheat region, and beautiful mountains and peaks in a golden and snow-capped setting." As she sped across Texas, she admired the "oil fields and great farm lands—fields of fruits and melons." When she dropped in on "matchless editor" Robert Vann in Pittsburgh, she praised his stunning and "palatial" home as "another achievement of my race." She had not forgotten her origins as a sharecropper's daughter, she assured readers. When she returned to Mayesville, South Carolina, "haunting memories" flooded back as she peeked through "the door of the little mission school that stood ajar to me years ago when I was shrouded in ignorance and darkness." Such experiences were the common chords in Bethune's life that resonated with so many black Americans.

Day to Day's readers also learned of the victories the Black Cabinet scored after the 1937 National Youth Administration (NYA) conference. In Texas, one college-training program served 150 African Americans of both genders from rural areas; it was the "most constructive we have put into operation." At one Kansas City site, Bethune observed 175 girls, "beautifully dressed, engaged in dressmaking, cooking, home management, dramatics, music appreciation, personal grooming, human engineering, community civics, and upholstery." A proud accomplishment for the race, she declared. "It was just grand." During a "rushing trip" through Florida, she reviewed black NYA projects as well as those sponsored by other New Deal agencies. They were all successful and had, she wrote, "brought another ray of hope and the knowledge that worthwhile things are happening."

Life in Washington, D.C., was a constant whirl, Bethune reported. The New Deal ran full throttle day and night. Her calendar was filled with important meetings and appointments as well as consultations with highly placed members of the administration, her Black Cabinet counterparts, and powerful leaders of the black community. Then, of course, there were the Roosevelts. "Wednesday at 4 p.m. into executive session with the President at the White House," she wrote in February 1938.

While promoting FDR and the New Deal, Bethune also used Day to Day to remind the administration it needed to do a lot more. In one column, she described the flood of letters she received from young African Americans desperate for education, highlighting the great racial divide in American schooling. As she traveled, she observed drastic inequalities throughout many parts of the nation. "I love Texas for the educational and economic opportunities afforded my people," she wrote, praising the program overseen by Lyndon Johnson, whom she came to know well. But she also made note of the state's disenfranchisement of African Americans. Of course, she insisted, blacks in the Lone Star State would eventually win the vote, and once politically empowered, they would push forward the entire African American community there. She also assured readers that her division would continue to provide work assistance to African Americans not included in the recovery. "Our office will do all in its power to preserve for as many Negro youth as possible the great advantage of this NYA program," she declared.

The bravado displayed in Day to Day reflected the formidable warrior Bethune was behind the scenes. She was determined to expand her educational and job training programs for black youths as far as possible. Her ties to the First Lady and her access to the White House (she claimed she met with FDR at least a dozen times a year) aided her causes considerably. But her later accounts also revealed that she experienced moments of overwhelming frustration. In the spring of 1937, when she discovered Congress had cut all NYA and Works Progress Administration (WPA) grants for black graduate students, she immediately demanded and got a meeting with the president. Her impatience spilled over as she laid out for FDR the "disaster that it would be for the potential leaders of the Negro people who were seeking training in various fields." As she talked, she grew more passionate, and she claimed that before she realized it, she was shaking her finger in the president's face. She apologized profusely. FDR paid it no mind, she declared; he "smiled quietly" and said, "I understand you thoroughly, Mrs. Bethune." She also reported that within the week, Congress had backed away.

Bethune's fame, in part fueled by Day to Day, continued to grow. A visit from Mary McLeod Bethune became an even more momentous event, as people clamored to see the nation's first African American federal administrator. At one stop she spoke to an auditorium "packed to its capacity," with people "standing and sitting on window sills." Many of her appearances were calculated to inspire black communities to call for more services and programs, intensifying the pressure on New Deal bosses to respond. Spreading demand for and excitement about NYA opportunities gave her (and her Black Cabinet colleagues) the needed leverage to appeal for more funding for black programs. By 1939, Bethune had been able to increase the number of black NYA local administrators in regions with significant African American populations. Student aid had increased. Job placement programs operated in eight states. Training centers had served 3,707 black youths, and 21,485 were employed on work projects.

Although more assistance was getting to more people, it barely skimmed the surface of the needs of black citizens. In 1939, Bethune reported that there were areas where nearly 60 percent of the black population still relied on direct relief. She continually implored Aubrey Williams to give her more resources. Every year, she requested an additional $100,000 for her budget. "I wish you would give me $200,000, but if you cannot, just give me $100,000 . . . [and] let me say where it will go," she told Williams once. "Let me be the boss of that." She often succeeded in getting more funds. But she wasn't exaggerating when she claimed it was never enough. Despite the advances made after the 1937

NYA conference, New Deal programs touched only a small portion of the millions of struggling African American citizens.

Bethune acutely felt the desperation of the populations she served. When she came into office, NYA aid was barely reaching African Americans. Most of what did trickle down went to boys and young men. Gender bias ran throughout all New Deal programs: getting men and boys back on their feet, since they were regarded as breadwinners, became the government's stated priority. In the black community, the reality was that many families relied either solely, equally, or in part on the earnings of women. While Bethune wanted more assistance for all African American youths, she also demanded more education and training programs for girls and women of all ages.

Reports from her field staff revealed the colossal needs of the black girls and young women who were seeking help from the NYA. At Alabama's Calhoun Colored School, a residential program enrolled forty-five teenage girls from farming families. All had come from surrounding, painfully destitute communities. "The soil is poor and the wages are low," reported one local black NYA supervisor. Many young women arrived at the school severely ill and malnourished. A number were illiterate. Once they were admitted, the NYA provided them with medical attention, academic and vocational classes, and on-campus jobs. After three months, most of the teens had gained weight (from two to twenty-two pounds), and one of the girls had emerged as the school's top student. Another NYA project—in Wilcox County, Alabama—offered an adult reading night class that drew women of all ages. Bethune's division also established a boarding program there to instruct teenage girls in health care, domestic skills, and "social and family relations." The girls received a stipend, and many spent it on their families, buying beds, furniture, fencing, and other essentials for their homes and farms. One girl purchased a stove—it was the first her family had ever owned. Another bought a sewing machine and sent it home. Her community had been relying on an old one that they all shared.

The work of Mary McLeod Bethune, like that of other black New Dealers, touched the individual lives of many African Americans in simple yet critical ways. Despite the successes, she knew that she could not let up on pressuring white public officials for action and that, in her position, she had wrestled the freedom to be as blunt as she felt was necessary. While delivering a public address in 1937, she stared directly at New York City politician Grover Whalen and declared, "Negroes [have] grown tired of getting the feet and the neck of the chicken of opportunity in this country and . . . [they want] some of the choice meat now." If anything, Mary McLeod Bethune's New Deal experiences empowered her to act even more boldly and even more decisively.

Although Bethune's NYA and Weaver's USHA received the most attention from the African American press and the black public, Al Smith's WPA division was the largest black program in the New Deal. The WPA, designed to put Americans back to work again, was the biggest work-relief agency in Washington. Within it, Smith pushed, prodded, and sometimes even duped his superiors into sending him funding for black jobs. He worked diligently to secure employment for as many unemployed African Americans as he could. He put black construction workers back to work, created posts for teachers, secured jobs for manual laborers on infrastructure projects, and funded initiatives that employed doctors, nurses, and other black professionals. He also spearheaded programs that offered employment to African American artists, writers, actors, and musicians.

Smith's office had been moved to the seventh floor of the stately Walker-Johnson Building, which overlooked the southern lawn of the White House. His staff consisted of a senior secretary, four office clerks, and two assistants—John Whitten, a Howard graduate; and Dutton Ferguson, a former journalist. It "hums with activity," one reporter observed, after a visit to the office in 1938. Visitors were lined up in the waiting area. Multiple telephones rang repeatedly. On one side of the office, several staff members were producing materials to be released to the press and the public. Sacks of mail arrived. Smith told the reporter that he answered an average of seven thousand letters a year. That may have been an exaggeration (Smith was known to embellish occasionally), but it accurately captured the persistent desperation of the black community. Working in Al Smith's office required a certain vitality and some creative thinking. "There is apparently no limit to the diversity of the needs of the underprivileged," the reporter commented. "Each day new problems challenge the staff's ingenuity."

Smith's goals were clear-cut: African American people wanted jobs, not public welfare, he told WPA chiefs and the press again and again. His first priority was to get African Americans back to work. But he also created vocational training programs and supported the expansion of black education. Creating temporary, unskilled jobs wasn't enough. Smith argued that African Americans needed to be prepared for permanent and stable employment after the economy recovered. When possible, he partnered with Bethune and the NYA; their missions often overlapped, and Smith was awestruck by the legendary educator. They also shared a southern, working-class background, making them, along with Henry Hunt, somewhat anomalous among a Black Cabinet dominated by members of the African American elite.

Smith continued to frequently tour WPA sites throughout the country. He investigated complaints of discrimination and the progress of his many and varied programs. In 1937, he covered fifteen states and logged twelve thousand miles while making thirty speeches and attending twelve conventions. He often screened *We Work Again*; he was intensely proud of the film. The office also prepared traveling exhibits to promote the various black WPA programs when Smith couldn't make a personal visit.

According to his reports, Al Smith's office was showing results. By 1939, he boasted, the WPA's African American division had hired four thousand black teachers, who instructed 181,000 students, in more than thirteen thousand schools and nurseries. He estimated that his programs had taught five hundred thousand African Americans how to read, and that by 1940, three hundred thousand black WPA workers had earned at least $15 million in wages. The precision of these figures was hard to verify. Al Smith, Mary McLeod Bethune, and Henry Hunt all complained that New Deal higher-ups refused to share information with them. When he couldn't get data, Smith made the best guess possible in order to make his case for support for his program.

In early 1937, Smith surveyed flood damage in black communities along the Mississippi and Ohio river valleys. When he returned to Washington, he admonished administration officials for rushing disaster assistance to the regions' white populations while ignoring the sufferings of black victims. That spring, despite some economic rebound and an increase in jobs, he warned that private-sector employers were passing up black workers, forcing African Americans to continue to depend on government relief jobs. Smith also documented the irregularities African Americans experienced when seeking help not only from his agency but from other New Deal programs. In the summer of 1938, he reported to his superiors that his office had received 167 complaints regarding discrimination in just one thirty-day period. Most revealed that local WPA officials were using various spurious excuses to reject African American applicants. In one locale, black residents reported being turned away if even one member of their household was earning wages of any kind, no matter how low. Although social security was hailed as a milestone in helping older Americans, it had drastically failed black citizens. Not only did the program specifically exclude domestic workers and farm laborers, local offices routinely rejected even those black applicants who met all the qualifications. Administrators insisted that they could not enroll anyone who could not produce official birth or marriage certificates. Such an interpretation of the rules specifically disadvantaged African Americans, since black births and marriages in the South very commonly went unrecorded by local officials.

Although they were outside his responsibilities, and his superiors rarely responded to even those complaints related to the WPA, Smith nonetheless insisted on documenting the broader failures of the New

Deal. The black public viewed his office as the center of all African American relief, and he received most of the information and protests related to the policies and programs that affected black citizens. Smith readily embraced his role as the voice of African Americans from all walks of life. When he couldn't get results from the inside, which was often, he leaked information to civil rights organizations and the African American press. "Aggressive members of the Black Cabinet make no apology for tipping the government's hand to the National Association for the Advancement of Colored People, or Urban League or any other pressure organization," he later revealed. This was especially the case when it appeared "that proposed government action is likely to be discriminatory and hurtful to Negroes." Al Smith embraced a charge that went beyond creating black job opportunities. Along with his fellow Black Cabinet members, he undertook the fight to block policies and programs that might sanction, and thus institutionalize, Jim Crow, disenfranchisement, and inequality as federal practice.

By FDR's second term, Smith had emerged as one of Washington's most important African American federal officeholders. He would never achieve the kind of fame garnered by the Ivy League–educated Robert Weaver or the captivating Mary McLeod Bethune. Frank and earthy, Smith lacked Weaver's smooth sophistication, and he could never match Bethune's magnetic charm and charisma. But as the wizard of black job relief, Al Smith took satisfaction in knowing he had made a difference in many African American lives—and that he was able to generate black jobs and open educational doors to young and old alike and do so on a much larger scale than his colleagues. For many African Americans, WPA programs meant salvation from starvation and despair.

While Al Smith savored his success, he never forgot those who struggled to get by in the American system. He would do whatever he could from inside to advance the people. "Improvement of race relations as a government function is as old as our government," he later wrote. "Its history is the history of our government." Smith thrived on challenging Washington to realize that race was central to the nation's story and that its obligation was to correct the past injustices of racism. But as a New Dealer he also paid the price. "Greying at the temples, lean and hungry looking, clever, minds his own business," was how he described himself at the age of only thirty-seven.

In the two years following FDR's reelection and the NYA conference, the Black Cabinet had made significant strides. In addition to the victories won by Hunt, Weaver, Hastie, Bethune, and Smith, there were other positive signs. The Blue Book, the recommendations from Bethune's 1937 NYA conference, had propelled an increase in black federal presence, and the number of African Americans working for the government surged. In January 1937, the Social Security Board's main office in Baltimore added over seventy African American employees. One study revealed that between June 1930 and June 1938, African Americans in federal jobs around the nation increased from approximately fifty thousand to eighty-two thousand. Most racial-affairs advisers expanded their office staffs significantly. Black Cabinet veterans and core leaders used some of these opportunities to hire noted race-relations experts in entry-level positions with the intention of eventually easing them into official advisory posts.

Yet there were also shortcomings within this growth. Most of the new positions were lower-level jobs with no influence at all. And the rise in the number of black federal employees came more from the expansion of the New Deal bureaucracy than from a genuine effort to integrate African Americans into government. The figures, when looked at closely, were troubling. Of the new African American employees, 90 percent were assigned to custodial service. Secretaries and clerks made up 9.5 percent, while racial-affairs advisers came in at a meager 0.5 percent.

But advancements took place beyond additional appointments and outside of the divisions overseen by the Black Cabinet core. The Civilian Conservation Corps, where Edgar G. Brown soldiered on, increased its enrollment of young black men. Before 1936, African Americans composed 6 percent of enrollees; by 1938, they had increased to 11 percent. A recent addition to the Black Cabinet, Joseph H. B. Evans, crusaded for more benefits for rural black families from the Farm Security Administration (FSA). He pressured field offices to hire more African American agents and, by 1940, 25 percent of families living in FSA farming communities—a few of them integrated—were African American. The FSA also added another new African American appointee, educator Constance E. H. Daniel. She was the second woman to join the Black Cabinet. A person of strong resolve, high expectations, and precision, Daniel undertook a careful analysis of her agency's programs to ensure that African Americans were receiving an equal share.

The enormous pressures and demands of federal posts, along with unending battles against racism, pushed Black Cabinet members to their limits. Even the energetic Bethune admitted to this. After attending a conference in Pennsylvania on a Friday, she missed her train back to Washington, D.C., dined with a friend at midnight, and finally made it home and to bed at three in the morning. Five hours later, at eight o'clock, she was off to the office to see Aubrey Williams and later to meet with Al Smith. "This is a busy and interesting life," Bethune told her readers in Day to Day.

Her itenerary reflected the breakneck pace that many black New Dealers sustained seven days a week for many years. Office work was constantly interrupted by field investigations. By 1939, Lawrence Oxley had visited all forty-eight states then in the union. Between June 1938 and June 1939, Bethune traveled thirty-eight thousand miles. Al Smith's schedule for a two-and-a-half-week period in 1937 characterized the feverish itineraries of black New Dealers. One trip started in Baltimore at two o'clock in the afternoon, when he addressed a gathering of 150 social workers, Public Works Administration administrators, and relief-project employees. Twenty-four hours later, he was in Pittsburgh at a black YMCA showing *We Work Again* and discussing his office's resources. An overnight train took him to Cleveland the next day for more screenings of his film and for speeches at two black churches and a settlement house. Over the next fifteen days, he toured black WPA sites in Toledo, Dayton, Saint Louis, Kansas City, Chicago, and Milwaukee.

The growth of programs after Roosevelt's reelection required more fieldwork and increased the duties of the Black Cabinet. As a result, its members were drawn away from the nation's capital and centers of power, which in turn reduced their influence in their agencies and hindered their ability to organize collective action.

A number of Black Cabinet members also remained active in civil rights organizations, and some continued to participate in community protests, making their lives even busier. Several even occupied leadership roles in external groups. Bethune, who had close ties to the NAACP's Walter White, served as vice president of both the NAACP and the Urban League, as a member of the Commission on Interracial Coopera-tion, and as president of the Association for the Study of Negro Life and History. She also continued as the head of the National Council of Negro Women. Eugene Kinckle Jones remained a vital presence among the Urban League's leaders. His duties in the Commerce Department were so light, he eventually began spending more time in New York City working on Urban League business. (As a result, he was forced out of his federal post in June 1937.) Bill Hastie maintained his affili-ations with the NAACP and the New Negro Alliance. Al Smith and several others also supported these organizations. Smith also joined Bill Hastie's mother, Roberta, and Bethune on the picket line in front of Peoples Drugs, a pharmacy that served the black community but refused to hire African Americans.

On a trip to Daytona Beach in July 1937, Bethune told readers of Day to Day that she was glad "to spend my 62nd birthday on my own porch." Like several other Black Cabinet members, she had left behind her family and home. Although revered by many African Americans as a symbolic mother, Bethune spent very little time with her family. She wasn't alone. Many in the African American brain trust found that their jobs impacted their home life. Newspapers reported rumors that

Al Smith and his wife, Leona, were having "domestic difficulties." Bill and Alma Hastie's marriage had also become strained. Robert Weaver became even more immersed in his job—public housing dominated his life. He worked long days in his office and spent weeks on the road conducting field investigations. Nights were devoted to drafting reports and studies on housing issues. Outside of his colleagues at the office, Bethune, his circle of poker buddies, and his wife, Weaver had almost no other contacts. Lawrence Oxley and Henry Hunt both left wives and children behind. In Washington, D.C., they lived like bachelors, in rented apartments or rooms.

Throughout 1937 and into 1938, Henry Hunt's calendar had grown fuller. He was on the road, often in Georgia attending to family matters and checking on the affairs of Fort Valley. He also monitored the Flint River development, which was shaping up to become one of the New Deal's most impressive resettlement projects. The *Pittsburgh Courier* already praised it as a "farmer's paradise." There on the river bottoms in middle Georgia, federally supported black farmers were transforming the land that generations of enslaved people had toiled on without compensation into a place where African Americans could experience the freedom and economic stability that came from tilling their own fields. In addition to farming necessities, the Flint River project also provided residents with access to a public health nurse, a home economics instructor, and an agricultural supervisor. On October 1, 1938, after eighteen months of planning and building, the community center was finished—it would house the project's school, which was staffed by five teachers and a principal.

That morning, as workers were putting the final touches on the community center, seventy-two-year-old Henry Hunt collapsed in his Washington, D.C., rented room. Within minutes he was dead; doctors determined he had suffered a massive heart attack. One friend remarked that Hunt had been suffering from "the strain of overwork." Bethune expressed "shock" at his loss; she praised Hunt as "courageous and unselfish." W. E. B. Du Bois took Hunt's death hard. In his tribute the NAACP leader praised Hunt for living a life of "sacrifice" so that the African American poor could achieve "happiness and comfort."

The week following Henry A. Hunt's death, the Flint River School opened its doors for the first time. More than three hundred African American students flooded in.

Chapter Nine

Thwarted

B Y THE time Franklin Delano Roosevelt started his second term, Kelly Miller had been a fixture in the District of Columbia's black community for over forty-five years. He had risen from slavery to become a pioneering educator at Howard University. Respected for his quick mind and his outspoken commitment to civil rights, he had established a reputation as a keen political observer. His membership in the first Black Cabinet and his long career as a newspaper columnist had secured his position as a wise political voice within black America. He had retired from Howard University in 1931 but remained an active member of the campus community. Although by 1937 Miller was seventy-four and losing his sight, he remained vigorous. When the weather was good, he could be found in his backyard, tending his rich and bountiful garden in overalls, pith helmet, starched white shirt, and bow tie. At other times, he retreated to his basement, where, surrounded by a massive library of books on topics ranging from literature to science, he sat at his typewriter churning out academic papers, articles, speeches, books, and his popular syndicated column, Kelly Miller Writes.

For several years, Miller had been a booster for both the New Deal and FDR. In his view, Roosevelt's victory had demonstrated the power of the black electorate. And, as he and his contemporaries at the turn of the twentieth century had predicted, the swing in black voting

from Republican to Democrat had forced some important concessions benefiting the community. But Miller and others continued to
warn Democrats not to rest too easy and assume that the black ballot
was exclusively theirs. The Democrats not only needed to continue to
address the needs of African Americans, they also had to do even more
to ensure black voters became regular members of the party's base.
Miller had long realized that politics was a delicate balancing act—a
game of give and take by both sides.

That was why, by the spring of 1937, he had become increasingly
impatient with Robert Vann.

Since leaving his government post, Vann had grown more vocally
critical of the Democrats. The editor blasted away at the party's congressional leadership, accusing it of cowardice on issues of race and of
lacking the grit required to push through anti-lynching legislation. In
the past, Vann had held back on expressing open criticism of the president. But in February 1937, FDR proposed to add more justices to the
Supreme Court, and Vann joined the forces that condemned that plan
as an unconstitutional abuse of executive power. Miller was appalled
at what he felt was Vann's fickle loyalty. Roosevelt's plan was perfectly
constitutional, Miller scolded the editor, and the effect would benefit
African Americans, since it would "liberalize the Supreme Court." Vann
blustered back: unlike Miller, he could be proud that he was no "'Yes
man' to President Roosevelt." Miller scoffed: "Since your sudden conversion [to the Democrats] I have followed your political course. . . . You
now seem to me to be executing a 'presto-change,' which, I am sure,
your many readers and admirers will find . . . difficult to understand."

Significant public opposition compelled FDR to withdraw his proposal. Nonetheless, Vann continued to grow more disenchanted with
both the president and the Democratic Party, especially as the midterm
elections of 1938 approached. He had hoped FDR would choose him
for the Virgin Islands judgeship, but it had gone to Bill Hastie. His
supporters floated his name for a seat on the Supreme Court. Even
Vann realized that was a long shot. As the 1938 midterm elections

approached, Vann's constant brawling with other black Democrats and his growing frustration with the White House's feeble race policies had increasingly relegated him to the party's fringe.

In October 1938, he arrived in Washington, D.C., fuming. Two issues critical to the African American community were at the forefront of his mind—the unmitigated suffering in black rural America and the U.S. military's continued segregation and unfair treatment of African Americans in the ranks. Determined to discuss these face-to-face with the president, Vann showed up at Mary McLeod Bethune's office. She attempted to calm him down, aware of how important it was to keep the newspaper editor in the fold. But she also agreed; the administration had failed African Americans on farm aid and in military policy, as well as in many other areas under the New Deal. Some weeks before Vann's visit, she had sent off a letter to the president encouraging him to take immediate steps to help black Americans by issuing "executive orders" and stern policy "suggestions to certain cabinet and department heads." Granting the Blue Book's core requests would facilitate "the solidifying of opinion among my people for the spirit of democracy which you so nobly represent." Doing nothing would only alienate black voters, she warned.

The White House had not heeded her advice. Now, Robert Vann had arrived at her office more agitated than ever. His newspaper, the *Pittsburgh Courier*, remained one of the most widely read among African Americans, and the November election was only weeks away. After talking with Bethune, Vann telephoned the White House and requested a meeting with the president. Immediately a secretary added him to FDR's official calendar. The White House response was so rapid it indicated that Vann's meeting must have been prearranged somehow by Bethune and Eleanor Roosevelt.

On Friday morning, October 28, the president arrived in the Oval Office at about ten thirty. He held a brief press conference to announce the appointment of a new assistant secretary of the treasury and then went into a series of very short meetings with New Deal officials.

Robert Vann arrived for his 11:45 A.M. appointment and was ushered in. Fifteen minutes later, the *Courier's* editor emerged. Would he take questions? reporters asked as he descended the White House steps. Yes, of course, Vann replied, knowing the spot where he stood was reserved for the administration's most important announcements. What was Roosevelt's reaction to Vann's proposals regarding relief for black farmers and the expansion of black opportunities in the U.S. military? asked one reporter. The president's "attitude" was "sympathetic," Vann stated. What should be done about the crisis in rural black America next? "I think we ought to obey the President's suggestions and have a very definite understanding with Secretary [of Agriculture] Wallace," Vann replied. Then he revealed that he had an important announcement to make. He would be voting Republican in Pennsylvania's midterm elections. "The best political joke in recent history," one white journalist quipped. "Deceitful and dishonest," huffed Democratic party leader, now Pennsylvania senator, Joe Guffey.

Election day in November 1938 came and went. In Vann's home state of Pennsylvania, the Republican slate won, but in most areas of the nation where African Americans could vote, they chose Democrats. While some white political pundits insisted there was evidence that the party's hold on the black vote was collapsing, Kelly Miller disagreed. The best measure of African American allegiances, he contended, could be found in an Illinois congressional race where both candidates were black, but victory had gone to the Democrat. Other reports also suggested that African Americans had stuck by the party of Roosevelt; there was a notable increase of black Democrats winning public office in several local precincts around the nation. In Pennsylvania, five African Americans took seats in the state assembly. This included the Works Progress Administration's Crystal Bird Fauset, who became the first black woman elected as a state legislator. Five more African Americans won local races in Saint Louis. In New York, one African American party leader insisted that black votes had put the Democratic incumbent for governor, Herbert H. Lehman, over the top. Kelly Miller predicted that the black ballot was destined to become even mightier as the Democrats continued to win races with it.

However, not all the news was good. During the midterm campaigns, FDR had launched a drive to force his Democratic opponents out of the House and Senate and replace them with New Deal liberals. Conservative anti–New Deal Democrats, many of them from the South, often joined forces with reactionary Republicans in what Joe Guffey called "the unholy alliance." These Democrat and Republican factions shared hostility toward government spending (especially on relief), the union movement, and the federal regulation of business and industry. They also agreed on an unofficial and longstanding practice by private businesses and employers that Guffey described as "the low wage policy." Paying marginalized populations like African Americans as little as possible was good for the American economy because it increased profits for big business and commercial agriculture, argued members of the unholy alliance. In their view, the New Deal's attempts to raise the standard of living by instituting fairer wages threatened big money's returns and would impede recovery. Guffey insisted that the South, which relied on "the continued subjection of the Negro in order to maintain a docile labor supply at low cost," was especially invested in protecting the "low wage policy." Bonded by their shared interests and attitudes, conservative Democrats crossed the aisle and voted with Republicans against New Deal legislation. In turn, the GOP paid back its Democratic allies by opposing anti-lynching laws, voting rights acts, and funding for relief programs addressing the needs of African Americans.

Roosevelt's efforts to purge his Democratic enemies failed spectacularly. All won reelection in 1938. And, alarmingly, the Republicans, who had been soundly thumped in the three previous elections, regained ground in both the House and the Senate. Roosevelt's inability to sway the election could be blamed in part on unemployment figures, which had been on a roller coaster. In 1937 joblessness had dropped to about

14 percent. Trying to balance the budget, Roosevelt had pulled back on relief, which sent the economy careening downward. In 1938, unemployment shot up to 20 percent. In a panic, the White House started flushing more money into several New Deal programs and, over the next year, the jobless rate declined to 17.2 percent. Throughout this time, FDR continually scuffled with the "unholy alliance," which had expanded in number and in power. Watching from the sidelines, the Black Cabinet grew more anxious.

Another grave worry enveloped the entire country. In the Pacific, Japan had escalated an aggressive campaign to secure more territory for its resource-strapped island nation. On the other side of the world, Adolf Hitler had ascended to power and embarked on a mission to reunite all Germanic peoples under one flag. Hitler's blueprint for world domination by the "Aryan" race, outlined in his political manifesto *Mein Kampf*, circulated widely. As international tensions intensified, the president appealed to Americans to unite, recognize common bonds, and put their divisions behind them. But FDR's calls for national harmony rang hollow in a country where black citizens, lacking political, social, and economic rights, lived in fear of deadly racial violence. As Robert Weaver pointed out, the United States' growing criticism of Hitler's actions and his philosophy demanded that Americans look inward and "question the racial policy of our own democracy."

The world turned even more somber in the spring of 1938 when Hitler annexed Austria. FDR struggled to craft a response to fascist aggression while confronting a stubborn isolationist strain within the American public. Vocal forces demanded that the United States not become involved in another world war; shedding American blood on foreign shores seemed unthinkable to many after World War I. South Dakota senator Gerald Nye's opinion—"let Europe resolve its own difficulties"—was shared by a good portion of Americans.

Yet preparedness became the keynote for the Roosevelt White House, which recognized the necessity of building up American defense. This resulted in an increase in government-funded employment. In the past,

African Americans had fought to secure a fair share of federal relief jobs; now they would also have to press the administration for equal inclusion in the expansion of the defense industry and the armed forces. Furthermore, the clock on FDR's second term was starting to run out. Although the Constitution placed no term limits on U.S. presidents, Roosevelt's predecessors had followed the tradition set by George Washington, who retired after two terms. Although the gains made under Roosevelt had been limited, they needed to be extended, protected, and institutionalized quickly, since it was not known who might occupy the White House next.

Bethune decided it was time to convene a second National Youth Administration (NYA) conference. It must be big, bold, and dramatic, she told the Black Cabinet. Her staff booked a large auditorium adjacent to the Department of Labor, and Bethune announced to the public that the gathering would run for three days in January 1939. Eleanor Roosevelt agreed again to be a special guest. Invitations went out to African American leaders across the nation. The guest list was double the size of that for the 1937 conference.

When he received his invitation, Robert Vann called his secretary into his office and dictated a response. "If I should come to your conference," he began, "I am very much afraid I would blurt right out to an embarrassing degree some of the things I know." The *Pittsburgh Courier*'s recent investigation of the New Deal in the black rural South had revealed the persistence of deplorable conditions perpetuated not only by racism but also by fraud routinely committed by local administrators. The conference should be dedicated to the interests of the majority of black Americans—and Vann pointed out that those were predominantly farmers. Bethune must, he demanded, take the case for the black farmer directly to Roosevelt and insist he act swiftly. If she was "afraid to do this," then she must step aside and yield to someone who had more courage. "You cannot afford to travel around the country and talk about the blessings of the New Deal unless there are some real blessings to talk about," Vann continued. "Fearing I might break up your conference, I prefer to stay away." He signed off with a warning: "If something is not done about it [New Deal neglect], I'm going to make a direct attack on the Administration at Washington."

On January 12, 1939, before 225 delegates, Bethune brought to order the NYA's second National Conference on the Problems of the Negro and Negro Youth. "We are calling you together to do two things: First to note our progress since the last conference, and second, to consider new developments and devise new approaches to the solution of our basic problems," she told the crowd. Since the last conference, fascism had spread, and the world had been engulfed in crises. "At a time like this when the basic principles of democracy are being challenged at home and abroad, when racial and religious hatreds are being engendered, it is vitally important that minority groups in this nation express anew their adherence to the fundamental principles of democracy." Let the spirit of American patriotism and unity infuse all discussions and solutions, she urged. But she also added:

> We recognize that no such "united democracy" can possibly exist unless this "common opportunity" is available to all Americans regardless of race, color, or creed. A "united patriotism" is the fruit of political equality, economic opportunity and the universal enjoyment of basic civil rights. Only when these objectives are fully achieved will our country be able to stand before the world as the unsullied champion of true democracy.

Democracy thrived only where liberties were reciprocal and shared by all. Bethune made clear that she was willing to wave the flag but was also fully aware that the president's appeal for Americans to come together was impossible if a portion of its citizens were denied, by law and by custom, their constitutional rights.

On the first day of the conference, late in the afternoon, Eleanor Roosevelt arrived, escorted by new Black Cabinet member William

Trent, who was Robert Weaver's assistant at the Housing Authority. She took a seat next to Bethune and listened to a panel presentation on African American youth. Then Bethune stood and introduced the First Lady as "a friend, a humanitarian, a woman who has set the pace for the service of womanhood in America and the world. The most humble child in the alley can stop her and speak to her and receive a smile."

As the crowd broke into applause, Eleanor Roosevelt rose. "Instead of just talking, I am going to ask if you will ask me questions," she said. "Now are there any questions?"

The First Lady's willingness to take any question both surprised and won over the crowd. Should black and white schools be equally funded? Absolutely, she stated; the purpose of public schools was to offer all students "the right to the same opportunities for education." Yes, she agreed, military service in the Army and Navy, and advancement within the ranks to officer status, should be open to all. Domestics and farmworkers absolutely deserved social security. On employment, she was passionate—everyone merited equal opportunity for all jobs: "It is a question of the right to work and the right to work should know no color line." What was her opinion on wage differentials? White New Dealers who contended blacks deserved lower pay because they were less efficient than whites were absolutely wrongheaded. "I think you labor under the same difficulties women labor under," she maintained. "Now women have to do, as a rule, in a given job, twice as well as men have to do. I think it is probably that a colored person must do his job, whatever it is, twice as well as perhaps the white person who is doing that same job."

"What are your views on anti-lynching legislation?" asked Charles C. Diggs Sr., who had won a seat as a state senator in Michigan in 1936. "I doubt very much whether the anti-lynching legislation would do away with lynching," Roosevelt replied. "But I would like to see it passed, because it puts us as a whole on record against something which we should certainly all of us, anywhere in the country, be against."

However, at one point during the session she cautiously added, "I don't want you to take any of the opinions that I give as representative of the Administration. They are representative of what I think as an individual." Despite her disclaimer, everyone present understood that the First Lady of the United States had offered a critically important endorsement of federal anti-lynching legislation.

However, audience members had to be somewhat deflated to hear the First Lady's complacency regarding segregation in federal buildings in Washington, D.C.: "I think the Federal Government is established in a city which is still largely a southern city . . . [and] like it or not, we cannot change things in a day." Still, overall, Roosevelt wowed the crowd. In part, she was riding high on a recent episode in which she had protested segregated seating at a Birmingham, Alabama, meeting she had attended with Bethune. There the two women had been barred from sitting next to each other, as Bethune was restricted to a blacks-only section. Rather than agree to sit in the section designated for whites, Eleanor Roosevelt took her chair and placed it in the middle of the empty aisle that divided the black and white attendees. Now, several weeks later, here she was at the second NYA conference, sitting by Bethune's side and engaging African American representatives from across the country respectfully and directly.

The hour-long question-and-answer session at the NYA's second conference concluded with hearty applause for the First Lady. For-rester Washington, who had continuously blasted the New Deal since his resignation from the Federal Emergency Relief Administration in 1934, then rose to speak. He had also been at the Birmingham meeting, he told those present, and had witnessed the First Lady's bravery. He offered a motion to "thank her for her moral courage then and the stand she has taken today for social justice for minority groups represented here."

It was approved enthusiastically.

Eleanor Roosevelt departed, and the delegates dug in to work. Over the next forty-eight hours, they pored over facts and figures, many

The Black Cabinet (1938). Front row, left to right: Ambrose Caliver, Roscoe Brown, Robert Weaver, Joseph H. B. Evans, Frank Horne, Mary McLeod Bethune, Lawrence A. Oxley, William J. Thompkins, Charles E. Hall, William I. Houston, Ralph E. Mizelle. Back row, left to right: Dewey R. Jones, Edgar Brown, J. Parker Prescott, Edward H. Lawson, Jr., J. Arthur Weiseger, Alfred Edgar Smith, Henry A. Hunt, John W. Whitten, Joseph R. Houchins. *Scurlock Studio Records, c. 1905–1904, Smithsonian Archives Center, National Museum of American History.*

Booker T. Washington and President Theodore Roosevelt review a parade at Tuskegee Institute (1905). Images, like this stereoscope card, of Washington and Roosevelt circulated to court African American support for the president. *Library of Congress, Prints and Photographs Division.*

Richard (R.W.) Thompson (1902). Journalist who coined the term the Black Cabinet in 1908. *Schomburg Center for Research in Black Culture, Manuscripts, Archives and Rare Books Division, New York Public Library.*

Ralph W(aldo) Tyler (1908). Leader of the first Black Cabinet under Theodore Roosevelt and William Howard Taft. *Schomburg Center for Research in Black Culture, Jean Blackwell Hutson Research and Reference Division, New York Public Library.*

Kelly Miller (1911). Dean of Arts and Sciences at Howard University, Miller was an informal member of the first Black Cabinet and a champion of the second Black Cabinet. *Scurlock Studio Records, c. 1905-1994, Smithsonian Archives Center, National Museum of American History.*

Robert Vann (center) with *Pittsburgh Courier* Assistant Editor Percival (P. L.) Prattis on the right (c. 1940). Attorney and newspaper publisher Vann led the crossover of African Americans from the Republican Party into the Democratic Party and became the first African American appointee in Franklin Delano Roosevelt's administration. *Percival L. Prattis Papers, ULS Archives and Special Collections, University of Pittsburgh.*

"Robert Vann: Champion of Justice" (1943). Part of a series of illustrations created by artist Charles Alston for the African American press to promote support for World War II. *Office of War Information, National Archives and Records Administration.*

Robert C. Weaver as a child (1911). Leader of the Black Cabinet under Franklin Delano Roosevelt, Weaver was born into the black elite of Washington D.C. and was raised in the integrated D.C. neighborhood of Brookland. *Schomburg Center for Research in Black Culture, Jean Blackwell Hutson Research and Reference Division, New York Public Library.*

Bottom row: Al (Alfred Edgar) Smith, Mamie Johnson Smith (mother), Henry Smith (brother). Top row: Kate Smith (sister), Jesse Rufus Smith (father), Shepherd Acre (cousin) (c. early 1910s). Born and raised in the south, Smith worked in a variety of blue-collar jobs as a youth and understood the struggles of working class people and the poor. *Alfred Edgar Smith Papers, Special Collections, University of Arkansas, Fayetteville.*

Robert Weaver and Executive Secretary of the Fair Employment Practice Committee Lawrence Cramer (1942). Weaver and Cramer pose in front of a plaque commemorating Executive Order 8802, which outlawed discrimination in defense and government employment and was achieved in part because of ongoing pressure from Black Cabinet members. *Farm Security Administration, Office of War Information Photograph Collection, Library of Congress.*

Al Smith, official Works Progress Administration portrait (c. 1930s). During the FDR administration, Smith ran the largest African American jobs program in the New Deal. *Alfred Edgar Smith Papers, Special Collections, University of Arkansas, Fayetteville.*

Al Smith, shown with his clerical staff in the Works Progress Administration office (c. 1930s). *Ralph J. Bunche Papers, Special Collections, Charles E. Young Library, University of California Los Angeles.*

Illustration: the masthead designed by Eugene Davidson for his 1934 syndicated column for black newspapers, that established the Black Cabinet of the FDR era in the public eye. *The Claude A. Barnett Papers: The Associated Negro Press, 1918–1967. Part 2: Associated Negro Press Organizational Files, 1920–1966, Chicago History Museum, Research Center.*

Robert Weaver with secretary Mary Pipes (1942). *Farm Security Administration, Office of War Information Photograph Collection, Library of Congress.*

William Hastie (1930). Born in Tennessee and raised in Washington, D.C., after graduating with a law degree from Harvard, Hastie returned to the nation's capital to practice and teach law as well as participate in civil rights activism. *Scurlock Studio Records, c. 1905-1994, Smithsonian Archives Center, National Museum of American History.*

William Hastie with Assistant Secretary of War Robert P. Patterson (1942). Appointed as a Civilian Aide to the Secretary of War, during World War II Hastie battled with War Department officials for integration and equal treatment of African American soldiers. *Farm Security Administration, Office of War Information Photograph Collection, Library of Congress.*

"William Hastie: Champion of Justice" (1943) by Charles Alston. *Office of War Information, National Archives and Records Administration.*

Mary McLeod Bethune (1910). Born in 1875 in South Carolina, Bethune pursued a career in teaching and established her own school in 1904 in Daytona Beach Florida. *Print Collections, State Library and Archives of Florida.*

Mary McLeod Bethune and Roberta Hastie (mother of William Hastie) picket outside a Peoples Drug Store with the New Negro Alliance in 1939, demanding that the chain hire African Americans. *Baltimore Afro-American.*

Mary McLeod Bethune (1943). Appointed by Franklin Delano Roosevelt to the National Youth Administration as the head of the African American division in 1936, Bethune was the first African American woman to become a federal administrator. *Farm Security Administration, Office of War Information Photograph Collection, Library of Congress.*

Clark Foreman. A white Georgian, Foreman was active in integrationist organizations and appointed to head up the Office of the Special Adviser on the Economic Status of Negroes in 1933. *Papers of Clark Foreman, Special Collections, University of Virginia.*

SHE KNOWS **THE BOSS'S** SECRETS

MISS LUCIA MAE PITTS, private secretary to Clark Foreman, special assistant to the administrator and director of power under the PWA. Miss Pitts, in this picture reflects a pensive mood which is adumbrative to her habit of giving careful consideration to all business matters while endeavoring to carry out her boss's orders right to the letter. She has knowledge of all his confidential matters and is loyal under all circumstances.

Lucia Mae Pitts. Appointed as Clark Foreman's secretary in 1933, Pitts became the first African American woman to work as a stenographer to a white federal administrator. Pitts became Foreman's right hand and he relied on her not only for clerical work but also advice regarding racial affairs, field investigations, and recommendations for hiring. She later also served as Robert Weaver's secretary. *Baltimore Afro-American.*

John P. Davis, left and U. Simpson Tate, right with A. Philip Randolph in the center (c. 1940). John P. Davis cofounded the Negro Industrial League with his childhood friend Robert Weaver. Later on he would join U. Simpson Tate and others to organize the National Negro Congress. They are pictured here with labor leader A. Philip Randolph. *Scurlock Studio Records, c. 1905-1994, Smithsonian Archives Center, National Museum of American History.*

A. Philip Randolph, 1942. The founder of the Brotherhood of Sleeping Car Porters and Maids, Randolph had close ties to several Black Cabinet members. Some in the Black Cabinet supported his call for a March on Washington in 1941. Although Randolph suspended his plans after Roosevelt signed Executive Order 8802, he would later join forces with Dr. Martin Luther King to carry out the March in 1963. *Photo: Gordon Parks, Prints and Photographs Division, Library of Congress, Washington, D.C.*

Elizabeth McDuffie. White House maid Elizabeth McDuffie served as a confidante and advocate for African American causes, and campaigned for FDR. *Elizabeth and Irvin McDuffie Papers, Archives Research Center, Robert W. Woodruff Library, Atlanta University.*

Irvin McDuffie. Franklin Delano Roosevelt's valet, McDuffie worked for the president for over a decade and became a close confidante. Along with his wife, he carried concerns from the black community and the Black Cabinet directly to the president. *Elizabeth and Irvin McDuffie Papers, Archives Research Center, Robert W. Woodruff Library, Atlanta University.*

President Franklin Delano Roosevelt visits the dedication of the Terrace Village housing project, Pittsburgh, PA, October 11, 1940. The low-income housing project was a product of the newly formed United States Housing Authority, where Robert Weaver fought for the inclusion of African Americans in the New Deal's housing policies. *Franklin Delano Roosevelt Library and Museum, National Archives and Records Administration.*

William J. Thompkins (Washington D.C. Recorder of Deeds) at far left and Franklin Roosevelt at groundbreaking for District of Columbia's Recorder's Office (1940). Unlike his predecessor Herbert Hoover, Roosevelt appeared at African American events and was photographed with African American leaders. *Franklin Delano Roosevelt Presidential Library and Museum, NARA.*

THE WHITE HOUSE
WASHINGTON

November 22, 1941

MEMO FOR THE PRESIDENT:

I have been asked to call your
attention to the importance of having a
Negro in a position who can actually confer
with the President occassionally on problems
that are pertinent to Negroes, and who can
have a very close affiliation with the
Under- Secretaries of the President as to
the Negro's cause.

E.R.

Memorandum from Eleanor Roosevelt to Franklin Roosevelt. The First Lady often communicated the black community's needs to the President through notes sometimes left on his bed table as a way to avoid White House secretaries antagonistic to African American causes. "MEMO FOR THE PRESIDENT: I have been asked to call your attention to the importance of having a Negro in a position who can actually confer with the President occasionally on problems that are pertinent to Negroes, and who can have a very close affiliation with the Under-Secretaries of the President as to the Negro's cause. E.R. No—any more than I can put in a Jew as such or a Spiritualist as such. Explain to Mrs. Bethune better to have a white person. F.D.R." *Franklin Delano Roosevelt Presidential Library and Museum, NARA.*

Franklin Roosevelt with White House Press Secretary Stephen Early (1941). A Virginian, Early was unsympathetic to African Americans and emerged as the Oval Office's guardian and often blocked black requests from getting to the president. *Franklin Delano Roosevelt Presidential Library and Museum, NARA.*

Franklin Delano Roosevelt with the White House Cabinet, 1941. *Farm Security Administration, Office of War Information Photograph Collection, Library of Congress.*

Eleanor Roosevelt visits a Des Moines, Iowa, WPA nursery (1936). Eleanor Roosevelt traveled the country and visited New Deal sites, including those that addressed black needs. *Franklin Delano Roosevelt Presidential Library and Museum, NARA.*

Aubrey Williams, Mary McLeod Bethune, and Eleanor Roosevelt at the National Youth Administration's Second Conference on the Problems of the Negro and Negro Youth (1939). The First Lady supported Bethune's NYA conferences of 1937 and 1939 organized by the Black Cabinet to expose the conditions facing not only African American youth but black people in general. *Alfred Edgar Smith Papers, Special Collections, University of Arkansas Library.*

Eleanor Roosevelt (second from left) visits Al Smith's Washington WPA staff (c. 1937). *Alfred Edgar Smith Papers, Special Collections, University of Arkansas, Fayetteville.*

An African American family moves into Sojourner Truth Homes of Detroit (1942). The area was a site of riots in 1942 and 1943, when whites attempted to terrorize the black community to prevent them from occupying homes in this Black Cabinet collaborative housing effort. *Farm Security Administration, Office of War Information Photograph Collection, Library of Congress.*

Farmer Jesse Stubbs works his land on Flint River Farms Project (1939). Flint River Farms offered black families land and the necessities for farming as a loan that they paid off with the earnings from their crops. *Farm Security Administration, Office of War Information Photograph Collection, Library of Congress.*

Flint River Farms School House surrounded by fields of oats (1939). Flint River provided education to hundreds of African American children and adults. *Farm Security Administration, Office of War Information Photograph Collection, Library of Congress.*

Mary McLeod Bethune, singer Marian Anderson, and defense workers at the launching of the SS Booker T. Washington (1943). Black Cabinet members played a critical role in advocating for African American employment in defense work. *Farm Security Administration, Office of War Information Photograph Collection, Library of Congress.*

Robert Weaver speaks after President Lyndon Baines Johnson swears him in as the first Secretary of Housing and Urban Development and as the first African American member of a White House Cabinet (1966). *Lyndon Baines Johnson Presidential Library, NARA.*

Black Cabinet and black leaders celebration of Robert Weaver's appointment as the head of the Housing and Home Finance Agency (1961). Left to right—first row: Frank Horne, Campbell Johnson, Robert Weaver, William Hastie, Robert Ming, Ralph Bunche. Second row: A. Maceo Smith, Booker T. McGraw, Frederick D. Patterson, Farrow Allen, Donald Wyatt, Ted Jones, Roy Wilkins, Ted Poston, William J. Trent, Ralph Lanier, Truman Gibson, Henry Lee Moon, Al Smith, Lawrence Oxley. *Schomburg Center for Research in Black Culture, Manuscripts, Archives and Rare Books Division, New York Public Library.*

supplied by the Black Cabinet. All black brain trusters were present and offered counsel "tactfully in the background." For three long days and nights, Bethune guided the conference. When a fight broke out on the floor, she laughingly interrupted: "Children, children. I'm an old, confused woman. I want you to help me. Let us forget this parliamentary business and get down to common sense." While Bethune, at sixty-three, was one of the more senior participants, there were others her age or older. But by her own admission, she was beginning to feel the strain of being a New Dealer. Still, she was exhilarated by the gathering. "My body was weary, but I wasn't tired. I was refreshed. There before me, thinking together, were some of the finest minds in this country," she later recalled.

In between sessions, participants from around the nation networked: D.C. recorder of deeds William Thompkins chatted with John Whitten, one of Al Smith's assistants at the Works Progress Administration. Robert Weaver joined Philadelphia attorney and civil rights leader Raymond Pace Alexander for a smoke. Bethune circulated through the throng, greeting participants and making introductions. Spying national Urban League figure Lester Granger, Bethune cornered him, "patted his hand," and lavished him with praise for his work on inner-city poverty. She then insisted that he chair the conference's findings committee. He hesitated; he didn't want to admit it, but he had planned to enjoy some D.C. nightlife while in town. Bethune persisted. He couldn't say no.

For the second day of the gathering, Bethune had been able to orchestrate an official appointment with the president. It had not been easy. Weeks before, she had written to Roosevelt asking whether she could bring a delegation to see him during the conference. FDR had instructed White House staffer Marvin McIntyre to handle the matter and speak with Aubrey Williams. The Kentucky-born McIntyre attempted to head off Bethune and plainly told Williams he thought such a meeting was needless. Growing impatient for a response, shortly before the conference, Bethune telephoned the White House and left the president a message, imploring that he "not fail" her. She got Williams to take her side; he convinced FDR it was vital that he receive Bethune and a group of conference participants.

At four o'clock on January 13, Bethune arrived at the Oval Office with the NAACP's Walter White, Howard University president Mordecai Johnson, and three other delegates. Bethune spoke first, telling Roosevelt that "progress had been made under the New Deal regime," but "many obstacles remained blocking full citizenship rights." Johnson then requested that the president personally act to help realize the goals emerging from the conference. Outside the usual pleasantries, there was no indication that FDR made any promises.

The following day, the committees presented their reports, and the conference attendees discussed the findings. All agreed: advances had been made in the previous two years, but they were extremely limited. The White House, cabinet heads, New Deal chiefs, and Congress had all failed to step up. But the Black Cabinet and the New Deal divisions led by Bethune, Smith, and Weaver had achieved some results. "These distinctive gains have been in some degree effected by certain significant governmental techniques," Bethune told the audience. "We would emphasize the importance of the presence of a growing number of trained and competent Negro executives in administrative and policy-making federal positions, especially in the ... 'New Deal' agencies." In addition to calling for more African American voices in the federal service, Bethune repeated the "immediate need" for federal anti-lynching laws, voting rights, education, jobs, and housing. Among the many other demands was a new proposal for "a national health program" that would cover all Americans. Conferencegoers also agreed to issue a statement reminding the government of its responsibility to bring "the democratic ideal within the grasp of the lowliest citizen, regardless of race, creed, or color."

As the final session neared its end, Robert Weaver appeared at the podium and took the microphone. A special-delivery letter had just arrived, he told the audience, and it was from the president. "My dear Mrs. Bethune, as your conference breaks up I want to congratulate all of you taking part in the sound and constructive efforts being made to have this meeting a real worthwhile one," Weaver read. "I was glad to have the talk with you and your conferees yesterday afternoon, as it gave me quite an insight into your aims and objectives. I sincerely hope that further progress will be made toward those great objectives for the betterment of your Race."

Roosevelt had adeptly crafted a noncommittal statement. And it implied that while the president had "hope" for "progress," somehow it was out of his hands.

Still the audience was buoyed by the president's letter, which validated, to a degree, the proceedings. The meeting wrapped up, and several delegates offered heartfelt tributes to Bethune. The crowd exploded with applause. A radiant Bethune stood and then lifted her hands and clasped them together in a gesture of victory. It was a sign of strength, of encouragement to fight on.

Bethune and the Black Cabinet received excellent press in the weeks after the gathering. The *New Journal and Guide*, an African American newspaper based in Norfolk, Virginia, ran a large pictorial section showing the delegates meeting, Eleanor Roosevelt answering questions with Bethune at her side, and various speakers addressing the assembly. The *Atlanta Daily World* praised the Black Cabinet as "a powerful force," and despite Robert Vann's refusal to support the conference, one *Pittsburgh Courier* columnist celebrated Bethune with a "Hats Off," hailing her as "our recognized First Lady of the Land." Many African American papers focused on Eleanor Roosevelt's appearance. ASK ME ANYTHING, read a caption for a photograph of the First Lady in the *Baltimore Afro-American*. "No hedging on her part or disposition to talk in circles," reported the *Pittsburgh Courier*. The *New York Age* headlined its story on the conference "First Lady for Anti-Lynch Law," but it also remarked: "We hope her husband will follow suit and also declare himself." To have the president's support for federal legislation outlawing lynching would make a powerful difference.

The president remained silent.

Eleanor Roosevelt's public resistance to racism continued to grow. About the time the second NYA conference took place, Howard University officials attempted to book Constitution Hall in Washington, D.C., for a concert featuring the famous African American contralto Marian Anderson. The deeply conservative Daughters of the American Revolution (DAR) controlled the hall, and their leadership immediately denied the request. When the First Lady, who belonged to the DAR, learned of the organization's obstruction, she was irate. She knew Anderson, who had supported the president in 1936, and had invited the singer to perform at the White House. Privately, Eleanor Roosevelt despaired over what to do. To not act would be read as an endorsement of segregation, which she had come to loathe. To protest might give her husband's enemies, primarily those in the South, a weapon to use in an attack on his administration and programs. She talked it over not only with Mary McLeod Bethune but also with the NAACP's Walter White and several other Black Cabinet members.

On February 27, 1939, Americans opened their papers to the First Lady's My Day column. "I have been debating in my mind for some time a question which I have had to debate with myself once or twice before," Eleanor Roosevelt wrote. "The question is, if you belong to an organization and disapprove of an action which is typical of a policy, should you resign or is it better to work for a changed point of view within that organization?" (She did not name the DAR specifically, but everyone following the news knew what she was referring to.) There was little she could do to influence "the organization" from within, but she could not "approve of their action." "Therefore," she announced, "I am resigning." Privately, she rebuked the head of the DAR in a letter: "You had an opportunity to lead in an enlightened way and it seems to me that your organization has failed."

Behind the scenes, Eleanor Roosevelt helped to reschedule Anderson's concert, which took place on the steps of the Lincoln Memorial on Easter Sunday, 1939. Several members of the Black Cabinet were present to witness Anderson's performance. When she began "My Country 'Tis of Thee," the crowd went silent. Robert Weaver remembered that "it was a moving experience . . . almost like a tribute."

As spring came in 1939, the Black Cabinet battled to maintain the momentum from the second NYA conference. A second Blue Book of the proceedings was issued, repeating many of the 1937 conference's calls for jobs, housing, education, voting rights, desegregation, health care, equal treatment under the law, anti-lynching legislation, and an end to police brutality. One correspondent for the *Baltimore Afro-American* praised the latest Blue Book for its thorough account of "how the other third (or tenth) lives—or does not live." In his mind, it would serve as "a handbook for all having an interest in the civic, social, and economic affairs of the country."

Bethune convinced Aubrey Williams to send a copy to each cabinet and agency head with a request that all respond to the conference's proposals. Upon receiving their copy, most upper-level administrators ignored it. Those who did respond registered reactions that ranged from bland acknowledgement to peevish defenses of their programs. The head of the Farm Credit Administration, Forrest Hill, insisted that the conference had unfairly characterized his division as failing. On the contrary, he insisted, his programs were working quite well for African Americans. The Civil Service Commission's leadership dismissed all recommendations for their agency as either "impractical" or too expensive. Robert Fechner recoiled at requests that the Civilian Conservation Corps recruit more black officers and desegregate its units. The suggestion that more African Americans be given command of camps was unfeasible because, he maintained, very few African Americans met the military's requirements for leadership. He added, "I cannot approve the recommendation for the establishment of interracial camps. After almost six years, I am convinced that segregation of negro and white enrollees is desirable not only for the junior enrollees but also for the war veterans." It was clear: many white New Dealers had no intention of taking either the first or the second Blue Book seriously. There was not only a lack of commitment but also a tenacious resistance to reforming New Deal policies and programs to reach more African Americans.

On April 5, Bethune called the Black Cabinet together for the first time since the January conference. Confronting the continued intransigence of many New Deal chiefs and a more conservative Congress, the group decided to marshal more external pressure in hopes of advancing its objectives. The members agreed to establish a network of state-level spokespeople to mobilize the black public behind the second Blue Book's recommendations. They also made attempts at organizing a committee of national African American leaders whose responsibilities would include lobbying Congress, tracking legislation affecting African Americans, and attending Capitol Hill hearings. Black Cabinet members pledged to use their connections with the NAACP and the Urban League to directly "push forward" the second conference's demands. Bethune and Weaver agreed to become the main recruiters of "other heads of National organizations" for the effort.

Efforts at organizing a Washington-based lobby and a nationwide network of representatives withered. In part, this was because Black Cabinet members' demanding jobs gave them little time to devote to such a grand vision. But the failure of the plan also resulted from the proliferation of challenges during 1939 that made their work and lives even more complicated.

The federal workplace had always been hostile to African Americans, and this hardly eased up during the later New Deal. Paradoxically, the implementation of legislation aimed at providing civil service employees with more federal protection produced more hardships for African Americans. Early in 1939, Roosevelt issued Executive Order 7915, which mandated extensive civil service reform. The Civil Service

Commission had been founded to ensure that a critical mass of government positions were nonpolitical—hiring for these jobs was based on examination and qualifications, not party fidelity. Many federal jobs, ranging from custodians to cabinet department employees, fell under the civil service. Ideally, it was the one area where fairness ruled. But the reality had been that favoritism still plagued the civil service, and Roosevelt's order was designed to end cronyism once and for all.

To assure African Americans that the executive order would benefit them, the Civil Service Commission sent its legal counsel, James O'Brien, to address John P. Davis's National Negro Congress, which he had cofounded with James Ford, a communist party organizer, in 1935. In opening remarks, O'Brien pronounced the executive order a leap forward, asserting that it outlawed racial bias in hiring and the workplace. Furthermore, he claimed, it streamlined the process for investigating allegations of discrimination against applicants or employees. He also assured the predominately black audience that, with the new regulations, there was "only one problem for the colored worker," and that rested in his or her ability.

Immediately, Robert Weaver challenged O'Brien. The order only prohibited discrimination on the basis of "political or religious opinions," not race, he pointed out. The process of arbitrating complaints of prejudicial treatment was not neutral. Rather, it would be carried out in the divisions from which the allegations arose. The order left in place the requirement that applicants submit photo identification and the long-standing rule that allowed supervisors to select any of the top three scorers on examinations. There was little in the executive order that would help African American people.

Indeed, after FDR's reforms went into effect, there was very little improvement for African Americans. Although the order required departments to promote from within, civil service bosses still passed over longtime African American employees and instead promoted or hired less-experienced white workers. When selecting new agents, the Federal Bureau of Investigation declined to consider longtime African

American messengers, many of whom were studying for law degrees. "Standard equipment for a young government messenger en route to work is a paper bag of lunch and a law book," Al Smith observed. Instead, openings for new G-men went to far less qualified whites with very little time on the federal employment clock.

Discrimination continued in the government's custodial ranks, as African Americans with twenty to thirty years on the job were routinely rejected for new positions regardless of their proven performance and capabilities. Some divisions used health screenings to block hiring or advancement. In one case, a federal hospital worker was rejected for a promotion because a government doctor reported she had "organic heart trouble." A Treasury Department clerk complained he had been passed over too; he was diagnosed with both a heart condition and a potential hernia. One laborer was turned down for a promotion because he had "bad kidneys, high sugar and albumen readings." All reported that their personal physicians had given them clean bills of health.

Black civil service employees were not only missing out on chances for advancement. Many, along with other nonclassified African American workers, were also being demoted or let go. In the spring of 1939, the National Park Service began to shift black carpenters, electricians, engineers, and other skilled African American employees into manual labor jobs, filling their vacated positions with whites. According to the *Baltimore Afro-American*, by February 1939 the park service was discharging two black employees every day.

Meanwhile, across the New Deal, divisions were responding to funding decreases in relief programs. Federal dollars were now being redirected into military preparedness should the United States be drawn into a war. The Senate cut $150 million out of the budget of the Works Progress Administration (WPA). The move was, in part, a jab at the president by his political foes, who intended to dismantle the New Deal. The "unholy alliance" of southern Democrats and their Republican allies made the WPA, the jewel of FDR's recovery programs, the main target of its attacks on the White House. Their beef against the WPA was twofold. First, advocates of limited government viewed it as an expensive folly that generated dependency; it exemplified the kind of liberalism and federal intervention that conservatives of both parties opposed. Second, they were convinced that the Roosevelt wing of the Democratic Party used WPA funding and jobs to leverage votes—especially black votes. While the White House denied that was the case, state-level Democratic leaders had indeed used WPA posts as patronage to ensure political support.

The forces determined to kill off the WPA discovered a powerful friend in none other than FDR's vice president, John Nance Garner. A hidebound southern conservative, he had become fed up, over FDR's two terms, with an administration that consigned him to the outer edges. Now, he came out in open support of the "unholy alliance" and personally agitated for drastic cuts to the WPA. Garner's own White House ambitions had begun to surface, and it was no secret that the vice president and his friends were determined to go further than dismantling the WPA. They believed that Roosevelt was going to seek a third term and that they could head him off by demolishing the New Deal.

Al Smith bore the brunt of the attack on the WPA. His office's mission—to furnish work relief to black Americans—made it an especially sore spot for the powerful white southern Democratic bloc. Smith's program remained one of the most effective in getting New Deal assistance to African Americans; it had become a point of pride in the black community. The WPA had provided jobs to African Americans throughout the nation. These opportunities allowed black citizens not only to get back on their feet but also, in many cases, to claim a degree of upward mobility. By offering education and training to African Americans young and old alike, the WPA empowered black neighborhoods. Because of this, the program presented a threat to southern Democrats and their allies. They continued to oppose the allocation of government resources to black citizens, fretting that the results would challenge what white society regarded as the proper place for African Americans.

Even before the second NYA conference in January, rumors that Smith's office was on the chopping block had begun to float around Washington, eventually making their way into the black press. In June, the ax fell partway. New Deal higher-ups pruned Smith's staff and eliminated his travel budget. Smith's responsibility for corresponding with black citizens requesting aid was transferred to other offices staffed by white clerks. The *Pittsburgh Courier* insisted that the assault on Smith was politically motivated, calculated to undermine the power of African Americans within the New Deal and swing the Democratic Party back under the thumb of the white South.

Never one to back down from a battle, Smith slugged back. He sent out press releases to newspapers promoting the effectiveness of his programs across the nation. In his 1939 annual report, Smith boasted: "The Works Progress Administration saved the unemployed Negro worker from privation and want, and in a great many instances from actual starvation." He claimed the WPA was readying African Americans for jobs in the private sector and the expanding defense industry. Smith asserted that his division was "the nation's best invest-ment during 1939."

Smith wasn't the only Black Cabinet member under siege. In spring, Lawrence Oxley learned that he was to be reassigned from the Labor Department to the Social Security Board. Although some of his white counterparts were also scheduled to move with him, it was much more than a transfer for Oxley. It would place him under a program known for its indifference to black Americans and would distance him from Secretary Frances Perkins and other upper-level Labor Department officials.

Oxley sent an urgent memo to the labor secretary outlining his many accomplishments, highlighting his political usefulness in the upcoming national campaigns, and pleading with her to reconsider. She did not, and in July, she sent him packing. Press releases put the best spin on his new position, announcing that it was "a well-merited recognition of the constructive service rendered by him in the field of conserving the interests and welfare of the Negro wage earner." But Oxley knew it was no step up.

The Black Cabinet also sustained the loss of some members in the first half of 1939. Bill Hastie had become exasperated in his judgeship and with the Virgin Islands' brand of racism. In February 1939, he announced he would resign and return to Howard as the dean of the university's law school. Al Smith's assistant John Whitten, without warning, received a pink slip. In the Farm Security Administration, one racial-affairs position had sat empty for months; political observers speculated that bosses there hoped that if they didn't fill it, the post would eventually disappear. Eugene Kinckle Jones's job also went unfilled; concern grew that the absence of a black adviser in the Commerce Department was setting back African American businesses. As the White House began shifting resources away from relief and toward defense, and as the next presidential campaign began to heat up, some speculated that soon there would be "wholesale dismissals" of African American racial-affairs advisers. The Black Cabinet was nearing its end, several journalists predicted.

In the summer of 1939, the Black Cabinet was further rocked by the passage of the Hatch Act, Congress's attempt to place political restrictions on federal employees. The bill's purpose was to draw a deeper divide between politics and federal jobs—to end political cronyism. It placed heavy restrictions on the dissemination of federal funds in programs where they could be used to purchase political loyalties. Designed in part to undermine the political influence of the New Deal, the Hatch Act especially targeted the WPA. Much of the bill was the handiwork of conservative Democrats still angry with Roosevelt for attempting to purge them.

Although the Hatch Act carried an antidiscrimination clause that outlawed hiring on the basis of race or political affiliation, there was little celebration for it among Black Cabinet members. The act made no provisions for the enforcement of its antidiscrimination mandate. It also threatened to suppress the Black Cabinet's activism. Specifically, it prohibited government employees from participating in political organizations or campaigns. This curtailed the electioneering of the Black Cabinet on behalf of Roosevelt and the Democrats. But there was also the possibility that it would be invoked to require the brain trusters to surrender their memberships in civil rights organizations, which were regarded as political by a number of governmental agencies, white federal officials, and white politicians. The broad wording in the Hatch Act endangered the very existence of the Black Cabinet—since the group itself could be interpreted as a political lobby.

In late summer 1939, after the Hatch Act had gone into effect, the U.S. Information Service sent a query to Mary McLeod Bethune. She was instructed to provide information about the history, purpose, and membership of an organization called the Federal Council on Negro Affairs—the formal name the Black Cabinet had adopted in 1936. Bethune's reply was short. She insisted that since the Federal Council was "an informal group of persons interested primarily in the welfare of Negro citizens in their relationship to the government," it couldn't be defined as an organization at all. If the group served any purpose, she asserted, it was to encourage efficiency in the workplace by "coordinating efforts and work of the Federal Government agencies represented in their [the council's] membership."

Some political observers worried that the Hatch Act would force Bethune, one of the Democratic Party's biggest drawing cards with African American voters, to resign from her government post so she could campaign in 1940. When confronted with the rumors, Bethune quickly dismissed them. "I am not in politics. I am here as an educator," she told the Associated Negro Press. "I am here as an interpreter of my people. I am here making contacts for them. I never make a political speech. I have never been asked to make one." And, she added, "I did not come here seeking a job, the job came seeking me." Of course, she would continue to speak on the New Deal, she assured reporters. That wasn't politics; it was her job as a government official. Would she support the Democrats in the next election? "I am in sympathy with the ideals of Franklin Delano Roosevelt," she stated. "But as far as the Democratic Party goes, I don't believe in them. I am with Franklin Delano Roosevelt as long as he holds to his present ideals."

It certainly was no violation of the Hatch Act for a federal employee to profess allegiance to a sitting president. But the new constraints exposed Bethune and other Black Cabinet members engaged in civil rights activism to another peril, that of being "red-baited"—being accused of communist sympathies and affiliations. The act stipulated that federal employees could not hold "membership in any political party or organization, which advocates the overthrow of our constitutional form of government in the United States." Individuals working for the federal government who violated that restriction were to be promptly terminated. American reactionaries, especially the southern Democratic caucus, had long attacked the civil rights movement by linking it to the radical left. They declared that communists and socialists and those who supported racial equality were one and the same. Advocating for voting rights and integration could be twisted into evidence of association with insurrectionists endeavoring to undermine the American government.

In the fall of 1939, Texas Democratic congressman Martin Dies announced he had compiled a list of more than five hundred names of suspected communists working in the government. A brazen racist who opposed FDR, the New Deal, and civil rights, Dies had assumed the chairmanship of the House Committee to Investigate Un-American Activities (later the House Un-American Activities Committee, or HUAC) the year before. Coming off a midterm election victory and planning a presidential bid himself, Dies had returned to Washington, D.C., determined to grab the public eye by hunting down all "subversives"—both fascists and communists— and preventing them from operating within the United States.

By the second half of 1939, Dies had trained his sights on the leading members of the African American community in the District of Columbia. According to the *Chicago Defender*, the congressman's list included, among others, African American activists, teachers, Howard University faculty members, and federal workers ranging from those on custodial crews to Black Cabinet members. Specifically, he alleged that Al Smith's assistant Dutton Ferguson and the Housing Authority's Charles Duke, who worked with Robert Weaver, were communists. (Both Ferguson and Duke were active in the Black Cabinet.) Several African American clerical workers, including Bethune's secretaries, Harriet West and Arabella Denniston, were also named. Eugene Davidson, whose column, The Black Cabinet in the New Deal, had brought the African American brain trust into the public eye, also found himself under investigation. But the most notable name on Dies's list was the grandmotherly, cane-wielding, devoutly religious Mary McLeod Bethune.

Bethune, Ferguson, Duke, and others found themselves in good company. Dies had also singled out the First Lady, Harold Ickes, and Frances Perkins as radicals. (Pure politics, Eleanor Roosevelt assured a nerve-racked Perkins through a friend.) When John P. Davis was called to testify, he blasted Dies for persecuting innocent Americans. If the congressman wanted to cleanse the nation of subversives, he suggested, he should spend his time prosecuting terrorist groups like the Ku Klux Klan, not those trying to better the lives of African Americans.

When his hearings concluded, Dies published the committee's findings in a flashy book entitled *The Trojan Horse in America*. In it, he sounded the alarm: communists and fascists were infiltrating all levels of American society. In a chapter devoted solely to black Americans, he argued that they were favored, unwitting targets for the radical left. "Communists believe that an appeal to racial prejudice and an exaggeration of grievances will gradually separate the two races into hostile camps and that the resulting clash will be a sort of auxiliary to the class struggle and civil war," he maintained. Asserting that the Soviets had planted black agents throughout the United States, he claimed they fostered racial intermixing at social events "arranged so that Negro men could dance with white partners"—a trick to dupe African Americans into demanding equality. Additionally, Dies alleged that "Communist Negroes" had been "placed in strategic positions in [government] organizations so that they may carry on the work of the Party under the guise of social and economic programs." To leave these malingerers—these black New Dealers—in their positions, Dies charged, put the country in danger of a race war.

When reporters sought his reaction to appearing on the Dies list, Dutton Ferguson remarked that the only thing that Dies got correct was the spelling of his name.

Although Dies failed in his attempts to openly prosecute black New Dealers, behind the scenes he would begin to pressure the FBI to investigate Mary McLeod Bethune for subversive activities and violating the Hatch Act. Whether or not she was aware of the congressman's actions was not clear. But his public accusations weighed heavily on her. Since the January conference, she seemed to grow increasingly drained. In addition to keeping the Black Cabinet moving ahead, she battled continually for increased resources for her division and to keep her college, perpetually in debt, from going broke. She also remained active in women's clubs and other programs to advance black women. In an attempt to circumvent the Hatch Act, she began to use the National Council of Negro Women (NCNW) as a cover under which she could operate politically. For civil and women's rights activities, she sent out letters on NCNW stationery and made her appearances on the council's behalf rather than as a National Youth Administration representative. But the constant work didn't seem to invigorate her as it had in the past. Her asthma had grown worse. Her famous stamina appeared to flag.

Much of Bethune's growing fatigue no doubt resulted from her constant struggle to keep the Black Cabinet unified. Under fire from all sides, with frustrations mounting, the coalition, fragile to begin with, started to weaken. For Bethune, the golden rule of cohesiveness rested on a longtime unspoken understanding in the black community—internal disputes were to be kept private; putting on the best public face and presenting a solid front was especially important when dealing with the white world. Not only did this practice promote solidarity, it protected black federal employees who could lose their jobs should their criticism of their bosses or the White House come out. Former journalist Dutton Ferguson had begun to handle public relations for the Black Cabinet and tried to help secure positive coverage for the group. But leaks regarding the brain trust's internal disagreements made it into the papers, revealing that the tide of discontent was rising and Bethune's control was slipping.

In early June 1939, after returning from the road, Bethune summoned members to meet. According to one account, the gathering was packed. The discussions remained "closed door" and the press was told it was a "purely routine" meeting. However, news that all was not well reached the public through the black press. Readers learned that Joseph H. B. Evans, an African American appointee with the Farm Security Administration, had vigorously condemned his division and its leadership. This news was a glimpse into the group's growing impatience. It was also an embarrassment that it was public.

According to press reports, black advisers' tempers flared now whenever they gathered. Members clashed throughout the summer of 1939. Bethune called a critical meeting in August to discuss whether to back Roosevelt should he run for a third term. The priority, one faction insisted, was to retain African American posts and voices in the federal government. The president must be supported, or the black federal presence would definitely end. One member disagreed. The Hatch Act prevented all present from publicly endorsing FDR—that would be politics, and they would certainly lose their jobs. Another black brain truster "blew up and read the riot act" to the group. No one should be restrained by "fear," that member contended, from taking a political position or standing up for what they believed would benefit the African American people.

Lawrence Oxley interrupted; he could not support any position put forward, he announced. It was a puzzling move, and the press speculated that his defiance was part of a scheme to dethrone Bethune. But the Black Cabinet's indomitable leader would not be ousted or derailed easily. She reasserted control. We must stand for the president, she forcefully told the group. FDR was the only option in the ongoing fight for equality.

In the end, the Black Cabinet agreed to "stand by Franklin Delano Roosevelt." The *Atlanta Daily World* reported that this was done only "half-heartedly."

Although Bethune carried the day, she had failed to restore harmony in the ranks. Skirmishes continued at subsequent meetings. Some Black Cabinet members declared they could no longer acquiesce to their New Deal bosses and openly contemplated Forrester Washington–style protest resignations. A bitter fight broke out at a November meeting, "when some members showing their uneasiness . . . spoke out of turn." Bethune scolded the group and imposed order.

The negative publicity not only indicated an upswing of internal strife within the Black Cabinet; it also demonstrated that Bethune's honeymoon with the African American press was nearing an end. She appeared now as a partisan figure, associated by her own design with the president. In turn, her close relationship with FDR increasingly transformed her and the Black Cabinet into targets. Black newspaper editors who had remained loyal to the GOP or who had become disenchanted with the president saw another opportunity to undermine the White House by running negative stories about Bethune and her Black Cabinet.

These editors included the Associated Negro Press's Claude Barnett, who had renewed his ties to the Republicans as the upcoming presidential campaign neared. In a May 1939 memorandum to the GOP, he assessed the important role black New Dealers played in the migration of African American votes over to the Democrats. "The New Deal has made use of the talents of many young Negroes in responsible governmental positions," Barnett observed. "Their activity in this regard overshadows anything which the Republicans did for decades." To counter this, the

Republicans had to undercut the black brain trust's influence. He reported that the Associated Negro Press wire service and several other black news sources were already turning out exposés on the failures of the Black Cabinet and New Deal programs. This assault needed to be sustained. "The personalities which have been selected by the administration have had halos built around their heads," Barnett asserted. "Those are being dissipated by factual reporting of their activities and exposition of their jealousies and bickerings and shortcomings. It is being done gradually and as occasion arises so as not to appear offensive."

By 1939, some African American news outlets previously sympathetic to Bethune accused her of being passive, ineffectual, and an accommodationist. One journalist reported that she had counseled her colleagues to soften their resistance to white New Deal bosses and had remarked to one disillusioned officeholder, "I have a job, so have you, why worry?" Some members of the press also turned on Bethune's Black Cabinet. The African American brain trust was "disillusioned" with the New Deal, a source claimed, and its members were experiencing "a general feeling of discomfort . . . as they see their offices shorn of authority and power with only a grandiose title remaining." They were simply "window-dressing." A Chicago publication alleged that all the Black Cabinet members cared about was their purportedly high salaries. "The sun shines and the hay-makers are industrious," it commented. "Prying them loose will be a job for Republicans upon their return but it will be a job quickly done." Retired Howard University administrator Emmett J. Scott insisted that the New Deal had been a disaster for the African American people. "With powers almost as great as those of Hitler, Stalin, and Mussolini, the Democratic Administration has winked at discrimination in the NRA, FHA, PWA, CCC, WPA, and a dozen other alphabetical set-ups," he wrote. "Worse, it has helped spread Jim-crowism over the country where it had never before existed, and Negro New Deal officeholders have approved of it by silence or hollow apology."

The shrewd Bethune knew how to play the political game just as well as anyone. For some time, she had fretted over the uptick in criticism of the Black Cabinet and negative coverage of New Deal race relations. In October 1939, she received a request from Aubrey Williams to stage a third conference. She refused. Virtually nothing substantial had been done to address the demands made by the previous two conferences, she told him. An honest meeting would only expose the shameful lack of action and result in humiliation for the Democrats and the president. What would help, she proffered, was for the White House to correct its poor record by expanding the ranks of black federal advisers and ordering the War Department to admit African Americans to military combat units. "This immediate action will prevent our having to answer many embarrassing questions which are already being posed by persons who look to us for guidance and leadership," she advised Williams. "We do not have sufficient ground to stand on to ward off the bombardment from the opposition. They see clearly the inadequacies in the numerous federal departments."

In November 1939, she followed up with a sternly worded letter to the president. The GOP was plotting to recapture African American support by pouring money into pockets of "purchasable" voters and plastering newspapers with "legitimate propaganda," she reported. The White House's ineffectual responses to black Americans, the increasing "Negrophobia" of white southern Democrats, and the failure to enact anti-lynching legislation provided fuel for the Republican crusade for black votes. She urged the president to respond immediately to the second conference's recommendations. "It is my conviction that it would be a serious mistake to believe that the Negro vote is irrevocably fixed in the Democratic ranks," she warned. "It would be equally a mistake to believe that not only the leaders of Negro opinion, but the rank and file are satisfied with the deal the Negro has received even under your administration."

The relationship between African Americans and the Democratic Party was also on Kelly Miller's mind. In his columns, Miller sounded the alarm over Republican efforts to take back the black vote. In the spring of 1939, he reported that the GOP had commissioned Ralph Bunche, an intimate of Weaver and Hastie, to study why African Americans had strayed from the party. Bunche had produced a long list of recommendations for the GOP to use in the upcoming campaign. This included appointing African Americans to key positions of federal influence, fighting for black voting rights in the South, extending civil rights to all, and pushing through an anti-lynching bill. Miller warned that if the party followed Bunche's recommendations, "the Negro will, of course, return to its former allegiance unless in the meantime the Democratic adversary is willing to call the hand of its Republican rival and do him one better." In Miller's mind, it would be a travesty if the GOP took back the black vote as well as the White House. Over the course of FDR's two terms, Miller had become a solid believer in New Deal liberalism, which he characterized as a "social gospel for the regeneration of an upset and bedeviled world."

For years, Miller had reigned as one of the last direct ties to Theodore Roosevelt's original Black Cabinet; he had witnessed the rise, the fall, and then the second rise of the group. As an elder in black politics, he had played an important role in promoting hope in the New Deal and confidence in its black brain trust. But despite his keen mind and still-vigorous pen, Miller was declining. In mid-December, he suffered a serious heart attack that left him bedridden. In an editorial published on December 23, he expressed optimism for the future. The black vote, he predicted, would be "unshakeable" from its new Democratic moorings. But he also admonished both the Democratic Party and the GOP for failing to fully support civil rights. "It is well for the Negro that the two parties are rival bidders for his support although neither party is willing to involve itself and assume the responsibility of enforcing the Constitutional Amendments," he wrote.

On December 29, 1939, six days after his last editorial ran in the *New York Age*, Kelly Miller died.

Shortly before Kelly Miller passed away, Al Smith paid the Black Cabinet pioneer a visit at his home. He asked the venerated professor what he considered to be his greatest accomplishment. According to Smith, "Miller pointed out the window and replied: 'I have planted what is now a full-grown tree.'"

With Kelly Miller's death the Black Cabinet lost its godfather, one of its biggest and longest-reigning champions. The previous year had been a rocky one for racial-affairs advisers as they wrestled with external opposition and internal disputes. As 1939 closed, the *Atlanta Daily World* reported that the group had been "held down and thwarted at most every turn." Although the future looked uncertain, Mary McLeod Bethune forged ahead. As 1940 dawned, she began mobilizing support for Joseph Gavagan's anti-lynching bill. In addition to attending House debates and almost getting thrown out for applauding one congressman's speech, she demanded the Black Cabinet join her in the fight. Bethune wasn't going to give up, and she was determined that her Black Cabinet colleagues continue by her side in the struggle to reconstruct America.

PART FOUR

Fighting on Two Fronts, 1940–1944

Chapter Ten

Keep 'Em Squirming

A T THE end of his life, Kelly Miller had become convinced that the African American vote would go Democratic in 1940, but Mary McLeod Bethune was not so sure. Early in the year, with the presidential race on the horizon, she had a long conversation with Democratic National Committee chair Jim Farley. She stressed the party's need to aggressively counter Republican propaganda and urged the speedy recruitment of an African American adviser to the DNC. Furthermore, she demanded that the Democrats make a high-profile appointment of a black public relations expert: "There is too much good which has been done by the New Deal for the Negro for us to sleep at the switch." She also met with white female Democratic party leaders and encouraged them to reach out to black women voters. The year would pass quickly. She urged the party to act expeditiously. The presidency and the Democratic majority in the House and Senate had to be protected.

During the winter of 1940, Bethune was back on the speaking circuit extolling the virtues of her National Youth Administration division, the New Deal, and Franklin Delano Roosevelt. But the four years of perpetual work and travel had taken its toll. She had visibly aged, and suffering from a persistent cough, she had grown weaker and weaker. In March, she headed back to Daytona Beach to celebrate the thirty-fifth anniversary of Bethune-Cookman College and to rest a bit. By early April, she was on the road again. A few weeks later, she returned to Washington, D.C., exhausted. Her cough had become even worse, and her asthma attacks more severe. On the advice of her doctor, she checked into Johns Hopkins University Hospital in April. It was nothing serious, the Associated Negro Press assured the black public.

The doctors had a different opinion. Chronic bronchitis and a serious, long-term sinus infection had worsened her asthma. She desperately needed sinus surgery, but she was too overweight and run-down to survive it. She would have to remain hospitalized and on a strict diet until it was safe to operate. She should expect to stay at least two months, the doctors informed her. Eleanor Roosevelt had flowers clipped from the White House gardens and sent to Bethune once a week. "I realize how much the inactivity will irk you," the First Lady wrote to her friend. The *Pittsburgh Courier* hoped she would "heed her physician's advice."

"Rest is the thing," doctors emphasized.

Bethune tried. Bouquets flowed in each day; she received "letters, cards, and telegrams from all over the country." From her window, she watched people moving about on the Hopkins campus. She listened to the radio and, she claimed, appreciated having "time for reading, meditation, and reflection."

But she was miserable. She longed to be in the thick of all the political intrigue. Times were uncertain. No one knew whether Roosevelt would run again. War was spreading throughout Asia and Europe. The U.S. government drove harder to expand its defense resources, cutting New Deal funding to increase the country's war chest.

Not everyone had recovered from the Depression, and those left behind, especially African Americans, would suffer if programs serving their communities were ended. From her hospital bed, Bethune struggled to protect the New Deal and to maintain the Black Cabinet's fragile cohesion. She dispatched orders to her assistants. She sent out missives pressuring the government to establish programs at black colleges to train airplane mechanics to serve in the expanding air corps. She ordered the Housing Authority's Charles Duke and Robert Weaver to work together and update the Black Cabinet's goals. Duke pleaded with her to relax and follow doctors' orders: "It seems that sometimes it is necessary for us to go to hospitals for needed rest."

Bethune had reason to be concerned about the Black Cabinet. For over a year, it had been on the verge of collapse. Bereft of her mediating influence, it further disintegrated while she remained sidelined; no one was willing to attempt a meeting of the whole group without her. Black Cabinet members returned to working in isolation or exclusively with their closest allies. There was little Bethune could do. In May, her physicians demanded she curtail all of her activities. An assistant arrived to sit by her side and shoo visitors away. "It was not easy to submit to the long treatment with my hands restless and mind so full of things to be done," Bethune confessed.

By late May 1940, Bethune had reportedly lost, according to the *Pittsburgh Courier*, twenty-two pounds, and doctors performed the operation. Although there were complications, Bethune was sent home in early June to finish recuperating. She announced she would be headed back to work soon. A cheery letter from Al Smith arrived: "This is to serve the double purpose of a warm welcome back to your desk and official duties and to assure you of my continued and intense interest in the [Black Cabinet's] program. . . . You must feel free to call on this office or me at any time." Sheepishly, he added a confession: he had not been working with his colleagues in the Black Cabinet. "Because of a life-long habit of working quietly and rather independently, it may appear that my spirit of cooperation flags a bit at times," he admitted. "But be assured that this is not so." Bethune invited him to come visit her at home: "You know I believe so firmly in you young men and your honest efforts in the cause you represent that my faith in you never lags."

Although Bethune hoped to spark the Black Cabinet back into action, she was only slowly regaining stamina after her surgery. But soon after her release from the hospital, she met with Eleanor Roosevelt. She handed the First Lady a memorandum that demanded not only equal opportunities for black men in the defense buildup but also the chance for black women to participate as well. Eleanor Roosevelt forwarded it to the president with the notation: "FDR— Desires and aspirations! ER."

This was more than "desires and aspirations," as the First Lady so breezily put it. Bethune recognized the gravity of the crisis sweeping the globe. She urged the federal government to draw from all resources and include all Americans as it readied the country in case of attack. It was wise counsel. In June 1940, Hitler moved into Paris, and France fell to Germany. As foreign affairs consumed more of Roosevelt's time and attention, the New Deal's three R's—relief, recovery, and reform— became lower (and lower) priorities. The president ordered the establishment of several new defense agencies, including the War Production Board (WPB), the Office of Emergency Management (OEM), and the National Defense Advisory Commission (NDAC). As the war in Europe worsened, FDR also began to shake up his cabinet, bringing in two seasoned military guns: Frank Knox, who had served as a Rough Rider under Theodore Roosevelt, was appointed secretary of the navy, and Colonel Henry L. Stimson, previously William Howard Taft's secretary of war and Herbert Hoover's secretary of state, returned to head the War Department. Both men were Republicans.

As federal dollars were channeled into defense priorities, most racial-affairs advisers found their divisions either dramatically reduced or terminated altogether. In 1940, several members of the Black Cabinet received notice that they were being transferred. Lawrence Oxley was reassigned to the Employment Security Board, a defense division within the Labor Department. William Trent, Weaver's assistant at the Housing Authority, was moved to the Federal Works Agency to consult on African American housing there. The government announced the transfers as if they were promotions to positions of more power, but the truth was quite the opposite. These new posts carried either no more or even less weight than the previous ones and placed many black New Dealers in undefined jobs in new divisions that were still in the process of being organized. Lucia Mae Pitts recalled it as a "hectic" time, when "agencies were fast organized, unorganized, disorganized, reorganized, snuffed out."

Of all of those affected, Robert Weaver probably lost most ground. The Rosenwald Fund's Will Alexander, who had been appointed to the National Defense Advisory Commission, insisted to its chief, former labor leader Sidney Hillman, that Weaver be hired to consult on defense housing and employment. Alexander presumed that Hillman would give Weaver full authority in negotiations over black employment with defense contractors. In July, Weaver accepted the NDAC position only to find his duties vaguely outlined. It turned out, as Alexander discovered, that Hillman "was very timid about the race question." The NDAC's head was convinced that big businesses would cooperate in defense preparedness only if their racist expectations went unchallenged. Hillman decided that Weaver had to be, as much as possible, restricted from acting in leadership roles.

Weaver refused to be straitjacketed and immediately begin battling to expand his responsibilities and influence within the NDAC. But it was almost as if he were starting again from scratch. By the time he left the Housing Authority, he had been overseeing a division with several assistants and a number of secretaries. At the NDAC, he was assigned to a small office and allocated funding for only one stenographer. He recruited Lucia Mae Pitts, whose agency was in the process of being dissolved. Eventually Weaver convinced Hillman to allow him to hire an assistant. He brought on Ted Poston, a widely respected journalist who wrote for the *New York Post* and *Pittsburgh Courier*.

Over in the beleaguered Works Progress Administration, Al Smith was nervous. During the previous year, he had fought to maintain African American work and training opportunities as well as to retool his division to address new realities. In a spring 1940 report, he maintained that his programs were preparing black workers to transition into the growing number of private-sector jobs. His division, Smith argued, was essential to war readiness. "Because of the necessity of strengthening our national defense, we must look to the strength of mind and body of all groups of citizens within the nation," he told the *New York Age*. "Upon what we do today for the children who will become citizens tomorrow, rests much of our hope of maintaining our democratic ideals and accomplishments." Smith predicted that a growing number of those in work relief would be "engaged in projects directly of national defense value," and many would be "eligible for special training for employment in defense industries."

Smith argued that the WPA was a training ground for the future. In his view, if his programs became synchronized with the defense buildup, the resulting new employment opportunities could be translated into long-range gains and economic stability for African Americans. Unlike most relief work, jobs in industry and in the military would outlast economic downturns and had the potential to become permanent. Even though he had often flown solo, Smith also believed that the struggle to secure equal access to federally fueled job growth demanded cooperation within the Black Cabinet. In his view, "the destiny of the Negro was in their hands."

Smith's efforts were part of a larger battle that engaged Black Cabinet members desperate to protect the New Deal from a death hastened by opposition, neglect, and distraction. As defense employment surged, American workers vacated relief jobs for new opportunities in factories and the armed forces. But defense contractors repeatedly rejected black workers. Generally, this was a product of a long tradition of racial discrimination practiced by industry bosses, but in some cases, white unions had interceded and actively blocked African Americans from new jobs.

With escalated defense spending, the country's economy finally showed the signs of a real recovery. Cuts in New Deal work relief, however, threatened to drive African Americans, who now dominated the rolls in these programs, back into a wholesale state of massive unemployment. The priority for Black Cabinet members still holding on to their posts in relief agencies was to make their programs permanent, yet that seemed increasingly less likely. The New Deal had been designed to be a temporary emergency response to the Great Depression, destined to end when prosperity returned. Furthermore, many whites had never accepted that they had to share resources with black citizens or that African Americans, because of their unique history and circumstances, merited programs tailored to their community's experiences.

The possibilities of keeping the New Deal largely intact looked increasingly grim as the GOP steamed ahead early in the presidential campaign. In June the party nominated Democrat-turned-Republican Wendell Willkie, a businessman and corporate lawyer. Generally, Willkie was regarded as a liberal, and he supported many New Deal reforms, such as Social Security, regulations on banking, and the protection of unions. But he opposed select relief and recovery programs that he believed extended the government's reach too far. Willkie had never held elective office, and he was a wild card on the issue of race. To court African Americans, the Republican Party's platform recycled Theodore Roosevelt's campaign slogan and promised African Americans "a square deal in the economic and political life of this nation." This included full civil, voting, and economic rights for all Americans, an end to lynching, and the desegregation of the military, civil service, and "all branches of the government." It was far more than the Democrats and Franklin D. Roosevelt had ever promised.

But as the Republicans rolled out their campaign, the question on everyone's mind was, would FDR run again?

Many bet that the president would not break with tradition to try for a third term. When, in late 1939, FDR's trusted valet, Irvin McDuffie, announced his departure from White House service, some insisted it was a sign that the president was preparing to retire. McDuffie seemed to confirm the speculation when he told prying reporters, "I just figured that with things as uncertain as they are, I'd better get me a regular job while the getting was good." In reality, according to the White House domestic staff, McDuffie had a drinking problem fueled, perhaps, by the stress of years of nonstop work. During the latter part of FDR's second term, Mcduffie's drinking had worsened, and on occasion he was too incapacitated to answer the president's call. Eleanor Roosevelt, whose father and brother had died of alcoholism, demanded that the president let McDuffie go. FDR finally agreed and arranged for McDuffie to take a position in the Treasury Department. The McDuffies moved out of the White House, but Elizabeth McDuffie kept her job and returned every day to work. Still, Irvin McDuffie's departure contributed to rumors that FDR's presidency was almost over.

Robert Vann had become certain that Roosevelt wouldn't run again. He wrote to Bethune in July 1940, livid over the president's refusal to meet with him to discuss "our proposal for integrating some of our people into the national defense." White House staffers had handed him off to the president's senior military aide, General Edwin M. "Pa" Watson, who hailed from Alabama. The president "was too busy" to meet, Watson told Vann. Vann insisted to Bethune that this was proof FDR was "not going to run because if he were going to run, he would find time to see people who could be of any assistance to him in getting some votes." Roosevelt was shedding "all the little annoying things," Vann ventured, so he could "retire in peace" to Hyde Park. "I feel that way about this whole thing myself," Vann admitted. "There is such a thing as getting tired of the load."

When Bethune replied, her tone sounded equally gloomy. She refrained from criticizing FDR but agreed with Vann on other points. The president seemed to be winding down. The Democrats were in disarray and drifting away from their African American constituents, she observed. The doors for social justice, civil rights, and improving black lives appeared to be slamming shut. "I really don't know what to work for," Bethune remarked wearily.

But Mary McLeod Bethune knew more than she was admitting.

Within the White House walls, the Roosevelt administration was bustling with activity. FDR remained preoccupied with defense mobilization efforts and an economy that was still depressed. Believing that the survival of the nation relied on stable and consistent leadership, the president and his advisers were orchestrating a "draft Roosevelt" movement. To assure the public that there were no pretensions toward tyranny on FDR's part, they all agreed that the push for a third term had to come from the delegates on the party's convention floor. It would not be easy. FDR had formidable challengers: vice president–turned–New Deal foe John Nance Garner and DNC chair Jim Farley, who opposed third terms, both ambitiously put themselves in the running for the nomination. When the Democrats convened in Chicago in July 1940, on the second night of the convention, with some help from Windy City pols, a spectacular demonstration for Roosevelt broke out on the floor. For over an hour, pro-Roosevelt delegates chanted "Roosevelt" and sang "Happy Days Are Here Again." It sealed the nomination for the president on the first ballot.

Roosevelt dumped Garner and picked a new running mate, Agriculture Secretary Henry Wallace. Jim Farley, an unsuccessful challenger for the nomination, stepped down from the leadership of the DNC. The loss of Farley triggered concern within the Black Cabinet and among African American political watchers. Although he never completely embraced the African American cause, he recognized the value of the black vote. Bethune had carved out a working relationship with Farley, and it had provided her with access deep into the Democratic Party core. Many speculated that with Farley gone, even if FDR won again, the Black Cabinet was through. "Following Jim Farley's swan song on Wednesday night one could hear the political gears of the Black Cabinet grating and shifting up and down South Parkway [Chicago] Thursday morning," commented one stringer for the Associated Negro Press.

While FDR's camp was in the process of securing the president's place on the ticket, Mary McLeod Bethune was doing some of her own backstage plotting on behalf of the Black Cabinet. Given her close friendship with the First Lady, Bethune must have known of the "draft Roosevelt" plan. She certainly was willing to play her part in getting

Roosevelt nominated and reelected. And she was determined to broker an early deal with the president.

Two days after she claimed to Vann she didn't know "what to work for" and two days before FDR was renominated, Bethune delivered a set of demands to the White House. They centered on African Americans and national defense. Readiness depended on the "enthusiastic support of citizens," she reminded FDR, and the "existence of racial discrimination" endangered that support. African Americans would be willing to step up to fight for their country, but they faced exclusion from and demeaning treatment by all branches of the military. They were not permitted to sign up for pilot training. Both the U.S. Army and the National Guard were segregated and refused to organize additional black units. African Americans already enlisted were denied combat training. There was growing disillusionment among African Americans as the military continued to relegate those in the ranks to "labor battalions."

In the past, White House responses, if they came at all, had been sluggish. But this time, replies to Bethune's requests came from General Watson only seventy-two hours later—notably, on the first day of the Democratic National Convention. The integration of the military was absolutely off the table, he informed her. But the administration would ask the army to organize eighteen new all-black units. Twelve would be noncombatant truck companies; the others included a field artillery regiment, an engineering regiment, two antiaircraft battalions, and one chemical field laboratory unit. Applications for the officers' corps would be accepted from African American reservists. There would be "at least one, and probably two schools for Negro pilots." In early August, Watson followed up with a letter to Bethune assuring her that the army would double the number of enlisted African American men. Furthermore, he promised that if the administration instituted a draft, black men would be called up in "the proper proportion" to their population.

Dealmaking with Roosevelt during past campaigns seemed to have produced some favorable results, and so far, negotiations looked promising. "Time to bargain with the major political parties is just prior to the election," Al Smith observed. Bethune wrote back, praising the White House's moves as "encouraging." She would hold up her end: "Our coming campaign has been most important in my mind. I am pointing all the strength and influence I have in that direction. God bless our President and give him continued courage and strength. We believe so fully in him."

Over in the WPA, Al Smith spent the summer of 1940 fighting to save his program. After his travel budget was cut, he could no longer carry out field investigations. For most of the previous year, he had guided African American programs remotely from Washington with information he collected from local WPA officials. He also had translated that data into reports and press releases broadcasting his office's successes.

As fall neared, Smith hatched a new, and risky, plan. "The government was an interesting place. Inside was very different from what it looked like outside," he remembered telling two good friends, regaling them with stories about the Black Cabinet. One was an editor for the *Chicago Defender*, and he urged Smith to start contributing a weekly column to the paper exposing Washington's underside and the state of African American affairs. "This is against regulations and I'll probably get thrown in jail," Smith responded. But mulling it over, he realized that by leaking information to civil rights organizations and African American journalists, he had already been "double crossing the government." If he could get away with it, his column would be an extension of what he and many of his Black Cabinet colleagues had already been doing for almost seven years. To protect Smith and his job, the *Defender* agreed to shield his identity. He entitled his column the "National Grapevine" and selected the pen name Charley Cherokee, a nod to his Native American ancestry. Eventually, most of his columns would end with, "Keep 'em squirming"—encouragement to his readers to fight on.

Charley Cherokee's National Grapevine began running in September 1940 and promised readers news, information, and gossip dug from the depths of the U.S. government. Each week, Smith used his alter ego to battle for the African American people. The Grapevine became a forum that allowed him to directly protest against the injustices ingrained in the Roosevelt administration as well as in American society at large. Written with a combination of outrage, sarcasm, and humor, it traveled across a wide terrain of issues, promoting African American causes and figures. On occasion Smith took on black leaders and even his Black Cabinet colleagues. He avoided detection by teasing his readers with speculation about the true identity of Charley Cherokee; sometimes he named other black journalists, his Black Cabinet colleagues, and even himself as the author. And despite his increasing disillusionment with the New Deal and its leadership, he often plugged the president and the Democrats.

One of the first issues Smith tackled was the military and its arrogance and racism. African American youth were "fighting for the right to fight," Charley Cherokee remarked. The army was, he reported, unnerved by African American enthusiasm for serving the country and was reeling over the thought of black pilots. "Gad! Sir, Negro Aviators indeed!" quipped Cherokee. War readiness had laid open the absurdity of the ideology of white supremacy: "One question mooted about in officers' clubs over Scotch and soda is whether or not to give the Negro a gun and teach him how to use it to kill white men or to leave him home with the women."

Smith also frequently promoted the Black Cabinet and its role in the fight for racial equality. Although at odds with many of his counterparts, Smith was devoted to the towering Bethune. He celebrated her as one of the "dark saints" who walked "the earth beside us." He also offered brief sketches of other African American New Dealers. Robert Weaver was "young, able, Harvardish." Edgar Brown was "determined," and it was best to "have him on your side," Cherokee advised. Lawrence Oxley, whom Smith loathed, was "energetic, bald, able speaker, self-satisfied."

Despite his respect for Bethune, Smith broke one of her cardinal rules and exposed the divisions within the Black Cabinet, likely using his columns to gain the upper hand in his disputes with his colleagues. In one column, he underscored that the African American brain trust believed that with global war escalating, "Negro workers must have more training and jobs" to have equal access to the expanding defense employment opportunities. But the breakup of New Deal agencies and the dispersal of Black Cabinet members into new and competing divisions, he revealed, had inflamed the already intense rivalries that dated back to the New Deal's earliest days. Several Black Cabinet members had become embroiled in a dispute over who should oversee the inclusion of African American workers in the defense industry, and Smith leaked the fight's details in his column. On the one side was Robert Weaver, who pushed for his office in the National Defense Advisory Commission to assume broad and absolute control. Opposing him was Lawrence Oxley, who felt he should have all the power in his post at the Employment Security Board. Smith's stance was that the WPA should be the main player. His point, and it was persuasive, was that his program had trained and placed black workers in jobs across the nation for years. But Smith was up against a wall of opposition. Weaver was a top leader in the Black Cabinet, and Oxley was a bare-knuckle political infighter. Moreover, Smith was barely hanging on at the WPA.

Smith's insight into the Black Cabinet, even if it served his own needs and resulted in damaging publicity, did keep the group in the public eye. Weekly, he tracked the individual activities and victories of its members. He did not sugarcoat internal disputes or deny that there were defeats. But at the same time, he drove home the message that racial-affairs advisers were working for African Americans. He also used his column to back the president. In September 1940, he highlighted FDR's role in the groundbreaking ceremony for the brand-new D.C. Recorder of Deeds Building. William Thompkins, who still oversaw the office, organized a home-style celebration with an old-fashioned fish fry that drew people from throughout the black community, as well as FDR. "Mr. President, every black man in America is behind you! If Hitler comes over here, we will stop him at the District line," pledged one speaker. Smith reported that the president "had a 'ball'" at the affair and even "laughed heartily when the engine of the steam shovel refused to start at his signal." Charley Cherokee did not just support the president; through his voice, Smith was able to subvert the Hatch Act prohibitions against campaigning by Black Cabinet members. He intimated that the black brain trust still backed FDR: "New Deal employees do not care for Willkie buttons or for bright young men who distribute them." He also told his readers not to forget that "Negroes used to be chased out of" Willkie's hometown of Elwood, Indiana.

Mary McLeod Bethune was also anxious to stump for the president. The team of racial-affairs advisers remained one of the president's biggest drawing cards with African American voters, and Bethune was determined to contribute to the third-term efforts. She attempted to steer around the Hatch Act but did not need to openly campaign for the president. Just her presence at meetings and community events combined with her sunny reports of the NYA's good doings served as endorsements of both Roosevelt and the New Deal.

By August, she had reemerged as the Bethune of old, racing from location to location. She made an appearance at the world's fair in New York City. She closed Chicago's Spiritual Song Festival with a dramatic reading. She gave a speech based on the book of Matthew to students and faculty at North Carolina's Palmer Memorial Institute. At a public meeting in Cleveland, Ohio, she discussed the challenges faced by African American children and teenagers and then toured NYA programs. Back in Washington, D.C., she announced that 44,700 African American youths would soon be receiving NYA jobs. "I have repeated to groups all over this land my belief that the National Youth Administration is leading the way to a new emancipation of Negro youth from the despair of denied opportunities for education, for guidance, for employment, and for recreation," Bethune declared. Her meaning was unambiguous. To preserve forward progress, African Americans needed to vote for Roosevelt.

Bethune's boldest and most strategic endorsement of the president came through press coverage that highlighted her close ties to Eleanor Roosevelt. It was a tactic that did not sit well with many campaign insiders. With the departure of Jim Farley, the atmosphere within the Roosevelt camp had changed dramatically. Harry Hopkins, who now headed the Commerce Department, emerged to lead the reelection effort. For Hopkins, the black vote was more of an afterthought than a priority. And in his ear was press secretary Stephen Early, who oversaw an Oval Office staff that remained dominated by southerners, including senior aide Marvin McIntyre. Over FDR's two terms, tensions between the First Lady and the staff had grown, especially over the issue of race. "I knew, for instance, that many of my racial beliefs and activities in the field of social work caused Stephen Early and Marvin McIntyre grave concern," Eleanor Roosevelt remembered. "They were afraid I would hurt my husband politically and socially, and I imagine thought I was doing many things without Franklin's knowledge and agreement." Indeed, Early, McIntyre, and others fumed to the president about the First Lady's sympathy for African American causes. They were particularly distressed by her commitment to the passage of a federal anti-lynching law, which they maintained would undermine Democrats' attempts to hold the white South.

Eleanor Roosevelt had become more resolute in her commitment to civil rights, and the campaign, in turn, attempted to reign her in. Later she recalled her refusal to back down from what she believed was right. "I always felt that if Franklin's re-election depended on such little things that I or any member of the family did," she wrote in her memoirs, "he could not be doing the job the people of the country wanted him to do."

Despite the hand-wringing of Early and McIntyre, Eleanor Roosevelt and Mary McLeod Bethune proudly publicized their friendship. During the fall campaign, the First Lady welcomed Bethune and a delegation from the National Council of Negro Women to the White House to discuss the challenges faced by black women. Eleanor Roosevelt joined Bethune and the NCNW at a New York meeting of A. Philip Randolph's Brotherhood of Sleeping Car Porters and Maids. When it came time for her to speak, Bethune praised the First Lady as "the personification of Democracy." The *Chicago Defender* and the *Pittsburgh Courier* ran shots of a smiling Mrs. Roosevelt posing at another appearance as she purchased a ticket for a Bethune-Cookman College fund-raising event. "I have great admiration for Mrs. Bethune and her devotion to her race, as well as her tact and wisdom in all she undertakes," the president's wife declared.

On the surface, Roosevelt and his reelection wagon rolled along merrily. But deeper down, the president's mood was serious as he watched war spread in Europe. The Germans commenced the Blitz, the relentless day-and-night bombing of London and other British cities. With the escalation of attacks on U.S. allies, Roosevelt took a drastic step and, on September 16, 1940, signed the Selective Service Act. For the first time in its history, the United States of America instituted a peacetime draft. While it was a risky move during an election year, FDR judged it necessary. "America stands at the crossroads of its destiny," Roosevelt wrote after signing the order. "A few weeks have seen great nations fall. We cannot remain indifferent to the philosophy of force now rampant in the world."

For most of August and into September, Bethune had floated the idea of having a committee of African Americans visit FDR to present its concerns about national defense. The announcement of the draft made it essential that the meeting happen as quickly as possible, and the NAACP's Walter White took the lead. Initially, he had planned for a delegation including himself, Mary McLeod Bethune, A. Philip Randolph, and Robert Vann to call on the president. After consulting with a well-placed campaign staffer, who hoped to use the visit to generate positive publicity with African American voters, he dropped Vann. Just weeks before, the *Pittsburgh Courier* editor had made his split with the Democrats formal. "We are not leaving Mr. Roosevelt," he insisted. "He has left us." He would be voting for Willkie.

Bethune also vanished from the list. Instead, her soon-to-be new aide, T. Arnold Hill, of the Urban League, was substituted. White, and possibly Bethune, had likely wagered that the political nature of the visit would put her in jeopardy of being fired for violating the Hatch Act. Hill's full-time appointment in her office had not been finalized, so he could be (and was) identified as a representative of the Urban League rather than the NYA. Still, White had regrets that Bethune would not be by his side. "I hope it will work out all right," White wrote to a campaign insider. "But I wonder if a wise choice was made in inviting Mr. Hill and not Mrs. Bethune. Mr. Hill is her assistant. There should have been a woman on the committee."

Although the campaign had seemed open, even eager, to having the president receive the group, when White attempted to schedule the meeting, Stephen Early brushed him off. The White House press secretary insisted that it would draw too much attention to the controversies surrounding race and defense and, as such, would offend white voters and put the president in an awkward position. In a letter to the DNC, Early blasted party staffers for supporting the meeting and thinking they could use it in the campaign. "The [Democratic National] Committee will keep hands off" the president's activities and election strategy, Early warned.

Roosevelt himself was doing his best to avoid the meeting by attempting to extract compromises from his military chiefs. Harold Ickes noted in his diary that FDR brought up integrating the troops at a cabinet meeting: "The President told Stimson that he was in favor of announcing that with respect to the Negroes who are conscripted, our policy will be to put them in units in proportion to their ratio in the general population, which is about ten per cent." In addition, Roosevelt made known his dissatisfaction with the military's plans to bar black draftees from combat and consign them exclusively to manual labor. African American men should be "given a chance" to join the air corps, Roosevelt argued, dismissing the objections of the Army Air Forces that black pilots would never be skilled enough to "qualify as first class aviators."

Secretary of War Stimson shot down all of the president's proposals. Using African American troops in combat would be a disaster, he insisted. He privately complained that during World War I some black soldiers in France "made perfect fools of themselves and one at least of the [black] Divisions behaved very badly. The others were turned into labor battalions." (This wasn't true; black regiments fought bravely under the French, since white U.S. military officers refused to command them.) African Americans, Stimson insisted, were fit to serve only as servants and laborers. And any suggestion of integration was absolutely out of the question.

Unable to schedule an appointment, White enlisted Eleanor Roosevelt's help. She sent a note to the president, insisting he meet with White, Randolph, and Hill to talk seriously about equal opportunities for African Americans in defense. "This is going to be very bad politically, besides being [wrong] intrinsically," she warned her husband. She advised him to sit down with the African American delegation with the intention of sincerely addressing its demands. Soon after, Walter White received a message from General Watson, confirming that the president would meet with the delegation for thirty minutes in the Oval Office. Also present would be the secretary of the navy, Frank Knox, and the assistant secretary of war, Robert Patterson. Stimson decided he was too busy to attend and was sending Patterson in his place.

On September 27, 1940, White, Hill, and Randolph gathered early, in Bill Hastie's home, to strategize ahead of the meeting. At Hill's suggestion, Hastie, along with Charles H. Houston and Robert Weaver, had distilled their demands into a memorandum that they would deliver to the president. The memo contained many of the requests that had appeared in the second Blue Book. It called for the incorporation of African Americans into all levels of military service and equal consideration for African Americans for war industry jobs funded by American tax dollars. Among other essentials was the demand that the U.S. Navy and the War Department appoint African Americans as advisers in civilian administrative posts with the authority to make and enforce policy.

At 11:30 A.M., Roosevelt welcomed White and his committee cheerfully. He had good news for them, he said. According to White, FDR then announced that "he had been pleasantly surprised a few days before by officials of the War Department stating to him, without solicitation on his part, that Negroes would be integrated into all branches of the armed service as well as service units." White was skeptical. He demanded specifics: Would more officer ranks be opened up to African Americans? Patterson replied that the War Department would appoint only African American reservists, veterans, and current members of Reserve Officers' Training Corps as officers. All others would be classified as enlisted men, regardless of their qualifications. Was this genuine inclusion, even in white combat units? White asked. Would Jim Crow be ended in all branches of the military? Together Knox, Patterson, and Roosevelt admitted that they hadn't considered either integration or using blacks in combat. It would be impossible, Patterson added. Mixing black and white recruits in southern combat regiments might put African Americans at risk. But, White observed, integration would be acceptable among troops in other parts of the nation. Patterson hesitated. The president took over, suggesting that if segregated divisions were deployed side by side in battle, the heat of battle would force the army to informally "'back into' the formation of units without segregation." Look into it, the president ordered Patterson.

Secretary Knox chimed in. Personally, he was in favor of the desegregation of American society, he stated. However, the navy would never integrate. It was unthinkable, he told the group, for blacks and whites "to live together on ships." Everyone present knew that blacks already served at sea as navy cooks and servants. How about assigning a naval band composed of black sailors to each ship as a way of building up good feelings and gradually beginning the process of desegregation? the president asked. Knox had no response.

The half hour that had been allotted for one of the most important issues facing the preparedness effort went by quickly. Roosevelt even granted the group five more minutes, but time ran out before anyone could bring up defense jobs. Staffers appeared, and White, Randolph, and Hill were escorted out.

White left anticipating a speedy announcement of new military policies that reflected at least some of the committee's requests. Yet the days began to pass, and no word came. Growing suspicious, he began to urge the administration to issue a statement. He called the White House several times, trying to reach General Watson or Stephen Early. Each time, he was told that they were either busy, at lunch, or with the president. Finally, growing anxious, White telegrammed Watson: PLEASE ADVISE IF YOU PLAN MAKING ANY STATEMENT. IF NOT, ADVISE WHAT I AM AT LIBERTY TO STATE. It was met with more silence.

White appealed to Aubrey Williams to intervene. Still the White House offered no response. Finally, Eleanor Roosevelt stepped in and secured permission for White to send out a report summarizing some of the delegation's demands. The administration required him to redact any mention of the integration of the military and a call the delegation had made for the incorporation of black civilian advisers in the War Department.

Much of the stalling was caused by FDR's struggles with his military brass. Knox threatened to hand in his resignation if the president ordered integration of the navy. Stimson dismissed any concession to African Americans as ill-conceived election-year pandering. He wrote in his diary that Patterson had described the meeting between the president and the African American delegation as "a rather amusing affair" with Roosevelt performing "gymnastics as to politics."

Finally, at an October 9 press conference, Stephen Early dropped word that the president had just approved a new War Department policy on African Americans. The armed forces would allow black men to fight and promised to provide them with some opportunities to advance as officers. But segregation would remain strictly the rule. "The policy of the War Dept. is not to intermingle colored and white enlisted personnel in the same regimental organizations," stated a press release distributed by Early. "This policy has proven satisfactory over a long period of years, and to make changes would produce situations destructive to morale and detrimental to preparations for national defense."

The new policy was a giant step backward. Segregation in the military had been the custom; now it was official. Furthermore, Early led reporters to believe that White, Randolph, and Hill had not only supported but also helped to develop the War Department's new policy. Driving the wound deeper, on the same day that Early announced military segregation would be the rule, the Congressman Joseph Gavagan's anti-lynching legislation died in the Senate after southerners threatened a filibuster. That afternoon, a group of Confederate veterans, guests of the president, performed the rebel yell, the South's battle cry, on the White House lawn.

Many in the African American community were outraged by the War Department's reaffirmation of Jim Crow. Some charged that White and his delegation had sold out the black community, and they bombarded the NAACP with letters of protest. White immediately issued denials and attempted to correct the record. Along with Randolph and Hill, he fired off a telegram to the president on October 10, insisting that the White House's actions were A STAB IN THE BACK OF DEMOCRACY and represented a SURRENDER SO COMPLETELY TO ENEMIES OF DEMOCRACY WHO WOULD DESTROY NATIONAL UNITY BY ADVOCATING SEGREGATION. White released the telegram and the delegation's original memo to all NAACP branches and African American newspapers. He demanded that Early admit he had misrepresented the African American delegation's role in discussions over the new policy and that the press secretary apologize.

Finally, after six days of silence, Robert Patterson telegrammed White offering to meet. After consulting with Thurgood Marshall and Bill Hastie, White wrote back, refusing the invitation and insisting that nothing short of an apology, a retraction, and a clarification, along with a revision in policy, was acceptable. Stephen Early then responded, urging the NAACP leader to reconsider and accept the opportunity to talk with Patterson. But, Early added, he wanted to be clear that his remarks at the press conference did not give "the impression that you had approved segregation or that you did not oppose it." He had no control over what journalists reported, and he was not going to apologize. "I do not feel, therefore," he concluded, "that the White House can be expected to correct implications for which it is not, in any way, responsible."

White was incensed, and the NAACP fired back. The organization urged African American newspapers and citizens to shower Roosevelt with objections to Early's deceitfulness and the War Department's affirmation of discrimination. The election neared, and the president should be reminded of that. "THE MOST EFFECTIVE ACTION . . . CAN BE TAKEN BETWEEN NOW AND ELECTION DAY—NOVEMBER 5," read a message from the NAACP. "THE QUICKER, THE BETTER. PROTEST! PROTEST AGAIN!!"

In the midst of this White House–generated crisis, Bethune decided to awaken the Black Cabinet. In a letter to the WPA's James Atkins, she lamented that because she had been "ill most of the year," the Black Cabinet had "not functioned regularly." But the New Deal, African Americans' equal inclusion in national defense, and the president's future were all endangered. Times now called for the African American brain trusters to reaffirm their commitment to each other and their willingness to work jointly on behalf of the African American people. Bethune personally telephoned each member of the Black Cabinet and invited them to gather on October 10 at the National Council of Negro Women's headquarters.

However, the many months of dormancy had allowed old antagonisms to fester. At the start of the meeting, Black Cabinet members immediately fell out over the prioritization of discussion topics and how to structure upcoming sessions. After the meeting, James Atkins wrote to Bethune blaming Weaver and the poker crowd for the discord.

"I would have to be charitable to speak complimentary of the rest of the talk of the 'Boys,'" whom Atkins characterized as having "the desire to be 'impressive' and to show how 'great'" they were during debate. He felt that the advice offered by the older generation, represented by William Thompkins and his allies, was far wiser. She remained optimistic, Bethune told Atkins. "Somehow I feel that our Council ought to do a lot of good," she responded, assuring him that efforts were under way to keep the group moving forward.

In the meantime, black journalists in the Republican camp used the military's new policy to pummel the president. PRESIDENT OKAYS JIM CROW, announced the *New York Age*. Willkie promised that under his administration, by contrast, segregation would "vanish." The *Cleveland Gazette* ran a front-page story titled, "Segregation! The South Shows Its Hand in the Control of the War Department." The *Pittsburgh Courier* charged that the White House's actions exposed "a sense of guilt and perhaps something worse . . . [since] the Administration felt it necessary to use the good name and reputation of Messrs. White, Randolph, and Hill to deflect" the fury of the African American community over the discriminatory policies adopted by the U.S. military. White, Randolph, and Hill, the paper asserted, were following Robert Vann's lead and "supporting the *Pittsburgh Courier's* campaign" for the equal incorporation of African Americans into national defense. To White that was probably a surprise, but he allowed Vann's assertion to stand. The newspaper editor had been diagnosed with cancer, and it was rapidly spreading. On October 24, less than two weeks before the election, the pioneering Black Cabinet member, who had become one of the administration's harshest critics, died.

Vann had steered waves of African American voters into the Democratic Party and, at the time of his death, was attempting to reverse the tide. The War Department's segregationist policies and Stephen Early's deceptive actions seemed to indicate the time had come for black citizens to swing back to the GOP. The possibility of losing the black vote induced panic in the Roosevelt camp. WPA head and FDR's chief strategist Harry Hopkins called Will Alexander to the White House for a meeting. "This fellow Willkie is about to beat the boss, and we damn well better do something about it," Hopkins declared, fretting over the potential of massive black defections. "The President has done more for these negroes in this country than anyone ever did since Lincoln," Hopkins continued. "It looks as though they are all going to go against him. You damn well better do something about that. If you care, tell me what to do." Alexander responded: White's delegation had placed demands before FDR, and they should be acted on, especially the call to place African Americans in policy-making positions in the War Department and defense agencies.

Mary McLeod Bethune offered the same advice when Eleanor Roosevelt asked her how to resolve the crisis.

It is very likely that Eleanor Roosevelt carried Bethune's message to FDR. She definitely told her husband that Stephen Early must make a public apology and correct the record on the White House meeting with White and his delegates. Roosevelt was already wrestling with a recalcitrant Early, along with the obstinate duo of Stimson and Knox. "There is a tremendous drive going on by the Negroes, taking advantage of the last weeks of the campaign in order to force the Army and Navy into doing things for their race which would not otherwise be done, and which are certainly not in the interest of sound national defense," Stimson commented in his diary. "But they are making such progress in their drive that the friends of Mr. Roosevelt are very much troubled and are asking us to do anything we can."

While Stimson may have been unhappily contemplating some compromises, on his end Secretary Knox was not. He stubbornly refused to consider appointing even one black adviser and continued to oppose enlisting black sailors, much less naval officers. Ranking African Americans as anything other than "mess men" or servants would destroy "teamwork, harmony, and ship efficiency" as well as "discipline," Knox insisted.

Knox never gave in. But Stimson did—somewhat. He approved the expansion of African Americans in the U.S. Army's officer corps. He also agreed to make some upper-level appointments in the War Department. He received three names, the result of collaboration between Walter White and the Black Cabinet. Major Campbell Johnson, a reservist overseeing Howard's ROTC, was recommended for an administrative position in the Selective Service. Colonel Benjamin O. Davis, who had just been passed over for promotion (unlike his white counterparts), was put forward for the rank of brigadier general. And Bill Hastie was identified as the most logical choice for an undersecretary's post in the War Department.

On October 25, Franklin Roosevelt wrote to White, Randolph, and Hill: "I regret that there has been so much misinterpretation of the Statement of the War Department Policy issued from the White House on October ninth. I regret that your own position, as well as the attitude of both the White House and the War Department has been misunderstood." He then listed some actions he had approved. Hastie would be nominated for an appointment under Stimson, not as an undersecretary but as a civilian aide. (It was a much lesser title but avoided the confirmation process.) The Selective Service System would call Johnson up for duty and install him as an official. African Americans would be admitted to combat units and given aviation training comparable to that of whites. Davis was not mentioned, nor was desegregating the military, and the White House made no promises to open up defense industry jobs to African Americans, but FDR did pledge that "further developments of policy" would be "forthcoming to ensure that Negroes are given fair treatment on a non-discriminatory basis."

On the heels of Roosevelt's letter came an apology, of sorts, from Stephen Early. Writing to White, the press secretary insisted:

There was no disposition or intention on my part, when I made the statement to the press, to cause you or your colleagues any embarrassment whatsoever. If the words I used have been interpreted by any newspaper writer in a way that embarrasses you or your associates, I am deeply regretful.

Still, Early went on to maintain that there was "nothing in anything that I said that could be used to indicate your approval of the policy or that either Mr. Hill or Mr. Randolph had given it their approval." Nonetheless, he assured White, he would set the record straight. With the election twelve days away, the Roosevelt campaign hoped the mess that Stephen Early had created had finally been cleaned up.

On October 28, 1940, the president, along with the First Lady, Stephen Early, and several staffers, headed to New York City for a long day of campaigning. The Democratic National Committee arranged for the president to speak in all five of the city's boroughs and at an evening rally at Madison Square Garden. Security was tight. During his 1932 campaign, Roosevelt had barely dodged an assassin's bullet. Now, in addition to the usual threats, there were rumors that the Axis powers (Germany, Italy, and Japan) had been rumbling about taking the president's life. Surrounded by five thousand New York City policemen, Roosevelt was not visibly concerned. Throughout the day, he appeared jovial—laughing, shaking hands, and smiling his way around the city. By evening, the presidential party had arrived at the rally, where in front of a cheering throng of twenty thousand, Roosevelt gave a rousing speech. Resurrecting the New Deal fighting spirit, he vowed to continue to stand up against the special interests of the rich and fight on for the people. "I should like to have it said of my first administration that in it the forces of selfishness and of lust of power met their match," he thundered. "I should like to have it said of my second administration that in it these forces met their master." The crowd roared with approval.

When the rally finished, Stephen Early rushed to Penn Station to catch the presidential train back to Washington. When he attempted to dash through security lines to board, a group of policemen blocked him. A scuffle broke out, and the press secretary kicked a patrolman named James M. Sloan. In the midst of the confusion, Early got a sympathetic police captain to wave him through.

Officer Sloan required medical attention. On top of his injuries, he was recovering from hernia surgery. A father of five, he was a decorated veteran officer. He was also one of the very few African Americans serving in the NYPD.

Reports of Early's latest offense began to circulate almost immediately. A *New York Amsterdam News* reporter followed Sloan to the hospital. According to him, Sloan alleged that Early had not only kicked him but also yelled, "Get out of my way, n----r!" The *New York Times* noted that the city's district attorney, Republican stalwart Thomas Dewey, had opened an investigation into Sloan's claims. Back in Washington the day after the rally, the White House press pool questioned Early about the incident. He shrugged it off. The officers had unjustifiably delayed him and had struck him first. When he "shoved" back, the black officer piled on. It was all overblown. He had not kicked Sloan, he scoffed; he had kneed him in the groin.

The election was just a week away, and Republicans jumped at the chance to use the incident to reclaim black votes. The Republican National Committee distributed a flyer with a photograph of bedridden patrolman Sloan warning: "NEGROES—if you want your President to be surrounded by Southern influences of this kind, vote for Roosevelt. If you want to be treated with respect, vote for WENDELL WILLKIE." Boxing champion Joe Louis, who was stumping for the Republicans, telegraphed news outlets: "If Mr. Steve Early kicked the colored policeman in New York, he pulled the foulest blow in boxing. . . . I don't see how colored people have any respect for Mr. Early after this."

Letters, telegrams, and petitions protesting Early's actions began to flow into the White House.

Early had little respect within the Black Cabinet. Bethune found him arrogant and condescending. Weaver dismissed him as "impetuous." Although she later professed to like Early, Eleanor Roosevelt deplored his "hot temper" and privately confessed that she found the attack on Sloan "distressing . . . not only from the campaign angle." Harold Ickes called for Early's resignation. Harry Hopkins insisted that would only make matters worse—Early had powerful supporters in the party, and the press secretary's departure would draw even more attention to the episode. Eventually, Early sent a letter of apology to the NYPD's commissioner and the patrolman (not naming Sloan directly) "who believes I was responsible for hurting him." Ickes blasted Early for his lack of sincerity: the letter was "trifling and grudging," hardly contrite at all.

Shortly after the Sloan incident, the phone rang at Robert Weaver's home late one night. On the other end was administration staffer Jonathan Daniels, the son of Josephus Daniels, FDR's former boss in the Department of the Navy. Early's actions gravely endangered the black community's trust in FDR, Daniels admitted to Weaver. He worried that it "could cost us the Negro vote." Could Weaver "get the boys together" immediately and compose a "stirring speech" for the president to deliver to rally African Americans back to his side? Weaver laughed. It would be hard to round everyone up on such short notice and so late at night, but he would do his best.

In truth, Ralph Bunche, Bill Hastie, and, according to some reports, Frank Horne and Ted Poston, among others, were already there, playing poker in Weaver's basement. The group tossed around possibilities and came up with a response. There would be no ghostwritten speech for the president. It was time for Roosevelt to address the requests that had been placed before him again and again. The military remained segregated. Colonel Davis had not received his promotion. The president hadn't even sealed the deal on the appointments he had promised the week before. Campbell Johnson had not been activated. Bill Hastie had delayed accepting the War Department appointment—he viewed it as more symbolic than real, and it came with the expectation he would loyally support the military's policy on segregation. "I was rather skeptical as to what [could be done by] a person with no authority of his own who I was sure the military did not want serving in the Secretary's office," Hastie later revealed.

Weaver telephoned Daniels the next morning. The Black Cabinet leader was adamant that the president had to stop talking and start acting. Only a "dramatic" announcement could begin to heal the many wounds inflicted by Early. Davis had to be promoted and fast; it would make him the first African American general in the U.S. Army. The appointments of Johnson and Hastie had to be immediately finalized. Hastie had to be permitted to accept his post with the understanding that he would be allowed to state publicly his opposition to War Department segregation. Ted Poston claimed that when Daniels heard Weaver's recommendations, he "almost fainted."

Poston also claimed that Roosevelt forced through Weaver's requests. To signal a commitment to the African American community, White House press releases went out to the black newspapers. In some black weeklies, the story of the Sloan incident ran side by side with the announcements of the appointments of Johnson, Davis, and Hastie. The *New York Age* was not fooled. It remarked that Davis's elevation in rank was "a political move to halt Negro voters" from abandoning the Democrats. Having just buried its crusading editor, the *Pittsburgh Courier* was more blunt. "Too Little Too Late," it declared. "The day has passed when colored Americans can be bribed by the appointment of two to three Negroes."

Still, winning the posts for Johnson, Davis, and Hastie was a victory that resulted from a collaborative effort by Black Cabinet members and leaders from outside of the government. Davis's promotion was historic, a milestone that came to be regarded with tremendous pride in the African American community. And the return of brilliant and principled Bill Hastie to federal service was also regarded as a reason to celebrate. "Through Hastie, we can fight toward the objective that we want," the NAACP's Roy Wilkins asserted. That objective was the integration of and fair treatment by the military—"the toughest department [on racial relations] in the whole government." Hastie's appointment also heartened Bethune. It would help the president on election day, she assured Eleanor Roosevelt. Hastie bolstered African Americans' hopes by issuing a statement after formally accepting his post. He remained and would remain "consistently opposed to any policy of discrimination and segregation" in the military. His goals were "to work effectively toward the integration of the Negro into the Army and to facilitate his placement, training, and promotion."

Two days before the election, on Sunday, November 3, 1940, Joe Louis visited Officer Sloan at his sickbed. No doubt the champ was caught off guard when Sloan confessed that he still planned on voting for Roosevelt. He bore no grudge against the president for the misdeed of another man, the officer explained. The next day, FDR signed an executive order banning the request for photographs of job applicants in federal hiring. It represented a hard-won step forward; both the first and second Black Cabinets had protested the practice. That same day, Harry Hopkins and Harold Ickes arranged for Marian Anderson to sing on the radio and endorse Roosevelt. Ickes worried, however, that her appearance was too late in the game to have much effect.

The following day, Americans went to the polls. FDR won his third term, handily beating Willkie in the electoral college and taking 54.7 percent of the popular vote.

Kelly Miller had been correct. Roosevelt and the Democrats had held onto the African American vote. Despite the missteps and insults, in most areas, FDR's percentages among black voters were the same as they had been in 1936. In some communities he had captured even more black votes. Despite years of neglect in the New Deal, compounded by Stephen Early's shocking behavior, the 1940 campaign transformed black voters from crossover Republicans into habitual Democrats.

The last-minute appointments of Hastie, Johnson, and Davis, pushed by the Weaver wing of the Black Cabinet, certainly helped draw black citizens again to Roosevelt. But there was also a perception that Franklin and Eleanor Roosevelt floated above the sins of the New Deal and the administration's staffers. As deeply flawed as they were, FDR and the New Deal had provided African Americans with more substantial assistance and more cause for hope than had ever been tendered by any previous administration. In the minds of many, Willkie represented big business and the other interests that triggered the nation's worst economic crisis. In contrast, Roosevelt still appeared to be a man of the people who had rescued the country from certain disaster. "Election day witnessed an uprising of common folks. Folks like you and me," Charley Cherokee wrote, reflecting on the 1940 election. "The little man was bigger when he spoke with a concerted voice. Hooray, for Democracy!"

Chapter Eleven

Mobilization

IN JANUARY 1941, the uncertainties of war loomed over the nation as Franklin Delano Roosevelt prepared to take the oath of office for the third time.

War was on Mary McLeod Bethune's mind. Up to the day of the election and throughout the weeks following, Bethune pressured FDR to make African American appointments. Black reserve officers must be called up immediately, she insisted. Colonel West Hamilton, a World War I veteran, should be given a post as quickly as possible. Civil rights attorney Hubert Delany was a loyal black Democrat, and he deserved a judgeship. She enlisted Eleanor Roosevelt to help her lobby. "What about these requests?" the First Lady jotted on a memo to her husband. Eventually Delany was seated as a family court judge in New York City. Colonel Hamilton was given the command of the 366th Infantry Regiment at Fort Devens, Massachusetts. In mid-December, the White House announced that the first black reserve officers had been called up from the District of Columbia. Three were assigned to Fort Dix, New Jersey, and six graduates of Howard University's ROTC were sent to Fort Benning, Georgia.

As 1941 dawned, Al Smith also saw some postelection compensation come his way. After two years of drastic cuts, funds began to trickle back into his office at the WPA (now called the Work Projects Administration), allowing him to begin rebuilding his staff, though the new resources fell far short of his needs. While white employees were quickly leaving the WPA for new defense jobs, Smith estimated that more than fifty thousand of their African American counterparts had been passed over for the growing opportunities in the federally subsidized industrial workforce. He protested to his superiors, but they gave him the cold shoulder. He took to his typewriter and, as Charley Cherokee, pounded away: "Negroes are getting some jobs, but damn few and mostly of an unskilled and temporary nature."

Over in his office, Robert Weaver was also pushing for defense jobs for African Americans. But he immediately ran into a major setback. Early in 1941, the White House designated his new agency, the National Defense Advisory Commission, for termination. Weaver and Lucia Mae Pitts followed Sidney Hillman over to the Office of Production Management (OPM). In just over four years, Weaver had served in four agencies, and this move was disheartening. Working with Hillman, who remained fainthearted when dealing with race relations, was frustrating. Later, Weaver would praise Hillman for bureaucratic smarts but lament that his boss failed to apply those skills in "getting action on Negro training and employment."

As 1941 opened, Bill Hastie began to settle into his new job in the War Department and build his staff. Among his new hires was the Chicago attorney Truman Gibson, who had fought against Windy City residential segregation on behalf of the Hansberry family in a local milestone case. Hastie decided to confront the military head-on; he and Gibson would work side by side to conduct a sweeping investigation of racial discrimination in the U.S. Army. Gibson became a poker night regular and remembered that with the world situation deteriorating, the discussions were somber: "Amid the haze of cigarette smoke, the clinking of ice in the drinks, and hand after hand of five-card stud, the table talk returned time and again to exploring avenues to influence federal policy on African Americans in the military." Gibson later recalled that Hastie and Weaver lectured him on the "duty, responsibility, and challenge" that came with being a Black Cabinet member.

The opening weeks of 1941 found the *Pittsburgh Courier*'s staff members still mourning the loss of their leader, Robert Vann. Jessie Vann, his wife, had a plaque memorializing her husband cast and hung in the *Courier*'s foyer; it read: FEARLESS CHAMPION OF RIGHTS. She spent the weeks following his death sitting in his desk chair in the stillness of his office. But as the New Year dawned, she decided that grieving alone was no way to honor her husband. She must carry on his work—African Americans must be treated equally in the rapidly multiplying defense programs. On January 4, 1941, the *Pittsburgh Courier* issued an urgent call to African Americans: "Prove that you love your race." It called for them to join the National Committee for Participation of Negroes in National Defense. A newly founded organization spearheaded by the *Courier* to demand that African Americans be hired in the defense industry, its supporters included, among others, Mary McLeod Bethune, Robert Weaver, and Bill Hastie. The *Courier* urged African American communities nationwide to organize mass protest meetings. "Negroes are being pushed further and further from all kinds of jobs," the paper warned. "The Federal Government won't help him [the black man]. The Unions won't help him. Industry and business spurn him. THE BLACK MAN HAS GOT TO HELP HIMSELF. That means YOU!"

The winter days of 1941 seemed long and grim. At home, Americans had suffered through eleven straight years of depression. Abroad, fascism had marched through Europe and was moving deeper into North Africa. Japan pushed into Asia and the Pacific. Uncertainty hung heavily over the nation.

On January 20, 1941, as a bundled crowd waited for the inaugural parade to begin, loudspeakers blared out a radio report that Adolf Hitler had met with Benito Mussolini. Once the procession began, Roosevelt sat stern-faced. There were no floats and no hometown bands. Instead, General George C. Marshall, the army chief of staff, escorted by the Fort Myer, Virginia, African American cavalry regiment, headed up wave after wave of soldiers and sailors marching to military cadence. The only reminders of the New Deal were the detachments of WPA, National Youth Administration, and Civilian Conservation Corps laborers. Reportedly, the president beamed his famous smile only twice: once when he caught sight of the CCC youths, and again when the WPA, consisting mostly of African American workers, stopped by the stand and saluted him by waving their caps. Otherwise his demeanor was solemn. During his inaugural message, the president weighed the seriousness of the times. A threat to the country's "spirit"—to its Democratic system—was spreading across the globe. Americans must make "every sacrifice" they could for "the cause of national defense." Now was the time to join together and pledge to "protect and perpetuate the integrity of democracy."

On February 1, 1941, just as Roosevelt's third term got underway, the *New York Age* reported that a gang of white laborers working on a defense project in Jacksonville, Florida, attacked and killed a black coworker. Someone had stolen the victim's shovel, and he was bludgeoned to death when he demanded it back. Several days later, the *Pittsburgh Courier* reported the death of a handcuffed black prisoner at the hands of a New Orleans policeman who was transporting him for trial. The officer insisted that he had been forced to shoot the detainee, who had, allegedly, instigated "a scuffle." A few weeks later, the press noted the death of Paul Mayo, a private in the black Tenth Cavalry unit stationed at West Point, New York. A white commanding officer explained that he had reprimanded Mayo for being disruptive, and the private had swung a belt at him. He was acting in self-defense, the officer claimed, when he shot Mayo dead. A local court ruled the death a justifiable homicide. At Fort Benning, Georgia, Private Felix Hall went missing. He was later found dead, hanging by a rope, with his hands and feet bound. Military police ruled Hall's death a suicide, though it bore all the telltale signs of a lynching. Protests followed. Investigators responded: the case was closed.

It was hard to reconcile the president's lofty calls for American solidarity with the continued brutalities and injustices perpetrated by police and other authorities against black Americans. Rather than compelling whites to acknowledge and correct racism's sins, the country's leaders expected African Americans to accept without protest—indeed, as part of their patriotic duty—discrimination, racial violence, and disenfranchisement. The burden of national unity fell on the shoulders of black citizens.

Serious external threats to democracy and disingenuous attempts at national consensus building accelerated the struggle for equal rights. Roosevelt and other white leaders attempted to contrast the United States with Nazi Germany. But the nation's refusal to take action against discrimination, to halt racial violence, and to denounce white supremacy laid bare the contradictions on the U.S. home front. In turn, in 1941 activism blossomed in black communities across the nation.

This rise in militant resistance to inequality took on various forms. In Chicago, Ernest Calloway refused his summons to serve in a segregated military. "When the United States Army denies me or any other Negro the right and opportunity to make an equal contribution to the welfare and defense of my country, it violates a basic right guaranteed to me by the Constitution," he told his draft board. Conversely, when black applicants showed up to register at a New York selective service office, they were all rejected. The NAACP branch there demanded that the decision be reversed. Protests extended beyond discrimination by the military. Black citizens in Raleigh, North Carolina, rallied to oppose the construction of a Jim Crow entrance at the city's new bus station. In Saint Louis, when blocked from federal jobs as carpenters and construction workers by a white union, African American carpenters took their grievances directly to government authorities. In Washington, D.C., Bill Hastie's wife, Alma, and his mother, Roberta, picketed a Safeway store that refused to hire African American clerks.

However, union leader A. Philip Randolph's efforts to mobilize the grassroots eclipsed all others. As the nation's top black labor leader, he had garnered deep respect for successfully unionizing black railway workers. He drew from Mahatma Gandhi's philosophy of nonviolent direct action, leading many to compare him to India's renowned leader. In a resonating voice, Randolph mesmerized audiences with appeals to the high ideals of social justice. Al Smith dubbed him "St. Philip," and Mary McLeod Bethune praised him as "gallant and courageous." (Randolph was a Bethune-Cookman alumnus and a longtime acquaintance.) Over the years, using strikes, collective bargaining, and people-driven protests, he had won important victories for his Brotherhood of Sleeping Car Porters and Maids.

In late 1940, just after the election, Randolph and his lieutenant, Milton Webster, climbed aboard a southbound train in Washington, D.C., and took their seats in the Jim Crow car. Randolph was pensive. Reflecting on his experiences as a member of the team that took black grievances directly to FDR the previous fall, he had decided that working within the system was ineffective. Nothing had been accomplished in terms of getting African American workers defense jobs. Dealing directly with "top representatives in government who could do something about racial biases" had been a waste of time. He felt that Roosevelt and his circle had no intention of addressing "many of the basic problems" that perpetuated racial oppression. He had begun to rethink his approach, Randolph told Webster. The struggle could not be carried forward solely by negotiations between black leaders and white power brokers. Rather, it must rise from and be fueled by the people.

If the Roosevelt administration did not immediately open up equal opportunity to African Americans, Randolph vowed to call for all black citizens to rally and march in Washington, D.C., on July 1, 1941.

As Randolph envisioned it, the March on Washington would be a peaceful demonstration—a "pilgrimage"—channeling the power of the masses to force the U.S. government to include African Americans in the defense industry, the pool of government jobs, and the military. Since it was clear that Congress would refuse to act, the goal was to force FDR to mandate antidiscrimination through executive order.

Randolph acknowledged the serious threat of fascism and believed the global crisis made a swift response imperative. But he stressed in his call to protest that "there can be no true national unity where one-tenth of the population are denied their basic rights as American citizens." In the past, other dispossessed Americans, including the poor, woman suffrage activists, and veterans, had marched on Washington. With threats of totalitarianism hanging heavily over the world, it was black Americans' turn to take their case directly to the nation's seat of power.

Randolph's proposal rapidly gained support, and he received endorsements from a variety of civil rights organizations as well as black leaders, including Black Cabinet confidants Walter White and Ralph Bunche. Journalist Eugene Davidson joined the march's steering group. The *Pittsburgh Courier*'s National Committee for Participation of Negroes in National Defense offered its backing. Chapters of what became known as the March on Washington Movement sprouted across the country. The predicted number of participants grew quickly from ten thousand to fifty thousand and then to one hundred thousand.

The march presented a serious dilemma for the Black Cabinet. On the one hand, Randolph's objectives complemented those the group pursued. But Randolph's aggressive approach diverged drastically from the Black Cabinet's strategies based on conciliatory, gradual, and hushed internal political maneuverings. Although he praised racial-affairs advisers as "honest, able, and courageous," Randolph believed their tactics lacked the potency necessary to force concessions from the federal government. Bethune, Weaver, and Hastie had all agitated for change in the military and in industrial hiring practices, yet "Negroes got no jobs," Randolph maintained. "The March-on-Washington was the last resort of a desperate people who had failed to get decisive results in the form of jobs in national defense through conferences, petitions, and appeals to leaders of government and private industry."

The proposed march triggered a debate within the Black Cabinet that divided the already fractured group even further. Several racial-affairs advisers immediately distanced themselves from the march. For them, Randolph's proposal was too extreme and too drastic. Exposing FDR's shaky record on race would undermine the White House and the president's reputation with black voters. Additionally, unveiling black discontent would imperil national unity during a time of cataclysmic global upheaval. Most Black Cabinet members had avoided open confrontation and some worried the march might create hard feelings and trigger a reduction of African Americans in the federal ranks.

Other Black Cabinet members insisted Randolph's plan could possibly result in "a fiasco." What if the demonstration failed to draw a critical mass of participants? some asked. Others worried it would actually attract the promised numbers and it might "get out of hand." Some insisted there was nothing to discuss. The Hatch Act precluded their support for an action so clearly political in nature. D.C. recorder of deeds William Thompkins pronounced the proposed march a folly and hit the road to speak out against it.

Among those leery of the March on Washington was Bethune. Protective of the president, as well as of her position with the White House, she insisted that the march would damage the administration, alienate white allies in the federal government, and set back the civil rights struggle. Bethune fought fellow members of the National Council of Negro Women (NCNW) who wanted the organization to officially endorse the march. She also tangled with Randolph, insisting that putting the spotlight on black Americans' discontent would hurt military preparedness. Randolph responded that national defense and unity could be secured only when African Americans asserted and won "their rights as equals with the white people in this country."

By May 1941, NCNW leaders had convinced Bethune that she had to support the march. In African American communities nationwide, the march had achieved sweeping popularity, and Bethune must have realized she had too much to lose by continuing her opposition. Consequently, she gave the march one of its biggest strategic boosts. In mid-May 1941, Bethune announced that the annual NCNW conference would be held from June 28 through June 30 in the District of

Columbia. "The hour has come for thought and action on the part of the womanhood of our country to the end that the Negro may participate fully in all phases of the National Defense program," she declared. Although she stopped short of a full public endorsement of the march, she had now positioned thousands of black women in Washington, D.C., to participate the day after their conference ended. At the same time, Bethune began working behind the scenes with Eleanor Roosevelt to head off the demonstration.

Like Bethune, Al Smith refrained from publicly endorsing the March on Washington Movement. As a part of the fragile WPA, Smith had to tread carefully. But that didn't stop Charley Cherokee, who plugged the demonstration in his columns. The movement was growing fast, he contended, updating readers as Randolph's plans unfolded during the spring. "An orderly march of protest in the nation's capital by a goodly representation of a tenth of the nation, will be impressive," he asserted. "[It] puts the world's model democracy in an uncomfortable position."

However, Bill Hastie not only openly supported the march, he helped plan it. Refusing to be intimidated by the Hatch Act, he had remained an active member of the NAACP's Washington, D.C., branch, which was the local lead organization for the March on Washington Movement. Additionally, he chaired the NAACP's National Legal Committee and, in that capacity, provided Randolph with counsel and advice. In May, Randolph announced that whites would be banned from participation, explaining his intention was to protect the demonstration from being taken over by white communists, who might use it for their political ends. The march must, Randolph emphasized, demonstrate the power of black self-determination. Hastie and Charles H. Houston objected. The District of Columbia's NAACP would pull out if the march did not welcome whites, they warned. "Exclusion of white people solely on the ground of race would be the color bar in reverse, the very thing you have fought against so long," Houston wrote to Randolph.

The March on Washington continued to gain momentum and generate excitement. Randolph's approach empowered African Americans around the nation; the movement felt fresh and energetic. "In this period of power politics," he told followers, "nothing counts but pressure and still more pressure, through the tactics and strategy of broad organized aggressive mass action behind the vital and important issues of the Negro." In various areas of the country, local March on Washington committees staged mass meetings, and black citizens began preparing for the trip to the capital. The march received broad endorsements from many black journalists and newspapers.

Of course, Randolph and others reminded the president, the march need not happen if the White House enacted broad reforms regarding African Americans and defense.

Although many applauded Randolph for igniting a new spirit of African American assertiveness, Al Smith insisted that the Black Cabinet deserved a good share of credit for laying its groundwork. "Orchids for the Negro Brain Trusters in Washington, those government executives sometimes referred to inelegantly as 'The Black Cabinet,'" wrote Charley Cherokee as the March on Washington neared. "Due mainly to their alertness, Negroes are at least waking up and fighting before they get left out of things rather than after, as has been the custom." This proactive approach had become the hallmark of those who worked from inside. Without the Black Cabinet to check the actions of Washington policy makers, Charley Cherokee pointed out, the government would have crafted programs and laws that deliberately institutionalized racism and federally protected Jim Crow. "The general practice was to detect potential injustices before they crystallized, and adjust inequalities before they were perpetrated," recalled Pauline Redmond Coggs, who worked under Bethune at the National Youth Administration. Although the Black Cabinet had been weakened over the previous year, Al Smith claimed that it continued to be "a powerful force both actually and potentially."

While the Black Cabinet may have been just as important for the government actions that it blocked as for the change it instituted,

Smith's appraisal of its collective power was certainly overstated. All new racial-affairs advisers were welcomed into the group, and by June 1941, membership in the Black Cabinet had reached nearly fifty. But the group existed mostly in name only. Collaborative efforts among the whole had evaporated, to a great degree because Bethune had been sidelined or unavailable. In the winter of 1941, illness forced her to retreat to Daytona Beach, and once she recovered, her travel itinerary kept her away from Washington for long stretches of time. Weaver made one attempt to chair a meeting in her absence, but hard feelings flared, and the session ended badly. As a result, throughout the year, members of the black brain trust retreated even further into their cliques, which, according to Charley Cherokee, were multiplying as the group's membership expanded.

At the same time, challenges to the Black Cabinet were proliferating, as core members fought off new forms of discrimination taking hold in federal war-readiness efforts. Bill Hastie took on the biggest and hardest fight as he relentlessly pressed the military to desegregate, even while being regularly demeaned by his bosses. Stimson condescendingly referred to Hastie as a "rather decent Negro." When Hastie pushed the secretary on the incorporation of African Americans into the air corps, Stimson sniffed back, "Mr. Hastie, is it not true that your people are basically agriculturalists?" Additionally, lower-level administrators blazed with open resentment against the military's only racial-affairs adviser. Hastie served the NAACP, not the War Department, they alleged. His goal, insisted one, was "to advance the colored race at the expense of the Army." When Hastie and Gibson were assigned to offices in the Munitions Building, some of the military brass there complained. The chief of staff of the army, General George C. Marshall, dismissed those objections. He also instructed aides to route all African American–related affairs through Hastie's office. Nonetheless, War Department officials ignored Marshall's order and routinely marked "not to be shown to Judge Hastie" on racial-affairs memos.

When it came to African American equality, both the army and the navy continued with their bitter opposition, leaving FDR hesitant to pressure either Henry Stimson or Frank Knox on desegregation. He feared that the two, both Republicans, might resign, hindering his efforts at bipartisanship and readiness. As Robert Weaver later observed, the president continued to hold back when it came to civil rights: "If he could have done it without losing other things, he might have done it, but if it meant losing something that he held up as a greater importance, he would hesitate to do it." In 1941, with war spreading, the white military brass steadfastly clung to its discriminatory racial traditions. Roosevelt was willing to tolerate Jim Crow in the military to appease Stimson and Knox and retain them in their positions.

However, defense industry employment was different. Unlike the military, defense contractors were not represented by cabinet secretaries. Big businesses' intense desire for a piece of the expanding federal budget and their need for labor provided an opening for the administration to pressure them to discard enshrined discriminatory hiring practices. FDR had hoped that Robert Weaver's inclusion in the Office of Production Management under Hillman would somehow appease Randolph and other March on Washington leaders. Likely with some prodding from Weaver, Hillman agreed to circulate a letter to all government-funded industries instructing them to include African Americans in their hiring pools. Bias against African American labor, Hillman wrote, was "extremely wasteful of our human resources and prevents a total effort for national defense."

Hillman's order seemed like a step forward. But in practice it did almost nothing to halt discrimination or alleviate black concerns. It lacked any specifics on enforcement or penalties for continued racial bias in hiring. Hillman's OPM cochair, William S. Knudsen, was fresh from his job as president of General Motors, a company notorious for discrimination. He refused to cosign the letter. So did other businessmen when asked to endorse the policy. Some African American political observers dismissed Hillman's missive as a meaningless publicity stunt.

Weaver fought with Hillman regularly over African American employment. Joined by Will Alexander, who was also working at the OPM, he pressed Hillman to demand that all defense contracts carry enforceable antidiscrimination clauses. But the OPM head consistently evaded his requests. Repeatedly, Weaver and Alexander forwarded examples of brazen prejudicial treatment of African Americans in industry to Hillman's office. There was no response, while, as Alexander recalled, "the complaints kept piling up."

Weaver not only had to wrangle with Hillman, in the field he had to coax business and factory owners to sign agreements that guaranteed that African Americans would be hired in fair proportion to the population. He met substantial defiance. Defense employers offered a long list of excuses for excluding African American workers. Black people did not possess the skills required for industrial jobs. Whites resented laboring side by side with them. Integrated workforces would hurt morale and slow down manufacturing. Most unions excluded black workers, and legislation prevented employers from hiring nonunion labor. "You almost never see Negroes in aircraft factories," *Fortune* magazine observed. "There is little concealment about the anti-Negro policy." The NAACP reported that one Kansas City aviation firm candidly admitted it had no intention of hiring black workers, "except as janitors."

Like other administration chiefs, Hillman viewed his racial-affairs adviser as little more than an advance man to promote the Roosevelt administration in black communities. Weaver gave interviews, released reports, and spoke to African American audiences around the nation on defense employment. Although he had begun his career as the pride of the black community, over the years the veteran Black Cabinet leader was increasingly viewed as a tool of the White House. Outspoken Howard University historian and civil rights activist Rayford Logan charged that Weaver and Bill Hastie not only were ineffective but were impeding the fight for equal treatment. "I fully endorse the appointment of these men, who are all personal friends of mine," he told an audience in Philadelphia. "But I feel, as do several others in Washington, that they are just being used as 'barriers' against 'pressure groups.'"

Weaver was determined not to allow himself to become a lackey for the administration and Hillman's OPM. He worked harder than ever, pounding on the doors of businessmen and factory owners, demanding they hire African Americans. In the spring of 1941, he reported some progress. In Joliet, Illinois, a factory manufacturing armaments agreed to set aside 15 percent of its positions for black applicants. A shipbuilder in Pennsylvania promised that 10 percent of his workforce would be African American. A remarkable 50 percent of the laborers at a Montgomery, Alabama, munitions plant were African American. (The downside to that news was that munitions jobs could be very dangerous.) Weaver also convinced Bell Aircraft to hire a few black construction workers and to accept African Americans at its vocational school. Curtiss-Wright, one of the larger airplane manufacturers, was employing only six black workers. But, Weaver pointed out, two were engineers, and the company also had accepted six African Americans into its training program. Weaver argued that the doors of industry were starting to open, but he also acknowledged that there was a long way to go.

Weaver later maintained that he used the threat of the March on Washington in his negotiations with defense contractors as a way to force them to hire African Americans and sign antidiscrimination agreements. Although at the time he remained publicly silent about the march, he later claimed he had quietly supported it and had kept close tabs on Randolph's movement. It must have been a topic of conversation with Bill Hastie and Charles H. Houston during poker nights. Additionally, Weaver later revealed he had supplied the March on Washington Movement with information on discrimination in industry that Randolph used to pressure the government. He also ordered his staff to conceal a portion of his office's achievements and to downplay successes. Too much good news about African American private-sector employment would give politicians more ammunition to use against the remnants of the New Deal. The worse the situation for black Americans appeared, the more Randolph and his movement could put the squeeze on the president for inclusion in the government's defense initiatives.

Eleanor Roosevelt knew A. Philip Randolph and thought well of him. With Bethune at her side, she had appeared at a meeting of the Brotherhood of Sleeping Car Porters and Maids in 1940. The First Lady and the black labor leader had different political approaches—she was a flag bearer for the liberal Democrats, and Randolph was a committed socialist—but they respected each other, and she admired him. Still, Eleanor Roosevelt regarded the March on Washington as ill-advised, and she became determined to make sure it didn't happen.

In late May, Sidney Hillman received an invitation to have lunch at the White House with the First Lady. Several other high-ranking administration chiefs would be there, including Aubrey Williams, she told him. She would send a car.

On May 29, 1941, Hillman waited in front of his office building for the White House chauffeur to pick him up. He was joined on the sidewalk by Robert Weaver and Will Alexander. When the car appeared, Hillman climbed in; much to his surprise, so did Weaver and Alexander. The First Lady had invited them too.

Lunch was in the White House dining room and was served by a team of African American butlers. The First Lady ate rapidly—as she usually did—and immediately got down to business, asking Aubrey Williams to report on the state of black employment. The situation was dire, he stated. Many African Americans had failed to recover under the New Deal. Now they were being left further behind by job discrimination in the war effort. "I'm interested in this employment. How are the employment things going in the defense industry?" the First Lady asked, as she turned to the OPM head. "Mr. Hillman, what do you have to say?" Hillman hesitated: "Well, I'm sure Dr. Alexander and Dr. Weaver won't agree with me. We haven't agreed on it." The First Lady grew impatient. "Well, go on and state your position so they can state theirs," she urged. Contrary to Williams's assertions, Hillman announced, all was well for African Americans in defense employment, at least in his agency.

The First Lady asked Weaver and Alexander for their impressions. "We disagreed strongly with him," Weaver remembered. There were numerous cases of prejudicial treatment of African Americans who sought defense work, Weaver told her. In his opinion, racial bias in the defense industry could be remedied only by "writing into the contract a nondiscrimination clause and requiring the contractors to enforce it." Despite some who suggested that the clauses created "difficulty," the reality was quite the opposite. They had been used successfully in New Deal housing contracts in two agencies, and there was no evidence they had negative results. And, Weaver suggested, with Alexander backing him up, rather than mandating equal opportunity on a contract-by-contract basis, fair treatment could be most powerfully instituted by an all-encompassing executive order.

Eleanor Roosevelt was satisfied. There was "some validity" to Weaver's argument, she observed. The president, she assured those gathered, was unaware of how bad conditions were for African Americans and the internal debates over racial prejudice in defense employment. She promised to bring the idea of an executive order "to his attention."

A few weeks later, in a meeting with Randolph, Walter White, and Aubrey Williams, Eleanor Roosevelt tried to convince the March on Washington leadership to call off the protest. (Reportedly, White House military aide General Watson despaired when he heard Williams was again present: "Hell, Williams will join them.") Randolph held his ground, refusing to call off the march unless the White House took definitive steps to stop discrimination through an executive order. We must lay the case directly before the president in a meeting, he insisted. Walter White observed that "with her usual honesty," Eleanor Roosevelt responded, "I think you are right." She promised to do what she could.

By June, with a little help from Bill Hastie pressuring the War Department from within, the meeting was on. Nonetheless, Secretary of War

Stimson was readying himself to reject Randolph's proposals, especially those regarding the integration of the military. Stimson ordered Hastie to compose a memorandum that he could use to prepare for the meeting. Hastie's brief was frank and matter-of-fact. He informed Stimson that he had spoken with Randolph, and because of "the failure of the President to take any coercive action with reference to racial discrimination" in the defense industry, the military, and federal employment, the march was going to happen. Be ready, Hastie counseled Stimson, to accept the consequences of inaction. In the absence of an executive order, all the White House and the military could do was seek more information about the march to prevent any "untoward incidents." The War Department needed to be prepared to call up Fort Dix's African American National Guard unit to oversee crowd control, he advised. Like most in the black community, he knew that the Washington, D.C., police department was dominated by white southerners who would not hesitate to take out their racial resentments on black marchers.

At two o'clock, on June 18, 1941, A. Philip Randolph and Walter White were ushered into the West Wing. In Roosevelt's office they found the president, Stimson, Robert Patterson, Knox, Hillman, and Knudsen, along with Aubrey Williams and Anna Rosenberg, who acted as a special adviser to the president. Randolph and White opened the meeting demanding the desegregation of the U.S. military. Both Stimson and Knox fought back, citing their usual reasons that integration was impossible. The president interrupted—his main concern was the March on Washington. "Walter," he said, "how many people will *really* march?" White assured him that the number would be large, at least one hundred thousand, if not more. "The President looked me full in the eye for a long time in an obvious effort to find out if I were bluffing or exaggerating," White remembered.

Then Roosevelt said, "What do you want me to do?"

Randolph made a moving appeal for an executive order to end the prejudicial and unfair treatment of African Americans in the defense industry.

After forty-five minutes of debate, FDR gave in. He dispatched the group to draft an executive order for him to sign.

On June 25, 1941, Roosevelt signed Executive Order 8802. It outlawed discrimination in hiring by the federal government and by defense contractors. Bias against anyone on the basis of "race, creed, color, or national origin" was outlawed in "all departments and agencies of the Government . . . concerned with vocational and training programs for defense production." A grievance board, known as the Fair Employment Practices Committee (FEPC), would investigate and adjudicate complaints of discrimination lodged against both defense employers and government agencies. All government contracts issued for defense work would carry antidiscrimination clauses.

The order failed to desegregate the military; Stimson and Knox were absolutely unyielding on the issue. It did offer progress on the job front, and from Randolph's view, that was the March on Washington Movement's top priority. But to keep the White House on notice, he announced that the march was "postponed," not canceled. He assured followers that it remained an option, especially should the administration renege at any point on its part of the deal.

Executive Order 8802 was widely celebrated in the African American community as a milestone. Kansas City's *Plaindealer* praised FDR for using the power of his office toward "a more definite approach to eradicating some of the political and social evils practiced and enforced against Negroes." It was black America's Magna Carta, some claimed. Mary McLeod Bethune sent an effusive letter to Eleanor Roosevelt. "I was most happy that we were able to ward off the March on Washington," she wrote, thanking the First Lady for her efforts. "Not since Abraham Lincoln spoke on the memorable day of the emancipation of the slaves has such a far-reaching Executive Order come forth for the benefit of my people." As she traveled the country, Bethune announced that "a new day is dawning" and urged audiences to seek out the opportunities promised by 8802. At one appearance, she assured a student group that "in spite of past disappointments we will be needed, and we must prepare ourselves. Our chance is coming here and now."

Bethune and other Black Cabinet members had reason to hail 8802. The president had finally imposed a federal order that explicitly outlawed the racist status quo, capturing many of the black brain trust's long-fought-for goals in policy and practices. Born out of the pioneering work by Weaver and Hastie in the Department of the Interior, 8802 was the first comprehensive federal act to ban discrimination both in federal hiring and in the government workplace. The establishment of the FEPC acknowledged what racial-affairs advisers had long insisted was paramount: it was not enough to forbid discrimination. There had to be a federal-level watchdog to hold defiant white employers accountable. In the past, Weaver and the few racial-affairs advisers surrounding him had acted to police workplaces and endeavor to make sure they were free of discrimination. Now 8802 obligated the U.S. government to use its full powers to protect federal workers and job seekers from prejudice based on race, religion, or national origin.

Nevertheless, as Black Cabinet member and Housing Authority specialist William Trent observed, the Roosevelt administration's growing federal reach had created tension. Federal intervention and the expansion of protection to include marginalized populations, such as African Americans, often clashed with local and state law or customs. To ensure all citizens' rights were equally secure, Trent argued, Washington was obligated to intercede and use "affirmative and, in many cases, positive action," to end discrimination. Trent likely was drawing from language taken from the New Deal's Wagner Act, officially the National Labor Relations Act, of 1935. Designed to protect American laborers, that legislation had mandated that an employer who violated workers' rights take "affirmative action" and offer redress and recompense to those who were treated unfairly. Trent was the first to apply the then-generic legal concept of affirmative action to the issue of racial discrimination. But in practice, the antidiscrimination clauses and the prima facie model forged by Weaver and Hastie marked the first time that affirmative action in principle had been applied to racial justice. In their capacity as racial-affairs advisers, Weaver and Hastie, followed by their Black Cabinet colleagues, had taken the first steps toward institutionalizing equal rights, rather than Jim Crow, as the norm for American society. The path the Black Cabinet had cleared during the New Deal now guided the present. And the African American brain trust was hopeful it would lay the groundwork for the future.

The celebration of the Black Cabinet's achievements, including its contribution to Executive Order 8802, was short-lived. In July 1941, the White House began assembling the Fair Employment Practices Committee. Although Robert Weaver, Al Smith, and even Lawrence Oxley were all charged with overseeing African American inclusion in defense employment, not a single member of the Black Cabinet was invited to join the committee. Rather, Roosevelt named a white southerner, journalist Mark Ethridge, to chair the group. The membership consisted of three white men—Philip Murray, of the Congress of Industrial Organizations; William Green, of the American Federation of Labor; and David Sarnoff, of the Radio Corporation of America—and two black men—Milton P. Webster, A. Philip Randolph's confidant; and Earl B. Dickerson, a Democrat and former Chicago alderman, who came with endorsements from both Bethune and Walter White. In August, the president appointed another white southerner, former governor of the Virgin Islands Lawrence Cramer, to serve as the FEPC's executive secretary, whose duty it was to head up the committee's day-to-day operations.

Almost immediately the FEPC, which Charley Cherokee labeled "a new headache" for the Black Cabinet, ran into complications. FDR's executive order did not specify the scope of the committee's investigatory powers or the penalties for those found guilty of discrimination. Furthermore, the committee was starved for funding, and its members, most of whom lived outside of Washington, D.C., couldn't meet regularly. As a result, the FEPC delegated most of the grievance process to officials in the states or agencies where the discrimination allegedly

occurred. FEPC regulations were resented by many locals, and allowing them to arbitrate alleged violations protected rather than policed
racial discrimination. Charley Cherokee insisted that even when complaints came forward at the federal level, "the agency usually assigns
its race relations officer to prove . . . it wasn't discrimination but just a
mistake." Demands from Black Cabinet members that FEPC rules be
taken seriously in the federal workplace resulted in "dirty looks" from
white federal bosses.

Of all Black Cabinet members, Robert Weaver, who had years of
experience investigating unfair employment practices, would have been
the most natural choice for a seat on the FEPC. Yet he had been
excluded. Walter White and A. Philip Randolph pressured committee
head Lawrence Cramer to keep the FEPC "completely independent of
any governmental agency," especially Hillman's OPM. "We are firmly
convinced that any such relationship between your committee and
the Office of Production Management might lead to conclusions or
opinions which could be harmful to your Committee, to the Office
of Production Management, and to the objectives of the President's
order." FEPC members concurred and voted to operate separately and
report directly to the president. The result not only blocked the diffident
Hillman and the obstinate Knudsen from having any control over the
committee but also completely marginalized Weaver.

It was burningly obvious to insiders that the troubling overlap between
the FEPC and Weaver's office at the OPM threatened to derail both
units. The "FEPC was a duplication which contributed to a dissipation
of effort," Lucia Mae Pitts charged. Weaver hashed out an agreement
with the FEPC that allowed him to set up contracts, but the committee
insisted on retaining complete control over the enforcement of 8802's
antidiscrimination directive. "There Weaver and I parted company with
them because we were sure that the only person that could enforce the
contract was the man who made the contract," Will Alexander recalled.
African American journalist Marjorie McKenzie agreed—FEPC committee members were unpaid advisers with no real authority to force

employers to cooperate with the executive order. It would be far better, she argued, to empower Weaver and his staff. Pitts insisted that vesting all responsibility for making and enforcing antidiscrimination contracts in Weaver would have been much more effective: "Our office was already there, doing the same work the FEPC was created to do. All that was needed was to clothe us and give us weapons." The redundancy between Weaver's office and the FEPC generated "continuous and considerable jockeying behind the scenes for position, with the advantage passing back and forth." The end result, Pitts contended, greatly hindered the fight against discrimination in war industries.

Weaver was not willing to be frozen out. From his view, he had started to win significant victories. Shortly after Roosevelt signed 8802, Weaver released a couple of positive reports. (They probably contained information he had previously suppressed to aid the March on Washington.) Ten Curtiss-Wright plants, Republic Aviation, and several West Coast shipbuilders had all agreed to hire black workers. After months of haggling, Weaver had also convinced New York's Brewster Aeronautical to admit some African American men to its training programs. Later discovering that Brewster had refused to employ its own black trainees, Weaver protested. The company eventually relented and hired six black sheet-metal workers.

Riding on his victories in midsummer 1941, Weaver convinced Cramer to let his staff review all complaints before they were sent to the members of the FEPC for action. Both Walter White and Claude Barnett, the powerful editor of Associated Negro Press, objected, insisting that Weaver should not be permitted oversight of antidiscrimination charges. Weaver was exaggerating his successes, they maintained. Charley Cherokee also made the same allegation, insisting that Weaver's claims were met with skepticism from the Urban League, the NAACP, John P. Davis's National Negro Congress, and Howard University's Emmett Scott, along with many other leaders and organizations. In reality, taking into consideration that industries with lucrative defense contracts were generating hundreds of thousands of jobs, not to mention enormous profits, Weaver's achievements were indeed thin, barely touching the lives of the millions of black citizens still trapped in poverty.

When the OPM highlighted its work with Brewster Aeronautical as a success, Walter White and Roy Wilkins went public with their criticism of Weaver. In an NAACP press release, they charged that he was "painting a rosy picture of a dark situation." The NAACP, they testified, had received several complaints that Brewster had turned away African Americans in favor of less-qualified whites. Weaver immediately went on the defensive. The black workers who had protested did not possess the skills required for Brewster's positions, he maintained. While prejudice against black workers could be found in all war industries, he wrote in one article, important gains were being made.

However, the statistics proved, and Weaver admitted, that blacks received a disproportionately small share of the employment opportunities generated by the increase in taxpayer-supported defense spending. Eventually, Weaver and White called a truce. But their clash left a lingering public impression that Weaver was a sellout.

Scrutiny and vocal disapproval of Weaver and the Black Cabinet were not new. But they were on the upswing throughout 1941. The escalation of grassroots protests and the triumphant result of the threat of the March on Washington made the Black Cabinet's methods of working within the system appear feeble and obsolete. Former Black Cabinet member Forrester Washington, well known for his criticism of the group, was back at it. He charged that racial-affairs advisers continued to be powerless "rubber stamps." The *Cleveland Gazette* dismissed Hastie and Weaver as White House "stooges." A *Chicago Defender* editorial, under the title "Betrayers," charged that Black Cabinet members sat timidly at their desks while Jim Crow ruled the military, blacks were excluded from defense work, and African American servicemen increasingly became targets of racial violence. Another *Defender* piece blasted Black Cabinet members for being nothing more than self-interested bureaucrats. They were "bought and paid for" and served only "as professional letter writers whose duty it is to satisfy Negro complaints by mail and keep protesting delegations, or discourage them, from storming the various government departments and White House with grievances." One contributor to the *Pittsburgh Courier* joined in: "If practical and immediate methods are not developed to meet equitable and democratic ultimatums, then the black cabinet ought to resign and go to the people. Then the people will begin to have faith in their leadership; then the white man will begin to respect it and know that we mean business."

Others came to the Black Cabinet's defense. A. Philip Randolph publicly commended Bethune, Hastie, and Weaver for fighting to bend the power of the government away from protecting white supremacy and privilege and toward extending civil rights and equality of opportunity to all Americans. Although some *Pittsburgh Courier* editorialists were critical of the Black Cabinet, others offered praise for black federal appointees. "They are not political stop gaps," wrote P. L. Prattis, who succeeded Robert Vann as the paper's editor. "Many of us recall the old Black Cabinets [of Theodore Roosevelt and William Howard Taft] not too pleasantly," he remarked. "They are gone. They had no power and, without special training, were of little service." The new Black Cabinet was filled with race-relations experts who were "digging in more deeply and broadly" into a federal government than any previous group.

Another writer in the *Pittsburgh Courier* maintained that the Black Cabinet wasn't to blame for the perpetuation of segregation, racial violence, and poverty. Rather, the burden fell on white officials in Washington who ignored recommendations from racial-affairs advisers while forcing them to "interpret" the administration's ill-conceived policies for black communities. The Black Cabinet was trapped in a "two-way attack." On the one side, "the Negro public kicks and accuses [them] . . . of being a rubber stamp." On the other, Black Cabinet members who spoke out in their posts were subjected to the wrath of white bosses who regarded them with suspicion for their loyalty to black people and accused racial-affairs advisers of "trying to get everything for the Negro." The *Courier* assured readers that some cabinet members, specifically Bethune and Hastie, did not hesitate "to criticize various administrative agencies for acts of discrimination and to even disagree publicly with the policies of their own agency or department."

Black Cabinet members could not defend themselves against their increasingly vocal critics. When they countered attacks by publicizing their accomplishments, it appeared as self-serving arrogance or White House puffery. Furthermore, many of the Black Cabinet's triumphs resulted from behind-the-scenes maneuvering, often executed with the help of internal favors, external forces, or strategic leaks. These achievements had to remain masked to protect the Black Cabinet's techniques and allies. The price the black brain trust paid was that many of its victories had to remain unacknowledged.

Still the Black Cabinet's presence had made and continued to make a difference. Increasing numbers of African Americans were joining the federal ranks. William Trent successfully convinced the Federal Works Agency to award contracts to African American builders, to hire a black labor lawyer, to devote more attention to African American housing, and to follow, as required, Executive Order 8802 in all its defense-related projects. Robert Weaver pointed out that while African Americans were hired for defense jobs in numbers far below their fair share, those who were employed were forging ahead in factory jobs with companies that previously refused to employ black workers. In 1941, James Atkins compelled his bosses at the WPA, representatives of the Selective Service System, and some white southern educators to abandon their stance that illiteracy was only a "Negro problem" and that teaching black Americans to read was a waste of time and resources. The military required all enlistees to be able to read and write, Atkins pointed out. Since illiteracy in the South cut across racial lines, the refusal to support reading programs hurt recruitment within the black and white populations. More funding to expand these educational programs, which welcomed all races, would remedy what could be a big problem should the United States be drawn into war. The administration agreed.

Mary McLeod Bethune also could claim a few triumphs in her division. In 1941, she got the okay to add more members to her National

Youth Administration staff. One of Bethune's new assistants, Dovey Johnson Roundtree, recalled that their office was always buzzing with activity. Roundtree was delighted to be working for Bethune. Her grandmother, a domestic worker active in women's clubs, knew Bethune and held the college president up as the model of proud and courageous black womanhood. "If Dr. Mary McLeod Bethune, child of slaves, could rise from poverty to command the attention of presidents . . . [my] granddaughters could do the same," Roundtree's grandmother insisted. While some, mostly male, African American journalists and leaders claimed that Bethune's political influence had passed its peak, her status with the African American masses, especially women, remained intact. In August, a female government worker filled in for Charley Cherokee, writing the National Grapevine column under the name "Edie." (It may have been Lucia Mae Pitts, who had previously worked for the *Chicago Defender*. This use of a guest columnist indicated that Charley Cherokee's true identity may have been known to at least some black Washington insiders.) In one column, Edie recounted the story of a visit to Bethune-Cookman by Eleanor Roosevelt. Just before the First Lady was to speak, a torrent of rain descended. According to the story, which would become legendary, Bethune stood up, raised her hands, and commanded the rain to stop. Reportedly it did. "More power to you, Mary!" Edie exclaimed.

Despite experiencing frequent lapses in health, Bethune continued as much as possible on the speaking circuit. She could still draw a crowd. At many stops, she urged African Americans to embrace both the struggle for civil rights and the fight to protect the nation against the global spread of fascism. She continued to stump for the New Deal and to insist that African Americans demand inclusion in all benefits offered by the government. But the pursuit of equality, she warned, must proceed under a banner of cooperation. "We must do all we can to preserve the spirit and morale, in spite of discrimination and handicaps that confront us in both industry and the general defense programs," she cautioned. "We must not fail America and as Americans, we must insist that America shall not fail us."

From her Washington, D.C., office, Bethune battled back what now became constant assaults on her hard-won NYA programs. Like Al Smith, she also attempted to maintain relevancy by driving her division toward readying participants for defense work. African American teens and young adults received instruction in welding, aviation and automotive repair, wood and metal work, canning, sewing, nursing, clerical skills, and electronics. One *Pittsburgh Courier* columnist praised Bethune's revamped programs as a "renaissance of industrial education" that was preparing young people for jobs in the new "power age." But overhauling vocational programs was costly, and the office constantly worried about funding. In September, Bethune's assistant T. Arnold Hill reported that the government planned to reallocate $30 million from the domestic budget to defense. "You can see," he told Bethune, "what devastating results this will have on our Negro program."

In October, attacks on the NYA intensified. The U.S. government's comptroller general, Lindsay C. Warren, alleged that an audit revealed numerous NYA "irregularities," including misappropriation of funds, the falsification of budget claims, and the manipulation of enrollees' ages to mask dwindling numbers of recruits in some areas. A former North Carolina congressman and avowed segregationist, Warren zeroed in on Bethune's Chicago aviation training program for black youths, insisting it was rampant with fraud. The *Pittsburgh Courier* observed that "some seem to feel that the charges are a direct challenge to the popularity and power of Mary McLeod Bethune." Her supporters, the paper warned, would wage "a bitter battle should the integrity of Mrs. Bethune be questioned or assailed."

Aubrey Williams labeled Warren's accusations a "smear" and called for a congressional investigation to prove they were unsubstantiated. Bethune urged her NYA boss along in the battle against the comptroller. One must read the Psalms for strength, she advised Williams. "Every fiber in us—the thousands of NYA trainees and workers throughout America—beats with confidence in you and admiration for the high ground you take in the administration of the program that has been entrusted to you," she told him. Eventually Williams prevailed, and Warren backed down.

At the same time, Bethune was juggling some challenges from inside her own office. With new staff came new conflicts; Bethune had assembled an impressive group of young and ambitious African American experts on race, activism, and education, and competition within the group was fierce. According to Charley Cherokee, Bethune had become concerned that "some of her choices [were] unwise." Several of the newcomers vied for her attention. Others reportedly had designs on her position. Worried about "double crossing," she began to withhold information from subordinates and seek counsel elsewhere. By the summer of 1941, she had decided her two biggest problems—her two most senior male advisers, Joseph H. B. Evans (who had been transferred from the Farm Securities Administration to her division earlier) and T. Arnold Hill— had to go. She didn't trust them and believed they were more focused on themselves and their careers than the cause. Hill had been "dumped" on Bethune, the *Pittsburgh Courier* claimed; it was well known he was hard to work with and had already fallen out with other members of the Black Cabinet. Nonetheless, Hill survived Bethune's attempt to get rid of him, protected by his ties to Tuskegee. But she did succeed in banishing Evans to Colorado as an NYA regional director.

With troublesome staff, and the NYA still under siege in Congress, Bethune shifted even more of her business from her government office to the National Council of Negro Women headquarters. The NAACP's Walter White and the Urban League's Lester Granger, as well as Eleanor Roosevelt, were frequent visitors. Dovey Johnson Roundtree was often called to work at Bethune's home above the NCNW's offices, where she remembered the Black Cabinet head continuing to forge "coalitions of every sort." As she had in the past, Bethune focused special attention on advancing black women. The March on Washington Movement had not protested against gender discrimination in the defense buildup, and Bethune was determined see the exclusion of black women corrected. "After white men and women and colored men have jobs, then people think about jobs for colored women," Edie had protested in the National Grapevine. As industry retooled for war, Bethune shifted more energies from Depression relief to securing a place for black women in national defense.

As war readiness accelerated, the armed services, along with many American industries, continued to shun women. However, from the summer into the fall of 1941, the international conflict assumed a staggering enormity, as both Germany and Japan expanded into new territories. Nazis and Russian forces were engaged in bitter battles in eastern Europe. Tensions escalated as the United States cut off all oil and gas exports to Japan. Secretary of War Stimson and military chiefs realized that to meet the threats, they would eventually have to institute a mass mobilization of all Americans, including women.

As a preliminary step, the War Department announced an October conference on women and preparedness, inviting representatives from the country's major women's organizations. When Bill Hastie realized that not a single African American woman had been invited, he protested and demanded Bethune be included. The War Department ignored him and proceeded ahead with its all-white gathering. Bethune responded with a "stinging rebuke" directed at Stimson and printed in the *Pittsburgh Courier*. "We are anxious for you to know that we want to be considered a part of our American democracy, not something apart from it. We know from experience that our interests are too often neglected, ignored, or scuttled unless we have effective representation in the formative stages of these projects and proposals," she stated. "We are not blind to what is happening. We are not humiliated. We are incensed."

Throughout 1941, independent action or ad hoc collaboration between various combinations of Black Cabinet members had become the group's dominant form of operation. Although Bethune assured the African American public that the black brain trust met weekly, Charley Cherokee revealed that the group rarely gathered as a whole. However, membership continued to swell. By late 1941 more than one hundred African American federal officials would identify as black brain trusters. Despite the barbs directed at the Black Cabinet, claiming one's place in it carried a certain enviable status.

But expansion came with a price. With the war came more employment for African Americans. All of those hired into white-collar administrative posts, even if they were lower-level desk jobs without advisory responsibilities, were welcomed into the cabinet. The increasingly larger membership was highlighted as a proud accomplishment of the black community and a way to encourage the administration to add more African Americans. But the size of the Black Cabinet made it unwieldy and impersonal. It also meant that meetings, especially with Charley Cherokee's leaks, no longer functioned as a place where racial-affairs advisers could speak frankly, hatch covert plans, and brainstorm on strategy. The rapid growth in African American appointees introduced new personalities and new agendas to the group. This shift made unity even harder to sustain and drove the brain trust's core to rely more than ever on its inner circles. Bethune leaned on the National Council of Negro Women. Weaver had his poker buddies. Hastie was among them, but he also looked to the NAACP for support in his fight with the War Department's higher-ups. Al Smith wrestled mostly alone, using his Charley Cherokee alter ego to take shots at almost everyone, Black Cabinet colleagues and white Washingtonians alike.

To add to the Black Cabinet's woes, its new additions included many younger members who were unwilling to pledge complete and unconditional loyalty to Mary McLeod Bethune. For them, she was too accommodating to the powers that be and too old-fashioned. A new split emerged, between those who supported the venerated Bethune and those who felt her time had passed. Rumors spread that an anti-Bethune faction was forming around the dynamic former Pennsylvania state legislator Crystal Bird Fauset. Accepting a post in the Office of Civilian Defense, Fauset was given an office next door to one occupied by the First Lady. Reportedly, Bethune had earlier rejected attempts to place Fauset in the NYA, and an intense rivalry had developed between the two women.

But for the old-timers in the Black Cabinet, divisions between new racial-affairs advisers and attempts to dethrone Bethune must have seemed minor. They had witnessed the devastation of the Great Depression sweep black America. Now they faced the pressing urgency of a bloody war waged by totalitarian powers. If the United States entered the conflict, the nation would, without hesitation, demand black lives be sacrificed for the cause.

On December 7, 1941, Japan attacked the U.S. base at Pearl Harbor. The next day, Bill Hastie arrived at the War Department and joined Truman Gibson for a meeting with African American journalists. The War Department had scheduled the meeting well before the attack and had planned to have Hastie and Gibson persuade black journalists to write more supportively of FDR and his administration. General George C. Marshall and Colonel E. R. Householder dropped in. They proudly announced the expansion of ROTC training for black youths and the formation of a new African American army unit. But Householder also confirmed that there would be no integration in the military. Hastie left dejected: "Because of the Japanese attack . . . I was no longer optimistic that it would be possible to persuade the military to eliminate existing racial segregation."

In another part of the capital, on the morning of December 8, Mary McLeod Bethune headed to the White House to speak at a meeting arranged weeks before by the First Lady. Eleanor Roosevelt had excused herself from the gathering; she and her husband had talked alone in his room until after midnight. Later Bethune released a call for unity: "I know that at a time like this, every Negro man, woman, and child will stand straight up without reservations to his responsibility to his country."

While Bethune was speaking at the White House, in his office, Robert Weaver was preparing telegrams to send out around the nation.

In them, he urged parents to enroll their sons in defense-work training programs sponsored by his office. One newspaper promoting Weaver's program stated: "The way is open; will you avail yourself of this opportunity and . . . be an asset to your country? Delay may mean fate for our future."

The morning after Pearl Harbor, Al Smith's WPA office was nearly deserted; almost everyone had headed over to the House of Representatives and was waiting to hear the president address an emergency session of Congress.

At noon, the president and the First Lady arrived in the House chambers. The audience was on its feet, and applause thundered as FDR took the rostrum. "Yesterday, December 7, 1941—a date which will live in infamy—the United States of America was suddenly and deliberately attacked by naval and air forces of the Empire of Japan," he began. Then he listed off the many areas throughout the Pacific also targeted by the Japanese, declaring that "the American people in their righteous might will win through to absolute victory."

Less than an hour later, the nation was at war.

"'War is Hell,' said Sherman," wrote Charley Cherokee. "Had he been colored he would have been more inclusive—so is peace! However, my chickadees, since we are in this mess up to our necks, let's smack the Axis' ears down pronto so we can get back to the important business of fighting Jim Crow. All together!"

Chapter Twelve

Mighty Struggle

S HORTLY AFTER Pearl Harbor, Mary McLeod Bethune summoned
all Black Cabinet members to an emergency meeting. Al Smith
declared it "historic"—it was the largest Black Cabinet meeting
ever, drawing fifty of the group's now more than one hundred members.
During the gathering, Smith, Lawrence Oxley, Edgar Brown, Frank
Horne, and William Thompkins all made stirring speeches. Then Mary
McLeod Bethune rose and issued an emotional call for unity and for
action. When she finished, she was joined by several longtime members,
and together they unveiled the Black Cabinet's plans to increase
African American opportunities in national defense, to end continued
discrimination in the civil service, and to rescue the remnants of the
New Deal, specifically the National Youth Administration and the
Civilian Conservation Corps. "Newcomers were fired with enthusiasm,"
Charley Cherokee reported. "'Twas rather swell. . . . For victory and
democracy, keep 'em squirming."

Black federal officials left the meeting inspired and with a renewed
sense of purpose. Never before had so much been on the line. The
vehement and open racial hostility Black Cabinet members had com-
bated in the past escalated once the nation entered the war. The most
immediate and biggest fight came over preserving the New Deal. The
"unholy alliance" of conservative anti–New Deal Democrats and reactionary Republicans was stronger than ever and steadfastly determined

to extinguish what was left of Franklin Delano Roosevelt's signature accomplishment. Although its programs had not done enough for black Americans, they had, thanks to the Black Cabinet, made significant changes in federal policy and black lives.

While the world descended further into war, in early 1942, the southern congressional bloc led a vote to defund the Work Projects Administration (WPA), the National Youth Administration (NYA), and the Civilian Conservation Corps (CCC). Furthermore, public housing programs, long regarded as suspicious because of their potential to unravel residential segregation, were also under attack. During one Capitol Hill hearing, Alabama Democrat Joe Starnes and Massachusetts Republican Richard B. Wigglesworth teamed up for an assault on the U.S. Housing Authority, which quickly mutated into a referendum against the Black Cabinet. "I do not see why we need racial relations set-ups in all of these agencies. We have never had them before," Wigglesworth complained. Starnes joined him: "They are put in there . . . to promote the idea that racial discrimination is being practiced." The Alabama congressman charged that Black Cabinet members were "special propagandist[s]" operating "at government expense." No prejudicial treatment existed, he maintained; it was entirely fabricated. The *Pittsburgh Courier* concluded that the attacks by Wigglesworth and Starnes were a part of a larger "effort to drive the Negro out of government."

FDR responded to the attempt to terminate the New Deal by doing what he could to shore up funding for its remnants. But the budgets for the WPA, NYA, and CCC were already greatly reduced, and their programs, especially in black communities, had begun to rapidly contract. Worried over their future, lower-level black administrators and assistants in the NYA and the WPA sought transfers to other agencies. Pauline Redmond Coggs left Bethune to work for Crystal Bird Fauset in Civilian Defense. The CCC's Edgar Brown began courting officials in the Office of Price Administration, which oversaw rationing programs and price controls, hoping they would take him before he lost his job. Some speculated that the black brain trust was at its end. "All told, the

'Black Cabinet' has fallen on evil days since the inception of the war," observed the *New York Amsterdam News* in January 1942.

In addition to facing threats from within the federal government, Black Cabinet members continued to be targets of criticism from a growing number of black political pundits. The do-nothing image that had long haunted the African American brain trust seemed to intensify as the nation was drawn into the war. Some black political observers insisted that the group's achievements were slim at best. Most of the criticism was directed at Bill Hastie, who was battling for equal treatment for African Americans in the U.S. military. Over the year since his appointment, there seemed to have been few tangible results. "The Negro press and public hasn't been fully informed as to Judge Hastie's duties," the *New York Age* declared. "But we think that his race expects him to be something more than a 'rubber stamp' official." Other sources continued to insist that the entire Black Cabinet was hapless, selfish, and opportunistic. One *Chicago Defender* columnist opined that African Americans "may be better off without ANY of these 'specialists' in Negro affairs."

Black Cabinet members answered back. Hastie and a few other racial-affairs advisers wrote to black newspapers defending their actions, but that did little to stop the bad press. "Veterans in the Black Cabinet . . . realize that part of holding a public office is having abuse directed at their heads," remarked Smith, writing as Charley Cherokee. While his National Grapevine continued to promote the group's accomplishments, his reports of the Black Cabinet's defeats and internal dissent made Charley Cherokee sometimes sound more like a doubter than a believer. Yet his willingness to criticize the group both obscured his identity and gave him more credibility when he came out in favor of the black brain trust. He insisted that his motives were pure. "Rest assured, as a fan who is secretary to a black cabinet member wrote, 'Charley gives it to his friends as well as enemies,'" he commented, "because as another said, 'if you can't get the truth in Negro papers, where can you get it?'" While on the road, Lawrence

Oxley tried to stand up for the Black Cabinet and almost got into a fistfight with a critic at a defense meeting to rally the black public. After returning to Washington, D.C., he received a stern reprimand from other racial-affairs advisers.

Mary McLeod Bethune decided to undertake an aggressive campaign to repair and raise the Black Cabinet's image. Fostering public confidence in the African American brain trust was essential to sustaining its members' roles as advocates within Washington's bureaucracy and to protecting their programs. Administration officials generally were ignorant of, and uninterested in, black public opinion. But when they felt it could benefit their aims in some way, they had consulted with racial-affairs advisers, viewing them as spokespeople for their race. If the Black Cabinet appeared to have lost the African American community's confidence, and it increasingly looked as if it had, many white federal officials might begin to regard racial-affairs advisers as dispensable. Members would lose their jobs and see their programs shuttered. Thousands and thousands of African Americans would lose out on government support. While the Black Cabinet had always been marginalized within the Roosevelt administration, its presence was far better than no black voice at the federal level at all.

In February, Bethune summarily announced to African American brain trusters that it was "time to issue a public statement regarding the Federal Council [Black Cabinet] and the responsibilities of Negro officials connected with the various government agencies." Racial-affairs advisers themselves must correct the record. "During the past months the Negro public has become increasingly critical of the Negro government officials," she stated. "Too frequently the criticisms have been based on misinformation." She demanded the Black Cabinet's lead members submit reports summarizing the purposes of their divisions and the various duties performed by their staffs. If African Americans were aware of the quiet actions being taken on their behalf, the cabinet's reputation certainly would be improved and advisers shielded from dismissal.

Bethune's idea didn't sit well with several key players in the Black Cabinet. Circulating a press release would be "a great mistake," Robert Weaver insisted. She must reconsider: "For the Federal Council to make such a statement would place its members immediately on the defensive and, I fear, would create more adverse than favorable opinion." Bill Hastie agreed: "I am convinced that any such publicity, to be effective, must come from persons outside of the government who cannot be accused of any personal interest." Constance Daniel of the Farm Security Administration outright refused to comply: "I have nothing at all to defend and prefer not to be included in any movement which might be in any way interpreted as an attempt to defend my employment in this or any other agency." The opposition was so intense that Bethune was forced to quickly abandon her plan.

Bethune had more success when she organized a public meeting of racial-affairs advisers and invited guests. On February 18, 1942, in the National Archives auditorium, the Black Cabinet hosted a screening of four films: the WPA's *We Work Again*, the FSA's *The Negro Farmer*, the NYA's *Youth-Building at Wilberforce*, and the Public Health Service's *Three Counties Against Syphilis*. These New Deal movies, done in documentary style, showed the progress made in the areas of industrial work, farming, education, and health. The intention was to use the event to educate newcomers in the tactics used by pioneering black brain trusters. "Many of our leaders and others interested in the Negro's struggle for participation in various government sponsored programs are unaware of some of the praiseworthy accomplishments of which we can boast," Bethune remarked. In uncertain times, she pointed out, it was important to celebrate the Black Cabinet's victories in the "mighty struggle in which the Negro is involved in America and as a part of America."

National Negro Congress leader (and Robert Weaver's former associate) John P. Davis attended the screenings. He praised Bethune for "a timely and thoughtful act on your part which deserves wide repetition among many groups and leaders of our people." Disappointingly, the meeting made nothing more than a ripple in the black press.

Bethune's campaign to convince the public of the Black Cabinet's continued relevance soon came to an abrupt halt. In early March, while visiting Daytona Beach, she fell ill again and took to her bed.

In Washington, D.C., Bethune's Black Cabinet colleagues carried on, each in his or her own division. But the Weaver crowd had also managed to push forward a collaborative project that cut across agency boundaries. Beginning in 1941 and into early 1942, Robert Weaver, Bill Hastie, William Trent, Ted Poston, and Frank Horne worked together on a Detroit public housing project that had been named the Sojourner Truth Homes, in honor of the famous female abolitionist. Using the combined influence of their positions in the Office of Production Management, the War Department, and the Housing Authority, they not only got the project off the ground but fought to ensure that African Americans would be allowed to live in it.

Like many other urban areas during World War II, Detroit witnessed a massive influx of new residents drawn to cities by industrial job growth. In particular for African Americans, the war sparked what was known as the Second Great Migration. Cities of the North, Midwest, and West offered not only new employment opportunities but also a chance to escape southern poverty, segregation, disenfranchisement, and racial violence. However, African American migrants seeking to build new lives immediately confronted serious housing shortages, as people of all races looking for defense work crowded into cities across the nation. To address the problem, the federal government had shifted resources away from low-income housing to focus on constructing new developments for defense employees. However, projects welcoming African Americans were met with vociferous and angry protests. Such was the case with the Sojourner Truth Homes. In Detroit, white residents organized strident opposition to the development and successfully enlisted support from their congressman, Rudolph Tenerowicz. Throughout the fall of 1941, Tenerowicz pummeled away at the project. By January 1942, he had successfully convinced housing administrators to declare that the homes would be reserved for white people.

Clark Foreman, no doubt in counsel with Robert Weaver and others, stepped in. He had been transferred to the Federal Works Agency, where he oversaw the construction of public housing. In early January, Foreman telegrammed the Detroit Housing Commission and directed it to accept African Americans at the Sojourner Truth Homes. Three hours later, the commission received a second telegram; this one, from Foreman's superiors, rescinded his order and re-designated the project as exclusively white. The next day, Foreman resigned. Reportedly, a powerful southern congressman had threatened to end all public housing programs if the FWA continued to employ Foreman. "Clark Foreman Loses [His] Head for Us," reported the *Pittsburgh Courier*. "It is the duty of every Negro man and woman in Detroit to let his representatives in congress . . . know how he or she feels about the axe which struck Foreman's neck."

Throughout January and February, the FWA had received protests from the NAACP, Detroit's black community, and Black Cabinet members over the exclusion of African Americans from the Sojourner Truth Homes. The pressure was so great, eventually local and federal authorities issued a new decision. They refused to integrate the project but they did agree to restrict it to African Americans. The new homes would be ready for occupancy on Saturday, February 28, 1942.

When the African American families selected for the Sojourner Truth Homes arrived on the morning of move-in day, they were met by an angry white mob numbering over seven hundred. Many of the whites were armed, and, joined by members of Detroit's police force, they blocked all entrances to the development. When the first moving truck attempted to cross, the driver was attacked, and the white crowd destroyed every piece of the furniture he was hauling. When he pleaded for help from the police, they advised him to "turn around and go back." Hearing rumors that whites intended to carry the violence into the black community, a group of African American men headed for the housing site and confronted the white protesters. Fighting broke out, and according to the *Pittsburgh Courier*, the police joined in, "using tear gas, swinging their clubs, and riding down the Negroes but not bothering the whites."

Over the next two days, the violence escalated and continued. White mobs stormed black neighborhoods, destroyed black property, and attacked African American residents throughout the city. When order was restored, on the third day, thirty-three African Americans had been hospitalized and ninety-five had been jailed. The Detroit police had arrested only five white people.

News of the white community's brazen attacks on Detroit's black citizens circulated throughout the country, both in the national press and on the radio. Many of the African Americans who had been accepted as residents of the Sojourner Truth project were now without homes. It was hardly what the White House wanted to hear at a time when the push for national unity had become a priority. And for the Black Cabinet members who had worked hard on the project, the violent clash represented a major setback.

Although authorities reestablished order in the city by Monday, March 2, it was an uneasy peace. Detroit's black population was adamant that it would not allow the city's white residents to continue to terrorize its community and insisted that African Americans be permitted to occupy the Sojourner Truth Homes. When the NAACP's Roy Wilkins arrived in the city, black residents told him that they were no longer interested in talking. Working within the system and negotiating with government officials had failed. "You polite people step down out of the picture and let us run it," Wilkins was told. "We will do battle." One black soldier remarked, "I might as well die here for democracy as on a foreign field against an enemy I do not know or have never seen."

Back in Washington, D.C., the Black Cabinet made the fight for the Sojourner Truth Homes a top priority. Weaver's circle agreed it had to move fast, and strategically, to preserve the project for African Americans. This went beyond Detroit—it was a battle to save housing programs for poor Americans nationwide. One unnamed Black Cabinet member earlier had told the *Pittsburgh Courier* that attacks on the New Deal and the focus on building homes for defense workers and military families meant that all low-income housing projects were "practically out."

Working in collaboration with the NAACP, Black Cabinet members began supplying national leaders, the black press, and Detroit's African American community with all the inside information related to the project that they could gather. Where they could, they pressured their division chiefs. They called for law enforcement to investigate the riot and for the prosecution of the white ringleaders. They reminded the administration that vile racist outbursts, like the one in Detroit, only destabilized national loyalty. Racial violence provided grist for the propaganda mills in Germany and Japan, which cited such episodes as examples of the weakness of American democracy.

The pressure by African Americans and white allies on the administration to act was overwhelming. Black Cabinet members, working all angles internally, refused to let the issue rest. Bethune was still bedridden in Florida. Crystal Bird Fauset stepped in and helped the Black Cabinet reach Eleanor Roosevelt. In early March, one Black Cabinet member triumphantly telegrammed Roy Wilkins: SOJOURNER TRUTH PLANNED FOR NEGRO OCCUPANCY AND THE DECISION TO THAT END IS STILL IN EFFECT. Despite this confirmation, members of Detroit's white community refused to accept that the project would be reserved for African Americans. The *Detroit Free Press* reported that some whites had hatched a "conspiracy . . . to prevent Negroes from occupying" the Sojourner Truth Homes. It also reported allegations that the Ku Klux Klan had organized protesters to picket the project and had burned a cross nearby. The Justice Department opened a probe and eventually confirmed that the KKK had played a lead role in inciting the riot and blocking African Americans from the project.

Still Rudolph Tenerowicz was unwilling to admit defeat. According to the *Pittsburgh Courier*, he continued as "one of the leaders in the fight to prevent Negroes from occupying" the Sojourner Truth Homes. In late April, he launched attacks on the black brain trust, accusing them of harboring communists in their ranks and demanding the House appoint a committee to investigate the Federal Housing Authority. He then took to the House floor and alleged that there was a special interest group operating within the federal government that had masterminded a scheme to unfairly privilege Detroit's black citizens. "I was astonished and surprised to learn of another agency—the black cabinet—at work in official Washington," Tenerowicz thundered. "I know of but one cabinet, the cabinet appointed by the President of the United States, and I am wondering who appoints this so-called black cabinet. . . . Is this so-called black cabinet to decide where all Negro housing projects are to be erected? How much pressure was exerted on [the U.S. Housing Authority] by this agency?"

Tenerowicz's last-minute attempt at excluding African Americans from the Sojourner Truth Homes failed. On April 29, at the behest of the White House, over two thousand fully armed "[national] guardsmen, state troopers, and city police" escorted fourteen black families as they took possession of their homes. "Dissension," the UPI story read, "was limited to catcalls and threats." Military forces and police authorities continued to patrol the community for months afterward as more black residents trickled into the project. Despite the continued tensions, Black Cabinet members would point to the Sojourner Truth Homes as one of their major victories. In a later interview, one member insisted, "If the Black Cabineteers had not kept the issue alive and in focus, the story could have ended in defeat."

During the early months of 1942, as the Black Cabinet battled in Washington, grassroots activism accelerated in African American communities nationwide. In New York City, the Mount Olivet Baptist Church called a meeting protesting civilian assaults on black soldiers, discrimination in the military, and lynching. It drew twelve hundred participants. Ten thousand African American citizens of Evansville, Indiana, petitioned the city government, insisting it overturn policies that barred African Americans from many local defense jobs and from attending a publicly funded vocational school. After the slaying of an African American soldier, Thomas P. Foster, by a police officer in Little Rock, Arkansas, the area's black ministers spearheaded a drive to have his murderer brought to justice. After reports that white MPs, local police, and townsfolk in Alexandria, Louisiana, had opened fire on black soldiers during a clash, protests erupted in black communities and in the black press. Bill Hastie conducted his own investigation into what became known as the "Lee Street Riot" and demanded the War Department stop "terrorism by civil authorities and local citizens." Although his superiors ignored him, Hastie persisted. In the winter of 1942, the *Pittsburgh Courier* announced the beginning of the "Double V" campaign, which called for "Victory over our enemies at home and victory over our enemies on the battlefields abroad." Support for the *Courier*'s crusade rapidly flourished, as many African American organizations and leaders endorsed it. Among them was Mary McLeod Bethune.

By the spring of 1942, as open protests increased, White House advisers decided that they needed to address African American discontent. Rather than seek advice from the Black Cabinet, the administration instead tapped several white defense agency leaders. Almost nine years had passed since Clark Foreman had arrived as the federal government's first racial-affairs adviser, and FDR's circle still, when it came to black issues, preferred the counsel of whites. Some of the white defense heads did, in turn, consult with African American brain trusters, but whether they acted on the feedback they were given was unclear. However, the end result was a proliferation of conflicting and competing proposals. "DIME A DOZEN are plans afloat in Washington to save the nation by saving the Negro," Charley Cherokee commented.

One of the first plans to come forward had originated with Bethune. In early January 1942, before she had taken ill, she had called a meeting with a highly select group of nongovernmental leaders to discuss African Americans in national defense. Out of that gathering had come a recommendation that the president appoint a special adviser on race relations who would report directly and solely to him. It essentially was an attempt to formalize the model of what she was already doing—acting as a go-between for the African American community with the White House. Bethune pushed the plan with Eleanor Roosevelt, but it ended up shelved. However, in the spring, when the White House began debating how to address African American needs and preserve black support for the war, Bethune's idea was revived. Although she may have seen herself in the role of presidential counselor on race relations, many preferred Bill Hastie's outspoken cousin, the revered Charles H. Houston, for the position.

By May, Bethune's proposal was eclipsed by the Fair Employment Practices Committee's "plan to end all plans," as Charley Cherokee described it. Although the committee had limped along for most of its nearly ten months of existence, its white leadership had easy access to the White House. In the later part of May, FEPC head Lawrence Cramer pitched the committee's plan directly to the president. It was inefficient to have racial-affairs divisions dispersed throughout the administration, Cramer insisted. African American problems could be better addressed if all black brain trusters and their programs were placed under the FEPC's supervision. To carry this out, he told Roosevelt, the FEPC's membership would need to be expanded. It also required an increased budget, more authority to punish violators of Executive Order 8802, and for the committee to be placed directly under the White House. These reforms would free the FEPC from layers of bureaucratic constraints, Cramer insisted, and allow it to function as a federal clearinghouse on all concerns related to black citizens.

The FEPC's proposal set off alarms in the Black Cabinet as well as within civil rights leadership circles. It sounded disturbingly similar to past proposals for a separate agency with exclusive oversight of African American affairs, an idea that had been rejected out of fear it would marginalize African American interests and disempower black appointees even further. Additionally, as a number of observers knew, the FEPC was barely functional, and many doubted it could fulfill its promise to act effectively and decisively to integrate black citizens into the defense industry. Hindered from the beginning by underfunding, internal squabbles, and a dysfunctional structure, the committee had begun to rely on public investigatory hearings as its main tactic to weed out discrimination. While the hearings generated much publicity, by spring of 1942 the FEPC had produced very few tangible gains for African Americans. Employers and unions generally ignored the committee's directives, and FEPC heads, worried about meeting production quotas, hesitated to yank contracts from factories that had violated 8802.

The FEPC's white membership was also a source of grave concern. It appeared that it was more interested in appeasing white southerners than in fighting for African Americans. At hearings in Birmingham, Alabama, committee chair Mark Ethridge insisted: "Negroes must recognize that there is no power in the world—not even in all the mechanized armies of the earth, Allies and Axis—which could force the southern white people to the abandonment of the principle of segregation."

Although they normally remained in the background, several Black Cabinet members publicly opposed the FEPC plan. Crystal Bird Fauset scoffed at the idea of working under the committee, insisting it would tie her hands in the Office of Civilian Defense. Bill Hastie had the same reservations; placing him under the FEPC would only create another barrier between his office and the military brass so stubbornly resentful of his presence. Robert Weaver also protested. Even though he was never one for publicity, Weaver openly declared that he was unwilling to work under Cramer. The FEPC head had repeatedly insisted that African Americans should not be assigned to work on race relations because, in his opinion, they were incapable of objectivity. Cramer's attitude not only endangered the incorporation of African American voices throughout the administration, it portended the creation of a Black Cabinet within the FEPC that was overseen by whites.

The FEPC's proposal was regarded as the most formidable, but a competing alternative had been also making the rounds—this one in secret. Ambassador to Liberia Lester Walton, a longtime black Democrat who was in Washington on leave, had begun promoting his own version of a "Bureau of Negro Affairs." Like the FEPC, Walton advocated for the consolidation of all programs that addressed African American affairs into a separate agency. But his plan was to place it under an African American head. He put himself forward as the best choice for the leader of the bureau, which presumably would consist of his own appointees. By April 1942, Walton had begun attempts to sell well-placed administration officials, including Vice President Henry Wallace, on his plan. Although Walton was controversial—many African American leaders regarded the former theatrical manager and journalist as underqualified and self-serving—his plan was taken seriously enough by upper-level officials that it was discussed at an official White House cabinet meeting.

In May, when the FEPC appeared with its competing proposal, Walton began pushing his plan by sending out confidential memoranda to select top Washington officials. But an office staffer made some extra copies of Walton's memos and got them into the hands of an African American messenger, who passed them on to Black Cabinet members. They were furious. In their view, the ambassador's actions were an underhanded attempt to eliminate them, and his vision of a black agency under his control would only impede the fight against institutional racism in the federal government.

A secret emergency meeting of the Black Cabinet was called. The delicate nature of conferring over a leaked and confidential government document required that attendance be limited to only the most trusted of the racial-affairs advisers—the core of the original black New Dealers. Certainly, the fear of being fired for using leaked information to subvert a proposal made by a government official weighed heavy on their minds. Yet, they were just as concerned with protecting the messenger who had alerted them to Walton's plan: the loyalty of black messengers had long benefited the Black Cabinet in its behind-the-scenes crusades.

Despite the veil of secrecy that enveloped the meeting, African American journalists sniffed out a few details. About a dozen Black Cabinet members turned out. A few core members skipped the meeting; they may have included Bethune, who was still battling health problems. Later, when pressed by State Department officials investigating the leak of Walton's plan, "no member [of the Black Cabinet] would make a statement and no one would name names of those who attended."

When the time was right, Al Smith let Charley Cherokee do the talking. The group, he revealed, had "consider[ed] the danger of too many 'plans' and how to best reemphasize the idea that the Negro merely wants democracy administered through every government agency." The Black Cabinet made it clear: Walton's plan and all the others in circulation were unacceptable. The members remained certain that the system they had fought for over the years, one in which African Americans were represented throughout all of the federal government, was best. To place black brain trusters in a separate division would only validate and extend, not challenge, segregation.

In an effort to stop Walton, someone leaked a copy of one of his internal memos to Claude Barnett of the Associated Negro Press. In turn, Barnett's wire service released news of Walton's proposed separate black agency to the black press. It resulted in embarrassingly negative coverage for the ambassador and his plan—which to the public smacked of opportunism and accommodation to white racism. But Black Cabinet members did not fare well either. The story of their opposition and their secret meeting made them look self-serving, duplicitous, and thin-skinned. The *New York Amsterdam News* eagerly exposed Walton's proposal but it also dismissed the Black Cabinet members as "'Big Negroes' in fat jobs."

At the same time, the hush-hush, select gathering of the Black Cabinet also deepened the divide that already existed among African Americans in federal posts. It drew an even clearer line between the core pioneers and the recent arrivals. The old-timers, for the most part, still controlled the leadership of the group. Hard feelings became only more intense when the core members cut the rookies, whose numbers had grown rapidly, out of their internal fights with the federal government and unilaterally decided to oppose both the FEPC and the Walton plans. From the original members' view, their exclusivity was justified. The Black Cabinet's most effective weapons for change—stealthy protests and hidden campaigns—could not be used in a large group. By the summer of 1942, there were two Black Cabinets. One included all black racial-affairs advisers, numbering more than one hundred. The other was a highly select group of about a dozen senior black New Dealers.

Possibly in an attempt to smooth over rising internal animosity, on June 10, 1942, Mary McLeod Bethune summoned all Black Cabinet members to discuss the various plans for handling African American affairs. The goodwill that had been generated just after Pearl Harbor had long since evaporated. Splits had only intensified during the intervening months. Many Black Cabinet members had dug themselves even deeper into their separate trenches as their struggles to secure funding for individual programs had become more desperate. Furthermore, a small contingent of FEPC representatives who had joined the Black Cabinet enthusiastically promoted their agency's plan. Well-known foes of Robert Weaver, they added another thorny barrier to cooperative efforts.

Bethune called the meeting to order, and immediately the brimming distrust among the factions flared openly. Despite her attempts to assert her authority and maintain civility, the discussion over the various plans became "torrid." When pushed, Bethune surprisingly refused to take a stand for or against any plan. Then the "newcomers" did the unthinkable—they staged a coup and took control of the group. There was, Charley Cherokee reported, "no pretense of a solid front." He blamed the chaos on Bethune, for her failure to steer the Black Cabinet toward a single conclusion. Unable to settle on an acceptable alternative to any of the proposals in play, the meeting ended. It was now, Charley Cherokee declared, "every man for himself."

Although there was no consensus after the June meeting, almost everyone agreed that Lester Walton's proposal for a separate bureau was a terrible idea. Key Black Cabinet members spoke out publicly against it. At its annual meeting, the NAACP voted to oppose it. Rather than continue to fight and further jeopardize his standing in black leadership circles, Walton backpedaled. When confronted by reporters, he insisted he had no intention of setting up a competing and separate Black Cabinet, commenting that "the whole affair was an unfortunate misunderstanding."

Yet victory against Walton came with a price. The *Pittsburgh Courier* observed that the chaotic debate over the various plans had "served to only strengthen the [FEPC] . . . and to make it the dominant factor in the Negro's life in the United States to the chagrin and disappointment of many smart boys," no doubt referring to Weaver and his crowd. By mid-June, the FEPC's proposal remained the most favored of the many proposals—at least among white Washington bureaucrats and a few black political observers. It was Robert Weaver, FEPC supporters claimed, who stood in the way and prevented the plan from moving ahead. One African American FEPC member insisted that Weaver was ineffective and his methods, based in statistical studies and honed during the New Deal, were now obsolete. Weaver defended his record. Defense employers would not respond to "abstract justice" he insisted, but they were persuaded by numbers—by "sound economic proof that the Negro is entitled to a real post in industry."

Even the White House was in disarray over what direction to take. Reportedly, at one point FDR devoted part of one of his official cabinet meetings to discussing the various proposals floating around. According to the *Pittsburgh Courier*, that meeting was also "stormy," and in the end the cabinet secretaries agreed that "all plans submitted for directing the welfare of the Negro [should be] thrown into the discard."

Finally, in early July, after months of debate, FDR came to a decision. There would be no special presidential adviser and no Bureau of Negro

Affairs, he announced. Racial-affairs advisers would continue their work in their separate agencies. The FEPC would not report directly to him. Instead, he placed it under the War Manpower Commission (WMC) and directed Cramer to report to its head, former Indiana governor Paul McNutt, a Democrat. He also ordered the FEPC to refer Executive Order 8802 investigations to Weaver's office. White House adviser Jonathan Daniels had convinced the president that Weaver's approach achieved the best results.

Many bristled when FDR placed the FEPC under McNutt's control. While McNutt was publicly supportive of African Americans, most black leaders viewed him as disingenuous. McNutt was a politician at heart, with White House aspirations, and he hoped to reel in support from below the Mason-Dixon Line. The NAACP charged that FDR's decision put the FEPC's future in the hands of "southern reactionaries" who would not hesitate to kill it by slashing its funding. Bethune sent congratulations to McNutt when he took over the FEPC. She was always eager to cultivate white administrators, and in the past McNutt had supported some of her NYA efforts. Nonetheless, she had reservations. She told one acquaintance that McNutt had won control over the committee by using "political pressure" and lamented, "it seems that the whole thing will not be as active, yet we cannot tell how things will work out." Almost no one could miss the fact that McNutt acquired the FEPC after it had held investigatory hearings in Alabama and white southerners had sent up a shrill outcry.

While FDR's decision preserved the Black Cabinet and its model of integrating black advisers throughout the federal government, it was a limited triumph. In fact, troubles for the African American brain trust had only multiplied. Bill Hastie, Mary McLeod Bethune, Al Smith, and Robert Weaver found their battles intensified. These struggles consumed each one of them, leaving little time to coordinate as they desperately hung on. That summer Bethune telephoned one Black Cabinet member to check on her colleagues. Why hadn't anyone reported in? she asked. "The boys are too busy with their own little problems," was the explanation.

For Bill Hastie, as for others, the problems were hardly little. He witnessed the military regress in the area of race relations. In several locations, African Americans who rushed to enlist after Pearl Harbor reported being turned away by both the army and the navy. The War Department initially ordered the Red Cross to refuse African American blood. After protests flooded in, the military acquiesced but still required that black and white blood be stored separately. African American military personnel, often required to travel long distances between bases, frequently endured racial insults from railroad workers and white passengers. As southbound trains traversed the Mason-Dixon Line, conductors demanded that black servicemen, like all other African Americans, surrender their seats to white riders and move to Jim Crow cars. The military was shot through with racism, from the white officer corps to white enlisted men. New York City patrolman James Sloan, who had been assaulted by Stephen Early during the 1940 campaign, was attacked by two white soldiers who attempted to beat him with his own nightstick on the streets of Harlem. Sloan, who was in plainclothes, wouldn't have it; he fought back, subdued the duo, and had them arrested.

Despite his pessimism after the United States entered the war, Hastie continued battling military racism. He persisted in his demands that the U.S. Army desegregate. "The traditional mores of the South have been widely accepted and adopted by the Army as the basis of policy and practice in matters affecting the Negro soldier," he protested in a report to military officials. "So long as we condone and appease un-American attitudes and practices within our own military and civilian life, we can never arouse ourselves to the exertion which the present emergency requires."

War Department heads repeatedly cold-shouldered Hastie and ignored his appeals for reform. Integration was not only impossible, they claimed, it was foolish. Mixing black and white troops would impact "discipline and morale" and drastically weaken the nation's defensive capabilities. "The Army cannot accomplish such a solution and should not be charged with the undertaking," General George C. Marshall, the army's chief of staff, told Secretary of War Henry L. Stimson. During a War Department meeting with the black press, Claude Barnett suggested that "perhaps war is a good time to forget racial differences" and urged the army "to experiment with a mixed battalion." One military official stiffened. The U.S. Army, he declared, was not "a sociological laboratory." He insisted that segregationist traditions must be upheld, and to abandon them "would result in ultimate defeat."

Adding to his mounting frustrations, Hastie encountered solid resistance to his field investigations of prejudice within the ranks. Receiving numerous letters from servicemen protesting discriminatory treatment, Hastie scheduled tours of bases with the intention of interviewing complainants. When he arrived, he was often informed by white officers that no soldiers had come forward to speak with him. All was well, they insisted, while concealing that they had denied those who had complained permission to leave their posts to meet with Hastie. Wise to the military's deceptions, Hastie leaked his own protests through Charley Cherokee.

Doing what he could, Hastie documented that African American GIs unquestionably lived and worked under deplorable conditions. "Humiliation was a fact of life for the black soldier," his assistant, Truman Gibson, reported. Despite earlier promises, the War Department had assembled very few black combat units. Instead, African American enlistees were assigned to KP (kitchen) duty, to building and cleaning latrines, and to transporting supplies and dangerous munitions. On bases that housed both black and white GIs, African Americans lived in segregated barracks, trained in separate areas, and were forbidden from using recreational facilities. In some areas, MPs (military police) commonly beat black servicemen and detained them on trumped-up charges. Seventy-five percent of African American troops assigned to basic training were sent to bases in the South, where they faced hostility and violence from local townsfolk and police. At Arkansas's Camp Robinson, some local white residents formed a mob and threatened to "clean out" all African American soldiers. Sixty of the division's men went AWOL (absent without leave) seeking safe shelter.

Hastie submitted pages and pages of reports and memoranda detailing the persistence of racial brutality and prejudice in the U.S. military. He pushed for extensive reforms. These included a ban on the use of racial slurs by white officers and enlisted men as well as the desegregation of military housing, recreational facilities, drinking fountains, and toilets. He also called for the addition of more black MPs and insisted that the nation's governors order state and local law enforcement to treat black soldiers with fairness and respect.

Hastie's demands went unanswered.

In April 1942, a riot broke out at New Jersey's Fort Dix, resulting in the death of two African American GIs and one white military policeman. The War Department quickly dispatched Hastie to a meeting in Puerto Rico. The military didn't want his advice—it wanted him out of the way.

"As I had anticipated," Hastie remembered, "I was not really welcomed by the military." His office had been relocated to the new Pentagon Building in Arlington. That effectively isolated him from his bosses and required him to travel in and out of an area known to be antagonistic to black Americans. Although he was supposed to be consulted on all African American matters, "that was as much honored in breach as it was in performance," he recalled. He often first heard of War Department decisions affecting black Americans from the press.

According to reports by African American journalists, Hastie had offered his resignation three times between 1941 and 1942, only to have the War Department repeatedly refuse to accept it. When confronted about the rumors, Hastie avoided either denying or confirming they were true. But he did allow the black press to spill information on his frustrations. An Associated Negro Press report revealed that Hastie had become dissatisfied "when he discovered that his recommendations were not being taken as he thought they should be and as he had been promised they would." The *Pittsburgh Courier* assured readers that Hastie had "acted on every issue which concerns us." It reported that Hastie and Gibson stuck with their jobs because they believed that quitting would set back "the racial cause [and] . . . not improve the situation." African Americans must show support for the Black Cabinet member as well as for his colleagues, the paper urged. "We all can help Hastie by applying this pressure. But they can't and won't tell us how."

The stress of the job began to take a visible toll on Bill Hastie. Charley Cherokee reported to his readers that War Department business had cost Hastie many sleepless nights. By the summer of 1942, the always trim Hastie had grown gaunt and looked drawn. Truman Gibson remarked on his boss's increasing moodiness and noted that he had stopped socializing with other Black Cabinet members. At home, his marriage was in a shambles, nearing divorce.

Bethune had also been struggling. She was out of action for most of the first six months of 1942, as she battled asthma and painful bouts of arthritis. Her leadership in the Black Cabinet had been undercut both by her long absences from Washington and by younger, more militant members who felt the group was too conservative and moved too slowly. But Bethune still wielded significant power. Despite rumors that Crystal Bird Fauset had taken her place with the First Lady, Bethune's ties to both Roosevelts remained strong. After FDR had signed Executive Order 8802, she wrote to him, promising, "my strength and influence are yours to the end." She had also reminded Eleanor Roosevelt that she anticipated she would remain the administration's central adviser on African American issues: "I want you to feel that you can always depend on me and if there is any suggestion or consultation I can give please let me know." The relationship between the First Lady and Bethune continued on as quid pro quo, the favors flowing in both directions. It allowed Bethune to remain a behind-the-scenes force even when she was ill.

Bethune made use of her connections with the First Lady when, in 1942, she assumed a lead role in the desperate crusade to save the life of twenty-five-year-old sharecropper Odell Waller. Convinced he had been cheated out of his portion of a summer harvest, in July of 1940, Waller confronted his landlord, Oscar Davis. The dispute got heated, and believing that Davis was going for a gun, Waller insisted that he had been forced to shoot first to defend himself. An all-white jury convicted Waller and sentenced him to death. For two years, Waller had awaited execution. But A. Philip Randolph, working with activist Anna Pauline "Pauli" Murray, had taken up his case, asserting that Virginia's poll taxes, which excluded blacks from voting and serving on juries, denied the sharecropper his constitutional right to a fair trial. While Waller was only one very poor black farmer, he represented numerous African Americans throughout the South who had been robbed of justice by a racially biased all-white court system.

By June 1942, Waller had run out of appeals. At Randolph's request, Bethune arranged a meeting between Eleanor Roosevelt and a delega-tion representing Waller. Shortly after, the First Lady called Virginia's governor and pleaded with him to spare the young man's life. He refused. On July 1, with the execution set for the next day, Waller's supporters appealed to Mrs. Roosevelt again, requesting that she intercede and ask her husband to issue a reprieve. Throughout the day, the First Lady repeatedly telephoned Harry Hopkins, who during the war had become one of FDR's central advisers. She demanded to be put through to the president. Each time, Hopkins insisted FDR was too preoccupied with war business to talk to her.

While Eleanor Roosevelt was trying to get to her husband, Bethune and Randolph, along with Pauli Murray and seven others, made their way to the White House. The Oval Office staff turned them away. For the rest of the day, they were referred from department to department. The delegation was able to see a member of the attorney general's staff, who insisted Waller's case was out of the Justice Department's hands; there had been unfairness in the past and there would be more in the future, he shrugged. When they appeared at the office of a powerful congressman, he sent out an assistant to intercept them. That staffer, Murray recalled, "displayed contempt for the delegation by picking up Mrs. Bethune's cane . . . and twirling it like a drum major's baton." At the Office of War Information, they found its head sympathetic but adamant that he could not help. When Bethune informed him that protesters were ready to picket the White House, his attitude hardened. Such demonstrations were "unadvisable," he grumbled.

For more than eight hours, the group rushed around the capital trying to save Odell Waller's life. At one point Bethune spotted Vice President Henry Wallace in the hallway of his office. Wallace saw her coming and tried to hurry off. Despite her fragile health, the sixty-nine-year-old Bethune ran after him. "I can do nothing," he told her as she cornered him. "It is out of my jurisdiction."

That evening, the group retreated to the NAACP's local headquarters waiting to hear from Eleanor Roosevelt. She had persisted throughout the day. "Mrs. Roosevelt . . . would not take 'No' for an answer," Harry Hopkins wrote in a White House memo. "The President finally got on the phone himself and told Mrs. Roosevelt that under no circumstances would he intervene with the Governor and urged very strongly that she say nothing about it." At eleven o'clock that night, she telephoned with the bad news. Within hours, Odell Waller died in the electric chair.

It was a heart-wrenching loss.

Bethune was determined to carry on by reminding the country of the hypocrisies exposed by the war. Unity to fight fascism went hand in hand with the struggle for social justice and civil rights. In a speech before the 1942 Southern Conference for Human Welfare, Bethune asked the crowd, "What are we fighting for?" For her, the answer was clear: "We are fighting for the perfection of the democracy of our own beloved America, and the extension of that perfected democracy to the ends of the world." According to Bethune's assistant, Dovey Johnson Roundtree, "somewhere in her mind's eye, beyond what she called 'foolish prejudices and discrimination,' Dr. Bethune saw an America so perfect, so filled with possibility, that it was worth dying for." At a June rally, Bethune urged the audience to fight on for "full freedom, justice, respect, and opportunity . . . you are no longer begging—you are insisting, because you realize that America, the only country you know and the country you love, cannot be preserved nine-tenths free and one-tenth oppressed."

Back at her office in Washington, D.C., Bethune scrambled to save her division at the National Youth Administration. Budget cuts had forced her to lay off staff. Seeing her programs shrinking, she had begun pushing for opportunities to fill the void that would be left by a downsized NYA. In a fight paralleling Hastie's battle for black men, Bethune had become determined to see that black women find an equal place in the U.S. military. For months, she lobbied the War Department to accept African American women in the Women's Army Corps (WAC). Bethune's goal was to see that black women were not consigned just to the enlisted ranks but, when qualified, received commissions as officers. This would require that they be admitted to officer training camps, which Bethune anticipated would follow the established practice for men and be integrated.

At first, military leaders recoiled at the idea of allowing black women to become WACs and were even more vexed by the suggestion that they institute female interracial officer training programs. But Bethune refused to hear *no* and recruited a very willing Eleanor Roosevelt to join her in the fight. With the First Lady applying enormous pressure, the military brass, eventually and very reluctantly, gave in and agreed to admit African American women to the WAC officer training school in Des Moines, Iowa. The first group of trainees would consist of 440 candidates, forty of whom would be black. While the camp would be integrated, the military underscored its intention to deploy African American women in racially separate units. In response, Bethune gave the military's plan only a "partial o.k." and declared her intention to carry on a battle to desegregate the WAC at all levels. She did successfully barter to be included in the recruitment of the inaugural class of WAC officers. But, in truth, before any deals were struck, she had informed her secretary Harriet West and her assistant Dovey Johnson Roundtree that they would be volunteering to attend the Des Moines WAC officer training program.

In August, Bethune was on hand for the opening of the training camp. She beamed with pride as the first group of African American women arrived. All had high school diplomas, and the majority possessed college degrees. The day represented a proud triumph for Bethune, who praised the integrated WAC officer training school as "democracy in action" and told the crowd, "We are seeking equal participation. We are not going to be agitators."

But once Bethune departed, Jim Crow took over. The camp's leadership relegated African American WACs to separate barracks, to blacks-only tables in the mess hall, and to a segregated recreation center. They were assigned to a separate platoon. Although they attended integrated classes and drilled with white women, they marched separately from their white comrades. But the women, both black and white, resisted and reached across the racial divide. White commanders discovered an interracial group of trainees swimming together in the camp's pool. An order came down restricting African American women to a separate pool time, one hour just before it was cleaned. One white officer encountered a group of black and white WACs eating dinner together at a Des Moines restaurant. He stormed over and shouted: "You darkies move those trays and sit where you belong."

After that incident, Dovey Johnson Roundtree and several others telegrammed Bethune detailing the various forms of discrimination that the camp had instituted. About the same time, a local Democratic leader also alerted Eleanor Roosevelt. Bethune dispatched black newspaperman and local attorney Charles Howard to investigate. Using the First Lady's name (at Bethune's urging), he gained access to the base. When he questioned base commanders about the young women's claims, they affirmed that they had separated black and white recruits and insisted that the army's policy required "segregation." The army, Howard pointed out to Bethune, had no such explicit policy for officer training. Furthermore, he added, Iowa was not a Jim Crow state and had outlawed discrimination in all dining establishments—that would cover even military cafeterias.

But the attempts made by Bethune and the First Lady to stop the prejudicial treatment of black recruits at the Des Moines base backfired. In the fall, Walter White reported to Bethune that white hostility had only worsened. Black instructors, who had previously taught white or integrated classes, were reassigned. Additionally, the army circulated press releases quoting Bethune's speech at the camp's opening, twisting it to imply that she had sanctioned the military's segregationist practices. Bethune pushed back, eventually forcing the army to promise to conduct an internal investigation. But in Des Moines, white commanders threatened Roundtree with prosecution for treason for leaking information about discrimination to Bethune. Soon afterward, Roundtree was transferred to a recruiting office—in the South. Segregation at Des Moines would remain the norm.

Meanwhile, Bethune was fighting on other fronts. Now more than ever, with the war raging abroad and racism raging at home, times called for black federal officials to come to the rescue. The *Chicago Defender* urged Bethune to resuscitate the Black Cabinet and make a practice of holding public meetings. She certainly must have considered it, but as autumn approached, her health began to fail again.

It worsened when Congressman Martin Dies pressed forward with his earlier charges that Bethune was a communist. The previous year, responding to the congressman's accusations, the FBI had opened a file on Bethune. The agency had interviewed various confidential informants, questioning them on her activities and allegiances. Clearly many of those who had spoken with the FBI were her coworkers, likely even her supervisors, in the NYA. Uniformly they all insisted that despite maintaining affiliations with a long list of left-leaning organizations, she was faithful to the president and the nation. Her association with these groups, one informant testified, was "to further the cause of the Negro race." She belonged to many and varied organizations; she was a "joiner," said another, who contended that Bethune credited the American democratic system for her rise from poverty to prominence. She was willing to accept support from communist groups for her various crusades and was "admired" by them, yet another informant stated. But she was using them to advance her goals and believed that black Americans would "see through" communist doctrines.

All agreed that Mary McLeod Bethune was a loyal American. But FBI director J. Edgar Hoover had already ordered that she be placed on the bureau's "custodial detention" list, where she was officially identified as a communist. The list had been compiled by the FBI at the order of the Justice Department and included the names of U.S. citizens regarded as a "danger" to national security. In case of a national emergency, the Justice Department and FBI planned to arrest and detain those listed until authorities determined that they posed no danger to the country.

Bethune was probably unaware that she was targeted for custodial detention, but nonetheless, throughout the year, she had battled rumors that she was a subversive. In the spring of 1942, the FBI had arrived at her home to interview her. She emphatically and repeatedly denied she was a communist or had any ties to communist or socialist organizations. At the end of the interview, when the special agent in charge asked her whether she had any statement to make, she spoke forcefully. "It startles me just a little to even have anyone surmise . . . from the role of my activities in life and from the things I do and stand for that there would be within my thinking any type of belief or action that would bring me under the rays of communistic ideas," she remarked. "It seems I have been so far removed from what my interpretation of a Communist is." She continued, "My great antagonism to communistic ideas . . . has been its irreverence to God. I am very spiritually guided and minded, and I am so far removed from that type of [communist] thinking."

That spring, the Justice Department informed the FBI that it had determined there was no need to continue a formal investigation of

Bethune and had exonerated her from any violation of the Hatch Act or other subversive activities. Still, the FBI continued to monitor her movements in the press and maintained her name on the custodial detention list. When public queries came forward, the agency refused to confirm or deny she was a communist, insisting that its findings were classified. With Dies's continued allegations, a cloud of suspicion hung over Bethune, and she began to sink under the pressure.

In the fall, Bethune headed home to Daytona Beach, and her health rapidly declined. "I have just heard that you are ill," wrote Eleanor Roosevelt. "I am sorry because I know how it must annoy you to be ill at this time." Bedridden throughout most of November and December, Bethune suffered an asthma attack so severe that she lost consciousness and nearly died. "Five doctors, nurses, and a noted asthma specialist" worked to revive her. "I have given of myself so fully and freely for others that I have neglected the nursing of my own strength," she wrote to the First Lady. Physicians restricted Bethune to her home. Eleanor Roosevelt sent her a box of treats from the White House kitchen.

Bethune's absence, the attacks on African American programs, and internal conflicts within the Black Cabinet left its members adrift in the latter part of 1942. Although more African Americans swelled the ranks of clerical workers and office assistants, the number of race-relations advisers thinned further. The New Deal programs where most advisers operated were subject to even more drastic budget reductions. Staffs working under both Bethune and Al Smith continued to shrink. In the summer, Congress terminated the CCC, which finally sent its racial-affairs adviser, Edgar Brown, packing. A few Black Cabinet members were called up by draft boards. Constance Daniel lost her job in the Department of Agriculture after she publicly complained about the Farm Security Administration's practice of using federal dollars to pay poll taxes for white southern farmers while denying requests from black farmers for the same assistance. The WPA's Dutton Ferguson left to take on the editorship of the Urban League's *Opportunity*. Over the previous year, Lawrence Oxley, who was still working for the Employment

Security Board, had been stripped of nearly all of his staff and had abandoned his efforts at securing jobs for African Americans. He now served exclusively in a public relations role, traveling about the country and giving talks on black labor.

Some offices shifted Washington-based appointees to field jobs, where they encountered even more hostility. One black Office of War Information representative in the South was "almost beaten to death by white police," Charley Cherokee reported. When Black Cabinet members demanded protection for African American field investigators, in some cases agency officials responded by eliminating their divisions and letting them go. The results were the termination of local programs for African Americans nationwide and the reduction of federal oversight in areas where discrimination was most likely to occur.

The fatigue that had set in over years of fighting racism from the inside compounded the Black Cabinet's struggle to stay alive and relevant during wartime. In many instances, the federal workplace had become even more hostile as the black workforce grew to meet the needs of wartime. The War Department segregated its burgeoning office staff; white workers were allowed to continue with a normal nine-to-five schedule, while African Americans were assigned to a new and separate graveyard shift. The Treasury Department mandated a similar policy. Charley Cherokee reported that black rank-and-file federal employees continued to be passed over for promotion and raises, and many positions still remained closed to them. The War Manpower Commission (WMC) prohibited African American administrators from interviewing white job applicants and supervising white workers. In the Bureau of Engraving's restroom, white women assaulted black women. It was a demoralizing time for Black Cabinet members, who had been battling for equal treatment throughout society and in the federal workplace for so long. When African American writer George Schuyler encountered two Black Cabinet members in New York City in the fall of 1942, both acknowledged their deep dismay. Schuyler reported that one admitted that he "loathed the whole Washington setup" and that he "saw the

Negro sinking farther and farther into segregation, with the color caste system becoming more and more rigid." The other, Schuyler claimed, was "an unusual man of character and training," who was "very unhappy because he took his job determined to set the world on fire and hasn't been able to raise a smudge."

The Black Cabinet's despondency may have been fed by the resurfacing of rumors that the FEPC was in the process of displacing it. The committee still operated under Paul McNutt, who had consolidated his power and expanded the reach of the War Manpower Commission by absorbing other programs into his agency. A number of New Deal and wartime divisions and their African American programs, including Bethune's National Youth Administration, were placed under his control. At the same time, his relationship with FEPC committee members was fraught with tension. McNutt had cut and then delayed approving the FEPC's operating budget, forcing it into a hiatus that lasted from summer into the fall. He consistently denied the committee's requests to meet with FDR. As a result, the FEPC began to collapse as members began to drift off or quit.

Among Black Cabinet members, Robert Weaver dealt most directly with McNutt, who was his most senior supervisor. Weaver's office had been in perpetual conflict with the FEPC over defense hiring and the enforcement of antidiscrimination agreements. As the year grew long, Black Cabinet insiders feared that McNutt was plotting to oust Weaver and then, after defanging the FEPC, turn over all of the responsibility for Executive Order 8802 to white administrators.

By the fall of 1942, the FEPC was in deep trouble. Crippled by a reduced budget, lack of administrative support, and poor leadership, committee members clashed constantly. But the one point they all agreed on was that Robert Weaver was in part to blame for their failure to achieve more for African American workers. The committee had long resented him as a rival and believed his approach to black employment was ineffective. Public denunciation of Weaver among some black leaders continued. His Harvard pedigree and scholarly demeanor only fed the impression that he was cold and condescending; an October speech reinforced the perception that he was out of touch and too accommodating. "Regardless of current practices and in spite of existing attitudes, Negroes will be used in many occupations in the months to come," he lectured a black audience in Cleveland, Ohio. "[It] is your responsibility as American citizens to do your best to win this war. This means that you must facilitate the maximum possible output of war goods in your present or your future employment." The problem was, as the *Chicago Defender* pointed out, Robert Weaver was "sagacious and efficient" but "not a politician."

According to Lucia Mae Pitts, FEPC members threated to resign en masse that fall unless Weaver was removed. Responding to their pressure, in October, McNutt clipped Weaver's wings. He transferred Weaver's staff, including his investigators, to the FEPC. Weaver was then assigned to a new and separate division and given the title "assistant to the director of operations" of the WMC. McNutt confined him to promoting training programs for black workers and nothing more.

McNutt's decision had effectively shorn the Black Cabinet's pioneering leader of nearly all of his influence within the federal government. Lucia Mae Pitts was "steaming mad." She had seen the rise of the Black Cabinet, beginning on that autumn day in October 1933 when Weaver arrived in Foreman's office for his interview. Now she couldn't bear to watch as the Black Cabinet fell into ruins. "I told Dr. Weaver on no uncertain terms how I felt and added that I would be looking for another job," she recalled. Weaver tried to convince her to stay, but this only made her more upset: "I couldn't see how he could stomach the situation, much less try to make me stomach it."

One year after Pearl Harbor, on December 7, 1942, Lucia Mae Pitts finished her last day on the job in Washington. Shortly afterward, as a heavy snowstorm enveloped Capitol Hill, she headed out of town, bound for Chicago in an old car with a leaky carburetor. She spent the holidays with family. For much of the next year, she searched for a new way to make her contribution to the struggle for equal rights. She applied to work for the Red Cross and was sent for a required physical examination. When she arrived she was told blacks could not be admitted to the waiting room and she was directed to sit in the hall. The job didn't work out. But she had been mulling over another option. "I had had the WAC bug in my bonnet ever since the bill creating it had passed in Congress but had held off enlisting, first because Bob Weaver had flattered my ego telling me he could not get along without me, and second because my oldest brother was dead set against it," she recalled. She finally sought out a local recruitment office and signed up. Just before Christmas 1943, she received her orders. In January she reported for duty at the Des Moines Women's Army Corps officer training camp.

Chapter Thirteen

Last of the Brain Trusters

IN JANUARY 1943, after a long rest in Daytona Beach, Mary McLeod Bethune returned to Washington. Back at her desk, she resumed control over her National Youth Administration programs but was still frail. Her asthma continued to plague her each morning, and the special inhaler concocted by her doctors did little to help. She now feared being alone, so her secretaries arranged to have someone with her at all times. Drained of energy, and always the careful politician, she avoided calling Black Cabinet meetings. Al Smith, using Charley Cherokee's pen, sorrowed over the continual plots to depose Bethune from the black brain trust's leadership. He reported that newer appointees had turned against one another in a competitive fray that made all previous internal divides seem tame.

For Al Smith, 1943 got off to a very bleak start. For most of the previous year, the Work Projects Administration had been gasping to stay alive. The war kicked the economy into high gear, and in the estimation of many, the Great Depression was over. With the expansion of industry and the military, the nation's unemployment rate dropped to just under 5 percent. But joblessness and poverty persisted in various areas, especially in black America. Even though some populations had not fully recovered from the Depression, FDR's opponents argued that the WPA had become obsolete and that it sapped away critical funds that could be used for the nation's defense. The midterm elections of the previous fall had increased Republicans' numbers in the House of Representatives, further emboldening the "unholy alliance's" campaigns against the New Deal and aid to African Americans. Certain that the new Congress would use its control over the federal budget to block his wartime policies, the president succumbed to the pressure of the anti–New Deal forces and ordered the WPA disbanded in early 1943.

Al Smith spent that January wrapping up his projects and packing up his office. Despite his ambivalence about his experiences working for the New Deal, he was proud of his accomplishments. There had been no revolutionary, large-scale change, he admitted. But for almost eight years, his division of the WPA had employed, trained, and educated a critical number of African Americans; and it had battled back starvation for many black families and laid the groundwork for many African Americans to move into the middle class. The WPA construction projects, many of which provided jobs to African Americans, had built schools, libraries, recreational facilities, and hospitals in black communities around the nation. In the National Grapevine, Charley Cherokee predicted African Americans would mark the WPA's "passing in thoughtful contemplation—it changed race history."

Charley Cherokee would live on for several more years. Believing that as the Black Cabinet began to shrink, more of the burden for lobbying the federal government for African Americans would fall on black journalists, Al Smith accepted an offer from the *Chicago Defender* to become the paper's official Washington, D.C., correspondent. He immediately ran into barriers as he attempted to report the news. Black reporters were excluded from White House press briefings and from the congressional press galleries. They were allowed to sit in the visitor section of the House and the Senate but, like other visitors, prohibited from taking notes. He gathered what news that he could and continued undercover as Charley Cherokee, exposing inequalities, digging up dirt, and dishing on Washington in his weekly National Grapevine column.

At the War Manpower Commission (WMC), as 1943 dawned, a dismayed Robert Weaver slogged along. He was weary of being forced to make boosterish speeches for the WMC and of sending off his facts and figures to other divisions to be used in their studies and programs. He had been completely cut out of the antidiscrimination enforcement activities of Fair Employment Practices Committee (FEPC), but Paul McNutt had ordered massive cuts to the committee's budget, so it was barely functioning anyway. Vocal condemnation of the WMC head and his interference with the FEPC had grown so loud that, early in the year, President Roosevelt announced another reorganization effort, which he promised would give new life to the committee. While Weaver awaited the outcome, likely hoping to be included in the action again, he joined "Hold Your Job," a campaign designed to prepare African Americans for the postwar job market, which was certain to become even more competitive once white soldiers became civilians again.

But Weaver grew tired of waiting. In spring, he offered his resignation. McNutt refused to accept it. McNutt was likely worried about his own image and feared that losing one of the federal government's most prominent racial-affairs advisers might adversely impact both the White House's unity efforts and his future in politics. Since Weaver and his wife had just adopted a baby boy, and there were few other employment prospects, the pioneering Black Cabinet leader reluctantly agreed to stay on.

By January 1943, Bill Hastie's job was also becoming increasingly unbearable. Over the previous months, his relationship with Secretary of War Henry Stimson and other department officials had grown icier. The previous fall, Hastie had discovered from newspaper reports that Assistant Secretary of War John McCloy had appointed his own committee to advise him on policies related to African Americans in the military. By the time Hastie learned of it, the committee had already been meeting for a month. He protested to Stimson—McCloy's act duplicated and hence would block his efforts. The war secretary brushed him off. Not too long afterward, Stimson privately complained about meetings with Hastie; their discussions "took a great deal of drain out of me," Stimson grumbled. He had accepted the black civilian aide only because of his value as a publicity tool, he told white associates. Now he had begun to think that Hastie's "usefulness was limited."

For very different reasons, Bill Hastie also began to wonder if his usefulness had run out.

When Bill Hastie made a recommendation, military leaders ignored it. When he pointed out discrimination, they discounted it. Yet, thoroughly committed to integration, he refused to be silenced. By 1943, he had been fighting the military brass for two years over the segregation of a pilot training program that they had organized at Tuskegee Institute. "To me the Air Force was the place where we should have made the most progress, because the Army Air Force was essentially new [and unrestrained by] traditions," Hastie later recalled. Despite his pressure for an integrated air corps, the War Department restricted the Tuskegee program to black enrollees. Some African Americans denounced it as a "Jim Crow squadron."

After the Tuskegee program got underway, Hastie began to receive complaints of discrimination by men enrolled there—they served under white officers who treated them with disrespect and brutality. Although Tuskegee Institute itself had always been integrated, the military had ordered its affiliated base to be segregated. As conditions worsened, Hastie dropped his campaign to integrate the base and focused on improving the living and training conditions there. He also began pressing for Tuskegee air corps graduates to be fully integrated into the Army Air Force's pilot divisions. This placed him in direct conflict with General Henry H. "Hap" Arnold, an aviation pioneer. Pilots formed a special brotherhood, Arnold argued, a relationship he thought was impossible to achieve across race lines. "Any participation of blacks in the Air Force had to be in completely separate units where everybody involved was black," Arnold declared.

Hastie continued to lobby the military to accept African Americans into integrated pilot training at air force bases other than Tuskegee. Over and over again, military leaders turned down his proposals. By

December 1942, Hastie was reduced to battling to preserve the one place where the military allowed integration, and that was in officer training schools. Over the months, he had tracked plans for a new air force officer training school at Jefferson Barracks, Missouri; he had obtained assurances from the War Department that the barracks would, like all other similar programs, enroll blacks and whites. But just before Christmas, while on the road doing field investigations, Hastie picked up a Saint Louis newspaper and was stunned to read that Jefferson Barracks had been restricted to black trainees. He was infuriated. Not only had the upper ranks deceived him; they had spread Jim Crow into places where it had never before existed.

On January 2, 1943, the *Pittsburgh Courier*'s front-page headline read, "'Hate Rule' at Tuskegee Air Base Charged to Col. Kimble." Characterizing Tuskegee as a "Hell Hole of Prejudice," the article exposed rampant discrimination at the base. The *Courier* revealed that it had long known about the abuse of the cadets at Tuskegee but had been withholding the story to support national unity. Now the time had come to air the truth: "It is no longer possible to help the boys training there, nor the country, by keeping quiet." The base, the story insisted, was in the grip of "Ku Klux Klanism." Tuskegee's commander, Colonel Frederick Kimble, banned fraternization between officers of different races and repeatedly passed over black veterans in favor of far less experienced whites for promotion. He had also ordered parts of the base, including all toilets, to be segregated. The second in command, Lieutenant Colonel John T. Hazard, was Kimble's "hatchet man," who enforced Jim Crow by "explosive cursing tantrums of temper." Morale among the patriotic black Tuskegee airmen was plummeting, and the *Courier* demanded that the War Department do something immediately.

On January 5, three days after the *Courier*'s story ran, Bill Hastie informed the War Department that he would resign from his position as civilian aide. "Changes of racial policy should be made but will not be made in response to advocacy within the Department but only as a result of strong and manifest public opinion," he wrote to Stimson. "Therefore, it has seemed to me that my present and future usefulness is greater as a private citizen who can express himself freely and publicly."

Hastie's resignation made the national news. Reporters clamored for comment, but he remained silent until he finally departed his post in early February 1943. Then he was eager to talk, confirming that his was a protest resignation. The War Department's deceptiveness about the segregation of Jefferson Barracks was just one example of a long and troubling pattern of military Jim Crowism. In a press release to the *Chicago Defender*, he disclosed that for more than two years the Army's ranking air commanders had refused to consult with him—it was punishment for his opposition to segregated pilot training. He also divulged that the War Department regarded the Tuskegee program as an "experiment"; its leadership doubted that African American men could become competent pilots or capable members of ground crews. Racism drove the military's policies and decision making. "This attitude is the result of wholly unscientific notions that race somehow controls a man's capacity and aptitudes," Hastie revealed.

Military leaders had also broken their promise that African Americans who completed the Tuskegee program would be allowed to fight, Hastie revealed. Instead, these trained pilots had been assigned to segregated squadrons and immediately grounded, relegated to "odd jobs and common labor." Pledging to continue his struggle on behalf of all black servicemen, Hastie stated that his decision to carry on his battle from outside came because he was convinced that "public opinion is still the strongest force in American life."

The African American press showered Hastie with praise for his resignation. The *Baltimore Afro-American* commended him as "courageous" for his "high sense of public responsibility." He had, the *Kansas City Call* reported, delivered "a severe blow at the sham, which pervades the War Department." The *Chicago Sunday Bee* predicted that Hastie's public departure from federal service would "dramatize the feelings and convictions of American Negroes who are daily irritated by the insults of racial injustices." Charley Cherokee reported that some believed Hastie had "done more for race relations inside and out of the Army than anything since the war started." Stimson was scurrying now, he alleged, to stop the rising tide of criticism. Will Alexander later observed that Hastie "rendered a greater service by resigning," since his actions generated "considerable trouble" for the secretary of war and his department. Indeed, military officials ordered their news-tracking service to gather the black press's reaction to Hastie's departure. It reported back: "The varied reactions of the Negro were all favorable and approved of his resignation."

In the short term, Hastie's strategy worked. By quitting the War Department he had created tremendous public pressure that forced military chiefs to act. They handed down transfer orders for Kimble and Hazard. One of the War Department's most progressive white officers, Colonel Noel Parrish, was sent in to take control of the Tuskegee camp. He immediately desegregated all base facilities, recruited more African American flight instructors, commenced combat training, and made attempts to improve troop morale. Many of the men praised the colonel and some insisted that his reforms paved the way for what would become the Tuskegee Airmen's later successes in the skies over Europe.

Yet, despite these steps forward, the military clung to segregation. Outside of integrated officer training in most locations, separation of the races remained enforced throughout the ranks.

In late February 1943, senior male members of the Black Cabinet gathered and roasted Hastie at a testimonial dinner. Joining in the celebration were Robert Weaver and his circle—which included Bill Trent, Ted Poston, and Frank Horne. Charles H. Houston, Al Smith, and Hastie's assistant, Truman Gibson, also took part. It was an evening of "ribbing" and "witticisms" over a hearty dinner followed by "scotch and tobacco." As the hour grew late, Hastie discussed his resignation. And the inevitable shoptalk eventually took over. The group contemplated "the besieged position of race relations in the government" and discussed what to do next.

In the following weeks and months, challenges faced by the Black Cabinet and its members grew more extreme. The fractured and unwieldy size of the group had terminated collective action. Bethune would not attempt to regenerate a united front. Physically it was too taxing, and she would not risk another public meeting at which she had to fight off new Black Cabinet members determined to push her out of the group's leadership. Her public position relied on maintaining an image as the venerated head of the African American brain trust.

Congress also continued to pose a grave danger to the Black Cabinet. Speculation that the House would soon eliminate most of the administration's racial-affairs advisers circulated through D.C. corridors. Alabama congressman Joe Starnes, who had attacked the Black Cabinet the previous year, called for the termination of housing specialists Bill Trent and Frank Horne and for the suspension of public housing programs. At one point, Starnes demanded that a list of all interracial housing projects be made public. Now safely on the outside, Bill Hastie was tapped to respond. In the black press, he condemned Starnes's action as a manipulation of white racial resentments and an irresponsible political ploy. He charged that publicizing the locations of integrated housing exposed residents to potentially life-threatening attacks by white supremacists.

Congressman Martin Dies also continued his crusade against specific members of the Black Cabinet. In a speech before the House in early 1943, he alleged that along with thirty-eight white federal employees, Bethune and the Treasury Department's racial-affairs adviser, William Pickens, were "dangerous red radicals." These "irresponsible, unrepresentative, crackpot and radical bureaucrats," he claimed, were controlling the federal government. Dies demanded that those he named be forced to appear before a congressional subcommittee for questioning.

Bethune sought help from Eleanor Roosevelt.

"I wanted to ask your opinion concerning the Dies attack. What must I do about it? It is beginning to annoy me," she wrote.

"If I were you I would get the most respectable white people I knew to write Mr. Dies and tell him they are outraged," the First Lady responded, adding, "I would write but I am a Communist too, so Mr. Dies says!"

Bethune turned to Charles H. Houston. He remained affiliated with the NAACP and continued to be one of the most respected black attorneys in the country. His first move was to rally public opinion. Working with the NAACP, he helped compose and distribute a national circular urging sympathetic congressional representatives to "vigorously oppose every attempt to stir up race or other prejudice" against African American advisers and their programs. Additionally, the NAACP called for African Americans to fight against the reelection of Dies and his congressional cronies. The black community must support Bethune and Pickens in their fight against red-baiting and in their efforts to retain their jobs, Houston insisted.

He also organized a letter-writing campaign on Bethune's behalf. The attacks on Bethune, he declared in his appeal, were "preposterous" and "reckless." They were a component of a larger assault on civil rights and African American women. "I do not believe that Mr. Dies himself thinks that Mrs. Bethune is a communist," Houston wrote to Bethune's supporters, black and white alike. "The trouble is that she is a black woman holding an important government position with influence in high government places, and for a black person to have such a position and such influence is to be ipso facto 'red' with Mr. Dies."

In response, more than one hundred letters—from educators, religious leaders, activists, philanthropists, and many others supporting Bethune—flooded into the congressional mailroom. The vast majority came from African Americans; despite Bethune's long history of good relations with whites, very few came to her aid. But among those from the black community was one from charter black brain trust member Forrester Washington. He condemned Dies for acting out of "ignorance, cowardice, or race hatred." To remove Bethune from office would be a disaster. She was a key figure in the administration's war "victory effort," Washington pointed out. "There is not a more important Negro in this country from the point of view of building morale, patriotism and character in general within the Negro race."

Dies refused to back down. In the spring of 1943, the House Un-American Activities Committee, charged with investigating his allegations, began to call the accused to closed-door hearings. William Pickens appeared first. According to the *Chicago Defender*, he testified for three solid hours. Reports indicated that Bethune's turn came sometime in April 1943. Given the confidential status of the inquiry, everyone involved remained tight-lipped. But Bethune had armed herself with a bold statement:

> If Rep. Dies sees fit to name me as a communist as a result of my outspoken belief in true democracy under our American form of government, my incessant efforts in seeking for all Americans the constitutionally guaranteed rights of full citizenship regardless of race, creed, or color, my endeavors to enlist the full cooperative strength of America in our victory efforts, then the names Mr. Dies chooses to apply are to me but tinkling cymbals and sounding brass.

Whether or not Bethune was able to deliver her remarks was never clear. But she and Pickens both escaped being formally charged as subversives. What went unsaid publicly, but what Dies as a congressman must have known, was that the year before, the FBI had already cleared her (and likely Pickens) of all charges of communist leanings. Dies's accusations were public theater designed to undermine Bethune, who had emerged as one of the nation's most important civil and women's rights leaders of the era.

Ironically, while Black Cabinet members faced some of their most venomous opponents and watched as their influence in government faded, they finally began to receive positive attention in the national white media. The coverage may have come from a boost by the White House as part of its drive for interracial wartime unity and as a celebration of the group's successful contributions to the African American struggle for equality. An *American Magazine* article, "Black Brain Trust," credited the Black Cabinet for crafting Executive Order 8802, establishing the Fair Employment Practices Committee, and creating opportunities for African Americans in the military, government, and defense industries. "The Black Cabinet," which appeared in *Common Sense*, a popular political publication, argued that with Bethune at the helm, the group had opened up more federal jobs for African Americans and compelled some unions to accept black members. Racial-affairs advisers, the article claimed, resisted being used "as a shield against pressure," and it added that Bill Hastie's protest resignation was evidence of internal resistance against the stubborn bigotry of white governmental administrators.

In his memoir *Washington Is Like That*, D.C. editor and publisher W. M. Kiplinger praised the Black Cabinet for its role in ending the civil service's discriminatory photo-identification hiring requirements and for integrating at least some federal government buildings and spaces. "It is really a revolution in Negro relations, accomplished with a minimum of publicity," he observed. African American journalist Roi Ottley, who reported for the *New York Amsterdam News* and the *Pittsburgh Courier*, also hailed the Black Cabinet for its victories in his widely circulated book *New World A-Coming*. He recounted the group's protest against White House press secretary Stephen Early's blunders during the 1940 election, its fight for the inclusion of African Americans in the Sojourner Truth Homes, and its battles on behalf of African American soldiers. Ottley maintained that the Black Cabinet opposed "anything that smacks of race separatism." But, as Ottley also observed, "much remains to be accomplished."

Washington-based white journalist Albert Hamilton agreed with Ottley's last observation. And he pointed to an alarming trend. During his third term, the president's days and nights were consumed with fighting the biggest war in human history. Whereas the New

Deal Roosevelt seemed approachable and filled with endless cheer, the World War II Roosevelt was remote and forever preoccupied. It was nearly impossible now to get to Roosevelt, even through the First Lady. Hamilton discovered what Black Cabinet members already knew: the president now sought counsel on African American issues from an inner circle of white advisers, which included white southerners Mark Ethridge and Lawrence Cramer (both from the FEPC) and longtime White House staffer Jonathan Daniels. "While all of these men have liberal reputations, the more militant Negroes, including many in the government, would not list them as effective advocates of Negro rights," Hamilton remarked.

In another troubling development, by spring of 1943, the administration began routinely selecting whites for racial-affairs posts in departments and agencies throughout the government. Among the new white appointees were Milton Starr, the proprietor of a chain of black theaters, who was consulting with the Office of War Information on African Americans in film; and Malcolm S. MacLean, formerly of Hampton Institute and fresh from a decidedly unsuccessful tenure at the FEPC, who had secured the post overseeing African American relations for the Department of the Navy. The White House justified its decision to turn to the "White Cabinet," as it was becoming known, by claiming that whites were ostensibly "less emotional and more objective in administering their posts when problems involving colored citizens arose."

Members of the black community stridently objected to the administration's increasing reliance on the White Cabinet. The Urban League's Pauline Redmond Coggs, formerly an assistant to Bethune, charged that white advisers would serve no good purpose. White northern liberals lacked an authentic understanding of black needs, and the white southern members were "infected with race jitters"; they blocked concessions to African Americans, arguing it was necessary to avoid a white backlash that would undermine the war effort. The *New Journal and Guide* of Norfolk, Virginia, denounced the White Cabinet's rise as just another effort at "keeping the Negro 'in his place.'" The empowerment of white advisers, the *New York Amsterdam News* insisted, was a "definite drive in Washington to eliminate the so-called Black Cabinet." The Urban League's Lester Granger rejected the White Cabinet and called for a "restoration" of the original black brain trust. "Time to Wake, Cabineteers," Charley Cherokee commanded.

In the middle of May 1943, the black press reported rumors that Bethune had called a meeting and made an attempt at resuscitating the Black Cabinet. Who attended and what was discussed remained confidential. But the events that followed hinted that the Weaver faction may have taken the lead and was aiming to use the might of the African American vote to regain what little power the members once possessed. Mindful of the Hatch Act and disdainful of the crude nature of political machinations, they proceeded gingerly and covertly.

On May 22, the *Chicago Defender*'s Harry McAlpin, formerly of Bethune's National Youth Administration, announced that he had conducted a survey of the black brain trust members and their opinions on the "growing unrest among Negro voters." He reported that it was "the consensus among the members of the 'black cabinet' that the Negro, in 1944, will be voting on men and issues rather than on party labels." Republicans had committed a long list of sins, it was true. But, McAlpin asserted, the White House had prioritized "expediency over principle" and increasingly neglected the black population to placate white southerners. FDR's administration had failed its newly converted African American base with "the gradual lessening of the influence of the 'black cabinet' and the usurpation of their advisory function by an appeasement minded group of 'white experts.'" The displacement of the Black Cabinet had forced African American voters to question their allegiance to the Democrats. African Americans had helped Roosevelt win three consecutive terms, and McAlpin cautioned both Democrats and Republicans against assuming that the black ballot was theirs to keep.

William Thompkins, the D.C. recorder of deeds, the last of the 1932 campaign's Big Four and a pioneering African American brain truster, was furious when he read what seemed to him to be the betrayal of the president and the Democrats by certain Black Cabinet members.

In early June, Thompkins gave an exclusive and gloves-off interview to Al Smith, openly reporting for the *Chicago Defender*. In it, Thompkins assailed the Weaver crowd as "Political Snobs" and fumed about their threat to break with the Democrats. No matter how anyone had obtained his or her job—through political payback, academic or activist credentials, or civil service channels—Thompkins insisted that those jobs were all tied to the fortunes of the Democratic Party and FDR. He dismissed the attitude held by many Black Cabinet members that party fidelity would sully their image as experts and representatives; he viewed it as foolish, naïve, and unrealistic. Even worse, Thompkins insisted, Weaver and his "fact-finding" had hurt the president rather than help black people. The data Weaver collected had been appropriated by FDR's critics and used against the White House. "Unless Roosevelt runs in 1944," Thompkins warned, "anything can happen." Loyalty to the president and his party was paramount to the survival of the Black Cabinet and to the uplift of the race. "It would be better if fair Harvard taught these Negro Ph.D.s a little politics, even if the dirty kind," Thompkins thundered. "As they are, they are no asset to either party and so far as government, the Negro public, and the Democratic Party are concerned, they live in a 49th state—the State of Inertia."

Thompkins's indignation provided just a hint of the multiple divides that blocked efforts to glue the Black Cabinet back together. In mid-June, Al Smith, as Charley Cherokee, reported that factions led by Bethune, Weaver, and Thompkins had been displaced by a "clique" composed of recent hires in the Housing Authority and the War Department. These newcomers were led by Bethune's former assistant T. Arnold Hill, who was believed by some to be positioning himself to unseat her and become the government's key adviser on all issues regarding African Americans.

Hill's maneuverings were the least of Robert Weaver's concerns. His troubles had been brewing for some time and were complicated by his ongoing conflicts with the War Manpower Commission's Paul McNutt. In spring 1943, McNutt exiled Weaver to the WMC's place-ment bureau and assigned him to report to a low-level administrator. This distanced Weaver even further from the higher authorities in the WMC, reducing his already limited effectiveness. Once word of Weaver's demotion reached the black public, protests immediately arose. "The administration is singularly blind," complained the *New York Age*, lobbying for Weaver to be restored to a position of full responsibility and influence. The *Chicago Defender* blasted McNutt for dispatching Weaver into a post where he was "enmeshed by a maze of irrelevant, unimportant functions." The move marked "the gradual but certain disintegration of the so-called Black Cabinet, the lone remaining vestige of liberal New Deal thinking."

The summer of 1943 brought dismal times. News from the battlefront was grim, the loss of American lives mounting as the war dragged on. Spirits sank, especially in the African American community, which faced one grave disappointment after another. Overcrowding in urban centers, continued discrimination in the military, and the persistent denial of civil rights heightened frustrations. The weather grew miser-ably hot, and riots exploded in several cities. One of the most serious occurred in Detroit, where racial tensions had been building since the previous conflict over the Sojourner Truth Homes. On June 20, 1943, white and black youths clashed at a local amusement park, and later in the evening, fights spread throughout the city. False reports alleging that black men were raping white women circulated among whites in the city. They formed mobs and attacked African Americans riding public transportation or enjoying a night out in Detroit's business and entertainment district. Black motorists were pulled from their cars and beaten. Police generally ignored victims' pleas for help.

But some black residents of Detroit, enraged by wartime inequali-ties, police brutality, and white violence, decided to fight back. A few assaulted white people on the streets, in their cars, and on the city's trolley system. Some threw rocks and bottles at police. In the black community, white businesses were ransacked and looted. Authorities sealed off the area, leaving those African Americans unable to reenter their neighborhoods and return to their homes at the mercy of white gangs, which now dominated the city's streets and byways. Local African American leaders demanded the city step in and stop the violence.

As morning dawned on June 21, the Detroit riot stretched into its second day, and authorities were unable to establish any kind of control. In Washington, D.C., Mary McLeod Bethune, likely acting on a request from Detroit's black leadership, urgently wrote to Eleanor Roosevelt, demanding an appointment with FDR and insisting that she was "thinking most sincerely now in terms of strength and guidance for our President." It is unlikely she got her meeting—FDR was in Hyde Park and seeing no one. The Detroit violence raged and the administration seemed to vanish from the public eye. Internally, uncertainty reigned, and White House advisers feared the wrong move would hurt the president. Bringing the crisis under control by deploying more troops seemed like the only solution—but, they worried, that might also backfire and result in worse bloodshed.

Bethune quickly turned to external sources to levy pressure on Roosevelt to act. She endorsed the Urban League's call for the president to use the power of his office to stop the riot. She also fired off her own public message to FDR, which she released to journalists. "A straight forward determined statement and program of action from you that will reach the core of this problem is imperative," she insisted. "We know you as the courageous leader who will not hesitate to act when the need of action is apparent."

As night fell in Detroit, thousands of whites gathered with the intention of breaking police lines and storming the black community. City and state officials compelled a divisional army commander to send troops, while the War Department and the president worked on issuing an official order. Even before the administration finally acted, U.S. soldiers used tear gas to drive rioters from the streets, finally restoring order to the city on the third day. In the end, twenty-five black people and nine white people lay dead. Seven hundred Detroit residents were injured, and the city estimated that it had sustained more than $2 million in damage to properties and businesses.

Detroit was not the only city that suffered from racial clashes that summer—violent white mobs had attacked minority communities in Harlem and Los Angeles. Black leaders called on FDR to assert his leadership and denounce these riots in a fireside chat. Worried that coming to the defense of African Americans would deepen white resentments and undermine the war effort, the president dodged their pleas.

Eventually the White House contrived a roundabout way to publicly denounce white urban mob violence. Congressman Vito Marcantonio of New York, whose district included parts of Harlem, wrote to Roosevelt with a strident condemnation of the race riots, protesting their damaging impact on African American communities and morale. Administration staffers seized the opportunity to circulate FDR's response in the press. "I share your feeling that the recent outbreaks of violence in widely spread parts of the country endanger our national unity and give comfort to our enemies. I am sure that every true American regrets this," the president wrote to the congressman in a letter that the White House released to journalists. Additionally, the administration also reported that Roosevelt had directed several agency chiefs, including Attorney General Francis Biddle, "to give special attention to the problem" of racial unrest in the nation.

Biddle was greatly respected by African Americans. He was a member of the NAACP and, even after he became U.S. attorney general in 1941, remained on the organization's national legal committee. Under his leadership, the Justice Department attempted to prosecute cases of lynching, debt peonage, and voting rights violations. In April 1943, Biddle tackled police brutality and pushed for indictments of three officers who had beaten a black prisoner named Robert Hall to death in Georgia. Yet Biddle's Justice Department had no racial-affairs adviser, and the attorney general often defended the White House against charges that it ignored African American concerns. In front of one black audience, he had praised the War Department for eliminating discrimination. That was probably a surprise not only to his listeners but also to the Black Cabinet and its former colleague Bill Hastie.

In early July, at a private meeting, Biddle criticized Detroit's white population as "short-sighted and narrow minded" and warned that its actions might "defeat some of the lofty purposes for which our soldiers are fighting and dying." During this time, Biddle was in the process of drafting a report to the president about the city's recent riot, in which he offered recommendations for preventing further racial clashes there and across the country. He insisted that much of the friction emerged from residential disputes and urged the administration to take steps to improve housing conditions nationwide. Biddle also recommended the establishment of a formal interdepartmental committee of representatives from all agencies dealing with African American affairs. A national educational campaign dedicated to promoting racial harmony would also help ease tensions, he added.

But Biddle also advised the administration to give "careful consideration . . . to limiting—and in some instances putting an end to—negro migrations into communities which cannot absorb them, either on account of their physical limitations or cultural backgrounds." The African American exodus from the South—the Second Great Migration—he implied, was the root cause of racial violence. Riots could be prevented if blacks were shut out of industrial jobs in cities where racial tensions simmered. This could be accomplished simply, Biddle suggested, if defense contractors were authorized to turn away potential black employees.

On July 15, 1943, Biddle delivered his report, marked confidential, to the White House.

A brave African American messenger working in the Justice Department made certain to get Biddle's report into the hands of the Black Cabinet leadership. Shortly afterward, a select group, likely headed by Weaver, gathered in secret to discuss how to thwart Biddle's plan to halt African American migration and exclude black applicants from defense jobs. The attorney general's recommendations threatened to unravel much of the progress in employment and housing that the Black Cabinet had fought for since the New Deal's heyday. If implemented, the plan would also be a flagrant denial of the constitutional rights of African Americans. The restriction of freedom of movement based on race echoed the era of slavery and, when African American mobility was completely constrained, tied to the whims of white masters or, in the case of free blacks, to local and state laws. Besides Japanese Americans, who were subjected to mass wartime internment, no other group of citizens was targeted for such an action. It called for a quick response.

As with the previous year's campaign against Lester Walton's "Bureau of Negro Affairs," the Black Cabinet's attempts to head off Biddle required extra care. The messenger who leaked Biddle's plan had to be shielded, as did Black Cabinet members participating in obstruction of a confidential proposal made directly to the president by the attorney general of the United States. Eventually they decided to fight back using public pressure. They leaked the attorney general's report to the *New York Post*, which ran a feature that quoted directly from it. (Black Cabinet member Ted Poston, a former *Post* reporter, likely opened the channel to the paper.) Other news outlets followed suit; the white newspaper *PM* and the African American *Chicago Defender* reprinted the complete text of Biddle's confidential report to the president.

The reaction from the African American community was swift. On behalf of the NAACP, Walter White telegrammed Roosevelt, condemning Biddle's recommendations as "obviously illegal, unsound, and destructive of public confidence. The inequality and injustice of the proposal are appalling." Kansas City's *Plaindealer* urged readers to commence protests immediately: "This [ban on black migration] is a condition that may exist before the end of this year, either quietly or openly. And we might as well start fighting this thing now." The *Pittsburgh Courier* called for its readers to write to the White House directly with their objections:

Tell the President curtailing the movement of workers from one section of the country to another on purely "racial" grounds is, in your opinion, little different from NAZIS curtailing the movement of workers in Germany purely on "racial" grounds; and that you regard such a proposal as the most REACTIONARY that has been made since the days of the notorious Black Laws.

The Urban League's Lester Granger declared Biddle's plan "unconstitutional" and condemned it as a double standard that allowed "white southerners to migrate and bring their social problems with them, but not Negro war workers."

When reporters sought comment from FDR, the White House denied that the president had any knowledge of Biddle's recommendations. Then the administration sent Biddle out to repair the damage. Attempting to sidestep the hot-button migration issue, the attorney general focused on assuring the black public that there was no intention of displacing the Black Cabinet with an interdepartmental committee. But members of the press demanded he respond to their questions about restricting the movement of black citizens. He refused to comment, stating that while confidential White House communications could not be discussed, he could promise that African Americans' civil liberties would be safeguarded. That seemed duplicitous, since at the same time, he was urging "responsible officials" to take stock of the capacities of their cities and towns to absorb newcomers "before taking any steps to fill the particular manpower requirements." Using the urban housing shortage, Biddle left the door open for African Americans to be barred from seeking a better life outside of the South through defense work.

Consequently, voices objecting to the Biddle plan grew only louder. Eventually the president, through a White House spokesman, issued promises that the administration would not restrict migration or direct employers to specifically discriminate against potential workers on the basis of race. Later the attorney general, whose reputation had suffered badly, blamed the White Cabinet for the proposal. He claimed he had only signed on to the plan at its members' behest.

Derailing the Biddle plan was an important triumph for Black Cabinet veterans who had survived years on the federal battlefield. But the victory was bittersweet. As they fought for this win, both Mary McLeod Bethune and Robert Weaver, the central leadership of the black brain trust, began desperate efforts to retain their posts and what was left of their influence within the Roosevelt administration.

Bethune's challenges had multiplied in number and severity throughout 1943. The previous winter, her doctors had forced her to resign the presidency of Bethune-Cookman College. She continued to serve as the cash-strapped institution's premier fund-raiser and even talked Eleanor Roosevelt into undertaking a brief speaking tour to support the campus. Bethune also still ruled over the National Council of Negro Women and used it to crusade for civil rights and equal treatment for African American women. At the same time, she remained in the center of a stormy struggle to preserve the National Youth Administration. By the summer of 1943, the NYA was one of the last surviving New Deal programs, a reminder of the liberal "common man" philosophy of the energetic and early days of the Roosevelt administration. Bethune remained thoroughly devoted to her agency and the ideals that had given it life. "I am classified as a New Dealer and have no apologies to make for that," she wrote to a friend. "I believe in the democratic and humane program of our New Deal leader, Franklin Delano Roosevelt." Even though the president and his advisers may have lost sight of their original mission, Bethune was sure of hers.

In the later part of June, the NYA ended up caught in a tug of war, with the House killing the agency only to have the Senate revive it. However, the Senate's reprieve was short-lived, as the House Committee on Appropriations circled back for another attack, this time on the NYA's budget. During committee hearings, Republican congressman John Taber of New York made the explosive and salacious claim that the youth of his state enrolled in NYA programs were engaged in interracial "sex affairs." The allegations of miscegenation set off alarms among southern white Democratic committee members who, in turn, joined their Republican counterparts and cut off all funding for the program. The NYA was dead.

In early July, Mary McLeod Bethune received her termination notice and orders to shut down all of her programs by the end of the month. Although she knew it was coming, nonetheless she was devastated. Bethune relished the power and prestige that came with her position. But she was also entirely devoted to the people and believed that the New Deal had been an opportunity for the nation to pursue a different path. Now she would have to dismiss more than two hundred black NYA field officials and suspend all job training, as well as paid stipends, for "tens of thousands" of African American teens and young adults. "Mary Bethune took the NYA fold-up pretty hard, and well she might," remarked Charley Cherokee. "Overnight 1,500 colored youth training for war jobs, cut off. . . . Colored people will feel it for a long time . . . [and] for southern colored kids with mechanical aptitude it's back to the kitchen and the ditch."

As Bethune was shutting down her program, she composed a final report of her accomplishments. It was an impressive list. For the first time in their lives, many African Americans, as NYA participants, had received proper nutrition and health care. Enrollees had been able to help feed and clothe their impoverished families. A significant number of young black Americans had received vocational training. Bethune's program had given people an opportunity for basic schooling and a chance to learn to read. Her scholarships had opened up higher education to many African American students. Black colleges and universities had received federal support to develop, sustain, and expand their curricula. Bethune's influence had reached well beyond the NYA. Through it she had forged opportunities for African American women to serve in the U.S. military. Her ascendance in Washington had allowed her to transform the Black Cabinet, for at least a time, into an effective voice for black citizens. Bethune had used that voice to further her vision of an inclusive and reconstructed nation, one freed from racism and sexism. While she achieved only a portion of the reform of America's race and gender relations she had hoped for, she had given it her all.

"I have felt like a mother at the burial of her murdered child," Bethune wrote to Eleanor Roosevelt. "It is hard to give NYA up. I think of the thousands of youth all over America who had no other chance but that they got through the National Youth Administration."

"I am just as sad as you are to have the National Youth Administration abolished. I feel it was our first step in providing education to those who could not afford to pay for it," Eleanor Roosevelt replied. "Perhaps after the war is over enough people will realize its value to demand its revival." The NYA's head, Aubrey Williams, himself out of a job, also attempted to lift Bethune's spirits: "You have been and are a source of strength and inspiration to young and old in the day-by-day job of making democracy a living thing for this nation." Charley Cherokee counseled Bethune to take solace in knowing that "she is the best thing that happened to the New Deal, and the government will be hollering for her again in the post-war time."

Bethune decided she wasn't going to wait for the war to end to get back into the fray. Almost immediately she appealed to Eleanor Roosevelt to help her find a new federal position. The First Lady was certainly aware of the political benefits that came with her association with America's most popular black female leader. And she also had a deep personal loyalty to Bethune. Eleanor Roosevelt knew that the sixty-eight-year-old was in poor health and in financial straits. The National Council of Negro Women allowed Bethune to continue to live in her home in the floors above its Washington, D.C., headquarters and waived her rent. With some prodding from Eleanor Roosevelt, Bethune-Cookman donor and successful businessman Marshall Field Jr. agreed to cover the salary of Bethune's secretary.

The now retired NYA administrator accepted all the help and was grateful. But, she insisted, she was eager to continue to work.

"Have you found anything for Mrs. Mary McLeod Bethune? E.R." read a memo the First Lady sent off to the president at the end of July 1943. Bethune asked about a job with the Fair Employment Practices Committee, but Eleanor Roosevelt's secretary replied that the committee had "no place important enough" for her. Why not appeal to White House adviser Jonathan Daniels for help? the First Lady suggested. In the past, such a request for a position for a well-respected African American leader would have gone to Bethune herself. It was an indication of the White Cabinet's ascendancy and the Black Cabinet's decline.

In August, Bethune still had no prospects, and in a face-saving announcement, she informed the public that she intended "to take some time to think through these various opportunities to make sure I am putting first things first. I shall, therefore, take some needed rest and make up my mind as to the thing that offers me the greatest opportunity for service at this stage of my life."

What the statement concealed was that her health was again deteriorating. In late August, a severe asthma attack sent her back to the hospital, where she remained for five weeks. Once released, despite remaining weakened, she resumed her push to get back into government. Perhaps, she suggested to Eleanor Roosevelt, she could be offered a job that she might refuse to maintain "prestige" with the African American community. That kind of political play was "dishonest," the First Lady objected. Still, she continued to search for some way for Bethune to make a comeback, lobbying both her husband and Jonathan Daniels without success. Eventually she turned to Will Alexander, who was barely hanging on at the War Manpower Commission. Bethune had "no source of income," she told him, asking whether he could help find someone who "could give her a little extra for her living expenses?" Alexander maintained there was nothing he could do.

Bethune's departure left Robert Weaver the last core member of the Black Cabinet still standing. In his new War Manpower Commission position, he was stuck with a job that had no purpose, no real responsibilities, and absolutely no power. Still, he looked for ways to contribute. In the summer of 1943, he spent time writing an article for the *Atlantic Monthly*. Deviating from his usual statistically heavy-handed fare, he reflected on the recent race riots and offered suggestions to head off further clashes. "We face the rise of racial disturbances because we have not taken preventative measures to avoid them," he observed. In the short term, African Americans needed a fair chance at defense jobs and to be treated equally in the military. But real changes depended on improving the economic position of black citizens both during and after the war. The system in place thrived and profited on a racial divide that pitted white and black laborers against each other. Whites were encouraged to embrace racism and blame their inability to get ahead on African Americans rather than on the employers who exploited workers of all races. Weaver hardly called for revolution—he was far too much of a traditionalist and a believer in capitalism. However, he reasoned, racial clashes could be averted, and racism rendered obsolete, if broad economic opportunity ended suffering and brought full employment to all Americans. The result would be a sustained and prosperous American economy.

In September 1943, after being sent out on the road, Weaver returned to his Washington, D.C., office to discover that McNutt had eliminated his new post and moved him into yet another position. Weaver was now assigned to negotiate cooperative relationships between the Fair Employment Practices Committee and the War Manpower Commission in local offices across the nation. While on the surface it looked as if he might have regained some authority, the reality was that his salary had been cut and he barely had enough of a budget to carry out his new charge. And this move was the closest McNutt could get to sending Weaver permanently out to the field without actually doing it. The result successfully removed the Black Cabinet leader from the sphere where he had exercised the most impact, both in the open and undercover. The *Baltimore Afro-American*, proclaiming Weaver the "Last of the Brain Trusters," reported that African American Washington insiders worried that with his demotion the end of the Black Cabinet was near.

In November, Weaver departed for a two-week tour of the West to finalize agreements between the FEPC and the WMC there. When he returned to Washington, he released a report of his trip: during the war, massive shifts in population had left U.S. cities without adequate residential options for African Americans, which had led to overcrowding and the expansion of racially segregated ghettos. He predicted that the nation's top postwar issue would be housing and that without adequate job opportunities, poverty and racial tensions would rise. He urged the federal government to expand federal housing, jobs, and home-loans programs for African Americans. The nation was at a fork in the road. This was a chance for Washington to use the lessons of the New Deal and the war to create a society in which citizens lived harmoniously, equally enjoying the fruits of democracy and a healthy economy.

Weaver's superiors never responded.

For more than a decade, Weaver had worked relentlessly for change within the federal government. But in late 1943, the thirty-six-year-old had become only more pessimistic about the possibilities for reform. "I didn't feel that I was making much progress but rather I was spending most of my time trying to hold the ground that I thought had already been achieved," he later remembered of those times.

On Christmas Day, 1943, Robert Weaver and his wife, Ella, opened up their home to celebrate with friends and family. Bill Hastie, whose first marriage had ended in divorce, brought his new bride, Beryl Lockhart. The year away from federal service had been good for the serious-minded Hastie. Shortly after the holidays, a Washington columnist spotted Hastie and his new wife at a D.C. nightspot and remarked that the former War Department official looked happy and well. Robert Weaver, so close to Hastie for so long, surely also noticed the change in his old friend, now freed from the constraints of a federal appointment.

In early January 1944, on the one-year anniversary of Hastie's resignation from the War Department, Weaver announced he was leaving his post at the War Manpower Commission. He had timed his departure to underscore his discontent with the federal government's approach to racial affairs, and to coincide with the beginning of the presidential election cycle. But unlike Hastie, even before he had left office Weaver talked freely about his disillusionment with the federal government. In a *Chicago Defender* interview, he said that a federal post had always been his life's goal, and that before the war started, he had never considered leaving government service. But times had changed. Reactionaries dominated Congress, and they had dismantled assistance for African Americans, many of whom still languished in economic despair. (Weaver's own studies revealed that African Americans still had not received wartime industrial employment in proportion to their population. Other investigations showed that those who stayed in the South were forced back into sharecropping or into low-paying jobs as farm laborers.) He also pointed out that racial-affairs advisers had been immobilized. States had assumed control over the remaining programs that might still address African American needs, a move sure to disadvantage black citizens even further. Like Bill Hastie, Weaver had become convinced of the "futility of the approach to the solution of [the] Negro's problems through the Federal Government." His departing advice was this: African American voters needed to "organize for the election of a liberal Congress in 1944, lest all New Deal gains be lost."

In February 1944, Robert Weaver packed up his family and left his hometown of Washington, D.C., for Chicago. There he would assume the leadership of the Mayor's Committee on Race Relations, which advised local government officials on African American concerns. While a member of Washington's Black Cabinet, he had been subjected to criticism from the black community for being too slow and too careerist as well as ineffective. But upon his departure, many voices of the community lamented his exit from the federal scene. Black news sources praised his academic credentials and reviewed his impressive résumé of federal posts; his achievements were a source of pride. Some sources highlighted Weaver as a pathbreaker: he had been hired for his scholarly expertise rather than for party loyalty. Certainly, many appreciated the fortitude it took for him to last for more than a decade as one of the few senior-level African American federal administrators. One *Pittsburgh Courier* editorialist celebrated Weaver's "technical" mastery—his ability to conduct surveys, synthesize information, and develop recommendations from raw data in the fight for improved African American employment and housing. The *Los Angeles Tribune* praised Weaver for his part in originating the practice of applying the prima facie model to expose racial discrimination and for pioneering the incorporation of antidiscrimination clauses in government contracts. By the paper's estimation, African Americans working on New Deal construction projects had taken home "three million dollars" in wages because Weaver had been there to fight for them.

Indeed, with Weaver's advocacy, African Americans had made strides. Some African Americans had secured employment in fields ranging from carpentry to architecture. Day laborers and farmers had benefited from his programs in the Department of the Interior, the United States Housing Authority, and war-era agencies. He had helped build better inner-city housing for black citizens; while housing projects fell below what he had envisioned for social uplift, at the time they provided a roof over the heads of many families that would have been homeless if not for his efforts. He had also battled for African American employment in defense plants. That alone opened a wide avenue of new job opportunities for black workers, especially women. African Americans stepped forward to take jobs in welding, shipfitting, and airplane repair, creating a whole new world of future possibilities. In December 1943, as Weaver contemplated his future, Dorothy Vaughan walked through one of the doors he had opened. A former math teacher, she started a new job as a data processor at Langley Memorial Aeronautical Laboratory in Hampton, Virginia. The office was segregated, and the bathrooms were divided by race. But Vaughan would persevere into the space age of the 1960s and work on NASA's Apollo program.

For some, the greatest cost of Weaver's departure was the death of the Black Cabinet. Although it had fallen on hard times in its final years, at critical movements, the African American brain trust had sprung back into action. As individuals, the members had approached their posts with dedication—their positions were opportunities to use their expertise, knowledge of the community, and power as insiders to push for change or block attacks on the African American community. "It was clear that the [African American] government advisors put the welfare of their people above their jobs," observed one journalist. Despite their rivalries and differences, at many critical turning points the men and women of the Black Cabinet had put the community first and united for the fight. Weaver had been on the front lines first and remained there the longest.

With Weaver gone, most of those left behind, the vast majority newcomers, were unable to muster any kind of collective action. And even if they had, the White House would not hear them. In late January 1944, Al Smith informed a Baltimore audience that "the black cabinet as a group can no longer reach the President"—which had been the case for a long time. But what was different, he told his listeners, was that black race-relations advisers had been completely eclipsed by the so-called White Cabinet. One editorialist for the *Pittsburgh Courier* concluded: "The period when bright, intelligent young Negroes were hired as experts to tell federal administrators how to do things, if not what to do, is all washed up."

In February, some hopeful news appeared. Shortly after Weaver's resignation, Harry McAlpin, who had moved on to report for the African American newspaper *Atlanta Daily World*, received notice that he would be regularly admitted to White House press conferences. At his first presidential briefing, Roosevelt shook hands with the pioneering reporter and former aide to Bethune, remarking "I'm glad to see you, McAlpin."

Then, in March 1944, African American news sources reported that Paul McNutt was begging Mary McLeod Bethune to take Weaver's vacant spot on the War Manpower Commission. Eleanor Roosevelt privately urged her to accept; it was "an opportunity" to "do a really good job," she told Bethune. But Bethune turned it down. The position's duties were only vaguely defined, a red flag, she told the *Pittsburgh Courier*, adding that she was uncomfortable reporting to the WMC's new race-relations boss—a white man.

Bethune's act was a last gasp of Black Cabinet resistance.

"The Black Cabinet was a power," Charley Cherokee declared in February 1944. "In spite of what you've heard and read, there were a dozen Negro advisers in government who could mold governmental policy in housing, employment, legal, justice, education, health and relief." But with the loss of "shrewd, histrionic Mary Bethune," "scholarly and obviously assured Bob Weaver," and "cultured Bill Hastie," it was over.

"May It Rest in Peace," Charley Cherokee wrote: "The Black Cabinet, chum, is dead."

PART FIVE

Vanishing Figures

Chapter Fourteen

·

No Resting

On April 12, 1945, Elizabeth McDuffie was dusting Franklin Delano Roosevelt's bedroom at the presidential retreat in Warm Springs, Georgia, while he waited for the morning papers. "The President looks tired," she remembered thinking. Roosevelt's previous year had been tense and hectic. In the fall, he had run for and won a fourth term; the African American vote again helped him retain the White House. Although the world war had stretched on, over the year it had turned in the Allies' favor. In February 1945, the president had journeyed to Yalta, in the Crimea, to meet with Britain's Winston Churchill and the Soviet Union's Joseph Stalin to begin planning for a postwar world.

"Tell McDuffie I didn't forget his birthday," FDR had called out to Elizabeth McDuffie, referring to her husband, his former valet. She stopped her work. They chatted about the weather. The Roosevelt family's Scottish terrier, Fala, wandered in. A few hours later, Elizabeth McDuffie passed by the parlor, where Roosevelt was working at a table. "The moment I looked in, the President sat back from his writing," she recalled. "He said something and smiled."

Later that day, while McDuffie was cleaning the guesthouse, Daisy Bonner, the cook at Warm Springs, appeared at the door: "Lizzie, the President may be dying."

McDuffie rushed back to the main house to find that Arthur Pretty-man, FDR's valet, had carried the unconscious president to the bedroom. Doctors were summoned, and they determined that Roosevelt had suffered a massive stroke. He lingered for two and a half hours, and then he was gone.

Eleanor Roosevelt had stayed behind in Washington and had gone out earlier in the day. When she returned, it was press secretary Stephen Early who informed her of the president's death. The First Lady took the news quietly. A few hours later, with Early by her side, she boarded a plane bound for Fort Benning, Georgia, and then made her way to the Roosevelt vacation home. At some point she learned that Lucy Mercer Rutherfurd, with whom FDR had carried on an affair, had also been at Warm Springs.

A stoic Eleanor Roosevelt carried on. The following morning, she led the presidential entourage as it boarded the special train, draped in black, bearing FDR's body on a long and somber ride back to Washington. Elizabeth McDuffie recalled that as the funeral cortege rolled slowly past, Americans from all walks of life, black and white, stood shoulder to shoulder along the railroad tracks, some with tears streaming—all in mournful silence. "I looked out at the crowds, all races, all ages, rich and poor," she wrote in *Ebony* magazine. "I lay in my berth with the curtains pulled back from the window and watched the lights and shadows of the passing countryside. In the midnight quiet, I looked out at the sharecroppers' cabins nested like old grey hens in the cotton fields. It was in a cabin like that I had been born."

On the other side of the Atlantic, Lucia Mae Pitts raced to attention when she heard morning reveille. For just over two months, she had been stationed with the Women's Army Corps in England, where her unit processed mail to and from American soldiers. She enjoyed being in England, surprised to find that the British warmly welcomed African American WACs into their homes, pubs, and businesses. But on that April morning, while she was standing in formation, her spirits sank when her sergeant announced: "We have just been informed of the death of President Roosevelt." She recalled shock and silence descending on the ranks. Some of the women began to weep. "I remember finally stamping my foot and saying out loud, 'Oh, no!'" Pitts wrote. "It hit me even harder, I think, for while I had never met the President in person, I had been a small part of his early efforts and naturally felt a closeness and loss."

The day FDR died, William Hastie was on the Howard University campus. As dean of the university's law school, he remained active in the NAACP and, while chairing the organization's legal committee, continued to fight against discrimination in the U.S. military. He learned of Roosevelt's passing in the late afternoon as the reports spread by word of mouth across campus. "The news of his death came to me, as I'm sure to the great majority of people, as a great surprise as well as shock," he recalled.

Mary McLeod Bethune was in Dallas, her health forcing her to travel with her personal physician, Dr. James Lowell Hall, by her side. Earlier in the day, she had made a speech at a college campus, and that evening was resting in the living room at a friend's house. Dr. Hall had been listening to the radio when reports of the president's death came over the air; he broke the news to Bethune as gently as possible, worried it might trigger an asthma attack. "I sat, stunned for ten minutes saying nothing to anybody," she recollected. "It was hard to realize he was gone." She then telegrammed her condolences to Eleanor Roosevelt. She caught a red-eye flight back to the capital, where White House officials arranged for her to appear on a special memorial radio broadcast the following night. "Today we breathe a sigh—we wipe a tear—we are filled with remorse," she told listeners. "Negroes shall confront their tomorrows with the stern resolution and conviction that he gave us in his time."

After Roosevelt's funeral train pulled into Washington's Union Station on April 14, Bethune made her way out to Constitution Avenue to watch the horse-drawn caisson carrying the president's remains pass on its way to the White House. Later that day, she arrived at the East

Room for the funeral services, the only African American to be invited. During the rites, the memories of her first meeting with FDR flooded back: "I recalled holding his hands and looking into his fine, strong face, and telling him how much the common people depended on him," she later wrote. "[I] found it impossible to restrain my feelings. I wept openly like a little child," she confessed. "On that day, I felt that something big and fine and brave had dropped out of the world, that we had lost our greatest leader."

Many African Americans agreed with Bethune, forgiving the president in death for his flaws and failures in life. Pitts felt FDR's death held a special significance for black citizens. She remembered Roosevelt as "the first President in the lifetime of many of us who seemed to care about us." The *Kansas City Call* lamented, "Negroes have lost the best friend they ever had in the White House." The *Pittsburgh Courier's* New York correspondent James Boyack recalled meeting the president at the White House with Robert Vann: "I immediately sensed his warm sympathy for the aspiration of all Americans. He did more for colored Americans than any other President since Lincoln." Howard University president Mordecai Johnson declared that "under the leadership of President Roosevelt we see the evidences of a great-hearted moral will, moving experimentally forward, under staggering difficulties, with a steady courage and a practical sagacity unparalleled in our time."

Walter White's praise was effusive: "We did not always see eye to eye on issues relating to the Negro or the reactionary southern leadership of his party but one never questioned the integrity and sincerity of his desire to secure, as far as possible for him to do so, the full fruits and benefits of democracy for all men whatever their color or creed." A gracious tribute came from William Hastie. "The loss is beyond calculation," he told the Associated Negro Press. "I feel that humanity has lost one of its greatest friends, America an outstanding statesman of all times, and the common man, a special benefactor."

Others paid a qualified homage to the fallen president. An African American YMCA leader remarked that "the sudden death of President Roosevelt has come as a great shock to the colored people of America, not because he was a special champion of their rights . . . but because he championed the rights of the common man." The Treasury Department's William Pickens observed that the First Lady was the one who would be most acutely missed. He declared the Roosevelts to be "the finest team that has ever yet occupied the White House." One *Pittsburgh Courier* editorial, echoing some of Robert Vann's bite, refused to succumb to sentimentality. The president, it reminded readers, had withheld his endorsement of anti-lynching and voting rights legislation because of his marriage to white southern Democrats and his continual fears that they would "endanger the approval of peace time and war appropriations."

For his part, Al Smith oscillated between misty-eyed mawkishness and steely-penned cynicism. "He's gone, chum, we're on our own," was Charley Cherokee's response to the news. "Franklin Roosevelt held us up for 13 years, now we have to stand on our own feet. And y'know, we can do it." But he also observed that Roosevelt's main contribution to African Americans rested in illuminating "what there is to be wanted," rather than actually securing those wants and needs for black citizens.

Despite the ambivalence over his legacy, a new narrative was born in the aftermath of FDR's sudden loss, as some argued that the president deserved credit for significant achievements on behalf of black America. A *Pittsburgh Courier* writer praised Roosevelt for mandating that all New Deal public works projects carry an antidiscrimination clause—"a provision that a certain percentage of Negroes must be employed." A number of voices hailed FDR for expanding Depression-era relief and recovery programs to include African American citizens. Others credited him with the establishment of the Fair Employment Practices Committee. One journalist insisted that FDR had instilled in African Americans "a new dignity, lifting them up in the scale of citizenship by improving their economic lot, and diminishing discrimination against them in the armed forces."

None of these tributes mentioned Robert Weaver, Bill Hastie, Al Smith, Mary McLeod Bethune, or Robert Vann. Nor was there any reference to the hard work and sacrifices made by the Black Cabinet to achieve the victories, now credited to FDR, that they had won for black Americans. Instead, the Black Cabinet itself came to be celebrated as yet another one of FDR's accomplishments. "Franklin Delano Roosevelt made a masterful stroke to enforce equal rights for Negroes in sharing the benefits of public relief by the organization of what is familiarly known as a 'black cabinet,' consisting of a group of Negro leaders who advised him about Negro affairs," one Associated Negro Press report claimed. Race-relations advisers had "positions of responsibility," and the emergence of the Black Cabinet marked "the first time in the history of America a President had openly concerned himself to such an extent with the welfare of Negro citizens." Cleveland's *Call and Post* maintained that the White House had "handpicked" the African American brain trust and that the Black Cabinet had been organized "to expand the opportunities of Negroes as well as keep the administration's fingers on the Negro's pulse in America."

In the wake of the president's death, the African American brain trust was rechristened "Roosevelt's Black Cabinet," and the president was eulogized as a human rights champion who used his office to further a vision of a nation based on social justice and equality for all. Bethune herself participated in this revisionist history during her radio appearance the night before FDR's funeral. "He came into high office at a critical time in the lives of all men and gave strength—and now his life—so that all men, irrespective of their creation, should live better," she told listeners. "It was no accident then that my people along with all other suffering minorities, should have been taken up into the arms of this humane Administrator of our government."

The refashioning of FDR's image, thanks in part to a few former black brain trusters as well as members of the black press, overwrote the reality that the Black Cabinet had been born of the efforts of African Americans who battled a reluctant president and an administration that was often explicitly hostile. Racial-affairs advisers had been forced upon FDR by the African American community, white liberal philanthropists, and vote-hungry Democratic leaders. The Black Cabinet was willed into existence by those very advisers who came together under Bethune and Weaver. The Black Cabinet existed because its members created and sustained it. It was never "Roosevelt's Black Cabinet." The president did not seek its members' advice. But as an autonomous and self-generated group, the Black Cabinet did force the changes that now became part of FDR's legacy on civil rights.

In part, the glossy appraisals of Roosevelt can be attributed to the emotional shock of his sudden death combined with the uncertainty of the times. Harry Truman, FDR's third vice president, would carry the country through the final months of the war and oversee victory in September 1945. African Americans were distrustful of the untested and tough-talking Truman, a Missourian whom Roosevelt had chosen in order to appease southern Democrats. Many feared the new president would be unsympathetic to black causes and to an African American presence in the Washington workplace. Political commentators speculated that the last of FDR's racial-affairs advisers would soon disappear from the federal ranks.

But the new administration brought some surprises. Truman had been a steadfast New Dealer and was committed to perpetuating portions of Roosevelt's policies. In April 1945, Truman appointed Mary McLeod Bethune to serve as a consultant to the World Security Conference, in San Francisco, a meeting at which the United Nations was officially organized. Several of the less influential Black Cabinet members had survived in their positions after Robert Weaver's departure, and under Truman, Frank Horne, Lawrence Oxley, William Pickens, Campbell Johnson, and Ambrose Caliver remained in government posts. But the new president, a product of midwestern machine politics, favored loyal African American Democrats over black experts and activists for new posts. "Politics replaces idealism," writer Roi Ottley commented on Truman's racial-affairs appointees. Although the African American press tracked the formation of a Truman Black Cabinet, there was no real effort by that administration's racial-affairs advisers to resurrect the collective action of the Roosevelt era.

Yet, in many ways, Truman's accomplishments overshadowed Roosevelt's record on race. Truman openly supported civil rights legislation and denounced racial discrimination. Bill Hastie attributed Truman's supportiveness to the Missourian's frankness, nurtured in the brawls of machine politics. Hastie also contended that Truman, unlike Roosevelt, "would not allow political considerations to cause him to disavow the position that he regarded as morally wrong." But Hastie was being generous. The value of the black vote was not lost on Harry Truman. Like FDR, he calculated his support of black Americans to coincide with his political ambitions and election cycles.

Truman's overtures to the African American community remained fairly steady throughout his years in office. In November 1945, he nominated Bill Hastie to serve as the governor of the Virgin Islands, the first African American to hold that post. Four years later, Hastie returned home to become the first African American appointed to serve as a judge on the United States Court of Appeals. Truman also established the Fair Employment Board to address prejudicial treatment in the civil service, recruiting early Black Cabinet member and Urban League official Eugene Kinckle Jones as one of its inaugural members. During the midterm elections of 1946, the White House organized the President's Committee on Civil Rights, a race-relations advisory group. Truman demanded that the committee explore how federal power might be used to end lynching. And while campaigning for president, Truman did what FDR refused to do: in 1948 he issued Executive Order 9981, desegregating the U.S. armed forces.

Still, the daily lives of most African Americans changed very little while Truman was in office. In 1946, Congress shut down the Fair Employment Practices Committee, and white soldiers arriving home quickly forced African American industrial workers out of their jobs. In postwar America, most black citizens lived in segregated neighborhoods and attended segregated schools. Poverty was the reality for many black families. In 1950, 80 percent of black workers were employed in low-paying, unskilled positions. That year, the unemployment rate for black men, at 6.4 percent, was almost twice that of white men. Despite the Great Migration, the majority of African Americans still resided in the South, earning their livings as either sharecroppers or farm laborers. One housing survey revealed that in 1950, 98 percent of black Americans in rural areas lived in dilapidated homes, many with no indoor plumbing. In those agricultural communities of the South, almost all African Americans were denied their constitutional right to vote. Although the president expressed hope that his Committee on Civil Rights might change white attitudes, violence against African Americans, including lynching, persisted, and the Ku Klux Klan continued with its campaigns of terror.

By the time of the 1952 presidential race, African Americans, even if they remained registered Republicans, had become regarded as a part of the Democrats' reliable and diverse base, composed of industrial workers and union members, farmers, Catholics, racial minorities, urbanites, and other New Deal liberals. But that coalition was not sturdy enough to hold on to the White House. With the help of the white South, Dwight D. Eisenhower retook the presidency for the GOP. In terms of civil rights, observers noted that a chill descended over the executive branch. Vice President Richard Nixon, never regarded as a friend to African Americans, was appointed to head up a special committee on race relations. In 1953, rumors circulated that Eugene Kinckle Jones would lose his seat on the Fair Employment Board to a loyal Republican. But before that could happen, the sixty-eight-year-old Jones died suddenly from a brain aneurysm.

Almost all the black federal officials who had been holdovers from the Roosevelt era were finally pushed out during the Eisenhower administration. Frank Horne, who had held on in the public housing division, was terminated in 1955. His superiors explained that they had to let him go because of deep and wide budget cuts, but Horne later revealed that his office was the only one hit by the purported reductions. No one had ever managed to oust the tenacious Lawrence Oxley, but as soon as he reached age seventy, the administration forced him into retirement.

Like other former Black Cabinet members, Horne and Oxley found new avenues to carry on the fight. Horne returned home to New York, where he was appointed the executive director of the city's Commission on Intergroup Relations. In 1960, he suffered a stroke that left him partially paralyzed. After recuperating, despite being wheelchair-bound, he served on New York City's Housing and Redevelopment Board. He remained active in the fair housing movement up until his death in 1974.

Lawrence Oxley told one interviewer that retirement was "the busiest and most productive" time in his public career. He became active in numerous organizations, including the Boy Scouts of America and the National Conference on Citizenship. Appointed the director of special projects for the National Council of Senior Citizens, he became an unrelenting advocate for a health-care program for the elderly that eventually would be widely known as Medicare. He also remained a committed Democrat. In 1973, when invited to a prayer breakfast with Richard Nixon, he took glee in rattling the then president. "I took hold of his hand just like he was a student," he chortled. "You are the seventh President to greet me in this spot in the White House," he told a visibly anxious Nixon.

While the majority of Black Cabinet members became Democratic partisans, some defected to the Republican Party. Most notable were Crystal Bird Fauset and Edgar Brown. Fauset's exit, which occurred after she lost her government post, was a result of her frustrations while working on Roosevelt's 1944 reelection campaign. It was a bitter break. The Democratic National Committee had not only ignored her pleas for the president to openly address the needs of African Americans but also failed to pay her a large chunk of her salary. But the final straw came when the administration turned down her proposal for a White House election-year conference on race relations. Believing that it might increase rather than resolve racial unrest, FDR had warned the First Lady away from endorsing the plan: "I would not encourage any announcement on future meetings on the Interracial subject. The less said about it, for the next few months, the less loss of life." When it became clear that the conference had been blocked, Fauset broke off her friendship with the First Lady and publicly endorsed Republican presidential candidate Thomas Dewey. Subsequently, Fauset rose within the Republican Party and campaigned for Eisenhower in the 1950s. She passed away in 1965.

After Edgar Brown lost his job with the Civilian Conservation Corps in 1942, he wasn't able to secure another position in the federal government, and he grew increasingly disillusioned with the Democrats. During the 1940s and into the 1950s, he split his time between Washington, D.C., and Chicago, where he inserted himself into local Republican circles. Brown continued to be a flamboyant and determined figure— although his unconventionality forced his former colleagues and many other black leaders to, as one put it, "avoid him like the plague." In 1944, Brown exchanged words with a white congressional doorman, resulting in fisticuffs that sent a bloodied Brown to the hospital. (Brown claimed the doorman had insulted him; the doorman insisted that Brown had attacked him with a shovel.) Although Brown ran for office in Chicago several times, he repeatedly lost. But he campaigned steadily for Windy City GOP candidates. During the 1950s, he drove Chicago's streets broadcasting his endorsements through a bullhorn attached to his car. On April 9, 1954, while canvasing neighborhoods for a Republican Senate candidate, he suffered a heart attack that sent his vehicle careening into a light pole. Emergency responders were unable to save him. Edgar Brown was fifty-six years old.

Just a little over a month after Edgar Brown passed away, in May 1954, the Supreme Court ruled school segregation unconstitutional in *Brown v. Board of Education of Topeka*. The decision overturned *Plessy v.*

Ferguson, the court's separate-but-equal mandate that had driven legal decisions on American race relations since 1896. Some credited William Hastie for laying the groundwork for the Brown decision, citing antidiscrimination cases he had argued on behalf of the NAACP in the mid-1940s. Certainly he had an impact on *Brown*'s lead attorney, his former student Thurgood Marshall. *Brown v. Board of Education* became a milestone in U.S. history, opening up the possibility for the integration of other public spaces and facilities. This challenge to American Jim Crow traditions spurred the movement for equal treatment of African Americans in all aspects of American society. The decision was celebrated across African American communities nationwide.

While Mary McLeod Bethune viewed it as a watershed, her enthusiasm was subdued. "I can see very little to be excited about," she wrote in the *Chicago Defender*. The Supreme Court was finally enforcing what had already been promised to all Americans in the Constitution, she observed. There would be vicious resistance mounted by "blind haters," she predicted, who would block integration and the citizenship rights of African Americans. "We must go about the business of implementing the decision," she stated. "This must be done with common sense and Christian forbearance. But it must be done! And within this simple fact lies the long road ahead."

The year of the *Brown v. Board of Education* decision, Bethune turned seventy-nine. After losing her government post in 1943, she continued with her campaigns for justice and equal treatment for African American men and women. During her years with the Roosevelt administration, she had come to view the African American struggle as part of a broader global battle. In her essay "Certain Inalienable Rights," she compared the civil rights crusade in the United States to both the American Revolution and to anti-colonialist movements around the world: "Just as the Colonists at the Boston Tea Party wanted 'out' from under tyranny and oppression and taxation without representation, the Chinese want 'out,' the Indians want 'out,' and the colored Americans want 'out.'" Refusing to be deterred by her chronic illnesses, Bethune continued to travel throughout the country and speak out against racism and sexism. She also carried her message to Haiti and Canada. In 1952, as a member of the U.S. delegation, she attended the inauguration of Liberia's new president. The trip was, she declared, "the fulfillment of a lifelong dream—to tread the soil of Africa from which my forebears came, and to stand erect, *in Africa*, on the soil of Liberia."

Yet, with the rise of the Cold War, the politics of reaction intensified as the hunt for subversives accelerated under Senator Joseph McCarthy. The enemies of African American equality persisted in their attempts to undermine civil rights by linking them with communism. Into the 1950s, Bethune remained a target of red-baiters. Always treading cautiously, she increasingly distanced herself from several friends on the left and in her speeches and writings denounced Marxist-influenced ideologies. Some criticized her actions as selfish and narrow-minded. But Bethune, always stubborn, refused to listen. And despite what seemed like a swing to the right, she continued to command significant respect from the grassroots of the black community.

In the spring of 1955, Bethune composed an essay, "My Last Will and Testament," for *Ebony* magazine. "Sometimes as I sit communing in my study, I feel that death is not far off. I am aware that it will overtake me before the greatest of my dreams—full equality of the Negro in our time—is realized," she wrote. Yet she was optimistic that African American youths would come together to build a new America. To those who would inherit the struggle, she left nine inspirational "principles and policies" that she identified as "represent[ing] the meaning of my life's work." They included "love," "hope," "confidence in one another," "a thirst for education," "respect for the uses of power," "faith," "racial dignity," "a desire to live harmoniously with your fellow men," and "finally, a responsibility to our young people." Foreseeing the brutal hostilities that those fighting for equality would continue to face, she advised civil rights activists to refuse to meet force with force. Only through peace, she contended, could the nation become whole. "Tomorrow a new Negro, unhindered by race taboos and shackles will benefit from more than 330 years of ceaseless striving and struggle," she predicted. "Theirs will be a better world. This I believe with all my heart."

On the afternoon of May 18, 1955, Mary McLeod Bethune sat rocking on the front porch of her Daytona Beach home. She pulled herself up from the chair. She crossed the threshold of her home.

Her heart stopped, and she died almost immediately.

"She was a great and good American and I will miss her very much for I valued her wisdom and goodness," Eleanor Roosevelt wrote to Bethune's son, Albert, remembering the woman who had become her mentor. "I will cherish the spirit she lived by and try to promote the causes she believed in."

In December 1955, seven months after Bethune passed away, the Reverend Martin Luther King Jr. took the helm of the Montgomery bus boycott. King was very familiar with Bethune—she had spoken at his father's church when he was a child. Educated at Morehouse College and the recipient of a divinity degree from Boston University, King had closely studied theologies of social uplift and nonviolent direct action. His philosophies and strategies, foreshadowed by Bethune, successfully compelled the Supreme Court to ban segregation in public transportation in 1956. From that point, waves of protest spread across the nation. Segregation in housing, transportation, schools, and other public spaces was challenged; equal access to the vote and to jobs was demanded. King would pay tribute to many of those who came before him, including Bethune. "There was a star in the sky of female leadership," King told a conference of ministers in 1959. "Mary McLeod Bethune grabbed it and used it."

In July 1959, as the civil rights movement accelerated, some of the original Black Cabinet members joined other African American Washington notables to celebrate the accomplishments of journalist Eugene Davidson. Over the years, the brain trust had made peace with Davidson, one of their staunchest critics, who had also brought them into the public eye in his 1934 series, The Black Cabinet in the New Deal. Davidson had served as the head of the District of Columbia's NAACP and would remain active in civil rights up until his death in 1976.

After the affair, the Black Cabinet old-timers drifted off to another location to catch up over drinks. They spent much of the evening reminiscing about their days with Roosevelt; several recounted their role in the proposed 1941 March on Washington and Executive Order 8802. "They revealed how this 'fighting group' gathered working ammunition and mapped out strategy for attacks on old Jim Crow," the *Pittsburgh Courier* reported. "They re-enacted those roundtable conferences with heads of industry and Government." There was common agreement that their sacrifices had been worth it, that they had paved the way for the new wave of protests and that African American people were finally "beginning to reap some of the benefits" of their efforts. They spent the waning hours debating the next steps in the fight for civil rights.

Two years later the group reunited again, in New York. "Dinner for Bob Weaver," read the January 1961 invitation. "Advice: stag, informal, and no publicity; just the gang getting together to honor one of its own." Hosted by the NAACP's Roy Wilkins, the occasion was President John F. Kennedy's appointment of Weaver to lead the Housing and Home Finance Agency. Wilkins had booked a posh dining room at the Waldorf-Astoria, and twenty of the surviving members of the Roosevelt-era Black Cabinet showed up that night. Among others, Frank Horne, Campbell Johnson, Ted Poston, Bill Trent, Truman Gibson, Al Smith, Lawrence Oxley, and old friend Ralph Bunche toasted and roasted Weaver, who was about to become the first African American to head a federal agency. After an elegant dinner, as the air grew heavy with smoke and talk, the group reminisced about the heyday of the Black Cabinet. "It had been an evening of stag humor enlivened by quips about end runs and broken field plays the group had successfully engineered in its efforts to outmaneuver the enemies of equal treatment," the *New York Times Magazine* reported. As Black Cabinet members, they had transformed the New Deal. They extended its benefits beyond white Americans and pushed its philosophy of democratic liberalism to go further than economic relief and recovery to embrace the reforming American society by challenging white racism. At the end of the Roosevelt years, their lives had taken them down different paths. But they had all been transformed by their experiences in their federal jobs. They all continued to fight against bigotry and for the rights of African Americans. At one point that night, the group gathered for a portrait with Robert Weaver who was, as he had been years before, right in the center.

Robert Weaver's return to Washington, D.C., had been long in the making. Since leaving in 1944, he had established a reputation as one of the nation's foremost experts on housing and inner cities. He had written two books—*Negro Labor: A National Problem* and *The Negro Ghetto*. Both were influenced by his experiences working in the FDR administration and grounded in his belief that the exercise of federal power was instrumental in conquering poverty and discrimination. In 1948, Weaver landed in Manhattan, where he served as vice chairman of New York City's Housing and Redevelopment Board and later in the governor's cabinet as the rent commissioner. The post-FDR Robert Weaver was far savvier about politics, and much of his newfound success came from his willingness to openly support the Democrats. No longer would he stand aloof from political scuffles and maneuverings. His willingness to play the game, his expertise, and his loyalty to the party opened up the doors for his return to the federal government.

Once back in Washington's federal ranks, Weaver poured himself into improving public housing and bettering the lives of those living in urban cores. It was an enormous task, in part because the federal government had not heeded his earlier warnings regarding inner cities and poverty. Since World War II's end, urban America and its populations had lagged far behind the rest of the country. As tax bases declined, maintenance and city services were cut. Segregation had persisted, locking African Americans into urban ghettos with limited job opportunities and poorly funded schools. City, state, and federal agencies had failed to provide housing projects with the budget needed for upkeep and improvement. Indeed, for the country's poor, which included a large portion of the African American citizenry, the Great Depression had never ended. Weaver saw a chance to correct these wrongs—an opportunity to apply the solutions he had been developing since he had cut his teeth in government service during the New Deal and World War II.

Now in his fifties, Weaver radiated the confidence of an old political hand. The *New York Times Magazine* described him as "a salty blend of realism, organizational talent, mental agility, and skill at unruffling feathers." Now "portly," he puffed away at his cigar and, when talking to the *Times* reporter, banged his fist on his desk to punctuate his points. He drove his staff hard, the magazine observed, with high expectations, long hours, and frigid disdain for error. Right off, Weaver and his team jumped in to formulate and push through new legislation designed to increase federal dollars going to cities for public housing, slum renewal, public transportation, and infrastructure. Weaver's proposals, in the form of the Housing Act of 1961, which expanded housing for low-income Americans, eventually got through Congress. But representatives had refused to incorporate an antidiscrimination mandate into the bill. Robert Weaver discovered that, in many ways, Washington had not changed much. Potentially, the Housing Act left open the possibility for African Americans to be left out again.

While it was pending, Weaver's housing bill had received an important boost from Eleanor Roosevelt, who wrote to John F. Kennedy directly, urging him to move it through Congress. Since leaving the White House, she had become more vocal about her support for civil rights and social justice. She had served as U.S. delegate to the United Nations and helped shape its Universal Declaration of Human Rights. Still, in many ways, she remained naïve about race. Reportedly, in 1948 she had backed the NAACP away from insisting on U.N. resolutions condemning the brutal treatment of black citizens of the United States. The title of her article "Some of My Best Friends Are Negroes," which appeared in *Ebony* magazine, certainly led some black readers to cringe when it appeared in 1953. Still, her willingness to make common cause with black citizens and support their struggle for equal treatment, as well as her long list of African American acquaintances (and friends), stood in defiance of segregation and racism.

Throughout the 1950s and into the early 1960s, Eleanor Roosevelt continued to support African American causes. She served on the NAACP's board of directors. When the Montgomery bus boycott began, she hosted a tea for Rosa Parks. She spoke out for Martin Luther King and praised his philosophy of nonviolence. She continued to use her privilege and position to push white political power brokers to act on civil rights agendas. But by 1962, she was seventy-eight and beginning to slow down. After a summer campaign appearance for a Democratic candidate in Harlem, she retreated to her New York apartment. A few months later, on November 7, 1962, aplastic anemia combined with chronic tuberculosis took her life. "Millions of Negroes mourned the passing of Mrs. Franklin Delano Roosevelt," the *Pittsburgh Courier* declared. "They mourned because her death reminded them of good words and deeds in furthering the concept and practice of practical democracy. . . . She gave Americans of all races and colors a living example of what interracial relations should be without mawkish sentimentality or condescension."

Insisting that the White House support Robert Weaver's housing legislation had been one of Eleanor Roosevelt's last acts in the final year of her life. Just short of two weeks after her death, Kennedy signed Executive Order 11063, which banned discrimination based on race, color, creed, or national origin in federal housing programs. The order was far more limited than Weaver would have liked; it did not apply to projects under construction or already completed and did not enact other protections against residential discrimination. But Robert F. Kennedy, the U.S. attorney general and the president's brother, convinced Weaver to accept the order as a beginning.

Despite these disappointments, Weaver seemed at ease as one of the nation's elite government officials. His life differed dramatically from the lives of those he served, as the head of national public housing programs. After he moved to New York in the 1950s, he and his wife, Ella, purchased a Park Avenue apartment and were welcomed into the social circles of the city's powerful and wealthy residents. A 1966 *Time* magazine profile remarked on Weaver's great passion for Manhattan, describing him as a "man who loves Broadway plays, savors his stereophonic collection of Liszt and Chopin piano concertos, relishes Italian food (his favorite is shrimp marinara), sips twelve-year-old bourbon when he works at home at night." After returning to Washington, he maintained his New York apartment. But in 1961, as a symbol of his faith in urban renewal, he rented a space in a black D.C. public housing project. He lasted only six months before trading it for an upscale apartment with a tony Washington address.

Yet, during this time, Robert Weaver faced the reality of personal suffering. His son, Robert Weaver Jr., had been a troubled youth. He ditched school often and at one point ran away from home. Instead of college, he did a stint in the military. By some reports, father and son had a strained relationship—the younger Weaver didn't live up to family expectations. It grew even more tense after Robert Jr. married a woman who did not meet his parents' approval. On November 7, 1962, he put a pistol to his head and pulled the trigger. He died immediately. Many speculated that the twenty-two-year-old Weaver had committed suicide. But the sole eyewitness, his wife, insisted it was an unfortunate accident resulting from a foolish game of Russian roulette.

Robert Weaver Sr. said little to friends about his son's death. He and Ella received a mountain of condolence cards. He threw them out and quickly returned to the office.

Weaver lost himself in his work, and the years ahead became some of the most productive of his long career in government. After Kennedy's assassination, President Lyndon Baines Johnson, a southerner and former New Deal administrator, drove forward civil rights reforms. Early in his career, LBJ had supported segregation; he had tangled with Juanita Saddler over the integration of the National Youth Administration in Texas. But he had also forged a close relationship with Mary McLeod Bethune. Bill Hastie told of witnessing a chance meeting between Bethune and Johnson during World War II. "She was in a crowded elevator and as the doors opened, they spotted each other immediately," Hastie recalled. "With arms outstretched there were outcries of 'Mary' 'Lyndon' as they embraced to the startled gaze of that crowd of Southern government workers. I was always convinced they were both acutely aware of the crowd, their surroundings, and their actions."

Although as a rising southern politician, Johnson had opposed civil rights laws, by the 1960s his stance had evolved. After he assumed the reins of the presidency in November 1963, he steered the Civil Rights Act of 1964 and the Voting Rights Act of 1965 through Congress. Johnson had been nurtured in the New Deal and maintained a vision of America as "the Great Society," a nation freed from both poverty and discrimination. He picked Thurgood Marshall as his solicitor general and then appointed him to the Supreme Court—making Marshall the court's first African American justice. In 1966, LBJ transformed Weaver's office into the Department of Housing and Urban Development and named Weaver as its first secretary. With that, Weaver became the first African American cabinet secretary in United States history.

Weaver made the cover of *Time* magazine, and his appointment was celebrated at a massive public reception hosted by the NAACP. Eight hundred guests greeted the new cabinet secretary in a receiving line and then adjourned to the Waldorf-Astoria's banquet room for tributes to the man who, over thirty years earlier, had joined the government under Harold Ickes and had forged a path for African Americans in federal service. Many surviving Black Cabinet members were present that night. It was the ultimate victory, long in coming, for the African American brain trust of the FDR years. With Weaver's appointment, the Black Cabinet finally had secured its place at the table with the White House's official cabinet.

A few weeks later, the Black Cabinet returned to the Waldorf for one last private celebration. The *Pittsburgh Courier* ran a 1938 portrait of the group with Bethune standing proudly in the middle, flanked by the men who composed the core membership of the Black Cabinet. "The singular thing about it all," the paper commented, "is that our children's children will remember these vanishing figures—as dignified pioneers in top-level Government jobs."

One of those vanishing figures, the woman who started it all, was Eva DeBoe Jones. By the 1960s, Jones was largely forgotten for her role engineering the meeting between Robert Vann and Joe Guffey that paved the way for African Americans to shift their votes to the Democratic Party. Living quietly in the same Pittsburgh public housing project since 1938, she had remained a staunch Democrat throughout the years, paying dearly for her loyalty. She retired from manicuring in 1942, at the age of sixty-five. For a few years, she drew Social Security and lived off a modest bequest from one of the Guffeys. She had inherited some land from family in Tennessee and sold it off to make ends meet. When that money ran out, with no other resources, she stopped paying her rent. That prompted an investigation by Pittsburgh's housing authority, which determined that Jones was destitute and, because she had no income, no longer qualified for low-income housing. She was rescued from eviction by a member of the authority's staff, who arranged for Jones to receive enough state aid to pay for living expenses, health care, a new pair of eyeglasses, and the rent on her apartment.

Eva DeBoe Jones, the unsung heroine, the woman who opened the door for the New Deal's Black Cabinet, died in her apartment on Valentine's Day in 1967.

Like Jones, the Black Cabinet and its story had begun to disappear from historical memory, replaced by a new narrative that traced the birth of the modern civil rights movement to the post–World War II activism of the younger generation. The black brain trust lingered in doctoral dissertations, master's theses, and occasional mentions in history books. There its members appeared as relics of the age of Franklin D. Roosevelt, their contributions judged to be limited to expanding the black presence in the federal workforce and bringing in black votes for the Democratic Party.

Lucia Mae Pitts was determined to see that the Black Cabinet and its achievements were not forgotten. Mustering out of the Women's Army Corps (WAC) in 1945, she eventually returned to Washington, D.C., as a secretary to Frank Horne. After Horne was forced out of office in the 1950s, Pitts worked in various federal race-relations divisions, eventually moving up to an administrative post in the public housing division. She stayed just long enough to witness Weaver's return and then, plagued by arthritis after years of typing, retired on disability in 1962. She remained in Washington, watching, as the civil rights movement rolled ahead with Martin Luther King's 1963 revival of A. Philip Randolph's March on Washington and the Johnson administration's equal rights legislation.

In Pitts's view, the civil rights movement under King was rooted in what she termed the "direct-action drive" that had commenced in the Roosevelt years. Seeing modern civil rights as a continuum, and troubled by the lack of credit given to the Black Cabinet, in 1964 Pitts got out her typewriter and, despite the pain, pounded out a manuscript, which she entitled "The Little Fire and How It Grew." In it, she intertwined her experiences as the first African American secretary to a white D.C. administrator with an account of the origins and accomplishments of the Black Cabinet. African American New Dealers, she contended, "had a great deal to do with the fire" that ignited change during the 1950s and 1960s. Reflecting on the hectic Roosevelt years, Pitts maintained that African Americans had the opportunity "for the first time to work officially and specifically inside the Federal Government to bring the Negro to the attention of the Government at large and the outside world too."

All the editors who read the manuscript rejected it. Although Pitts was an eyewitness to race relations during the FDR years, one reviewer suggested that a better account could be found in a biography of white New Deal liberal Will Alexander.

Pitts moved to California, an easier climate, where she self-published a memoir of her experiences as a pioneering WAC. Reflecting on her own contributions to the Black Cabinet and the movement for African American equality, Pitts insisted that despite the roadblocks and frustrations, the satisfactions had outweighed the sacrifices. She asserted that the combined efforts of inside pressure and external protest had set the stage for change in the 1960s. "I believe that *many* things have to be done in many ways, sometimes simultaneously to accomplish our purpose, and all of us cannot do all of them," she wrote. She lived out the rest of her life in Los Angeles, where she passed away, at the age of seventy-one, in 1973.

Lawrence Oxley would die that year as well—he was buried with military honors in Arlington National Cemetery. Shortly before his death, he also reflected on his Black Cabinet years—choosing to forget any hard feelings. "I doubt that any recognized Negro leader in this country was not in accord with what we were trying to do," Oxley reflected. "I can't think of anybody that said that Mary Bethune was wrong or so and so was wrong, I think that is what made the so-called Black Cabinet so important, because we could get together."

In 1971, William Hastie retired after almost forty years of public service. The legal sage of the Black Cabinet had seen the federal antidiscrimination policies that he had innovated during the Roosevelt years reawakened as the foundation for equal rights legislation and the affirmative action programs of the 1960s and 1970s. Before stepping down from the bench, he had risen to become the chief justice of the U.S. Court of Appeals for the Third Circuit. He had decided to leave his position as a protest against the Nixon administration's "inexcusable delay" in filling an open seat on his court. Returning to private life, Hastie continued to be active in the NAACP and remained a vocal integrationist.

When speaking to those who came calling for his memories of his Black Cabinet years, Bill Hastie singled out the leadership of Mary McLeod Bethune. He recounted how Bethune had ferried the Black Cabinet's requests and recommendations to Eleanor Roosevelt, who had stealthily dodged Oval Office gatekeepers to get them to the president. Although Hastie remembered Bethune with relish and admiration, he hesitated to say much more about his Black Cabinet years. "I have great reluctance talking about that period because it was the first opportunity since slavery for this country to really break the bonds which shackle Black people," he told one interviewer. "We were young and not politically seasoned. We or they failed to seize the moment." Although Eleanor Roosevelt and Harold Ickes, along with a few agency heads, had supported the Black Cabinet and its goals, Hastie maintained that most of the administration had expressed very little concern for African Americans or equal rights. There were some victories, he conceded, but overall, he viewed his early years in federal service with regret and as a "disappointment."

Nonetheless, the enduringly unpretentious Hastie had been a pathbreaker, and he remained in great demand as a speaker during the years after his retirement. On April 14, 1976, he was preparing for one of these appearances when he decided to unwind with a round of golf. While on the green, he collapsed and died of a heart attack. Bill Hastie was seventy-one years old. The *Pittsburgh Courier* remarked that the shock of his passing was felt keenly, "across the nation and in foreign lands." Many voices paid tribute to the respected jurist as an "early civil rights leader" and praised him for his many firsts, for his willingness to stand up to the federal government over the U.S. military's Jim Crow practices, and for his brilliance on the bench. *Jet* magazine hailed Hastie as the man who "turned American jurisprudence around."

Bill Hastie's death left Al Smith and Robert Weaver as the last remaining senior members of the Black Cabinet. Unlike Hastie and Weaver, Al Smith had received little attention during his post-Roosevelt years. But like his colleagues, he continued the fight for equal rights. In 1944,

Smith helped found the Capital Press Club, composed of African American newsmen who covered the Washington beat but were excluded from national news correspondents' organizations. He wrote for both the *Negro Digest* and *Ebony* until the government recruited him as a press officer in the Federal Civil Defense Administration's office in Michigan. In 1954, Smith landed a new position as the race-relations adviser to the Federal Housing Administration's northeastern region. When John F. Kennedy took office, Smith headed back to Washington to take a racial-affairs post in the Department of Labor. He worked there until 1965, when, at the age of sixty-two, he decided to retire. He spent the next years quietly, working in his garden and spending time with his second wife, Lula, whom he had married during World War II.

When interviewers sought him out, Smith, always the colorful raconteur, reveled in relating stories of past battles and subterfuge. He bragged about *We Work Again*, and he claimed he eluded the FBI in its attempts to unmask the true identity of Charley Cherokee, chuckling over duping unwitting white administrators. He often grumbled about never finding acceptance within Weaver's circle.

While Smith admitted that in its collective efforts the Black Cabinet had fallen short, he also maintained that its members had made important contributions within their individual federal agencies. Smith was frank about the Roosevelt administration's incompetence and apathy when it came to handling matters of race. "I wasn't dry behind my ears, and I was supposed to know everything there was to know about Negroes," he told the *New York Times*. "It amazed me the way the Government was run." He lived to be eighty-three years old and died in 1986.

By the 1980s, Robert Weaver had been long retired from government work. During his comeback years under Kennedy and Johnson, he was able to realize many of the goals that he had pursued during his initial go-around in the Roosevelt administration. First as housing administrator and then as cabinet secretary, he successfully demanded increases in the federal budget for public housing. He required that new projects incorporate more aesthetic designs, arguing that the boxy, nondescript architecture that dominated federal housing negatively impacted the emotional state of residents. He established a rent-subsidy program for the elderly and secured funding to help restore small businesses in redevelopment zones. Many called Robert Weaver the "master builder" of Johnson's Great Society.

But after Richard Nixon's election in 1968, Weaver exited the White House cabinet, and many of his programs collapsed as the new administration shifted priorities away from inner-city renewal. Returning to Manhattan, he worked with local government officials to help steer the city through the recession of the 1970s, but he spent most of the rest of his career in academic ivory towers. He taught at Columbia University, New York University, and Hunter College. He served as president of Baruch College of the City University of New York. He generally abstained from entering the political debates of the 1980s and 1990s but spoke out against the Reagan administration's rollback of support for public housing and refusal to enforce fair-housing laws. But for the most part, Weaver lived quietly, hosting friends at his Park Avenue apartment and traveling with his wife, Ella. She passed away in 1991. Friends knew that despite Weaver's dispassionate facade, the loss devastated him.

In 1992, filmmaker Henry Hampton and his production team interviewed Robert Weaver for the multipart documentary film series *The Great Depression*. For over an hour and a half, eighty-five-year-old Weaver recounted the desperate times of the nation's worst financial meltdown, the chaos of the New Deal, and the fight for African American inclusion in federal programs. There, in his memories, lived Harold Ickes, the "old curmudgeon," under whom Weaver and his associates had pioneered equal protection for African Americans by instituting the earliest forms of federal antidiscrimination policies. A vigorous and charismatic FDR—"a great President"—struggled and fell short of his full potential, never embracing civil rights, as he timidly placated the southern Democratic bloc. Eleanor Roosevelt was a genuine ally; she became "distraught . . . whenever instances of discrimination, gross discrimination, would be brought to her attention from any source." The memory of "Mrs. Bethune" still burned brightly. Using her friendship with the First Lady, she forged the desperately needed channel to the White House for the Black Cabinet.

"If you were to explain to a young person what it meant for you to be a part of the New Deal, what would you want them to understand?" the interviewer asked. "I would want them to understand that the New Deal represented a new situation vis-à-vis the importance of government in the lives of average citizens in this country," Weaver replied, with his characteristic formality. The shift of the U.S. government to democratic New Deal liberalism and federal intervention introduced "the seeds of getting new developments, new approaches, and new regulations which would assist and help the people who were in need and that included of course African Americans."

"Do you feel that you were part of a movement to make government more responsible?" the questioner asked the last of the Black Cabinet's stalwarts. "Yes, but I didn't think that I was a major part of it. I thought that I was among those who were participating in that activity, but I didn't think I was the captain of . . . the troops going over the hill," he answered, with a smile that countered the modesty of his claims.

In 1997, four months short of his ninetieth birthday, Robert Weaver died in his Park Avenue apartment. His passing received national attention. Around the country, news outlets applauded him for his pioneering contributions, both as the first African American to serve in a White House cabinet and as the moving force behind the Black Cabinet of the Roosevelt years. "History Will Remember Him," read the headline in San Francisco's *Sun-Reporter*. The article noted, "Although not well known to blacks of this time, Weaver should be accorded the same high regard that blacks hold for Philip Randolph and Bethune. These three, along with perhaps W. E. B. Du Bois, deserve a place in black history as three hard fighters in the pursuit of equality."

Robert Weaver, Bill Hastie, Al Smith, Mary McLeod Bethune, and Robert Vann, along with Lawrence Oxley, Eugene Kinckle Jones, Edgar

Brown, Henry Hunt, Forrester Washington, Frank Horne, Lucia Mae
Pitts, and their colleagues, left an enduring legacy of activism pursued
both inside and outside of government. While these members of the
Black Cabinet diverged in background and approach, all agreed on
two key points: they shared a common goal in securing human rights
and social justice for African Americans; and they all maintained faith
that American democracy and its system of government provided the
framework through which that goal could be achieved.

The African American brain trust refused to allow the New Deal to
be, as Eleanor Roosevelt once described it, "nothing more than an effort
to preserve our economic system." Black Cabinet members contributed both individually and collectively to the evolution of the modern
liberalism that sprouted from the New Deal—one that provided the
groundwork for not only the realignment of race relations but also
the redefinition of the government's responsibility to all its citizens.
They held up the mirror that exposed the contradictions of American
ideals and the nation's racism as it fought Nazism during World War
II. They led African Americans out of the Republican Party and into
a new alliance with the Democrats, which over time transformed that
party. The era of Roosevelt was, without a doubt, far richer and more
wide-reaching because of the Black Cabinet.

Imperfect in their union, the men and women of the Black Cabinet
remained clear in their vision. Regardless of their rivalries and divisions,
the members, individually and collaboratively, steered, prodded, and
pushed the United States into taking a journey toward becoming a more
inclusive nation. Their contributions compelled change in American
political culture and the nation's federal institutions. The country's
slow and continuing transformation, its renewed reconstruction, would
not be completed during their lifetimes, but their presence had been
critical to its birth.

In 1954, reflecting on *Brown v. Board of Education* and the banning of
segregation in public schools, Bethune called for all freedom fighters
to soldier on. Her long years in the struggle provided her with a special

ability to weave the past, the present, and the future together. Capturing the central goal that had driven not only her personal crusade but also that of the Black Cabinet, she urged next generations to take up the charge and continue the battle.

"And it would be a serious and calamitous mistake for any person to relax vigilance in our struggle to build a moral state," she wrote, commanding: "Let there be no resting at the oars."

NOTES

Prologue

xi "faith and prayer." Edwin Embree, *13 Against the Odds* (New York: Viking Press, 1944), 9.

xii "FDR's Black Cabinet." *Philadelphia Tribune*, March 29, 1934.

xii "First Lady of Our Negro Nation." *New York Age*, September 21, 1940.

xii "I know what." Dora Byron, "From 'Cabin in the Cotton,'" *Opportunity*, April 1936, 106–107, 125.

xiv "string him up" and "Don't look." Rackman Holt, "Biography of Bethune and corrections," chapter 1, 1–21; MMB-bio. Rackman Holt began working on a biography of Bethune in the 1940s. Correspondence indicates that Holt worked closely with Bethune, and Bethune read and remarked on chapter drafts. This file contains a draft of the biography, the correspondence, and corrections offered by Bethune. The final biography would not appear in print until 1964.

xv "Ma" and "her boys." "Robert C. Weaver," in Katie Lochheim and Jonathan Dembo, eds., *The Making of the New Deal* (Cambridge, MA: Harvard University Press, 1983), 262–63.

xv "If you do that again," "quiet and dignified," "nodded," and "Thank you." *Pittsburgh Courier*, January 27, 1940.

xvii "Each time." *Pittsburgh Courier*, January 27, 1940.

xix "The principle." Mary McLeod Bethune, "Closed Doors (1936)," in *Mary McLeod Bethune: Building a Better World, Essays and Selected Documents*, Audrey McCluskey and Elaine Smith, eds. (Bloomington: Indiana University Press, 1999), 211.

xix "Then armed." Bethune, "Clarifying Our Vision with Facts (1938)," in *Mary McLeod Bethune: Building a Better World*, 215.

CHAPTER ONE

3   "talkfests." *Washington Bee*, February 8, 1921.

4   "He could not." Byron, "Cabin," 107.

4   "race woman," "civil rights minded," and "Most of our neighbors." Gilbert Ware, *William Hastie: Grace under Pressure* (New York: Oxford University Press, 1985), 4. For a discussion of "race woman," see Gerald Horne, *Race Woman: The Lives of Shirley Graham Du Bois* (New York: New York University Press, 2000), 63.

5   "talented tenth." Wendell Pritchett, *Robert Clifton Weaver and the American City: The Life and Times of an Urban Reformer* (Chicago: University of Chicago Press, 2008), 8–9.

6   "Black Cabinet." *Washington Bee*, August 8, 1908.

6   "'epicurean' in its 'gastronomic delicacies.'" *New York Age*, March 12, 1908.

6   "The addresses were," "I came among you," and "Today we enjoy." Ibid.

7   "Party of Lincoln" and "evil." Eric Foner, *Reconstruction: America's Unfinished Revolution, 1863–1877* (New York: Perennial Classics, 2002), 30, 417.

11 "Lightning Calculator." Alfred E. Smith, "America's Greatest Unknown Negro," *Negro Digest*, April 1940, 42–46.

11 "Lily Whites." Richard B. Sherman, *The Republican Party and Black America: From McKinley to Hoover, 1896–1933* (Charlottesville: University Press of Virginia, 1973), 4–8.

13 "Rough Rider." Ibid., 23–25.

13 "of the strenuous life" and "high moral courage." *Colored American*, April 12, 1902.

14 "talked at." Deborah H. Davis, *Guest of Honor: Booker T. Washington, Theodore Roosevelt, and the White House Dinner That Shocked the Nation* (New York: Atria, 2013), 202.

15 "Equality." Lithograph by C. H. Thomas and P. H. Lacey, 1903, in Louis R. Harlan, *Booker T. Washington in Perspective: Essays of Louis R. Harlan*, Raymond Smock, ed. (Oxford: University of Mississippi Press, 2006), photo section.

15 "Tuskegee Machine." Louis R. Harlan, *Booker T. Washington: The Wizard of Tuskegee, 1901–1915*, vol. 2 (New York: Oxford University Press, 1983), viii.

15 "Booker T. Washington was," "Whatever patronage," and "the master hand." *Baltimore Afro-American*, January 30, 1937.

16 "Ralph Tyler always." *Washington Bee*, April 10, 1915.

17 "He knew how." Ibid.

17 "Jim Crow corner." Constance McLaughlin Green, *The Secret City: A History of Race Relations in the Nation's Capital* (Princeton, NJ: Princeton University Press, 1967), 166.

18 "criminality." Harlan, *Wizard*, 319–20.

18 "This message" Kelly Miller, *Race Adjustment: Essays on the Negro in America*, 2nd ed. (New York: Neale Publishing Company, 1909), 300.

19 "Le Cabinet Noir." Armand Mattelart, *Mapping World Communication: War, Progress, Culture* (Minneapolis: University of Minnesota Press, 1994), 7.

19 "*The [Washington] Bee* respectfully." *Washington Bee*, February 13, 1909.

19 "sans respect for." *Washington Bee*, February 8, 1921.

20 "If . . . you can" and "But I shall." David Levering Lewis, *W. E. B. Du Bois, 1868–1919: Biography of a Race* (New York: Macmillan, 1994), 341.

20 "IS IT TRUE?" *Washington Bee*, August 8, 1908.

20 "He is a friend." *The Indianapolis Freeman*, June 27, 1908.

21 "Any recognition" and "be pursued when." *Inaugural Addresses of the Presidents of the United States from George Washington 1789 to Richard Milhous Nixon 1969* (Washington, D.C.: U.S. Government Printing Office, 1969), 169.

21 "Black what?" "Black Cabinet," "And who and," and "The surprising." *Baltimore Afro-American*, April 24, 1909.

21 "imaginary." Ibid., February 6, 1909.

22 "I believe in your" and "Negroes who have." Booker T. Washington to William Howard Taft, June 18, 1909, *Booker T. Washington Papers, 1909–1911*, vol. 10, Louis Harlan, Geraldine McTigue, and Nan E. Woodruff, eds. (Champaign: University of Illinois Press, 1981), 138–40.

22 "The matter of." William Howard Taft to Booker T. Washington, June 24, 1909, ibid, 140.

23 "The Sage of the." *Washington Bee*, July 8, 1911.

23 "Outside of dining" and "no service." Ibid., October 29, 1910.

23 "Politically there is," "merely figurative," and "resume their talkfest." Ibid., January 14, 1911.

23 "grouchy and dyspeptic." Quoted from *Indianapolis Freeman* in *Washington Bee*, December 14, 1912.

24 "Practically all the time" and "which we made plain." Harlan, *Wizard*, 351.

24 "told him that the." Ibid., 352.

25 "I can't" and "I am not." Ibid.

25 "disgraceful" and "The address." *Baltimore Afro-American*, April 13, 1912.

25 "revolted and told him." *Indianapolis Star*, June 20, 1912.

26 "I hope that." *Baltimore Afro-American*, August 31, 1912.

27 "consolation dinner." *Washington Bee*, November 30, 1912.

27 "all reveled" and "[Wilson] feels he." Ibid.

29 "There ran by me" and "caught the Negro." David Levering Lewis, *When Harlem Was in Vogue* (New York: Vintage Books, 1982), 19.

29 "As an American," "foul play," and "fair play." *New York Age*, June 12, 1913.

30 "I peeped in" and "There wasn't even." *Washington Bee*, June 14, 1913.

30 "scattered to the." Ibid., May 24, 1913.

30 "For the Black Cabinet" and "here's rosemary." Ibid., April 12, 1913.

30 "Well, there will." Ibid., November 18, 1916.

30 "the famine." Ibid., February 8, 1921.

31 "racial amalgamation." W. E. B. Du Bois, "President Harding and Social Equality," *Crisis*, December 1921, 53–56.

32 "expensive" and "indispensable." *Indianapolis Freeman*, quoted in *Cleveland Gazette*, September 6, 1924.

32 "To supplement our" and "When Queen Cotton." Richard Wright, *12 Million Black Voices* (New York: Basic Books, 1941; reprinted 2008), 54–58.

33 "During his whole public." *New York Times*, October 6, 1929.

33 "the halcyon years." *Washington Bee*, February 8, 1921.

34 "a woman to." *Baltimore Afro-American*, September 20, 1930.

35 "We long to see" and "It's on furlough." *Capitol Plaindealer* (Topeka, KS), February 15, 1918.

Chapter Two

36 "pleasant" and "sensible." Joseph Alsop and Robert Kintner, "The Guffey: Biography of a Boss, New Style," *Saturday Evening Post*, March 26, 1938, 5–7.

38 "Mrs. Miller, Mr. Vann'd." Ibid., 5.

40 "Once having found" and "the individual." Andrew Buni, *Robert L. Vann of the Pittsburgh Courier* (Pittsburgh: University of Pittsburgh Press, 1974), 12.

40 "good fellow." *Philadelphia Tribune*, April 12, 1934.

40 "shrewd and calculating." Ibid.

41 "I'll see you." *Baltimore Afro-American*, August 25, 1936.

41 "disloyal and bitter." M. Hawkins, Publicity Committee, Colored Voters Division, 1928 Campaign, "Confidential comments on loyalty," n.d.; "Negro Newspapers: Their Political Affiliations and Attitudes during Period 1930–1932," n.d.; CBP RNC28.

41 "You can't take" and "You've got to." Alsop and Kintner, "Guffey," 5–6.

42 "Negro division." Joseph Johnson to Stephen Early, July 28, 1939; FDR-RR, reel 2.

42   "The Patriot and the Partisan," "blind," and "The Republican Party." *Pittsburgh Courier*, September 17, 1932.

43   "The only true gauge," "I see millions of," and "I, for one." Ibid.

43   "the Big Four." *Baltimore Afro-American*, August 25, 1936.

44   "adopted son." Roger Biles, *The South and the New Deal* (Lexington: University Press of Kentucky, 2015), 126.

45   "nothing to be afraid of," "a man whose," "I believe in equal," "the last of," "For most of us," and "But we know it." *Pittsburgh Courier*, November 5, 1932.

46   "PRESIDENT HOOVER OFFERS." Republican National Committee, "President Hoover Offers New Deal to Colored Race," ca. October 1932; CBP RNC28.

46   Colored Voters League and "Florida Negroes." *Pittsburgh Courier*, October 6, 1928.

47   "slightly appalled." Holt, "Biography of Bethune and corrections," 150; MMB-bio.

47   "excited at being." Ibid.

47   "Hey there, Auntie." Blanche Wiesen Cook. *Eleanor Roosevelt: The Defining Years, 1933–1938*, vol. 2. (New York: Penguin Books, 1999), 162. Bethune's versions of this story differed throughout the years. She often related it as having occurred at the White House. In other cases, she claimed it had occurred on trains. It is possible, given the constant displays of white public racism of the era, that it occurred many times. Audrey Thomas McCluskey, "Introduction," in Mary McLeod Bethune, *Mary McLeod Bethune: Building a Better*, 11.

48   "I want you." Joyce A. Hanson, *Mary McLeod Bethune and Black Women's Political Activism* (Columbia: University of Missouri Press, 2003), 124.

48   "She predicted." *Baltimore Afro-American*, October 22, 1932.

48   "I am using." Hanson, *Bethune*, 124.

48   "The country was." *New York Times*, November 9, 1932.

49–50   "the only organization" and "President Hoover has done." James Napier to Claude Barnett, September 7, 1932; CBP Survey32.

50   "For the first time." *Plaindealer* (Kansas City, KS), November 18, 1932.

50   "Negro Ballot Seen as Key to Victory." *New York Amsterdam News*, November 9, 1932.

50   "a splendid revolt." Arthur Krock, "Did the Negro Revolt?," *Journal of Negro Life* (January 1933), 19, 28.

51   "One thing is" and "No longer." *Baltimore Afro-American*, November 12, 1932.

51   "It is an open" and "I doubt that they." Nancy J. Weiss, *Farewell to the Party of Lincoln: Black Politics in the Age of FDR* (Princeton, NJ: Princeton University Press, 1983), 33.

51 "tests." *Plaindealer* (Kansas City, KS), November 18, 1932.

51 "I, for a long time." Ibid., February 3, 1933.

51 "a fair, impartial." Ibid.

52 "Before you say." Alsop and Kintner, "Guffey," 6.

53 "From end to end." *Pittsburgh Courier*, December 17, 1932.

53 "Men with families up." Ibid.

53 "OUR ECONOMIC SYSTEM." *Wyandotte (KS) Echo*, January 20, 1933.

54 "I wouldn't say." Weiss, *Farewell*, 35.

54 "the only thing." *Inaugural Addresses*, 235.

54 "a shaft of bright." *Pittsburgh Courier*, March 11, 1933.

55 "when these colored contingents" and "them a snappy." Ibid.

56 "We Do Our Part." David M. Kennedy, *Freedom from Fear: The American People in Depression and War* (New York: Oxford University Press, 1999), 183.

56 "I would not." *Baltimore Afro-American*, April 20, 1933.

56 "Since a few months." Ibid.

57 "the colored people." Letter: Julian Rainey to Louis Howe, April 17, 1933; FDR-RR, reel 1.

57 "not seeing any." Letter: Louis Howe to Julian Rainey, April 20, 1933; FDR-RR, reel 1.

57 "No news now." *Plaindealer* (Kansas City, KS), May 12, 1933.

59 "never seen." Buni, *Vann*, 206.

59 "Is the Negro." *Plaindealer* (Kansas City, KS), June 23, 1933.

59 "sitting at a." "The Rosenwald Conference," *Crisis*, July 1933, 156–57.

62 "a stuffed shirt." FBI Report: "Robert Clifton Weaver," Special Inquiry: Lester Granger Interview, January 30, 1965, Weaver FBI File.

63 "masterful." *Pittsburgh Courier*, July 29, 1933.

63 "Throughout the nation" and "we will see the." *Plaindealer* (Kansas City, KS), August 4, 1933.

63 "Negro Removal Act." William Pickens, "NRA—Negro Removal Act?" *The World Tomorrow*, September 28, 1933, 539–40.

63 "Second Amenia." Eben Miller, *Born along the Color Line: The 1933 Amenia Conference and the Rise of a National Civil Rights Movement* (New York: Oxford University Press, 2012), 3, 56.

64 "chiefly on paper," "individuals of intelligence," and "not representative." W. E. B. Du Bois to Myra Colson Callis, August 28, 1933, *W. E. B. Du Bois Papers, Series 1A, General Correspondence*, Special Collections and University Archives, University of Massachusetts Amherst Libraries; MS 312.

64 "I am told." Roy Wilkins to Claude Barnett, August 10, 1933; CBP FDR/ NRA.

64 "When anyone got," "reformed Democracy," and "full and indiscriminatory." W. E. B. Du Bois, "Youth and Age at Amenia," *Crisis*, October 1933, 226–28.

65 "Young Negro Brain Trust" and "the demands." *New York Amsterdam News*, September 20, 1933.

65 "certainly the Negroes." *Pittsburgh Courier*, August 26, 1933.

CHAPTER THREE

70 "a new kind of slavery." *Plaindealer* (Kansas City, KS), August 11, 1933.

70 "The lash of prejudice" and "I have not brooded." A. H. Raskin, "Washington Gets 'The Weaver Treatment,'" *New York Times Magazine*, May 14, 1961, 35.

71 "The way to offset" and "was to be awfully." "Cities: Hope for the Heart," *Time*, March 4, 1966, 31.

71 "a puritan." Alma Rene Williams, "Robert C. Weaver: From the Black Cabinet to the President's Cabinet," PhD diss., Washington University, 1978, 3–4.

72 "no question" and "would do well." Ware, *William Hastie: Grace*, 9.

72 "Stop that evil game." Peggy Mann, *Ralph Bunche: UN Peacemaker* (New York: Coward, McCann and Geoghegan, 1975), 51–52.

73 "didn't think that." Pritchett, *Robert Clifton Weaver*, 27–28.

73 "The High Wage Theory." Robert C. Weaver, "The High Wage Theory of Prosperity," PhD diss., Harvard University, 1934.

74 "Brain Trust" and "ready to work." *Pittsburgh Courier*, August 26, 1933.

74 "I had grown up" and "I had known." Transcript, Robert C. Weaver interview, February 15, 1992, *The Great Depression Interviews*, Blackside, Inc. accessed November 15, 2015, http://digital.wustl.edu/cgi/t/text/text-idx?c=gds;cc=gds;rgn =main;view=text;idno=wea00031.00880.064.

74 "Although there is grave need" and "Past experiences with." Williams, "Robert C. Weaver," 21.

75 "was a sort" and "perhaps the next." Will W. Alexander, *The Reminiscences of Will W. Alexander* (New York: Columbia University Oral History Collection, 1952), [typescript/microfiche] 367–68.

75 "We are frank" and "That is the." *Baltimore Afro-American*, September 16, 1933.

76 "It was certainly bad." *Chicago Defender*, September 16, 1933.

76 "Will the New Deal." Jessie O. Thomas, "Will the New Deal Be a Square Deal for the Negro?" *Opportunity*, October 1933, 308–11.

76 "The people who" and "bitterly fought by." Roy Wilkins to Claude Barnett, August 22, 29, 1933; CBP FDR/NRA.

76 "time" and "not ripe." *Baltimore Afro-American*, September 9, 1933.

77 "terrible, barbaric." Clark Foreman, Transcript, oral history interview by Jacquelyn Hall and William Finger, November 16, 1974, Documenting the American South (University of North Carolina at Chapel Hill), Oral Histories of the American South collection, p. 23, accessed February 14, 2008. http://docsouth.unc.edu/sohp/B-0003/B-0003.html.

78 "That was my" and "from southern tradition." Ibid., p. 4.

78 "If he [Foreman] waked up," "billy goat," "just butt," and "That young fellow's." Alexander, *Reminiscences*, 370–71.

78 "Many white people." Thomas, "Will the New Deal," 308.

79 "stoic." Lucia Mae Pitts, Manuscript, ch. 5, p. 2, *Manuscript and Letters*, State Historical Society of Wisconsin, Madison, microfilm edition, 1981.

80 "My ambition had been" and "Most Negroes have felt." Ibid., ch. 4, p. 20.

80 "rude." Foreman, transcript, oral history interview, p. 23.

80 "unbending," "I felt it was," and "I did not know." Pitts, Manuscript, prologue, 11.

81 "hectic and busy." Ibid., ch. 2, p. 22.

81 "He walks the." *New Journal and Guide* (Norfolk, VA), May 12, 1934.

82 "twice a day." Foreman, transcript, oral history interview, p. 23.

82 "got kicked out" and "kicked him out." Alexander, *Reminiscences*, 370–71.

82 "Well now, Mr. Foreman," "Well, Major," and "It would never." Foreman, transcript, oral history interview, p. 26.

82 "The Colonel showed." Clark Foreman to Harold Ickes, November 7, 1933, Harold Ickes Office Files, 1933–42, Department of Interior Record Group 48, *New Deal Agencies and Black America* (Frederick, MD: University Publications of America, 1983), microfilm: reel 7.

82 "Had a rather rough." Alexander, *Reminiscences*, 371–72.

84 "The appointment of" and "[Jones] had nothing." *Atlanta Daily World*, April 27, 1934.

85 "Credit to Race." *New York Daily News*, October 28, 1933.

85 "one of the." *New York Times*, October 19, 1933.

86 "Some may question." *New York Age*, November 25, 1933.

86 "the study of." *New York Times*, October 19, 1933.

86 "The burden is" and "if he makes." *Negro Star* (Wichita, KS), October 6, 1933.

86 "a conservative estimate." *Pittsburgh Courier*, November 11, 1933.

87 "The city Negro" and "The farm is the." *New York Times*, October 22, 1933.

88 "The work of." *Pittsburgh Courier*, October 21, 1933.

89 "pace the floor," "Will you two," and "You're driving." Pitts, Manuscript, ch. 1, p. 9.

89 "Do you work" and "Where?" Foreman, transcript, oral history interview, p. 24.

90 "I believe that," Pritchett, *Weaver*, 45.

90 "no more than." Ibid.

91 "We are anxious that." *Baltimore Afro-American*, November 18, 1933.

91 "a little short guy," "sort of pompous," and "liked to speak." Ibid., 37.

91 "pay off political debts." Lochheim and Dembo, *The Making*, 262.

93 "Here you had" and "This meant that." Weaver, *The Great Depression Interviews*.

93 "Too often when." National Urban League "Special Memorandum on the Social Adjustment of Negroes in the United States submitted to the President, Franklin Roosevelt," April 15, 1933, Department of Commerce Record Group 40, *New Deal Agencies and Black America*, reel 18.

95 "a national Negro organization" and "discrimination exercised against." Robert C. Weaver, "An Experiment in Negro Labor," *Opportunity*, October 1936, 295–98.

96 "Don't Buy Where." Henry Louis Gates Jr., *African American Lives* (New York: Oxford University Press, 2004), 381.

96 "advisory committee" and "with the government." Letter: Robert R. Moton to Harold Ickes, December 19, 1933; FGR-Ickes.

96 "strong, sensible, and tactful." Ray Stannard Baker, "The New Head of Tuskegee," *The World's Work*, vol. 31, Walter Hines Page and Arthur W. Page, eds. (New York: Doubleday, 1916), 527–31.

97 "It is no fiction" and "And when the." Robert R. Moton to Harold Ickes, December 19, 1933; FRG-Ickes.

97 "With a multitude" and "the public is at." Ibid.

98 "very great psychological," "carefully selected," and "as much as." Clark Foreman memorandum to Harold Ickes, December 22, 1933; FRG-Ickes.

99 "Do you work here?" "Yes," "Would you mind," "No. This is," and "She looked as if." Ware, *William Hastie: Grace*, 82.

99 "Good afternoon, ladies." Ibid.

CHAPTER FOUR

100 "a mind that can see." Ware, *William Hastie: Grace*, 30.

100 "they can't Jim Crow." Ibid., 4.

100 "After all" and "no deeper satisfaction." Ibid., 5.

101 "It is where" and "that the services of." Ibid., 29.

102 "secret meeting." *Baltimore Afro-American*, December 16, 1933.

103 "I assume no." Ibid.

103 "No Negro supported" and "All Negroes who." Letter: Clark Foreman to Harold Ickes, December 13, 1933, Harold Ickes Office Files, 1933–42, Department of Interior Record Group 48, *New Deal Agencies and Black America*, reel 7.

104 "thousands of forgotten." *Philadelphia Tribune*, December 21, 1933.

104 "Are you also situated," "not very satisfactory," and "I don't know." *Baltimore Afro-American*, December 16, 1933.

104 "I do not see" and "If we did." Ibid.

104 "The Negroes are treated." Ibid.

105 "Dr. [Alexander] Sachs has," "This was crazy," and "We would be playing." Ibid.

105 "an indication of." *Philadelphia Tribune*, December 21, 1933.

105 "I cannot believe." Robert Vann memorandum to Louis Howe, December 15, 1933; FDR-RR, reel 1.

107 "raw deal." *Baltimore Afro-American*, March 10, 1934.

107 "I think there is no." William H. Hastie, Transcript: Oral history interview by Jerry N. Hess, 53; Harry S. Truman Library and Museum. January 5, 1972, accessed May 28, 2014, https://www.trumanlibrary.org/oralhist/hastie.htm.

108 "What do you boys want?" *Baltimore Afro-American*, September 2, 1933.

108 "Under the Roosevelts" and "You were invited to." Lillian Rogers Parks, with Frances Spatz Leighton, *My Thirty Years Backstairs at the White House* (1961; reprint: Bronx, NY; Ishi Press, 2008), 235.

109 "weren't hard to please." Alonzo Fields, *My 21 Years in the White House* (New York: Coward-McCann, 1961), 50.

110 "I didn't know anyone." *Pittsburgh Courier*, January 7, 1933.

110 "Lizzie treated FDR." Lillian Rogers Parks, with Frances Spatz Leighton, *The Roosevelts: A Family in Turmoil* (Englewood Cliffs, NJ: Prentice Hall, 1981), 20.

110 "Doll." Ibid., 86.

110 "was democratic without." Elizabeth McDuffie, "FDR Was My Boss," *Ebony* April 1962, 69.

111 "He [FDR] had no." Parks, *The Roosevelts*, 20.

111 "SASOCPA" and "self-appointed." McDuffie, "FDR," 65.

112 "a mistake," "establish a precedent," and "correlate their work." Harold Ickes memorandum to Clark Foreman, January 2, 1934; FRG-Ickes.

113 "formulate general principles." Clark Foreman to Mr. Secretary [Daniel Roper], January 2, 1934; FRG-Jones.

114 "The Black Cabinet in the New Deal." *Philadelphia Tribune*, March 29, 1934.

115 "Roosevelt is the hub." Ibid., April 5, 1934.

115 "The New Deal is a revolution" and "a cool, collected." Ibid., March 29, 1934.

115 "Where is the Negro." Ibid.

115 "He has the illusions" and "but [he] likes to." *Philadelphia Tribune*, April 12, 1934.

116 "the sharecroppers' woes" and "a colorless old." Ibid., April 19, 1934.

116 "honest," "statesmanlike," "race-interested," "absurd and illogical," and "He likes too." Ibid., *Atlanta Daily World*, April 27, 1934.

116 "New Deal Personalities." *New Journal and Guide* (Norfolk, VA), April 21, 1934.

116 "quite distinguished looking." Ibid., May 19, 1934.

117 "all southern cooking." Ibid., March 31, 1934.

117 "He has a keen" and "good looking." Ibid., April 7, 1934.

117 "Dr. Foreman, sincere, immature," "protected," and "As a leader." *Atlanta Daily World*, May 10, 1934.

117 "team player," "establishment of a," and "unusual service." *Plaindealer* (Kansas City, KS), May 4, 1934.

117 "powerful influences." Davidson to Barnett, May 1, 1934; CBP-Davidson.

118 were "far from." Barnett to Davidson, May 17, 1934; CBP-Davidson.

118 "youthful." *New Journal and Guide* (Norfolk, VA), May 12, 1934.

118 "'FDR's Negro Brain Trust,'" "a body of highly trained," "The Negro stands," "They must blaze the way," and "and show the race." *Atlanta Daily World*, July 8, 1934.

119 "ginger-colored n-----." *Baltimore Afro-American*, January 5, 1935; Memorandum, September 27, 1933; FDR-RR, reel 1.

120 "be able to serve your people" and "Alaska, Howard." *Chicago Defender*, November 25, 1933.

121 "We met frequently." Lochheim and Dembo, *The Making*, 264.

121 "sometimes earthy, sometimes sly." Raskin, "Washington," 16.

121 "They wiped me out" and "Bunche taught me how." Truman K. Gibson Jr., with Steven Huntley, *Knocking down Barriers: My Fight for Black America* (Evanston, IL: Northwestern University Press, 2005), 81.

121 "feverish discussions of." Raskin, "Washington," 33.

122 "There were obvious" and "We shared ideas." "William Hastie Oral History," in Mariagnes Lattimer, "The Black Cabinet: The Study of Personal Commitment and Political Involvement by Blacks During the New Deal," PhD diss., Union Institute and University, 1974, form B #9.

122 "doubted that anyone." Minutes: First Inter-departmental Group Meeting, February 7, 1934, 8; FGR-Ickes34.

122 "had very little." Ibid., 7.

123 "displacement of Negro workers" and "violations . . . and intimidation." Ibid., 6.

123 "illiteracy" and "fear." Ibid., 7.

124 "creative program." Ibid., 3.

125 "of discrimination and other." Minutes: Second Inter-departmental Group Meeting, March 2, 1934, 3; FGR-Ickes.

125 "Can you deny that?" Ibid., 4.

126 "would be amazed." Ibid., 6.

126 "demanding jobs and relief." Inter-departmental Group: Report of the Agricultural Committee, March 30, 1934, 15; FGR-Ickes34.

127 "intimidation of the Negroes." Inter-departmental Group: Report on Negro Labor, April 18, 1934, 1; FGR-Ickes34.

127 "it allowed them." Ibid., 7.

127 "cooperation" "superfluous" and "acknowledge that there is." Minutes: Third Inter-departmental Group Meeting, March 30, 1934, 4, FRG-Ickes.

129 "establishes fact." David M. Gillmor, *Mass Communication Law: Cases and Comment* (Belmont, CA: Wadsworth Publishing, 1998), 256.

129 "caused some resentment" and "positive." Robert C. Weaver, transcript, oral history interview by Joe B. Frantz, November 19, 1968, p. 10, Lyndon Baines Johnson Presidential Library, Austin, TX; FRG-Weaver.

129 "a revolution in thought." Minutes: Fourth Inter-departmental Group Meeting, June 1, 1934, 3; FGR-Ickes34.

129 "It occurred to us" and "that a possible solution." Ibid., 7.

130 "special pressure of." Ibid., 9.

130 "touching on politics." Ibid., 11.

130 "touching on policies." Ibid.

130 "After all, some of us." Ibid., 12–13.

131 "to take advantage" and "The Negro has got." *Baltimore Afro-American*, November 4, 1934.

CHAPTER FIVE

132 "The Democrats are in!" *Pittsburgh Courier*, June 23, 1934.

133 "I'm an Ozark hillbilly," "A Pioneer's Pioneer: Al Smith," *Oracle*, Summer 1974, 1.

133 "foolishness," "fed all the livestock," and "If you never." Patricia A. Frank, "'Keep 'Em Squirming!' Alfred Edgar Smith, Charley Cherokee, and Race Relations 1933–1943." MA thesis, University of Arkansas, 1993, 7.

134 his body was "cut down." *Galena (KS) Evening Times*, June 21, 1933.

134 "the great number of." *Evening News* (Wilkes-Barre, PA), June 20, 1913.

134 "a new world." *New York Times*, July 21, 1933.

134 "The Elimination of the Negro." Frank, "'Keep 'em Squirming!'" 19.

135 "Do something with these." "A Pioneer's Pioneer," 3.

135 "Mister Roosevelt, Dear Colonel" and "I ain't got nowhere." *Pittsburgh Courier*, May 5, 1934.

135 "The feeling the white race." W. B. Smith to Forrester Washington, July 27, 1934; FRG-Smith.

135 "Please tell me" and "I know the United States." Jake Adams to Mr. [Hugh S.] Johnson, July 7, 1934; FRG-Smith.

136 "with its old slave quarters." *Pittsburgh Courier*, May 5, 1934.

136 "I'm Sylvester Harris," "A man is," and "Sylvester, I'll investigate." *New York Age*, March 10, 1934.

136 "a nigger down here" and "De White House gentleman." *Salt Lake Tribune* (Salt Lake City, UT), March 1, 1934.

137 "misquoted." *Pittsburgh Courier*, March 10, 1934.

138 "Mr. Speaker," "I . . . take peculiar," and "It has been increasingly evident." Ibid., August 11, 1934.

138 "we can have no group," "well-known colored leaders," and "little cabinet." Ibid.

139 "better deal." ANP News Release, April 23, 1934, 2–3; CBP-FED.

139 "Despite the shortcomings" and "without it the colored." *Baltimore Afro-American*, June 2, 1934.

139 "The immediate effect," "President Roosevelt," and "The colored workers serving." Ibid., July 28, 1934.

139 "a new and more," "refused to be licked," "smiling through," and "Do not go back." Ibid., May 17, 1934.

139 "colored welfare and citizens.'" ANP News Release, April 4, 1934, p. 3–4; CBP-FED.

140 "destitute Negro family." *Pittsburgh Courier*, April, 7, 1934.

140 "protest resignation." *Philadelphia Tribune*, August 16, 1934.

141 "Mr. Jones' bid," "new blood," and "Nothing had been done." *Chicago Defender*, August 25, 1934.

142 "I'm not used to." Ibid.

142 "In my mind" and "I believe that." Letter: Leo E. Allen to Barnett, August 2, 1934; CBP-FDR/NRA.

143 "glitter and glamor of" and "common man." Letter: Claude Barnett to Henry P. Fletcher, July 26, 1934; CBP-FDR/NRA.

143 "reliable," "disband," and "the President is." *New York Amsterdam News*, October 13, 1934.

143 "Not on Way Out." *New Journal and Guide*, (Norfolk, VA), October 20, 1934.

144 "young people are." *Baltimore Afro-American*, October 20, 1934.

145 "It is a," "Revolting because of," "economic exploitation," and "terrified Negroes." *Pittsburgh Courier*, December 1, 1934.

145 "the effect of such" and "the whole." Letter: Walter White to Harold Ickes, November 26, 1934; FRG-Ickes34.

145–146 "I considered jobs," "I meant what," "Advisers can do," and "There are numerous." *New Journal and Guide* (Norfolk, VA), November 3, 1934.

146 "Where a large number," and "[The president] made;" Weaver, *The Great Depression Interviews*.

146 "Folks flocked to see" and "A lot of them, moved." *Pittsburgh Courier*, November 17, 1934.

146 "awakening" and "if Abraham Lincoln." Ibid., November 24, 1934.

147 "Race Gains Posts." Ibid., November 17, 1934.

147 "Hand Me Down." *Plaindealer* (Kansas City, KS), November 23, 1934.

148 "spineless," "political parasites," "intellectual flies," "the courage and manhood," and "NOTHING." *Chicago Defender*, February 9, 16, 1935.

148 "sleeping at [the] switch." *New Journal and Guide* (Norfolk, VA), January 19, 1935.

148 "The only thing" and "The job of the." *New York Age*, March 23, 1935.

149 "Young man" and "You'll do fine." Pritchett, *Weaver*, 55.

150 "Weaver treatment," "marked by a," and "yeast, excitement." Raskin, "Washington," 30.

150 "I had all of." Weaver, *The Great Depression Interviews*.

152 "Rosenwald list." "A Pioneer's Pioneer," 4.

152 "Weaver's boys were more." Jane Motz, "The Black Cabinet: Negroes in the Administration of Franklin D. Roosevelt," MA thesis, University of Delaware, 1964, 25.

152 "considered us children" and "interested in mainly." Lattimer, "The Black Cabinet," 11.

152 "Bickerings and petty jealousies" and "Each had." *New Journal and Guide* (Norfolk, VA), January 25, 1937.

153 "the Coloured Serenader." Ibid., May 5, 1934.

153 "locality development." Yolanda Burwell, "Lawrence Oxley and Locality Development: Black Self-Help in North Carolina, 1925–1928," *Journal of Community Practice* 2, no. 4. (1996): 49–69.

154 "never have any more." Alexander, *Reminiscences*, 369.

154 "head S.O.B. of all" and "buttering his own." Jonathan Scott Holloway, *Confronting the Veil: Abram Harris, Jr., E. Franklin Frazier, and Ralph Bunche, 1919–1941* (Chapel Hill: University of North Carolina Press, 2003), 170–71.

154 "indiscreet" and "unfit for office." *Baltimore Afro-American*, August 18, 1934.

154 "knew how to." Alexander, *Reminiscences*, 369.

154 "It is important that." Memorandum: Lawrence Oxley to Frances Perkins, December 14, 1934; FRG-Oxley.

155 "If you are making," "you must be," "this is a," and "you people." Memorandum: Lawrence Oxley to A. F. Hinrichs, March 18, 1936; FRG-Labor.

155 "distinctly communistic in" and "seemed to be." Memorandum: Lawrence Oxley to Mr. Humphrey, July 26, 1935, in *Hearing Held before House Committee on Un-American Activities*, vol. 3, October–November, 1938 (Washington, D.C.: U.S. Government Printing Office, 1938), 2149.

156 "I come from" and "There the race." Jonathan Scott Holloway, "Ralph Bunche and the Responsibilities of the Public Intellectual," *Journal of Negro Education* (Spring 2004): 128.

156 "remarkable courage." Claude Barnett to [Ernie] Johnson, January 9, 1943; CBP-Brown.

156 "rantings did more harm." *Pittsburgh Courier*, April 17, 1954.

156 "sundown town." James W. Loewen, *Sundown Towns: A Hidden Dimension of American Racism* (New York: New Press, 2013), 372.

158 "his conduct was." Calvin W. Gower, "The Struggle of Blacks for Leadership Positions in the Civilian Conservation Corps: 1933–1942," *Journal of Negro History* (April 1976): 132.

158 "I hope you." Memorandum: FDR to Mr. Fechner, June 8, 1935; FDR-RR, reel 2.

158 "I agree with you." Cross References: Fechner, Hon. Robert, July 6, 1935; FDR-RR, reel 2.

158 "I am quite certain" and "and I do not." Letter: Harold Ickes to Robert Fechner, September 26, 1935, "CCC Negro Foremen" file, Box 700, General Correspondence of the Director, NAACP, *The Papers of the NAACP: General Correspondence of the Director, NAACP*, Record Group 35, National Archives, College Park, MD [microfilm].

159 "Segregation is not discrimination." Letter: Robert Fechner to Thomas Griffith, September 21, 1935, ibid.

159 "He seems to be." Gower, "Struggle," 132.

160 "bull thrower." *Chicago Defender*, May 23, 1942.

160 "iron rim" of the "wheel." *Philadelphia Tribune*, April 5, 1934.

160 "relations of the races." James A. Atkins, *The Age of Jim Crow* (New York: Vantage Press, 1964), 237.

161 "night riding." "A Hint to 'Night Riders,'" Columbia, South Carolina, October 17, 1939; MMB-NYA3.

161 "Employ White Men." *Baltimore Afro-American*, June 2, 1934.

162 "Mr. President" and "cant sign my name." Letter: [Anonymous] to Hon. Franklin Delano Roosevelt, October 19, 1935. Quoted in Robert McElvaine, Down and Out in the Great Depression: Letters from the Forgotten Man (Chapel Hill: University of North Carolina Press, 1983), 83.

162 "You gather your" and "The car you are." Kathleen A. Hauke, *Ted Poston: Pioneer American Journalist* (Athens: University of Georgia Press, 1998), 82–83.

162 "Lower-13." "A Pioneer's Pioneer," 9.

163 "You know what" and "That light-complexioned." Atkins, *Age*, 213.

163 "shock, disbelief." Pitts, Manuscript," ch. 3, p. 3.

163 "The United States Government." *Baltimore Afro-American*, February 11, 1939.

163 "Conditions on the job" and "blood boils." *Baltimore Afro-American*, July 1, 1939.

CHAPTER SIX

169 "Mrs. Bethune has always." "Mrs. Bethune: Spingarn Medalist," *Crisis*, July 1935, 202.

170 "My mother said when." Charles S. Johnson, "Interview with Bethune (1940)," in Mary McLeod Bethune, *Mary McLeod Bethune: Building a Better World*, 38.

170 "My ideas were different." Embree, *13 Against*, 12.

171 "Put that down" and "I thought." Ibid., 10–11.

171 "bitter disappointment." Holt, "Biography of Bethune and corrections," ch. 3, p. 12.

172 "This married life" and "The birth of." Embree, *13 Against*, 15.

173 "Mrs. Bethune was tough." "Edward Rodriguez Oral History," in Lattimer, "The Black Cabinet," form B #1, 2.

174 "Lifting as We Climb." Paula Giddings, *When and Where I Enter: The Impact of Black Women on Race and Sex in America* (New York: William Morrow, 1984), 95.

174 "adopt as its policy." *Pittsburgh Courier*, March 4, 1933.

175 "vile form," "deliberate and definite," "those in high," "new generation," and "action by collective." *Los Angeles Times*, December 7, 1933.

175 "President Roosevelt has touched" and "It looks like." *Pittsburgh Courier*, December 16, 1933.

175 "President Roosevelt deserves" and "May I thank." Ibid., March 10, 1934.

175 "When I read those," "We must," "the thunder," and "rushed over." Ibid., May 19, 1934.

176 "There is a great happiness in my heart." All quotes from the speech are in Bethune, "Response, Twenty-first Spingarn Medalist (1935)," in Mary McLeod Bethune, *Mary McLeod Bethune: Building a Better*, 112–15.

177 "The two women" and "You will understand." Mary Poole, *The Segregated Origins of Social Security: African Americans and the Welfare State* (Chapel Hill: University of North Carolina Press, 2006), 97.

177 "The black heroes like" and "But Mary McLeod Bethune." Jeannette Smythe, "Memories of Mary McLeod Bethune," *Washington Post*, July 13, 1974.

179 "progressing rapidly." *New York Age*, November 11, 1935.

179 "I have no inferiority." Genevieve Forbes Herrick, "Queen Mary: Champion of Negro Women," *Negro Digest*, December 1950, 50.

179 "her worth and the" and "determination." Embree, *13 Against*, 20.

179 "spiritual power," "eloquence," and "Few people." Clark Foreman to Rackman Holt, February 25, 1948; MMB-Holt.

179 "I looked out" and "It was at that." "William Hastie Oral History," in Lattimer, "The Black Cabinet," form B #9.

180 "Those of us" and "must realize." Mary McLeod Bethune, "Certain Inalienable Rights (1944)," in Mary McLeod Bethune, *Mary McLeod Bethune: Building a Better*, 25.

180 "vitally important," "genuine approval," and "the Cabinet." Letter: Mary McLeod Bethune to Congressman Arthur W. Mitchell, February 9, 1935, in *Hearing on Industrial Commission on Negro Affairs before the Committee on the Judiciary, House of Representatives.* H.R. 5733 (Washington, D.C.: U.S. Government Printing Office, 1935), 29.

181 "wards of the Government," "Negroes are not," and "their problems considered." Memorandum: Charles H. Houston to the Committee on the Judiciary, June 21, 1935, in ibid., 39.

181 administrative assistant in charge of "Negro Affairs." Elaine Smith, "Mary McLeod Bethune and the National Youth Administration," in *Clio Was a Woman: Studies in the History of American Women* (Washington, D.C.: Conference on Women's History, 1976), 154.

182 "The failure to have" and "As long as our." Juanita Saddler, "Report Covering First Six Months of Work of the Office of Negro Affairs, National Youth Administration," ca. June 1936, 4; NYA-35-36.

183 "The fact that the Government." B. Joyce Ross, "Mary McLeod Bethune and the National Youth Administration: A Case Study of Power Relationships

in the Black Cabinet of Franklin D. Roosevelt," *Journal of Negro History*, January 1975, 11.

184 "a very high I.Q.," "The Negro vote," and "It is highly probable." *Baltimore Afro-American*, December 14, 1935.

184 "I'm not doing anything." Buni, *Vann*, 221.

185 "running down the driveway" and "walking arm and arm." J. B. West and Mary Lynn Kotz, *Upstairs at the White House: My Life with the First Ladies* (New York: Coward, McCann and Geoghegan, 1973), 31–32.

185 "In those days." Alonzo Fields, "21 Years in the White House," *Ebony*, October 1982, 64.

186 *"contact is the thing."* "Mrs. M Mc Bethune on the Federal Council on Negro Affairs," November 29, 1939, *Ralph Bunche Papers*, Young Research Library, University of California, Los Angeles, folder 5, box 34.

186 "I never dreamed they." Eleanor Roosevelt, "Some of My Best Friends Are Negroes," February 1953, reprinted in *Ebony*, November 1975, 74.

186 "greatly influenced Eleanor Roosevelt." Parks, *The Roosevelts*, xii.

187 "give Bethune a peck." Joseph P. Lash, *Eleanor and Franklin* (New York: W. W. Norton, 1971), 662.

187 "Eleanor Roosevelt was a." "William Hastie Oral History," in Lattimer, "The Black Cabinet," form B #9.

187 "opportunist." Richard Bardolph, *The Negro Vanguard* (New York: Rinehart, 1959), 139.

187 "My thoughts are of." Letter: Mary McLeod Bethune to Eleanor Roosevelt, February 19, 1942; ER-MMB.

187 "Dear Mrs. Bethune." Letter: Eleanor Roosevelt to Mary McLeod Bethune, March 13, 1942; ER-MMB.

187 "warm and intimate." Lattimer, "The Black Cabinet," 7, 19.

187–188 "Always, of course," "She laid down," "ahead of its time," and "threatened both races." Dovey Johnson Roundtree and Katie McCabe, *Justice Older Than Law: The Life of Dovey Johnson Roundtree* (Jackson: University of Mississippi Press, 2009), 47–48.

188 "taking over the White House." Ralph Bunche, *The Political Status of the Negro in the Age of FDR* (Chicago: University of Chicago Press, 1973), 97.

188 *"NOT* visit the colored" and "such a visit." Memorandum: Stephen Early to Eleanor Roosevelt, March 20, 1936: ER-SE.

189 "You can't get on," "Do you know," and "that the day has." *Baltimore Afro-American*, January 7, 1939.

189–190   "meant real salvation," "We are bringing life," "Mrs. Bethune," and "I am glad." Mary McLeod Bethune, "My Secret Talks with FDR," *Ebony*, April 1949, 45–46.

190   "Think of serving." "Mary Bethune. Cotton Picker's Daughter. Now Heads Negro NYA Work," unsourced, n.d.; MMB-Clips-1.

190   "I visualized dozens." Bethune, "My Secret," 46.

190   "beaming" and "Aubrey . . . Mrs. Bethune." Ibid., 47.

191   "Dog House Education," "fine, brick school," "cracker box," and "bare and rain-eroded gully." Frank Horne, "Dog House Education," ca. 1936, 1–13; Letter: Frank Horne to Harold Ickes, June 27, 1936; FRG-Interior.

191   "There is a big job" and "Your service." Weiss, *Farewell*, 151.

191   "when she [Bethune] asks." Rackham Holt, *Mary McLeod Bethune: A Biography* (New York: Doubleday, 1964), 213.

191   "its great beehive," "make plans and give," and "brotherly love." *Pittsburgh Courier*, August 1, 1936.

192   "I was in awe." John Hope Franklin, *A Mirror to America: The Autobiography of John Hope Franklin* (New York: Farrar, Straus and Giroux, 2005), 69–70.

193   "Great Emancipator's" and "THE CONTINUATION OF." Weiss, *Farewell*, 190.

193   "I'd rather vote for" and "any black man who." James J. Kenneally, "Black Republicans During the New Deal: The Role of Joseph W. Martin, Jr.," *The Review of Politics* (Winter 1993): 123.

193   "The *negroes* of this country." Memorandum: Eleanor Roosevelt to Mr. Howe, "Political organization suggestions for 1936," n.d.; ER1.

194   "I know about" and "I will have another." James Farley to Eleanor Roosevelt, July 20, 1936: ER-JF2.

195   "They [the Democrats] do not" and "They are compelled." *Baltimore Afro-American*, September 12, 1936.

195   "Roosevelt has given the." *Pittsburgh Courier*, March 21, 1936.

195–196   "Distinguished leaders of our," "She has seen to it," "economic improvement," "hundreds of our brightest," and "of high authority." *New York Amsterdam News*, October 17, 1936.

196–197   "plans for the full integration," "The responsibility rests," "I feel," and "We must think." "First Meeting of the Federal Council on Negro Affairs," August 7, 1936, Washington, D.C.; MMB-NYA35-39.

197   "Three years ago," "their responsibility," "to the burning," and "Let us forget." Ibid.

198   "Mrs. Bethune has few equals." *New Journal and Guide* (Norfolk, VA), December 26, 1936.

CHAPTER SEVEN

199 "no stone unturned." *Chicago Defender*, February 6, 1937.

199 "Good Will," "In all her talks," and "She also emphasized." *New York Age*, September 12, 1936.

200 "I believe in the dignity" and "Do your work." *Capitol Plaindealer* (Topeka, KS), November 1, 1936.

200 "Do what you can." Weiss, *Farewell*, 197–98.

200 "optimistic in his outlook" and "to realize and." *Capitol Plaindealer* (Topeka, KS), November 1, 1936.

201 *Interesting Facts about the Negro and the WPA* and *We Work Again*. Alfred Edgar Smith, "Report of Activities," October 1936; NARA-WPA.

202 "The money does not" and "The colored voter." *Baltimore Afro-American*, October 3, 1936.

202 "As the campaign" and "humane attitude toward." *Capitol Plaindealer* (Topeka, KS), September 20, 1936.

202 "not only have hundreds." *Kansas American* (Topeka, KS), October 16, 1936.

203 "THE WAY TO JUDGE," "Facts and Figures," "300,000 Negroes [have been]," "Right and Regular," and "the most considerate friend." *Pittsburgh Courier*, October 24, 1936.

203 "Negro women . . . are." Smith, "Report of Activities"; NARA-WPA.

204 "ward[s] of the federal." Simon Topping, *Lincoln's Lost Legacy: The Republican Party and the African American Vote* (Gainesville: University Press of Florida, 2008), 40.

205 "made her way" and "broad smiles and friendly." *Pittsburgh Courier*, October 31, 1936.

205 "Among American citizens" and "there should be no." Ibid.

205 "The leaders of the Republican." *Kansas American* (Topeka, KS), October 16, 1936.

205 "President Roosevelt is the man." *Baltimore Afro-American*, July 18, 1936.

205 "The Negro vote stood." *Pittsburgh Courier*, November 7, 1936.

206 "The new mobility" and "Negroes, however, must wisely." *New York Age*, November 14, 1936.

207 "provocative." Letter: White to Bethune, November 30, 1936. In NAACP, *The Papers of the NAACP: The Campaign for Educational Equality*, 1913–1965, series A, (Frederick, MD: University Publications of America, 1981), reel 5, part 3.

207 "the minimum basic objectives." Walter White, "Points to be taken up at Mrs. Bethune's Conference in Washington," December 17, 1936, ibid.

207 "farm tenants and" and "more federal appointments." Ibid.

209 "He had lived in," "He did not have," and "was not a champion." Weaver, *The Great Depression Interviews*.

209 "More than once" and "But FDR usually." Bethune, "My Secret," 44.

209 "I did not choose" and "The Southerners by reason." Walter White, *A Man Called White: Autobiography of Walter White* (Athens: University of Georgia Press, 1995), 169–70.

209 "You know, Mrs. Bethune" and "That day will come." Bethune, "My Secret," 44.

210 "practical politics and how." Ibid.

210 "With a President planning" and "with one mind." *Pittsburgh Courier*, January 23, 1937.

210 "National Conference on the Problems of the Negro and Negro Youth"; MMB-NYA35-39.

211 "roared with applause." *Baltimore Afro-American*, January 9, 1937.

211 "This may be your" and "low standard." Ibid.

211 "We are all equal." Ibid.

211 "You have somebody." Holt, "Biography," 168.

212 "because of the danger." "National Conference on the Problems of the Negro and Negro Youth," "Recommendations: Increased Opportunity for Employment and Economic Security, Adequate Educational and Recreational Opportunity, Improved Health and Housing Conditions, and Security of Life and Equal Protection under the Law," January 6, 7, 8, 1937, p. 10; MMB-NC37.

213 "I feel that colored," "I have a feeling," and "I don't know." *Baltimore Afro-American*, January 16, 1937.

213 "The Country opens wide," "twelve million," "a challenge," and "loyalty." Letter: Mary McLeod Bethune to Franklin Delano Roosevelt, January 18, 1937, "National Conference on the Problems of the Negro and Negro Youth," January 22, 1937; MMB-NC37.

214 "The recommendations" and "There was no mincing." "Problems of Race Before President," *Crisis*, February 1937, 46, 62.

214 "Let us clearly." Letter: Mary McLeod Bethune to Charles H. Houston, January 14, 1937, NAACP, *The Papers of the NAACP: The Campaign for Educational Equality, 1913–1965*, series A, part 3 [microfilm].

214 "race relations and the." Letter: Charles H. Houston to Aubrey Williams, January 15, 1937, ibid.

215 "Despite the tremendous efforts" and "the mass Negro population." "National Conference on the Problems of the Negro and Negro Youth," "Recommendations:

Increased Opportunity for Employment and Economic Security," January 6, 7, 8, 1937, Washington, D.C., 13; MMB-NC37.

215 "technique" and "forward step." Holt, *Mary McLeod Bethune*, 200–201.

215 "a single, clearly stated." *New Journal and Guide* (Norfolk, VA), January 23, 1937.

216 "old-fashion galoshes," "Reserved," "just take one of those," "I do not necessarily," and "I will just go up here." *Pittsburgh Courier*, February 6, 1937.

216 "I see one-third of." Franklin D. Roosevelt, "Second Inaugural Address," January 20, 1937, in *Inaugural Addresses of the Presidents of the United States*, 240–43.

217 "The inauguration address was," "dream was realized," and "They were not." *Pittsburgh Courier*, February 6, 1937.

217 "stayed at home playing." *Chicago Defender*, January 30, 1937.

218 "Mary," "We have never," "I am Mrs.," "we are not so," and "Did we know each." Holt, "Biography," 171.

218 "there had been no" and "smiled," *Baltimore Afro-American*, February 20, 1937.

218 "There was no one" and "I spoke to the." "The Contribution of the National Youth Administration to the Development of Negro Youth," NYA press release, April 15, 1937; MMB-NC37.

219 "I found the President," "He was well informed," and "I feel." *Chicago Defender*, February 20, 1937.

219 "the conference to me." *Baltimore Afro-American*, January 16, 1937.

219 "Negro Angel" and "never before in." "Negro Angel," *Literary Digest*, March 6, 1937, 8–9.

219 "the most sought after." Jesse O. Thomas, "Another Woman Steals the Show," unattributed; MMB-Scrap2.

219 "the Booker T. Washington" and "Mary McLeod Bethune's." *Chicago Defender*, February 6, 1937.

219–220 "Our greatest hope is" and "Our only objective." Letter: Mary McLeod Bethune to Laurence J. W. Hayes, August 26, 1938; MMB-NYA38-42.

220 "backbiting." *New Journal and Guide* (Norfolk, VA), January 23, 1937.

220 "All for one and." *Chicago Defender*, February 6, 1943.

220 "Strong wills and fiery" and "Only the tact." *Chicago Defender*, June 21, 1941.

220–221 "cotton picking parties," "Those cotton picking," "social relationships," and "During those stages of." Mary McLeod Bethune interview by Daniel Williams, n.d., pp. 1, 4; MMB-writings.

221 "only on the call." *Chicago Defender*, June 21, 1941.

222 "opinion was sought and." Ibid., February 6, 1943.

222 "He was a thorough." Williams, "Weaver," 62.

222 "a forum where problems." Lochheim and Dembo, *The Making*, 263.

222 "a counsel of strategy" and "confidential inside information." *Chicago Defender*, June 21, 1943.

223 "That's the answer we'll give." Motz, "The Black Cabinet," 70.

223 "They probably would call." "Interview with Lawrence A. Oxley by Debra Newman," April 23, 1972, 21; NARA-Oxley.

223 "trying to do a." Bethune to Hayes, August 26, 1938; MMB-NYA38-42.

224 "two pairs of eye glasses" and "at home." *Chicago Defender*, January 17, 1942.

224 "To us she was." Lochheim and Dembo, *The Making*, 263.

224 "She had contacts." Weiss, *Farewell*, 148.

224 "practically hand in glove" and "You tell me." Ibid., 145.

225 "a dictator." Motz, "The Black Cabinet," 22.

225 "There is something about the." Elmer Anderson Carter, "A Modern Matriarch," *Survey Graphic* n.d.; MMB-Scrap2.

225 "not a drop of." Embree, *13 Against*, 15.

226 "would always bow and." Alonzo Fields, "21 Years in the White House," *Ebony*, October 1982, 64.

226 "Ma Bethune." Motz, "The Black Cabinet," 22.

226 "the titular head." Lattimer, "The Black Cabinet," 40.

226 "the most marvelous gift." Lochheim and Dembo, *The Making*, 262. This statement was originally made by the Urban League's Lester Granger. See Holt, *Mary McLeod Bethune*, 216.

226 "flattery" and "shame." Lochheim and Dembo, *The Making*, 262.

227 "I chat and deal" and "I never felt any." Bethune interview by Williams, n.d., 3.

227 "A lot of people." Weiss, *Farewell*, 142.

227 "There is today a" and "for the Negro." *Pittsburgh Courier*, December 5, 1936.

227 "We saw in her." Rachel Robinson, with Lee Daniels, *Jackie Robinson: An Intimate Portrait* (New York: Harry N. Abrams, 1996), 52.

228 "served with such competence," "being received with," "resplendent with sparkling," and "a veritable banquet." "Mrs. Bethune Guest at White House Tea," unsourced, ca. December 17, 1937; MMB-Scrap2.

228 "In all that great group" and "So, while I." Holt, "Biography," 174.

CHAPTER EIGHT

230 "straight-forward" and "self-effacing." Frank Horne, "Henry A. Hunt, Sixteenth Spingarn Medalist," *Crisis*, August 1930, 261.

230 "no one [else] in." W. E. B. Du Bois, "The Significance of Henry A. Hunt," Fort Valley State College, Fort Valley, Georgia, October 10, 1940, 24–25, *W. E. B.*

Du Bois Papers [MS 312]. Special Collections and University Archives, University of Massachusetts Amherst Libraries.

230 "feeling a kinship." H. A. Hunt, "The Negro as a Farmer," in *Twentieth Century Negro Literature; Or, A Cyclopedia of Thought on the Vital Topics Relating to the American Negro*, Daniel Wallace Culp, ed. (Atlanta: J. L. Nichols, 1902), 396.

231 "to take a stand" and "an opportunity for." Du Bois, "The Significance," 7.

231 "of culture, of accuracy." Horne, "Hunt," 261.

231 "The negress was lynched." *Cincinnati Enquirer*, quoted in "Lynched a Woman," *Crisis*, August 1912, 196.

232 "Those who do not" and "It is not a." Elmer A. Carter, "Henry A. Hunt," *Opportunity*, December 1938, 323.

232 "had arisen, if at all." Hunt, "The Negro," 395.

232 "There must be that." Ibid., 396.

233 "institutions for social reform." Du Bois, "The Significance," 23.

233 "Instead of big." *Atlanta Constitution*, October 6, 1931.

237 "would be an extremely." FDR Memorandum to Stanley Read, August 31, 1935; FDR-RR, reel 2.

239 "blunder." *Los Angeles Times*, March 2, 1937.

239 "a judicial point." Ware, *William Hastie: Grace*, 86.

239 "He was not only" and "he was arrogant." Harold Ickes, "My Twelve Years with F.D.R.," *Saturday Evening Post* (June 26, 1948), 81.

239 "imposing delegations." Ibid.

240 The Washington Merry-Go-Round. *Galena (KS) Evening Times*, March 12, 1937.

240 "The appointment of" and "Under President F. D. Roosevelt's." *Baltimore Afro-American*, April 24, 1937.

240 "to remove me from." "William Hastie Oral History," in Lattimer, "The Black Cabinet," form B #9, 4.

241 "Not only does the person." Robert Weaver, "The Negro in a Program of Public Housing," *Opportunity*, July 1938, 200.

242 "with filth and foul air." Wright, *12 Million*, 106.

243 "one of the outstanding examples." Weaver, transcript, oral history interview, LBJ Library, 9.

243 "Indeed, the USHA." Gunnar Myrdal, *An American Dilemma: The Negro Problem and American Democracy*, vol. 1. (1944; reprint: New Brunswick, NJ: Transaction Publishers, 2009), 350.

244 "worrying the rest of us." *Negro Star* (Wichita, KS), November 18, 1938.

244 "It will not be." Robert C. Weaver, "Racial Policy in Public Housing," *Phylon* (2nd Quarter 1940), 156.

244 "The initial approach" and "Though one may." Robert Weaver, "Racial Minorities and Public Housing," *Proceedings of the National Conference of Social Work* (New York: Columbia University Press, 1940), 291.

245 "Eva Jones has stuck by." James W. Gerard, *My First Eighty-Three Years in America: The Memoirs of James W. Gerard* (New York: Doubleday, 1951), 328.

245 "This kind of work." *Delaware County (PA) Daily Times*, October 11, 1940.

245 "another phase of democracy." *News-Herald* (Franklin, PA), October 11, 1940.

245 Day to Day. *Pittsburgh Courier*, March 13, 1937.

246 My Day. Cook, *Eleanor Roosevelt*, vol. 2, 290.

246 "The beautiful 'daylight train'" and "orange groves." *Pittsburgh Courier*, May 14, 1938.

246 "oil fields and great." Ibid., August 14, 1937.

246 "matchless editor," "palatial," and "another achievement." Ibid., March 13, 1937.

246 "haunting memories" and "the door of the." Ibid., June 18, 1938.

246 "most constructive we have." Ibid., August 14, 1937.

246 "beautifully dressed, engaged in." Ibid., May 28, 1938.

246 "rushing trip" and "brought another ray." Ibid., September 17, 1938.

247 "Wednesday at 4 p.m." Ibid., February 26, 1938.

247 "I love Texas." Ibid., August 14, 1937.

247 "Our office will do." Ibid., June 19, 1937.

248 "disaster that it would," "smiled quietly," and "I understand you." Bethune, "My Secret," 50.

248 "packed to its capacity" and "standing and sitting." *Pittsburgh Courier*, May 28, 1938.

248 "I wish you would" and "Let me be." Allen Francis Kifer, "The Negro under the New Deal." PhD diss., University of Wisconsin, 1961, 137.

249 "The soil is poor." "Report from Dollie T. Rogers," Calhoun School, Alabama, n.d.; *New Deal Agencies and Black America*, reel 6.

249 "social and family relations." Mary McLeod Bethune, "Report, May 1939," *New Deal Agencies and Black America*, reel 6.

250 "Negroes [have] grown tired." *New York Age*, January 30, 1937.

250–251 "hums with activity," "There is apparently no," and "Each day new." *Atlanta Daily World*, July 18, 1937.

253 "Aggressive members of" and "that proposed government." Alfred Edgar Smith, "Educational Programs for the Improvement of Race Relations: Government Agencies," *Journal of Negro Education* 13, no. 3: 364–65.

253 "Improvement of race" and "Its history is." Ibid., 361.

254 "Greying at the temples." *Chicago Defender*, September 28, 1940.

255 "This is a busy." *Pittsburgh Courier*, November 6, 1937.

256 "to spend my 62nd." Ibid., July 17, 1937.

257 "domestic difficulties." *New York Amsterdam News*, January 7, 1939.

257 "farmer's paradise." *Pittsburgh Courier*, May 21, 1938.

257 "the strain of overwork." George A. Kuyper, "Henry A. Hunt: Good Shepherd," *The Southern Workman*, December 1938, 373–75.

257 "shock" and "courageous and unselfish." *Pittsburgh Courier*, October 29, 1938.

258 "sacrifice" and "happiness and comfort." Du Bois, "The Significance," 29.

CHAPTER NINE

259 Kelly Miller Writes. *Pittsburgh Courier*, December 9, 1933.

260 "liberalize the Supreme Court." *New York Age*, May 21, 1937.

260 "'Yes man' to President Roosevelt." *Philadelphia Tribune*, March 11, 1937.

260 "Since your sudden conversion." *New York Age*, March 6, 1937.

261 "within the bounds" and "in the solidifying of." Mary McLeod Bethune to the President, n.d.; MMB-FDR.

262 sympathetic attitude and "I think we ought." *Pittsburgh Courier*, November 11, 1938.

262 "The best political joke." *Lincoln (NE) Journal Star*, November 1, 1938.

262 "Deceitful and dishonest." "Black Purge," *Time*, October 31, 1938.

263 "the unholy alliance," "low wage policy," and "the continued subjection." Joseph F. Guffey, *Seventy Years on the Red Fire Wagon: From Tilden to Truman Through New Freedom and New Deal* (Pittsburgh: privately published, 1952), 148–49.

264 "question the racial policy of." Weaver, "Racial Policy," 149.

264 "let Europe resolve its." Gerald P. Nye, "Yes, Says Nye," *New York Times*, January 14, 1940.

265–266 "If I should come," "I am very," "afraid to do this," "You cannot afford," and "If something is not." Robert L. Vann to Mary McLeod Bethune, January 11, 1939; MMB-NYA36-39.

266 "We are calling you together" and "At a time like this." *The Proceedings of the Second National Conference on the Problems of the Negro and Negro Youth*, January 12, 13, 14, 1939, Washington, D.C., Opening Session, 11; FRG-Conf2.

266 "We recognize that no." Ibid.

267 "a friend, a humanitarian." Ibid., 81.

267 "Instead of just talking" and "Now are there any." Ibid., Remarks of Mrs. Franklin Delano Roosevelt.

267 "the right to the same." Ibid., 83.

267 "It is a question," "I think you labor," and "Now women." Ibid., 89.

267 "What are your views." Ibid., 82.

267 "I doubt very much" and "But I would." Ibid., 82.

268 "I don't want you." Ibid., 83.

268 "I think the Federal." Ibid., 89.

268 "thank her for her." Ibid., 89–90.

269 "tactfully in the background." *Atlanta Daily World*, January 21, 1939.

269 "Children, children. I'm an old." Holt, *Mary McLeod Bethune*, 216–17.

269 "My body was weary." Mary McLeod Bethune, "Negroes Not Camouflaging Any More," unattributed clip, n.d.; MMB-Clips-2.

269 "patted his hand." Holt, *Mary McLeod Bethune*, 216.

270 "not fail." Cross References: Aubrey Williams, December 30, 1938; FDR-RR, reel 3.

270 "progress had been made." *Baltimore Afro-American*, January 21, 1939.

270 "These distinctive gains," "We would emphasize," "immediate need," and "a national health." *The Proceedings of the Second National Conference on the Problems of the Negro and Negro Youth*, January 12, 13, 14, 1939, *The Summary Statement of the Evaluation Committee Reports*, 32; FRG-Conf2.

270 "the democratic ideal within." Ibid., 33.

271 "My dear Mrs. Bethune" and "I was glad to." Letter: Franklin D. Roosevelt to Mrs. Bethune, January 14, 1939, ibid., 2.

271 "a powerful force." *Atlanta Daily World*, January 21, 1939.

271 "Hats Off" and "our recognized First Lady of the Land." *Pittsburgh Courier*, January 21, 1939.

271 ASK ME ANYTHING. *Baltimore Afro-American*, January 21, 1939.

271 "No hedging on her part." *Pittsburgh Courier*, February 4, 1939.

271 "First Lady for Anti-Lynch" and "We hope her husband." *New York Age*, January 21, 1939.

272 "I have been debating" and "The question is." *Pittsburgh Press*, February 27, 1939.

272 "the organization," "approve of their action," and "Therefore." Ibid.

272 "You had an opportunity." Eleanor Roosevelt to Mrs. Henry M. Robert Jr., February 26, 1939, NARA. Accessed June 10, 2014. https://www.archives.gov/exhibits/american_originals/eleanor.html.

273 "it was a moving experience." Weaver, *The Great Depression Interviews*.

273 "how the other third" and "a handbook." *Baltimore Afro-American*, May 20, 1939.

273 "impractical." Harry Mitchell to Aubrey Williams, April 11, 1939; MMB-NYA39.

273 "I cannot approve the." Robert Fechner to Aubrey Williams, March 15, 1939; MMB-NYA39.

274 "push forward" and "other heads of." "Meeting of the Federal Council on Negro Affairs," April 5, 1939; MMB-NYA39. Notes for this meeting are some of the few surviving documents of the Black Cabinet's gatherings.

275 "only one problem for." *Baltimore Afro-American*, December 17, 1938.

275 "political or religious opinions." Ibid.

276 "Standard equipment for." *Chicago Defender*, October 19, 1940.

276 "organic heart trouble" and "bad kidneys, high sugar." *Baltimore Afro-American*, March 11, 1939.

276 carpenters, electricians, engineers. Ibid., May 13, 1939.

278 "The Works Progress Administration saved." *New York Age*, July 15, 1939.

278 "the nation's best." "WIDESPREAD BENEFITS DERIVED BY NEGROES FROM WPA IN 1939 ARE REVIEWED BY AFRO-AMERICAN STAFF ADVISOR," Federal Works Agency Press Release, February 2, 1940; FRG-FWA.

278 "a well-merited recognition of." *New York Age*, July 15, 1939.

279 "wholesale dismissals." *Baltimore Afro-American*, June 10, 1939.

280 "an informal group" and "coordinating efforts and work." Mary McLeod Bethune to Miss C. M. Edmunds, September 29, 1939; MMB-NYA35-39.

280–281 "I am not in politics," "I am here as," "I did not come," "I am in sympathy," and "But as far." *Atlanta Daily World*, July 16, 1939.

281 "membership in any." David H. Rosenbloom, *Federal Service and the Constitution, Second Edition: The Development of the Public Employment Relationship* (Washington, D.C.: Georgetown University Press, 2014), 113.

281 "subversives." William Gellerman, *Martin Dies* (New York: Da Capo Press, 1972), 93.

282 "Communists believe that an." Martin Dies, *The Trojan Horse in America* (New York: Dodd, Mead, 1940), 119.

282 "arranged so that." Ibid., 119–20.

283 "Communist Negroes" and "placed in strategic positions." Ibid., 120.

284 "closed door" and "purely routine." *Plaindealer* (Kansas City, KS), June 2, 1939.

284 "blew up and read the," "fear," "stand by," and "half-heartedly." *Atlanta Daily World*, August 10, 1939.

285 "when some members showing." Ibid., December 4, 1939.

285 "The New Deal has" and "Their activity in." Memorandum: Claude Barnett, May 19, 1939; CBP-Camp40.

286 "The personalities which have" and "Those are being dissipated." Ibid.

286   "I have a job," "disillusioned," "a general feeling of discomfort," and "window-dressing." *Atlanta Daily World*, August 10, 1939.

286   "The sun shines and" "Prying them loose." *Metropolitan Post* (Chicago), November 19, 1939.

286   "With powers almost as" and "Worse, it has helped." *New York Age*, September 9, 1939.

287   "This immediate action will" and "We do not have sufficient." Mary McLeod Bethune memorandum to Aubrey Williams, October 17, 1939; MMB-NYA39.

287   "purchasable," "legitimate propaganda," "Negrophobia," "It is my conviction," and "It would be equally." Mary McLeod Bethune to My Dear Mr. President, November 27, 1939; MMB-NYA39.

288   "the Negro will." *New York Age*, April 8, 1939, October 14, 1939.

288   "social gospel for the." Ibid., August 19, 1939.

288   "unshakeable." Ibid., December 23, 1939.

288   "It is well for." Ibid.

289   "Miller pointed out." Smith, "America's Greatest Unknown Negro," 46.

289   "held down and thwarted." *Atlanta Daily World*, December 4, 1939.

CHAPTER TEN

293   "There is too much." "Talk Over with Mr. Farley," n.d.; MMB-FDR.

294   "I realize how much." Lash, *Eleanor and Franklin*, 662.

294   she "would heed" and "Rest is the." *Pittsburgh Courier*, April 20, 1940.

294   "letters, cards, and telegrams" and "time for reading." *New York Age*, June 1, 1940.

295   "It seems that sometimes." Letter: Chas. S. Duke to Mrs. Mary McLeod Bethune, May 11, 1940; MMB-NYA38-42.

295   "It was not easy." *New York Age*, June 1, 1940.

295   "This is to serve" and "Because of a life-long." Alfred Edgar Smith to Mrs. Mary McLeod Bethune, June 6, 1940; MMB-NYA38-42.

295   "You know I believe." Letter: Mary McLeod Bethune to Alfred E. Smith, June 11, 1940; MMB-NYA38-42.

296   "FDR—Desires and aspirations!" Quoted in Memorandum: Jim Rowe to FDR, June 12, 1940; FDR-RR, reel 3.

296–297   "hectic" and "agencies were fast." Pitts, Manuscript, ch. 4, p. 1.

297   "was very timid about." Alexander, *Reminiscences*, 669.

297–298   "Because of the necessity" and "Upon what we do." *New York Age*, July 20, 1940.

298   "will be engaged in." *New York Age*, August 10, 1940.

298   "The destiny of the." *Chicago Defender*, September 28, 1940.

299   "a square deal in" and "all branches of government." Weiss, *Farewell*, 270.

299   "I just figured." *Sedalia (MO) Democrat*, April 24, 1940.

300   "our proposal for integrating," "was too busy," "not going to run," "all the little," "retire in peace," "I feel that," and "There is such." Robert L. Vann to Mrs. Mary McLeod Bethune, July 5, 1940; MMB-NYA40-44.

300   "I really don't know." Letter: Mary McLeod Bethune to Robert L. Vann, July 10, 1940; MMB-NYA40-45.

301   "draft Roosevelt." Susan Dunn, *1940: FDR, Willkie, Lindbergh, Hitler: The Election amid the Storm* (New Haven, CT: Yale University Press, 2013), 132.

301   "Roosevelt" and "Happy Days Are Here Again." Ibid., 138.

301   "Following Jim Farley's swan song." *Philadelphia Tribune*, July 25, 1940.

302   "enthusiastic support of," "existence of racial discrimination," and "labor battalions." Bethune to General Edwin Watson, July 12, 1940; FDR-RR, reel 3.

302   "at least one." Memorandum: WBS to General Watson, July 15, 1940; FDR-RR, reel 3. WBS was likely then Colonel Walter Bedell Smith who served on General George C. Marshall's staff. See D. K. R. Crosswell, *Beetle: The Life of General Walter Bedell Smith* (Lexington: University Press of Kentucky, 2010), 206–10.

302   "the proper proportion." General Edwin Watson to Mary McLeod Bethune, August 8, 1940; FDR-RR, reel 3.

303   "Time to bargain with." *Chicago Defender*, November 16, 1940.

303   "encouraging" and "Our coming campaign has." Mary McLeod Bethune to General Edwin Watson, August 16, 1940; FDR-RR, reel 3.

303   "The government was," "This is against," and "double crossing." Frank, "'Keep 'Em Squirming!'" 74.

303   "National Grapevine." *Chicago Defender*, September 14, 1940.

303   "Keep 'em squirming." Ibid., September 6, 1941.

304   "fighting for the right to fight," "Gad! Sir," and "One question mooted about." Ibid., September 14, 1940.

304   "dark saints" and "the earth beside us." Ibid., November 21, 1942.

304   "young, able, Harvardish." Ibid., September 28, 1940.

304   "determined" and "have him on your side." Ibid., September 14, 1940.

304   "energetic, bald, able speaker, self-satisfied." Ibid., September 28, 1940.

305   "Negro workers must have." Ibid.

305   "Mr. President, every black man," "had a 'ball,'" and "laughed heartily when." Ibid., October 12, 1940.

306   "New Deal employees do" and "Negroes used to be." Ibid., November 2, 1940.

306 "I have repeated to groups." Ibid., October 26, 1940.

307 "I knew, for instance." Eleanor Roosevelt, *This I Remember* (New York: Harper and Brothers), 1949, 164.

307 "They were afraid I." Ibid.

307 "I always felt that" and "he could not be." Ibid.

308 "the personification of Democracy." *Pittsburgh Courier*, September 28, 1940.

308 "I have great admiration." *Chicago Defender*, August 17, 1940.

308 "America stands at the crossroads" and "A few weeks have." Franklin Delano Roosevelt, *The Public Papers and Addresses of Franklin Delano Roosevelt*, 1940 volume (New York: Macmillan, 1941), 430.

309 "We are not leaving." *Pittsburgh Post-Gazette*, October 22, 1940.

309 "I hope it will" and "But I wonder if." Letter: Walter White to Dave Niles, September 19, 21, 1940; NAACP-WHConf.

309 "The [Democratic National] Committee." Cross References: Oscar R. Ewing, September 18, 1940; FDR-RR, reel 3.

309–310 "the President told Stimson," "given a chance," and "qualify as first class." Harold L. Ickes, *The Secret Diary of Harold L. Ickes: The Lowering Clouds, 1939–1941* (New York: Simon and Schuster, 1955), 32.

310 "made perfect fools of." Lash, *Eleanor and Franklin*, 671.

310 "This is going to." Ibid., 670.

311 "he had been pleasantly," "to 'back into,'" and "to live together." Notes: Conference at the White House, "Discrimination Against Negros in the Armed Forces of the United States," Friday, September 27, 1940; NAACP-WHConf.

312 "PLEASE ADVISE IF YOU." Telegram: Walter White to Edwin M. Watson, September 30, 1940; NAACP-WHConf.

312 "a rather amusing affair" and "gymnastics as to politics." Lash, *Eleanor and Franklin*, 671.

313 "The policy of the War" and "This policy has proven." "Mr. Early's Press Conference," October 9, 1940; NAACP-WHConf. "War Department Policy in Regards to Negroes," ca. October 9, 1940; FDR-RR, reel 3.

313 "A STAB IN THE" and "SURRENDER SO COMPLETELY TO." Telegram: Walter White to Franklin D. Roosevelt, October 10, 1940; NAACP-WHConf.

314 "the impression that you" and "I do not feel." Letter: Stephen Early to Walter White, October 18, 1940; NAACP-WHConf.

314 "THE MOST EFFECTIVE ACTION" and "THE QUICKER, THE BETTER." Press Service of the National Association for the Advancement of Colored People, "White House Charged with Trickery in Announcing Jim Crow Policy of Army," October 11,

1940; "Nation-wide Meetings Protest Against Army Jim Crow Policy," October 18, 1940; NAACP-WHConf.

314 "ill most of the year" and "not functioned." Letter: Mary McLeod Bethune to James Atkins, October 22, 1940; MMB-NYA38-42.

315 "I would have to." Letter: James Atkins to Mary McLeod Bethune, October 14, 1940; MMB-NYA38-42.

315 "Somehow I feel that." Letter: Mary McLeod Bethune to James Atkins, October 22, 1940; MMB-NYA38-42.

315 "PRESIDENT OKAYS JIM CROW." *New York Age*, October 19, 1940.

315 "vanish." Ibid.

315 "Segregation! The South Shows." *Cleveland Gazette*, October 12, 1940.

315 "a sense of guilt" and "supporting the *Pittsburgh Courier*'s." *Pittsburgh Courier*, October 19, 1940.

316 "This fellow Willkie." Alexander, *Reminiscences*, 359.

316 "The President has done." Ibid., 360.

316 "There is a tremendous" and "But they are making." Phillip McGuire, *He, Too, Spoke for Democracy: Judge Hastie, World War II, and the Black Soldier* (New York: Greenwood Press, 1988), 9–10.

316 "mess men," "teamwork, harmony," and "discipline." Letter: Frank Knox to John A. Kenney, October 23, 1940; NARA-Hastie.

317 "I regret that there has." Letter: Franklin D. Roosevelt to Walter White, October 25, 1940; FGR-Ickes.

317 "further developments." Ibid.

317 "There was no disposition." Letter: Stephen Early to Walter White, October 25, 1940; FGR-Ickes.

318 "nothing in anything." Ibid.

318 "I should like to have it said." H. W. Brands, *Traitor to His Class: The Privileged Life of Franklin Delano Roosevelt* (New York: Anchor Books, 2008), 454.

319 "Get out of my." *New York Amsterdam News*, November 2, 1940.

319 "shoved." *New York Times*, October 30, 1940.

319 "NEGROES—If you want." "Negro Kicked in Groin by President's Press Secretary," ca. October 1940; CBP-Rep36-60.

319 "If Mr. Steve Early kicked." *New York Amsterdam News*, November 2, 1940.

319 "impetuous." Weaver, transcript, oral history interview, LBJ Library, 8.

319 "hot temper" and "distressing . . . not only." Lash, *Eleanor and Franklin*, 673.

320 "who believes I was." *Atlanta Daily World*, November 2, 1940.

320 "trifling and grudging." Ickes, *Secret Diary: Lowering Clouds*, 362.

320 "could cost us the Negro," "get the boys together," and "stirring speech." Weaver, transcript, oral history interview, LBJ Library, 8.

320 "I was rather skeptical." Ware, *William Hastie: Grace*, 97.

321 "dramatic." Ted Poston, "The 'Black Cabinet' in Action," *Negro Digest*, March 1962, 23.

321 "almost fainted." Ibid.

321 "a political move." *New York Age*, November 2, 1940.

321 "Too Little Too" and "The day has passed." *Pittsburgh Courier*, November 2, 1940.

321 "Through Hastie, we can" and "the toughest." McGuire, *He, Too*, 13.

321–322 "consistently opposed to any" and "to work effectively." *Pittsburgh Courier*, November 2, 1940.

323 "Election day witnessed" and "The little man was." *Chicago Defender*, November 16, 1940.

CHAPTER ELEVEN

324 "What about these." Cross References: Mary McLeod Bethune, October 28, 1940; FDR-RR, reel 3.

325 "Negroes are getting." *Chicago Defender*, May 24, 1941.

325 "getting action on Negro." Weaver, transcript, oral history interview, LBJ Library, 12–13.

325 "Amid the haze of" and "duty, responsibility, and challenge." Gibson, *Knocking Down*, 80–81. Gibson had represented the Hansberrys, whose youngest daughter, Lorraine, later told of her family's struggle to integrate their neighborhood in the play *Raisin in the Sun*.

326 FEARLESS CHAMPION OF RIGHTS. *Pittsburgh Courier*, January 4, 1941.

326 "Prove that you love," "Negroes are being pushed," and "The Federal Government won't." Ibid.

327 "spirit," "every sacrifice," "the cause of," and "protect and perpetuate." *Inaugural Addresses*, 246–47.

327 "a scuffle." *Pittsburgh Courier*, February 8, 1941.

328 "When the United States." Ibid., January 11, 1941.

329 "St. Philip." *Chicago Defender*, May 29, 1943.

329 "gallant and courageous." *Pittsburgh Courier*, October 29, 1938.

329 "top representatives in government." Cornelius L. Bynum, *A. Philip Randolph and the Struggle for Civil Rights* (Urbana: University of Illinois Press, 2010), 164.

329 "many of the basic." Ibid.

329 "pilgrimage" and "there can be no true." *New York Age*, January 25, 1941.

330 "honest, able, and courageous," "Negroes got no jobs," and "The March-on-Washington." A. Philip Randolph, "National Negro March-on-Washington Committee," Press Release, ca. July 1941; NAACP-FEPC.

331 "a fiasco" and "get out of hand." Motz, "The Black Cabinet," 94.

331 "their rights as equals." Beth Tompkins Bates, *Pullman Porters and the Rise of Protest Politics in Black America* (Chapel Hill: University of North Carolina Press, 2001), 167.

332 "The hour has come." *Pittsburgh Courier*, May 17, 1941.

332 "An orderly march of" and "[It] puts the world's." *Chicago Defender*, May 31, 1941.

332 "Exclusion of white people." Charles H. Houston to A. Philip Randolph, May 20, 1941; NAACP-MOW.

333 "In this period of power" and "nothing counts but pressure." *Plaindealer* (Kansas City, KS), May 23, 1941.

333 "Orchids for the Negro" and "Due mainly to their." *Chicago Defender*, June 21, 1941.

333 "The general practice was." Pauline Redmond Coggs, "Race Relations Advisors—Quislings or Messiahs?" *Opportunity*, July 1942, 112–14.

333 "a powerful force." *Chicago Defender*, June 21, 1941.

334 "rather decent Negro." Ware, *William Hastie: Grace*, 98.

334 "Mr. Hastie, is it not." Hastie, transcript: oral history interview, Truman Library, 29.

334 "to advance the colored race." Ware, *William Hastie: Grace*, 102.

334 "not to be shown." Ibid., 103.

335 "If he could have." Weaver, *The Great Depression Interviews*.

335 "extremely wasteful of our." Sidney Hillman: To all Holders of Defense Contracts, April 11, 1941; NAACP-FEPC.

336 "the complaints kept." Alexander, *Reminiscences*, 673.

336 "You almost never see" and "There is little concealment." *Fortune*, quoted in Robert C. Weaver, "With the Negro's Help," *Atlantic Monthly*, June 1942, 701.

336 "except as janitors." "Along the NAACP Battlefront," *Crisis*, July 1941, 229.

336–337 "I fully endorse the appointment" and "But I feel." *Pittsburgh Courier*, February 22, 1941.

338 "I'm interested in this," "Mr. Hillman, what," and "Well, I'm sure." Alexander, *Reminiscences*, 674.

338–339 "Well, go on and" and "We disagreed strongly." Ibid., 675.

339 "writing into a contract" and "difficulty." Ibid.

339 "some validity" and "to his attention." Weaver, *The Great Depression Interviews*.

339 "Hell, Williams will join." Lash, *Eleanor and Franklin*, 676.

339 "with her usual honesty" and "I think you are." White, *A Man Called*, 190.

340 "the failure of the." Memorandum: William H. Hastie to [Henry Stimson] the Secretary of War, June 17, 1941; NARA-MOW.

340 "untoward incidents." Ibid.

340 "Walter," "how many people," "The President looked me," and "What do you want." White, *A Man Called*, 192.

341 "race, creed, color" and "all departments and agencies." "Executive Order 8802, June 25, 1941," in Albert P. Blaustein and Robert L. Zangrando, eds., *Civil Rights and African Americans: A Documentary History* (Evanston, IL: Northwestern University Press, 1968), 358.

341 "postponed." Letter: A. Philip Randolph to William Hastie, August 7, 1941; NARA-MOW.

341 "a more definite approach." *Plaindealer* (Kansas City, KS), August 4, 1941.

341 Magna Carta. *Chicago Defender*, July 5, 1941.

341 "I was most happy" and "Not since Abraham Lincoln." Letter: Mary McLeod Bethune to Eleanor Roosevelt, July 10, 1941, in Mary McLeod Bethune, *Mary McLeod Bethune: Building a Better*, 240–41.

341 "a new day is dawning." Mary McLeod Bethune, "The Negro and National Defense (1941)," ibid., 244.

342 "in spite of past." *Pittsburgh Courier*, August 2, 1941.

342 "affirmative and, in many cases." W. J. Trent Jr., "Federal Sanctions Directed Against Racial Discrimination," *Phlyon* (2nd Quarter 1942), 171–82.

342 "affirmative action." Martha West, "The Historical Roots of Affirmative Action," *Berkeley La Raza Journal* 10, no. 2 (1998), 607–30.

343–344 "a new headache," "the agency usually assigns," and "dirty looks." *Chicago Defender*, December 20, 1941.

344 "completely independent of" and "We are firmly convinced." Letter: Walter White and A. Philip Randolph to Committee on Fair Employment Practices, August 7, 1941; NAACP-FEPC.

344 "FEPC was a duplication." Pitts, Manuscript, ch. 4, p. 14.

344 "There Weaver and I." Alexander, *Reminiscences*, 678.

345 "Our office was already" and "continuous and considerable." Pitts, Manuscript, ch. 4, p. 14.

346 "painting a rosy picture." Pritchett, *Weaver*, 98.

346 "rubber stamps." *Pittsburgh Courier*, January 18, 1941.

346 "stooges." *Cleveland Gazette*, September 20, 1941.

346 "Betrayers." *Chicago Defender*, October 18, 1941.

346 "bought and paid for" and "as professional letter writers whose." Ibid., October 11, 1941.

347 "If practical and immediate methods." *Pittsburgh Courier*, September 20, 1941.

347 "They are not," "Many of us recall," "They are gone," and "digging in more deeply." *Pittsburgh Courier*, April 26, 1941.

347 "interpret," "two-way attack," and "the Negro public kicks." *Pittsburgh Courier*, December 13, 1941.

347 "trying to get everything for the Negro." Ibid.

347 "to criticize various administrative." Ibid.

348 "Negro problem." Atkins, *Age*, 248.

349 "If Dr. Mary McLeod Bethune." Roundtree, *Justice*, 14.

349 "More power to you." *Chicago Defender*, August 9, 1941.

349 "We must do all" and "We must not fail America." Bethune, "The Negro and National Defense," 244.

350 "renaissance of industrial education" and "power age." *Pittsburgh Courier*, April 19, 1941.

350 "You can see." Memorandum: T. Arnold Hill to Mary McLeod Bethune, November 7, 194; MMB-NYA40-44.

350 "irregularities." *Greenfield (IN) Daily Reporter*, October 18, 1941.

350 "some seem to feel," "a bitter battle," and "smear." *Pittsburgh Courier*, October 18, 1941.

350 "Every fiber in us." Letter: Mary McLeod Bethune to Aubrey Williams, October 8, 1941; MMB-NYA37-41.

351 "fears some of" and "double crossing." *Chicago Defender*, August 9, 1941.

351 "dumped." *Pittsburgh Courier*, July 24, 1943.

351 "coalitions of every sort." Roundtree, *Justice*, 46.

351 "After white men and." *Chicago Defender*, August 9, 1941.

352 "stinging rebuke," "We are anxious for," and "We are not blind." *Pittsburgh Courier*, October 25, 1941.

354 "Because of the Japanese." McGuire, *He, Too*, 28.

354 "I know that at." *Pittsburgh Courier*, December 13, 1941.

355 "The way is open." *Negro Star* (Wichita, KS), December 12, 1941.

355 "Yesterday, December 7" and "the American people." Doris Kearns Goodwin, *No Ordinary Time: Franklin and Eleanor Roosevelt: The Home Front in World War II* (New York: Simon and Schuster, 1994), 295.

355 "'War is Hell'" and "Had he been colored." *Chicago Defender*, December 20, 1941.

CHAPTER TWELVE

356 "historic," "Newcomers were fired," and "'Twas rather swell." *Chicago Defender*, December 20, 1941.

357 "I do not see why," "They are put in there," "special propagandist[s]," and "at government expense." *Pittsburgh Courier*, January 31, 1942.

357 "All told, the." *New York Amsterdam News*, January 31, 1942.

358 "The Negro press and public" and "But we think that." *New York Age*, December 27, 1941.

358 "may be better off." *Chicago Defender*, July 18, 1942.

358 "Veterans in the Black Cabinet." Ibid., November 15, 1941.

358 "Rest assured" and "because as another said." *Chicago Defender*, October 10, 1943.

359 "time to issue," "During the past months," and "Too frequently the." Letter: Mary McLeod Bethune to William J. Trent, February 12, 1942; MMB-NYA42.

360 "a great mistake" and "For the Federal Council." Letter: Robert C. Weaver to Mary McLeod Bethune, February 16, 1942; ibid.

360 "I am convinced that." Letter: William H. Hastie to Mary McLeod Bethune, February 16, 1942; ibid.

360 "I have nothing at all." Constance Daniel to Mary McLeod Bethune, date not legible, *New Deal Agencies and Black America*, reel 8.

360: "Many of our leaders." Letter: Mary McLeod Bethune to "Dear Friend," February 12, 1942; MMB-NYA42.

360 "mighty struggle in which." Ibid.

360 "a timely and thoughtful." Letter: John P. Davis to Mary McLeod Bethune, February 18, 1942; ibid.

361 Second Great Migration. Stephen Grant Meyer, *As Long as They Don't Move Next Door: Segregation and Racial Conflict in American Neighborhoods* (Lanham, MD: Rowman and Littlefield, 2001), 64.

362 "Clark Foreman Loses [His] Head" and "It is the duty." *Pittsburgh Courier*, January 17, 1942.

362 "turn around and go." Meyer, *As Long*, 69.

363 "using tear gas." *Pittsburgh Courier*, March 7, 1942.

363 "You polite people." Memorandum for Files: Roy Wilkins, March 5, 1942; NAACP-STH.

363 "I might as well." *New York Age*, April 25, 1942.

364 "practically out." *Pittsburgh Courier*, January 17, 1942.

364 SOJOURNER TRUTH PLANNED. Telegram: Robert R. Taylor to Roy Wilkins, March 7, 1942; NAACP-STH.

364 "conspiracy . . . to prevent." Detroit Free Press, March 10, 1942.

365 "I was astonished and." Pittsburgh Courier, May 2, 1942.

365 "I know of but" and "Is this so-called." Call and Post (Cleveland, OH), May 2, 1942.

365 "[national] guardsmen, state troopers." New York Daily News, April 30, 1942.

365 "if the Black Cabineteers." Motz, "The Black Cabinet," 50.

366 "terrorism by civil authorities and local citizens." Memorandum: Civilian Aide [William H. Hastie] to Under Secretary of War [Robert Patterson], January 23, 1942. NARA-Hastie.

366 "Double V" and "Victory over our enemies." Pittsburgh Courier, February 14, 1942.

366 "DIME A DOZEN." Chicago Defender, May 30, 1942.

367 "plan to end all." Ibid., July 4, 1942.

368 "Negroes must recognize." New York Age, July 25, 1942.

369 "Bureau of Negro Affairs." Pittsburgh Courier, June 13, 1942.

370 "no member [of the Black Cabinet]." New York Amsterdam News, June 6, 1942.

370 "consider[ed] the danger of." Chicago Defender, May 30, 1942.

370 "'Big Negroes' in fat." New York Amsterdam News, June 6, 1942.

371 "torrid" and "newcomers." Chicago Defender, June 20, 1942.

371 "no pretense of" and "every man for himself." Ibid., July 4, 1942.

372 "the whole affair was." New York Amsterdam News, June 6, 1942.

372 "served to only strengthen." Pittsburgh Courier, June 13, 1942.

372 "abstract justice" and "sound economic proof that." William A. H. Birnie, "Black Brain Trust," American Magazine, January 1943, 95.

372 "stormy" and "all plans submitted." Pittsburgh Courier, June 13, 1942.

373 "southern reactionaries." "FEPC Is Captured by the South," Crisis, September 1942, 279.

373 "political pressure" and "it seems that." Letter: Mary McLeod Bethune to Robert Durr, August 5, 1942; MMB-NYA42.

374 "The boys are too." Chicago Defender, September 5, 1942.

374 "The traditional mores of." Gibson, Knocking Down, 82–83.

374 "So long as we condone." Ibid., 85.

375 "discipline and morale" and "The Army cannot." Ibid., 86.

375 "perhaps war is a." Baltimore Afro-American, December 13, 1942.

375 "to experiment." Ibid.

375 "a sociological laboratory" and "would result in ultimate." Ware, *William Hastie: Grace*, 101.

375 "Humiliation was a fact." Gibson, *Knocking Down*, 83.

376 "clean out." *Pittsburgh Courier*, August 30, 1941.

376 "As I had anticipated," "I was not really," and "that was honored in breach as it." Hastie, transcript: oral history interview, Truman Library, 15–16.

376 "when he discovered." *New York Amsterdam News*, January 31, 1942.

377 "acted on every," "the racial cause," and "We all can help." *Pittsburgh Courier*, January 24, 1942.

377 "my strength and influence." Letter: Mary McLeod Bethune to Franklin D. Roosevelt, November 28, 1941, in Mary McLeod Bethune, *Mary McLeod Bethune: Building a Better*, 122–23.

377 "I want you to feel." Letter: Mary McLeod Bethune to Eleanor Roosevelt, April 22, 1941, ibid., 120–21.

379 "displayed contempt for the." Patricia Bell-Scott, *The Firebrand and the First Lady: Pauli Murray, Eleanor Roosevelt, and the Struggle for Social Justice* (New York: Alfred A. Knopf, 2016), 90.

379 "unadvisable." *New York Age*, July 11, 1942.

379 "I can do nothing" and "It is out." Belinda Robnett, *How Long? How Long? African American Women in the Struggle for Civil Rights* (New York: Oxford University Press, 2000), 48.

379 "Mrs. Roosevelt . . . would" and "The President finally." Lash, *Eleanor and Franklin*, 854.

379 "What are we fighting" and "We are fighting for." Bethune, "What Are We Fighting For? (1942)," in Mary McLeod Bethune, *Mary McLeod Bethune: Building a Better*, 247.

379 "Somewhere in her mind's." Roundtree, *Justice*, 52.

380 "full freedom, justice, respect." *Pittsburgh Courier*, June 27, 1942.

380 "partial o.k." *Chicago Defender*, June 6, 1942.

381 "democracy in action" and "We are seeking equal." Roundtree, *Justice*, 57.

381 "You darkies move those." Ibid., 60.

382 "segregation." Memorandum: Charles P. Howard to Mary McLeod Bethune, August 26, 27, 1942; MMB-NYA42.

383 "to further the cause," "joiner," "admired," and "see through." E. A. Murphy, "Report: Mary McLeod Bethune," January 24, 1942; Mary McLeod Bethune FBI File, vol. 1.

383 "custodial detention" and "danger." "Custodial Detention Card: Mary McLeod Bethune," December 12, 1941; ibid.

383 "It startles me just" and "It seems I have." Galin N. Willis, "Mary McLeod Bethune Interviewed under Oath," April 14, 1942; ibid.

384 "I have just heard" and "I am sorry." Letter: Eleanor Roosevelt to Mrs. [Mary McLeod] Bethune, November 23, 1942; ER-MMB.

3.84 "Five doctors, nurses" and "I have given of." Letter: Mary McLeod Bethune to Eleanor Roosevelt, November 30, 1942; ibid.

385 "almost beaten to death." *Chicago Defender*, September 19, 1942.

385 "loathed the whole," "saw the Negro sinking," "an unusual man of," and "very unhappy because he." *Pittsburgh Courier*, October 31, 1942.

387 "Regardless of current" and "[It] is your responsibility." *New York Age*, October 17, 1942.

387 "sagacious and efficient" and "not a politician." *Chicago Defender*, July 10, 1942.

387 "steaming mad." Pitts, Manuscript, ch. 4, p. 24.

387 "I told Dr. Weaver" and "I couldn't see." Ibid.

388 "I had had the WAC." Ibid., ch. 5, p. 18.

Chapter Thirteen

390 "passing in thoughtful contemplation." *Chicago Defender*, December 5, 1942.

391 "Hold Your Job." *Pittsburgh Courier*, June 19, 1943.

391 "took a great deal." McGuire, *He, Too*, 43.

392 "usefulness was limited." Ibid.

392 "To me the Air Force." Hastie, transcript: oral history interview, Truman Library, 19.

392 "Jim Crow squadron." *Chicago Defender*, February 15, 1941.

392 "Any participation of blacks." Hastie, transcript: oral history interview, Truman Library, 21.

393 "'Hate Rule' at Tuskegee," "Hell Hole of," "It is no longer," and "Ku Klux Klanism." *Pittsburgh Courier*, January 2, 1943.

393 "hatchet man" and "explosive cursing tantrums." Ibid.

393–394 "Changes of racial policy" and "Therefore, it has seemed." Gibson, *Knocking Down*, 106.

394 "experiment" and "This attitude is the." *Chicago Defender*, February 6, 1943.

394 "odd jobs and common" and "public opinion is still." Ibid.

394 "courageous" and "high sense of" *Baltimore Afro-American*, February 6, 1943.

394 "a severe blow." *Kansas City (MO) Call*, January 29, 1943.

394 "dramatize the feelings and." *Chicago Sunday Bee*, January 31, 1943.

395 "done more for race." *Chicago Defender*, February 13, 1943.

395 "rendered a greater service" and "considerable trouble." Alexander, *Reminiscences*, 361.

395 "The varied reactions." Memorandum: To Chief, Analysis Branch, "Negro Press Trend," February 8, 1943; NARA-Hastie.

395–396 "ribbing" "witticisms" "scotch and tobacco" and "the besieged." *Chicago Defender*, March 6, 1943.

396 "dangerous red radicals." *Negro Star* (Wichita, KS), February 26, 1943.

396 "irresponsible, unrepresentative." *New York Times*, February 2, 1943.

397 "I wanted to ask." Letter: Mary McLeod Bethune to Eleanor Roosevelt, February 5, 1943; ER-MMB2.

397 "If I were you" and "I would write but." Letter: Eleanor Roosevelt to Mary McLeod Bethune, February 13, 1943; ibid.

397 "vigorously oppose every attempt." Memorandum: Walter White, ca. February 1943; MMB-Dies.

397 "preposterous," "reckless," "I do not think," and "The trouble is that." Letter: Charles Hamilton Houston, March 20, 1943; ibid.

397–398 "ignorance, cowardice," "victory effort," and "There is not a." Letter: Forrester Washington to Honorable John H. Kerr, March 26, 1943; MMB-Dies2.

398 "If Rep. Dies sees fit." "Statement of Mary Mcleod Bethune Re Dies Accusation of Being a Communist," n.d.; MMB-Dies.

399 "Black Brain Trust." Birnie, "Black Brain Trust," 36–37, 94–95.

399 "The Black Cabinet" and "as a shield against." Albert W. Hamilton, "The Black Cabinet," *Common Sense* 12 (1943), 97–99.

399 "It is really a revolution." Willard M. Kiplinger, *Washington Is Like That* (New York: Harper and Brothers, 1942), 148.

399 "anything that smacks" and "much remains." Roi Ottley, *New World A-Coming: Inside Black America* (Boston: Houghton-Mifflin, 1943), 254–55.

400 "While all of these." Hamilton, "The Black Cabinet," 98.

400 "The White Cabinet." Ibid.

400 "less emotional and more." *Pittsburgh Courier*, May 8, 1943.

400 "infected with race jitters." Redmond Coggs, "Race Relations Advisors," 114.

401 "keeping the Negro." *New Journal and Guide* (Norfolk, VA), March 12, 1943.

401 "definite drive in." *New York Amsterdam News*, March 20, 1943.

401 "restoration." Ibid.

401 "Time to Wake." *Chicago Defender*, February 6, 1943.

401 "growing unrest," "the consensus among the," "expediency over principle," and "the gradual lessening of." Ibid., May 22, 1943.

402 "Political Snobs." Ibid., June 12, 1943.

402 "fact-finding," "Unless Roosevelt runs in," "It would be better," and "As they are." Ibid.

402 "clique." Ibid.

403 "The administration is." *New York Age*, August 7, 1943.

403 "enmeshed by a maze" and "the gradual but certain." *Chicago Defender*, July 10, 1943.

404 "thinking most sincerely now." Letter: Mary McLeod Bethune to Eleanor Roosevelt, June 21, 1943; ER-MMB2.

404 "A straight forward determined" and "We know you." *Pittsburgh Courier*, July 3, 1943.

405 "I share your feeling." Ibid., July 24, 1943.

405 "to give special attention to." *New York Times*, July 22, 1943.

406 "short-sighted and narrow" and "defeat some of the." *Pittsburgh Courier*, July 10, 1943.

406 "careful consideration . . . to." *Chicago Defender*, August 21, 1943.

407 "obviously illegal, unsound." "Along the NAACP Battlefront," *Crisis*, September 1943, 280.

407 "This [ban on black migration] is." *Plaindealer* (Kansas City, KS), August 20, 1943.

408 "Tell the President curtailing." *Pittsburgh Courier*, August 21, 1943.

408 "unconstitutional" and "white southerners to." *Chicago Defender*, August 21, 1943.

408 "responsible officials" and "before taking any steps." "Along the NAACP Battlefront," *The Crisis*, September 1943, 280.

409 "I am classified as" and "I believe in the." Letter: Mary McLeod Bethune to Dr. Gordon B. Hancock, October 12, 1942; MMB-NYA42.

410 "sex affairs." *Pittsburgh Courier*, July 10, 1943.

410 "tens of thousands." *Pittsburgh Courier*, June 26, 1943.

410 "Mary Bethune took" and "Overnight 1,500." *Chicago Defender*, July 17, 1943.

411 "I have felt like" and "It is hard." Letter: Mary McLeod Bethune to Eleanor Roosevelt, July 6, 1943; ER-MMB2.

411 "I am just as" and "Perhaps after the war." Letter: Eleanor Roosevelt to Mary McLeod Bethune, July 21, 1943; ER-MMB2.

411 "You have been and." Letter: Aubrey Williams to Mary McLeod Bethune, July 9, 1943; MMB-NYA40-45.

411 "she is the best thing." *Chicago Defender*, August 14, 1943.

412 "Have you found." Memorandum for the President, E.R. [Eleanor Roosevelt], July 21, 1943; ER-MMB2.

412 "no place important enough." Letter: Secretary to Mrs. Roosevelt to Mrs. Bethune, August 19, 1943; ER-MMB2.

412 "to take some time." *Pittsburgh Courier*, August 8, 1943.

412 "prestige" and "dishonest." Letter: Eleanor Roosevelt to Mary McLeod Bethune, December 20, 1943; ER-MMB2.

412 "no source of income" and "could give her." Letter: Eleanor Roosevelt to Will Alexander, February 1, 1944; ER-WA.

413 "We face the rise." Robert C. Weaver, "The Negro Comes of Age in Industry," *Atlantic Monthly*, September 1943, 54–59.

413 "Last of the Brain Trusters." *Baltimore Afro-American*, September 4, 1943.

414 "I didn't feel that." Weaver, transcript, oral history interview, LBJ Library, 17.

415 "futility of the approach" and "organize for the election." *Chicago Defender*, January 15, 1943.

416 "technical." *Pittsburgh Courier*, February 5, 1944.

416 "three million." *Los Angeles Tribune*, January 31, 1944.

417 "It was clear that." *Atlanta Daily World*, April 28, 1942.

417 "the black cabinet as." *Baltimore Afro-American*, January 22, 1943.

417 The period when bright." *Pittsburgh Courier*, February 5, 1944.

417 "I'm glad to see." Donald A. Ritchie, *Reporting from Washington: The History of the Washington Press Corps* (New York: Oxford University Press, 2005), 33.

417 "an opportunity" and "do a really." Letter: Eleanor Roosevelt to Mary McLeod Bethune, February 15, 1944; MMB-ER2.

418 "The Black Cabinet was," "In spite of what," "shrewd, histrionic Mary," "scholarly and obviously," and "cultured Bill Hastie." *Chicago Defender*, February 12, 1944.

418 "May it Rest" and "The Black Cabinet, chum." Ibid.

Chapter Fourteen

421 "The President looks," "Tell McDuffie," "The moment I," and "Lizzie, the President." McDuffie, "FDR," 64–65.

422 "I looked out" and "I lay in my." Ibid., 65.

422 "We have just been." Lucia Mae Pitts, *One Negro WAC's Story* (Los Angeles: Lucia Mae Pitts, 1968), 13.

423 "I remember finally" and "It hit me even." Ibid.

423 "The news of his." Hastie, transcript: oral history interview, Truman Library, 33.

423 "I sat, stunned" and "It was hard to." Bethune, "My Secret," 51.

423 "Today we breathe." Mary McLeod Bethune, "Speech Broadcast over Blue Network," April 13, 1945; MMB-Radio.

424   "I recalled holding," "I found it impossible to," and "On that day." Bethune, "My Secret," 51.

424   "the first President in." Pitts, *One Negro WAC's*, 51.

424   "Negroes have lost the." *Kansas City (MO) Call*, quoted in *Atlanta Daily World*, April 15, 1945.

424   "at the White House." *Pittsburgh Courier*, April 21, 1945.

424   "under the leadership of." *Atlanta Daily World*, April 15, 1945.

424   "We did not always." *Chicago Defender*, April 21, 1945.

424   "The loss is" and "I feel that." *Atlanta Daily World*, April 15, 1945.

425   "the sudden death of," "the finest team that," and "endanger the approval of." *Pittsburgh Courier*, April 21, 1945.

425   "He's gone, chum," "Franklin Roosevelt held us," and "what there is to." *Chicago Defender*, April 21, 1945.

425   "a provision that a." *Pittsburgh Courier*, April 21, 1945.

425   "a new dignity." *Baltimore Afro-American*, April 17, 1945.

426   "Franklin Delano Roosevelt made," "positions of responsibility," and "the first time in." *Atlanta Daily World*, April 15, 1945.

426   "handpicked" and "to expand the opportunities." *Call and Post* (Cleveland, OH), April 28, 1945.

426   "He came into high office" and "It was no accident." Bethune, "Speech Broadcast."

428   "Politics replaces idealism." Roi Ottley, "Truman's New Black Cabinet," *Ebony*, August 1949, 15.

428   "would not allow political." Hastie, transcript: oral history interview, Truman Library, 54.

430   "the busiest and." "Lawrence A. Oxley," *Living Church*, June 28, 1964, 19.

430   "I took hold of" and "You are the seventh." Lawrence A. Oxley, "Interview," 1973, 14; NARA-Oxley.

431   "I would not encourage." Memorandum: F.D.R. to Mrs. Roosevelt, ca. June 1944; ER-CBF.

431   "avoid him like the." Memorandum: Ernie Johnson to Claude A. Barnett, January 4, 1944; CBP-Brown.

432   "I can see very," "blind haters," and "We must go about." *Chicago Defender*, May 29, 1954.

432   "This must be done." Ibid.

432   "Certain Inalienable Rights" and "Just as the Colonists." Mary McLeod Bethune, "Certain Inalienable Rights (1944)," in Mary McLeod Bethune, *Mary McLeod Bethune: Building a Better*, 25.

433 "the fulfillment of a." Mary McLeod Bethune, "Holistic Living: Yes, I Went to Africa (1952)," in ibid., 274.

433 all quotes from "My Last Will and Testament." Mary McLeod Bethune, "My Last Will and Testament," *Ebony*, August 1955, 105–10.

434 "She was a great" and "I will cherish." Letter: Eleanor Roosevelt to Albert Bethune, May 20, 1955; MMB-ERCorr.

434 "There was a star" and "Mary McLeod Bethune grabbed." Martin Luther King, "Address at Public Meeting of the Southern Christian Ministers Conference of Mississippi," September 13, 1959, in *The Papers of Martin Luther King Jr.: Threshold of a New Decade, January 1959–December 1960* (Berkeley: University of California Press, 2005), 285.

435 "They revealed how this," "They re-enacted those roundtable," and "beginning to reap some." *Pittsburgh Courier*, August 11, 1959.

435 "Dinner for Bob Weaver" and "Advice: stag, informal." Hauke, *Poston*, 155.

435 "It had been an evening." Raskin, "Washington Gets," 16.

437 "a salty blend of realism" and "portly." Ibid.

437 "Some of My Best." Roosevelt, "Some of My Best Friends Are Negroes."

438 "Millions of Negroes mourned" and "They mourned because." *Pittsburgh Courier*, November 24, 1962.

439 "man who loves Broadway." "Cities: Hope for the Heart," 29–33.

440 "She was in a" and "With arms outstretched." Lattimer, "The Black Cabinet, Hastie Oral History," form B #9.

440 "the Great Society." Philip A. Klinkner with Rogers M. Smith, *The Unsteady March: The Rise and Decline of Racial Equality in America* (Chicago: University of Chicago Press, 1999), 278.

441 "The singular thing" and "is that our." *Pittsburgh Courier*, June 25, 1966.

442 "direct-action drive." Pitts, Manuscript, epilogue, 5.

442 "The Little Fire and How." Letter: Lucia Mae Pitts to John Dizikes, February 26, 1965, in ibid.

442 "had a great deal." Pitts, Manuscript, introduction, 5.

442 "for the first time to." Ibid., 3.

443 "I believe that *many*." Ibid., ch. 5, p. 16.

443 "I doubt that any" and "I can't think of." Oxley, "Interview," 21.

443 "inexcusable delay." *New York Times*, December 31, 1970.

444 "I have a great," "We were young," and "disappointment." Lattimer, "The Black Cabinet, Hastie Oral History," 42, form B #9.

444 "across the nation and." *Pittsburgh Courier*, April 24, 1976.

444   "early civil rights leader." *Bakersfield Californian*, April 15, 1976.

444   "turned American jurisprudence." "Judge Hastie, First Black Federal Jurist, Dead at 71," *Jet*, April 29, 1976, 5.

445   "I wasn't dry behind" and "It amazed me the." *New York Times*, July 21, 1982.

446   "master builder." "Dr. Robert C. Weaver, 89, First Black Cabinet Member, Succumbs in Manhattan," *Jet*, August 4, 1997, 57.

446–447   "old curmudgeon," "a great President," "distraught . . . whenever instances," and "Mrs. Bethune." Weaver, *The Great Depression Interviews*.

447   "If you were to explain" and "I would want." Ibid.

447   "the seeds of getting," "Do you feel that," and "Yes, but I didn't." Ibid.

447   "History Will Remember" and "Although not well known." *Sun-Reporter* (San Francisco, CA), July 24, 1977.

448   "nothing more than an." Roosevelt, *This I*, 347–48.

448   "And it would be" and "Let there be no." *Chicago Defender*, May 29, 1954.

BIBLIOGRAPHY

ABBREVIATIONS

CBP: Claude Barnett Papers
ER: Eleanor Roosevelt
FDR: Franklin Delano Roosevelt
FRG: Federal Records Group
MMB: Mary McLeod Bethune
NARA: National Archives and Records Administration

NEWSPAPERS AND WIRE SERVICES

The *Anniston (AL) Star*
Associated Negro Press (ANP)
The *Atlanta Constitution*
Atlanta Daily World
The *Bakersfield Californian*
The *Baltimore Afro-American*
The *Bismarck Tribune*
The *Broad Ax (Salt Lake City, UT)*
The *Brooklyn (NY) Daily Eagle*
The *Brownsville (TX) Herald*
Call and Post (Cleveland, OH)
Cambridge (MA) Chronicle
The *Capitol Plaindealer (Topeka, KS)*
The *Chicago Defender*
Chicago Sunday Bee

Chicago Tribune
The *Cincinnati Enquirer*
The *Cleveland Gazette*
Delaware County (PA) Daily Times
The *Des Moines Register*
Detroit Free Press
The *Evening News (Wilkes-Barre, PA)*
Galena (KS) Evening Times
Greeley (CO) Daily Tribune
Greenfield (IN) Daily Reporter
Indianapolis Freeman
The *Indianapolis Star*
Kansas American (Topeka, KS)
The *Kansas City (MO) Call*
Lincoln (NE) Journal Star

Los Angeles Times
Los Angeles Tribune
The Macon (GA) Telegraph
Metropolitan Post (Chicago)
The Negro Star (Wichita, KS)
The New Journal and Guide (Norfolk, VA)
New York Age
New York Amsterdam News
New York Daily News
New York Post
The New York Times
The News and Observer (Raleigh, NC)
The News-Herald (Franklin, PA)
The Philadelphia Tribune

The Pittsburgh Courier
Pittsburgh Post-Gazette
The Pittsburgh Press
The Plain Dealer (Cleveland, OH)
Topeka (KS) Plaindealer
Plaindealer (Kansas City, KS)
The Robesonian (Lumberton, NC)
The Salt Lake Tribune (Salt Lake City, UT)
Sedalia (MO) Democrat
The Sun-Reporter (San Francisco, CA)
The Tulsa (OK) Star
The Washington Bee
The Washington Post
The Wyandotte (KS) Echo

Periodicals

The Colored American
The Crisis
Opportunity
The Southern Workman
Time

Government and Public Documents (Miscellaneous)

Arlington National Cemetery. Interments database. Accessed March 28, 2016. http://public.mapper.army.mil/ANC/ANCWeb/PublicWMV/ancWeb.html.

Bureau of Labor Statistics. *Historical Statistics of the United States, Colonial Times to 1970. Part I: Series D 85-86 Unemployment: 1890–1970.* Washington, D.C.: U.S. Government Printing Office, 1975.

Carded Records Showing Military Service of Soldiers Who Fought in Confederate Organizations, Compiled 1903–1927, Documenting the Period 1861–1865; Catalog ID: 586957; Record Group #: 109; Roll #: 7, NARA.

City Directories, 1822–1995 [database online]. Provo, UT: Ancestry.com Operations, 2011:
Boston, Massachusetts, 1905, 1909, 1910, 1917.
Washington, D.C., 1888, 1891, 1893, 1933–1945.

Salem, Massachusetts, 1886, 1890.

Cambridge, Massachusetts, 1894.

Compiled Service Records for Confederate Soldiers Who Served from Organizations from the State of Virginia, Record Group 109, NARA; "Mortimer Weaver," Case Files of the "Turner-Baker papers," relating to investigations of subversive activities in the Civil War, Record Group 94, reel 89, NARA.

Draft Registration Cards, 1917–1918, May 29, 1917, U.S., World War I Draft Registration Cards, 1917–1918 [database online]. Provo, UT: Ancestry.com Operations Inc., 2005.

Federal Bureau of Investigation Files: NARA, College Park, Maryland.

   Mary McLeod Bethune, #101-HQ-1823

   Robert C. Weaver, #1349465

Hearing Held Before House Committee on Un-American Activities. Vol. 3, October–November, 1938. Washington, D.C.: U.S. Government Printing Office, 1938.

Hearing on Industrial Commission on Negro Affairs Before the Committee on the Judiciary, House of Representatives. H.R. 5733. Washington, D.C.: U.S. Government Printing Office, 1935.

Inaugural Addresses of the Presidents of the United States from George Washington 1789 to Richard Milhous Nixon 1969. Washington, D.C.: U.S. Government Printing Office, 1969.

Kirby, John B., Robert Lester, and Dale Reynolds, eds. *New Deal Agencies and Black America in the 1930s.* Frederick, MD: University Publications of America, 1983. Microfilm.

Massachusetts, Death Records, 1841–1915 [database online]. Provo, UT: Ancestry.com Operations, 2013.

Massachusetts, Marriage Records, 1840–1915 [database online]. Provo, UT: Ancestry. com Operations, 2013.

New York, Military Service Cards, 1816–1979 [database online]. Provo, UT: Ancestry. com Operations, 2012.

Passport Applications, NARA, Ancestry.com. U.S. Passport Applications, 1795–1925 [database online]. Provo, UT: Ancestry.com Operations, 2007.

State of California Death Index, Ancestry.com, Provo, UT: Ancestry.com Operations, 2000.

Tennessee, Delayed Birth Records, 1869–1909 [database online]. Provo, UT: Ancestry.com.

U.S. City Directories, 1822–1995 [database online]. Provo, UT: Ancestry.com Operations, 2011.

U.S. Federal Censuses: Washington, D.C., National Archives and Records Administration [database online]. Provo, UT: Ancestry.com Operations, 2012.

   1850: Fairfield, South Carolina.

1860:   Fairfield, South Carolina.

1870:   Sparta, Georgia.

1880:   Wilson County, Tennessee.
         Fauquier County, Virginia.
         Boston, Massachusetts.
         Hancock County, Georgia.

1900:   Chicago, Illinois.
         Boston, Massachusetts.
         Sandoval, Illinois.

1910:   Chattanooga, Tennessee.
         Boston, Massachusetts.
         Sandoval, Illinois.
         Guthrie City, Oklahoma.
         Hot Springs, Arkansas.

1930:   Pittsburgh, Pennsylvania.
         Raleigh City, North Carolina.

1940:   Washington, D.C.
         Nashville, Tennessee.

U.S. Social Security Death Index, 1935–2014 [database online]. Provo, UT: Ancestry. com Operations, 2011.

We Work Again. Works Progress Administration and Pathé News, 1937.

PROQUEST DIGITAL FILES AND ABBREVIATIONS (IDENTIFIED BY MODULE, COLLECTION, ARCHIVE, FILE TITLE, FOLDER SUBJECT DATE, AND FILE NUMBER)

1. *Module: Black Freedom Struggle in the 20th Century. Organizational Records and Personal Papers. Part 1.*

Collection: Barnett, Claude A. Papers. Chicago Historical Society, 2011.
     The Claude A. Barnett Papers: The Associated Negro Press, 1918–1967.
         Part 1: Associated Negro Press News Releases, 1928–1964. Series
         A: 1928–1944.
             "Political events in the U.S. Virgin Islands and Haiti." 1934.
         001583_008_0774. [CBP-FED]
     The Claude A. Barnett Papers: The Associated Negro Press, 1918–1967.
         Part 2: Associated Negro Press Organizational Files, 1920–1966.
             "Eugene Davidson." 1931–1934. 001599_005_0117.
         [CBP-Davidson]

The Claude A. Barnett Papers: The Associated Negro Press, 1918–1967.
    Part 3: Subject Files on Black Americans, 1918–1967. Series C:
    Economic Conditions, 1918–1966.
        "Correspondence regarding federal aid programs to states."
    1932–1936. 001589_010_0839. [CBP Aid]
The Claude A. Barnett Papers: The Associated Negro Press, 1918–1967.
    Part 3: Subject Files on Black Americans, 1918–1967. Series H:
    Politics and Law, 1920–1966.
        "Attorneys and black leaders surveyed." 1932. 001594_
    002_0093. [CBP Survey32]
        "Edgar G. Brown." 1938–1954. 001594_009_0564.
    [CBP-Brown]
        "Hoover presidential campaign." 1928. 001594_ 001_0869.
    [CBP RNC28]
        "Hoover's White House conference." 1932. 001594_
    005_0215. [CBP Hoover 1932]
        "Political climate of 1939, including Federal employment,
    Anti-Lynching Bill." 1939. 001594_002_0881. [CBP-Camp40]
        "Republican Party and presidential election materials." 1936–
    1960. 001594_005_0136. [CBP-Rep36-60]
        "Republican Party on presidential election of 1940." 1940–
    1942. 001594_005_0470. [CBP-Rep40]
        "Republican Party pamphlets and handbills." 1932.
    001594_005_0001. [CBP RNC32]
        "Roosevelt administration and New Deal programs." 1933–
    1935. 001594_002_0444. [CBP FDR/NRA]

2. *Module: Black Freedom Struggle in the 20th Century. Federal Government Records.*

Collection: Civil Rights During the Johnson Administration, 1963–1969. Part
    III: Oral Histories. Presidential Library: Lyndon Baines Johnson Library,
    Austin, Texas.
        "Robert C. Weaver, Interview." 1968. 001343_003_0878.
    [FRG-Weaver]
Collection: New Deal Agencies and Black America. National Archives: Agency
    Record Groups.
        "Alfred Edgar Smith. Unemployment Relief." 1934–1938.
    001398_012_0090. [FGR-Smith]

"Civilian Conservation Corps Correspondence." 1933–1940. 001398_008_0814. [FGR-CCC]

"Conferences, Second National NYA Conference." 1939. 001398_004_0070. [FRG-NC2]

"Department of Commerce Division of Negro Affairs office activity." 1940. 001398_018_0648. [NARA-Comm]

"Discrimination Against Negroes, TVA." 1934–1937. 001398_013_0440. [FRG-Weaver-TVA]

"Eugene Kinckle Jones." 1933–1941. 001398_ 018_0231. [FRG-Jones]

"Farm Credit Administration." 1934–1936. 001398_ 012_0512. [FRG-FCA]

"Federal Works Agency: Work Projects Administration Press releases." 1939–1940. 001398_021_0635. [FRG-FWA]

"Forrester B. Washington Report." 1934. 001398_020_0896. [FRG-Washington]

"Frances Perkins, Correspondence, Black Workers." 1934–1939. 001398_013_0320. [FRG-Oxley]

"Harold Ickes Correspondence." 1933–1943. 001398_ 007_0765. [FGR-Ickes]

"Harold L. Ickes, Correspondence." 1934–1935. 001398_ 008_0001. [FGR-Ickes34]

"Joint Committee on National Recovery." 1934–1936. 001398_014_0849. [FRG-Joint]

"Lawrence A. Oxley Interview." 1973. 001398_ 009_0857. [NARA-Oxley]

"Lawrence A. Oxley—special report." 1939. 001398_ 017_0370. [FRG-Oxley-Report]

"Negro Affairs: Department of Labor." 1933–1936. 001398_017_0001. [FRG-Labor]

"NYA, Conference, remarks, press." 1936–1940. 001398_ 002_0165. [FRG-NYA-misc.]

"NYA, Documents." 1935–1936. 001398_003_0055. [NYA-35-36]

"Proceedings: Second National NYA Conference." 1939. 001398_015_0135. [FRG-Conf2]

"Report of Works Progress Administration." 1934–1937. 001398_020_0362. [NARA-WPA]

"U.S. Department of Interior Racial discrimination." 1935–1936. 01398_008_0123. [FRG-Interior]

"Works Progress Administration correspondence." 1933–1934. 001398_020_0744. [FRG-WPA]

Collection: African Americans in the Military. Part 2: Subject Files of Judge William Hastie, Civilian Aide to the Secretary of War, D–M, N–Z. NARA, College Park, Maryland.

"Censorship of African American newspapers." 1940–1943. 102613_015_0001. [NARA-press]

"Discrimination in civilian employment, Robert C. Weaver." 1940–1944. 102613_032_0521. [NARA-Weaver]

"March on Washington: Negro." 1941. 102178_015_0764. [NARA-MOW]

"William H. Hastie resignation." 1942–1943. 102178_018_0367. [NARA-Hastie]

Collection: Mary McLeod Bethune Papers: The Bethune Foundation Collection. Part 3: Subject Files, 1939–1955. Mary McLeod Bethune Foundation Archive, Bethune-Cookman College campus, Daytona Beach, Florida. Copyright, 2011: Bethune-Cookman College, Inc.

"Eleanor Roosevelt, NAACP." 1944–1955. 001392_017_0607. [MMB-ERCorr]

"NAACP correspondence." 1942–1949. 001392_014_0527. [MMB-NAACP]

"National Youth Administration and First Conference." 1935–1939. 001392_016_0555. [MMB-NYA35-39]

"Writings of Mary McLeod Bethune." 1937–1949. 001392_009_0039. [MMB-writings]

Collection: Mary McLeod Bethune Papers: The Bethune Foundation Collection, Part 2: Correspondence Files, 1914–1955. Personal Papers: Mary McLeod Bethune Foundation Archive, Bethune-Cookman College campus, Daytona Beach, Florida.

"Dies Committee investigation." 1943. 001390_004_0001. [MMB-Dies]

"Dies Committee, including opposition." 1943. 001390_003_0894. [MMB-Dies2]

"National Youth Administration correspondence." 1936–1939. 001390_007_0693. [MMB-NYA36-39]

"National Youth Administration correspondence." 1938–1942. 001390_007_0866. [MMB-NYA38-42]

"National Youth Administration correspondence." 1940–1944. 001390_007-0750. [MMB-NYA40-44]

"Rackham Holt correspondence." 1948–1954. 001390_005_0486. [MMB-Holt]

"Walter White Correspondence." 1936–1954. 001390_012_0790. [MMB-WW]

Collection: Mary McLeod Bethune Papers: The Bethune Foundation Collection. Part I: Writings, Diaries, Scrapbooks, Biographical Materials, and Files on the National Youth Administration and Women's Organizations, 1918–1955. Mary McLeod Bethune Papers, Bethune-Cookman College Archives, Daytona Beach, Florida.

"Biographical Sketches/résumé." 1944–1954. 001387_001_0021 27. [MMB-Sketches]

"Mary McLeod Bethune, Clippings." 1933–1945. 001387_008_0209. [MMB-Clips-1]

"Mary McLeod Bethune, Clippings 2." 1933–1944. 001387_008_0057. [MB-Clips-2]

"Mary McLeod Bethune, Scrapbook 2." 1936–1940. 001387_007_0190. [MMB-Scrap2]

"National Conference on the Problems of Negro and Negro Youth." 1937. 001387_012_0001. [MMB-NC37]

"National Youth Administration correspondence." 1939. 001387_010_0288. [MMB-NYA39]

"National Youth administration correspondence." 1937–1941. 001387_010_0525. [MMB-NYA37-41]

"National Youth Administration correspondence." 1942. 001387_010_0657. [MMB-NYA42]

"National Youth Administration correspondence, January–March 1943." 1943. 001387_010_0800. [MMB-NYA43]

"National Youth Administration correspondence, Mary McLeod Bethune, Franklin D. Roosevelt." 1918–1955. 001387_011_0270. [MMB-FDR]

"National Youth Administration, Eleanor Roosevelt." 1938. 001387_010_0222. [MMB-NYA38]

"Rackham Holt, Biography of Bethune and corrections." 001387_001_0304. [MMB-bio]

"Radio broadcasts and interviews." 1918–1955. 001387_
010_0125. [MMB-Radio]

3. *Module: NAACP Papers. The NAACP's Major Campaigns: Education, Voting, Housing,
Employment, Armed Forces.*

Collection: Papers of the NAACP. Part 13: NAACP and Labor. Series B: Coop-
eration with Organized Labor, 1940–1955. Library of Congress. National
Association for the Advancement of Colored People, 2012.
"Employment discrimination in national defense indus-
tries, White House conference." 1940. 001434_025_0001.
[NAACP-WHConf]
"Federal Employment, FEPC and March on Washington."
1941. 001434_011_0554. [NAACP-FEPC]
"March on Washington Committee." 1941.
001434_023_0001. [NAACP-MOW]
"March on Washington, including employment discrimina-
tion." 1940–1941. 001434_023_0001. [NAACP-MOW2]
"War Production Board and War Manpower Commission."
1942. 001432_021_0124. [NAACP-WMC]
Collection: Papers of the NAACP. Part 05: Campaign Against Residential Segrega-
tion, 1914–1955.
"Sojourner Truth Homes." 1942. 001521_005_0070.
[NAACP-STH]

FRANKLIN AND ELEANOR ROOSEVELT PAPERS

Roosevelt, Eleanor. The Selected Digitized Correspondence of Eleanor Roose-
velt, 1933–1945. Series I: Franklin D. Roosevelt Presidential Library and
Museum.
Alexander, Will [ER-WA]
Bethune, Mary McLeod, letters, 1942 [ER-MMB]
Bethune, Mary McLeod, letters, 1943–1945 [ER-MMB2]
Early, Stephen [ER-SE]
Farley, James [2] [ER-JF2]
Fauset, Crystal Bird [ER-CBF]
Roosevelt, Eleanor [1] [ER1]
Williams, Aubrey [ER-AW]

Roosevelt, Eleanor, to Mrs. Henry M. Roberts Jr. February 26, 1939. American Originals Collection, National Archives and Records Administration. Accessed June 10, 2014. https://www.archives.gov/exhibits/american_originals/elea-nor.html.

Roosevelt, Franklin Delano. *Franklin D. Roosevelt and Race Relations*. Woodbridge, CT: Primary Source, 2007. Microfilm. [FDR-RR]

Roosevelt, Franklin Delano. "Franklin D. Roosevelt Day by Day" [office calendar]. Pare Lorentz Center at Franklin Delano Roosevelt Presidential Library and Museum. Accessed September 16, 2014. http://www.fdrlibrary.marist.edu/daybyday/daylog/october-28th-1938/.

Roosevelt, Franklin Delano. *The Public Papers and Addresses of Franklin Delano Roosevelt*. 1940 volume. New York: Macmillan, 1941.

PRIMARY SOURCE ARTICLES AND BOOK CHAPTERS

Alsop, Joseph, and Robert Kintner. "The Guffey: Biography of a Boss, New Style," *Saturday Evening Post*, March 26, 1938, 5–7.

Bethune, Mary McLeod. "My Last Will and Testament." *Ebony*, August 1955, 105–10.

———. "My Secret Talks with FDR." *Ebony*, April 1949, 45–46.

Birnie, William A. H. "Black Brain Trust." *American Magazine*, January 1943, 36–37, 94–95.

"Black Purge." *Time*, October 31, 1938.

Byron, Dora. "From 'Cabin in the Cotton.'" *Opportunity*, April 1936, 106-107, 125.

Carter, Elmer. "Henry A. Hunt." *Opportunity*, December 1938, 323.

"Cities for the Heart." *Time*, March 4, 1966, 29–33.

"Dr. Robert C. Weaver, 89, First Black Cabinet Member, Succumbs in Manhattan," *Jet*, August 4, 1997, 57.

Du Bois, W. E. B. "President Harding and Social Equality." *Crisis*, December 1921, 53–56.

———. "The Significance of Henry A. Hunt." Founder's Day Address, Fort Valley State College, Fort Valley, Georgia, October 10, 1940, 24–25.

———. "Youth and Age at Amenia." *Crisis*, October 1933, 226–28.

"FEPC Is Captured by the South." *Crisis*, September 1942, 279.

Fields, Alonzo. "21 Years in the White House." *Ebony*, October 1982, 60–66.

Hamilton, Albert W. "The Black Cabinet." *Common Sense* 12 (1943): 97–99.

Hastie, William H. "A Look at the NAACP." *Crisis*, September 1939, 263–64, 274.

Herrick, Genevieve Forbes. "Queen Mary: Champion of Negro Women." *Negro Digest*, December 1950, 32–39.

Hunt, H. A. "The Negro as a Farmer." In *Twentieth Century Negro Literature; Or, A Cyclopedia of Thought on the Vital Topics Relating to the American Negro*. Daniel Wallace Culp, ed., 394–98. Atlanta: J. L. Nichols, 1902.

Ickes, Harold. "My Twelve Years with F.D.R." *Saturday Evening Post*, June 26, 1948, 36–37, 79–83.

"Judge Hastie, First Black Federal Jurist, Dead at 71," *Jet*, April 29, 1976, 5.

Krock, Arthur. "Did the Negro Revolt?" *Journal of Negro Life*, January 1933, 19, 28.

Kuyper, George A. "Henry A. Hunt: Good Shepherd." *Southern Workman*, December 1938, 373–75.

"Lawrence A. Oxley." *Living Church*, June 28, 1964, 19.

"Lynched a Woman." *Crisis*, August 1912, 196.

McDuffie, Elizabeth. "FDR Was My Boss." *Ebony*, April 1962, 73–74.

"Mrs. Bethune: Spingarn Medalist." *Crisis*, July 1935, 202.

"Negro Angel." *Literary Digest*, March 6, 1937, 8–9.

"New Deal Personalities." *Oracle*, June 1934, 6.

Nye, Gerald P. "Yes, Says Nye." *New York Times*, January 14, 1940.

Ottley, Roi. "Truman's New Black Cabinet." *Ebony*, August 1949, 15–18.

Oxley, Lawrence. "Negro Welfare and Progress in North Carolina." *Southern Workman*, November 1925, 515–19.

Pickens, William. "NRA—Negro Removal Act?" *World Tomorrow*, September 28, 1933, 539–40.

"A Pioneer's Pioneer: Al Smith." *Oracle*, Summer 1974, 1–11.

Poston, Ted. "The 'Black Cabinet' in Action." *Negro Digest*, March 1962, 22–25.

Raskin, A. H. "Washington Gets 'The Weaver Treatment.'" *New York Times Magazine*, May 14, 1961, 16, 30, 33, 35–36.

Redmond Coggs, Pauline. "Race Relations Advisors—Quislings or Messiahs?" *Opportunity*, July 1942, 112–14.

Roosevelt, Eleanor. "Some of My Best Friends Are Negroes." February 1953; reprinted: *Ebony*, November 1975, 73–78.

"The Rosenwald Conference." *Crisis*, July 1933, 156–57.

Smith, Alfred Edgar. "America's Greatest Unknown Negro." *Negro Digest*, April 1940, 42–46.

———. "Educational Programs for the Improvement of Race Relations: Government Agencies." *Journal of Negro Education* 13, no. 3, 361–66.

Thomas, Jessie O. "Will the New Deal Be a Square Deal for the Negro?" *Opportunity*, October 1933, 308–11.

Trent, W[illiam] J., Jr. "Federal Sanctions Directed Against Racial Discrimination."
    Phlyon, 2nd quarter, 1942, 171–82.

Weaver, Robert C. "An Experiment in Negro Labor." *Opportunity*, October 1936,
    295–98.

———. "The Negro Comes of Age in Industry." *Atlantic Monthly*, September 1943,
    54–59.

———. "The Negro in a Program of Public Housing." *Opportunity*, July 1938,
    198–203.

———. "The New Deal and the Negro: A Look at the Facts." *Opportunity*, July
    1935, 200–2.

———. "Racial Employment Trends in National Defense." *Phlyon*, 4th quarter,
    1941, 337–58.

———. "Racial Employment Trends in National Defense, Part II." *Phylon*, 1st
    quarter, 1942, 22–30.

———. "Racial Minorities and Public Housing." In *Proceedings of the National Con-
    ference of Social Work*, 289–96. New York: Columbia University Press, 1940.

———. "Racial Policy in Public Housing." *Phylon*, 2nd quarter, 1940, 151–57.

———. "With the Negro's Help." *Atlantic Monthly*, June 1942, 696–706.

EDITED COLLECTIONS

Bethune, Mary McLeod. *Mary McLeod Bethune: Building a Better World, Essays and Selected
    Documents.* Audrey McCluskey and Elaine Smith, eds. Bloomington: Indiana
    University Press, 1999.

Bunche, Ralph. *Ralph J. Bunche: Selected Speeches and Writings.* Ann Arbor: University of
    Michigan Press, 1995.

Lochheim, Katie, with Jonathan Dembo, eds. *The Making of the New Deal: Insiders Speak.*
    Cambridge, MA: Harvard University Press, 1983.

McElvaine, Robert S. *Down and Out in the Great Depression: Letters from the Forgotten Man.*
    Chapel Hill: University of North Carolina Press, 1983.

The Negro Problem: A Series of Articles by Representative Negroes of To-Day. New York: James
    Pott, 1903.

PAPERS (PRINT, ONLINE, AND MICROFILM)

Bunche, Ralph. Ralph J. Bunche Papers, 1927–1971. Young Research Library,
    University of California, Los Angeles.

Du Bois, W. E. B. *W. E. B. Du Bois Papers. Series 1A, General Correspondence.* W. E. B. Du Bois, Special Collections and University Archives, University of Massachusetts Amherst Libraries; MS 312. Accessed February 2, 2013. http://credo.library. umass.edu/view/full/mums312-b065-i095.

King, Martin Luther, Jr. *The Papers of Martin Luther King Jr.: Threshold of a New Decade, January 1959–December 1960.* Berkeley: University of California Press, 2005.

NAACP. The Papers of the NAACP: The Campaign for Educational Equality, 1913–1965. Series A, Part 3. Frederick, Md: University Publications of America, 1981 [microfilm].

NAACP. The Papers of the NAACP: General Correspondence of the Director, NAACP, Record Group 35. NARA, College Park, Md [microfilm].

Washington, Booker T. *Booker T. Washington Papers, 1909–1911.* Vol 10. Louis Harlan, Geraldine McTigue, and Nan E. Woodruff, eds. Champaign: University of Illinois Press, 1981.

Memoirs, Interviews, and Oral Histories

Alexander, Will W. *The Reminiscences of Will W. Alexander.* New York: Columbia University Oral History Collection, 1952 [typescript/microfiche].

Atkins, James A. *The Age of Jim Crow.* New York: Vantage Press, 1964.

Dancy, John C. *Sand Against the Wind: The Memoirs of John C. Dancy.* Detroit: Detroit Urban League, 1966.

Douglass, Frederick. *The Life and Times of Frederick Douglass.* 1892; reprint, New York: Collier Books, 1962.

Fields, Alonzo. *My 21 Years in the White House.* New York: Coward-McCann, 1961.

Foreman, Clark. Transcript, oral history interview by Jacquelyn Hall and William Finger, November 16, 1974. Documenting the American South (University of North Carolina at Chapel Hill), Oral Histories of the American South collection. Accessed February 14, 2008. http://docsouth.unc.edu/sohp/ B-0003/B-0003.html.

Gerard, James W. *My First Eighty-Three Years in America: The Memoirs of James W. Gerard.* New York: Doubleday, 1951.

Gibson, Truman K., Jr., with Steve Huntley. *Knocking down Barriers: My Fight for Black America.* Evanston, IL: Northwestern University Press, 2005.

Guffey, Joseph F. *Seventy Years on the Red Fire Wagon: From Tilden to Truman Through New Freedom and New Deal.* Pittsburgh: privately published, 1952.

510

510

BIBLIOGRAPHY

510

BIBLIOGRAPHY

Hastie, William H. Transcript, oral history interview by Jerry N. Hess. Harry S. Truman Library and Museum. January 5, 1972. Accessed May 28, 2014. https://www.trumanlibrary.org/oralhist/hastie.htm.

Ickes, Harold L. *The Secret Diary of Harold L. Ickes: The Inside Struggle, 1936–1939*. New York: Simon and Schuster, 1954.

———. *The Secret Diary of Harold L. Ickes: The Lowering Clouds, 1939–1941*. New York: Simon and Schuster, 1955.

Lochheim, Katie, with Jonathan Dembo, eds. *The Making of the New Deal: Insiders Speak*. Cambridge, MA: Harvard University Press, 1983.

Murray, Pauli. *The Autobiography of a Black Activist, Feminist, Lawyer, Priest, and Poet*. Knoxville: University of Tennessee Press, 1989.

Nash, Philleo. Transcript, oral history interview by Jerry N. Hess. August 17, 1966. Harry S. Truman Library and Museum, Accessed October 7, 2016. http://www.trumanlibrary.org/oralhist/nash2.htm#68.

Parks, Lillian Rogers, with Frances Spatz Leighton. *My Thirty Years Backstairs at the White House*. 1961; reprint: Bronx, NY: Ishi Press, 2008.

———. *The Roosevelts: A Family in Turmoil*. Englewood Cliffs, NJ: Prentice Hall, 1981.

Pitts, Lucia Mae. *Manuscript and Letters*. Madison: State Historical Society of Wisconsin. Microfilm edition, 1981.

———. *One Negro WAC's Story*. Los Angeles: Lucia Mae Pitts, 1968.

Robinson, Rachel, with Lee Daniels. *Jackie Robinson: An Intimate Portrait*. New York: Harry N. Abrams, 1996.

Roosevelt, Eleanor. *This I Remember*. New York: Harper and Brothers, 1949.

Roundtree, Dovey Johnson, and Katie McCabe. *Justice Older Than Law: The Life of Dovey Johnson Roundtree*. Jackson: University of Mississippi Press, 2009.

Thomas, Jessie O. *My Story in Black and White: The Autobiography of Jesse O. Thomas*. New York: Exposition Press, 1967.

Weaver, Robert C. Transcript, interview conducted by Blackside, Inc., on February 15, 1992, for *The Great Depression Interviews*. Washington University Libraries, Film and Media Archive, Henry Hampton Collection. Accessed November 15, 2015. http://digital.wustl.edu/cgi/t/text/text-idx?c=gds;cc=gds;rgn=main;view=text;idno=wea00031.00880.064.

———. Transcript, oral history interview by Joe B. Frantz. November 19, 1968. Austin, TX: Lyndon Baines Johnson Presidential Library.

West, J. B., and Mary Lynn Kotz. *Upstairs at the White House: My Life with the First Ladies*. New York: Coward, McCann and Geoghegan, 1973.

White, Walter. *A Man Called White: Autobiography of Walter White.* Athens: University of Georgia Press, 1995.

Primary Source Books and Pamphlets

Dies, Martin. *The Trojan Horse in America.* New York: Dodd, Mead, 1940.

Johnson, Charles S. *The Economic Status of Negroes: Summary and Analysis of the Materials Presented at the Conference on the Economic Status of the Negro Held in Washington, D.C.* Nashville, TN: Fisk University Press, 1933.

Miller, Kelly. *Race Adjustment: Essays on the Negro in America,* 2nd ed. New York: Neale Publishing Company, 1909.

National Conference on the Problems of the Negro and Negro Youth. Held January 6, 7, 8, 1937. Washington, D.C.: The Conference, 1937.

Second National Conference on the Problems of the Negro and Negro Youth. Held January 12, 13, 14, 1939. Washington D.C.: Second National Conference on the Problems of the Negro and Negro Youth, 1939.

Weaver, Robert C. *The Negro Ghetto.* New York: Harcourt, Brace, 1948.

————. *Negro Labor: A National Problem.* New York: Harcourt Brace, 1946.

Secondary Sources

Articles

Anderson, James D. "Philanthropy in the Shaping of Black Industrial Education Schools: The Fort Valley Case, 1902–1938." *Review Journal of Philosophy and Social Science,* Winter 1978, 184–209.

Baker, Ray Stannard. "The New Head of Tuskegee." In *The World's Work,* vol. 31. Walter Hines Page and Arthur W. Page, eds., 528. New York: Doubleday and Page, 1916.

Barrow, Frederica H. "Forrester Blanchard Washington and His Advocacy for African Americans in the New Deal." *Social Work,* July 2007, 201–8.

Bellamy, Donnie. "Henry Alexander Hunt's Crusade for Quality Public Education of Black Georgians." *Negro Education Review,* April 1977, 85–94.

————. "Henry A. Hunt and Black Agricultural Leadership in the New South." *Journal of Negro History,* October 1974, 464–79.

"Brother Lawrence A. Oxley." *BPD Update Online* 25, no. 3 (Fall 2003). Accessed February 17, 2009. http://www.betaphi.com/oxley.htm.

Burwell, Yolanda. "Lawrence Oxley and Locality Development: Black Self-Help in North Carolina, 1925–1928." *Journal of Community Practice* 2, no. 4 (1996), 49–69.

Butler, Sara A. "Ground Breaking in New Deal Washington, D.C.: Art, Patronage, and Race at the Recorder of Deeds Building." *Winterthur Portfolio*, Winter 2011, 277–320.

Collins, William. "Race, Roosevelt, and Wartime Production: Fair Employment in World War II Labor Markets." *American Economic Review*, March 2001, 272–86.

Derber, Milton. "The New Deal and Labor." In *The New Deal*, vol. 1, John Braeman, Robert H. Bremner, and David Brody, eds., 123. Columbus: Ohio State University Press, 1975.

"Evan P. Howell by a Georgian." *Georgia Historical Quarterly*, March 1917, 52–57.

Gower, Calvin W. "The Struggle of Blacks for Leadership Positions in the Civilian Conservation Corps: 1933–1942." *Journal of Negro History*, April 1976, 123–35.

Hargrove, Tasha, and Robert Zabawa, "The Physical and Social Environment of African American Agricultural Communities of the New Deal Resettlement Administration." In *Land and Power: Sustainable Agriculture and African Americans; A Collection of Essays from the 2007 Black Environmental Thought Conference*. Jeffrey L. Jordan, Edward Pennick, Walter A. Hill, and Robert Zabawa, eds., 113. Waldorf, MD: Sustainable Agriculture Publications, 2007.

"Henry Alexander Hunt." *Journal of Negro History*, January 1939, 135–36.

Holley, David. "The Negro in the New Deal Resettlement Program." *Agricultural History*, July 1971, 179–84.

Holloway, Jonathan Scott. "Ralph Bunche and the Responsibilities of the Public Intellectual." *Journal of Negro Education*, Spring 2004, 125–35.

"In Memoriam: Robert C. Weaver, 1907–1997." *Journal of Blacks in Higher Education*, Autumn 1997, 116.

Kenneally, James J. "Black Republicans During the New Deal: The Role of Joseph W. Martin, Jr." *Review of Politics*, Winter 1993, 117–39.

Kremer, Greg. "William J. Thompkins: African American Physician, Politician, and Publisher." *Missouri Historical Review*, April 2007, 168–82.

Lorenz, Alfred Lawrence. "Ralph W. Tyler: The Unknown Correspondent of World War I." *Journalism History*, Spring 2005, 2–12.

McGuire, Phillip. "Judge Hastie, World War II, and Army Racism." *Journal of Negro History*, October 1977, 351–62.

———. "Judge William H. Hastie and Army Recruitment, 1940–1945." *Military Affairs*, April 1978, 75–79.

Meier, August. "The Racial and Educational Philosophy of Kelly Miller, 1895–1915." *Journal of Negro Education*, Spring 1960, 121–27.

Muncy, Robyn. "Women, Gender, and Politics in the New Deal Government: Josephine Roche and the Federal Security Agency." *Journal of Women's History*, Fall 2009, 60–83.

Ross, B. Joyce. "Mary McLeod Bethune and the National Youth Administration: A Case Study of Power Relationships in the Black Cabinet of Franklin D. Roosevelt." *Journal of Negro History*, January 1975, 1–28.

Salinas, Andrew. "Edgar G. Brown Papers, 1937–1981." Amistad Research Center. Accessed August 5, 2012. http://www.amistadresearchcenter.org/archon/ ?p=creators/creator&id=443.

Simpson, William M. "A Tale Untold? The Alexandria Lee Street Riot (January 10, 1942)." *Louisiana History*, Spring 1994, 133–49.

Smith, Elaine. "Mary McLeod Bethune." In *Black Women in America: A Historical Encyclopedia*. Darlene Clarke Hine and Elsa Barkley Brown, eds. 113–27. Brooklyn, NY: Carlson Publications, 1993.

———. "Mary McLeod Bethune and the National Youth Administration." In *Clio Was a Woman: Studies in the History of American Women*, 151–52. Washington, D.C.: Conference on Women's History, 1976.

Smythe, Jeannette. "Memories of Mary McLeod Bethune." *Washington Post*, July 13, 1974.

Swain, Martha W. "Miller, Emma Guffey." In *American National Biography Online*. New York: Oxford University Press and American Council of Learned Societies, 2000. Accessed November 25, 2012. http://www.anb.org/ articles/07/07-00203.html.

Topping, Simon. "'Turning Their Pictures of Abraham Lincoln to the Wall': The Republican Party and Black America in the Election of 1936." *Irish Journal of American Studies* 8 (1999), 35–59.

"United Government Employees." In *Encyclopedia of U.S. Labor and Working Class History*, Eric Arnesen, ed., 1428. London: Taylor and Francis, 2007.

Weems, Robert. "'The Right Man': James A. Jackson and the Origins of U.S. Government Interest in Black Business." *Enterprise and Society* 6, no. 2 (June 2005), 254–77.

West, Martha. "The Historical Roots of Affirmative Action." *Berkeley La Raza Journal* 10, no. 2 (1998), 607–30.

Wolgemuth, Kathleen. "Woodrow Wilson and Federal Segregation." *Journal of Negro History* 44 (1959), 158–73.

Books

Alexander, Adele Logan. *Ambiguous Lives: Free Women of Color in Rural Georgia, 1789–1879.* Fayetteville: University of Arkansas Press, 1991.

Alter, Jonathan. *The Defining Moment: FDR's First Hundred Days and the Triumph of Hope.* New York: Simon and Schuster, 2006.

Armfield, Felix L. *Eugene Kinckle Jones: The National Urban League and Black Social Work, 1910–1940.* Urbana: University of Illinois Press, 2012.

Arsneault, Raymond. *The Sound of Freedom: Marian Anderson, The Lincoln Memorial, and the Concert That Awakened America.* New York: Bloomsbury Publishing, 2010.

Asch, Chris Myers, and George Derek Musgrove. *Chocolate City: A History of Race and Democracy in the Nation's Capital.* Chapel Hill: University of North Carolina Press, 2017.

Avery, Sheldon. *Up from Washington: William Pickens and the Negro Struggle for Equality, 1900–1954.* Newark: University of Delaware Press, 1989.

Barbeau, Arthur E., and Florette Henri, *The Unknown Solders: African-American Troops in World War I.* New York: Da Capo Press, 1996.

Barber, Lucy Grace. *Marching on Washington: The Forging of an American Political Tradition.* Berkeley: University of California Press, 2002.

Bardolph, Richard. *The Negro Vanguard.* New York: Rinehart, 1959.

Bates, Beth Tompkins. *Pullman Porters and the Rise of Protest Politics in Black America, 1925–1945.* Chapel Hill: University of North Carolina Press, 2001.

Bell-Scott, Patricia. *The Firebrand and the First Lady: Pauli Murray, Eleanor Roosevelt, and the Struggle for Social Justice.* New York: Alfred A. Knopf, 2016.

Berlin, Ira. *Slaves Without Masters: The Free Negro in the Antebellum South.* New York: Oxford University Press, 1981.

Biles, Roger. *The South and the New Deal.* Lexington: University Press of Kentucky, 2015.

Blain, Keisha. *Set the World on Fire: Black Nationalist Women and the Global Struggle for Freedom.* Philadelphia: University of Pennsylvania Press, 2018.

Blakely, Robert J., and Marcus Shepard. *Earl B. Dickerson: A Voice for Freedom and Equality.* Evanston, IL: Northwestern University Press, 2006.

Blaustein, Albert P., and Robert L. Zangrando, eds. *Civil Rights and African Americans: A Documentary History.* Evanston, IL: Northwestern University Press, 1968.

Bodnar, John, Roger Simon, and Michael P. Weber. *Lives of Their Own: Blacks, Italians, and Poles in Pittsburgh, 1900–1960.* Chicago: University of Illinois Press, 1982.

Brands, H. W. *Traitor to His Class: The Privileged Life of Franklin Delano Roosevelt.* New York: Anchor Books, 2008.

Brinkerhoff, J. H. O. *Brinkerhoff's History of Marion County, Illinois*. Indianapolis, IN: F. Bowen, 1909.

Brundage, William Fitzhugh. *Lynching in the New South: Georgia and Virginia, 1880–1930*. Chicago: University of Illinois Press, 1993.

Buckley, Gale Lumet. *The Hornes: An American Family*. New York: Applause Books, 1986.

Bunche, Ralph. *The Political Status of the Negro in the Age of FDR*. Chicago: University of Chicago Press, 1973.

Buni, Andrew. *Robert L. Vann of the* Pittsburgh Courier. Pittsburgh: University of Pittsburgh Press, 1974.

Bynum, Cornelius L. *A. Philip Randolph and the Struggle for Civil Rights*. Chicago: University of Illinois Press, 2010.

Capeci, Dominic, Jr. *The Harlem Riot of 1943*. Philadelphia: Temple University Press, 1977.

Chafe, William H. *Civilities and Civil Rights: Greensboro, North Carolina, and the Black Struggle*. New York: Oxford University Press, 1981.

Clive, Alan. *State of War: Michigan in World War II*. Ann Arbor: University of Michigan Press, 1979.

Cook, Blanche Wiesen. *Eleanor Roosevelt*. Vol. 1, *The Early Years, 1884–1933*. New York: Penguin Books, 1992.

———. *Eleanor Roosevelt*. Vol. 2, *The Defining Years, 1933–1938*. New York: Penguin Books, 1999.

———. *Eleanor Roosevelt*. Vol. 3, *The War Years and After, 1939–1962*. New York: Viking Books, 2016.

Crosswell, D. K. R. *Beetle: The Life of General Walter Bedell Smith*. Lexington: University Press of Kentucky, 2010.

Cullinane, Michael Patrick. *Liberty and American Anti-Imperialism, 1898–1909*. New York: Palgrave Macmillan, 2012.

Curtis, Susan. *Colored Memories: A Biographer's Quest for the Elusive Lester A. Walton*. Columbia: University of Missouri Press, 2008.

Davin, Eric Leif. *Crucible of Freedom: Workers' Democracy in the Industrial Heartland*. Lanham, MD: Lexington Books, 2010.

Davis, Deborah H. *Guest of Honor: Booker T. Washington, Theodore Roosevelt, and the White House Dinner That Shocked the Nation*. New York: Atria, 2013.

De Ferrari, John. *Historic Restaurants of Washington, D.C.* Charleston, SC: American Palate, 2013.

Djata, Sundiata A. *Blacks at the Net: Black Achievement in the History of Tennis*, vol. 1. Syracuse, NY: Syracuse University Press, 2006.

Downey, Kristin. *The Woman behind the New Deal: The Life of Frances Perkins, FDR's Secretary of Labor and His Moral Conscience.* New York: Doubleday, 2009.

Dray, Phillip. *Capitol Men: The Epic Story of Reconstruction Through the Lives of the First Black Congressmen.* New York: Mariner Books, 2008.

Dudziak, Mary L. *Cold War Civil Rights: Race and the Image of American Democracy.* Princeton, NJ: Princeton University Press, 2000.

Dunn, Susan. *1940: FDR, Willkie, Lindbergh, Hitler: The Election amid the Storm.* New Haven, CT: Yale University Press, 2013.

———. *Roosevelt's Purge: How FDR Fought to Change the Democratic Party.* Cambridge, MA: Harvard University Press, 2010.

DuRocher, Kristina. *Raising Racists: The Socialization of White Children in the Jim Crow South.* Lexington: University Press of Kentucky, 2011.

Dyer, Thomas G. *Theodore Roosevelt and the Idea of Race.* Baton Rouge: Louisiana State University Press, 1980.

Dykeman, Wilma, and James Stokely. *Seeds of Southern Change: The Life of Will Alexander.* Chicago: University of Chicago Press, 1962.

Embree, Edwin. *13 Against the Odds.* New York: Viking Press, 1944.

Fleming, George Thornton. *History of Pittsburgh and Environs.* New York: American Historical Society, 1922.

Foner, Eric. *Reconstruction: America's Unfinished Revolution, 1863–1877.* New York: Perennial Classics, 2002.

Fouche, Rayvon. *Black Inventors in the Age of Segregation: Granville T. Woods, Lewis H. Latimer, and Shelby J. Davidson.* Baltimore, MD: Johns Hopkins University Press, 2005.

Franklin, John Hope. *From Slavery to Freedom: A History of Negro Americans*, 6th ed. New York: Alfred A. Knopf, 1988.

———. *A Mirror to America: The Autobiography of John Hope Franklin.* New York: Farrar, Straus and Giroux, 2005.

Gates, Henry Louis, Jr. *African American Lives.* New York: Oxford University Press, 2004.

Gatewood, Willard B. *Aristocrats of Color: The Black Elite, 1880–1920.* Fayetteville: University of Arkansas Press, 2000.

Gellerman, William. *Martin Dies.* New York: Da Capo Press, 1972.

Gellman, Erik S. *Death Blow to Jim Crow: The National Negro Congress and the Rise of Militant Civil Rights.* Chapel Hill: University of North Carolina Press, 2012.

Giddings, Paula. *Ida: A Sword Among Lions and the Campaign Against Lynching.* New York: Amistad, 2008.

————. *When and Where I Enter: The Impact of Black Women on Race and Sex in America.* New York: William Morrow, 1984.

Gillmor, David, M. *Mass Communication Law: Cases and Comment.* Belmont, CA: Wadsworth Publishing, 1998.

Goodwin, Doris Kearns. *No Ordinary Time: Franklin and Eleanor Roosevelt: The Home Front in World War II.* New York: Simon and Schuster, 1994.

Gottlieb, Peter. *Making Their Own Way: Southern Blacks' Migration to Pittsburgh, 1916–1930.* Chicago: University of Illinois Press, 1987.

Green, Constance McLaughlin. *The Secret City: A History of Race Relations in the Nation's Capital.* Princeton, NJ: Princeton University Press, 1967.

Hahn, Stephen. *A Nation under Our Feet: Black Political Struggle in the Rural South from Slavery to the Great Migration.* Cambridge, MA: Harvard University Press, 2003.

Hanson, Joyce A. *Mary McLeod Bethune and Black Women's Political Activism.* Columbia: University of Missouri Press, 2003.

Harlan, Louis R. *Booker T. Washington in Perspective: Essays of Louis R. Harlan.* Raymond Smock, ed. Oxford: University of Mississippi Press, 2006.

————. *Booker T. Washington.* Vol. 2, *The Wizard of Tuskegee, 1901–1915.* New York: Oxford University Press, 1983.

Hauke, Kathleen A. *Ted Poston: Pioneer American Journalist.* Athens: University of Georgia Press, 1998.

Hayes, Laurence J. W. *The Negro Federal Government Worker: A Study in His Classification Status in the District of Columbia, 1883–1938.* Washington, D.C.: Howard University, 1941.

Hollie, Donna Tyler, Brett M. Tyler, and Karen Hughes White. *African Americans of Fauquier County.* Charleston, SC: Arcadia, 2009.

Holloway, Jonathan Scott. *Confronting the Veil: Abram Harris, Jr., E. Franklin Frazier, and Ralph Bunche, 1919–1941.* Chapel Hill: University of North Carolina Press, 2003.

Holt, Rackham. *Mary McLeod Bethune: A Biography.* New York: Doubleday, 1964.

Holt, Thomas. *Black over White: Negro Political Leadership in South Carolina during Reconstruction.* Chicago: University of Illinois Press, 1979.

Homan, Lynn, and Thomas Reilly. *Black Knights: The Story of the Tuskegee Airmen.* Gretna, LA: Pelican Publishing, 2001.

Honey, Maureen. *Shadowed Dreams: Women's Poetry of the Harlem Renaissance.* New Brunswick, NJ: Rutgers University Press, 2006.

Horne, Gerald. *Race Woman: The Lives of Shirley Graham Du Bois.* New York: New York University Press, 2000.

James, Rawn, Jr. *The Double V: How Wars, Protest, and Harry Truman Desegregated America's Military.* New York: Bloomsbury Publishing, 2014.

Janken, Kenneth Robert. *Rayford W. Logan and the Dilemma of the African American Intellectual.* Amherst: University of Massachusetts Press, 1997.

———. *Walter White: Mr. NAACP.* Chapel Hill: University of North Carolina Press, 2006.

Jones, Ida E. *The Heart of the Race Problem: The Life of Kelly Miller.* Littleton, MA: Tapestry Press, Ltd., 2011.

Jones, William P. *The March on Washington.* New York: W. W. Norton, 2013.

Keith, Caroline H. *"For Hell and a Brown Mule": The Biography of Senator Millard E. Tydings.* Lanham, MD: Madison Books, 1991.

Kelley, Robin D. G. *Hammer and Hoe: Alabama Communists During the Great Depression.* Chapel Hill: University of North Carolina Press, 1990.

Kennedy, David M. *Freedom from Fear: The American People in Depression and War.* New York: Oxford University Press, 1999.

Kersten, Andrew Edmund. *A. Philip Randolph: A Life in the Vanguard.* Lanham, MD: Rowman and Littlefield, 2007.

Kirk, John A. *Beyond Little Rock: The Origins and Legacies of the Central High Crisis.* Fayetteville, AR: University of Arkansas Press, 2007.

Kirby, John. *Black Americans in the Roosevelt Era: Liberalism and Race.* Knoxville: University of Tennessee Press, 1982.

Klara, Robert. *FDR's Funeral Train: A Betrayed Widow, a Soviet Spy, and a Presidency in the Balance.* New York: Palgrave Macmillan, 2010.

King, Desmond. *Separate and Unequal: Black Americans and the U.S. Federal Government.* New York: Oxford University Press, 1997.

Kiplinger, Willard M. *Washington Is Like That.* New York: Harper and Brothers, 1942.

Klinkner, Philip A., with Rogers M. Smith. *The Unsteady March: The Rise and Decline of Racial Equality in America.* Chicago: University of Chicago Press, 1999.

Kotlowski, Dean J. *Paul V. McNutt and the Age of FDR.* Bloomington: Indiana University Press, 2015.

Kousser, J. Morgan. *The Shaping of Southern Politics: Suffrage Restriction and the Establishment of the One-Party South, 1880–1910.* New Haven, CT: Yale University Press, 1974.

Kryder, Daniel. *Divided Arsenal: Race and the American State during World War II.* New York: Cambridge University Press, 2001.

Lash, Joseph P. *Eleanor and Franklin.* New York: W. W. Norton, 1971.

Leuchtenburg, William. *Franklin D. Roosevelt and the New Deal: 1932–1940.* New York: Harper and Row, 1978.

Levin, Linda Lotridge. *The Making of FDR: The Story of Stephen T. Early, America's First Modern Press Secretary.* New York: Prometheus Books, 2009.

Lewis, David Levering. *W. E. B. Du Bois, 1868–1919: Biography of a Race.* New York: Macmillan, 1994.

———. *W. E. B. Du Bois, 1919–1963: The Fight for Equality and the American Century.* New York: Henry Holt, 2000.

———. *When Harlem Was in Vogue.* New York: Vintage Books, 1982.

Lions, Zelda, and Gordon W. Allport. *Seventy-Five Years of Continuing Education: The Prospect Union Association.* Cambridge, MA: Cambridge Historical Society, 1967.

Lisio, Donald J. *Hoover, Blacks, and Lily Whites: A Study of Southern Strategies.* Chapel Hill: University of North Carolina Press, 1985.

Loewen, James W. *Sundown Towns: A Hidden Dimension of American Racism.* New York: New Press, 2013.

Lusane, Clarence. *The Black History of the White House.* San Francisco: City Lights Open Media, 2011.

Mann, Peggy. *Ralph Bunche: UN Peacemaker.* New York: Coward, McCann and Geoghegan, 1975.

Marable, Manning. *Race, Reform and Rebellion: The Second Reconstruction, 1945–1990,* 3rd ed. Oxford: University Press of Mississippi, 2007.

Mattelart, Armand. *Mapping World Communication: War, Progress, Culture.* Minneapolis: University of Minnesota Press, 1994.

McElvaine, Robert S. *The Great Depression: America, 1929–1941.* New York: Times Books, 1993.

McFeely, William S. *Frederick Douglass.* New York: Simon and Schuster, 1991.

McGuire, Phillip. *He, Too, Spoke for Democracy: Judge Hastie, World War II, and the Black Soldier.* New York: Greenwood Press, 1988.

McNeil, Genna Rae. *Groundwork: Charles Hamilton Houston and the Struggle for Civil Rights.* Philadelphia: University of Pennsylvania Press, 1983.

Meyer, Stephen Grant. *As Long as They Don't Move Next Door: Segregation and Racial Conflict in American Neighborhoods.* Lanham, MD: Rowman and Littlefield, 2001.

Miller, Eben. *Born Along the Color Line: The 1933 Amenia Conference and the Rise of a National Civil Rights Movement.* New York: Oxford University Press, 2012.

Mitchell, Ethan. *The Defender: How the Legendary Black Newspaper Changed America.* New York: Houghton Mifflin Harcourt, 2016.

Moe, Richard. *Roosevelt's Second Act: The Election of 1940 and the Politics of War.* New York: Oxford University Press, 2013.

Moore, Jacqueline. *Leading the Race: The Transformation of the Black Elite in the Nation's Capital, 1880–1920.* Charlottesville: University of Virginia Press, 1999.

Myrdal, Gunnar. *An American Dilemma: The Negro Problem and Modern Democracy,* vol. 1. 1944; reprint: New Brunswick, NJ: Transaction Publishers, 2009.

———. *An American Dilemma: The Negro Problem and Modern Democracy*, vol. 2. 1944; reprint: New Brunswick, NJ: Transaction Publishers, 2009.

Nalty, Bernard C. *Strength for the Fight: A History of Black Americans in the Military*. New York: Simon and Schuster, 1989.

Newton, Michael. *Unsolved Civil Rights Murder Cases, 1934–1970*. Jefferson, NC: McFarland, 2016.

Norton, Mary Beth, et al. *A People and a Nation: A History of the United States*. Vol. 2, *Since 1865*, 6th ed. New York: Houghton Mifflin, 2003.

Ottley, Roi. *New World A-Coming: Inside Black America*. Boston: Houghton-Mifflin, 1943.

Poole, Mary. *The Segregated Origins of Social Security: African Americans and the Welfare State*. Chapel Hill: University of North Carolina Press, 2006.

Pottker, Jan. *Sara and Eleanor: The Story of Sara Delano Roosevelt and Her Daughter-in-Law, Eleanor Roosevelt*. New York: St. Martin's Press, 2014.

Pritchett, Wendell E. *Robert Clifton Weaver and the American City: The Life and Times of an Urban Reformer*. Chicago: University of Chicago Press, 2008.

Reed, Merl E. *Seedtime for the Modern Civil Rights Movement: The President's Committee on Fair Employment Practice, 1941–1946*. Baton Rouge: Louisiana State University Press, 1991.

Ritchie, Donald. *Electing FDR: The New Deal Campaign of 1932*. Lawrence: University of Kansas Press, 2007.

———. *Reporting from Washington: The History of the Washington Press Corps*. New York: Oxford University Press, 2005.

Robnett, Belinda. *How Long? How Long? African American Women in the Struggle for Civil Rights*. New York: Oxford University Press, 2000.

Roeder, George H. *The Censored War: American Visual Experience during World War Two*. New Haven, CT: Yale University Press, 1993.

Rosenbloom, David H. *Federal Service and the Constitution: The Development of the Public Employment Relationship*, 2nd ed. Washington, D.C.: Georgetown University Press, 2014.

Rupp, Leila J., and Verta Taylor. *Survival in the Doldrums: The American Women's Rights Movement, 1945 to the 1960s*. New York: Oxford University Press, 1987.

Salmond, John A. *Southern Rebel: The Life and Times of Aubrey Willis Williams, 1890–1965*. Chapel Hill: University of North Carolina Press, 1983.

Sherman, Richard B. *The Case of Odell Waller and Virginia Justice*. Knoxville: University of Tennessee Press, 1992.

———. *The Republican Party and Black America: From McKinley to Hoover, 1896–1933*. Charlottesville: University Press of Virginia, 1973.

Sitkoff, Harvard. *A New Deal for Blacks: The Emergence of Civil Rights as a National Issue: The Depression Decade*. New York: Oxford University Press, 1978.

Smith, J. Clay, Jr. *Emancipation: The Making of the Black Lawyer, 1844–1944*. Philadelphia: University of Pennsylvania Press, 1993.

Smith, Jean Edward. *FDR*. New York: Random House, 2008.

Sollors, Werner, Caldwell Titcomb, and Thomas A. Underwood, eds. *Blacks at Harvard: A Documentary History of African-American Experience at Harvard and Radcliffe*. New York: New York University Press, 1993.

Stave, Bruce. *The New Deal and the Last Hurrah: Pittsburgh Machine Politics*. Pittsburgh: University of Pittsburgh Press, 1970.

Stewart, Alison. *First Class: The Legacy of Dunbar, America's First Black Public High School*. Chicago: Lawrence Hill Books, 2013.

Sullivan, Patricia. *Days of Hope: Race and Democracy in the New Deal Era*. Chapel Hill: University of North Carolina Press, 1996.

———. *Lift Every Voice: The NAACP and the Making of the Civil Rights Movement*. New York: Free Press, 2009.

Taylor, Quintard. *In Search of the Racial Frontier: African Americans in the American West, 1528–1990*. New York: W. W. Norton, 1999.

Topping, Simon. *Lincoln's Lost Legacy: The Republican Party and the African American Vote*. Gainesville: University Press of Florida, 2008.

Trotter, Joe W., and Jared N. Day. *Race and Renaissance: African Americans in Pittsburgh Since World War II*. Pittsburgh: University of Pittsburgh Press, 2010.

Vale, Lawrence J. *Purging the Poorest: Public Housing and the Design Politics of Twice-Cleared Communities*. Chicago: University of Chicago Press, 2013.

Ware, Gilbert. *William Hastie: Grace Under Pressure*. New York: Oxford University Press, 1985.

Watkins, T. H. *The Hungry Years: A Narrative History of the Great Depression*. New York: Macmillan, 2000.

Weems, Robert, and Louis A. Randolph. *Business in Black and White: American Presidents and Black Entrepreneurs in the Twentieth Century*. New York: New York University Press, 2009.

Weiss, Nancy J. *Farewell to the Party of Lincoln: Black Politics in the Age of FDR*. Princeton, NJ: Princeton University Press, 1983.

Williamson, Joel. *Crucible of Race: Black-White Relations in the American South since Emancipation*. New York: Oxford University Press, 1984.

Wilson, Woodrow. *A History of the American People*. 5 vols. New York: Harper and Brothers, 1903.

Wolters, Raymond. *Negroes and the Great Depression.* New York: Greenwood Press, 1970.

Wright, Richard. *12 Million Black Voices.* New York: Basic Books, 1941; reprinted 2008.

Wynn, Neil A. *The African American Experience During World War II.* Lanham, MD: Rowman and Littlefield, 2010.

Yellin, Eric. *Racism in the Nation's Service: Government Works and the Color Line in Woodrow Wilson's America.* Chapel Hill: University of North Carolina Press, 2013.

Zaki, Hoda. *Civil Rights and Politics at Hampton Institute: The Legacy of Alonzo G. Moron.* Urbana: University of Illinois Press, 2007.

Theses and Dissertations

Barrow, Frederica Harrison. "The Social Welfare Career and Contributions of Forrester Blanchard Washington: A Life Course Analysis." PhD diss., Howard University, 2002.

Coulibaly, Sylvie. "Kelly Miller, 1895–1939: Portrait of an African American Intellectual." PhD diss., Emory University, 2006.

Frank, Patricia A. "'Keep 'Em Squirming!' Alfred Edgar Smith, Charley Cherokee, and Race Relations, 1933–1943." MA thesis, University of Arkansas, 1993.

Grothaus, Larry Henry. "The Negro in Missouri Politics, 1890–1941." PhD diss., University of Missouri, 1970.

Kifer, Allen Francis. "The Negro Under the New Deal." PhD diss., University of Wisconsin, 1961.

Lattimer, Mariagnes. "The Black Cabinet: The Study of Personal Commitment and Political Involvement by Blacks During the New Deal." PhD diss., Union Institute and University, 1974.

McGruder, Larry. "Kelly Miller: The Life and Thoughts of a Black Intellectual." PhD diss., Miami University, 1984.

Motz, Jane. "The Black Cabinet: Negroes in the Administration of Franklin D. Roosevelt." MA thesis, University of Delaware, 1964.

Okie, William Thomas. "'Everything Is Peaches down in Georgia': Culture and Agriculture in the American South." PhD diss., University of Georgia, 2012.

Washington, Forrester. "A Study of Organized Social Agencies Among Negroes in New York City." MA thesis, Columbia University, 1916.

Weaver, Robert C. "The High Wage Theory of Prosperity." PhD diss., Harvard University, 1934.

Williams, Alma Rene. "Robert C. Weaver: From the Black Cabinet to the President's Cabinet." PhD diss., Washington University, 1978.

ACKNOWLEDGMENTS

In January 2008, ninety-six-year-old civil rights leader Dorothy Height, a protégé of Mary McLeod Bethune, reflected on the election of Barack Obama to the presidency of the United States and told the *New York Times*, "It took a lot of people a lot of work to make this happen." When I read that, I decided to set aside a project I had been working on to write a book about the Black Cabinet during the era of Franklin Delano Roosevelt. The Black Cabinet often gets a brief mention in textbooks as an accomplishment credited to FDR. But I had a hunch, and it proved true, that the Black Cabinet was self-generated and self-directed and was very much a part of building the bridge to the White House for President Barack Obama. At its height, the Black Cabinet included a large number of African American federal officials. My goal became to write a collective biography of the core members of the black brain trust of the era of Franklin Delano Roosevelt and explore how their lives intersected for this short but extremely important period of U.S. history.

For a historian, it has been an honor to spend the last twelve years with the members of the Black Cabinet. Their successes and failures offer lessons to subsequent generations. The Black Cabinet has taught me about patience and perseverance. And it also has taught me to never lose hope.

Researching and writing about the Black Cabinet, a clandestine and unofficial group that kept few written records and operated primarily out of the public eye, was a task that I could never have accomplished without the support of those I mention below.

There were numerous archivists and librarians that helped me take this journey. My thanks go out to the librarians at California State

University San Marcos: Debbie Blair, Rosa Castro, Judith Downie, and Teresa Roudenbush. I am also grateful to Klara Charlton of Union Institute and University, Kirsten Strigel Carter of the FDR Presidential Library and Museum, Simon Eliot of UCLA's Special Collections, Jessica Hartman and Noah Shankin of the National Archives, Kay Peterson of the Smithsonian Institute, Meredith McDonough of Alabama Department of Archives and History, Elizabeth Ratigan of the Kiplinger Research Library of the Historical Society of Washington, D.C., and Judith Silva, Archivist at Slippery Rock University. Thank you to Ida Jones of Howard University for her insights and her important work on Kelly Miller. Thanks also to Joellen ElBashir and Clifford Muse of Howard University's Moorland-Spingarn Library and Emory Tolbert of Howard University's Department of History. I appreciate also the assistance I received from Amber D. Anderson of the Archives Center at Atlanta University, Linden Anderson of the Schomburg Center for Research in Black Culture, Laura Brooks of the University of Pittsburgh, Craig Simpson of the Washington Area Spark historic website, Sheila Scott, Savannah Wood, and Nick Mazyeh of the *Baltimore Afro-American*, Geoffrey Stark of the University of Arkansas Special Collections archives, and Penny White of the Special Collections at the University of Virginia.

Thanks to Penelope Lattimer for permission to use the oral histories conducted by her mother, Mariagnes Lattimer, which are included in her doctoral dissertation on the Black Cabinet. Many, many thanks to Christy DeBoe Hicks and Kathy DeBoe, the great-grandnieces of Eva DeBoe Jones, for sharing the memories of their aunt.

I am indebted to mentors, colleagues, and friends who took time out of their busy lives to read this manuscript. Thank you to Michael Fitzgerald, Linda B. Hall, Cindy King, Chana Lee, Edward Reynolds, and Richard Weiss. My gratitude to Judy Kutulas for reading several versions and for her unfailing encouragement. I have benefited over many years from conversations and guidance from Ben Holman, Robert and Ardelle Matthews, Dorothy Smith, and George Walker Smith. Monica McCormick was one of the people who gave me my start in

> aiffort>8 >iscriminat

writing, and I'm forever indebted to her. Margaret Washington's influence continues to shape the work I do.

I appreciate the support I have received from California State University San Marcos. I am grateful to my students for teaching me so much. Students who assisted in research on this project include Denise Kane, Joy Miller, Amanda Regan, Chelsea Snover, and Charla Wilson; and those who offered insights include Mayela Caro, and Sarah Wolk-Fitzgerald. I am grateful to CSUSM faculty who have over many years supported me, encouraged me, and urged me on: my appreciation goes to David Avalos, Staci Beavers, Jeff Charles, Ann Elwood, Carmen Nava, Kim Quinney, Linda Shaw, and Zhiwei Xiao.

I am lucky to have so many friends who have seen me through this and other projects. Thanks to Belynda Bady, Diana Brooking, Ernesto Chavez, Sharon Coleman, Monte Kugal, Larry Goldstein, Valerie Matsumoto, Amanda Podany, Jerry Podany, and Nan Yamane for many years of friendship and great conversations. I am grateful to the following people for their special friendship: Alysia Allen, Stacey Barney, Kevin and Jillian Goff, Joanna and Mike O'Neill, Caitlin and Gilah Sexton, Candace Van Dall, and Becky and Patrick Van Zant. To the dog-walking crowd, thanks for cheering me on: Yoshiko and Hiro Inoue and Peg, Sarah Fitzgerald and Snoopy, Nicole Mulich and Jack, Pat and Bill Walker and Greta and Kahlua, and Nancy and Walter Clark and Max. Thank you Mike and Toni Dunn, Karen and Owen O'Gara, and Barbara and Jack Roland for all your kindness and constant support.

I greatly appreciate the opportunity to be associated with Grove Press, a publisher that has never shied away from pushing for positive change. My editor, Amy Hundley, nurtured this project over the years, and I am so grateful she gave me the chance and the space to tell this story. I am also appreciative of George Gibson for his editorial contributions and his support. I am grateful to publisher Morgan Entrekin for his support of this project. Thanks also to managing editor Julia Berner-Tobin, publicity director Deb Seager, copyeditor Amy K. Hughes, proofreader Alicia Burns, editorial assistants Dhyana Taylor and Savannah Johnston, Publicity

Manager Justina Batchelor, and Production Director Sal Destro. It takes a lot of people to create a book and I appreciate the Grove team very much. A special thanks goes to Gretchen Mergenthaler who designed the book's beautiful cover that captures the gravity of *The Black Cabinet*'s history.

Thank you to my agent, Victoria Sanders, for her many years of support and advice. Also I am grateful to Bernadette Baker-Baughman and Jessica Spivey of Victoria Sanders and Associates for all the work they have done.

Richard Newman, the walking and talking encyclopedia of African American history (and gossip of all forms), died long before I even thought of doing this project. But he remains a beacon for me, and I wrote this book with him in mind.

My family has always encouraged me. Thanks to my Aunt Nancy Watts Peck and my Uncle Bill Watts (who didn't live to see this project in its final form but who never failed to ask me how it was going). I had the great fortune to grow up in a large extended family with cousins who have been like brothers and sisters to me. Julie, Martha, Debbie, Peggy, Rose, Cheri, Donna, Stephanie, Heather, Wes, Damion, Alan, Doug, Russ, Rick, Jonathan, Jim, Kevin, and Steve—I appreciate you all so much. To my sister, Becky Watts Woo, and her family, Don, Sarah, and Abby, I am grateful to have you in my life. I labor to follow in the footsteps of my dad, Thomas Watts, who dedicated his life to social change through education. My mom, Doris Watts, is the one person who has read everything I ever wrote, and I am grateful to her for teaching me the love of writing.

Two rescue dogs have seen me through this book. Right now, the steadfast, and usually far more assertive than necessary, Fred is sleeping not under but on the desk where I write. But before Fred, there was Kirby. I adopted him from a shelter and discovered he had been used for seven years—his whole life—in animal testing. He lived for only two years into this project. But he embraced his new life, and I was so lucky to know and learn from such an open heart.

INDEX

Federal Emergency Relief Administration
(FERA), 113–114, 124, 164
federal government positions. *See also* specific
individuals
accomplishments of Second Black Cabinet,
254
the Big Four pressure F. Roosevelt, 56–57
black officials targeted by white supremacists, 12–13
"black posts," 10
civil service and, 10–11, 274–276
decrease in, during 1920s, 31
Douglass and, 10
increase in workplace segregation, 23
Johnson's appointments, 440
Kennedy's appointment of Weaver, 435
F. Roosevelt's appointments of blacks, 52,
79–80, 88–90, 94, 95–96, 113–114,
143, 190, 195–196, 238
T. Roosevelt's appointments of blacks, 3, 5,
10, 14–16, 17
F. Roosevelt's appointments of whites for
racial-affairs posts, 400
F. Roosevelt's appointments of white South-
ern loyalists, 107
F. Roosevelt's dismissal of black Hoover
appointees, 55
Rosenwald Fund, 59–61, 75, 76, 92, 133
in the South, 22
Taft's appointments of blacks, 21, 22–23
Truman's appointments of blacks, 427–428
R. Weaver's attempts to secure, 74
in White House, 47
Wilson's removal of blacks, 29
Ferguson, Dutton, 250, 282, 283, 284
Fields, Alonzo, 225–226
Ford, James, 275
Foreman, Clark
appointed Special Adviser on the Economic
Status of Negroes, 75
background, 77–78
on Bethune, 179
blacks hired by, 77, 79–80, 88–90, 94
on blacks returning to farms, 87
characteristics, 78, 81, 117, 118
Commerce Department conference on
economic problems of blacks, 83
Du Bois and, 77–78
efforts to expand New Deal programs to
blacks, 82–83
1934 election, 139

NRA and, 102–106
Pitts's initial attitude toward, 80–81
as "race traitor," 81–82
on racism in New Deal programs, 78–79
resignation, 145–146
Second Black Cabinet, 96–97, 125,
129–130, 131
Sojourner Truth Homes, 362
R. Weaver interview, 88–90
Fortune, 336
Fort Valley Industrial and Training School,
230, 231
Fort Valley Message, 234
Foster, Thomas P., 366
Frankfurter, Felix, 96, 101
Franklin, John Hope, 192
Frazier, E. Franklin, 60
Frothingham, Elizabeth, 47

Garfield, James, 10
Garner, John Nance, 44–45, 48, 277, 301
Gavagan, Joseph A., xiii, 137–138
gender discrimination, 225, 226–227, 249,
351–352, 380
Georgia Woman's World, 183–184, 188
Gibson, Truman, 354, 374, 377
GOP, 7. *See also* Republican Party
Grand Old Party (GOP). *See* Republican Party
Granger, Lester, 226, 269, 401, 408
Gray's Cafe, 6–7, 27
Great Depression
deepening of, 53
effect on blacks, 32–33, 36–37, 53, 60,
69–70, 86, 135
Hoover and, 32, 37
Green, William, 343
Guffey, Joe
Anslinger and, 119
black vote and, 41
1934 election, 137
Farley and black grassroots organizations, 52
on 1938 election, 262, 263
patronage positions from F. Roosevelt, 51, 52
Vann and, 38, 41–42
Guthrie, George W., 36

Haith, Ella, 151
Hall, Felix, 327
Hall, Robert, 405
Hamilton, Albert, 399–400
Hamilton.West, 324